MASTERING
HARDWARE AND NETWORKING

Dr. Ajay Rana
Ph.D (CSE), M.Tech (CSE), MBA (Gold Medalist (Twice))
Director: Amity Technical Placement Centre,
Amity University, U.P

Dr. Ajit Mittal
M. Com, Ph.D (U.P.), MBA (Finance)
Professor: Amity International Business School,
Amity University, Noida

KHANNA BOOK PUBLISHING CO. (P) LTD.
Publisher of Engineering and Computer Books
4C/4344, Ansari Road, Darya Ganj, New Delhi-110002
Phone : 011-23244447-48 **Mobile:** +91-9910909320
E-mail : contact@khannabooks.com
Website : www.khannabooks.com

Dear Readers,

To prevent the piracy, this book is secured with HIGH SECURITY HOLOGRAM on the front title cover. In case you don't find the hologram on the front cover title, please write us to at contact@khannabooks.com or whatsapp us at +91-99109 09320 and avail special gift voucher for yourself.

Specimen of Hologram on front Cover title:

Moreover, there is a SPECIAL DISCOUNT COUPON for you with EVERY HOLOGRAM.

How to avail this SPECIAL DISCOUNT:

Step 1: Scratch the hologram
Step 2: Under the scratch area, your "coupon code" is available
Step 3: Logon to www.khannabooks.com
Step 4: Use your "coupon code" in the shopping cart and get your copy at a special discount
Step 5: Enjoy your reading!

Thanks,
Khanna Publishing House

MASTERING HARDWARE AND NETWORKING
by **Dr. Ajit Mittal, Dr. Ajay Rana**

ISBN: 978-81-90645-12-6

Edition: 2026

To view complete list of books, please scan the QR Code:

Published by:
Khanna Book Publishing Co. (P) Ltd.
CIN: U22110DL1998PTC095547

Visit us at: www.khannabooks.com
Write us at: contact@khannabooks.com

Printed in Bharat.

How This Book is Arranged

This book is one from the series of books produced by the publishers to let the students and learning community know about the various aspects of the computers in general. The aim of the series is to educate them through easy and simple method. Indeed the series is to create a master in you!

Hardware and Networking form the basic cores of the computer knowledge, not only for the users but also for the people who are there to take care of the compuer system. They are the ones who would become Hardware Engineers. The book is divided into three sections:

1. Computer System
2. Hardware
3. Networking

SECTION 1: COMPUTER SYSTEM

It has only one chapter and it tells you about the basics of the computer system.

Chapter 1: It goes through the various classifications of the computers. Basic computer hardware and software are also discussed. It also tells you about the things which computer cannot do and what are its usages.

SECTION 2: HARDWARE

It the main section of the book and traces the various aspects of the hardware components which can be attached to the computer. Some of them are compulsory and some are optional. It has the following chapters:

Chapter 2: It tells you about mouse. Its various options, working and about the various buttons on the mouse. It also talks about the installaion of the mouse and its troubleshooting.

Chapter 3: Scanner is used for scanning both text and graphics. This chapter discusses the various type of scanners used and the working of the scanner on the whole.

Chapter 4: Keyboard is the most important part of the computer system. It the basic input device of the computer. In this chapter, the various keys of the keyboard are totally explained. Installing of keyboard is also discussed. It also talks about the methods to keep the keyboard healty, free of dust, etc.

Chapter 5: Monitor is like the TV, it shows the results on the screen. This chapter discusses the monitor's adavantages and disadvantages, various type of cards used to get displays, problems which can occur while using the monitor. It also talks about the modern technology used in Monitors.

Chapter 6: Printers are used to get an hard copy of the result of the processing of the data in the computer. This chapter discusses the various type of printers in use, their installation, their preventive maintainence and the modern print technology being used these days.

Chapter 7: For computers, the importance of input and output devices is very high. The most common removable input/output device in use, these days, is CD-ROM. This chapter discusses the various options available and their usage. It also talks about the advantages and disadvantages of the disks.

Chapter 8: Hard disk drives are the fixed input/output devices. Its working is explained in this chapter. Various new and advanced version of the hard disk are also explained here. As usual, installation and troubleshooting are also discussed.

Chapter 9: Floppy disk drives are on the way out and are becoming obselete, but, they are discussed here to show how they used to work and their various other aspects.

Chapter 10: Processors form the main computer part where all the working of the computer takes place. In this chapter, most of the new technologies are explained.

Chapter 11: Motherboard is the heart of all the chips which are used in the computer. This chapter talks about all the chips which are there, mainly, BIOS,CMOS battery, Bus Slots, Memory units, I/O chips, etc.

Chapter 12: Power supply is the main connection between the external power supply and the power which is fed to the various chips. Various type of power supplies are explained here.

Chapter 13: BIOS is used for giving a start to the computer. It has various options of settings and the initial house-warming which has to be done, before starting the computer. This chapter gives you an introduction to the various options which are available here.

Chapter 14: Beep codes are there to give sort of warning signals to you when you do something wrong. The various beep codes available are shown here.

Chapter 15: Memory is the main strength of the computer processing. This chapter shows the various types of memories available and their usage.

Chapter 16: Various input/output devices are used in computer. To run you need to have their respective interfaces too. This chapter shows the various input output device interfaces available.

Chapter 17: It shows how you can, if the need be, install the computer on your own. Though it is just to give you an idea, not that you can become an expert using this.

Chapter 18: It tallks about the various new devices which are there in the market, as a result of the various researches which keep on going. The chapter talks about Zip Drive, DVD ROM, Web camera, Modem and Flash Disk.

Chapter 19: Computer is afterall a machine and can fail at sometime. This chapter talks about the various sources available for recovering the data, once the computer fails. Though these are not foolproof, but, are useful.

SECTION 1: NETWORKING

This section discusses the various aspects of networking. It has the following chapters:

Chapter 20: Networking is all about communicating between the computers. This chapter talks about the various types of equipments used for transmission of data. It talks about, Data Transmission Techniques, Communication Channels, Bandwidth channesl, Buffers and Protocols, Serial and Parallel Interface, Methods of Data Transmission, Communication Processors, Transmission Modes, etc.

Chapter 21: This chapter talks about Network Technology on the whole. Among others it discusses the various types of networks used, various topologies used, etc. Applications of networing are also discussed.

Chapter 22: Most important to networking is the method of designing the network, which can be used by you. This chapter talks about that while mentioning about the hardware, wiring, computers, etc., to be used.

Chapter 23: When you have Networking, the security becomes a must. This chapter discusses about the various aspects of the network security.

Chapter 24: This chapter discusses about Network Architecture. Various topics covered are: ARCnet Specifications, Etherenet Specifications and Token Ring Specifications.

Chapter 25: This chapter covers Network Connectivity. Variuous topics covered are: Network Connectivity Devices, NICs, Hubs, Modes and Routers.

Chapter 26: This chapter discusses about Network Administration Security. Various aspects covered are: Server Chief Technology and Server Management, Raid Management and Mirroring, Hauffman Code and Cryptography.

Chapter 27: This chapter covers Wireless Networking. Various topics covered are: Wireless LAN, Bluetooth, etc.

We are indeed debited to our publishers Khanna Book Publishing Co. Pvt. Ltd., specially Sheetal Khanna for their suggestions and encouragement given in producing this book.

Suggestions for improvement of the book are indeed welcome.

Authors

CONTENTS

Section 1 — Computer System

Section 2 — Hardware

Section 3 — Networking

Section 1
Computer System

This section includes information about Computers.

1 Computer System

Computer Age

Though the first fully operational electronic computer was introduced to the world in 1946, but the historian assumes the starting of a computer age from 1951, when first commercial computer UNIVAC was introduced. The remarkable thing about the computer age is that so much has happened in so much short time. We have leapfrogged four generations of technology in about 50 years - a span of time whose events are within the memories of many people today. The first three computer generations are pinned to three technological developments:

1. vacuum tube
2. transistor and
3. integrated circuit

Each has drastically changed the nature and size of computers. We define the timing of each generation according to the beginning of commercial delivery of the hardware technology. Defining subsequent generations has become more complicated because the entire industry has become more complicated.

Characteristics of Computers

A computer can be judged by various factor, among them are:

Speed

Computers provide the processing speed essential to our fast-paced society. The quick service we have come to expect - for bank withdrawals, telephone calls, and travel reservations, to name a few - is made possible by computers. Businesses depend on the speedy processing computers to handle high volume activities such as balancing ledgers and designing products.

The smallest unit of time in the human experience is, realistically, the second. Computer operations - for example, the execution of an instruction, such as multiplying pay-rate with numbers of hours worked - are measured in milliseconds, microsecond, nanoseconds and picoseconds (one thousandth, one millionth, one billionth, and one trillionth of a second respectively).

Although all computers are fast, but there is a wide diversity of computer speeds. The execution of an instruction on a very slow computer may be measured in less than a millisecond. Most computer can execute an instruction measured in microseconds range, but still to be broken in the picosecond barrier.

A computer speed is generally expressed in megahertz (MHz), millions of machine cycles per second. Thus a PC (Personal Computer) listed at 100 MHz has a processor capable of handling 100 million machine cycles per second. Another measure of computer speed is MIPS (one million instructions per second). MIPS is often a more accurate measure than clock speed, because some computers can use each tick of the clock more efficiently than others.

A third measure of speed is the megaflops (MFLOPS), which stands for one million floating point operations per second. It measures the ability of the computer to perform complex mathematical operations.

Accuracy

Errors do occur in computer based information systems, but precious few can be directly attributed to the computer system itself. The vast majority can be traced to a program logic error, a procedural error, or erroneous data. These are human errors. High accuracy implies small error, but accuracy is contrasted with precision e.g. three places of decimals properly computed are less precise but more accurate than four places of decimals containing an error. The accuracy of the results obtained from computer mainly depends on the method of programming and the way the results are interprted.

Reliability

Computers are extremely reliable. Where reliability is the measurement of the performance of a computer, measured against some predetermined standard for operation without the failure of it.

Reliability Of Computer = Serviceable Time/Serviceable Time + Down Time

where serviceable time is the total time during which a computer is in a state where it can operate normally, including time when the computer is idle, but not the time when it is unattended. Down time is the time when a computer is inoperable due to a machine fault.

Computer systems are particularly adept at repetitive tasks. They donot take sick leave and tea breaks, and they seldom complain anything below 99.9% serviceable time, the time when the computer system is in operation, is usually unacceptable. For some companies, any down time is unacceptable. These companies provide backup computers that take over automatically if the main computer fails.

Provides a Capability that would otherwise be Impossible

Computers operate on very high speed on data so that they can produce results in seconds, which is not possible otherwise. For example, computer can be used to provide management with up-to-the minute figures on all aspects of its business. This information can go long way in taking decisions by management.

Similary, computers enable companies to provide customers with instanteneous services, such as airline flight availability and charge account status. The result is that these companies can offer far more customer services than would be impossible without the computer.

Storage Capability

Since, various computer media can store millions of characters of data in a condensed form, there is a tremendous savings in the storage area required to maintain the vital records necessary in a business environment.

Intangable Benefits

There are many companies that utilize computers for intangible benefits such as flexibility, ability to accomodate growth, and the psychological factor that may give them a competitive edge in attracting consumers to buy their products or services.

Reduced Cost

With the ever-increasing advances being made in the state of the art, the cost of computer equipment has dropped drastically over the years. Hardware costs have been decreasing at an estimated anual rate of 30%. Thus, companies that at one time could not justify the cost of acquiring their own computer system may now find it not only feasible to acquire a system, but cost-effective as well.

Brief History of Computers

Would you not like to know how the present day computers were invented? Well, they were not like these from very beginning. These have been developed over the years. In the early days people started exchanging goods and in this process they felt the need of counting. This was done with the help of stones. Each stone represented a single unit. Stones could be counted before giving or taking the things.

Next, they started drawing lines on wall or on sand before selling or purchasing the goods. It was a simple but a lengthy process for large numbers. So even this was abolished later.

Then in 3000 B.C., Abacus was invented by the **Chinese**. Later it was modified by **Egyptians** and **Indians**. Let us see how this **Abacus** looks like, it is shown here.

Abacus

It is a rectangular wooden frame with rods and rounded moveable beads which are used for counting. It has **10 rods** with **7 beads** in each. Each rod has 2 sections, upper and lower. In lower section there are 5 beads representing a single unit. Upper section has 2 beads representing number 5 each. The beads move on the rods from one end to other end and the resultant number is represented by the beads at the centre.

After this lots of developments took place. This is mentioned here year wise.

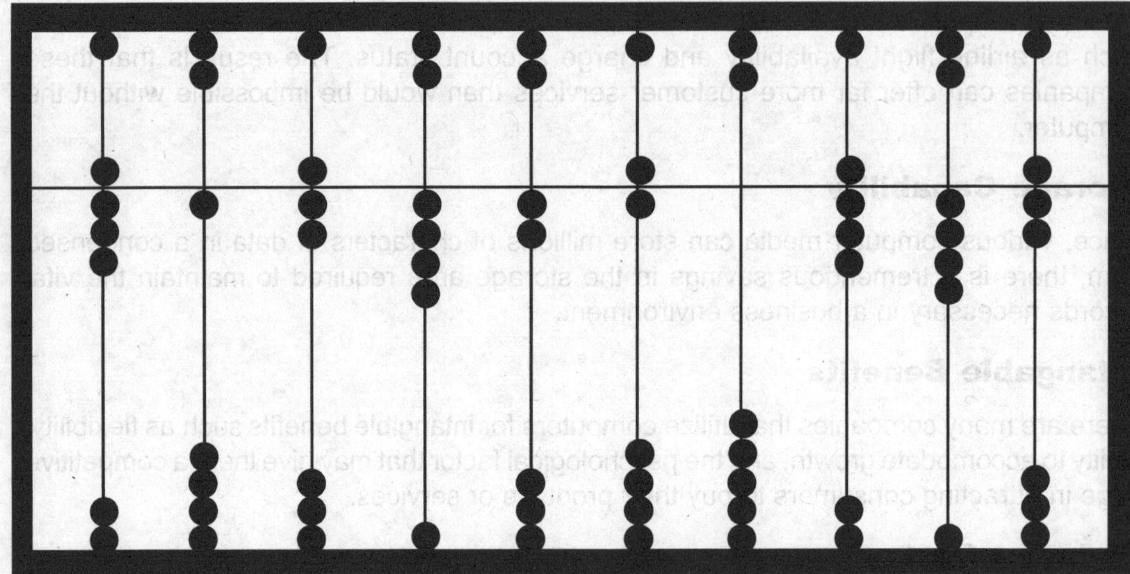

Other Computer Developments

1617- **John Napier** invented a machine which consisted of a set of numbered rods for doing multiplications. *Each rod contained digits from 1 to 9.*

1642- A famous French mathematician **Blaise Pascal** developed the first mechanical calculating machine. This machine had a number of teeth and wheels connected together by chains. Numbers were fed into the machine by dialing them on the wheels. It could add and do multiplications.

1671- Ad Gofried Leibrietzi – Modified or improved the Pascal's machine.

1792 – 1871 Charles Babbage, an English Mathematician, designed a machine, named **Difference Engine**. In 1833- 34, Babbage invented another machine with an automatic computing mechanism. He named it **Analytical Engine**. This machine could store the data in **Memory**, which became the base of Modern Computers. This is why he is known as the **Father of Computers**.

1880- **Herman Hollerith**, a mathematician, invented a Tabulating Machine by using punch cards for the census (calculation of population) in USA. The cards used to have holes for different answers. When these cards passed through this machine, the machine could detect holes on cards, recognize numbers and it could make required calculations.

1930-1939 During the IInd World War, Computers were utilized in military operations for decoding secret messages and creating designs for aircrafts. They were nicknamed **Z1** and **Z2** machines.

1940- IBM had made a computer and named it **Harvard Mark–I**. It worked electro mechanically without any manual efforts. It could perform three addition operations and one subtraction operation per second. As multiplication, it could perform one operation per second. It was a first computer and was also called **A**utomatic **S**equence **C**ontrolled **C**omputer (ASCC).

1946- **ENIAC** computer was developed in 1946. This was based on Mark 1, which was developed by **Howard Aitken** and **Grace Hopper** in 1930.

Technical Evolution of Computers

Development of computer is usually measured in terms of computer generations, which show how over the periods computer has changed effectively. Computer generations can be derived on the basis of the various methods used in the making of the computer.

	Generations	*Based on*	*Period*
(i)	First Generation	**Electronic Valves**	1950
(ii)	Second Generation	**Transistors**	1960
(iii)	Third Generation	**Integrated Circuits**	1965
(iv)	Fourth Generation	**Microprocessors**	1975
(v)	Fifth Generation	**Large Scale Integrated Systems**	1980

First Generation Computers

J.P. Eckert and J.W. Muchly developed the first electronic computer known as ENIAC. The other computers which come into this category are NIVAC, EDVAC, UNIVAC etc.

Second Generation Computers

Second Generation Computers were based on transistor (transfer resistor) technology which replaced the vacuum tubes. Examples of second generation computers are: UNIVAC 1108, IBM 700, 1401, CDC-1604, 3600.

Third Generation Computers

The transistors used in second generation were then replaced with Integrated Circuits (ICs) or chip. Example: IBM –360, 370, ICL–1900.

Fourth Generation Computers

These computers were based upon the development of Large Scale Integration (LSI). Examples: INTEL 4004 Apple Series I and II, Spectrum 7.

Fifth Generation Computers

Fifth Generation Computers focused on connectivity. This method of connecting of computers is called Networking.

Categories of Commercial Computers

Computers can be classified into two categories:

- Classification according to the logic used
- Classification according to the size.

Classification according to the logic used

Analog Computer

Analog computers are in which numerical magnitudes are represented by physical quantities, such as electric current, voltage or resistance, mechanical movements etc. Analog computers accepts data and then process it to produce analog data.

Analog computer are machines designed to perform arithmetical functions upon numbers where the numbers are represented by physical quantity. For example, in mechanical analog computers the number are often represented by physical dimensions of the members forming the various functional units for instance by the angular rotation of the shaft or gear wheels.

In electrical analog machines voltages are used to represent the input variables.

Essentially an analog computer must be able to accept inputs which vary with respect to time, and directly apply these inputs to various devices within the computer which perform the computing operations of addition, subtraction, multiplication, division and integration. The output from the system may be in the form of a graph produced by a plotting pen or a trace on a cathode-ray tube. The computing units of analog computers are able to respond immediately to the changes which they detect in the input variable and the connection of these various units in a particular fashion can cause an analog computer to perform very complex arithmetical functions at high speed while the actual process under study is in operation.

The ability to operate in real time mode means that analog computers has many application in the scientific and industrial fields in simulating various physical systems or automatically controlling industrial processes. They are widely used for research into design problems. Analog computers are used in manufacturing units where temperatures, pressure or flow of liquids are to be monitored continuously. It also used at service station where gasoline pump contains an analog processor that connect fuel flow measurements into quantity and price values.

Digital Computers

A digital computer operates on data in the form of digits, rather than the physical quantities used in analog computers. That is, its input must be discrete rather than continuous and may consist of combinations of numbers, characters and special symbols, written in appropriate programming language. Computers generate digital signals representing bit patterns, whereas standard telephone lines were designed to handle analog signals in the form of voices and other sound patterns to use telephone for data communication digital signals need to be converted to an analog format.

Originally digital computers were mechanical devices employing cogs, gears and levers, they now depend upon electronic technique enabling them to deal automatically with a wide range of problems at a very high speeds. Some of the earlier digital computing devices were developed from punched card machines and the program was set up by means of connections on a plugboard, machines of this category are generally referred to as calculators, rather than computers.

Modern digital computers are usually based on the binary notation, numbers and letters being coded into group of digits consisting only of 1 or 0. Each of these digits is represented in an electronic circuit or magnetic store by a component in an on or off state. For example, passing current or not passing current, magnetized or not magnetized. Data in this form is processed in the CPU of the computer by gates (switches) which obey the instructions of the program.

The individual operations performed by a digital computer are very simple arithmetic or logical processes involving the manipulation of the bits in words or characters of information. The great power of any digital computer rets in the ability to store large volumes of data and to perform these various functions at extremely high speed. Arithmetic and logical circuits for processing data in binary form are constructed from simple basic units designed to perform the operations of Boolean algebra AND, OR, NOT etc. These simple units are used as building blocks in constructing the complex logic and control circuits required.

General purpose digital computers

It is also known as all purpose digital computer. Theoretically it can be used for any type of application. e.g., computers that are used for payroll, graphs, analysis etc.

Special purpose digital computers

A digital computer designed to solve problems of a restricted type. That is, special-purpose digital computer is designed to be especially efficient in a certain class of applications. For example, computers installed in washing machines.

Classification according to size

Computers come in sizes from tiny to monstrous, in both appearance and power. The size of a computer that a person or an organization needs depends on the computing environments. Clearly, the National Weather service provided by Meteorological Department of India keeping watch on the weather fronts of many continents has requirements different from those of a two wheeler dealer's service department that is trying to keep track of its parts inventory. And the requirements of both of them are different from the needs of a salesperson using a small laptop computer to record client orders on a sales trip.

In general the classification of computers can be characterized by cost, size, storage capacity, number of users and processing speed. In many cases, there is a considerable amount of overlapping of these characteristics. So broadly, computers can be classified as

- Super Computers
- Mainframe Computers
- Mini Computers
- Workstations
- Micro Computers or Personal Computers

Supercomputers, the biggest of all, have greater computing capacities than mainframe computers. Mainframe computers have grater computing capacities than minicomputers and Minicomputers have greater computing capacities than microcomputers. Rapid advances in computer technology have blurred what used to be distinguishing characteristics (physical size, cost, memory capacity and so on).

Large Computer Systems

These are sometime called the mainframe computers too.

Super Computers

The speed of a computer is limited by two things,

1. the switching time
2. the time taken by an electric pulse to go from one part of the computer to another.

The Switching time may be thought of as the time a transistor takes to go from a conducting state to nonconducting state or vice versa. Since the switching time is now only of one thousand millionth of a second, the time an electric pulse takes to travel from one part of the computer to another is becoming a more serious limitation.

Nothing can travel faster than the speed of light and light can only travel one foot in a thousand millionth of a second. Thus it is not feasible to increase the speed of sequential computer (e.g. PCs, mainframe etc.) made with a single processor beyond a limit. The only alternative for achieving higher speed of computing is to use many processors to work in parallel. Also it is very important that everything is made as small as possible and the memory does not require too much space.

One of the problems with packing a very large numbers of silicon chips into a small space is that they use power and this means a lot of heat is generated in this space. An elaborate cooling system is a very important part of a supercomputer.

Mainframe Computers

Next step down from supercomputers, in terms of speed and storage capacity are mainframes. Mainframes are large, relatively expensive machines that offer extensive problem-solving capabilities. It can have memory capacities measured in gigabytes and more. The largest mainframes can process well over 100 MIPS. Their operating systems usually handle multiple applications within a timesharing environment. This provides many users with the ability to perform different processing tasks Data storage is primarily on hard disks, with tapes used as backup. Mainframe is a large computer, in particular one to which other computers can be connected so that they can share facilities the mainframe provides. e.g; a System/370 computing system to which personal computers are attached so that they can upload and download programs and data.

The term mainframe usually refers to hardware only : main storage, execution circuitry and peripheral units. Mainframe word-length may be 48, 60 or 64 bits. It has got a system memory (ie; RAM) of 64 to 256 MB, hard disk of capacity 1 -10 GB or more and processing speed of 30 - 100 Millions of Instructions per seconds. A substantial amount of peripherals can be attached to mainframe computer.

Mainframe computers are designed to handle tremendous amount of input, output and storage. Mainframe computers often act as host computers i.e., computers that serve as central receiving and switching computers in regional or national computer networks. Mainframe act as a database server, that is, the database is controlled by mainframe computer that can handle the input and output needs of all terminals connected to it.

Mini Computers

The next step down from mainframe computers, in terms of speed and storage capacity are minicomputers. It is an intermediate - size computer that can perform the same kind of applications as a mainframe but has less storage capacity, processing power and speed than a mainframe.

It is functionally intermediate between a microcomputer and a mainframe. Minicomputers are floor-standing or desktop devices, frequently connected to a mainframe to perform subsidiary operations. They are priced for purchase by smaller businesses and are sufficiently compact to be located in a typical office environment. When Digital Equipment Corporation (DEC) began shipping its PDP series computer in the early 1960s the press dubbed these machines, minicomputers, because of their small size compared to other computers of the day.

Some minicomputers are uniprocessor systems whereas some are multiprocessor system. The processing speed lies in the range 10 -30 MIPS. Memory capacity lies in the range of

8 - 256 MB and can easily range into gigabytes of temporary storage. Minicomputers have operating systems with multitasking and network capabilities enabling them to serve more than one user. It serves as a centralized storehouse for cluster of workstations or as a network server.

For example, a team of architects working on different subsystem within the same building could be directly linked to the office minicomputer that maintains everyone's files and documentation. A mini computer can support more than 100 terminals. Generally, the processing speeds and related capabilities of minicomputers exceed those of microcomputers and more peripheral devices can be attached to them. Minicomputer also tend to have more sophisticated operating systems than microcomputers and can usually be programmed in a wider variety of programming languages.

Small Computer Systems

The following computers are generally grouped into this.

Supermini

The term supermini has been coined to describe minis at the top of the size-price scale. It is a large minicomputer. Physically it is a 32-bit minicomputer which support more simultaneous users (one hundred or more) and more peripheral devices and large memories than previous minicomputer.

Workstations

Between minicomputers and microcomputer in terms of processing power is a class of computers known as workstations. A workstation looks like a personal computer and is typically used by only one person, much as is a personal computer. Although workstations are still more powerful than the average personal computer, the difference is the capabilities of these types of machines.

Microcomputers And Personal Computers

The microcomputer is a scaled-down version of the mainframe. Microcomputer is a digital computer whose processing unit consists of one or more microprocessors, one or more input/output units and sufficient memory to execute instructions. The essential components of a microcomputer are often contained within a single enclosure. Microcomputers are usually desktop or portable devices with a display, a keyboard and tape disk and diskette storage, they are designed primarily for stand-alone operation but can be used as workstations in terminal emulation mode. Every microcomputer is capable of performing jobs once handled by only the largest computers. A typical microcomputer memory unit stores upto 64 MB of data. Processing speeds of microcomputer are measured in megahertz instead of MIPS. A microcomputer running at 90 MHz is faster than one running at 33 MHz and works at approximately 90 MIPS.

The terms microcomputer and personal computer are interchangeable however, PC-which stands for personal computer-has a more specific meaning. In 1981, IBM called its first microcomputer the IBM PC. Within a few years, many companies were copying the IBM design creating "clones" or "compatibles" that aimed at functioning just like the original. For this reason, the term PC has come to mean the family of computers that includes IBMs and compatibles.

Personal computer is a type of microcomputer primarily intended for stand-alone use by an individual. It is a desktop, floor - standing or portable microcomputer that usually consists of a system unit a display monitor, a keyboard, one or more diskette drives, internal hard disk storage, and an optional printer. PCs are designed primarily to give independent computing power to a single user and are inexpensively priced for purchase by individuals or small businesses. A few of the major personal computer manufacturers are APPLE, IBM, Compaq, Dell, AST and Hewlett-Packard.

Supermicros

The upper-end machines used by workers such as engineers, financial traders and graphics designers are small enough to fit on a desk top but approach the power of a mainframe.

Computer Hardware

Computer as mentioned earlier, is a device which has consists of various parts. The main parts of the computer are: Monitor, Keyboard and Central Processing Unit. The physical components of a computer system, such as the computer itself, its modules and peripherals (the input/output devices and auxilary storage units) are called hardware. It consists of:

Processor Unit

The heart of any computer system is the processor unit, which consists of primary storage, arithmetic-logic and control elements. These would be taken up later.

Input Devices

Input is the process of entering and translating incoming data into machine readable form so that they can be processed by the computer. Any hardware item that is attached to the main unit of a computer that houses the Central Processing Unit (CPU) is referred to as peripheral device. An input device is a peripheral device through which data are entered and transformed into machines readable form. For example, punch cards, keyboard, scanner, etc.

Output Devices

Output is the process of translating data, in machine readable form into a form understandable to humans or readable by machines. The information that is the result of processing is also often referred to as outputs. An output device is a peripheral device that allows a computer to communicate information to humans or another machine by accepting data from the computer and transforming them into a usable form.

Output that can be understood by humans can be categorized as:

Hard Copy: Output such as paper that can be read immediately or stored and read later.

Soft Copy: Screen displayed output, which cannot be saved.

Computer Software

Software is a program which cannot be seen but tell the computer what results to produce and a program is a set of instructions given to the computer to perform a certain task. There are two main types of software, namely:

(i) Application Software and **(ii) System Software**

System Software

The software used to operate and maintain a computer system and also used by a programmer to develop application software is known as **System Software**. It is written in a language which handles the computer hardware directly, whereas the application software works through the system software.

The Operating Systems like DOS, Windows fall into this category. Their job is not only to run the system but also to maintain it. Every comptuter system must have system software to make it work, without system software a computer cannot work.

Operating System (OS)

An operating system (OS) is a set of computer programs that manage the hardware and software resources of a computer. It processes raw data which is given to the computer as input. It then allocates and manages the tasks of the internal system resources of the computer. It is the operating system which performs basic tasks such as controlling and allocating memory, prioritizing system requests, controlling input and output devices, facilitating networking and managing file systems.

Most operating systems come with an application that provides an interface to the operating system managed resources. These applications have had command line interpreters as a basic user interface, but more recently have been implemented as a Graphical User Interface (GUI) for ease of operation.

Operating Environments and shells

These are software programs that run top of the operating system and acts as homogenous user-interface between the applications and the operating system. They provide more facilities for input/output then the operating system. For example, Microsoft Windows on DOS, X-Windows for Unix, etc.

Device Drivers

These are special programs to extend the capabilities of operating system in order to support more Input/Output devices like Mouse, Tape drives, etc.

Disk Directory and File Management Utilities

These are utility programs generated to manage data. These programs provide a good user-interface to ease the process of maintaining the files, directories and other system related settings.

Application Software

The computer does different type of jobs and for these different jobs, different applications are used. Each application needs to have its own set of programs and these programs combine together to form an Application Software. For example railway-ticketing, telephone-bill printing, salary and wages calculation, etc.

Application Software are of two types: **Ready Made Software** (Pre written application packages) and **Customized Software** (User written application packages).

User written application packages

User writing application packages are those that are designed and coded by the users of the package for their own use. For example, Payroll program, and Inventory control program for specific organization, etc.

Pre written application packages

Pre-written application packages are those packages that have been written by another person or group and made available to computer users. The following have been the most popular of these packages.

Word Processor

Word processor allows you to play with words. You can create documents, edit them, decorate them, add tables, graphs, pictures to them, etc., using a word processing program. Popular word processing programs are: Microsoft Word, Wordstar, WordPerfect, etc.

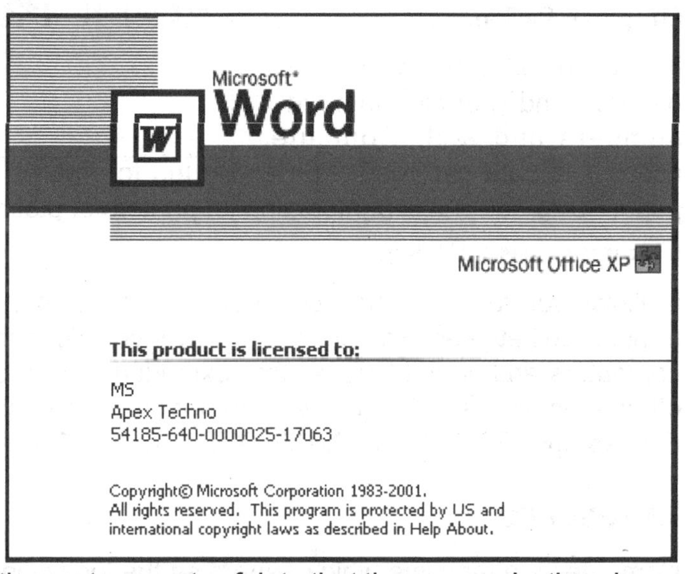

Data Manager

It stores, organizes, manipulates, retrieves, displays and prints data. Data Managers are important to Corporations and Central/State Governments as they keep track of the vast amounts of data that these organizations have to gather and store. Common among them are:

Database Management System (DBMS): A database is an integrated collection of well defined data and information, centrally controlled in all its aspects, created and stored in a typical structure for an organisation. In an organisation, the database could be, one or more, depending upon the needs and the operations of the organisation. The data structure and its storage should be such that it facilitates shareability, availability, evolvability and integrity of the data. The database separates a design of the information system from the data design and its management.

Relational Database Management System (RDBMS): A relational database management system (RDBMS), such as Access, stores data in related tables. For instance, a table containing employee data (names and addresses) may be related to a table containing payroll data (pay date, pay amount, and cheque number). Queries allow the user to ask complex questions (such as "What is the sum of all paychecks issued to Amitabh Bachchan in 2007") from these related tables, with the answers displayed as on-screen forms and printed reports.

Electronic Spreadsheet

A spreadsheet is a matrix of rows and columns. These columns and rows are used for entering text and numbers, which can then be used for calculations. An ideal software for accounting purposes and is very widely used for creating balance sheet, etc.

Graphics Packages

These are used for working with pictures and graphics instead of numbers and text. Computer-accessible data can readily be converted to graphic form on the screen as well as on paper using dot-matrix printers, ink-jet printers or plotters.

Communication Packages

It allows you to send and receive data over communication lines. The data/text can be transferred between two points, or it may involve communication through out a network of computers and work stations. Text extended at one office can be sent electronically to other sites. Users at these sites can retrieve and examine the text at their convenience. For example, PC-TALK, NICMAIL, Xpad, Radix, XTALK, etc.

Liveware

Computer is a machine which generates the logical information after processing the raw data. But, above all it is the human which controls the whole process. Unless a human instruction is given, a computer cannot do anything. It cannot accept input, generate output without human intervention or programming. Thus, we say that the most important part of the computer is Liveware, i.e., the human being.

What computers cannot do

Though we have read earlier that computer can do most of the things, but, it cannot do everything. Few of the things which it cannot do are:

1. They need to be programmed for running.

2. They don't know how to program themselves.
3. They cannot interpret the outputs.
4. They cannot take any decisions.
5. They cannot decided what input to take.

The Need for Computer Literacy

There was a time when students wanted to learn computers, just to get jobs in US. Slowly it changed and computers became the IN thing. Everybody wanted to learn computers. Since, computers were used everywhere, a computer literate was finding it easier to get the job. While on other hand, girls, who were not planning to take up jobs, wanted to add an extra qualifications in their matrimonial status. But, all this has changed now. The jobs are plenty in India only. Computer knowledge has become the basic information need. Most of the graduate and post-graduate syllabus have computer related course.

What is it enough? No. The computer knowledge has to be given at basic level, i.e., Schools. I do not say that computers are not taught at schools. But, whatever is taught is not enough. It is still treated as an elective subject. Moreover, there is dearth of good computer teachers around. All schools want a good teacher first, i.e., they should have a B.Ed degree, even if they do not have MCA. Good teachers cannot teach good computers. Teachers who are good at computers, take up computer related jobs, like, software development, which is more attractive.

To make the computer education reach the masses, somebody has to devise a method to make the computer education, more user friendly. In fact, everyone from publisher to school to teacher to student, everyone should have a say in the development of this method. Only then it will succeed.

Computer Limitations

Despite being the most powerful machine available to us these days, the computer still has its own limitations. Some it does perform abnormally, due to some reasons or others which may be baffling to the users. To ensure that the computers work normally, we have to see that the following are taken care of:

Programs must be Reliable

The most common problems faced by computers come from the use of faulty software. These are the software which are usually called the Pirated software. One person buys the original software and makes copies of them for others to use. It is possible that while copying something or the other is missed and you would not know about it immediately. Most of the popular computer software are subjected to the vigorous tests before releasing in public. It can be possible that a particular eventuality is not taken care of and that occurs for some unknown reason. This can give problem.

Application Logic must be Understood

Computer works on logic, if your logic is wrong, it will give bad results. It is like chess, where making a move you have to mentally sit on the opposite side and think of all the possible moves, before making your own move. Similarly, a program has to look into all the possible situations.

Uses and Impact of Computers

There are lots of uses of computers. In fact, in our everyday life it is used in almost every step. Some of the places where it is used is listed below.

Business and Industry: For most of the companies, all the work relating to accounts is now done on computers, for accuracy and speediness. You can even have your correspondence on it. Computers are finding their place in automizing the production process too.

Health care: Lots of research in medicine is done using computers. Doctors now a days can see the complete inside of the human beings using the computers, which results in no fault operations.

Education: Computers can help in teaching too. In fact this books on computers was created using computers. Most of the schools now use computers for accounting, students record management, papers preparation and even results compilation.

Humanities: In recent years, computer usage has increased in people having interests in history, literature, music, graphics, arts and other branches of humanities.They use it to:

- ease manuscript preparation
- translate texts from one natural language to another
- conduct studies that would otherwise be impractical
- apply artistic talents to a new medium, and
- discover significant stylistic patterns in text.

Science and Technology: All the movements of the satellites are controlled using computers. Using computers and satellites you can predict the weather for the next few days. In fact, the biggest computer in India is with the Meteorological Department of India, at New Delhi.

Recreation and Entertainment: There are various programs available in computers which allow you to create animations. By learning about them you can become an expert animator. You may even make a movie of your own. Computers are used in cinema halls too, for tickets printing and seat allocation.

Government: America has used the computers in defence for the fullest with pin pointing the position of enemy targets. Most of the missiles these days are computer controlled. Government uses it planning and other information too.

Section 2
Hardware

This section includes information about the following:

- Mouse
- Scaners
- Keyboard
- Monitors
- Printers
- Optical Media
- Hard Disk Drives
- Floppy Disk Drives
- Processor
- Motherboard
- Power Supplies
- BIOS
- Beep Codes
- Buses and Memory
- I/O Interfaces
- Computer Installation
- New Computer Devices
- Data Recovery and BIOS Updating

2 Mouse

Introduction

In computing, a mouse functions as a pointing device by detecting two-dimensional motion relative to its supporting surface. Physically, a mouse consists of a small case, held under one of the user's hands, with one or more buttons. It sometimes features other elements, such as "wheels", which allow the user to perform various system-dependent operations, or extra buttons or features can add more control or dimensional input. The mouse's motion typically translates into the motion of a pointer on a display.

The name mouse, coined at the Stanford Research Institute, derives from the resemblance of early models (which had a cord attached to the rear part of the device, suggesting the idea of a tail) to the common mouse.

The first marketed integrated mouse — shipped as a part of a computer and intended for personal computer navigation — came with the Xerox 8010 Star Information System in 1981.

Mechanical Mice

Operating a mechanical mouse.

1: Moving the mouse turns the ball.

2: X and Y rollers grip the ball and transfer movement.

3: Optical encoding disks include light holes.

4: Infrared LEDs shine through the disks.

5: Sensors gather light pulses to convert to X and Y velocities.

Bill English, builder of Engelbart's original mouse, invented the so-called ball mouse in 1972 while working for Xerox PARC. The ball-mouse replaced the external wheels with a single ball that could rotate in any direction. It came as part of the hardware package of the Xerox Alto computer. Perpendicular chopper wheels housed inside the mouse's body chopped beams of light on the way to light sensors, thus detecting in their turn the motion of the ball. This variant of the mouse resembled an inverted trackball and became the predominant form used with personal computers throughout the 1980s and 1990s. The Xerox PARC group also settled on the modern technique of using both hands to type on a full-size keyboard and grabbing the mouse when required.

The ball mouse utilizes two rollers rolling against two sides of the ball. One roller detects the horizontal motion of the mouse and other the vertical motion. The motion of these two rollers causes two disc-like encoder wheels to rotate, interrupting optical beams to generate electrical signals. The mouse sends these signals to the computer system by means of connecting wires. The driver software in the system converts the signals into motion of the mouse pointer along X and Y axes on the screen.

Ball mice and wheel mice were manufactured for Xerox by Jack Hawley, doing business as The Mouse House in Berkeley, California, starting in 1975.

Based on another invention by Jack Hawley, proprietor of the Mouse House, Honeywell produced another type of mechanical mouse. Instead of a ball, it had two wheels rotating at off axes. Keytronic later produced a similar product.

Modern computer mice took form at the École polytechnique fédérale de Lausanne (EPFL) under the inspiration of Professor Jean-Daniel Nicoud and at the hands of engineer and watchmaker André Guignard. This new design incorporated a single hard rubber mouseball and three buttons, and remained a common design until the mainstream adoption of the scroll-wheel mouse during the 1990s.

Another type of mechanical mouse, the “analog mouse” (now generally regarded as obsolete), uses potentiometers rather than encoder wheels, and is typically designed to be plug-compatible with an analog joystick. The “Color Mouse,” originally marketed by Radio Shack for their Color Computer (but also usable on MS-DOS machines equipped with analog joystick ports, provided the software accepted joystick input) was the best-known example.

Optical Mice

An optical mouse uses a light-emitting diode and photodiodes to detect movement relative to the underlying surface, rather than moving some of its parts — as in a mechanical mouse.

Early Optical Mice

Early optical mice, circa 1980, came in two different varieties:

Some, such as those invented by Steve Kirsch of Mouse Systems Corporation, used an infrared LED and a four-quadrant infrared sensor to detect grid lines printed with infrared absorbing ink on a special metallic surface. Predictive algorithms in the CPU of the mouse calculated the speed and direction over the grid.

Others, invented by Richard F. Lyon and sold by Xerox, used a 16-pixel visible-light image sensor with integrated motion detection on the same chip and tracked the motion of light dots in a dark field of a printed paper or similar mouse pad. These two mouse types had very different behaviors, as the Kirsch mouse used an x-y coordinate system embedded in the pad, and would not work correctly when the pad was rotated, while the Lyon mouse used the x-y coordinate system of the mouse body, as mechanical mice do.

Modern Optical Mice

Modern surface-independent optical mice work by using an optoelectronic sensor to take successive pictures of the surface on which the mouse operates. As computing power grew cheaper, it became possible to embed more powerful special-purpose image-processing chips in the mouse itself. This advance enabled the mouse to detect relative motion on a wide variety of surfaces, translating the movement of the mouse into the movement of the pointer and eliminating the need for a special mouse-pad.

This advance paved the way for widespread adoption of optical mice. Optical mice illuminate the surface that they track over, using an LED or a laser diode. Changes between one frame and the next are processed by the image processing part of the chip and translated into movement on the two axes using an optical flow estimation algorithm. For example, the Avago Technologies ADNS-2610 optical mouse sensor processes 1512 frames per second: each frame consisting of a rectangular array of 18×18 pixels, and each pixel can sense 64 different levels of gray.

Laser Mice

The laser mouse uses an infrared laser diode instead of an LED to illuminate the surface beneath their sensor. As early as 1998, Sun Microsystems provided a laser mouse with their Sun SPARCstation servers and workstations. However, laser mice did not enter the mainstream market until 2004, when Logitech, in partnership with Agilent Technologies, introduced its MX 1000 laser mouse. This mouse uses a small infrared laser instead of an LED and has significantly increased the resolution of the image taken by the mouse. The laser enables around 20 times more surface tracking power to the surface features used for navigation compared to conventional optical mice, via interference effects. While the implementation of a laser slightly increases sensitivity and resolution, the main advantage comes from power usage.

Power-saving in Optical Mice

Manufacturers often engineer their optical mice — especially battery-powered wireless models — to save power when possible. In order to do this, the mouse blinks the laser or LED when in standby-mode (Each mouse has a different standby time). This function may also increase the laser / LED life. Mice designed specifically for gamers, such as the Logitech G5 or the Razer Copperhead, often lack this feature in an attempt to reduce latency and to improve responsiveness.

Optical versus Mechanical Mice

The Logitech iFeel optical mouse uses a red LED to project light onto the tracking surface.

Unlike mechanical mice, which can become clogged with lint, optical mice have no rolling parts; therefore, they do not require maintenance other than removing debris that might collect under the light emitter. However, they generally cannot track on glossy and transparent surfaces, including some mouse-pads, sometimes causing the cursor to drift unpredictably during operation. Mice with less image-processing power also have problems tracking fast movement, though high-end mice can track at 2 m/s (80 inches per second) and faster.

Some models of laser mice can track on glossy and transparent surfaces, and have a much higher sensitivity than either their mechanical or optical counterparts. Such models of laser mice cost more than LED based or mechanical mice.

As of 2006, mechanical mice have lower average power demands than their optical counterparts. This typically has no practical impact for users of cabled mice (except possibly those used with battery-powered computers, such as notebook models), but has an impact on battery-powered wireless models.

Optical models will outperform mechanical mice on uneven, slick, soft, sticky, or loose surfaces, and generally in mobile situations lacking mouse pads. Because optical mice render movement based on an image which the LED illuminates, use with multi-colored mouse pads may result in unreliable performance; however, laser mice do not suffer these problems and will track on such surfaces. The advent of affordable high-speed, low-resolution cameras and the integrated logic in optical mice provides an ideal laboratory for experimentation on next-generation input-devices. Experimenters can obtain low-cost components simply by taking apart a working mouse and changing the optics or by writing new software.

Inertial Mice

Inertial mice use a tuning fork or other accelerometer (US Patent 4787051) to detect movement for every axis supported. Usually cordless, they often have a switch to deactivate the movement circuitry between use, allowing the user freedom of movement without affecting the pointer position. A patent for an inertial mouse claims that such mice consume less power than optically based mice, and offer increased sensitivity, reduced weight and increased ease-of-use.

3D Mice

Also known as flying mice, bats, or wands, these devices generally function through ultrasound. Probably the best known example would be 3DConnexion/Logitech's SpaceMouse from the early 1990s.

In the late 1990s Kantek introduced the 3D RingMouse. This wireless mouse was worn on a ring around a finger, which enabled the thumb to access three buttons. The mouse was tracked in three dimensions by a base station. Despite a certain appeal, it was finally discontinued because it did not provide sufficient resolution.

A recent consumer 3D pointing device is the Wii Remote. While primarily a motion-sensing device (that is, it can determine its orientation and direction of movement), Wii Remote can also detect its spatial position by comparing the distance and position of the lights from the

IR emitter using its integrated IR camera (since the nunchuk lacks a camera, it can only tell its current heading and orientation). The obvious drawback to this approach is that it can only produce spatial coordinates while its camera can see the sensor bar.

Double Mouse

Double mouse allow for two mice to be used by both hands as input devices such as when operating various graphics and multimedia applications.

How to Use the Mouse

There are three simple techniques — clicking, double-clicking and dragging

Clicking

To click on something with the mouse means to move the pointer or cursor to the item on the screen and to press the release the mouse button once.

Double-Clicking

Press and release the mouse button twice in rapid succession.

Dragging

After positioning the mouse pointer over the item, then depress the button and hold it down as you move the mouse.

How Mouse Works

A mouse has a ball inside of it that extends just below the housing of thc mouse itself. When you slide the mouse around on a flat surface such as a desktop or mouse pad the ball rolls. Movement of the mouse result in a corresponding movement of the pointer on the screen.

On two sides of the ball at 90 angle each other are two small rollers or wheels that spin to match the speed of the ball. Sensors detect how much each roller spins and send this information to the computer in the form of changes to the current pointer position.

Like the keyboard, a mouse does not actually send a message directly to the program that

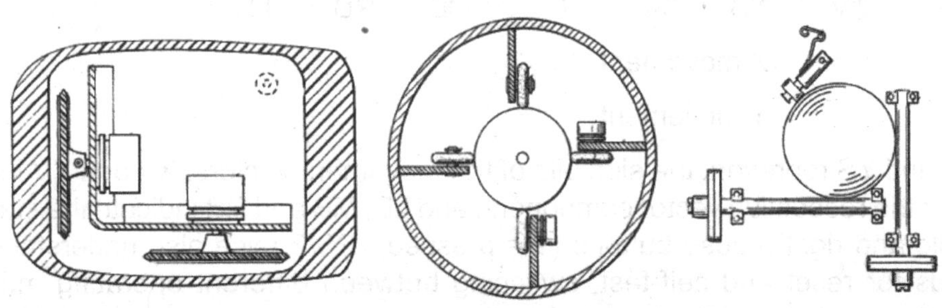

Mouse Diagram

the computer is running. Rather it sends an interrupt request to the CPU. The program that is running checks regularly to see whether a mouse event has occurred or not.

Connectivity and Communication Protocols

To transmit their input, typical cabled mice use a thin electrical cord terminating in a standard connector, such as RS-232C, PS/2, ADB or USB. Cordless mice instead transmit data via infrared radiation (see IrDA) or radio (including Bluetooth or WiFi), although many such cordless interfaces are themselves connected through the aforementioned wired serial buses.

While the electrical interface and the format of the data transmitted by commonly available mice is currently standardized on USB, in the past it varied between different manufacturers. A bus mouse used a dedicated interface card for connection to an IBM PC or compatible computer.

Serial Interface and Protocol

Standard PC mice once used the RS-232C serial port via a D-subminiature connector, which provided power to run the mouse's circuits as well as data on mouse movements. The Mouse Systems Corporation version used a five-byte protocol and supported three buttons. The Microsoft version used an incompatible three-byte protocol and only allowed for two buttons. Due to the incompatibility, some manufacturers sold serial mice with a mode switch: "PC" for MSC mode, "MS" for Microsoft mode.

PS/2 Interface and Protocol

With the arrival of the IBM PS/2 personal-computer series in 1987, IBM introduced the eponymous PS/2 interface for mice and keyboards, which other manufacturers rapidly adopted. The most visible change was the use of a round 6-pin mini-DIN, in lieu of the former 5-pin connector. In default mode (called stream mode) a PS/2 mouse communicates motion, and the state of each button, by means of 3-byte packets.[28] For any motion, button press or button release event, a PS/2 mouse sends, over a bi-directional serial port, a sequence of three bytes, with the following format:

	Bit 7	Bit 6	Bit 5	Bit 4	Bit 3	Bit 2	Bit 1	Bit 0
Byte 1	YV	XV	YS	XS	1	MB	RB	LB
Byte 2			X movement					
Byte 3			Y movement					

Here, XS and YS represent the sign bits of the movement vectors, XV and YV indicate an overflow in the respective vector component, and LB, MB and RB indicate the status of the left, middle and right mouse buttons (1 = pressed). PS/2 mice also understand several commands for reset and self-test, switching between different operating modes, and changing the resolution of the reported motion vectors.

Extensions: IntelliMouse and others

A Microsoft IntelliMouse relies on an extension of the PS/2 protocol: the ImPS/2 or IMPS/2 protocol (the abbreviation combines the concepts of "IntelliMouse" and "PS/2"). It initially operates in standard PS/2 format, for backwards compatibility. After the host sends a special command sequence, it switches to an extended format in which a fourth byte carries information about wheel movements. The IntelliMouse Explorer works analogously, with the difference that its 4-byte packets also allow for two additional buttons (for a total of five).

The Typhoon mouse uses 6-byte packets which can appear as a sequence of two standard 3-byte packets, such that ordinary PS/2 driver can handle them.

Mouse-vendors also use other extended formats, often without providing public documentation.

For 3D or 6DOF input, vendors have made many extensions both to the hardware and to software. In the late 90's Logitech created ultrasound based tracking which gave 3D input to a few millimeters accuracy, which worked well as an input device but failed as a money making product.

Advantages and Disadvantages of Mouse

Advantages

1. It is simple device and very easy to use.
2. It is not that very expensive.
3. It moves the cursor faster than the arrow keys of keyboard do.

Drawbacks of a Mouse

1. The movement of the cursor is not very sensitive to movement of mouse.
2. If the contact between wheels and mouse pad is lost, the cursor does not move.
3. It is not useful in word-processing or in computer programming applications.
4. It requires space on tabletop or other hard surface to roll.
5. It requires serial port for connection with computer system.

A recent development in the wireless mouse or remote mouse, which works on transmission of infrared or radio waves.

Installing Mouse

A mouse connects to one of the serial ports, such as COM1 or COM2 on your computer. This is one of the most simple and commonly used mouse.

To replace or to install a serial mouse, perform these steps.

- First of all check if you have a spare serial port for the mouse. If you do not have a spare serial port, then you need to first install a serial interface board or a multi I/O board into your computer.

If you have a spare serial port or if you are replacing an already available serial mouse then perform the following steps:

- Power off the PC's main system unit.
- Remove the existing mouse by removing the mouse from the serial port.
- Select the new serial port into which you want to install a new mouse, connect the new mouse into the port. Sometime you may require 9 to 25 pin or 25 to 9 pin converter to connect the mouse to the available serial port.
- Power on your system, update your mouse driver and other software as necessary. Test the mouse.

Buttons

In contrast to the motion-sensing mechanism, the mouse's buttons have changed little over the years, varying mostly in shape, number, and placement. Engelbart's very first mouse had a single button; Xerox PARC soon designed a three-button model, but reduced the count to two for Xerox products. After experimenting with 4-button prototypes Apple reduced it back to one button with the Macintosh in 1984, while Unix workstations from Sun and others used three buttons. OEM bundled mice usually have between one and three buttons, although in the aftermarket many mice have always had five or more.

The three-button scrollmouse has become the most commonly available design. As of 2007 (and roughly since the late 1990s), users most commonly employ the second button to invoke a contextual menu in the computer's software user interface, which contains options specifically tailored to the interface element over which the mouse pointer currently sits. By default, the primary mouse button sits located on the left-hand side of the mouse, for the benefit of right-handed users; left-handed users can usually reverse this configuration via software.

On systems with three-button mice, pressing the center button (a middle click) typically opens a system-wide noncontextual menu. In the X Window System, middle-clicking by default pastes the contents of the primary buffer at the pointer's position. Many users of two-button mice emulate a three-button mouse by clicking both the right and left buttons simultaneously.

Additional buttons

Aftermarket manufacturers have long built mice with five or more buttons. Depending on the user's preferences and software environment, the extra buttons may allow forward and backward web-navigation, scrolling through a browser's history, or other functions, including mouse related functions like quick-changing the mouse's resolution/sensitivity. As with similar features in keyboards, however, not all software supports these functions.

The additional buttons become especially useful in computer games, where quick and easy access to a wide variety of functions (for example, weapon-switching in first-person shooters) can give a player an advantage. Because software can map mouse-buttons to virtually any function, keystroke, application or switch, extra buttons can make working with such a mouse more efficient and easier.

In the matter of the number of buttons, Douglas Engelbart favored the view “as many as possible”. The prototype that popularised the idea of three buttons as standard had that number only because “we could not find anywhere to fit any more switches”.

Wheels

The scroll wheel, a notably different form of mouse-button, consists of a small wheel that the user can rotate to provide immediate one-dimensional input. Usually, this input translates into “scrolling” up or down within the active window or GUI-element . The scroll wheel can provide convenience, especially when navigating a long document. The scroll wheel nearly always includes a third (center) button. Under many Microsoft Windows applications, appropriate pressure on the wheel activates autoscrolling, and in conjunction with the control key (Ctrl) may give the capability of zooming in and out; applications that support this feature include Adobe Reader, Microsoft Word, Internet Explorer, Opera, Mozilla Firefox and Mulberry. Some applications also allow the user to scroll left and right by pressing the shift key while using the mouse wheel.

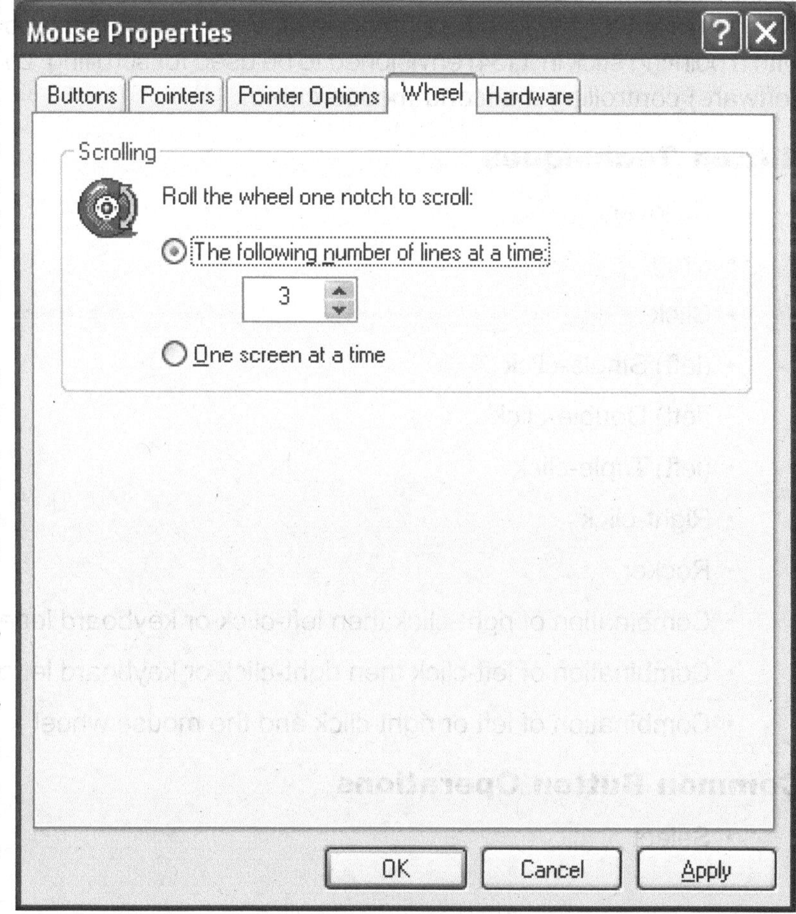

Note that scrollwheels almost always function more as two switches, rotating only in discrete “clicks” rather than actually acting as a third analog axis.

Manufacturers may refer to scroll-wheels by different names for branding purposes; Genius, for example, usually brand their scroll-wheel-equipped products “Netscroll”.

Mouse Systems introduced the scroll-wheel commercially in 1995, marketing it as the Mouse Systems ProAgio and Genius EasyScroll. However, mainstream adoption of the scroll wheel mouse did not occur until Microsoft released the Microsoft IntelliMouse in 1996. It became a commercial success in 1997 when their Microsoft Office application suite and their Internet Explorer browser started supporting its wheel-scrolling feature. Since then the scroll wheel has become a standard feature of many mouse models.

Some mouse models have two wheels, separately assigned to horizontal and vertical scrolling. Designs exist which make use of a "rocker" button instead of a wheel — a pivoting button that a user can press at the top or bottom, simulating "up" and "down" respectively. A peculiar early example was a mouse by Saitek which had a joystick-style hatswitch on it.

A more recent form of mouse wheel is the tilt-wheel. Tilt wheels are essentially conventional mouse wheels that have been modified with a pair of sensors articulated to the tilting mechanism. These sensors are mapped, by default, to horizontal scrolling.

A third variety of built-in scrolling device, the scroll ball, essentially consists of a trackball embedded in the upper surface of the mouse. The user can scroll in all possible directions in very much the same way as with the actual mouse, and in some mice, can use it as a trackball. Mice featuring a scroll ball include Apple's Mighty Mouse and the IOGEAR 4D Web Cruiser Optical Scroll Ball Mouse. IBM's ergonomics laboratory designed a mouse with a pointing stick in it,[34] envisioned to be used for scrolling, zooming or (with appropriate software) controlling a second mouse cursor.

Button Techniques

- Rollover
- Drag
- Click
- (left) Single-click
- (left) Double-click
- (left) Triple-click
- Right-click
- Rocker
- Combination of right-click then left-click or keyboard letter
- Combination of left-click then right-click or keyboard letter
- Combination of left or right-click and the mouse wheel

Common Button Operations

- Select

- Launch an application
- Display a menu
  - Drag and drop
  - Cut/copy to the clipboard
  - Paste from the clipboard

Mouse Speed

The computer industry often measures mouse sensitivity in terms of counts per inch (CPI), commonly expressed less correctly as dots per inch (DPI) — the number of steps the mouse will report when it moves one inch. In early mice, this specification was called pulses per inch (ppi). If the default mouse-tracking condition involves moving the pointer by one screen-pixel or dot on-screen per reported step, then the CPI does equate to DPI: dots of pointer motion per inch of mouse motion. The CPI or DPI as reported by manufacturers depends on how they make the mouse; the higher the CPI, the faster the pointer moves with mouse movement. However, software can adjust the mouse sensitivity, making the cursor move faster or slower than its DPI. Current software can *change the speed of the* pointer dynamically, taking into account the mouse's absolute speed and the movement from the last stop-point. Different software may name the settings "acceleration" or "speed" — referring respectively to "threshold" and "pointer precision".

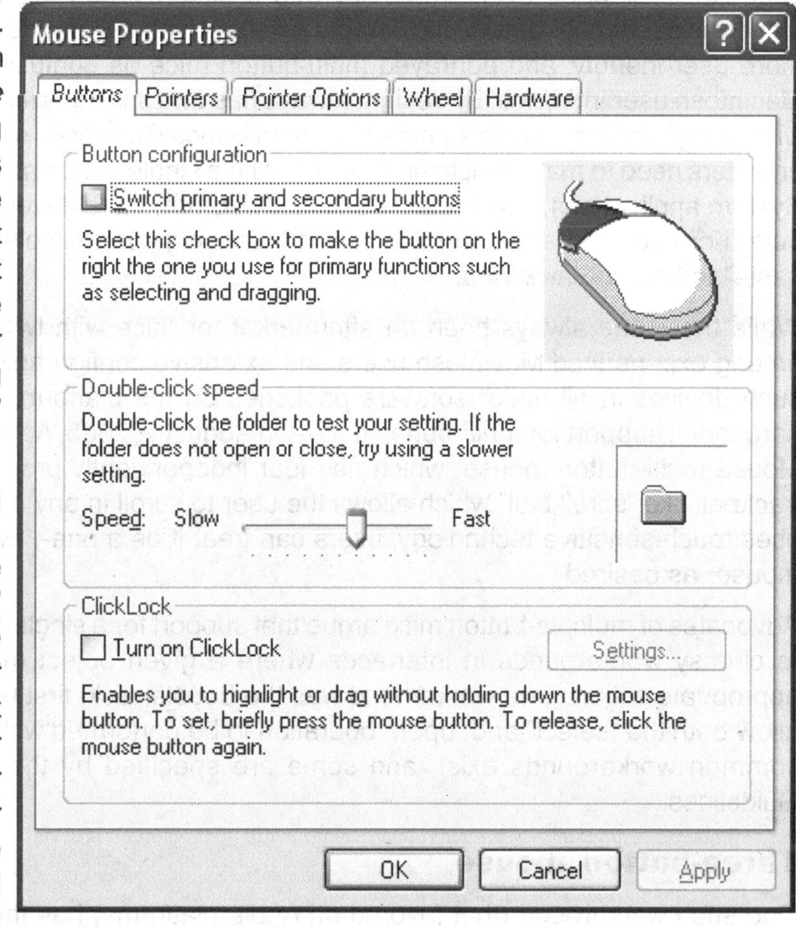

For simple software, when the mouse starts to move, the software will count the number of "counts" received from the mouse and will move the pointer across the screen by that number of pixels (or multiplied by a factor f1=1,2,3). So, the pointer will move slowly on the screen, having a good precision. When the movement of the mouse reaches the value set for "threshold", the software will start to move the pointer more quickly; thus for each number n of counts received from the mouse, the pointer may move (f2 x n) pixels, where f2=2,3...10. Usually, the user can set the value of f2 by changing the "acceleration" setting.

Operating systems sometimes apply acceleration, referred to as "ballistics", to the motion reported by the mouse. For example, versions of Windows prior to Windows XP doubled reported values above a configurable threshold, and then optionally doubled them again above a second configurable threshold. These doublings applied separately in the X and Y directions, resulting in very nonlinear response. For example one can see how the things work in Microsoft Windows NT. Starting with Windows XP OS version of Microsoft and many OS versions for Apple Macintosh, computers use a smoother ballistics calculation that compensates for screen-resolution and has better linearity.

One, Two or Three Buttons?

The issue of whether pack-in bundled mice "should" have exactly one button or more than one has attracted an enormous amount of controversy. From the first Macintosh until late 2005 Apple shipped every computer with a single-button mouse, whereas most other platforms used multi-button mice. Apple and its advocates promoted single-button mice as more user-friendly, and portrayed multi-button mice as confusing for novice users. The Macintosh user interface, by design, always has and still does make all functions available with a single-button mouse. Apple's Human Interface Guidelines still specify that all software-providers need to make functions available with a single button mouse. However, X Window System applications, which Mac OS X can also run, have developed with the use of two-button or even three-button mice in mind, causing even simple operations like "cut and paste" to become awkward.

While there has always been an aftermarket for mice with two, three, or more buttons among experienced Macintosh users and extensive configurable support to complement such devices in all major software packages on the platform, Mac OS X shipped with hardcoded support for multi-button mice. On August 2, 2005, Apple introduced their Mighty Mouse multi-button mouse, which has four independently-programmable buttons and a trackball-like "scroll ball" which allows the user to scroll in any direction. Since the mouse uses touch-sensitive technology, users can treat it as a one-, two-, three-, or four-button mouse, as desired.

Advocates of multiple-button mice argue that support for a single-button mouse often leads to clumsy workarounds in interfaces where a given object may have more than one appropriate action. One workaround was the double click, first used on the Apple Lisa, to allow both the "select" and "open" operation to be performed with a single button. Several common workarounds exist, and some are specified by the Apple Human Interface Guidelines.

Three-button mouse

One such workaround (that favored on Apple platforms) has the user hold down one or more keys on the keyboard before pressing the mouse button (typically control on a Macintosh for contextual menus). This has the disadvantage that it requires that both the user's hands be engaged. It also requires that the user perform actions on completely separate devices in concert; that is, holding a key on the keyboard while pressing a button on the mouse. This can be a difficult task for a disabled user, although can be remedied by allowing keys to stick so that they do not need to be pressed down.

Another involves the press-and-hold technique. In a press-and-hold, the user presses and holds the single button. After a certain period, software perceives the button press not as a single click but as a separate action. This has two drawbacks: first, a slow user may press-and-hold inadvertently. Second, the user must wait for the software to detect the click as a press-and-hold, otherwise the system might interpret the button-depression as a single click. Furthermore, the remedies for these two drawbacks conflict with each other: the longer the lag time, the more the user must wait; and the shorter the lag time, the more likely it becomes that some user will accidentally press-and-hold when meaning to click. Studies have found all of the above workarounds less usable than additional mouse buttons for experienced users.

Most machines running Unix or a Unix-like operating system run the X Window System which almost always encourages a three-button mouse. X numbers the buttons by convention. This allows user instructions to apply to mice or pointing devices that do not use conventional button placement. For example, a left handed user may reverse the buttons, usually with a software setting. With non-conventional button placement, user directions that say "left mouse button" or "right mouse button" are confusing. The ground-breaking Xerox Parc Alto and Dorado computers from the mid-1970s used three-button mice, and each button was assigned a color. Red was used for the left (or primary) button, yellow for the middle (secondary), and blue for the right (meta or tertiary). This naming convention lives on in some SmallTalk environments, such as Squeak, and can be less confusing than the right, middle and left designations.

Acorn's RISC OS based computers necessarily use all three mouse buttons throughout their WIMP based GUI. RISC OS refers to the three buttons (from left to right) as Select, Menu and Adjust. Select functions in the same way as the "Primary" mouse button in other operating systems. Menu will bring up a context-sensitive menu appropriate for the position of the mouse pointer, and this often provides the only means of activating this menu. This menu in most applications equates to the "Application Menu" found at the top of the screen in Mac OS, and underneath the window title under Microsoft Windows. Adjust serves for selecting multiple items in the "Filer" desktop, and for altering parameters of objects within applications — although its exact function usually depends on the programmer.

Troubleshooting Mouse

If you experience problems with your mouse, the problem could be because of the mouse, mouse driver software, the application software you are using, cables or the main system itself. So, before you throw away your mouse, try the following troubleshooting techniques:

- Make sure the mouse cable is correctly connected to its port.
- Turn your PC's system unit power off and back on and see if the error disappears.
- If you have a second mouse available, turn off your PC's power and connect the new mouse. Power the PC back on to see if the error disappears.
- Try the mouse on some other system where a mouse of the same type is working without any trouble.
- Some software do not support mouse. Try mouse with a program that is known to support the mouse.
- Make sure the mouse device driver being used is correct one and is setup correctly.
- If the mouse is a serial mouse, try using a second serial port. You might need to update the mouse device driver to use the second serial port.
- If you are using a bus mouse, make sure that the mouse adapter card is properly seated in its expansion slot.

3 Scanner

Image and Text Scanner

In computing, a scanner is a device that analyzes images, printed text, or handwriting, or an object (such as an ornament) and converts it to a digital image. Most scanners today are variations of the desktop (or flatbed) scanner. The flatbed scanner is the most common in offices. Hand-held scanners, where the device is moved by hand, were briefly popular but are now not used due to the difficulty of obtaining a high-quality image. Both these types of scanners use charge-coupled device (CCD) or Contact Image Sensor (CIS) as the image sensor, whereas older drum scanners use a photomultiplier tube as the image sensor.

Another category of scanner is a rotary scanner, used for high-speed document scanning. This is another kind of drum scanner, but it uses a CCD array instead of a photomultiplier.

Other types of scanners are planetary scanners, which take photographs of books and documents, and 3D scanners, for producing three-dimensional models of objects, but these types of scanner are considerably more expensive than other types of scanners.

Another category of scanner are digital camera scanners, which are based on the concept of reprographic cameras. Due to increasing resolution and new features such as anti-shakc, digital cameras have become an attractive alternative to regular scanners. While still containing disadvantages compared to traditional scanners, digital cameras offer unmatched advantages in speed and portability.

Types

There are different types of scanners, depending on the user's purposes. Described below are the most commonly used types that can be found in the market:

Drum

Drum scanners capture image information with photomultiplier tubes (PMT), rather than the charge-coupled-device (CCD) arrays found in flatbed scanners and inexpensive film scanners. Reflective and transmissive originals are mounted on an acrylic cylinder, the scanner drum, which rotates at high speed while it passes the object being scanned in front of precision optics that deliver image information to the PMTs.

Most modern color drum scanners use 3 matched PMTs, which read red, blue, and green light respectively. Light from the original artwork is split into separate red, blue, and green beams in the optical bench of the scanner. The drum scanner gets its name from the large glass drum on which the original artwork is mounted for scanning: they usually take11"x17" documents, but maximum size varies by manufacturer. One of the unique features of drum scanners is the ability to control sample area and aperture size independently. The sample size is the area that the scanner encoder reads to create an individual pixel. The aperture is the actual opening that allows light into the optical bench of the scanner. The ability to control aperture and sample size separately is particularly useful for smoothing film grain when scanning black-and white and color negative originals.

While drum scanners are capable of scanning both reflective and transmissive artwork, a good-quality flatbed scanner can produce excellent scans from reflective artwork. As a result, drum scanners are rarely used to scan prints now that high quality inexpensive flatbed scanners are readily available. Film, however, is where drum scanners continue to be the tool of choice for high-end applications. Because film can be wet-mounted to the scanner drum and because of the exceptional sensitivity of the PMTs, drum scanners are capable of capturing very subtle details in film originals.

Currently only a few companies continue to manufacture drum scanners. While prices of both new and used units have come down over the last decade, they still require a considerable monetary investment when compared to CCD flatbed and film scanners. However, drum scanners remain in demand due to their capacity to produce scans that are superior in resolution, color gradation, and value structure. Also, since drum scanners are capable of resolutions up to 12,000 PPI, their use is generally recommended when a scanned image is going to be enlarged.

In most current graphic-arts operations, very-high-quality flatbed scanners have replaced drum scanners, being both less expensive and faster. However, drum scanners continue to be used in high-end applications, such as museum-quality archiving of photographs and print production of high-quality books and magazine advertisements. In addition, due to the greater availability of pre-owned units many fine-art photographers are acquiring drum scanners, which has created a new niche market for the machines.

The first image scanner ever developed was a drum scanner. It was built in 1957 at the US National Bureau of Standards by a team led by Russell Kirsch. The first image ever scanned on this machine was a 5 cm square photograph of Kirsch's then-three-month-old son, Walden. The black and white image had a resolution of 176 pixels on a side.

Flatbed

A flatbed scanner is usually composed of a glass pane (or platen), under which there is a bright light (often xenon or cold cathode fluorescent) which illuminates the pane, and a moving optical array, whether CCD or CIS. Color scanners typically contain three rows (arrays) of sensors with red, green, and blue filters. Images to be scanned are placed face down on the glass, an opaque cover is lowered over it to exclude ambient light, and the sensor array and light source move across the pane, reading the entire area. An image is therefore visible to the charge-coupled device only because of the light it reflects. Transparent images do not work in this way, and require special accessories that illuminate them from the upper side. Many scanners offer this as an option.

Film

"Slide" (positive) or negative film can be scanned in equipment specially manufactured for this purpose. Usually, uncut film strips of up to six frames, or four mounted slides, are inserted in a carrier, which is moved by a stepper motor across a lens and CCD sensor inside the scanner. Some models even have adaptors for APS film cassettes. Dedicated film scanners often offer better resolution than flatbed scanners, partly because they do not need to scan large areas.

Hand

Hand scanners are manual devices that are dragged across the surface of the image to be scanned. Scanning documents in this manner requires a steady hand, as an uneven scanning rate would produce distorted images - a little light on the scanner would indicate if the motion was too fast. They typically have a "start" button, which is held by the user for the duration of the scan; some switches to set the optical resolution; and a roller, which generates a clock pulse for synchronisation with the computer. Most hand scanners were monochrome, and produced light from an array of green LEDs to illuminate the image. A typical hand scanner also had a small window through which the document being scanned could be viewed. They were popular during the early 1990s and usually had a proprietary interface module specific to a particular type of computer, usually an Atari ST or Commodore Amiga.

Quality

Scanners typically read red-green-blue color (RGB) data from the array. This data is then processed with some proprietary algorithm to correct for different exposure conditions and sent to the computer, via the device's input/output interface (usually SCSI or LPT in machines pre-dating the USB standard). Color depth varies depending on the scanning array characteristics, but is usually at least 24 bits. High quality models have 48 bits or more color depth. The other qualifying parameter for a scanner is its resolution, measured in pixels per inch (ppi), sometimes more accurately referred to as samples per inch (spi). Instead of using the scanner's true optical resolution, the only meaningful parameter, manufacturers like to refer to the interpolated resolution, which is much higher thanks to software interpolation. As of 2004, a good flatbed scanner has an optical resolution of 1600–3200 ppi, high-end flatbed scanners can scan up to 5400 ppi, and a good drum scanner has an optical resolution of 8000–14,000 ppi.

Manufacturers often claim interpolated resolutions as high as 19,200 ppi; but such numbers carry little meaningful value, because the number of possible interpolated pixels is unlimited.

The higher the resolution, the larger the file. In most cases, there is a trade-off between manageable file size and level of detail. The third important parameter for a scanner is its density range. A high density range means that the scanner is able to reproduce shadow details and brightness details in one scan.

Colour Models

Colour models are closely related to bit depth. Greyscale goes up to 8-bit, which renders 256 shades. Colour images are multiples of 8-bit channels. RGB, the normal model for computer graphics, goes up to 24-bit (three 8-bit channels for red, green, and blue). CMYK, the standard for printing colour images, is a 32-bit model.

RGB Colour

Red, green and blue are the primary colours of light. The human eye responds to stimuli from varying RGB wavelengths and renders the appropriate signals to the brain so that we perceive such colours as cherry, mauve and beige. Most of the scanners use an RGB colour model for recording digital image data. RGB colours is called additive because colours throughout the spectrum are created by adding varying intensities of red, green, and blue light to black (no light). These intensities vary from 255 (full intensity) to 0. Each colour channel has 256 variations and their combinations allow creating a total of 16,777,216 colours. A combination of R:255 G:255 B:255 creates white, while R:0 G:0 B:0 is black (no light).

CMYK Colour

Cyan, magenta and yellow are the secondary colours of RGB and are opposites. When RGB light strikes an object, the amount of cyan, magenta and yellow in the object's pigmentation affects how much light is reflected back (it's the reflected light that we see). Cyan absorbs red light, magenta absorbs green light and yellow absorbs blue light. The degree of absorption depends on the amount of pigment or, in printing terms, the amount of CMY ink. This is why CMYK is considered subtractive; the colours displayed by CMYK are the result of subtracting varying amounts of red, green, and blue light.

In the example below, a printed object composed of 39% cyan, 47% magenta, 0% yellow and 1% black (which absorbs all light) would reflect back 60% red light, 52% green light, and 99% blue light.

Installing Scanner

To install a scanner follow the steps below:

(*i*) Parallel Port Scanner

1. Shutdown system.
2. Hook parallel connector to printer port of your computer. If you have a SCSI scanner, or USB simply hook into one of those ports.
3. Unlock scanner head. This is usually done underneath scanner of on sides by power switch.

4. Plug in power for scanner boot system up Windows will recognize new device and hardware manager will appear.

(*ii*) SCSI Scanner

1. If you have a SCSI scanner first cover installing the SCSI Adapter Card.
2. Make sure and refer to your adapters documentation for jumper settings. You will want to set the jumpers if any before we install the adapter.
3. Turn Off PC and unplug from outlet.
4. Remove case cover
5. Unscrew a slot on case for adapter card
6. Connect any necessary internal cables. (drives)
7. Align card with Bus slot and seat evenly. Be careful of any catching the cards ports on anything.
8. Tighten down card snug
9. Close case
10. Hook up power

(*iii*) USB Scanner

1. This one is very simple. You will simply plug in with computer running and install a driver for it.
2. Exit all programs running.
3. With only windows running plug in your scanner into the USB port
4. Give windows a few seconds
5. you should be brought to a hardware wizard
6. Now you are ready to load a driver for it.

Computer Connection

Scanning the document is only one part of the process. For the scanned image to be useful, it must be transferred from the scanner to an application running on the computer. There are two basic issues: (1) how the scanner is physically connected to the computer and (2) how the application retrieves the information from the scanner.

Physical Connection to the Computer

The amount of data generated by a scanner can be very large: a 600 DPI 9"x11" (slightly larger than A4 paper) uncompressed 24-bit image consumes about 100 megabytes of uncompressed data in transfer and storage on the host computer. Recent scanners can generate this volume of data in a matter of seconds, making a fast connection desirable. There are four common connections used by scanners:

- Parallel - Connecting through a parallel port is the slowest common transfer method. Early scanners had parallel port connections that could not transfer data faster than 70 kilobytes/second. The primary advantage of the parallel port connection was economy — it avoided adding an interface card to the computer.
- Small Computer System Interface (SCSI), which is supported by most computers only via an additional SCSI interface card. Some SCSI scanners are supplied together with a dedicated SCSI card for a PC, although any SCSI controller can be used. During the evolution of the SCSI standard speeds increased, with backwards compatibility; a SCSI connection can transfer data at the highest speed which both the controller and the device support. SCSI has been largely replaced by USB and Firewire, one or both of which are directly supported by most computers, and which are easier to set up than SCSI.
- Universal Serial Bus (USB) scanners can transfer data quickly, and they are easier to use and cheaper than SCSI devices. The early USB 1.1 standard could transfer data at only 1.5 megabytes per second (slower than SCSI), but the later USB 2.0 standard can theoretically transfer up to 60 megabytes per second (although everyday rates are much lower), resulting in faster operation.
- FireWire is an interface that is much faster than USB 1.1 and comparable to USB 2.0. FireWire speeds are 25, 50, and 100 megabytes per second (but a device may not support all speeds). There's also a newer 400 megabyte per second speed.

Applications Programming Interface

An application such as Adobe Photoshop must communicate with the scanner. There are many different scanners, and many of those scanners use different protocols. In order to simplify applications programming, some Applications Programming Interfaces ("API") were developed. The API presents a uniform interface to the scanner. This means that the application does not need to know the specific details of the scanner in order to access it directly. For example, Adobe Photoshop supports the TWAIN standard; consequently, (in an ideal world) Photoshop can acquire an image from any scanner that also supports TWAIN.

In practice, there are often problems with an application communicating with a scanner. Either the application or the scanner manufacturer (or both) may have faults in their implementation of the API.

Typically, the API is implemented as a dynamically linked library. Each scanner manufacturer provides software that translates the API procedure calls into primitive commands that are issued to a hardware controller (such as the SCSI, USB, or FireWire controller). The manufacturer's part of the API is commonly called a device driver, but that designation is not strictly accurate: the API does not run in kernel mode and does not directly access the device.

Some scanner manufacturers will offer more than one API.

- Most scanners use the TWAIN API. The TWAIN API, originally used for low-end and home-use equipment, is now widely used for large-volume scanning.

Other scanner API's are

- ISIS, created by Pixel Translations, which still uses SCSI-II for performance reasons, is used by large, departmental-scale, machines.
- SANE (Scanner Access Now Easy) is a free/open source API for accessing scanners. Originally developed for Unix and Linux operating systems, it has been ported to OS/2, Mac OS X, and Microsoft Windows. Unlike TWAIN, SANE does not handle the user interface. This allows batch scans and transparent network access without any special support from the device driver.
- Windows Image Acquistion ("WIA") is an API provided by Microsoft.

Bundled Applications

In addition to the API, many scanners come bundled with other software. Typically, a scanning utility, some type of image-editing application (such as Photoshop), and OCR software. OCR, or optical character recognition, software makes possible the conversion of graphical images of text into standard text that can be edited using common word-processing and text-editing software. OCR utilises an averaging algorithm to determine the character shape, then matches that shape to a corresponding letter or number.

Output Data

The scanned result is a non-compressed RGB image, which can be transferred to a computer's memory. Some scanners compress and clean up the image using embedded firmware. Once on the computer, the image can be processed with a raster graphics program (such as Photoshop or the GIMP) and saved on a storage device (such as a hard disk).

In common use, scanned pictures are stored on a computer's hard disk, normally in image formats such as JPEG, TIFF, Bitmap, and PNG. Some scanners can also be used to capture editable text, so long as the text can be read by the computer in a discernable font. This process is called Optical Character Recognition (OCR).

Document Processing

The scanning or digitization of paper documents for storage makes different requirements of the scanning equipment used than scanning of pictures for reproduction. While documents can be scanned on general-purpose scanners, it is more efficiently performed on dedicated document scanners manufactured by Atiz Innovation, Böwe Bell & Howell, Canon, Epson, Fujitsu, HP, Kodak and other companies.

When scanning large quantities of documents, speed and paper-handling is very important, but the resolution of the scan will normally be much lower than for good reproduction of pictures.

Document scanners have document feeders, usually larger than those sometimes found on copiers or all-purpose scanners. Scans are made at high speed, perhaps 20 to 150 pages per minute, often in grayscale, although many scanners support color. Many scanners can scan both sides of double-sided originals (duplex operation). Sophisticated document scanners have firmware of software that cleans up scans of text as they are produced, eliminating accidental marks and sharpening type; this would be unacceptable for photographic work, where marks cannot reliably be distinguished from desired fine detail. Files created are compressed as they are made.

The resolution used is usually from 150 to 300 dpi, although the hardware may be capable of somewhat higher resolution; this produces images of text good enough to read and for optical character recognition (OCR), without the higher demands on storage space required by higher-resolution images.

Document scans are often processed using OCR technology to create editable and searchable files. Most scanners use ISIS or Twain device drivers to scan documents into TIFF format so that the scanned pages can be fed into a document management system that will handle the archiving and retrieval of the scanned pages. Lossy JPEG compression, which is very efficient for pictures, is undesirable for text documents, as slanted straight edges take on a jagged appearance, and solid black (or other color) text on a light background compresses well with lossless compression formats.

While paper feeding and scanning can be done automatically and quickly, preparation and indexing are necessary and require much work by humans. Preparation involves manually inspecting the papers to be scanned and making sure that they are in order, unfolded, without staples or anything else that might jam the scanner.

Indexing involves associating keywords to files so that they can be retrieved by content. This process can sometimes be automated to some extent, but is likely to involve manual labour. One common practice is the use of barcode-recognition technology: during preparation, barcode sheets with folder names are inserted into the document files, folders, and document groups. Using automatic batch scanning, the documents are saved into the appropriate folders, and an index is created for integration into document-management software systems.

A specialized form of document scanning is book scanning. Technical difficulties arise from the books usually being bound and sometimes fragile and irreplaceable, but some manufacturers have developed specialized machinery to deal with this. For instance, Atiz DIY scanner uses a V-shaped cradle and a V-shaped transparent platen to handle brittle books. Often special robotic mechanisms are used to automate the page turning and scanning process.

4 Keyboard

Introduction

Physically, a keyboard is an arrangement of rectangular buttons, or keys. A keyboard typically has characters engraved or printed on the keys; in most cases, each press of a key corresponds to a single written symbol. However, to produce some symbols requires pressing and holding several keys simultaneously or in sequence; other keys do not produce any symbol, but instead affect the operation of the computer or the keyboard itself. See input method editor.

A majority of all keyboard keys produce letters, numbers or signs (characters) that are appropriate for the operator's language. Other keys can produce actions when pressed, and other actions are available by the simultaneous pressing of more than one action key.

Keyboards with Extra Keys

There are various keyboards available in the market, which have different keys.

Multimedia Keyboards

Multimedia keyboards offer special keys for accessing music, web, and other oft-used programs. They also usually have other convenient controls, such as a mute button, volume buttons or knob, and standby (sleep) button.

Gaming Keyboards

Some gaming keyboards offer extra function keys which can be programmed with keystroke macros. For example, ctrl+shift+y could be a keystroke that is frequently used in a certain computer game. But it is a physically awkward (or, at least, annoying) combination for the hands to reach for repeatedly. It may be very useful to assign that keystroke combination to one function key. Some keyboards have a keypad full of "G keys" to the left of the QWERTY keyboard for this purpose. The keystroke macros can be reprogrammed at will.

The development of these keyboards was spurred by gaming, but the concept can also be very convenient in non-gaming applications, such as office work. Any keystroke combination that is awkward or annoying but frequently needed can be replaced with a "G key". The meaning of the "G key" press can automatically change depending on which application has focus, thus extending the number of macros available given a certain limited number of G keys.

Virtual keyboards

A relatively new type of keyboard, the I-Tech Virtual Laser Keyboard, works by projecting an image of a full-size keyboard onto a surface. Sensors in the projection unit identify which key is being "pressed" and relay the signals to a computer or personal digital assistant.

Keyboard Layout Alternatives to QWERTY

As explained above, the QWERTY layout was a legacy from mechanical typewriters. In contrast, some keyboard layouts are specifically designed for speed. The most common is the Dvorak layout; more recently, layouts such as Colemak have been developed to improve on Dvorak and to be easier to learn for existing QWERTY users. The fastest keyboard so far is the stenotype — some people who use a stenotype type faster than 300 words per minute.

How Computer Accepts Input from the Keyboard

When we press a key on a keyboard key say the letter S, then a tiny computer chip inside either the computer or the keyboard called the keyboard controller, takes a note that a key has been pressed and places a code into part of its memory buffer, indicating which key was pressed. This code is called the key's Scan Code (identifying number). Now without specifying what has happened the keyboard controller signals (*i.e.*, sends interrupt) the computer processing components that something has happened at the keyboard. The keyboard controller sends an interrupt request to the CPU (using the interrupt number 9 assigned to the keyboard interrupt) when it receives a complete keystroke.

Interrupts cause the CPU to put aside what it is doing and jump to an interrupt handling program. In this case the interrupt handles an integral part of the ROM-BIO software. When the computer's processing components receive an interrupt request, the program that is controlling the computer at that moment evaluates the request to determine the appropriate response. In the case of a key press, the program reads the memory location in the keyboard buffer that contains the scan code of the key that was pressed and places the keyboard letter in the computer's main memory.

The keyboard buffer can actually store a number of keystrokes at once. This is necessary because some time elapses between the pressing of a key and the computer's reading of that key from the keyboard buffer. Also programmers must put instructions into their programs to read keystrokes and program might be doing something else when the key is pressed.

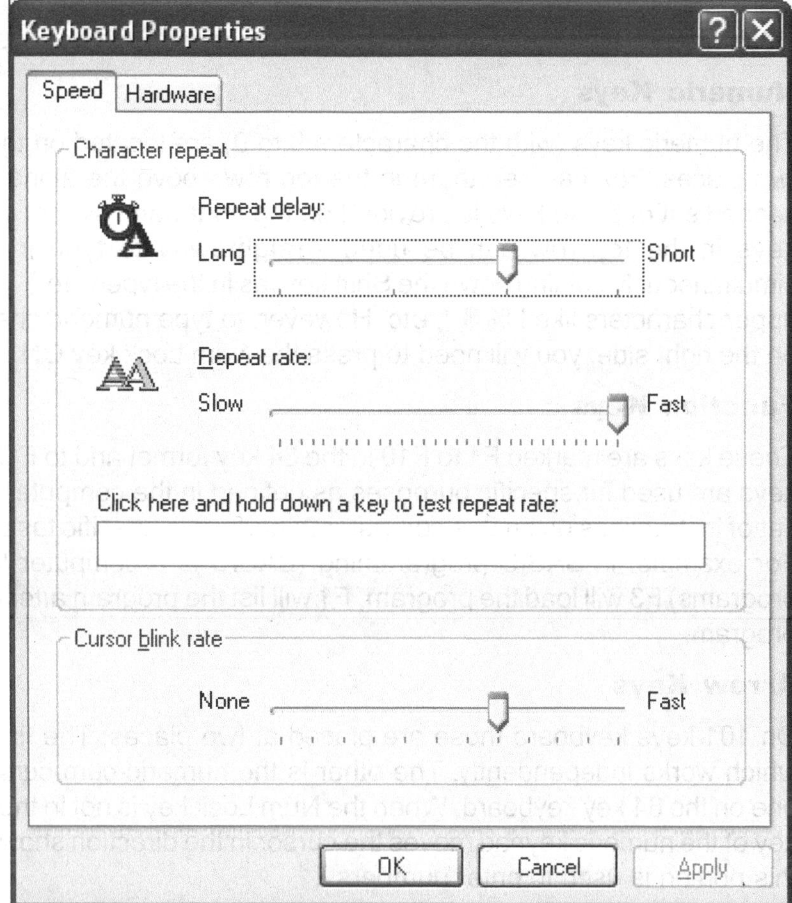

With the keystrokes stored in a buffer the program can react to them when convenient. Because reading the keyboard to get the scan code of a key action is a function of software, we can reassign scan codes to represent different letters or symbols.

Various Keys of the Keyboard

There are more keys on computer keyboard than on typewriter. Most commonly used keyboards has **101 keys** and more. With XT, 84 key keyboard was used but it has now become obsolete. The 101 key keyboard has the important keys:

Alphabetic Keys

These are alphabet keys from a to z. As in typewriter, you can use Shift to make them capital, *i.e.*, ABCDE, etc. So if you press a b c d e …. etc. With Shift key already pressed, you will get A B C D E …. etc. Similar results can be obtained by putting CAPS LOCK key ON.

a = a

Shift + a = A

For typing A, you press Shift key and then while keeping Shift key pressed, press the "a". Otherwise for typing a, you don't need to press the Shift key, just press the a key.

Numeric Keys

The numeric keys (with the characters 0 to 9) are located on the computer's keyboard at two places. You can see them in the top row above the alpha keys (as in typewriter). A second set of these keys is provided on the right-hand side of the keyboard. The numeric keys in the top row can be used straightaway to type in numeric characters. By simultaneously holding down the Shift key (as in the typewriter), you can also type in special upper characters like ! % $ *, etc. However, to type numeric characters by using the keys on the right side, you will need to press the Num Lock key ON.

Function Keys

These keys are marked F1 to F10 in the 84 key format and to F12 in the 101 format. These keys are used for specific purposes as defined in the computer (a computer program is a set of instructions given to a computer to perform a specific task) which you may be using. For example, in BASIC programming (BASIC is a computer language used for writing programs) F3 will load the program, F1 will list the program after loading and F2 will run the program.

Arrow Keys

On 101 keys keyboard these are placed at two places. The first is called the cursor pad which works independently. The other is the numeric-cum-cursor pad. It is similar to the one on the 84 key keyboard. When the Num Lock key is not in the ON position, pressing the key of the numeric keypad moves the cursor in the direction shown on each key. Otherwise, this portion is used to enter numbers.

Installing Keyboard

1. Position the keyboard cable over the connector, and pull the keyboard slightly to the right so the cable is not bent. Hold the cable as close as possible to the connector and press straight down. Press the cable firmly into the connector.
2. Flip the keyboard over and insert the small tabs at the bottom of the keyboard into the openings in the PowerBook case.
3. Pull down on the keyboard release tabs (located to the left of the F1 and F9 keys) and then press down on the top portion of the keyboard.
4. Let go of the keyboard release tabs to secure the keyboard in place.
5. Replace the PowerBook battery or plug in the power adapter.
6. Restart the computer.

Removing the Installed Keyboard

1. Place your computer on a clean, flat surface.

2. Shut down your computer, remove the battery from the expansion bay, and disconnect the power adapter, modem, and any other cables connected to the computer.

3. Make sure that the keyboard locking screw is not in the locked position. Your new PowerBook comes with the keyboard unlocked, so unless you or someone else locked the keyboard, you can skip this step.

4. Release the keyboard by pulling down on the keyboard release tabs (located to the left of the F1 and F9 keys) until the top portion of the keyboard pops up.

5. Lift the top portion of the PowerBook keyboard up slightly near the top row of keys and pull it back far enough to release the small tabs that hold the bottom of the keyboard in place.

6. Flip the keyboard over and lay it on the palm rests.

7. Touch a metal surface inside the computer to discharge any static electricity.

8. Grasp the keyboard cable as close as possible to the connector and pull up to disconnect the keyboard from the logic board. Rock the cable carefully if additional leverage is needed.

Troubleshooting Keyboard

Most of the problem faced in keyboard operation can be divided into two categories:

- complete non-operation of the keyboard and .
- broken or stuck keys

First problem could be either because of a broken connection between the keyboard and the system or because of some problem in the keyboard or the main system itself. If you find that your keyboard is not working then to see if the problem is with the keyboard or the main system you can try a different working keyboard on your system.

If the new keyboard is also not working then the problem most probably is with the main system. If the new keyboard is working properly then the problem is with your old keyboard. You can also try your old keyboard on some other machine to make sure that the fault is really with the keyboard.

When the keyboard of a system is not working then some of the points that must be checked are:

- Some old keyboards have a small switch at their bottom side to select the operating mode of the keyboard. Using this switch one can select either XT (8088/8086) or AT (80286) operating mode.
- Many old computers have a keyboard lock on the front panel. This lock disables the keyboard. Forgetting to unlock this lock, or not properly unlocking this could be one reason of the keyboard not working.

- Another problem could be the connector from lock to the motherboard coming loose at the lock or the motherboard side.
- The keyboard socket on the motherboard—into which the keyboard is plugged—is often one of the reason of keyboard failure. This socket sometimes become loose and may not connect properly with the keyboard. A loose socket may give intermittent problems in the keyboard operation.
- Check the connection between the socket and the motherboard. Check for any loose solder on motherboard.
- Check the keyboard cable. Open the keyboard, remove the cable and using a Multi-meter test each wire for continuity and cross-connection. If some fault is found then replace the cable.

5 Monitor

Introduction

A computer display monitor, usually called simply a monitor, is a piece of electrical equipment which displays viewable images generated by a computer without producing a permanent record. The word "monitor" is used in other contexts; in particular in television broadcasting, where a television picture is displayed to a high standard. A computer display device is usually either a cathode ray tube or some form of flat panel such as a TFT LCD. The monitor comprises the display device, circuitry to generate a picture from electronic signals sent by the computer, and an enclosure or case. Within the computer, either as an integral part or a plugged-in interface, there is circuitry to convert internal data to a format compatible with a monitor.

Imaging Technologies

As with television, several different hardware technologies exist for displaying computer-generated output:

- Liquid crystal display (LCD). TFT LCDs are the most popular display device for new computers in the Western world.
- Passive LCD gives poor contrast and slow response, and other image defects. These were used in some laptops until the mid 1990s.
- TFT Thin Film Transistor LCDs give much better picture quality in several respects. All modern LCD monitors are TFT.
- Cathode ray tube (CRT)
- Standard raster scan computer monitors
- Vector displays, as used on the Vectrex, many scientific and radar applications, and several early arcade machines (notably Asteroids - always implemented using CRT displays due to requirement for a deflection system, though can be emulated on any raster-based display.
- Television receivers were used by most early personal and home computers, connecting composite video to the television set using a modulator Image quality was reduced by the additional steps of composite video ? modulator ? TV tuner ? composite video.

- Plasma display
- Surface-conduction electron-emitter display (SED)
- Video projector - implemented using LCD, CRT, or other technologies. Recent consumer-level video projectors are almost exclusively LCD based.
- Organic light-emitting diode (OLED) display
- Penetron military aircraft displays

Cathode Ray Tube

The CRT or cathode ray tube, is the picture tube of a monitor. The back of the tube has a negatively charged cathode. The electron gun shoots electrons down the tube and onto a charged screen. The screen is coated with a pattern of dots that glow when struck by the electron stream. Each cluster of three dots, one of each color, is one pixel.
The Image on the monitor screen is usually made up from at least tens of thousands of such tiny dots glowing on command from the computer. The closer together the pixels are, the sharper the image on screen can be. The distance between pixels on a computer monitor screen is called its dot pitch and is measured in millimeters. Most monitors have a dot pitch of 0.28 mm or less.

There are two electromagnets around the collar of the tube which deflect the electron beam. The beam scans across the top of the monitor from left to right, is then blanked and moved back to the left-hand side slightly below the previous trace (on the next scan line), scans across the second line and so on until the bottom right of the screen is reached. The beam is again blanked, and moved back to the top left to start again. This process draws a complete picture, typically 50 to 100 times a second. The number of times in one second that the electron gun redraws the entire image is called the refresh rate and is measured in hertz (cycles per second). It is common, particularly in lower-priced equipment, for all the odd-numbered lines of an image to be traced, and then all the even-numbered lines; the circuitry of such an interlaced display need be capable of only half the speed of a non-interlaced display. An interlaced display, particularly at a relatively low refresh rate, can appear to some observers to flicker, and may cause eyestrain and nausea.

Performance Measurements

The performance parameters of a monitor are:

- Luminance, measured in candelas per square metre (cd/m²).
- Viewable image size, measured diagonally. For CRT the viewable size is one inch (25 mm) smaller then the tube itself.
- Dot pitch. Describes the distance between pixels of the same color in millimetres. In general, the lower the dot pitch (e.g. 0.24 mm, which is also 240 micrometres), the sharper the picture will appear.

- Response time. The amount of time a pixel in an LCD monitor takes to go from active (black) to inactive (white) and back to active (black) again. It is measured in milliseconds (ms). Lower numbers mean faster transitions and therefore fewer visible image artifacts.
- Contrast ratio. The contrast ratio is defined as the ratio of the luminosity of the brightest color (white) to that of the darkest color (black) that the monitor is capable of producing.
- Refresh rate. The number of times in a second that a display is illuminated.
- Power consumption, measured in watts (W).
- Aspect ratio, which is the horizontal size compared to the vertical size, e.g. 4:3 is the standard aspect ratio, so that a screen with a width of 1024 pixels will have a height of 768 pixels. A widescreen display can have an aspect ratio of 16:9, which means a display that is 1024 pixels wide will have a height of 576 pixels.
- Display resolution. The number of distinct pixels in each dimension that can be displayed.

CRT

- High contrast ratio
- High speed response
- Full range light output level control
- Large size
- Large weight
- Most produce geometric distortion
- Greater power consumption than LCD.
- Prone to moire effect at highest resolution
- Can display natively in almost any resolution
- Intolerant of damp conditions
- Small risk of implosion (due to internal vacuum) if the picture tube glass is broken

Passive LCD

- Very poor contrast ratio (eg 20:1)
- High visible noise if used in more than 8 colour mode (3 bit colour depth).
- Very slow response (moving images barely viewable)
- Some suffer horizontal & vertical ghosting
- Very small size

- Very low weight
- Very low power consumption
- Lower cost than TFT LCDs.
- Zero geometric distortion

TFT LCD

More or less all modern LCD monitors are the TFT type.

- Medium contrast ratio
- Response rates vary from one model to another, slower screens will show smearing on moving images
- Very small size
- Very low weight
- Very low power consumption
- Higher cost than Passive LCD or CRT.
- Zero geometric distortion
- LCDs of both types only have one native resolution. Displaying other resolutions requires conversion & interpolation, which often degrades image quality.

Plasma

- High operating temperature can be painful to touch
- Prone to burn-in
- No geometric distortion
- Highest cost option
- High power consumption

Penetron

- Only found in military aircraft
- 2 colour display
- See through
- Orders of magnitude more expensive than the other display technologies listed here.

Advantages and Disadvantages of various Displays

Advantages of LCDS

1. Low power consumption and cost
2. Small size

Disadvantages of LCDs

1. LCD do not emit light so the image has very little contrast
2. Resolution is poor
3. Screen is susceptible to glare so the optimum viewing angle is very narrow

Advantages of Plasma Display

1. Resolution is good
2. Glare is less
3. Flickering is absent
4. Images are brighter than CRT

Disadvantages of Plasma Display

1. Uses lot of power
2. The technology is costly
3. Only a single colour is available (reddish orange)

Advantages of Terminals

1. They are relatively inexpensive.
2. Terminals are usually connected on line to a mainframe. This enables users to enter data directly into a processing system, thereby increasing the timeliness of data input and eliminating the need for intermediary storage media viz., floppy disks.
3. User's ability to correct errors or to alter data that has already been typed.
4. Its ability to enter data to computer system from remote sites.
5. Terminals extend the use of the computer to various places of work. They are widely used for such tasks as control, entering orders, updating accounts and seat reservations.

   They can be sited at various points on a factory floor to record and receive information on different stages of an industrial process.

Disadvantages of Terminals

1. Terminal dependency on the main server. If the main server goes down the connected terminals are useless.
2. Long hour work at visual display terminals are unhealthy i.e.; can cause strain in eyes, pain in wrist and back.

3. Terminals can not store data or create backup copies of data input, thereby forcing the user to rekey the original input data if it is lost.

Dots and Pixels

The images displayed on a PC's monitor are created from a pattern of dots in much the same way as the photographs in a newspaper. Dots are shaded lighter or darker so that your eyes can form a visual image from them. The CRT creates these dots from the phosphor on the back of its screen using masking methods that isolate each dot so that it can be illuminated by an electron gun.

A monochrome or single color, monitor has phosphor of only one color, so that when the phosphor dots are illuminated, the text and graphic image is a single color on a contrasting background. Typically, the background is black and the display color is green, amber or white.

The image produced on a color monitor is created by illuminated small triangles of phosphor dots called picture elements or pixels for short. In the CRT, one-third of the dots are red dots, one-third are green dots and one-third are blue dots. These different colored dots are interspersed evenly on the screen so that a dot of each color can be grouped with a dot of each of the other colors to form a triangle or pixel.

A color CRT has three electron guns that are used to light up the phosphors in each pixel. The combinations and intensities used to illuminate the phosphors define the image produced on the screen. The electron guns sweep over the pixels from side to side, one row at a time, to create or refresh the displayed image.

LCD displays are of two different types: passive matrix and active matrix. A passive matrix display has a layer of LCD elements on a grid (matrix) of wires. When current is applied to the wire intersections, the diodes (pixels) are lighted.

A passive matrix refreshes the display by applying current to the pixels at a fixed refresh rate. Active matrix displays control each LCD elements (diode) individually with one or more transistors that continually refresh each element of the display.

Resolution

The number of pixels on a monitor, whether CRT or LCD, determine the amount of detail that can be used to create and image. As the number of pixels increases, the better the image resolution a monitor can produce. The number of pixels on a monitor is its resolution, which is expressed in the number of pixels on each row of the display and the number of rows of pixels on the display.

For example, the VGA standard resolution is 640 x 480 which is read as 640 by 480. This means that the monitor has 640 pixels arranged horizontally on each row of pixels and 480 vertical rows of pixels. A monitor with 640 x 480 resolution uses 307,200 (640 times 480) pixels to create displayed images.

The following table shows the resolutions most commonly supported by today's monitors.

Resolution	Total Pixels Used
640 x 480	307,200
800 x 600	480,000
1024 x 768	786,432
1280 x 1024	1,310,720
1600 x 1200	1,920,000

Larger size monitors, such as 19- or 21-inch have trouble displaying smaller resolutions and on most smaller monitors, such as a 14- or 15- inch monitor, higher resolutions don't have the image quality you desire. It is always best to match the monitor and its resolution to your needs.

Because of their construction, LCD displays have natural resolutions that are set by the number of pixels on each line of the display. This is why an LCD display must often reduce the size of the display area to reproduce images in resolutions lower than its natural one.

For example, a 12.1 inch LCD monitor (800 x 600 resolution) has 800 pixels on each row of its display. If the resolution to 640 x 480, it is not possible to evenly represent 640 pixels with 800 pixels and produce clear text or images. So, the display image area is reduced to 10.4 inches for the 640 x 480 image.

However, as the natural resolution and the size of the display get larger, reproducing lower resolutions become much easier in the standard screen area. Table 16-3 illustrates how LCD displays adjust for resolutions other than their natural resolution. In the table, small means the display is reduced, full means it is the natural resolution and linear means that the user must scroll up and down and left and right to see all of the displayed image.

Monitor Size and Resolution

As the space available to hold more pixels increases, so does the monitor's ability to handle higher resolutions. This is not a hard and fast rule, but in general it holds true. Another factor in this equation is the age of the monitor. Most newer monitors can display higher resolutions than many older and larger monitors.

Higher resolutions use smaller pixels and when applied on a smaller monitor, may require a magnifying glass to read the screen. A 15 – inch monitor may support 1280 x 1-24 resolution, but you may never actually use it. In fact, you may never actually use the highest resolution available on any monitor smaller than a 19-inch monitor. On the other hand, lower resolutions look better on smaller monitors. Larger monitors display lower resolutions in pixel blocks that can really detract from the image on the screen

Natural Resolution	640 x 480	800 x 600	1024 x 768
640 x 480	Full	Linear	Linear
800 x 600	Small	Full	Linear

1024 x 768	Small	Small	Full

Color Depth

In addition to its resolution, the color depth of a monitor is another very important characteristic, depending on your needs. The color depth of a monitor is the maximum number of colors that it can display. The color depth is represented as the number of bits required to hold the number of colors in the color depth.

For example, an 8 – bit color depth has a maximum of 256 colors, because that is the highest value that can be written in 8-bits. In binary numbers, the range of numbers available in 8 bits is 0000000 to 11111111 or the range in decimal numbers of 0 to 255, which represents different 256 colors. The colors included in the color palette for a particular color depth are represented in the binary values stored in the number of bits available. The following table lists the number of colors associated with each of the color depths, which are also called bit depths, supported on current monitors.

Colour Depth (in bits)	*Colours Available*	*Common Name*
1	2	Monochrome
4	16	VGA Standard
8	256	256-colour
16	65,536	High colour
18	262,144	LCD colour
24	16,777,216	True Colour (24-bit)
32	4,294,967,296	True Colour (32-bit)

Depending on the PC, video card and monitor, either 24-bit or 32-bit is typically designated as True Color setting. The number of colors that 32-bit color, which is popular with 3D video accelerator systems, can develop is perhaps overkill. The human eye cannot distinguish beyond 16 million or so colors. Above that the eye may have difficulty discerning the color distinction of two adjacent pixels.

Refresh Rate

Another key settings on a video system is its refresh rate or the number of times per second that the screen is entirely redrawn. The refresh rate is actually a function of the video card and indicates how many times per second the data used by the monitor to refresh the displayed image is sent. The phosphor on the CRT's screen begins to dim almost immediately, so the electron gun must sweep back over each pixel a number of times per second to keep the display sharp and bright. A low refresh rate can make the CRT screen flicker and can cause eye fatigue and headaches.

You definitely want a monitor that supports a refresh rate of 75Hz (Hertz) or faster, especially a higher resolutions and color depths. LCD displays do not have refresh rate issues. Because of the way LCD technology works, it can provide stable images at 60Hz and sometimes less. To see the refresh rate on your monitor or to check to see what it is set at, follow the steps used above to display the Display Properties Settings window. Click on the Advanced button to display the Properties window for the video adapter in your PC. Select the Adapter tab. The Refresh rate is selected from a list box that is located about in the middle of the window. On most Windows 9x or Windows 2000 systems, the refresh rate is likely set to Optimal.

If you change the refresh rate and the result is a distorted or blurry image, reboot your PC into Windows Safe Mode and reset the refresh rate.

Video Display Standards

Video display standards are developed more to define the capabilities of video cards than they are for monitors, but by listing the video standards to which the monitor is compatible, its capabilities in terms of color depth and resolution are automatically defined. What differentiates one video display standard from another is the resolution it supports, how it creates text characters, whether it is color or monochrome and its color depth, color palette, refresh rate, scan rates and bandwidth. The following table lists the resolution and color depths of the VGA and SVGA video standards, the two most commonly used standards today.

Standard	*Name*	*Resolution*	*Colour Depth*
VGA	Video Graphics Array	640 x 480	16
		320 x 200	256
SVGA	Super VGA	800 x 600	16
		1024 x 768	256
		1280 x 1024	256
		1600 x 1200	256

Over the years, several video display standards have been used. Here are a few of the more popular ones:

Monochrome Display Adapter (MDA)

This standard displayed only text data in only one color on a solid contrasting background.

Color Graphics Adapter (CGA)

This standard provided the first color graphics support. CGA supports 2 or 4 colors out of a 16- color palette on a 640 x 200 resolution.

Monochrome Graphics Adapter (MGA)

Also known as Hercules Graphics. Developed by Hercules Graphics corporation, this incorporated graphics into the monochrome display. It supported a 720 x 350 resolution for text and a 720 x 348 resolution for graphics, both in monochrome.

Enhanced Graphics Adapter (EGA)

This standard improved the text and graphics display capabilities of the CGA standard. EGA supported graphics with a 640 x 350 resolution and up to 16 colors from 64 – color palette.

Video Graphics Array (VGA)

VGA is now the de facto graphics standard for all monitors, video cards and software. It supports a range of resolutions and color depths, as shown in table 6-5 including 640 x 480 which is commonly known as VGA standard resolution.

Super VGA (SVGA)

SVGA is a collection of standards that defines graphics above the VGA standard. SVGA is commonly linked to the 800 x 600 resolution and 256 colors. Most manufacturers consider SVGA the current standard.

Of the video display standards listed above, only VGA and SVGA are in common use today. The others were part of the video standards evolution and each new standard was an improvement on the last. You may encounter other video display standards, such as XGA (Extended Graphics Array) or UVGA (Ultra VGA), which are loosely defined standards that vary from manufacturer to manufacturer.

The VGA (Video Graphics Array) display standard is considered the base standard for video display systems today. Virtually all current monitors and video cards support the VGA standard. It is the default standard for Windows and almost all other operating systems and device drives that interact directly with the video system.

Video Cards

In general, the video card processes the graphics data produced by software running on the PC and prepares it for use by the monitor for converting it from digital data to an analog signal. The video card also sends out the data needed by the monitor to refresh the image or renew it as it changes.

Video cards, graphics cards and accelerator cards are all names for the adapter card inside the PC that is responsible for generating the signals that tell the monitor what to display. The relationship between the video card and the monitor should be carefully matched. These two device must be compatible in terms of the signal used to communicate to the monitor, the type of connector used to connect them together, the video display standards they support and their speed.

Problems of Monitors

Dead pixels

A fraction of all LCD monitors are produced with "dead pixels". Due to the desire for affordable monitors, most manufacturers sell monitors with dead pixels. Almost all manufacturers have clauses in their warranties which claim monitors with fewer than some number of dead pixels is not broken and will not be replaced. The dead pixels are usually stuck with the green, red, and/or blue subpixels either individually always stuck on or off.

Like image persistence, this can sometimes be partially or fully reversed by using the same method listed below, however the chance of success is far lower than with a "stuck" pixel. It can also sometimes be repaired by physically flicking the pixel, however it is always a possibility for someone to use too much force and rupture the weak screen internals doing this.

Stuck pixels

LCD monitors, while lacking phosphor screens and thus immune to phosphor burn-in, have a similar condition known as image persistence, where the pixels of the LCD monitor can "remember" a particular color and become "stuck" and unable to change. Unlike phosphor burn-in, however, image persistence can sometimes be reversed partially or completely. This is accomplished by rapidly displaying varying colors to "wake up" the stuck pixels.

Phosphor burn-in

Phosphor burn-in is localised aging of the phosphor layer of a CRT screen where it has displayed a static bright image for many years. This results in a faint permanent image on the screen, even when powered off. In severe cases it can even be possible to read some of the text, though this only occurs where the displayed text remained the same for years.

This was once a relatively common phenomenon in single purpose business computers. It can still be an issue with CRT displays when used to display the same image for years at a time, but modern computers aren't normally used this way any more, so the problem is not a significant issue today, with CRTs.

The size of the issue seems to have become exaggerated in popular opinion. The only systems that suffered the defect were ones displaying the same image for years, and with these the presence of burn-in was not a noticeable effect when in use, since it coincided with the displayed image perfectly. Also such systems were inevitably functional rather than eye candy, so even visible slight damage that occurred when reusing a heavily used business monitor for another business app was a trivial cosmetic issue. It only became a significant issue in 3 situations:

- when some heavily used monitors were reused at home,
- or re-used for display purposes
- in some high security applications (but only those where the high security data displayed did not change for years at a time).

Screen savers were developed as a means to avoid burn-in, but are redundant for CRTs today, despite their popularity. The problem does not occur with multitasking systems, and powering down the display after a period of non-use is as effective and has additional benefits, such as increasing monitor life and reducing power use.

Phosphor Burn-in can be gradually removed on damaged CRT displays by displaying an all white screen with brightness & contrast turned up full. This is a slow procedure, and is usually but not always effective.

Plasma burn-in

Burn-in has re-emerged as an issue with plasma displays, which are much more vulnerable to this than CRTs. Screen savers with moving images may be used with these to minimise localised burn. Periodic change of the colour scheme in use also helps reduce the issue.

Black level misadjustment

User misadjustment of black level is common. This alters the colour displayed with most darker colours.

A testcard image may be used to set the image black level correctly. On CRT monitors

- Black level is set with the 'brightness' control
- White level is set with the 'contrast' control
- Sometimes black level can need readjustment after setting white level.

The naming of CRT controls is historic, and in some cases counterintuitive.

Glare

Glare is a problem caused by the relationship between lighting and screen, or by using monitors in bright sunlight. LCDs and flat screen CRTs are less prone to this than conventional curved CRTs, and trinitron CRTs, which are curved on one axis only, are less prone to it than other CRTs curved on both axes.

If the problem persists despite moving the monitor or adjusting lighting, a filter using a mesh of very fine black wires may be placed on the screen to reduce glare and improve contrast. These filters were popular in the late 1980s. They do also reduce light output, which can occasionally be an issue.

Color misregistration

With exceptions of DLP, most display technologies, especially LCD, have an inherent misregistration of the color channels, that is, the centres of the red, green, and blue dots do not line up perfectly. Subpixel rendering depends on this misalignment; technologies making use of this include the Apple II from 1976, and more recently Microsoft (ClearType, 1998) and XFree86 (X Rendering Extension).

Incomplete spectrum

RGB displays produce most of the visible colour spectrum, but not all. This can be a problem where good colour matching to non-RGB images is needed. This issue is common to all monitor technologies with 3 colour channels.

Troubleshooting Monitor

The monitor's glass screen is the component on a PC that should be cleaned the most often the monitor screen produces a lot of static electricity that attracts and hold dust and flying lint. If the screen becomes covered with dust, it can strain your eyes to view the screen for extended periods. The following steps detail how you can safely keep the glass screen and the monitor itself clean and bright:

1. Before cleaning the monitor, switch its power off and unplug it from its power source. There is really no need to disconnect it from the PC. After turning the monitor off, wait a few minutes before beginning to clean it. Do not wear an ESD ground strap when working with a monitor, even to clean it.
2. Using compressed air, clean away any dust on the top of the monitor's case. Point the air stream to blow across the top of the monitor, not directly down on it, to prevent dust from blowing into the monitor's vents. Never open and remove the cover of a monitor! There is an extremely high voltage hazard inside every monitor, regardless of its size.
3. Use a soft cloth and either isopropyl alcohol or a general-purpose no-rinse cleaner to clean the outside of the monitor case. The alcohol is probably a better choice because it will not create a safety hazard if it's inadvertently dripped inside the case.
4. Use and antistatic cleaner of a Scotch-Brite HPEC for electronics cloth to clean the glass of the monitor. Never use an ammonia-based glass cleaner on the monitor glass. The monitor screen is coated with filtering chemicals to help improve the image and reduce eyestrain. Using a harsh cleaner can remove these coatings, harming the monitor and potentially harming you. Never use water or a liquid cleaner to wash the monitor's glass with the power on. Water is an excellent conductor of electricity and if your hand makes sufficient contact with the screen your could be the ground for the electricity in the monitor.
5. Reconnect the monitor and test the video. If nothing displays, check the power switch, the power cord, the video connection and the brightness and contrast settings any of which could have been accidentally disloaded, moved or turned while you were cleaning the case.

Modern Technology

Analog RGB monitors

Most modern computer displays can show thousands or millions of different colors in the RGB color space by varying red, green, and blue signals in continuously variable intensities.

Digital and Analog combination

Many monitors have analog signal relay, but some more recent models (mostly LCD screens) support digital input signals. It is a common misconception that all computer monitors are digital. For several years, televisions, composite monitors, and computer displays have been significantly different. However, as TVs have become more versatile, the distinction has blurred.

Multi-head monitor

Some users use more than one monitor. The displays can operate in multiple modes. One of the most common spreads the entire desktop over all of the monitors, which thus act as one big desktop. The X Window System refers to this as Xinerama.

Virtual displays

The X Window System provides configuration mechanisms for using a single hardware monitor for rendering multiple virtual displays, as controlled (for example) with the Unix DISPLAY global variable or with the -display command option.

Power saving

More or less all modern monitors contain a power saving mode they will switch to if they receive no video input signal. Modern operating systems can thus power down a monitor after a specified period of inactivity. Typical lifetime cost savings outweight the cost of implementation. This also extends the service life of the monitor.

Some monitors will also switch themselves completely off after a time period on standby.

Some laptops have a dimmed screen mode they can use to extend battery life.

Directional screen

Narrow viewing angle screens are used in some security conscious applications.

Touch screen

These monitors use touching of the screen as an input method. Items can be selected or moved with a finger, and finger gestures may be used to convey commands. This does however mean the screen needs frequent cleaning due to image degradation from fingerprints.

Power Options for Monitor

You can set the power options for the monitor from the Control Panel, Display options. Follow the following steps to do the same.

1. Move the mouse over empty region in Desktop and click the right mouse button. A shortcut menu appears.
2. Click at the Properties.
3. A Display Properties dialog box appears with four tabs just below the title bar.
4. Move the mouse over the Screen Saver too and click the left mouse button.

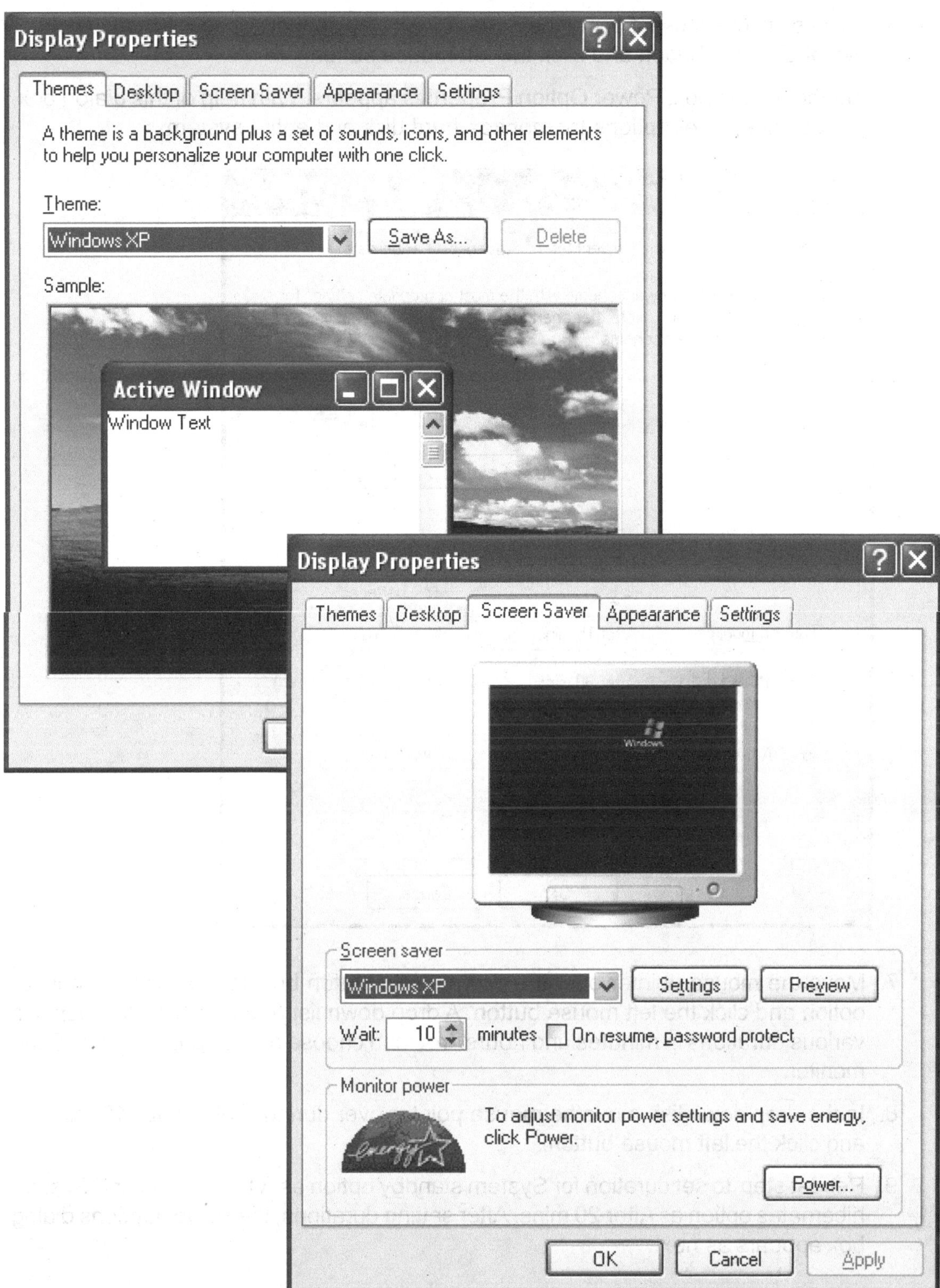
Display Properties
Themes
Desktop
Screen Saver
Appearance
Settings
A theme is a background plus a set of sounds, icons, and other elements to help you personalize your computer with one click.
Theme:
Windows XP
Save As...
Delete
Sample:
Active Window
Window Text
Display Properties
Themes
Desktop
Screen Saver
Appearance
Settings
Screen saver
Windows XP
Settings
Preview
Wait: 10 minutes
On resume, password protect
Monitor power
To adjust monitor power settings and save energy, click Power.
Power...
OK
Cancel
Apply

5. Various options present under the Screen Saver tab appear. Move the mouse pointer over the Power button and click the left mouse button.
6. Another dialog box, Power Option Properties appears. With help of this dialog box, you can set power options for monitor, hard disk and entire system.

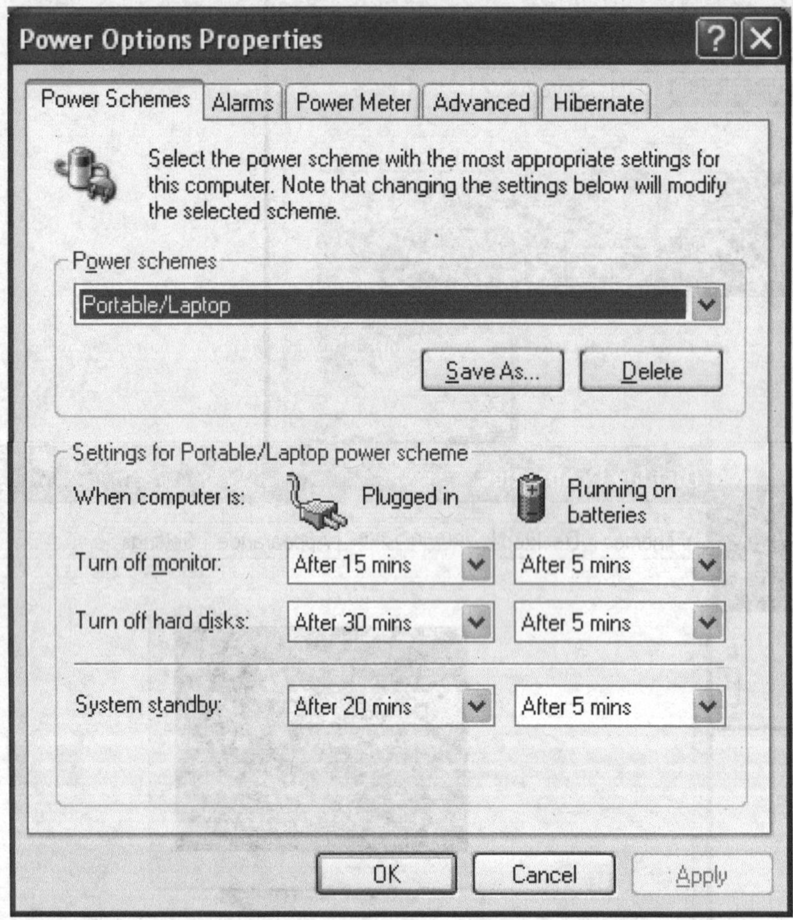

7. Move the mouse pointer over the down arrow button beside the Turn off monitor option and click the left mouse button. A drop down list appears. This list displays various durations in minutes and hours. You can choose any duration to turn off the monitor.
8. In the drop down list, movethe mouse pointer over during. Selec After 10 minutes and click the left mouse button.
9. Repeat step to set duration for System standby option as After 10 mins and System hibernates option as After 20 mins. After setting durations, the Power Options dialog box appears as next.

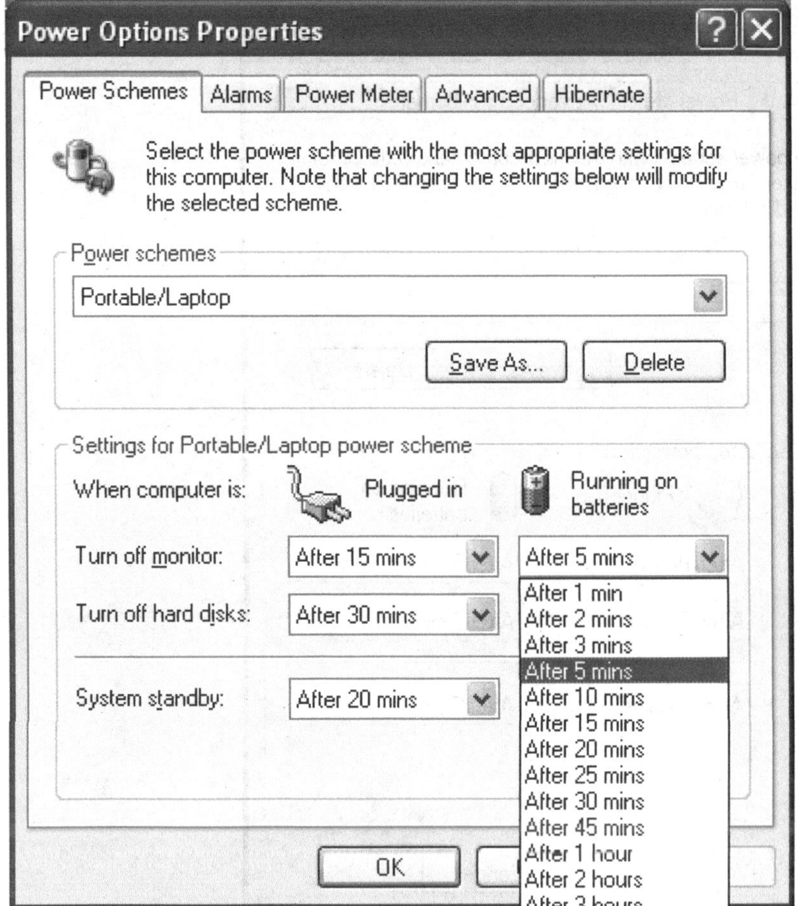

Saving Power Scheme

After setting otions in Power Options Properties dialog box, you can save all options under a new powe scheme. By doing so, you can personalize power options for your computer. Le us now undertake the following steps and learn to save a power scheme.

1. Start with previos image. Move the mouse pointer over the Save As button and click the left mouse button.
2. A Save Scheme dialog box appears with some default name to save the power scheme.
3. Type some new name for power scheme which you can remember easily. For instance, type Portable/ Laptop as new name for power scheme.
4. After typing the name, move the

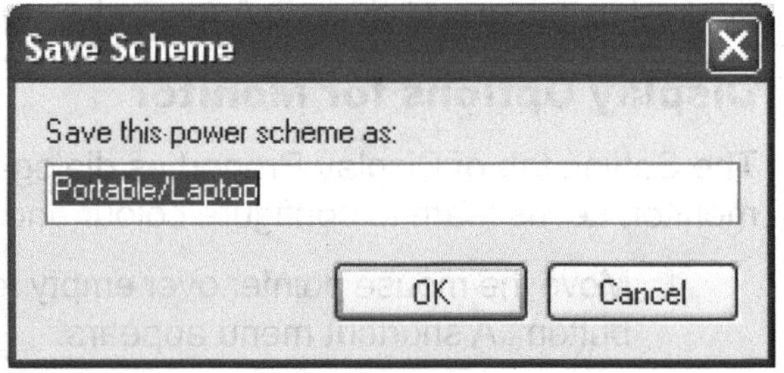

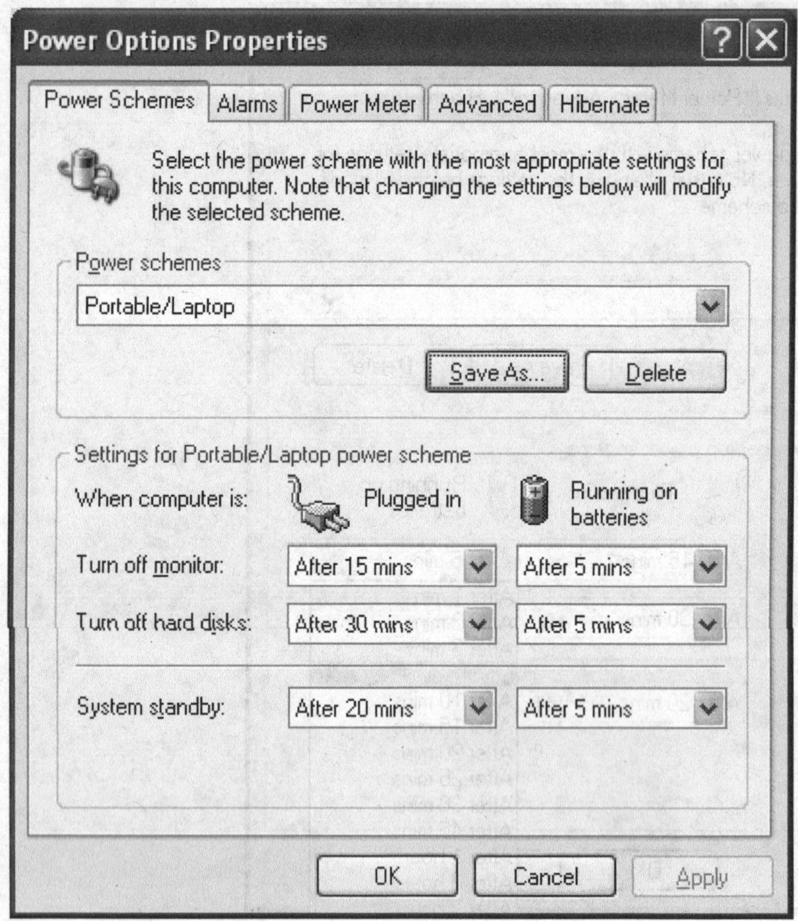

mouse pointer over the Ok button, present in Save Scheme dialog box, and click the left mouse button.

5. The Power Options Properties dialog box reappears. Move the mouse pointer over the Apply button and click the left mouse button. Similarly, move the mouse pointer over the Ok button and click the left mouse button.
6. At last, Display Properties dialog box appears. Repeat step 5, i.e., click at Apply and then on Ok buttons of Display Properties dialog box.

If you want to make changes in My PC Power Scheme then simply set new values for desired option and click on to Apply button and Ok.

Display Options for Monitor

The Setting tab of Display Properties dialog box is used to set colour and resolution for a monitor. Let us learn to configure colour and resolution for a monitor.

1. Move the mouse pointer over empty region in the Desktop and click the right mouse button . A shortcut menu appears.

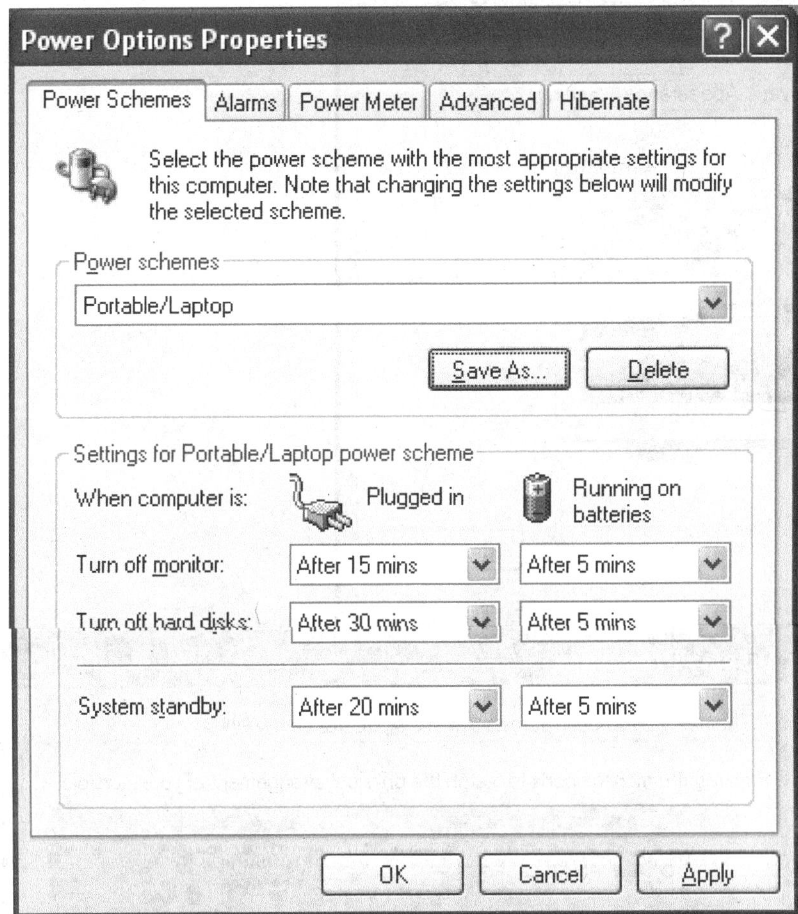

2. Inside shortcut menu, click on the Properties option.
3. A Display Properties dialog box appears. Move the mouse pointer over the Settings tab and click the left mouse button. Various options present under Settings tab appear.
4. To adjust the screen resolution, move the mouse pointer over slider present under Screen resolution option and clock the left mouse button. Keeping left mouse button pressed, drag the slider towards Less (to reduce the screen resolution) to More (to increase the screen resolution).
5. After setting screen resolution, select quality for colours from Color quality option. To do so, move the mouse over the down arrow button under the Color quality option and click the left mouse button. A drop down list appears. Move the mouse pointer over the desired colour quality. For instance, move the mouse pointer over Medium (16 bit) option and click the left mouse button. This sets the desired option on monitor.

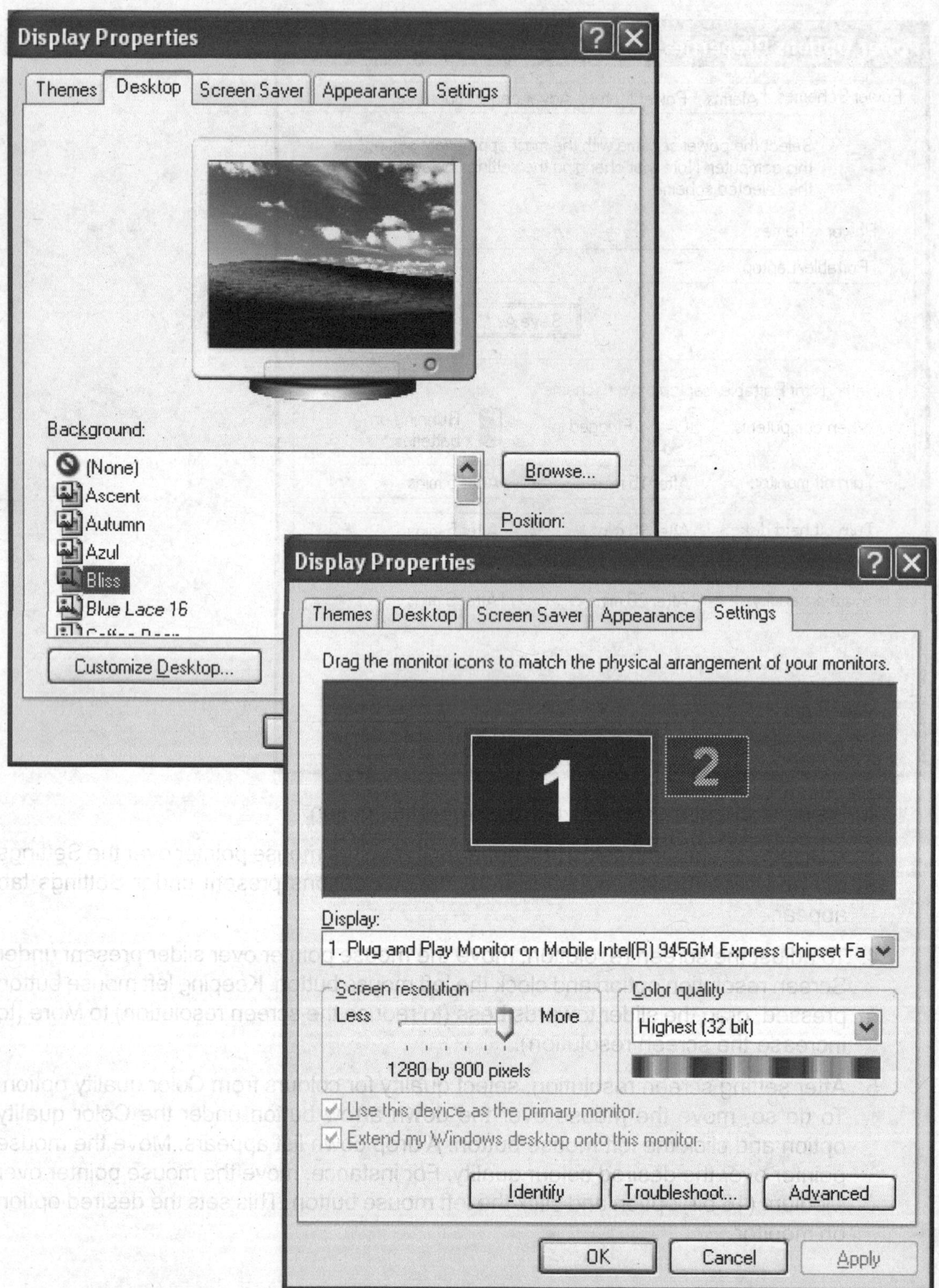

Display Properties
Themes
Desktop
Screen Saver
Appearance
Settings
Background:
(None)
Ascent
Autumn
Azul
Bliss
Blue Lace 16
Browse...
Position:
Customize Desktop...
Display Properties
Themes
Desktop
Screen Saver
Appearance
Settings
Drag the monitor icons to match the physical arrangement of your monitors.
1
2
Display:
1. Plug and Play Monitor on Mobile Intel(R) 945GM Express Chipset Fa
Screen resolution
Less
More
1280 by 800 pixels
Color quality
Highest (32 bit)
Use this device as the primary monitor.
Extend my Windows desktop onto this monitor.
Identify
Troubleshoot...
Advanced
OK
Cancel
Apply

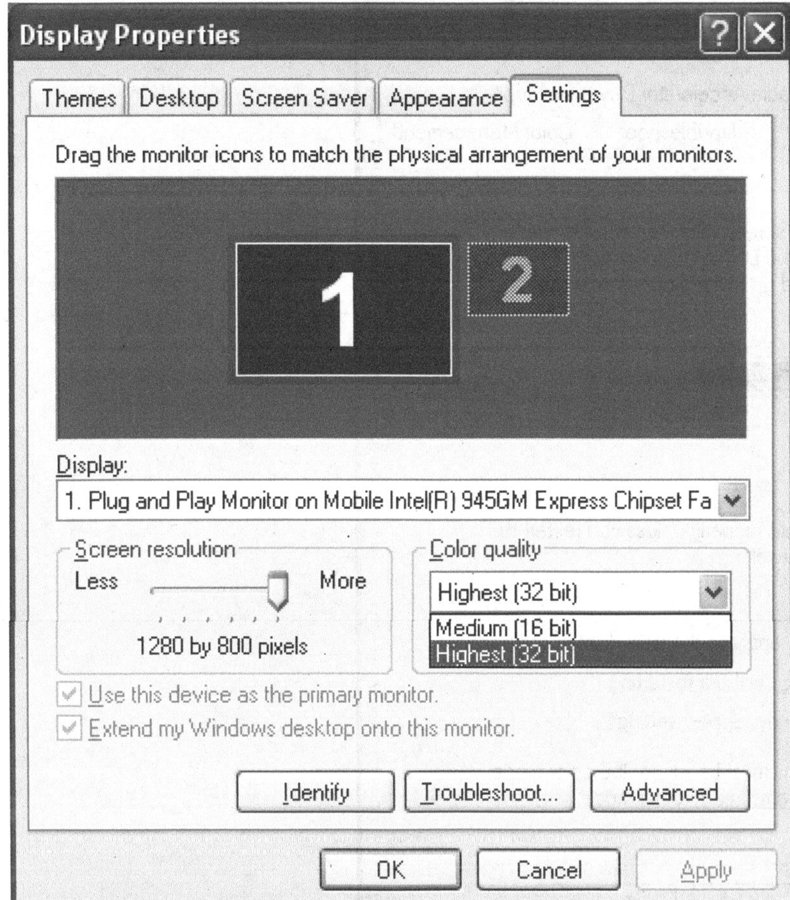

Advance Display Options for Monitor

The Advance button in Settings tab of Display Properties dialog box is used to configure advace options for a monitor. Advance options may include setting refresh rate for monitor, updating or removing driver, setting colour management for a monitor and troubleshoot problems related to a monitor. Let us now undertake following steps and learn to use advance options for a monitor.

1. In Settings tab of Display Properties dialog box, move the mouse pointer over the Advanced button and click the left mouse button.

2. An advance dialog box for monitor is installed on your computer appears. By default, the General tab appears first. The title bar of this dialog box displays text Plug and Play alongwith the name of the manufacturer which provides driver and other software support for monitor.

3. The DPI setting option in General tab is used to increase or decrease the size of screen. Increasing the DPI increases the size of every object on your screen. Similarly, on decreasing sizes of objects on screen are reduced. Let us now learn

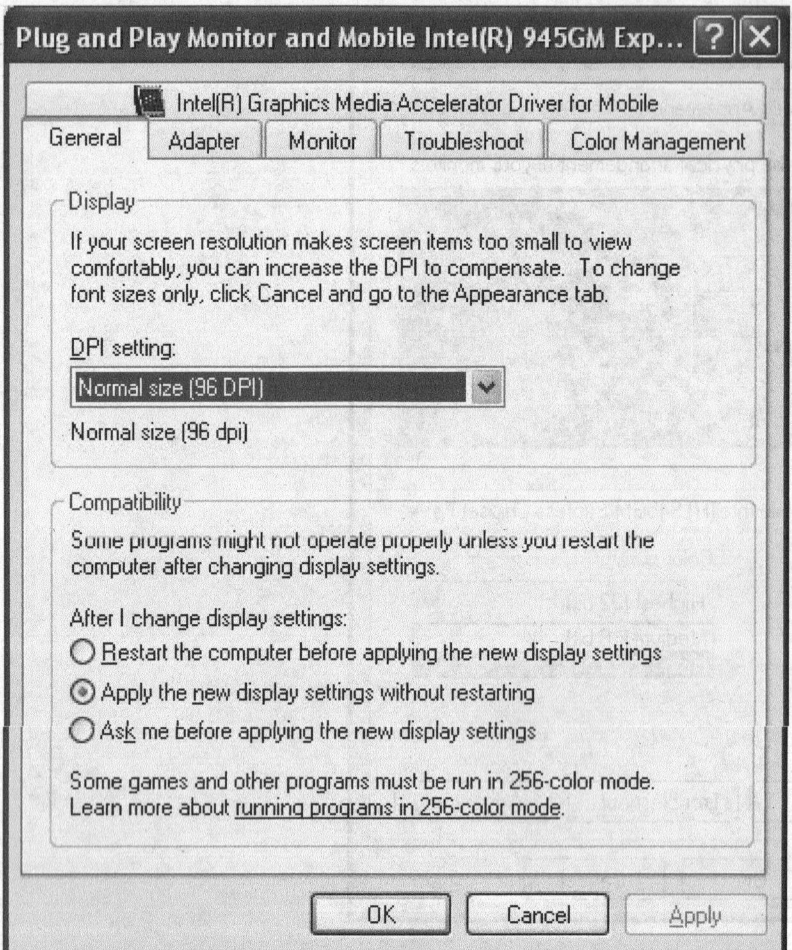

to change the DPI setting for monitor. To do so, move the mouse pointer over the down arrow button, present under the DPI setting option, and click the left mouse button. A drop down list appears.

4. Mouse the mouse pointer over the Custom setting option and click the left mouse.
5. A Custom DPI Setting dialog box appears. This dialog box contains an edit box with a down arrow button and a ruler. You can use:
   - Edit box to type value to increase or decrease the DPI level.
   - Down arrow button to display a pre-defined drop down list for DPI level.
   - Ruler to increase or decrease the DPI level. To do so, move the mouse pointer over ruler and click the left mouse button. Keeping it pressed, drag the mouse pointer towards the right side. As you move the pointer, the scale moves and value in edit box increases. After attaining the desired DPI level, release the mouse button.

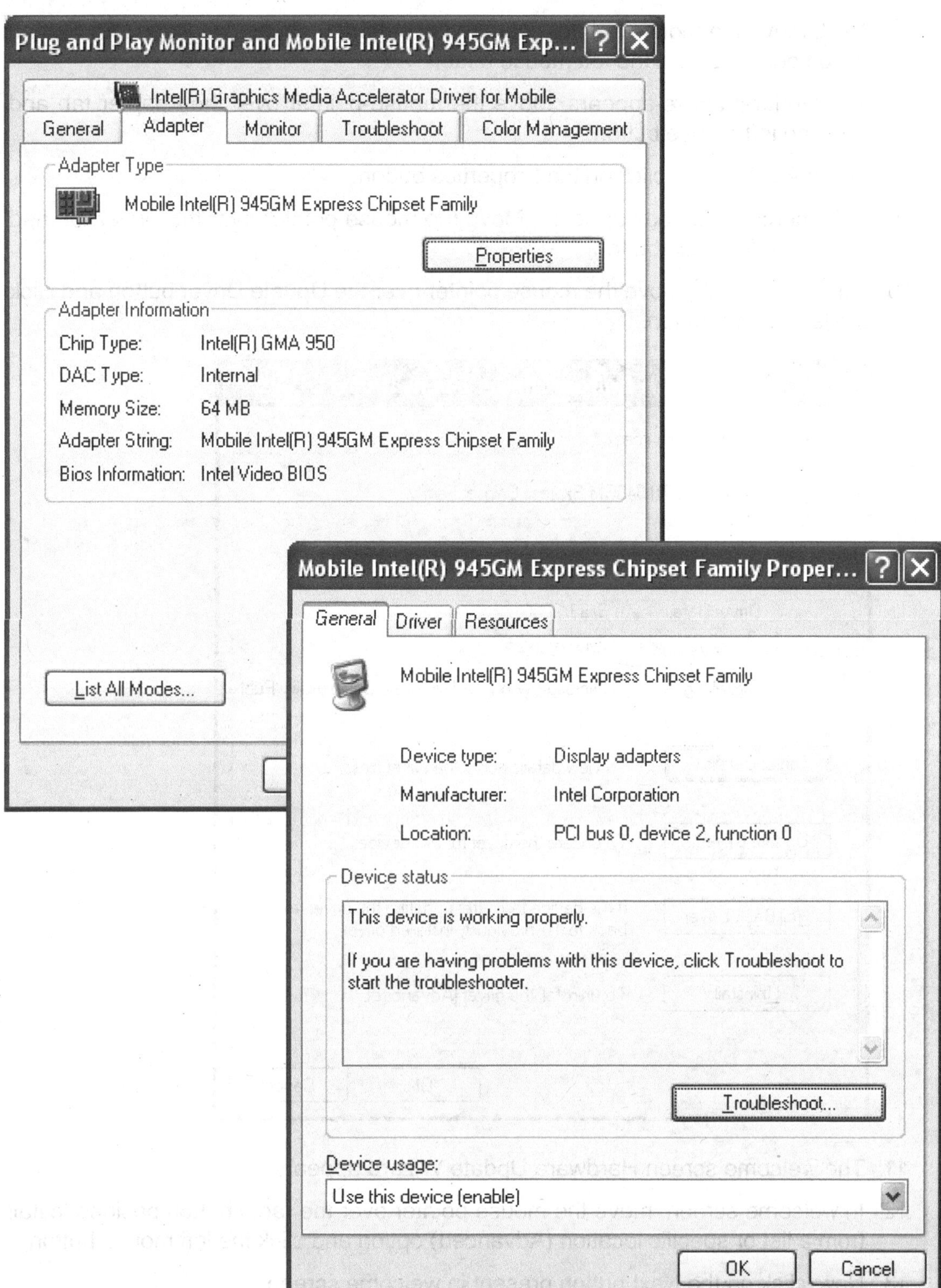
Plug and Play Monitor and Mobile Intel(R) 945GM Exp...
Intel(R) Graphics Media Accelerator Driver for Mobile
General
Adapter
Monitor
Troubleshoot
Color Management
Adapter Type
Mobile Intel(R) 945GM Express Chipset Family
Properties
Adapter Information
Chip Type: Intel(R) GMA 950
DAC Type: Internal
Memory Size: 64 MB
Adapter String: Mobile Intel(R) 945GM Express Chipset Family
Bios Information: Intel Video BIOS
List All Modes...
Mobile Intel(R) 945GM Express Chipset Family Proper...
General
Driver
Resources
Mobile Intel(R) 945GM Express Chipset Family
Device type: Display adapters
Manufacturer: Intel Corporation
Location: PCI bus 0, device 2, function 0
Device status
This device is working properly.
If you are having problems with this device, click Troubleshoot to start the troubleshooter.
Troubleshoot...
Device usage:
Use this device (enable)
OK
Cancel

6. Next, move the mouse pointer over the Ok button, present in Custom DPI Setting dialog box, and click the left mouse button.
7. The General tab re-appears. Move the mouse-pointer over the Adapter tab and click the left mouse button.
8. Under Adapter tab, click on the Properties button.
9. A Properties dialg box appears. Move the mouse pointer over the Driver tab and click the left mouse button.
10. Under Driver tab, move the mouse pointer over the Update Driver button and click the left mouse button.

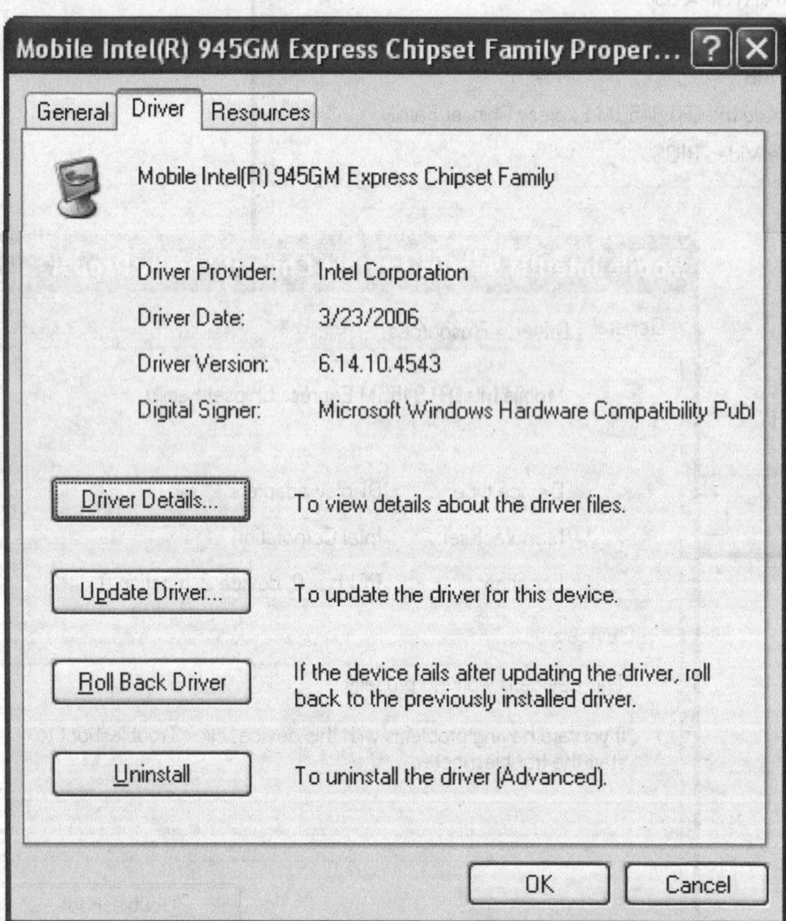

11. The welcome screen Hardware Update Wizard appears.
12. In welcome screen, move the mouse pointer over the radio button besides Install from a list or specific location (Advanced) option and click the left mouse button.
13. Now, click on the Next button present in welcome screen.

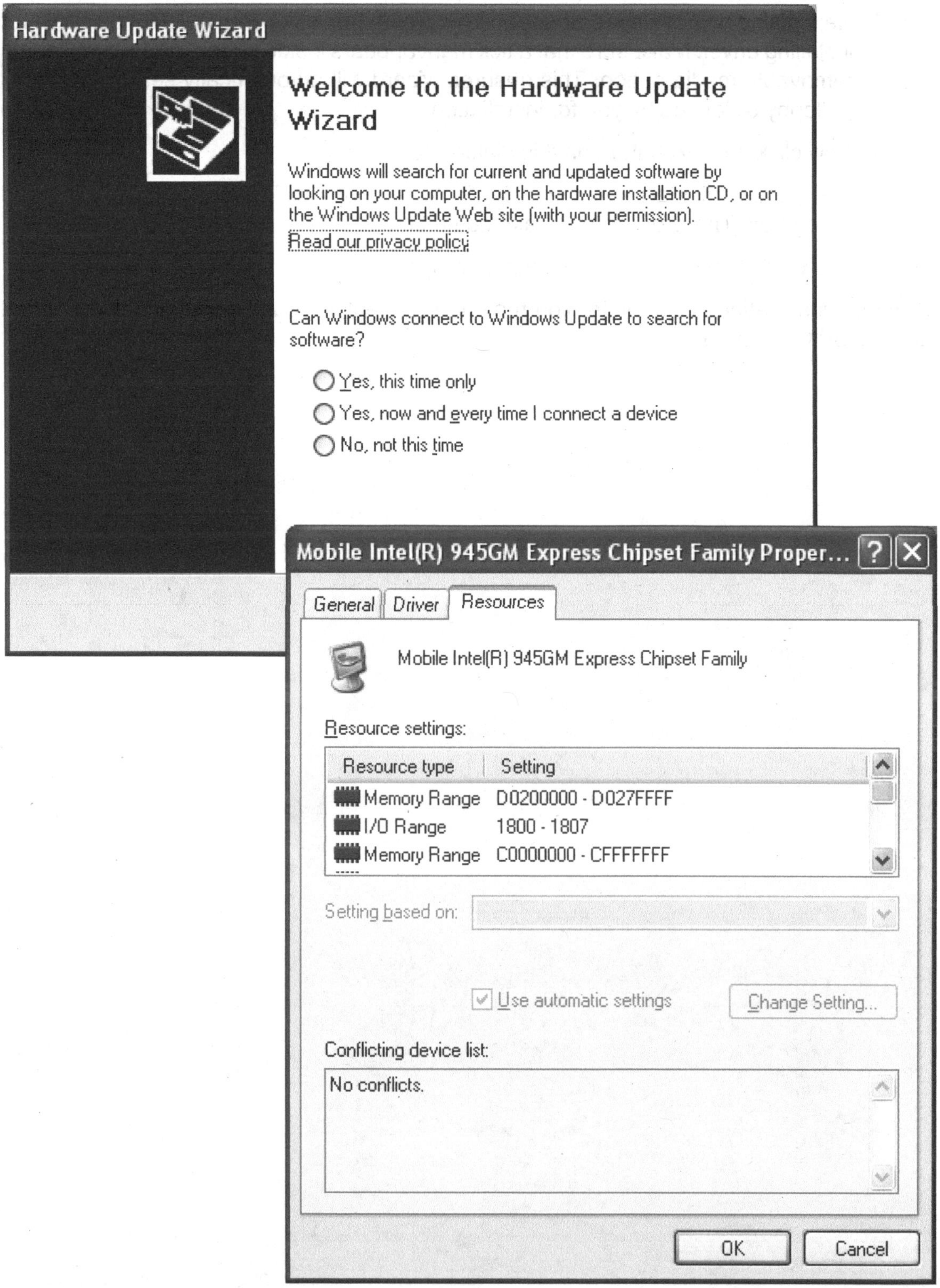

Hardware Update Wizard

Welcome to the Hardware Update Wizard

Windows will search for current and updated software by looking on your computer, on the hardware installation CD, or on the Windows Update Web site (with your permission).
Read our privacy policy

Can Windows connect to Windows Update to search for software?

- Yes, this time only
- Yes, now and every time I connect a device
- No, not this time

Mobile Intel(R) 945GM Express Chipset Family Proper...

General | Driver | Resources

Mobile Intel(R) 945GM Express Chipset Family

Resource settings:

Resource type	Setting
Memory Range	D0200000 - D027FFFF
I/O Range	1800 - 1807
Memory Range	C0000000 - CFFFFFFF

Setting based on:

Use automatic settings — Change Setting...

Conflicting device list:

No conflicts.

OK | Cancel

14. Next dialog box of wizard appears. This dialog box asks you to select a source for installing driver. Make sure that a tick mark appears inside check box beside Search removable media option. This ensures wizard will automatically search CD-ROM or floppy disk used by you for installation.
15. Now click on Next button on this dialog box.
16. The wizard will start searching CD-ROM or floppy disk used for installation and dialog box. The process may take some time.
17. The wizard will start the installation process.

Once the installation is complete, you may need to restart your computer. Save all work and restart the computer.

6 Printer

Introduction

A computer printer, or more commonly a printer, produces a hard copy (permanent human-readable text and/or graphics) of documents stored in electronic form, usually on physical print media such as paper or transparencies. Many printers are primarily used as local computer peripherals, and are attached by a printer cable to a computer which serves as a document source. Some printers, commonly known as network printers, have built-in network interfaces (typically wireless or Ethernet), and can serve as a hardcopy device for any user on the network. Individual printers are often designed to support both local and network connected users at the same time.

In addition, many modern printers can directly interface to electronic media such as memory sticks or memory cards, or to image capture devices such as digital cameras, scanners; some printers are combined with a scanners and/or fax machines in a single unit. Printers that include non-printing features are sometimes called Multi-Function Printers (MFP) or Multi-Function Devices (MFD).

A printer which is combined with a scanner can function as a photocopier if so designed. Most MFPs include printing, scanning, and copying among their features.

Printers are designed for low-volume, short-turnaround print jobs; requiring virtually no setup time to achieve a hard copy of a given document. However, printers are generally slow devices (30 pages per minute is considered fast; and many consumer printers are far slower than that), and the cost-per-page is relatively high.

In contrast, the printing press (which serves much the same function), is designed and optimized for high-volume print jobs such as newspaper print runs—printing presses are capable of hundreds of pages per minute or more, and have an incremental cost-per-page which is a fraction of that of printers.

The printing press remains the machine of choice for high-volume, professional publishing. However, as printers have improved in quality and performance, many jobs which used to be done by professional print shops are now done by users on local printers; see desktop publishing.

The world's first computer printer was a 19th century mechanically driven apparatus invented by Charles Babbage for his Difference Engine.

Printing Technology

Printers are routinely classified by the underlying print technology they employ; numerous such technologies have been developed over the years.

The choice of print engine has a substantial effect on what jobs a printer is suitable for, as different technologies are capable of different levels of image/text quality, print speed, low cost, noise; in addition, some technologies are inappropriate for certain types of physical media (such as carbon paper or transparencies).

Another aspect of printer technology that is often forgotten is resistance to alteration: liquid ink such as from an inkjet head or fabric ribbon becomes absorbed by the paper fibers, so documents printed with liquid ink are more difficult to alter than documents printed with toner or solid inks, which do not penetrate below the paper surface.

Checks should either be printed with liquid ink or on special "check paper with toner anchorage". For similar reasons carbon film ribbons for IBM Selectric typewriters bore labels warning against using them to type negotiable instruments such as checks. The machine-readable lower portion of a check, however, must be printed using MICR toner or ink. Banks and other clearing houses employ automation equipment that relies on the magnetic flux from these specially printed characters to function properly.

Various Features of Printers

Modes

Some printers operate in a number of different modes that trade off print quality for speed. These modes vary with the technology used by the printer.

Three of the most common modes for impact dot matrix printers are draft, near letter quality, and letter quality. Draft mode delivers the highest speed and the lowest quality. To achieve the highest possible speed, in draft mode the printers move their print heads faster than they can fire to print at each dot position on the paper. Typically, in draft mode these printers can blacken only every other dot. The thinly laid dots give text and graphics a characteristic gray look in draft mode. Near letter quality mode slows the print head so that text characters can be rendered without the machine gun, separated dots look of draft mode. Because the dot density is higher, characters appear fully black and are easier to read. Letter quality mode slows printing further, often using two or more passes to give as much detail as possible to each individual character. The printer concentrates on detail work, adding serifs and variable line weights to characters to make them look more like commercially printed text.

Color

Printers start with the primaries when it comes to color. They start with inks corresponding to the three primary colors—red, yellow, and blue. If you want anything beyond those, the printer must find some way of mixing them together. This mixing can be physical or optical.

The physical mixing of colors requires that two or more colors of ink actually mix together while they are wet. Printer inks are, however, designed to dry rapidly so the colors to be mixed must be applied simultaneously or in quick succession. Few printers rely on the physical mixing of inks to increase the number of colors they produce.

Optical mixing takes place in either of two ways. One color of ink can be applied over another (that has already dried), or the colors can be applied adjacent to one another.

Applied multiple layers of color require that the inks be to some degree transparent, as a truly opaque ink would obscure the first color to be applied. Most modern printer inks are transparent, which allows them to be used on transparencies for overhead projection as well as paper. The exact hue of a transparent ink is, of course, dependent on the color of the medium it is applied to.

Optical mixing also takes place when dots of two or more colors are intermixed. If the dots are so close together than the eye cannot individually resolve each one, their colors blend together on the retina, blending the individual hues together. Most PC color printers take advantage of this kind of optical mixing by dithering

Print Engines

The actual mechanism that forms an image on paper is called the print engine. Each uses a somewhat different physical principle to put ink on paper. Although each technology has its strengths, weaknesses, and idiosyncrasies, you might not be able to tell the difference between the pages they print. Careful attention to detail has pushed quality up to a level where the paper rather than the printer is the chief limit on resolution, and color comes close to photographic, falling short only on the depth that only a thick gelatin coating makes possible. In making those images, however, the various print engine technologies work differently at different speeds, at different noise levels, and with different requirements. These differences can make one style of print engine a better choice for your particular application than others.

Impact Printers

A printer in which printing is the result of mechanically striking the printing medium. An impact printer makes contact with the paper to produce an image. The impact may be produced by a print hammer character, like that of a typewriter key striking a ribbon against the paper or by a print hammer hitting paper and ribbon against a character.

An impact printer must be used if printing a multiple copy report so that the duplicate copies will receive the imprint.

Impact printers are of following types:

Solid Font

A complete character, such as on a typewriter key, strikes a carbon ribbon or other inked surface against paper to produce an image of the character. The solid-font characters are mounted on one of several types of printing heads such as a ball, wheel or cup.

Advantage

- The advantage of a solid-font over non-solid is that they give the best quality formed character images.

Disadvantage

- Solid-font print heads are usually slower than other types.

Dot-Matrix Printer

In it the individual characters are formed by a matrix of wires or styluses. Dot-matrix printers are also called serial printers. The images are formed by a print head that is composed of a series of little print hammers that look like the heads of pins. The print head usually has nine pins or 24 pines. The bottom 2 pins are used to form the descenders of lower case letters viz., p, q, g and y. Many expensive dot-matrix printers do not provide descenders, but print quality is improved when they are used.

The modern minimal printer uses an impact dot matrix print engine. The heart of the machine is a mechanical print head that shuttles back and forth across the width of the paper. A number of thin print wires act as the hammers that squeeze ink from a fabric or Mylar ribbon to paper.

Working Principle of Dot Matrix Printer

In most impact dot matrix printers, a seemingly complex but efficient mechanism controls each of the print wires. The print wire normally is held away from the ribbon and paper, and against the force of a spring, by a strong permanent magnet. The magnet is wrapped with a coil of wire that forms an electromagnet, wound so that its polarity is the opposite of that of the permanent magnet.

To fire the print wire against the ribbon and paper, this electromagnet is energized (under computer control, of course), and its field neutralizes that of the permanent magnet. Without the force of the permanent magnet holding the print wire back, the spring forcefully jabs the print wire out against the ribbon, squeezing ink onto the paper. After the print wire makes its dot, the electromagnet is de-energized and the permanent magnet pulls the print wire back to its idle position, ready to fire again. The Mechanical Section or DMP is shown next.

The two-magnets-and-spring approach is designed with one primary purpose—to hold the print wire away from the paper (and out of harm's way) when no power is supplied to the printer and the print head. The complexity is justified .by the protection it affords the delicate print wires.

The print head of a dot matrix printer is made from a number of these print wire mechanisms. Most first generation personal computer printers and many current machines use nine wires arrayed in a vertical column. To produce high quality, the second generation of these machines increased the number of print wires to 18 or 24. These often are arranged in parallel rows with the print wires vertically staggered, although some machines use different arrangements. Because the larger number of print wires fit into the same space (and print

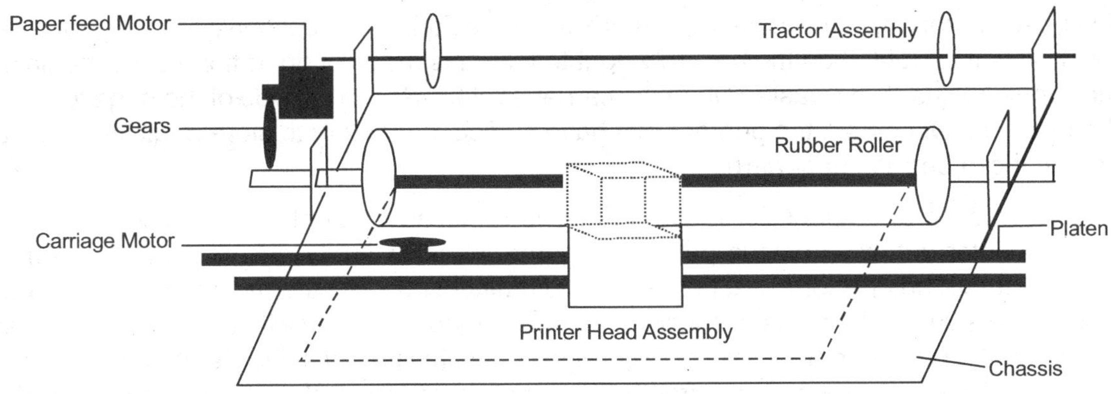

Mechanical Section of DMP

at the same character height), they can pack more detail into what they print. Because they are often finer than the print wires of lesser endowed machines, the multitude of print wires also promises higher resolution.

No matter the number of print wires, the print head moves horizontally as a unit across the paper to print a line of characters or graphics. Each wire fires as necessary to form the individual characters or the appropriate dots for the graphic image. The impact of each wire is precisely timed so that it falls on exactly the right position in the matrix. The wires fire on the fly—the print head never pauses until it reaches the other side of the paper.

When computer sends series of hex data in hex format this code type of data represents the character to be printed with the help of printer this data may be punctuation mark tabs, enter and various other types of keyboard words that are sent to the printer by the computer. These codes are first of all stored into buffer Ram or memory because usually printer is a slower device as compare to computer so printer sends this data slowly when the printer Ram is full of the data then printer sends the acknowledgement signals to the computer so that computer can stop sending more data to the printer. The codes stored into the buffer Ram of printer are hexal decimal numbers in the form of binary and these codes represent alphabets like A, B, C in both types of formats capital and small also codes indicate various character and special symbols after storing data the printer microprocessor will send this data to the print head so that a definite print out can be taken. Electrical signals from the microprocessor are amplified and travel to particular circuits to the head which contain 9 pins or 24 pins called printing pins that are erroring in state lines one and of each pins is connected to an electromagnetic the current from the microprocessor activates the magnetic and creates a magnetic field around the so line.

Oid (electromagnet) which repels a magnetic on the end of the pin causing the pin to strike the surface of the ribbon.

The moving pin strikes a ribbon which is coated with ink the impact of pin is used to create a dot on the surface on paper. Due to impact action DMP is also called impact type of printer. The force of impact transfer ink from ribbon to paper surface.

To speed operation, some impact dot matrix machines print bi-directionally, rattling out one row from left to right, then the next row right to left. This mode of operation saves the time that would ordinarily be wasted when the carriage returns to the left side of the page to start the next line. Of course, the printer must have sufficient memory to store a full line of text so that it can be read backwards.

Adding color to an impact dot matrix printer is relatively straightforward. The color the impact printer actually prints is governed by the ink in or on its ribbon. Although some manufacturers build color impact printer using multiple ribbons, the most successful (and least expensive) designed used special multi-colored ribbons lined with three or four bands corresponding to the primary colors. To change colors, the printer shifts the ribbon vertically so a differently hued band lies in front of the print wires. Most of the time the printer will render a row in one color, shift ribbon colors, then go across the same row in a different color. Of course, the color ribbon costs more and does not last as long as its monochrome equivalent.

As with their typewriter progenitors, all impact dot matrix printers have a number of desirable qualities. Owing to their heritage of more than a century of engineering refinement, they represent a mature technology. Their designs and functions are relatively straightforward and familiar.

Impact technology takes the lead when you share one of the most common business needs, making multi-part forms. Impact printers can hammer an impression not just through a ribbon, but through several sheets of paper as well. Slide a carbon between the sheets or, better yet, treat the paper for non-carbon duplicates, and you get multiple, guaranteed identical copies with a single pass through the mechanism. For a number of business applications—for example the generation of charge receipts—exact carbon copies are a necessity, and impact printing is an absolute requirement. The output from DMP is in the form of dots.

Principal of DMP

The head of DMP works on the basic of electromagnetic induction.

The DOT MATRIX PRINTER (DMP) is an example of Impact printer because while printing the printer head comes in contact with the printing paper. Printer is a simple device consists of mechanical section and Electronic section. It has two sections in electronics.

1. Power Supply Unit (PSU)
2. Logic Card.

Dot Matrix Printer consists of the following:

Power Switch

The power switch is used to turn power to the printer on and off. It is on the left side near the back.

Tractors

The tractors are the sprockets that feed continuous fan-folded paper into the printer and keep the paper properly aligned.

Platen

The platen is the hard steel rod on which the cartridge assembly move.

Paper Feed Knob

The paper feed knob turns the platen. By turning this knob, you can manually feed the paper. Please do not rotate this knob when the printer is powered on.

Paper Select Lever

The paper select lever adjusts the pressure on the platen according to the type and thickness of paper.

Top Cover

The top cover protects the MSP printer from dirt and dust as well as reducing the sound level while printing. The top cover helps hold the paper against the platen when the tractor is installed in the "push" position. The top cover has special beveled edge for tearing off the paper.

Single-Sheet Guide/Paper Separator

The single-sheet guide is used for loading single sheets of paper. It also acts as a paper separator (in the down position) when using continuous paper.

Paper Thickness Lever

The paper thickness lever adjusts the print head to accommodate different paper thickness and types of forms. You can also increase the life of your ribbon by adjusting this lever.

Paper Park Lever

The paper park lever adjusts the printer's tractor mechanism for switching between continuous paper and single sheets, without having to manually remove the continuous paper.

Pressure Release Lever

The pressure release lever is used when you have the tractor mechanism installed in the push position or when you are feeding single sheets. It improves the paper feeding and hence quality of graphics printing.

Control Panel

The control panel is located on the right front of the MSP. It consists of four tactile switches and six lights to indicate the printer status.

On Line Light

The online light is built into the online switch. When this light glows, the printer is online and is ready to work.

Font Lights

The font lights indicate which typeface one is currently using. Selections include: Draft, High sped draft, NLQ Roman, NLQ Sans serif and NLQ Script. By pressing the FONT switch when the printer is OFGFLINE, you can scroll through the options and the lights will indicate, which one is to be selected.

Pitch Lights

These lights indicated the character pitch you are using. By pressing the switch wile the printer is OFFLINE, you can scroll through the options such as Pica Elite and condensed.

ONLINE Switch

Pressing the switch toggles the printer between ONLINE and OFFLINE states.

OFFLINE Mode

Micro line feed (reverse): While holding the ONLINE switch press LF/FF switch. Each time one presses, the printer reverses the paper in micro steps (1/72 Inch).

In MENU mode

Save: Press ONLINE switch to save the current filed selection in the non-volatile memory of the printer. While powering on.

Configuration reset: Hold the ONLINE switch and power on the printer to reset the content's of the non-volatile memory to the factory default settings.

Self-Test Of DMP Printer

1. With the paper loaded on the printer and the power switch- OFF, plug the power cord into an electrical outlet
2. While holding down the LF/FF switch, turn ON the power switch.
3. If you want to interrupt the self-test, press the ONLINE switch.
4. To resume, press ONLINE switch again.
5. If you want to stop the self-test, turn the power switch OFF. The printer will continue printing until you turn the printer OFF.

Connecting Printer with Computer

Computer and Printer communicate by means of a cable, which is usually sold separately. Each computer uses a slightly different cable so you'll need one made specifically for your computer. The cable one needs is called a Centronics parallel printer cable or a parallel printer interface cable as shown in next two figures. It's possible to purchase a cable with

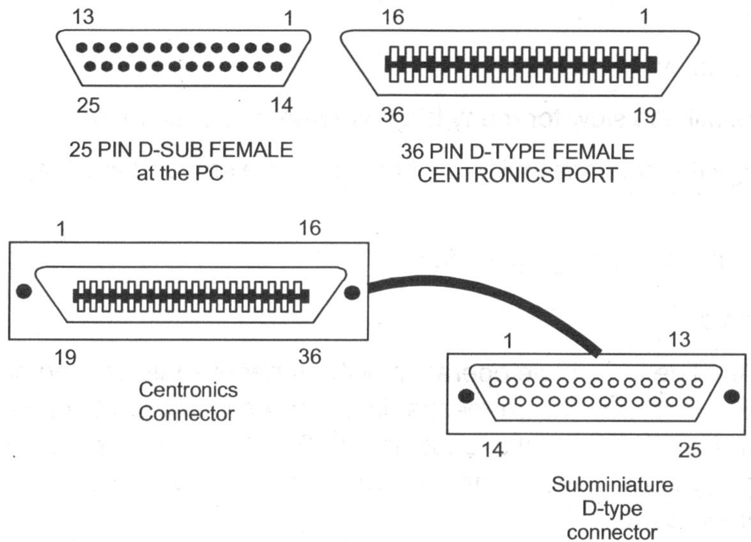

Parallel and Centronics Port

the connector attached perpendicular to the cable; this allows you to place the printer close to a wall.

Drawbacks

1. Their speed limitation is slow as compared to line printers.
2. Their print resolutions are inferior to the daisywheel printers.
3. These printers may not be able to print graphic objects adequately but can handle applications such as accounting, personnel and payroll very well.

Daisywheel Printers

A serial impact printer in which the printing element is a plastic hub that has a large number of flexible radial spokes, each spoke having one or more different raised printing characters, the wheel is rotated as it is moved horizontally step by step under computer control, and stops when a desired character is in a desired print position so a hammer can drive that character against an inked ribbon.

Daisy Wheel Printers are slower than dot-matrix printers, but they produce a high-resolution output. This high-resolution output is often called letter quality printing because it is suitable for business letters and memos. You can print in as may type fonts or foreign languages on a daisywheel printer as there are print wheels to fit your particular model of machine.

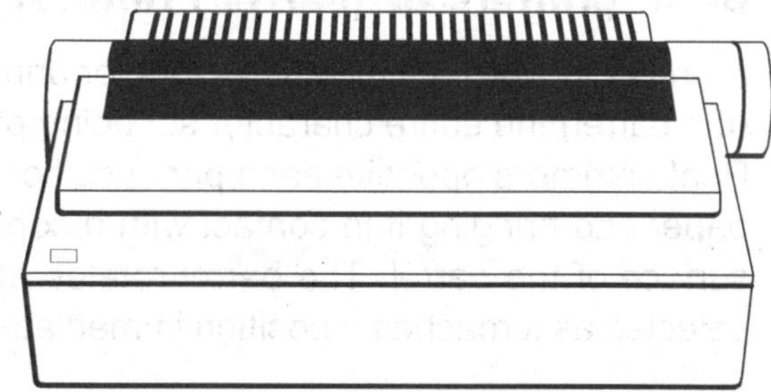

It is also called as a smart printer because of its bi-directional printing and built-in microprocessor control features.

Disadvantages

1. They are noisy
2. They are still too slow for many large volume output situations.
3. To change the typeface style, machine has to be stopped and then the print wheel is changed.
4. They cannot produce graphic output.

Line Printers

It prints an entire line in a single operation without necessarily printing one character at a time. These are generally electro-mechanical devices which print complete lines of print, up to 160 characters in width, at speeds about 300 to 2000 lines per minute. Line printers are used primarily in the mini/mainframe processing environment. Examples of line-at-a-time impact printers are:

1. Chain Printers
2. Band Printers and
3. Drum Printers

Chain Printers

It is a high-speed printer in which the type are carried by the links of a revolving chain. As the characters on the print chain revolve in a horizontal loop, a desired character eventually aligns in a given column. At this instant, the hammer strikes the paper forcing the page into the inked ribbon and the ribbon against the character thus creating the desired symbol on the print page. The chain is cycled continuously until a complete print line has been formed. The print page is then advanced one line and the process is repeated.

Band Printers

On a band printer, several similar sets of fully formed characters are embossed on a horizontal band that is continuously moving in front of the print hammers. In band printer, the paper is momentarily stopped and, as the desired character passes over a given column, the hammer activates, pressing the ribbon against the paper to form the image. It is a line printer that uses band of type characters as its printing mechanism.

Drum printers or (barrel Printers)

A printer in which all the characters for printing are placed round the surface of a cylinder (the barrel) the entire character set being placed round the cylinder at each print position. Print hammers opposite each print position can be activated by the computer striking the paper and bringing it in contact with a continuous ink ribbon between the paper and the surface of the barrel. The barrel rotates at high speed, the appropriate character being selected as it reaches a position immediately opposite the print hammers. A complete line of output is printed for each revolution of the drum since all the characters in each set pass their print stations during revolution.

Non-Impact Printers

Printers that do not strike characters against ribbon or paper when they print, are non-impact printers. Example of non-impact printers include

1. Ink-jet printers
2. Laser printers

These printers makes much less noise than impact printers.

If you are using a non-impact printer, do not try to print on multiple-part carbon forms: because no impact is being made on the paper you will end up with no copies.

A drum printer uses 80 or more character sets embossed on a cylindrical drum. A separate hammer for each character set forces the print page into an inked ribbon and the character when the character aligns at the print position.

Advantages of Non-impact Printers

1. They are faster and quieter
2. They have got the ability to change typefaces automatically and their ability to produce high-quality graphics.

Ink-jet Printers

It uses a technique of projecting droplets of ink at paper to form the required image. Ink-jet printer create an image directly on paper by spraying ink through as many as 64 tiny nozzles. It provides a print resolution of around 360 dots per inch.

The InkJet printers consist of a special nozzle type head. Ink passes through ionic chamber (special) Ink charges in this chamber. The charged ink is passed through the given to electrical field and variation is done in electronic field the charges shape come in the drop.

The ink is passed through the special ink chamber so as to provide it with the charge the changed ink drop when ejected through the nozzle has to pass through various deflection field produced by deflecting coils which are controlled by logic circuit. The charge in drop after passing through this field attains the necessary shape on the paper.

Today's most popular personal printers use inkjet print engines. The odd name "inkjet" actually describes the printing technology. The outlook of inkjet printer is shown here. It sprays droplets of ink onto paper-it works well enough to deliver image sharpness on a par with most other output technologies.

In essence, the inkjet printer is a line printer, little more than a dot matrix printer with the hammer impact removed. Instead of a hammer pounding ink onto paper, the inkjet flings it into place from tiny nozzles, each one corresponding to a print wire of the impact dot matrix printer. The motive force can be an electromagnet or, as is more likely today, a piezoelectric crystal (a thin crystal that bends when electricity is applied across it). A sharp, digital pulse of electricity causes the crystal to twitch and force ink through the nozzle into its flight to paper. The types of inkjet engines are commonplace: thermal, piezoelectric, and phase-change.

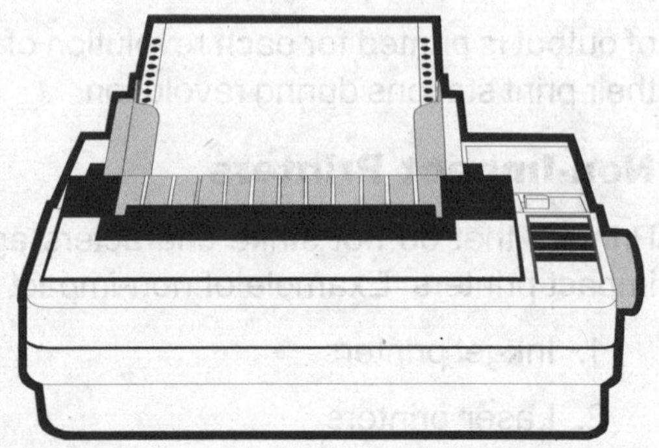

At heart, the basic technology of all three kinds of inkjets is the same. The machines rely on the combination of the small orifice in the nozzle and the surface tension of liquid ink to prevent a constant dibble from the jets. Instead of oozing out, the ink puckers around the hole in the inkjet the same way that droplets of water bead up on a waxy surface. The tiny ink droplets scrunch together rather than spreading out or flowing from the nozzle because the attraction of the molecules in the ink (or water) is stronger than the force of gravity. The inkjet engine needs to apply some force to break the surface tension and force the ink out, and that's where the differences in inkjet technologies arise.

InkJet printers are mostly used medium type of printers between Laser and DMP. These are very small type of printers, which provide higher resolution as compare to DMP cost of inkjet printers is the cost of DMP so we can say that these are the cheaply used printers with respect to DMP but the per page cost of InkJet printer must higher then the DMP. These printers are void ally used because lost of these printers is best speed is also best and quality is also some much better DMP and Laser. The print out taken with the help of InkJet printer is all most same with that taken with a Laser another quality of inkjet is that these printers print very silently but high amount of noise is associated with DMP so we can say that InkJet printer is the best for there similarly to Laser printers the InkJet printer really works better then a DMP also InkJet have print head that can travel approach the width of page that can print the almost line with one pass.

This mechanical movement puts inkjet printer in the same category as the DMP. As the inkjet printer print character by character so the speed of inkjet printer is specified in character per second. Usually it is 100 to 200 characters per second the main different between resolutions of a printer is defined as number of dots per inch. The main different between inkjet printer and DMP is the inkjet printer head an inkjet printer spits all through ink on the surface of paper to produce a print out but its technology is much better as compare to DMP.

An inkjet is attached to the head which moves across the width of paper which is the colored data is given to the print head contains four ink cartages one for Red, Blue, Yellow, Black and each cartages of printer head is made up of ink filled chambers each attached to a nozzle smaller than hair. An electrical current flows to thin resistances at the bottom of all the color that printer will use to form a small section of a word or picture. A resistance used here is called film type resistance when current passes through the resistance a high amount of heat is produced it will occur. The temperature produced here is more than 900^{0}f only for a second. The ink jets boiled due to this and forms a bubble of vapor. As the vapor expands it pushes ink through the nozzle. The vapor of printer in the form of a drop jet at the tip of nozzle. The drop jet over comes the pressure of the bubble forces the drop Jet over to the paper. The volume of the ink is above one million of a drop of water from an eyedropper. A typical character is formed by twenty drops across and 30 high.

How printer colors are Created

All colors are made up of different combinations of light we see all the wavelength that make white light through a prism a white light is broken into various color by the prism. The various colors are called spectrum. The spectrum is a mixture of colors. Different mixture of primary color can create any color from the spectrum by either enabling colors or subtracting. Color mixing is of two types additive color mixing subtractive color mixing. Additive color mixing is used to create colors and television. Computer monitors and in movies. Three colors Red, Green, Blue are used to produce all other colors.

Subtractive color Mixing

Reflection properties are used. All color printer use small dots of four inks to make various shades are made by learning dots of unprinted while some printers uses this type of process. Most common color computer can operate up to 3001. But now a day's printer of 700 DPI and 1440 DPI are also used.

Advantages

1. Many of ink-jet printers can also be programmed to print unusual symbols, *e.g.*, Japanese or Chinese characters.
2. It provide an excellent middle ground between dot-matrix and laser printers.
3. Multiple-nozzle print heads enables them to print in several colours.

Disadvantages

1. They can only create one character at a time and therefore cannot match the print speed of line printers.
2. They are expensive

Laser Printers

The one revolution that has changed the faces of both offices and forests around the world was the photocopier. Trees plummet by the millions to provide fodder for the duplicate, triplicate, megaplicate. Today's non-impact, bi-image laser printer owes its life to this technology. The outlook of Laser Printer shown here.

At heart, the laser printer principle is simple. Some materials react to light in strange ways. Selenium and some complex organic compounds modify their electrical conductivity in response to exposure to light. Both copiers and laser printers capitalize on this photoelectric effect by focusing an optical image on a photo-conductive drum that has been given a static electrical charge. The charge drains away from the conductive areas that have been struck by light but persists in the dark areas. A special pigment called a toner is then spread across the drum, and the toner sticks to the charged areas. A roller squeezes paper against the drum to transfer the pigment to the paper. The pigment gets bonded to the paper by heating or "fusing" it.

The laser printer actually evolved from the photocopier. Rather than the familiar electrostatic Xerox machine, however, the true ancestor of the laser printer was a similar competing process called electro-photography, which used a bright light to capture an image and make it visible with a fine carbon-based toner. The process was developed during the 1960s by Keizo Yamaji at Canon. The first commercial application of the technology, called New Process to distinguish it from the old process (xerography), was a Canon photocopier released in 1968.

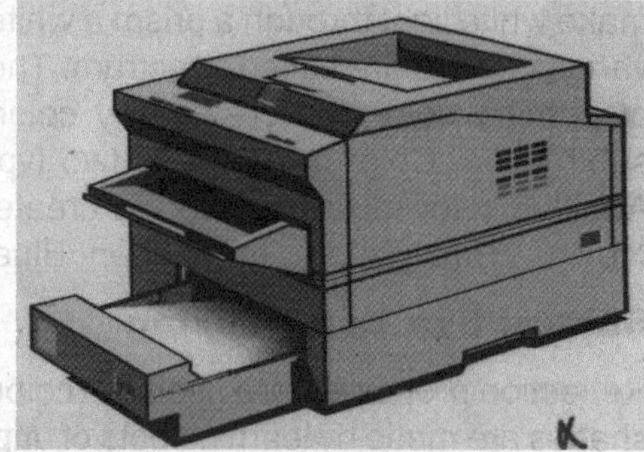

The first true laser printer was a demonstration unit, made by Canon in 1975, that was based on a modified photocopier. The first commercial PC laser printer came in 1984 v/hen Hewlett-Packard introduced its first LaserJet, which was based on the Canon CX engine. At heart, it and all later lasers use the same process, a kind of heat set, light inspired offset printing.

The magic in a laser printer is forming the image by making a laser beam scan back and forth across the imaging drum. The trick, well known to stage magicians, is to use mirrors. A small rotating mirror reflects the laser across the drum, tracing each scan line across it. The drum rotates to advance to the next scan line, synchronized to the flying beam of laser light. To make the light and dark pattern of the image, the laser beam is modulated on and off. It's rapidly switched on for light areas, off for dark areas, one minuscule dot at a time to form a bit image.

The major variations on laser printing differ only in the light beam and how it is modulated. LCD-shutter printers, for example, put an electronic shutter (or an array of them) between a constant light source (which need not be a laser) and the imaging drum to modulate the beam. LED printers modulates ordinary Light-Emitting Diodes as their optical source. In any case, these machines rely on the same electro-photographic process as the laser printer to carry out the actual printing process.

The basic laser printer mechanism requires more than just a beam and a drum. In fact, it involves several drums or rollers, as many as six in a single-color printer and more in color machines. Each has a specific role in the printing process. The Mechanical Section of Laser Printer is shown here.

The imaging drum, often termed the OPC for optical photoconductor, must first be charged before it will accept an image. A special roller called the charging roller applies the electrostatic charge uniformly across the OPC.

After the full width of an area of the OPC gets its charge, it rotates in front of the modulated light beam. As the beam scans across the OPC drum and the drum turns; the system creates an electrostatic replica of the page to be printed.

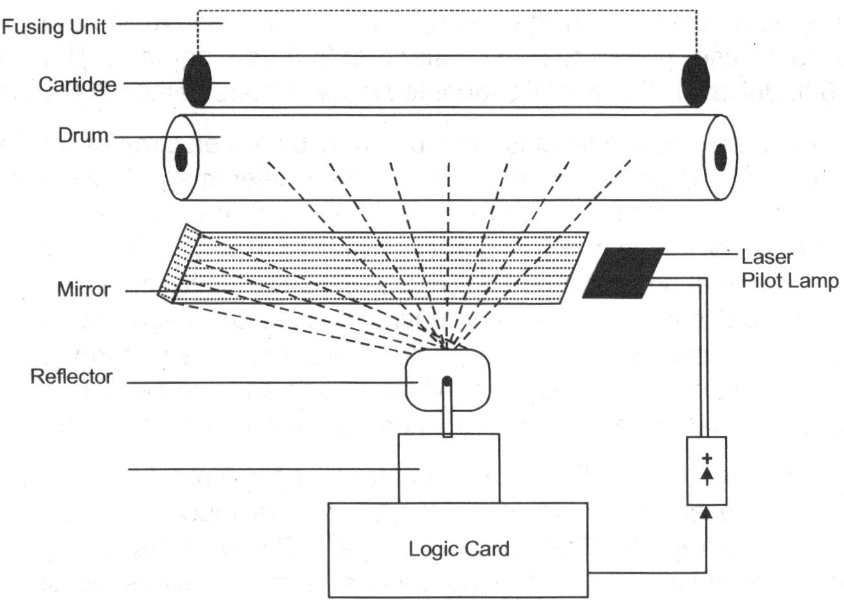

Mechanism of Laser Printer

To form a visible image, a developing roller then dusts the OPC drum with particles of toner. The light-struck areas with an electrostatic charge attract and hold the toner against the drum. The unexposed parts of the drum do not.

The printer rolls the paper between the OPC drum and a transfer roller, which has a strong electrostatic charge that attracts the toner off the drum. Because the paper is between the transfer roller and the OPC drum, the toner collects on the paper in accord with the pattern that was formed by the modulated laser. At this point only a slight electrostatic charge holds the toner to the paper.

To make the image permanent, the printer squeezes the paper between a fuser and backup roller. As the paper passes through, the printer heats the fuser to a high temperature—on the order of 350 degrees Fahrenheit (200 degrees Celsius). The heat of the fuser and the pressure from the backup roller melt the toner and stick it permanently on the paper. The completed page rolls out of the printer.

Meanwhile, the OPC drum continues to spin, wiping the already-printed area against a cleaning blade that scrapes any leftover toner from it. As the drum rotates around to the charging roller again, the process repeats. Early lasers used OPC drums large enough to hold an entire single-page image. Modern machines use smaller rollers that form the image as a continuous process.

Although individual manufacturers may alter this basic layout to fit a particular package or to refine the process, the technology used by all laser machines is essentially the same. At a given resolution level, the results produced by most mechanisms is about the same, too. You need an eye loupe to see the differences. The major difference is that manufacturers have progressively refined both the mechanism and the electronics to produce higher resolutions Basic laser printer resolution starts at 300 dots per inch. The mainstream is now at the 600 dpi level. The-best PC-oriented laser printers boast 1200 dpi resolution.

In most lasers, the resolution level is fixed primarily by the electronics inside the printer. The most important part of the control circuitry is the Raster Image Processor, also known as the RIP. The job of the RIP is to translate the string of characters or other printing commands into the bit image that the printer transfers to paper. In effect, the RIP works like a video board, interpreting drawing commands (a single letter in a print stream is actually a drawing command to print that letter), computing the position of each dot on the page, and pushing the appropriate value into the printer's memory. The memory of the printer is arranged in a raster just like the raster of a video screen and one memory cell—a single bit in the typical black and white laser printer—corresponds to each dot position on paper.

The RIP itself may, by design, limit a laser printer to a given resolution. Some early laser printers made this constraint into an advantage, allowing resolution upgrades through after-market products that replaced the printer's internal RIP and controlled the printer and its laser through a video input. The video input earns its name because its signal is applied directly to the light source in the laser in raster scanned form (like a television image), bypassing most of the printer's electronics. The add-in processor can modulate the laser at higher rates to create higher resolutions.

Moving from 300 dpi to 600 dpi and 1200 dpi means more than changing the RIP and adding memory, however. The higher resolutions also demand improved toner formulations because, at high resolutions, the size of toner particles limits sharpness much as the size of print wires limits impact dot matrix resolution. With higher resolution laser printers, it becomes increasingly important to get the right toner, particularly if you have toner cartridges refilled. The wrong toner limits resolution just as a fuzzy ribbon limits the quality of impact printer output.

Adding color to a laser printer is more than dumping a few more colors of toner. The laser must separately image each of its three or four primary colors and transfer the toner corresponding to each to the paper. The imaging process for each color requires forming an entire image by passing it past the OPC drum. Forming a complete image consequently requires three or four passes of the drum.

Exactly what constitutes a pass varies among manufacturers. Most color laser printers use three or four distinct passes of each sheet of paper. The paper rolls around the drum and makes four complete turns. Each color gets images separately on the drum, then separately transferred to the sheet. The printer wipes the drum clean between passes.

So-called "one-pass" printing, pioneered by Hewlett-Packard, still requires the drum to make four complete passes as each color gets separately scanned on the drum, and toner is dusted on the drum separately for each color. The paper, however, only passes once through the machine to accept the full color image at once and to have all four colors fused together onto the paper. The first three colors merely transfer to the drum. After the last color—black—gets coated on the drum, the printer runs the paper through and transfers the toner to it. The paper thus makes a single pass through the printer, hence the "one-pass" name.

This single-pass laser technology yields no real speed advantage. The photoconductor drum still spins around the same number of times as a four-pass printer. The speed at which the drum turns and the number of turns it makes determines engine speed, so the one-pass process doesn't make a significant performance increase.

The advantage to one-pass color laser printing comes in the registration of the separate color images. With conventional color laser systems, the alignment of the paper must be critically maintained for all four passes in order for all the colors to properly line up. With the one-pass system, paper alignment is not a problem. Only the drum needs to maintain its alignment, which is easy to do because it is part of the mechanism rather than an interloper from the outside world.

No matter the number of passes, adding color in laser printing subtracts speed. In general, color laser speed falls to one-quarter the monochrome speed of a similar engine because of the requirement of four passes. (With three-pass printing, speed falls to one-third the monochrome rate). For example, a printer rated at 12 pages per minute in monochrome will deliver about 3 ppm in color. Even allowing for this slowdown, however, color lasers are usually faster than other color page printers. They are also often quieter. Compared to thermal wax transfer printers, a popular high quality color technology, they are also economical because a laser uses toner only for the actual printed image. Thermal wax machines need a full page of ink for each page printed no matter the density of the image.

Working of Laser Printer

1. Eraser Lamp clears residual charge from drum
2. Main corona puts-6KV charge on drum surface
3. Laser beam selectively hits parts of the EP drum, making that part conductive. The conductive part loses voltage, dropping from –600V to –100V.
4. Developer Roller Squeezes Toner (represented by the #4 area) into a uniform layer on the EP drum. The parts that are charged to -6KV, however, repel the toner. Toner only remains where the laser has touched, as it is the most positively charged part of the drum.
5. The paper is pulled under the drum, which now contains the desired image written in toner. A second corona, drawing the toner from the drum to the paper.
6. The image now only sits on the paper as fine, dust-like toner. The toner must be fixed to the page. The fuser roller actually melts the toner into the page with heat at a temperature of 180 degrees C.

Cartridges

Laser printers use up a bit of their mechanism with every page they print. The organic photoconductor drum on which images are made gradually wears out. (A new drum material,

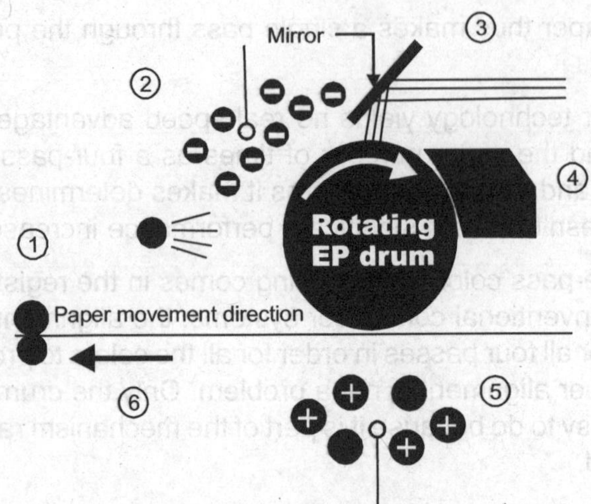

Working of Laser Printer

silicon, is supposed to last for the life of the printer, but few printer models currently use silicon drums.) In addition, the charging corona or other parts may also need to be periodically replaced. And, of course, you need toner.

Laser printer manufacturers have taken various approaches to replacing these consumables. Hewlett-Packard's LaserJets, for example, are designed with one-piece cartridges that contain both the drum and toner. The whole assembly is replaced as a single unit when the toner runs out. Other laser printers are designed so that the toner, drum, and sometimes the fuser, can be replaced individually.

The makers of the latter style of printer contend that the drum lasts for many times more copies than a single shot of toner, so dumping the drum before its time is wasteful. On the other hand, the all-in-one cartridge folks contend that they design their drums to last only as long as the toner.

Surprisingly, from a cost standpoint the choice of technology does not appear to make a difference. (From an ecological standpoint, however, the individual replacement scheme still makes more sense.)

A similar situation reigns among inkjet printers. Some designs incorporate the print head nozzles into the ink cartridge. Others make the nozzles a separately replaceable item. Although the latter should have a cost advantage and a convenience disadvantage, as a practical matter the differences are not significant.

A more important issue to consider with inkjets is single versus separate cartridges for ink colors. Many printers, typically the less expensive models, use a single cartridge for all three primary ink colors. If you use all three colors equally, this is a convenient arrangement. Most of the time, however, one color will run out before another and force you to scrap a cartridge still holding a supply of two colors of rather expensive ink. If you are frugal or simply appalled at the price of inkjet ink, you'll want a separate cartridge for each ink color.

Refilling

One way to tiptoe around the high cost of laser printer consumables is to get toner or ink cartridges refilled. Most manufacturers do not recommend this—because they have no control over the quality of the toner, they can't guarantee that someone else's replacement works right in their machines. Besides, they miss the profits in selling the toner or ink.

Quality really can be an issue, however. The Resolution Enhancement technology of the HP's LaserJet III series, for example, requires toner with a particle size smaller than that of toner used by other printers. You cannot tell the difference in toner just by looking at it—but you can when blotchy gray pages pour out of the printer. When you get cartridges refilled, you must be sure to get the proper toner quality

Printer Control

To make what you see on paper resemble what you preview on your monitor screen, your printer requires guidance from your computer and your software to tell it exactly how to make a printout look. The computer must send the printer a series of instructions, either to control the most intimate operation of the dumb printer or to coax special features from the brainy machine.

The instructions from the computer must be embedded in the character stream because that is the only data connection between the printer and its host. These embedded instructions can take on any of several forms.

Character Mode

In printing text from your PC, a printer receives a stream of ASCII code characters. The printer matches those characters to one of the fonts in its memory, which may be ROM or RAM. It then uses the pattern from memory to control the placement of bits on paper. All commands to the printer guide the formation and arrangement of these characters.

Because the entire process is oriented toward making characters, the commands to the printer are gauged in terms of characters and lines of text. Most commands deal with fonts and character positioning. For example, the printer may have several fonts in memory and use specific commands to select each one. Other commands tell the printer to emphasize characters or to slant them into italics. Placement commands tell the printer where to put the characters including how to space them.

The printer's interface uses the same signals to carry character data as well as commands. The printer needs some way to distinguish one from the other so that it doesn't print its commands on paper garbled with the text you actually want to see as hard copy. To prevent this confusion, most printers use a combination of two ideas for their commands: special control characters that code commands that also tell the printer not to print the character symbol; and escape sequences, a series of characters preceded by a special command telling the printer not to print the command characters.

Advantages of Laser Printers

1. Very high speed

2. Low noise level
3. Very high image quality
4. Excellent graphics capabilities
5. A variety of type sizes and styles
6. Uses standard, inexpensive copy paper which is loaded into a paper tray.

Thermal Printers

The thermal printers (a non-impact) is an alternative to the other serial printers. Heat elements produce dot-matrix images on heat-sensitive paper. Some fax machines use technique similar to thermal printers to produce documents on heat-sensitive paper. Output on thermal paper fades quickly when exposed to light, but the hardware is often inexpensive.

Advantages

- The advantages include compact size, limited noise, and low purchase price.

Disadvantages

- The major disadvantage is the cost of the heat-sensitive paper.

A thermal printer uses heated dot-matrix wires to print output on specially treated paper.

Electrostatic Printers

Electrostatic printers are devices in which the parts of paper which are to be printed are electrostatically charged, and attract a fine dust which is then fused to the paper by the application of heat. An electrostatic printer may be used in some instances as a plotter.

Some properties associated with printers.

Spooling and Printer Buffers

The term spooling is derived from the expression Simultaneous Peripheral Operation On Line. Spooling is a temporary storage of input and output on high-speed input-output devices, which helps in reducing processing delays when transferring data between peripheral equipment and the processors of a computer. The speed of the printers is incredibly slow as compared with the processing speed of the computers to which they are connected. Which makes CPU to sit idle during printing process. To overcome this, two approaches are used.

Spooler Program

It allows the processor to alternate between processing a user's ongoing activity and controlling the printing process. Of course disk space or a dedicated block of primary storage must be available to store the text to be printed by the spooler.

Printer Buffer Hardware

It is an additional storage device that can accept text to be printed as fast as the computer can send it. The buffer then slowly releases the test data to match the printer's speed while the computer is free to do other things.

Printer Installation

Windows Millennium/98/95 Installation Instructions

1. Click the Windows Start button.
2. Choose Settings, and then click Printers.
3. Double-click the Add Printer icon.

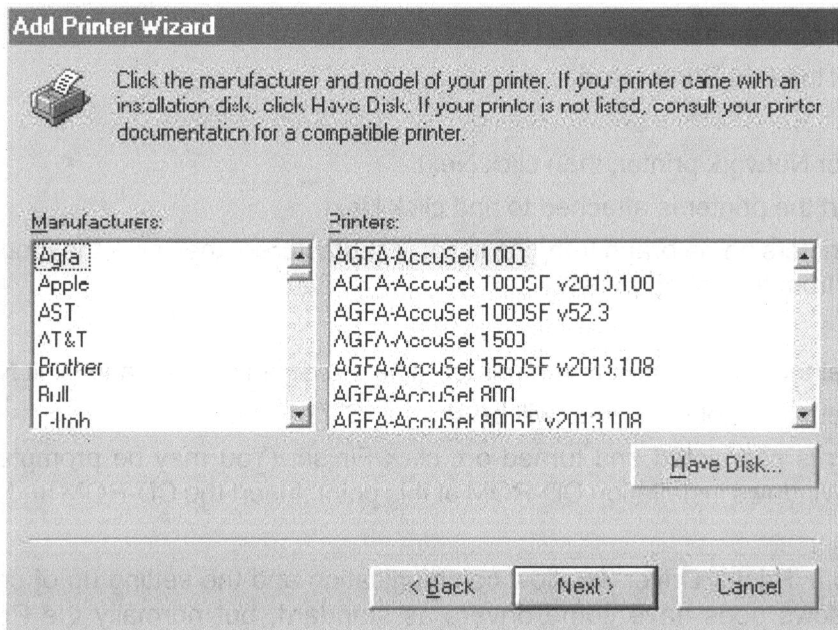

4. Click Next.
5. A screen may appear asking you "How is the printer attached to your computer?" Click local, then click Next.
6. Click your printers name brand from the list of Manufacturers then click the model of your printer from the list of printers.

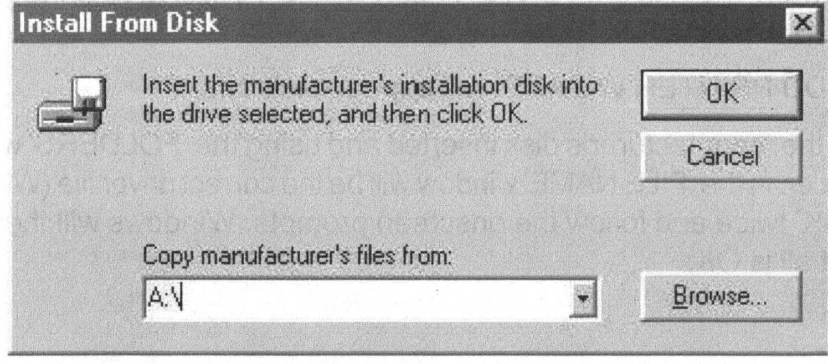

7. Click Next.
8. Click the port the printer is attached to and click Next.
9. Choose whether or not you want the printer to be the default printer and click Next.
10. If the printer is connected and turned on, click Finish. (You may be prompted to insert your Windows installation CD-ROM at this point. Insert the CD-ROM and click OK.)

Windows 2000 Installation Instructions

1. Click the Windows Start button.
2. Choose Settings, then click Printers.
3. Double-click the Add Printer icon.
4. Click Next.
5. Click Local or Network printer, then click Next.
6. Click the port the printer is attached to and click Next.
7. Click your printers name brand from the list of Manufacturers then click the model of your printer from the list of printers.
8. Click Next.
9. Choose whether or not you want the printer to be the default printer and click Next.
10. Choose whether or not the printer will be shared. Click Next.
11. If the printer is connected and turned on, click Finish. (You may be prompted to insert your Windows installation CD-ROM at this point. Insert the CD-ROM and click OK.)

Windows requires a 'Printer Driver' to allow communication and the setting up of printer parameters. Windows does have some drivers as standard, but normally the Printer manufacturer will supply a driver disk with the printer.

A printer can be installed one of three ways. Either

- Let Windows 'PLUG and PLAY' install it;
- Run the '*setup*' on the printer driver disk;
- By double clicking on the 'ADD PRINTER' icon in the PRINTERS window. *i.e*, START>SETTINGS>PRINTERS

Once this is done the 'ADD PRINTER WIZARD' will appear click 'NEXT'

Select the drive that has the manufacturer's disk inserted and using the 'FOLDERS' window browse to the relevant folder. In the 'FILE NAME' window will be the correct driver file (Windows selects the file!) Click 'OK' twice and follow the onscreen prompts. Windows will then print a test page to verify that all is OK.

Troubleshooting Printer

Here are a few simple techniques that will solve many printer problems.

1. Reboot your computer. This generally solves most printing problems.

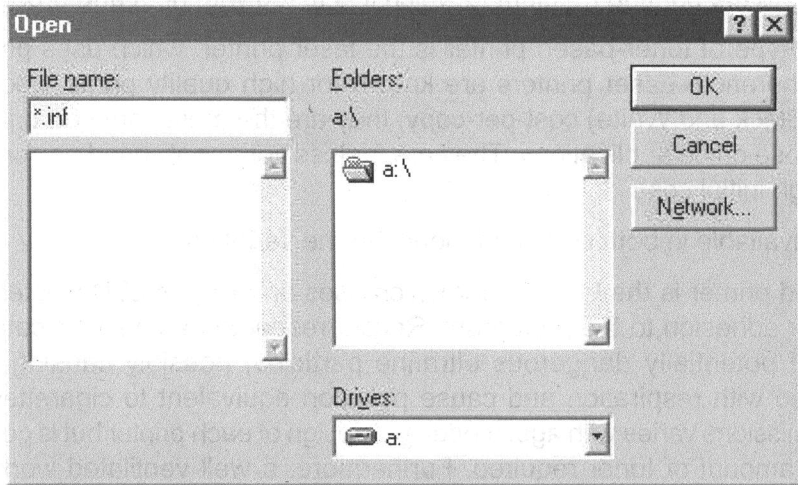

2. If it's not printing, or you're getting a message about the Fax printer, change your default printer: Start — Settings — Printers/Faxes. Right-click the printer you want, and then select (left-click) Set as Default.
3. Check and make sure all connections going to and coming from the printer are firmly in place.
4. Check that the printer is on-line:

    (*i*) Start — Settings — Printers, right-click the printer.

    (*ii*) If there isn't a checkmark by "Set as Default", left-click that option to select it.
5. Print a test page. If that prints and the application you are using doesn't, you probably will need to contact the application's vendor for support.
6. Turn off your printer for 10 seconds and turn it back on. Make a note of any error messages or flashing lights when the printer is turned back on.
7. If your printer is connected directly to another computer, try rebooting that computer. If your printer is connected to a JetDirect box, try unplugging the Jet Direct box for 10 seconds.
8. You may wish to uninstall and then re-install your printer.

Modern print technology

The following printing technologies are routinely found in modern printers:

Toner-based Printers

Toner-based printers work using the Xerographic principle that is at work in most photocopiers: by adhering toner to a light-sensitive print drum, then using static electricity to transfer the toner to the printing medium to which it is fused with heat and pressure.

The most common type of toner-based printer is the laser printer, which uses precision lasers to cause adherence. Laser printers are known for high quality prints, good print speed, and a low (Black and White) cost-per-copy; they are the most common printer for many general-purpose office applications. They are far less commonly used as consumer printers due to a high initial cost.

Laser printers are available in both color and monochrome varieties.

Another toner based printer is the LED printer which uses an array of LEDs instead of a laser to cause toner adhesion to the print drum. Recent research has also indicated that Laser printers emit potentially dangerous ultrafine particles, possibly causing health problems associated with respiration and cause pollution equivalent to cigarettes. The degree of particle emissions varies with age, model and design of each printer but is generally proportional to the amount of toner required. Furthermore, a well ventilated workspace would allow such ultrafine particles to disperse thus reducing the health side effects.

Liquid Inkjet Printers

Inkjet printers spray very small, precise amounts (usually a few picolitres) of ink onto the media. These droplets of ink will carry a slight electrical charge. The placement of the ink on the page is then determined by the charge of a cathode and electrode between which the ink moves towards the paper. Inkjet printing (and the related bubble-jet technology) are the most common -quality inkjet printers are inexpensive to produce.

Virtually all modern inkjet printers are color devices; some, known as photo printers, include extra pigments to better reproduce the color gamut needed for high-quality photographic prints (and are additionally capable of printing on photographic card stock, as opposed to plain office paper).

Inkjet printers consist of nozzles that produce very small ink bubbles that turn into tiny droplets of ink. The dots formed are the size of tiny pixels. Ink-jet printers can print high quality text and graphics. They are also almost silent in operation. Inkjet printers have a much lower initial cost than do laser printers, but have a much higher cost-per-copy, as the ink needs to be frequently replaced.

In addition, consumer printer manufacturers have adapted a business model similar to that employed by manufacturers of razors; the printers themselves are frequently sold below cost, and the ink is then sold at a high markup.

Various legal and technological means are employed to try and force users to only purchase ink from the manufacturer (thus leading to vendor lock-in); however there is a thriving aftermarket for such things as third-party ink cartridges (new or refurbished) and refill kits.

Inkjet printers are also far slower than laser printers. Inkjet printers also have the disadvantage that pages must be allowed to dry before being aggressively handled; premature handling can cause the inks (which are adhered to the page in liquid form) to run.

Solid ink printers

Solid Ink printers, also known as phase-change printers, are a type of thermal transfer printer. They use solid sticks of CMYK colored ink (similar in consistency to candle wax), which are melted and fed into a piezo crystal operated print-head. The printhead sprays the ink on a rotating, oil coated drum. The paper then passes over the print drum, at which time the image is transferred, or transfixed, to the page.

Solid ink printers are most commonly used as color office printers, and are excellent at printing on transparencies and other non-porous media. Solid ink printers can produce excellent results. Acquisition and operating costs are similar to laser printers. Drawbacks of the technology include high power consumption and long warm-up times from a cold state.

Also, some users complain that the resulting prints are difficult to write on (the wax tends to repel inks from pens), and are difficult to feed through Automatic Document Feeders, but these traits have been significantly reduced in later models. In addition, this type of printer is only available from one manufacturer, Xerox, manufactured as part of their Xerox Phaser office printer line. Previously, solid ink printers were manufactured by Tektronix, but Tek sold the printing business to Xerox in 2001

Dye-sublimation Printers

A dye-sublimation printer (or dye-sub printer) is a printer which employs a printing process that uses heat to transfer dye to a medium such as a plastic card, paper or canvas. The process is usually to lay one color at a time using a ribbon that has color panels. Dye-sub printers are intended primarily for high-quality color applications, including color photography; and are less well-suited for text. While once the province of high-end print shops, dye-sublimation printers are now increasingly used as dedicated consumer photo printers.

Inkless Printers

Inkless printers use paper with colorless dye crystals embedded between the two outer layers of the paper. When the printer is turned on, heat from the drum causes the crystals to colorize at different rates and become visible. The technology was worked on by Zink Imaging and is now available (2007). Because of the way it prints, the printer can be as small as a business card, the images are waterproof, and in fact, one product slated for release by Zink Imaging is a digital camera with a printer built into it. Xerox is also working on an inkless printer which will use a special reusable paper coated with a few micrometres of UV light sensitive chemicals. The printer will use a special UV light bar which will be able to write and erase the paper. As of early 2007 this technology is still in development and the text on the printed pages can only last between 16-24 hours before fading.

Preventive Maintenance of Printers

Before starting the troubleshooting we must first examine or check some preventive maintenance steps that can keep our printer in good working condition. The main steps preventive maintenance is.

1. Clean the paper path, ribbon path, and head assembling movement path with a dry soft Cloth we can also use the soft brush for this purpose.
2. Clean the outer surface of printer time to time so that printer; can be kept free from dust.
3. Clean the printer roller time to time with soft cloth so that it is kept free from dust and rust.
4. If you clean time to time and oil the printer then we can avoid expenses repair
5. Check for loose belt because in some DMP the print head is connected to the motor with the help of belt if be it is loose then replace it.
6. Lubricating (oiling) of head assembling mechanism will keep the printer away from heaving unnecessary fault.
7. Do not extra oiling the various part of printer because extra oiling can cause serious fault in a printer due to dusted so for log life of printer its head must be kept cool as can it is possible. If your printer has fraction feed and tractor feed then do not use both these at the same time. If you use both them the paper feeding will not be paper and the paper may get struck in side the printer.

7 Optical Media

Introduction

CD-ROM (an abbreviation of "Compact Disc read-only memory") is a Compact Disc that contains data accessible by a computer. While the Compact Disc format was originally designed for music storage and playback, the format was later adapted to hold any form of binary data. CD-ROMs are popularly used to distribute computer software, including games and multimedia applications, though any data can be stored (up to the capacity limit of a disc). Some CDs hold both computer data and audio with the latter capable of being played on a CD player, whilst data (such as software or digital video) is only usable on a computer (such as PC CD-ROMs). These are called Enhanced CDs.

Although many people use lowercase letters in this acronym, proper presentation is in all capital letters with a hyphen between CD and ROM. It was also suggested by some, especially soon after the technology was first released, that CD-ROM was an acronym for "Compact Disc read-only-media", or that it was a more 'correct' definition. This was not the intention of the original team who developed the CD-ROM, and common acceptance of the 'memory' definition is now almost universal. This is probably in no small part due to the widespread use of other 'ROM' acronyms such as Flash-ROMs and EEPROMs where 'memory' is the correct term.

Media

CD-ROM discs are identical in appearance to audio CDs, and data is stored and retrieved in a very similar manner (only differing from audio CDs in the standards used to store the data). Discs are made from a 1.2 mm thick disc of polycarbonate plastic, with a thin layer of aluminum to make a reflective surface. The most common size of CD-ROM disc is 120 mm in diameter, though the smaller Mini CD standard with an 80 mm diameter, as well as numerous non-standard sizes and shapes (e.g. business card-sized media) are also available.

Data is stored on the disc as a series of microscopic indentations ("pits", with the gaps between them referred to as "lands"). A laser is shone onto the reflective surface of the disc to read the pattern of pits and lands. Because the depth of the pits is approximately one-quarter to one-sixth of the wavelength of the laser light used to read the disc, the reflected beam's phase is shifted in relation to the incoming beam, causing destructive interference and reducing the reflected beam's intensity. This pattern of changing intensity of the reflected beam is converted into binary data.

Standards

There are several formats used for data stored on compact discs, known collectively as the Rainbow Books. These include the original Red Book standards for CD audio, White Book and Yellow Book CD-ROM. The ECMA-130 standard, which gives a thorough description of the physics and physical layer of the CD-ROM, inclusive of CIRC and Eight-to-Fourteen Modulation, can be downloaded from.

ISO 9660 defines the standard file system of a CD-ROM, although it is due to be replaced by ISO 13490. UDF format is used on user-writeable CD-R and CD-RW discs that are intended to be extended or overwritten. The bootable CD specification, to make a CD emulate a hard disk or floppy, is called El Torito. Apparently named this because its design originated in an El Torito restaurant in Irvine, California.

CD-ROM format

A CD-ROM sector contains 2352 bytes, divided into 98 24-byte frames. The CD-ROM is, in essence, a data disk, which cannot rely on error concealment, and therefore requires a higher reliability of the retrieved data. In order to achieve improved error correction and detection, a CD-ROM has a third layer of Reed-Solomon error correction.[1] A Mode-1 CD-ROM, which has the full three layers of error correction data, contains a net 2048 bytes of the available 2352 per sector. In a Mode-2 CD-ROM, which is mostly used for video files, there are 2336 user-available bytes per sector. The net byte rate of a Mode-1 CD-ROM, based on comparison to CDDA audio standards, is 44.1k/s×4B×2048/2352 = 153.6 kB/s. The playing time is 74 minutes, or 4440 seconds, so that the net capacity of a Mode-1 CD-ROM is 682 MB.

A 1x speed CD drive reads 75 consecutive sectors per second.

CD sector contents

- A standard 74 min CD contains 333,000 blocks or · sectors.
- Each sector is 2352 bytes, and contains 2048 bytes of PC (MODE1) Data, 2336 bytes of PSX/VCD (MODE2) Data, or 2352 bytes of AUDIO.
- The difference between sector size and data content are the Headers info and the Error Correction Codes, that are big for Data (high precision required), small for VCD (standard for video) and none for audio.
- If extracting the disc in RAW format (standard for creating images) always extract 2352 bytes per sector, not 2048/2336/2352 bytes depending on data type (basically, extracting the whole sector). This fact has two main consequences:

- Recording data CDs at very high speed (40x) can be done without losing information. However, as audio CDs do not contain a third layer of error correction codes, recording these at high speed may result in more unrecoverable errors or 'clicks' in the audio.
- On a 74 minute CD, one can fit larger images using RAW mode, up to 333,000 × 2352 = 783,216,000 bytes (747 MiB). This is the upper limit for RAW images created on a 74 min or 650 MiB Red Book CD. The 14.8% increase is due to the discarding of error correction data
- Please note that an image size is always a multiple of 2352 bytes (the size of a block) when extracting in RAW mode.

Structure of CD-ROM Drive

The CD-ROM has two sections namely Mechanical Section and the Electronics Section.

The center of the drive is a cast aluminum or rigid frame assembly. As with other drives, the frame is the single primary structure for mounting the drive's mechanical and electronic components The front panel consists of lid, volume control, and eject button attached to the frame, and offering a fixed reference slot for CD insertion and removal.

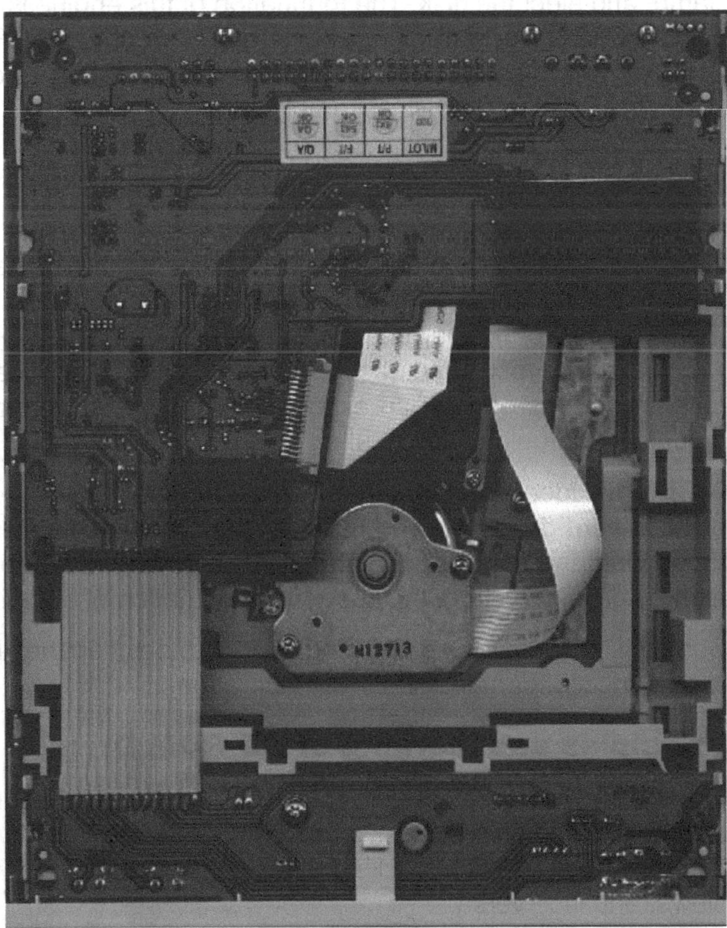

The main PC board, handles the drive control and interfacing, and the headphone PC board, which provides an audio jack for headphones. The main CD subassembly called a drive engine, which uses to hold eject, spin, and read the disk. This interchangeability is part of the genius of CD-ROM drives—a single sub-assembly performs 80 percent of the work. Sony, Philips, and Toshiba are the major manufacturers of CD-ROM engines, but other companies, such as IBM and Ikka, are also producing engines.

The engine features a series of mechanisms that accept,

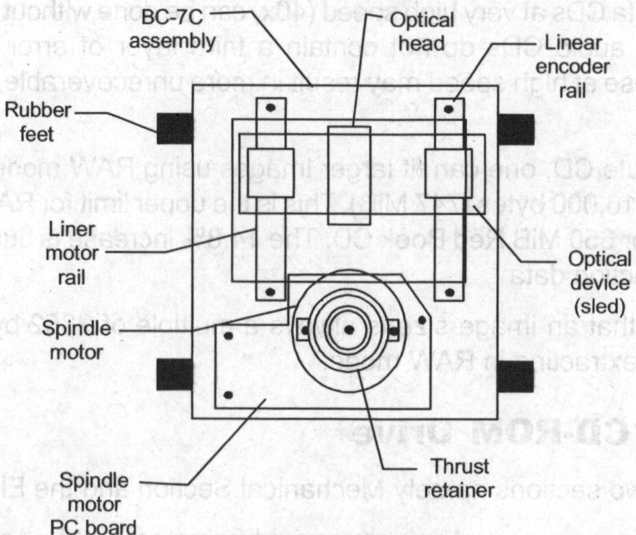

Assembly of CD-ROM Drive

clamp, and eject the disk. The foundation of this engine is the BC-7C assembly. It acts as a sub-frame, the sub-frame is shock-mounted with four rubber feet to cushion the engine from minor bumps and ordinary handling as shown in the figure 5.27 below. The slider assembly, loading chassis assembly, and the cover shield provide the mechanical action needed to accept the disk and clamp it into place over the drive spindle, as well as to free the disk and eject it on demand. A motor/ gear assembly drives the load unload mechanics. The work of spinning and reading a disk is handled under the engine.

A spindle motor is mounted on the sub-frame and connected to a spindle motor PC board. The most important part of the CD engine is the optical device that contains the 780-nm (nanometer) 0.6-mW gallium aluminum arsenide (GaAIAs) laser diode and detector, along with the optical focus and tracking components. The optical device slides along two guide rails and shines through an exposed hole in the sub-frame. This combination of device mounting and guide rails is called a full form check.

A CD drive ideally requires a linear motor to act much like the voice coil motor used to position hard-drive R/W heads. By altering the signal driving a sled motor and constantly measuring and adjusting the sled's position, a sled can be made to track very smoothly along a disk—free from the sudden, jerky motion of stepping motors.

Some CD drives still use stepping motors to position the sled. The drive's main PC board is responsible for managing these operations.

Principles and Working of CD-ROM Drive

CD-ROM/CD-R drives are impressive pieces of engineering. The drive accept standard-sized disks and spin the disk at a Constant Linear Velocity (CLV)—that is, the disk speed varies inversely with the tracking radius. As tracking approaches the disk edge, disk speeds slows, and vice versa.

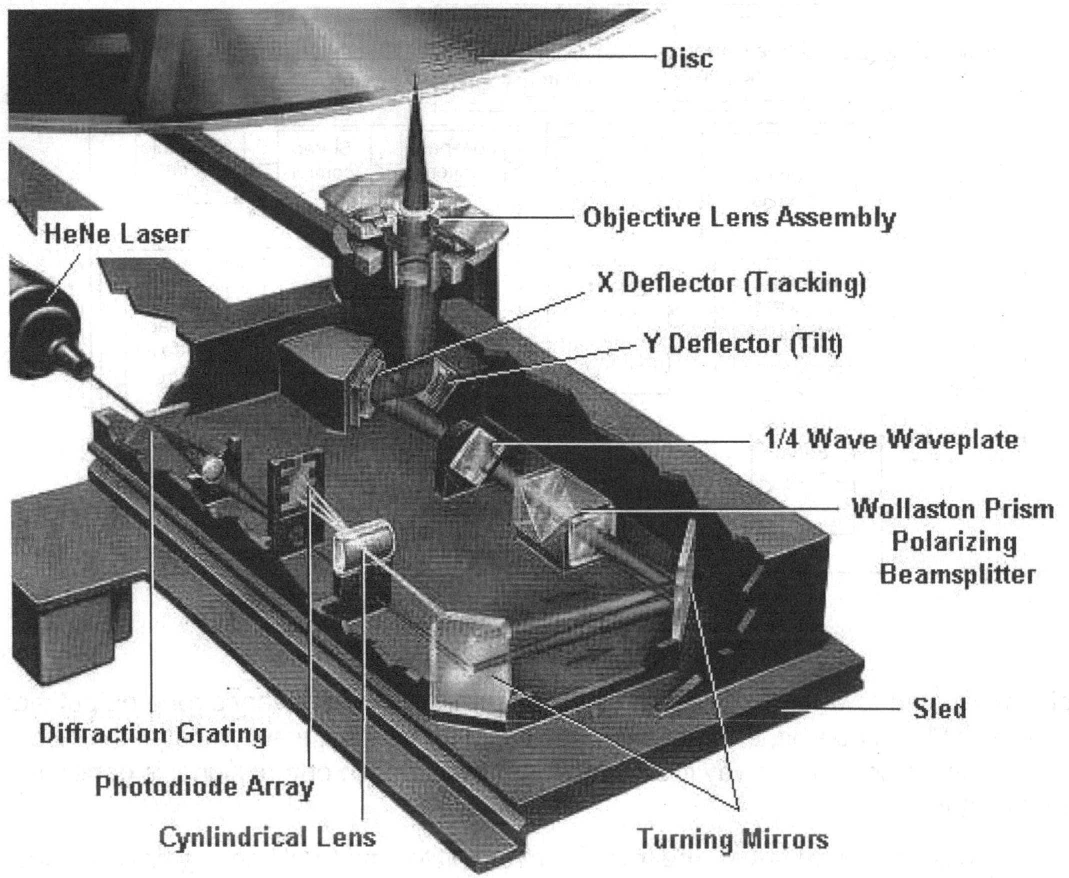

Mechanical Section of CD-ROM Drive

Keep in mind that CLV is different than the Constant Angular Velocity (CAV) method used by floppy and hard drives, which moves the media at a constant speed. The purpose of CLV is to ensure that CD data is read at a constant rate. A drive must be able to follow the spiral data path on a spinning CD-ROM. The drive electronics must be able to detect and correct any unforeseen data errors in real time, operate reliably over a long working life.

CDs are not segregated into concentric tracks and sectors as magnetic media is. Instead, CDs are recorded as a single, continuous spiral track running from the spindle to the lead out area. Each pit is about 0.12 mm (micrometers deep and 0.6 mm wide. Pits and lands can range from 0.9 to 3.3 mm in length. Approximately 1.6 mm are between each iteration of the spiral. Given these microscopic dimensions, a CDROM disc offers about 16,000 tracks per inch (TPI). During playback, CDs use a highly focused laser beam and laser detector to sense the presence or absence of pits.

The laser/detector pair is mounted on a carriage, which follows the spiral track across the CD. A laser is directed at the underside of the CD, where it penetrates more than 1 mm of clear plastic before shining on the reflective surface. When laser light strikes a land, the

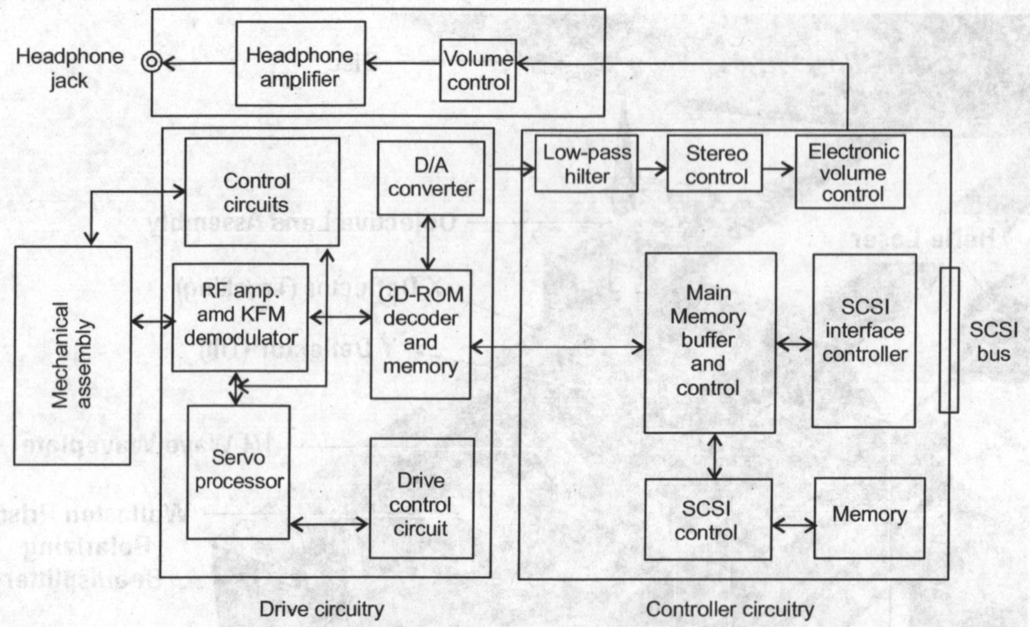

Block diagram of CD-ROM Drive

light is reflected toward the detector, which, in turn, produces a very strong output signal. As laser light strikes a pit, the light is slightly out of focus. As a result, most of the incoming laser energy is scattered away in all directions, so very little output signal is generated by the detector.

As with floppy and hard drives, the transition from pit to land (and back again) corresponds to binary levels, not the presence or absence of a pit or land. The analog light signal returned by the detector must be converted to logic levels and decoded. A process known as Eight-to-Fourteen Modulation (EFM) is very common with CD-ROMs.

EFM and Data Storage

A complex decoding process is necessary to convert the arcane sequence of pits and lands into meaningful binary information. The technique of EFM is used with CD-ROMs. For hard-disk drives, such techniques as 2.7 RLL encoding can be used to place a large number of bits into a limited number of flux transitions. The same is true for CDs using EFM.

User data, error-correction information, address information, and synchronization patterns are all contained in a bit stream that is represented by pits and lands. Magnetic media encodes bits as flux transitions—not the discrete orientation of any magnetic area. The same concept holds true with CD-ROMs, where binary 1s and 0s do not correspond to pits or lands. A binary 1 is represented wherever a transition (pit to land or land to pit) occurs. The length of a pit or land represents the number of binary 0s.

The EFM encoding technique equates each byte (8 bits) with a 14-bit sequence (called a symbol), where each binary. 1 must be separated by at least two binary 0s.

A CD-ROM frame is composed of 24 synchronization bits, 14 control bits, 24 of the 14-bit data symbols you saw previously, and eight complete 14-bit Error-Correction (EC) symbols. Each symbol is separated by additional three merge bits, bringing the total number of bits in the frame to 588.

Thus, 24 bytes of data is represented by 588 bits on a CD-ROM, expressed as a number of pits and lands. There are 98 frames in a data block, so each block carries (98 x 24) = 2048 bytes (2352 with error correction, synchronization, and address bytes).

The basic CD-ROM can deliver 153.6 KB of data (75 blocks) per second to its host controller.

CD-ROM Capacity

A standard 120 mm CD-ROM holds 650 or 700 MiB of data. To put this storage capacity into context, the average novel contains 60,000 words. Assume that average word length is 10 letters and that each letter occupies one byte.

A novel therefore might occupy 600,000 bytes (600 kB, without layout information). One CD can therefore contain over 1,000 novels. If each novel occupies at least one centimetre of bookshelf space, then one CD can contain the equivalent of over ten metres of bookshelf. However, textual data can be compressed by more than a factor of ten, using compression algorithms, so a CD-ROM can accommodate at least 100 metres of bookshelf space.

In comparison a single layer DVD contains 4.4 GB of data, nearly 7 times the amount of a CD-ROM.

Capacities of Compact Disc types

Type	Sectors	Data max size		Audio max size		Time
	(MB)		(MiB)	(MB)	(MiB)	(min)
8 cm	94,500	193.536	~ 184.6	222.264	~ 212.0	21
283,500	580.608	~ 553.7	666.792	~ 635.9	63	
650 MB	333,000	681.984	~ 650.3	783.216	~ 746.9	74
700 MB	360,000	737.280	~ 703.1	846.720	~ 807.4	80
800 MB	405,000	829.440	~ 791.0	952.560	~ 908.4	90
900 MB	445,500	912.384	~ 870.1	1,047.816	~ 999.3	99

Note: Megabyte (MB) and minute (min) values are exact.

CD capacities are always given in binary units, although decimal SI prefixes are usually used: a "700 MB" CD has a nominal capacity of about 700 MiB. DVD capacities, on the other hand, are given in decimal units: a "4.7 GB" DVD has a nominal capacity of about 4.38 GiB.

Installing of CD Drive

The following procedure outlines the installation of a CDROM drive.

1. Disconnect the power to the computer.
2. Configure the appropriate master/slave settings or SCSI ID for the drive.
3. Insert the drive into an available drive bay.
4. Screw in the 4 screws — 2 on each side of the bay.
5. If the drive is an IDE, connect the IDE cable to the drive. There should be a stripe along 1 edge of the cable. This stripe denotes pin 1. Pin 1 on the drive is usually closest to the power connector on the drive, however, you should consult the manufacturers documentation. Then connect the signal cable to the motherboard ID1 or ID2 interface making sure to note the pin 1 orientation there as well. If the drive is a SCSI drive, a SCSI cable would be connected from the drive to a SCSI controller card.
6. Connect one of the power supply's power connectors to the drive.

Troubleshooting CD-ROM Drives

The troubleshooting steps for CD-ROM and DVD drives are nearly identical to those of an HDD system. The connections and data paths are very similar. Basically, three levels of troubleshooting apply to CD-ROM problems. These are the configuration level, the operating system level, and the hardware level.In most systems, the CD-ROM and DVD drives share a controller or host adapter with the hard disk drive. Therefore, verify their Master/Slave jumper settings to ensure they are set correctly. Normally, the CD-ROM or DVD drive should be set up as the master on the secondary IDE channel.

In this manner, each drive has its own communications channel and does not need to share. If three or four IDE devices are installed in the system, you must determine which devices can share the channels most effectively. In many systems, the CD-ROM and DVD drives share a controller or host adapter with the hard disk drive. Therefore, if the hard drive is working and the CD-ROM drive is not, the likelihood that the problem is in the CD-ROM or DVD drive unit is very high.

DVD

DVD stand stands for digital video disc or digital versatile disc, is the next generation of optical disc storage technology. It is bigger, faster CD that can hold cinema-like view, better-than-CD audio, and compatriot CD data. Using a DVD you can have home entertainment, computers, and business information with a single digital format. The DVD will eventually replace audio/video CD, videotape, laserdisc, CD-ROM, and video game cartridges.

There are various variations of DVD; DVD-ROM or DVD-R are physical formats and DVD-Video or DVD-Audio are application formats. DVD-ROM is the base format that holds data. Physical format of DVD-ROM includes recordable variations DVD-R, DVD-RAM, DVD-

RW, and DVD-RW. The application formats include DVD-Video, DVD-Video Recording, DVD-Audio, DVD-Audio Recording, DVD Stream Recording, and SACD.

Storage Capacity of DVDs

DVDs are of the same diameter and thickness as CDs, and they are made using some of the same materials and manufacturing methods. Like a CD, the data on a DVD is encoded in the form of small pits and bumps in the track of the disc. A DVD is composed of several layers of plastic, totalling about 1.2 millimeters thick. Each layer is created by injection molding polycarbonate plastic. This process forms a disc that has microscopic bumps arranged as a single, continuous and extremely long spiral track of data.

Once the clear pieces of polycarbonate are formed, a thin reflective layer is sputtered onto the disc, covering the bumps. Aluminium is used behind the inner layers, but a semi-reflective gold layer is used for the outer layers, allowing the laser to focus through the outer and onto the inner layers. After all the layers are made, each one is coated with lacquer, squeezed together and cured under infrared light.

For single-sides discs, the label is silk-screened onto the nonreadable side. Double-sided discs are printed only on the nonredable area near the hold in the middle. If you could lift the data track off a single layer of a DVD, and stretch it out into a straight line, it would be almost 7.5 miles long. A double-sided, double-layer DVD would have 30 miles of data.

Multi-Layer Storage

To increase the storage capacity, a DVD can have up to four layers, two on each side. The laser that reads the disc can actually focus on the second layer through the first layer. Here is a list of the capacities of different forms of DVDs:

DVD disc capacity

Physical size	Single layer capacity GB	GiB	Dual/Double layer capacity GB	GiB
12 cm, single sided	4.7	4.38	8.5	7.92
12 cm, double sided	9.4	8.75	17.1	15.93
8 cm, single sided	1.4	1.30	2.6	2.42
8 cm, double sided	2.8	2.61	5.2	4.84

Note: GB here means gigabyte, equal to 10^9 (or 1,000,000,000) bytes. Many programs will display gibibyte (GiB), equal to 2^{30} (or 1,073,741,824) bytes.

Example: A disc with 8.5 GB capacity is equivalent to: (8.5 × 1,000,000,000) / 1,073,741,824 H" 7.92 GiB.

Size Note: There is a difference in size between + and - DL DVD formats. For example, the 12 cm single sided disk has capacities:

Disk Type	Sectors	bytes	GB	GiB
DVD-R SL	2,298,496	4,707,319,808	4.7	4.384
DVD+R SL	2,295,104	4,700,372,992	4.7	4.378
DVD-R DL	4,171,712	8,543,666,176	8.5	7.957
DVD+R DL	4,173,824	8,547,991,552	8.5	7.961

Capacity Nomenclature

The four basic types of DVD are referred to by their capacity in gigabytes, rounded up to the nearest integer.

DVD type	Name
Single sided, single layer	DVD-5
Single sided, dual layer	DVD-9
Double sided, single layer	DVD-10
Double sided, dual layer	DVD-18

Another format in limited use is a double sided DVD with one side comprising a single layer of data while the opposite side comprises two layers of data (effectively a DVD-5 on one side bonded to a DVD-9 on the other). This format holds approximately 12.3 GB of data and is known as DVD-14.

Various ROM Drives

According to needs and developments, the ROM has also changed over the years. With the advent of DVDs the option to read and write on it has also added the needed. Various combinations available available are:

CD ROM Drive

It is the simple CD ROM drive which can read all the simple CD ROM formats. But no option of writing to the CD ROM.

DVD ROM Drive

Drive which can read the DVD drive but cannot write DVD but create CD ROM.

DVD Writer

Drive which can read all type of CD ROM including the DVD and write too on DVD ROMs.

Combo Drive

A Combo drive is a type of optical drive that combines CD-R/CD-RW recording capability with the ability to read (but not write) DVD media. The term was popularized by Apple Computer as a name for the low-end substitute for their high-end SuperDrive, which was designed to both read and write DVD and DVD recordable media. The device was created as a mid-range option between a CD burner and a DVD burner, which at the time the combo drive was introduced was generally an expensive option costing in excess of US$300 a unit.

Combo drives are becoming less and less common on new systems, though they do occasionally appear in lieu of CD-only drives on low-end computers to lower production and sale costs. The cost difference between a combo drive and DVD burner has been steadily declining in recent years, so most new PCs (except for the low-end budget computers) have a DVD burner (which also reads and writes CDs).

In Apple computers, only the bottom of the range MacBooks and Mac minis have combo drives.

Recordable Disk:Write Once, Read Many (WORM)

As with the CD, once data have been etched into the surface of a WORM disk they can not be changed. WORM is an ideal medium for making a permanent record of data, *i.e.*, it can be a feasible alternative to magnetic tape for archival storage.

For example, many banks use WORM disks to store a record of each day's transactions. The transactions are written to an optical disk and become a permanent record that can be read but never altered.

Another popular application of WORM disks is in information systems, that require the merging of text and images that do not change for a period of time. A good example is an "electronic catalog".

A customer can pursue a retailer's electronic catalog on a VDT, or perhaps a PC, and see the item while he reads about it and, with a few keystrokes the customer can order the item as well.

Erasable Disks: Magneto-Optical Disks

A hybrid disk, called magneto-optical (MO), combines the best features of magnetic and optical disk technologies. A magneto-optical disk has the high-volume capacity of an optical disk but can be written over as a magnetic disk. The disk surface is coated with plastic and embedded with magnetically sensitive metallic crystals.

To write data, laser beam melts a tiny spot on the plastic surface and a magnet aligns the crystal before the plastic cools. The crystal are placed in such a way that some reflect lights and others do not. Later on, when the data is read by a laser beam, only the crystals that reflect light are picked up.

Advantages

1. Instead of using 15 to 20 diskettes an entire suite of programs and data could reside on a single CD-ROM.
2. CD-ROM are not vulnerable to magnetic fields which can destroy the data on a diskette.
3. Optical media are extremely durable and reliable under normal use. Because the surface of the disk (sealed in its plastic coating) is never touched by anything but light and because the medium itself is virtually unaffected by moisture on temperature conditions.
4. One reason optical technology is so reliable is that the read head is several millimeters away from the disk surface.

However there are two main reasons that prevent CD drives from totally displacing hard devices:

One reason is that CD drives are still slow. A drive that meets the multimedia PC2 standard for performance only has to move 900 KB of data per second. A good hard drive, by comparison, transfers 10 MB of data per second. Whereas on time scale the internal hard drive can find the data your application asks for in 10 msec, and on the other side CD-ROM drive takes upto 300 msec for the same task.

The other reason is that you can not write to portions of a writable CD-ROM that already have data written to them. You can add to data that was written to the disk in an earlier session but you can't delete or change what is already there.

Disadvantages

1. Magneto-optical disks are too expensive and do not offer anywhere near the kind of reliability that users have come to expect of magnetic media.
2. The access time in magneto-optical disks are relatively slow, about the same as a low-end, Winchester disk.
3. As optical disk technology matures to offer reliable, cost-effective, read/write operation, it eventually may dominate secondary storage in the future as magnetic disks and tape to today.

8 Hard Disk Drive

Introduction

A hard disk drive (HDD), commonly referred to as a hard drive, hard disk or fixed disk drive, is a non-volatile storage device which stores digitally encoded data on rapidly rotating platters with magnetic surfaces. Strictly speaking, "drive" refers to a device distinct from its medium, such as a tape drive and its tape, or a floppy disk drive and its floppy disk. Early HDDs had removable media; however, an HDD today is typically a sealed unit (with filtered vent hole to equalize air pressure) with fixed media.

Strictly speaking, an HDD is a rigid-disk drive, although it is probably never referred to as such. By way of comparison, a so-called "floppy" drive (more formally, a diskette drive) has a disc that is flexible. Originally, the term "hard" was temporary slang, substituting "hard" for "rigid", before these drives had an established and universally-agreed-upon name. Some time ago, IBM's internal company term for an HDD was "file".

HDDs were originally developed for use with computers. In the 21st century, applications for HDDs have expanded beyond computers to include digital video recorders, digital audio players, personal digital assistants, digital cameras and video game consoles. In 2005 the first mobile phones to include HDDs were introduced by Samsung and Nokia. The need for large-scale, reliable storage, independent of a particular device, led to the introduction of configurations such as RAID arrays, network attached storage (NAS) systems and storage area network (SAN) systems that provide efficient and reliable access to large volumes of data.

Technology

HDDs record data by magnetizing ferromagnetic material directionally, to represent either a 0 or a 1 binary digit. They read the data back by detecting the magnetization of the material. A typical HDD design consists of a spindle which holds one or more flat circular disks called platters, onto which the data is recorded. The platters are made from a non-magnetic material, usually aluminum alloy or glass, and are coated with a thin layer of magnetic material. Older disks used iron(III) oxide as the magnetic material, but current disks use a cobalt-based alloy.

The platters are spun at very high speeds. Information is written to a platter as it rotates past devices called read-and-write heads that operate very close (tens of nanometers in new drives) over the magnetic surface. The read-and-write head is used to detect and modify the magnetization of the material immediately under it. There is one head for each magnetic platter surface on the spindle, mounted on a common arm. An actuator arm (or access arm) moves the heads on an arc (roughly radially) across the platters as they spin, allowing each head to access almost the entire surface of the platter as it spins. The arm is moved using a voice coil actuator or (in older designs) a stepper motor. Stepper motors were outside the head-disk chamber, and preceded voice-coil drives. The latter, for a while, had a structure similar to that of a loudspeaker; the coil and heads moved in a straight line, along a radius of the platters. The present-day structure differs in several respects from that of the earlier voice-coil drives, but the same interaction between the coil and magnetic field still applies, and the term is still used.

Older drives read the data on the platter by sensing the rate of change of the magnetism in the head; these heads had small coils, and worked (in principle) much like magnetic-tape playback heads, although not in contact with the recording surface. As data density increased, read heads using magnetoresistance (MR) came into use; the electrical resistance of the head changed according to the strength of the magnetism from the platter. Later development made use of spintronics; in these heads, the magnetoresistive effect was comparatively huge, compared to that of earlier types, and was dubbed "giant" magnetoresistance (GMR) referreing to the degree of effect, not the physical size; the heads themselves are extremely tiny, too small to see without a microscope. GMR read heads are now commonplace.

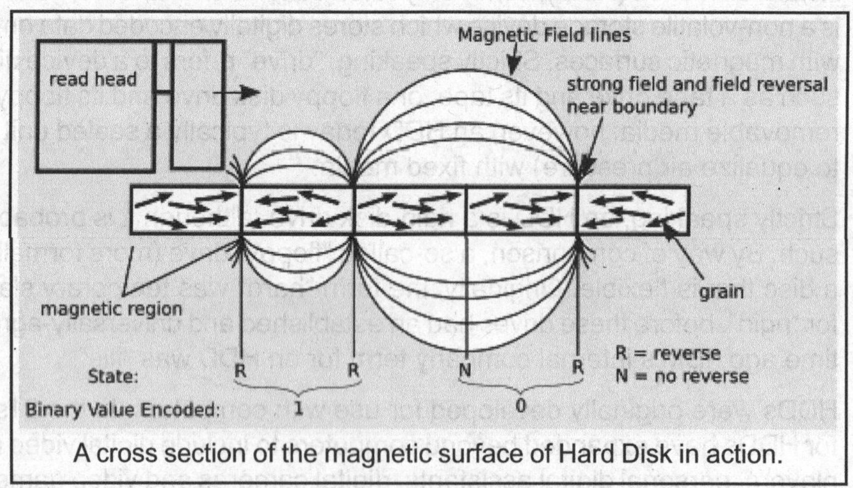

A cross section of the magnetic surface of Hard Disk in action.

HD heads are kept from contacting the platter surface by the air that is extremely close to the platter; that air moves at, or close to, the platter speed. The record and playback head are mounted on a block called a slider, and the surface next to the platter is shaped to keep it just barely out of contact. It's a type of air bearing.

The magnetic surface of each platter is conceptually divided into many small sub-micrometre-sized magnetic regions, each of which is used to encode a single binary unit of information. In today's HDDs each of these magnetic regions is composed of a few hundred magnetic grains. Each magnetic region forms a magnetic dipole which generates a highly localized magnetic field nearby. The write head magnetizes a region by generating a strong local magnetic field nearby. Early HDDs used an electromagnet both to generate this field and to read the data by using electromagnetic induction. Later versions of inductive heads included metal in Gap (MIG) heads and thin film heads. In today's heads, the read and write elements are separate but in close proximity on the head portion of an actuator arm. The read element is typically magneto-resistive while the write element is typically thin-film inductive.

In modern drives, the small size of the magnetic regions creates the danger that their magnetic state be lost because of thermal effects. To counter this, the platters are coated with two parallel magnetic layers, separated by a 3-atom-thick layer of the non-magnetic element ruthenium, and the two layers are magnetized in opposite orientation, thus reinforcing each other. Another technology used to overcome thermal effects to allow greater recording densities is perpendicular recording, which has been used in many hard drives as of 2007.

Working of Hard Disk

Disks are rotated continuously so that read/write heads mounted on movable or fixed arms can read or write programs or data to and from the disk. The Hard Disk Drive can be classified into two sections Mechanical Section and Electronic Section. The Mechanical Section consists of the followings which are explained accordingly.

Spindle Motor : One part of a hard disk, around which the platters rotate.

Disk drive : The motor that actually rotates the disk, plus the read/write heads and associated mechanisms, usually in a mountable housing. Sometimes, it is used synonymously to mean the entire disk subsystem

Platters : The platters are no. of disks made of aluminum or plastic coated with a magnetic material. The data is stored on the platter.

Read/Write Head : The part of the hard disk which writes data to or reads data from a platter It functions like a coiled wire that reacts to a changing magnetic field by producing a minute current that can be detected and amplified by the electronics of the disk drive.

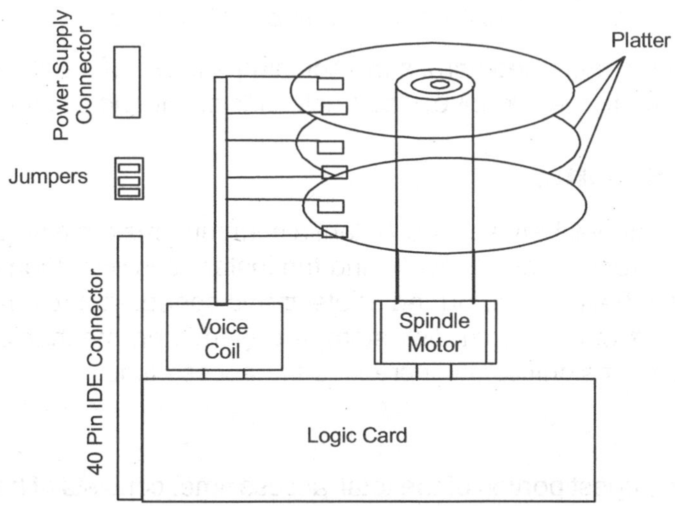

HDD Showing Platters and R/W Heads

Head Actuator : In a disk drive, the mechanism which moves the read/write head radially across the surface of the platter of the disk drive.

Electronic Section of HDD : The Electronic Section consists of a Logic card which controls the stepper and the spindle motors and the read/write heads of the disk it has 40 pin IDE interface data cable connector and a 4 pin D-type Power supply connector.

Sector : The basic storage unit on a hard disk. On most modern hard disks, sectors are 512 bytes each, four sectors make up a cluster, and there are 17 to 34 sectors in a track although newer drives may have a different number of sectors.

Track : The circular path traced across the spinning surface of a disk platter by the read/ write head inside the hard-disk drive. The track consists of one or more clusters.

Disk Access Time

Access time is the interval between the instant a computer makes a request for transfer of data from a disk-storage device to RAM and the instant this operation is completed. The access of data from RAM is performed at electronic speeds-approximately the speed of light. But the access of data from disk storage depends on mechanical apparatus. Any mechanical movement significantly increases the access time.

Seek Time

The seek time, the largest portion of the total access time, consists of how long it takes the access arm (mechanical) to move the read/write head to the desired track or cylinder. Some hard disk drives have two sets of access arms, one for reading and writing on the inside tracks and another for the outside tracks.

Two independent sets of access arms significantly reduce the average seek time because they have a shorter distance to move and can move while the other is reading or writing.

Rotational Delay Time

The rotational delay time is the time it takes for the appropriate data to be positioned under the read/write head. On the average, it would be half the time it takes for one revolution of the disk or about 8 msec for a hard disk spinning at 3600 rpm.

Transmission Time

The transmission time i.e; the time it takes to transmit the data or RAM, is negligible.

Disk Access Time = Seek time + rotational delay time + transmission time

How to minimize the seek time

If records of a file stored on disk are to be accessed sequentially, then access time can be minimized by properly allocating disk space to the file. Assume the file requires 10 tracks of space. Rather than allocating 10 tracks on one surface to the file, space should be allocated to tracks on one cylinder, thereby minimizing the arm movement required to access the records.

Advance Technology Attachment

Shown next is the ATA = AT bus Attachment which has been developed by Western Digital, Conner, Seagate and Quantum.

Average Access Time

The time (in milliseconds) that a disk drive takes to find the right track in response to a request (the seek time), plus the time it takes to get to the right place on the track (the latency).

Arial Density

The amount of data which can be stored in one area of a Hard Disk or Floppy.

Interleaving

A hard-disk term which describes a method of arranging disk sectors to compensate for relatively slow computers Spreads sectors apart instead of arranging them consecutively. For example, 3:1 interleaving means your system reads one out of every three tracks on one rotation. The time required for the extra spin lets the read/write head catch up with the disk drive, which might otherwise outrun the head's ability to read the data

Cluster

A cluster is the minimum amount of space used to store a file. If the cluster size for operating system is 256 bytes even a 1-byte file takes up 256 bytes worth of space.

Recording Data on Disk

Data can be recorded on disk tracks with or without the use of keys. A key is a label that is used to identify a particular record. A key is required whenever the location of the record can't be specified exactly. Layout of the fields on a track in disk storage when data is recorded without the use of keys can be as given below:

- BT: beginning of track
- G: fields are separated by a gap
- HA: home address consists of 4 fields
- TC: track condition signals as to whether the track is operative or defective
- CY: cylinder number
- HD: Head number
- EC: Error checking code which tells whether the data is read/write correctly or not.
- TDR: Track descriptor record, serves to indicate an alternative track if the given track is defective.

Many disk systems contain spare tracks that are used as alternates whenever a track becomes defective; this avoids the necessity of terminating a job in the middle or re creating an entire file because of difficulty with one or two tracks.

Record

The data are often consists of hundreds of characters, and thus is much longer than the identification and control fields which preceded it on the track. Data is recorded with associated keys. In many disk systems the length of the key is limited to 255 bytes. Key field makes it possible to check the identification of a record in the disk control unit before it is transferred to the central processor, thus conserving central processor time.

Capacity and Access Speed

PC hard disk drive capacity (in GB). The vertical axis is logarithmic, so the fit line corresponds to exponential growth.

Using rigid disks and sealing the unit allows much tighter tolerances than in a floppy disk drive. Consequently, hard disk drives can store much more data than floppy disk drives and can access and transmit it faster. As of January 2008:

- A typical desktop HDD, might store between 120 and 300 GBs of data (based on US market data, rotate at 7,200 revolutions per minute (RPM) and have a media transfer rate of 1 Gbit/s or higher.

- The highest capacity HDDs are 1TB.
- The fastest "enterprise" HDDs spin at 10,000 or 15,000 rpm, and can achieve sequential media transfer speeds above 1.6 Gbit/s. Drives running at 10,000 or 15,000 rpm use smaller platters because of air drag and therefore generally have lower capacity than the highest capacity desktop drives.
- Mobile, i.e., laptop HDDs, which are physically smaller than their desktop and enterprise counterparts, tend to be slower and have less capacity. A typical mobile HDD spins at 5,400 rpm, with 7,200 rpm models available for a slight price premium. Because of the smaller disks, mobile HDDs generally have lower capacity than the highest capacity desktop drives.

The exponential increases in disk space and data access speeds of HDDs have enabled the commercial viability of consumer products that require large storage capacities, such as digital video recorders and digital audio players. In addition, the availability of vast amounts of cheap storage has made viable a variety of web-based services with extraordinary capacity requirements, such as free-of-charge web search and email (Google, Yahoo!, etc.).

The main way to decrease access time is to increase rotational speed, while the main way to increase throughput and storage capacity is to increase areal density. A vice president of Seagate Technology projects a future growth in disk density of 40% per year.[13] Access times have not kept up with throughput increases, which themselves have not kept up with growth in storage capacity.

As of 2006, some disk drives use perpendicular recording technology to increase recording density and throughput.

Capacity Measurements

The capacity of an HDD can be calculated by multiplying the number of cylinders by the number of heads by the number of sectors by the number of bytes/sector (most commonly 512). Drives with ATA interface bigger and more than eight gigabytes behave as if they were structured into 16383 cylinders, 16 heads, and 63 sectors, for compatibility with older operating systems. Unlike in the 1980s, the cylinder, head, sector (C/H/S) counts reported to the CPU by a modern ATA drive are no longer actual physical parameters since the reported numbers are constrained by historic operating-system interfaces and with zone bit recording the actual number of sectors varies by zone. Disks with SCSI interface address each sector with a unique integer number; the operating system remains ignorant of their head or cylinder count.

The old C/H/S scheme has been replaced by logical block addressing. In some cases, to try to "force-fit" the C/H/S scheme to large-capacity drives, the number of heads was given as 64, although no drive has anywhere near 32 platters.

Hard disk drive manufacturers specify disk capacity using the SI prefixes mega-, giga- and tera-, and their abbreviations M, G and T. Byte is typically abbreviated B.

Some operating-system tools report capacity using the same abbreviations but actually use binary prefixes.

For instance, the prefix mega-, which normally means 10^6 (1,000,000), in the context of data storage can mean 2^{20} (1,048,576), which is nearly 5% more. Similar usage has been applied to prefixes of greater magnitude. This results in a discrepancy between the disk manufacturer's stated capacity and the apparent capacity of the drive when examined through some operating-system tools. The difference becomes even more noticeable (7%) for a gigabyte.

For example, Microsoft Windows reports disk capacity both in decimal-based units to 12 or more significant digits and with binary-based units to three significant digits. Thus a disk specified by a disk manufacturer as a 30 GB disk might have its capacity reported by Windows 2000 both as "30,065,098,568 bytes" and "28.0 GB". The disk manufacturer used the SI definition of "giga", 10^9 to arrive at 30 GB; however, because the utilities provided by Windows define a gigabyte as 1,073,741,824 bytes (2^{30} bytes, often referred to as a gibibyte, or GiB), the operating system reports capacity of the disk drive as (only) 28.0 GB.

Form factors

The earliest "form factor" hard disk drives inherited their dimensions from floppy-disk drives (FDDs), so that either could be mounted in chassis slots, and thus the HDD form factors became colloquially named after the corresponding FDD types. "Form factor" compatibility continued after the 3½ in size even though floppy disk drives with new smaller dimensions ceased to be offered.

- "8 inch" drive: (9.5 in x 4.624 in x 14.25 in = 241.3 mm x 117.5 mm x 362 mm)

  In 1979, Shugart Associates' SA1000 was the first form factor compatible HDD, having the same dimensions and a compatible interface to the 8" FDD. Both "full height" and "half height" (2.313 in) versions were available.

- "5¼ inch" drive: (5.75 in x 1.63 in x 8 in = 146.1 mm x 41.4 mm x 203 mm)

  This smaller form factor, first used in an HDD by Seagate in 1980, was the same size as full height 5¼-inch diameter FDD, i.e., 3.25 inches high. This is twice as high as commonly used today; i.e., 1.63 in = 41.4 mm ("half height"). Most desktop models of drives for optical 120 mm disks (· DVD, · CD) use the half height 5¼" dimension, but it fell out of fashion for HDDs. The Quantum "Bigfoot" HDD was the last to use it in the late 1990s, with "low-profile" (~25 mm) and "ultra-low-profile" (~20 mm) high versions.

- "3½ inch" drive: (4 in x 1 in x 5.75 in = 101.6 mm x 25.4 mm x 146 mm)

  This smaller form factor, first used in an HDD by Rodime in 1984, was the same size as the "half height" 3½ FDD, i.e., 1.63 inches high. Today has been largely superseded by 1-inch high "slimline" or "low-profile" versions of this form factor which is used by most desktop HDDs.

- "2½ inch" drive: (2.75 in x 0.374 in x 3.945 in = 69.85 mm x 9.5 mm x 100 mm)

  This smaller form factor was introduced by PrairieTek in 1988; there is no corresponding FDD. It is widely used today for hard-disk drives in mobile devices (laptops, music players, etc.). Today, the dominant height of this form factor is 9.5 mm, but there were also 19 mm, 17 mm, and 12.5 mm high variants in use.

- "1.8 inch" drive: (54 mm × 8 mm × 71 mm)

  This form factor, originally introduced by Integral Peripherals in 1993, has evolved into the ATA-7 LIF with dimensions as stated. It is increasingly used in digital audio players and subnotebooks. An original variant exists for 2–5 GB sized HDDs that fit directly into a · PC card expansion slot.

- "1 inch" drive: (42.8 mm × 5 mm × 36.4 mm)

  This form factor was introduced in 1999 as ·IBM's· Microdrive to fit inside a CF Type II slot. Samsung calls the same form factor "1.3 inch" drive in its product literature.

- "0.85 inch" drive: (24 mm × 5 mm × 32 mm)

  Toshiba announced this form factor in January 2004 for use in mobile phones and similar applications, including SD/MMC slot compatible HDDs optimized for video storage on 4G handsets. Toshiba currently sells a 4 GB (MK4001MTD) and 8 GB (MK8003MTD) version and holds the Guinness World Record for the smallest harddisk drive.

Major manufacturers discontinued the development of new products for the 1-inch (=1.3-inch) and 0.85-inch form factors in 2007, due to falling prices of flash memory, although Samsung introduced in 2008 with the SpinPoint A1 another 1.3-inch drive.

The inch-based nickname of all these form factors usually do not indicate any actual product dimension (which are for more recent form factors specified in millimeters), but just roughly indicate a size relative to disk diameters, in the interest of historic continuity.

Access and interfaces

Hard disk drives are accessed over one of a number of bus types, including parallel ATA (PATA, also called IDE or EIDE), Serial ATA (SATA), SCSI, Serial Attached SCSI (SAS), and Fibre Channel. Bridge circuitry is sometimes used to connect hard disk drives to buses that they cannot communicate with natively, such as IEEE 1394 and USB.

Back in the days of the ST-506 interface, the data encoding scheme was also important. The first ST-506 disks used Modified Frequency Modulation (MFM) encoding, and transferred data at a rate of 5 megabits per second. Later on, controllers using 2,7 RLL (or just "RLL") encoding increased the transfer rate by 50%, to 7.5 megabits per second; this also increased disk capacity by fifty percent.

Many ST-506 interface disk drives were only specified by the manufacturer to run at the lower MFM data rate, while other models (usually more expensive versions of the same basic disk drive) were specified to run at the higher RLL data rate. In some cases, a disk drive had sufficient margin to allow the MFM specified model to run at the faster RLL data rate; however, this was often unreliable and was not recommended. (An RLL-certified disk drive could run on a MFM controller, but with 1/3 less data capacity and speed.)

Enhanced Small Disk Interface (ESDI) also supported multiple data rates (ESDI disks always used 2,7 RLL, but at 10, 15 or 20 megabits per second), but this was usually negotiated automatically by the disk drive and controller; most of the time, however, 15 or 20 megabit ESDI disk drives weren't downward compatible (i.e. a 15 or 20 megabit disk drive wouldn't run on a 10 megabit controller). ESDI disk drives typically also had jumpers to set the number of sectors per track and (in some cases) sector size.

SCSI originally had just one speed, 5 MHz (for a maximum data rate of five megabytes per second), but later this was increased dramatically. The SCSI bus speed had no bearing on the disk's internal speed because of buffering between the SCSI bus and the disk drive's internal data bus; however, many early disk drives had very small buffers, and thus had to be reformatted to a different interleave (just like ST-506 disks) when used on slow computers, such as early IBM PC compatibles and early Apple Macintoshes.

ATA disks have typically had no problems with interleave or data rate, due to their controller design, but many early models were incompatible with each other and couldn't run in a master/slave setup (two disks on the same cable). This was mostly remedied by the mid-1990s, when ATA's specification was standardised and the details began to be cleaned up, but still causes problems occasionally (especially with CD-ROM and DVD-ROM disks, and when mixing Ultra DMA and non-UDMA devices).

Serial ATA does away with master/slave setups entirely, placing each disk on its own channel (with its own set of I/O ports) instead.

FireWire/IEEE 1394 and USB(1.0/2.0) HDDs are external units containing generally ATA or SCSI disks with ports on the back allowing very simple and effective expansion and mobility. Most FireWire/IEEE 1394 models are able to daisy-chain in order to continue adding peripherals without requiring additional ports on the computer itself.

Disk Interface Families used in Personal Computers

Notable families of disk interfaces include:

- Historical bit serial interfaces — connected to a hard disk drive controller with three cables, one for data, one for control and one for power. The HDD controller provided significant functions such as serial to parallel conversion, data separation and track formatting, and required matching to the drive in order to assure reliability.
- ST506 used MFM (Modified Frequency Modulation) for the data encoding method.
- ST412 was available in either MFM or RLL (Run Length Limited) variants.

- Enhanced Small Disk Interface (ESDI) was an interface developed by Maxtor to allow faster communication between the PC and the disk than MFM or RLL.
- Modern bit serial interfaces — connect to a host bus adapter (today typically integrated into the " south bridge") with two cables, one for data/control and one for power.
- Fibre Channel (FC), is a successor to parallel SCSI interface on enterprise market. It is a serial protocol. In disk drives usually the Fibre Channel Arbitrated Loop (FC-AL) connection topology is used. FC has much broader usage than mere disk interfaces, it is the cornerstone of storage area networks (SANs). Recently other protocols for this field, like iSCSI and ATA over Ethernet have been developed as well. Confusingly, drives usually use copper twisted-pair cables for Fibre Channel, not fibre optics. The latter are traditionally reserved for larger devices, such as servers or disk array controllers.
- Serial ATA (SATA). The SATA data cable has one data pair for differential transmission of data to the device, and one pair for differential receiving from the device, just like EIA-422. That requires that data be transmitted serially. The same differential signaling system is used in RS485, LocalTalk, USB, Firewire, and differential SCSI.
- Serial Attached SCSI (SAS). The SAS is a new generation serial communication protocol for devices designed to allow for much higher speed data transfers and is compatible with SATA. SAS uses serial communication instead of the parallel method found in traditional SCSI devices but still uses SCSI commands.
- Word serial interfaces — connect to a host bus adapter (today typically integrated into the "south bridge") with two cables, one for data/control and one for power. The earliest versions of these interfaces typically had a 16 bit parallel data transfer to/from the drive and there are 8 and 32 bit variants. Modern versions have serial data transfer. The word nature of data transfer makes the design of a host bus adapter significantly simpler than that of the precursor HDD controller.
- Integrated Drive Electronics (IDE), later renamed to ATA, and then later to PATA ("parallel ATA", to distinguish it from the new Serial ATA). The original name reflected the innovative integration of HDD controller with HDD itself, which was not found in earlier disks. Moving the HDD controller from the interface card to the disk drive helped to standardize interfaces, including reducing the cost and complexity. The 40 pin IDE/ATA connection of PATA transfers 16 bits of data at a time on the data cable. The data cable was originally 40 conductor, but later higher speed requirements for data transfer to and from the hard drive led to an "ultra DMA" mode, known as UDMA, which required an 80 conductor variant of the same cable; the other conductors provided the grounding necessary for enhanced high-speed signal quality. The interface for 80 pin only has 39 pins, the missing pin acting as a key to prevent incorrect insertion of the connector to an incompatible socket, a common cause of disk and controller damage.

- EIDE was an unofficial update (by Western Digital) to the original IDE standard, with the key improvement being the use of direct memory access (DMA) to transfer data between the disk and the computer without the involvement of the CPU, an improvement later adopted by the official ATA standards.

  By directly transferring data between memory and disk, DMA does not require the CPU/program/operating system to leave other tasks idle while the data transfer occurs.
- Small Computer System Interface (SCSI), originally named SASI for Shugart Associates System Interface, was an early competitor of ESDI. SCSI disks were standard on servers, workstations, and Apple Macintosh computers through the mid-90s, by which time most models had been transitioned to IDE (and later, SATA) family disks. Only in 2005 did the capacity of SCSI disks fall behind IDE disk technology, though the highest-performance disks are still available in SCSI and Fibre Channel only.

  The length limitations of the data cable allows for external SCSI devices. Originally SCSI data cables used single ended data transmission, but server class SCSI could use differential transmission, either low voltage differential (LVD) or high voltage differential (HVD).

Hard Disk Enhancements

Hard disk drives are accessed over one of a number of bus types, including ATA (IDE, EIDE), Serial ATA (SATA), SCSI, SAS, and Fibre Channel. Bridge circuitry is sometimes used to connect hard disk drives to busses that they cannot communicate with natively, such as IEEE 1394 and USB. Back in the days of the ST-506 interface, the data encoding scheme was also important. The first ST-506 disks used Modified Frequency Modulation (MFM) encoding, and transferred data at a rate of 5 megabits per second. Later on, controllers using 2,7 RLL (or just "RLL") encoding increased the transfer rate by fifty percent, to 7.5 megabits per second; it also increased disk capacity by fifty percent.

Many ST-506 interface disk drives were only specified by the manufacturer to run at the lower MFM data rate, while other models (usually more expensive versions of the same basic disk drive) were specified to run at the higher RLL data rate. In some cases, a disk drive had sufficient margin to allow the MFM specified model to run at the faster RLL data rate; however, this was often unreliable and was not recommended. (An RLL-certified disk drive could run on a MFM controller, but with 1/3 less data capacity and speed.)

Enhanced Small Disk Interface (ESDI) also supported multiple data rates (ESDI disks always used 2,7 RLL, but at 10, 15 or 20 megabits per second), but this was usually negotiated automatically by the disk drive and controller; most of the time, however, 15 or 20 megabit ESDI disk drives weren't downward compatible (i.e. a 15 or 20 megabit disk drive wouldn't run on a 10 megabit controller). ESDI disk drives typically also had jumpers to set the number of sectors per track and (in some cases) sector size.

SCSI originally had just one speed, 5 MHz (for a maximum data rate of 5 megabytes per second), but later this was increased dramatically. The SCSI bus speed had no bearing on the disk's internal speed because of buffering between the SCSI bus and the disk drive's internal data bus; however, many early disk drives had very small buffers, and thus had to be reformatted to a different interleave (just like ST-506 disks) when used on slow computers, such as early IBM PC compatibles and early Apple Macintoshes.

ATA disks have typically had no problems with interleave or data rate, due to their controller design, but many early models were incompatible with each other and couldn't run in a master/slave setup (two disks on the same cable). This was mostly remedied by the mid-1990s, when ATA's specification was standardised and the details began to be cleaned up, but still causes problems occasionally (especially with CD-ROM and DVD-ROM disks, and when mixing Ultra DMA and non-UDMA devices).

Serial ATA does away with master/slave setups entirely, placing each disk on its own channel (with its own set of I/O ports) instead. FireWire/IEEE 1394 and USB(1.0/2.0) hard disks are external units containing generally ATA or SCSI disks with ports on the back allowing very simple and effective expansion and mobility. Most FireWire/IEEE 1394 models are able to daisy-chain in order to continue adding peripherals without requiring additional ports on the computer itself.

Acronym	Meaning	Description
SASI	Shugart Associates System Interface	Predecessor to SCSI
SCSI	Small Computer System Interface	Bus oriented that handles concurrent operations.
ST 506		Seagate interface
ST-412		Seagate interface (minor improvement over ST-506)
ESDI	Enhanced Small Disk Interface	Faster and more integrated than ST-412/506, but still backwards compatible
ATA	Advanced Technology Attachment	Successor to ST-412/506/ESDI by integrating the disk controller completely onto the device. Incapable of concurrent operations.

eSATA

Standardized in mid-2004, eSATA defined separate cables, connectors, and revised electrical requirements for external applications:

- Minimum transmit potential increased: Range is 500–600 mV instead of 400–600 mV.
- Minimum receive potential decreased: Range is 240–600 mV instead of 325–600 mV.
- Identical protocol and logical signaling (link/transport-layer and above), allowing native SATA devices to be deployed in external enclosures with minimal modification
- Maximum cable length of 2 m (USB and FireWire allow longer distances.)

Aimed at the consumer market, eSATA enters an external storage market already served by the USB and FireWire interfaces. Most external hard disk drive cases with FireWire or USB interfaces use either PATA or SATA drives and "bridges" to translate between the drives' interfaces and the enclosures' external ports, and this bridging incurs some inefficiency. In the case of USB 2.0, protocol overhead limits the maximum effective bandwidth to a fraction of USB's physical signalling rate. With modern hard disk drives, USB's transfer rate is a bottleneck.

FireWire, with its isochronous transfer mode, is more efficient, such that even in its slower variant, FireWire 400 (IEEE 1394a), the effective transfer rate is significantly faster than that of USB 2.0, but this can still be a bottleneck for fast drives or RAIDs. Some single disks can transfer well over 70 MB/s during real use, well in excess of USB 2.0's or the older FireWire 400's abilities. Finally, some low-level drive features, such as S.M.A.R.T., are not usable through USB or FireWire bridging. eSATA does not suffer from these issues.

eSATA will likely co-exist alongside USB 2.0 and FireWire storage for several reasons. The ubiquity of USB ports on all mass-market computers, and FireWire ports on many consumer electronic appliances, guarantee a large market for USB and FireWire storage. For small form-factor devices (such as external 2.5" disks), a PC-hosted USB or FireWire link supplies sufficient power to operate the device. Where a PC-hosted port is concerned, eSATA connectors cannot supply power, and would therefore be more cumbersome to use.

As of 2007, few computer motherboards have eSATA connectors. Non-equipped desktops can be upgraded with the installation of an eSATA host bus adapter (HBA), while notebooks can be upgraded with Cardbus or ExpressCard versions of an eSATA HBA. Also available are passive eSATA-to-SATA bracket/cable-adapters.

With passive-adapters, the maximum cable length is reduced to 1 meter, due to the absence of compliant eSATA signal levels. Full SATA speed for external disks (115 MB/s) have been measured with external RAID enclosures.

eSATA is likely to be ignored by the enterprise and server market, which has already standardized on the separately-developed Serial Attached SCSI (SAS) interface, which has extra features for remote management, link redundancy, and link monitoring.

SATA vs SCSI

SCSI currently offers transfer rates higher than SATA, but is a more complex bus usually resulting in higher manufacturing cost. Some drive manufacturers offer longer warranties for SCSI devices, however, indicating a possibly higher manufacturing quality control of SCSI devices compared to PATA/SATA devices. SCSI buses also allow connection of several drives (using multiple channels, 7 or 15 on each channel) whereas SATA only allows one per channel.

SATA 3.0 Gbit/s offers a maximum bandwidth of 300 MB/s per device compared to SCSI with a maximum of 320 MB/s. Also, SCSI drives provide greater sustained throughput than SATA drives because of disconnect-reconnect and aggregating performance. SATA devices are generally compatible with SAS enclosures and adapters, while SCSI devices cannot be directly connected to a SATA bus.

SCSI hardware is used in enterprises for server purposes, partially due to higher cost of drives and adapters, and partially due to market reasons. The MTBF of SATA drives is usually about 150,000 hours, while SCSI drives are rated for upwards of 1,500,000 hours.

SAS (Serial Attached SCSI) vs Parallel SCSI

- SAS uses Serial transfer protocol to interface multiple devices hence lesser signaling overhead than parallel SCSI, resulting in higher speed.
- No bus contention as SAS bus is point-to-point while SCSI bus is multidrop. Each device is connected by a dedicated bus to the initiator. Connection through expanders may appear to cause some contention, but this is transparent to the initiator.
- SAS has no termination issues and does not require terminator packs like parallel SCSI.
- SAS eliminates clock skew.
- SAS supports higher number of devices (> 16384) while Parallel SCSI limits it to 8, 16, or 32.
- SAS supports higher transfer speed (1.5, 3.0 or 6.0 Gbit/s). The speed is realized on each initiator-target connection, hence higher throughput whereas in parallel SCSI the speed is shared across the entire multidrop bus.
- SAS controllers typically support SATA devices.
- SAS uses SCSI commands to interface with SAS End devices.

SAS vs SATA

- SATA devices are uniquely identified by their port number connected to the Host bus adapter while SAS devices are uniquely identifed by their World Wide Name (WWN).
- Most SAS drives provide Tagged Command Queuing, while most newer SATA drives provide Native Command Queuing, each of which has its pros and cons.
- SATA follows the ATA command set and thus only supports hard drives and CD/DVD drives. In theory, SAS also supports numerous other devices including scanners and printers. However, this advantage could also be moot, as most such devices have also found alternative paths via such buses as USB, IEEE 1394, and Ethernet.
- SAS hardware allows multipath I/O to devices while SATA does not. An effort is underway to use port multipliers to achieve multipathing with SATA II.
- SATA is marketed as a general-purpose successor to Parallel ATA and is now common in the consumer market, while the more expensive SAS is marketed for critical server applications.

- SAS error recovery and reporting are much cleaner than SATA.
- SAS uses higher signaling voltages (800-1600mv TX, 275-1600mv RX) than SATA (400-600mv TX, 325-600mv RX). When SAS is mixed with SATA, the SAS drives run at SATA-voltages. One reason for this higher voltage is so SAS may be used in server backplanes.
- Because of its higher signaling voltages, SAS can use cables up to 8 m (25 ft) long, SATA is limited to 1 m (3 ft).

External SATA

Standardized in mid-2004, eSATA defined separate cables, connectors, and revised electrical requirements for external applications:

- Minimum transmit potential increased: Range is 500–600 mV instead of 400–600 mV.
- Minimum receive potential decreased: Range is 240–600 mV instead of 325–600 mV.
- Identical protocol and logical signaling (link/transport-layer and above), allowing native SATA devices to be deployed in external enclosures with minimal modification
- Maximum cable length of 2m (USB and FireWire allow longer distances.)

Aimed at the consumer market, eSATA enters an external storage market already served by the USB and FireWire interfaces. Most external hard disk drive cases with FireWire or USB interfaces use either PATA or SATA drives and "bridges" to translate between the drives' interfaces and the enclosures' external ports,[citation needed] and this bridging incurs some inefficiency. In the case of USB 2.0, protocol overhead limits the maximum effective bandwidth to a fraction of USB's physical signalling rate. With modern hard disk drives, USB's transfer rate is a bottleneck. FireWire, with its isochronous transfer mode, is more efficient, such that even in its slower variant, FireWire 400 (IEEE 1394a), the effective transfer rate is significantly faster than that of USB 2.0, but this can still be a bottleneck for fast drives or RAID arrays. Some single disks can transfer well over 90 MB/s during real use, well in excess of USB 2.0's or the older FireWire 400's abilities. Finally, some low-level drive features, such as S.M.A.R.T., are not usable through USB or FireWire bridging. eSATA does not suffer from these issues.

eSATA will likely co-exist alongside USB 2.0 and FireWire storage for several reasons. The ubiquity of USB ports on all mass-market computers, and FireWire ports on many consumer electronic appliances, guarantee a large market for USB and FireWire storage.[citation needed] For small form-factor devices (such as external 2.5" (70 mm) disks), a PC-hosted USB or FireWire link supplies sufficient power to operate the device. Where a PC-hosted port is concerned, eSATA connectors cannot supply power, and would therefore be more cumbersome to use.

As of 2007, an eSATA external drive enclosure will typically ship with a passive eSATA-to-SATA bracket/cable-adapter to install on desktops that lack an eSATA port or that need another. Desktops can also be upgraded with the installation of an eSATA host bus adapter (HBA), while notebooks can be upgraded with Cardbus or ExpressCard versions of an eSATA HBA. With passive-adapters, the maximum cable length is reduced to 1 meter, due to the absence of compliant eSATA signal levels. Full SATA speed for external disks (115 MB/s) have been measured with external RAID enclosures.

eSATA is likely to be ignored by the enterprise and server market, which has already standardized on the separately-developed Serial Attached SCSI (SAS) interface, which has extra features for remote management, link redundancy, and link monitoring.

Prior to the final eSATA specification, there were a number of products designed for external connections of SATA drives. Some of these use the internal SATA connector or even connectors designed for other interface specifications, such as FireWire. These products are not eSATA compliant. The final eSATA specification features a specific connector designed for rough manipulation. It's similar to the regular SATA connector, but with reinforcements in both the male and female sides, inspired by the USB connector. It's harder to unplug and can withstand a cable being yanked or wiggled. On a SATA connector, this kind of action will break the male side of the connection (the hard drive or host adapter), rendering the device unusable. With an eSATA connector, considerably more force is needed to damage the connector, and even in this situation, only the female side (the cable itself) will break, possibly leaving the male usable.

Cables and Connectors

The SATA power and data cables are the most noticeable change from Parallel ATA. Unlike Parallel ATA, the same physical connectors are used on 3.5-in (90 mm) desktop hard disks and 2.5-in (70 mm) notebook disks; this eliminates the need for a mechanical adapter when using a notebook drive in a desktop computer.

Pin #	Function
1	Ground
2	A+
3	A"
4	Ground
5	B"
6	B+
7	Ground

The SATA standard defines a data cable with seven conductors (3 grounds and 4 active data lines in two pairs) and 8 mm wide wafer connectors on each end. SATA cables can be up to 1 m (39 in) long. PATA ribbon cables, in comparison, carry either 40- or 80-conductor wires and are limited to 45 cm (18 in) in length by the PATA specification (however, cables up to 90 cm (36 in) are readily available). Thus, SATA connectors and cables are easier to fit in closed spaces and reduce obstructions to air cooling. However, they are more susceptible to accidental unplugging.

A 7-pin Serial ATA data cable.

Pin #	Function
1-3	3.3V
4-6	Ground
7-9	5V
10	Ground
11	Staggered spinup(in supporting drives)
12	Ground
13-15	12V

The SATA standard also specifies a new power connector. Like the data cable, it is wafer-based, but its wider 15-pin shape prevents accidental misidentification and forced insertion of the wrong connector type. Native SATA devices favor the SATA power-connector over the old four-pin Molex connector (found on all PATA equipment), although some SATA drives retain older 4-pin Molex.

The SATA/power connector has been criticized for its poor robustness—the thin plastic tops of the connectors (see power connector picture at right) can break due to shearing force when the user pulls the plug at a non-orthogonal angle. The seemingly large number of pins are used to supply three different voltages: 3.3 V, 5 V, and 12 V. Each voltage is supplied by three pins ganged together, while ground is provided by five pins. Pin 11 is used in newer drives for staggered spinup. The supply pins are ganged together because the small pins by themselves cannot supply sufficient current for some devices. One pin from each of the three voltages is also used for hotplugging.

Adaptors are available to convert a 4-pin Molex connector to SATA power connector. However, because the 4-pin Molex connectors do not provide 3.3 V power, these adapters provide only 5 V and 12 V power and leave the 3.3 V lines disconnected.

This precludes the use of such adapters with drives that require 3.3 V power. Understanding this, drive manufacturers have largely left the 3.3 V power lines unused. However, without 3.3 V power, the SATA device may not be able to implement hotplugging as mentioned in the previous paragraph.

Installation of HDD

The following procedure outlines the installation of a hard disk.

1. Disconnect the power to the computer.
2. Configure the appropriate master/slave settings or SCSI ID for the drive.

3. Insert the drive into an available drive bay. If the drive is too small for the bay, you will need a mounting kit.
4. Screw in the 4 screws - 2 on each side of the bay.
5. If the drive is an IDE disk, connect the IDE cable to the drive. There should be a stripe along 1 edge of the cable. This stripe denotes pin 1. Pin 1 on the drive is usually closest to the power connector on the drive, however, you should consult the manufacturers documentation. Then connect the signal cable to the motherboard ID1 or ID2 interface making sure to note the pin 1 orientation there as well. If the drive is a SCSI drive, a SCSI cable would be connected from the drive to a SCSI controller card.
6. Connect one of the power supply's power connectors to the drive.

Once the drive has been installed it must be configured for use in the following steps:

1. CMOS configuration-Newer BIOSes autodetection features will do this automatically. Otherwise, enter the setup utility during boot up and configure the drive.
2. Certain older drives types must be low-level formatted. Do not do this on IDE drives!
3. Partition the drive-Using the DOS utility FDISK, the drive can be partitioned into logical drives. The disk must contain an active primary partition that will be the C drive. An extended partition may also be created if desired. In Windows NT, the Disk Administrator program is used instead of FDISK. The size of the partitions can be set to a desired size, however, note the following:
   - Windows 95 Rev A(FAT16) only supported partitions up to 2GB in size.
   - Windows 95/98 OSR2(FAT32) supported drives up to 8GB.
   - Even if the OS supports larger partition sizes, the BIOS must also support logical block addressing (LBA) or the maximum partition that you will be able to create will be either 504 or 528 MB.
4. Once the disk has been partitioned, it must then be formatted. This can be done using the DOS format utility.

Due to the magnetic nature of hard disks, they should remain clear of magnetic fields.

Troubleshooting Hard Disk Drives

Symptoms associated with hard disk drive failures include the following:

1. An Invalid Media Type message appears, indicating the controller cannot find a recognizable track/sector pattern on the drive.
2. A No Boot Record Found, a Nonsystem Disk or Disk Error, or an Invalid System Disk message appears, indicating that the system boot files are not located in the root directory of the drive.
3. The video display is active, but the HDD's activity light remains on and no bootup occurs, indicating that the HDD's CMOS configuration information is incorrect.

4. The front panel indicator lights are visible, and the display is present on the monitor screen, but there is no disk drive action and no bootup.
5. The computer boots up to a system disk in the A drive, but not to the hard drive, indicating that the system files on the hard disk drive (HDD) are missing or have become corrupt.
6. The computer does not boot up when turned on.
7. An IBM-compatible 17xx error code is produced on the display.
8. No motor sounds are produced by the HDD while the computer is running.
9. A HDD Controller Failure message appears, indicating a failure to verify hard disk setup by system configuration file error.
10. A C: or D: Fixed Disk Drive error message appears, indicating a hard disk CMOS setup failure.
11. An Out of Disk Space message appears.
12. A Missing Operating System or a Hard Drive Boot Failure message appears.
13. A Current Drive No Longer Valid message appears, indicating that the HDD's CMOS configuration information is incorrect or has become corrupt.

9 Floppy Disk Drive

Introduction

A floppy disk is a data storage medium that is composed of a disk of thin, flexible ("floppy") magnetic storage medium encased in a square or rectangular plastic shell. Floppy disks are read and written by a floppy disk drive or FDD, the initials of which should not be confused with "fixed disk drive", which is another term for a hard disk drive. Invented by IBM, floppy disks in 8", 5.25", and 3.5" formats enjoyed many years as a popular and ubiquitous form of data storage and exchange, from the middle 1970s to the late 1990s. However, they have now been largely superseded by flash and optical storage devices while e-mail has become the preferred method of exchanging small to medium size digital files.

Types of Floppy Disks

Floppies come in two physical sizes:

5 1/4 inch and

3 1/2 inch.

The size refers to the diameter of the disk, not to the capacity.

The 5 1/4" type is encased in a flexible vinyl envelope with an oval cutout that allows the read/write head to access the disk.

The density of the disk is a measure of the quantity of the disk surface: the higher the density, the more closely the iron-oxide particles are packed and the more data the disk can store. The disk itself is made of soft flexible mylar plastic with a magnetically sensitive iron oxide coating. The coating is present on both sides, even for single-sided disks that are intended to be recorded on only one side. The second side of a single-sided disk may not have its second side finished, polished and tested but it still has the same coating.

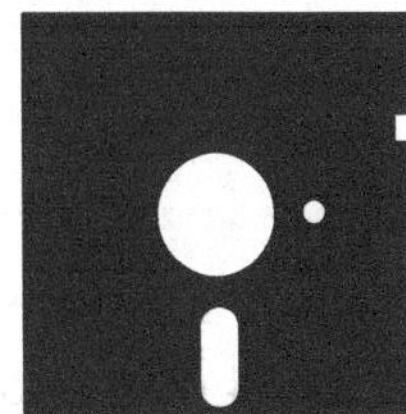

These days 5.25 inch disks (1.2 MB capacity) are used primarily in older computers although some people buy optional 5.25" disk drives for their new PCs to be able to read and write to the old disks. 3.5 inch type is encased in a hard plastic shell with a sliding metal cover. When the disk is inserted into the drive, the cover slides back to expose the disk to the read/write head. The term floppy disk refers to the disk inside, not to the square plastic protector.

The 3.5 inch size floppy disk come in three capacities:

1. double density
2. high density and
3. very high density

Floppy Disk Drives

A disk drive designed to read and write data to a floppy disk for transfer to and from a computer. It can be classified into two sections Mechanical Section and Electronic Section. A Floppy Drive consist of the following:

The following two figures show the block diagram of Floppy Disk Drive and real outlay of Floppy Disk Drive.

Mechanical Section

1. Two Motors : (*i*) Stepper Motor
   (*ii*) Spindle Motor
2. Read/Write Heads (Head zero and head one)
3. Chassis
4. HUB
5. Plastic Jaw
6. Head Actuator

Electronic Section

7. Two cards (*i*) Servo Card
   (*ii*) Logic Card
8. Four Sensor : (*i*) Track Zero Sensor
   (*ii*) Index Hole Sensor
   (*iii*) Write Protect Sensor
   (*iv*) Lock Sensor
9. 34 pin floppy drive connector
10. 4 pin power supply connector

Various parts of the Floppy Disk drive, as shown in the figure are:

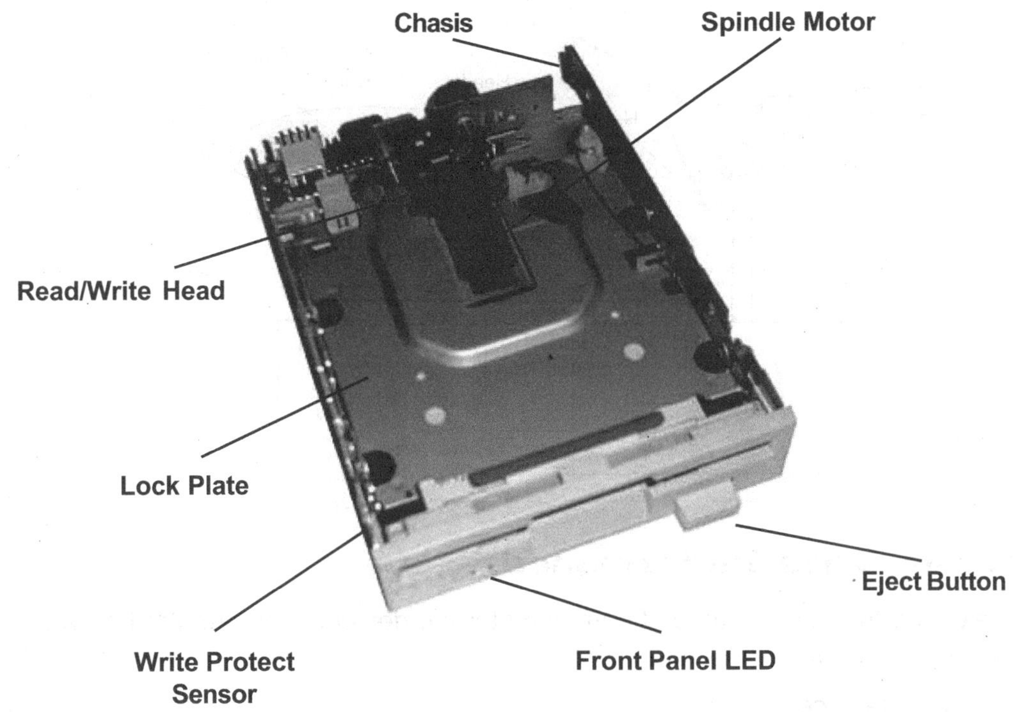

Spindle Motor : This motor is used to rotate the floppy disk at 360 revolutions per minute (RPM) so that the sectors can come under the read/write head.

Stepper Motor : This motor is used to move the read/write head over the tracks of the disk, it takes step pulses to move to the next track or previous track.

Read/Write Head : The Read/Write head are used to write and read information on the media *i.e.,* floppy, It works on ,the principle of electromagnetism.

Chassis : This is the base for the other parts, which are assembled on it.

Hub : The hub is used to hold the floppy at spindle hole and rotate it at 360 rpm.

Head Actuator : In a disk drive, the mechanism that moves the read/write head radially across the surface of the disk drive.

Plastic Jaw : This is used to hold the floppy at the spindle hole when it is inside the disk, so that it can rotate.

Lock Plate : The lock plate is used to lock the floppy inside the disk.

Electronic Section of FDD : The Electronics section of FDD consists of Two Cards Logic card and Servo card. The Logic card is used to control the stepper motor and the Read/Write Heads and the Servo card is used to control the spindle motor's rpm.

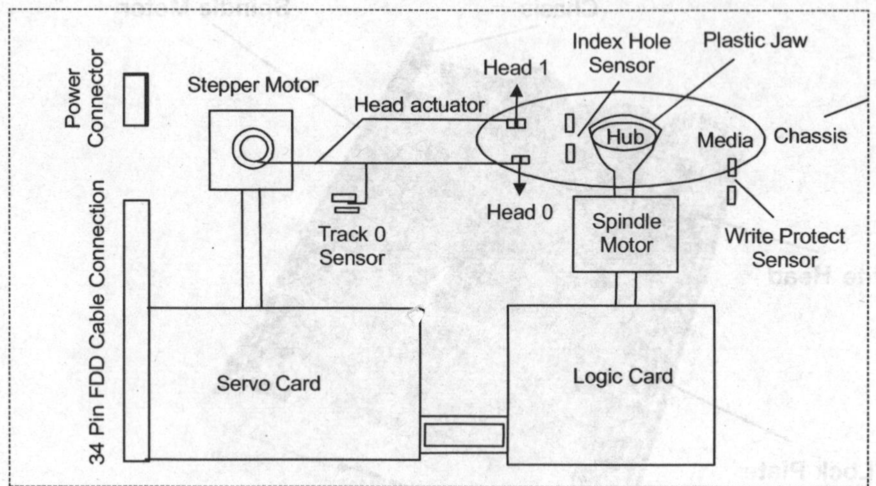

Measuring Drive Performance

When evaluating the performance of common storage devices, you need to be aware of two common measures:

1. The average access time and
2. The data-transfer rate.

Average Access Time

The average access time of a device is the amount of time it takes the device to position its read/write heads over any spot on the recording medium. Access time is the combination of two factors:

1. the speed at which the disk spins (in RPM) and
2. time the read/write head takes to move the heads from one track to another.

Access time is measured in msec. (1/1000 second), so the maximum access time for floppy disks = 60/30 * 1000/1 = 200 m secs.

Average Data Transfer Rate

It implies at which rate drive can transfer data, *i.e.*, how long it takes to read or write data. For data-transfer rates, the unit of time is almost always the second, but units of data may be measured in bytes, KB or MB. Disk controllers coordinate the flow of data to and from the computer and disk drive. They are often connected to the system as an expansion card and can control the flow of data to several drives.

Drive Interface Standards

Another important factor in determining how quickly a drive can read and write data is the type of controller that the drive uses. A disk controller is connected directly to the computer's bus on some computers, the disk controller is an integral part of the computer's main motherboard. On others, the controller is an expansion board that connects to the bus by plugging into one of the computer's expansion slots.

Integrated Drive Electronics (IDE)

The IDE interface places most of the controller's circuitry on the drive itself to provide a simpler interface with the computer. IDE is capable of providing data-transfer rates of about 1 MB per second under ideal conditions.

Enhanced Small Device Interface (ESDI)

It encodes the data on the drive instead of on the controller card. This results in a higher degree of reliability - which in turn allows for higher speeds. ESDI is capable of transferring data at rate of 3 MB per second.

Small Computer System Interface (SCSI)

It takes an approach to interfacing peripheral devices. Because the original concept of SCSI was to provide peripherals access to the computer's bus, one way to think of SCSI is as an extension of the computer's bus. One benefit of SCSI is that bringing the computer's bus directly into the drive improves efficiency greatly. Because a SCSI interface is essentially an extension of a computer's bus, it can accommodate multiple devices — as many as the bus can handle. Most current implementations of SCSI limit the number of devices to seven.

Internal Structure of a Floppy Disk

The outermost track of any disc is called track zero. Track zero is very important for any disk. It is responsible for booting of a computer, for storing the details of directories and files stored inside the disk.

Track zero has four parts:

1. Master Boot Record (MBR): It stores all the information of the operating system through which the floppy disk is formatted.
2. Dos Boot Record (DBR): It is used to store all the system files, which are required for booting of the computer There are three system files, which are required to boot a computer and they are
    i. IO.SYS
    ii. MSDOS.SYS
    iii. COMMAND.COM
3. Directory Structure (DS): It stores the information of all the directories and files stored inside the disk, such as, Directory name, File name, Size of the files and the date and time of the creation or modification of file etc.
4. File Allocation Table (FAT): It is very-very important part of track zero. It stores all the

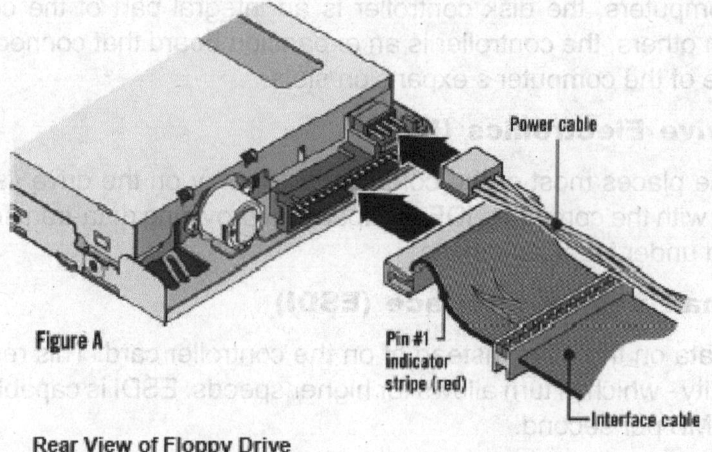

Rear View of Floppy Drive

information about the file and directory stored inside the disk such as track number, sector number and side number It is just like an index of a text book.

Installation of Floppy Disk Drives (FDD)

1. Power off and unplug the computer.
2. Detach all devices, *e.g.*, printer, keyboard, monitor.
3. Remove the computer cover. Refer to your computer system manual.
4. If you are replacing an existing drive, note how the drive is connected. For installation of a second drive or a new drive, go to Step 11.
5. Unplug the four pin power cable and the 34 pin flat interface cable.
6. Remove the screws mounting the old drive and carefully remove the unit.
7. Mount the Imation floppy drive using the screws supplied with the kit.
8. Attach the existing flat interface cable making certain that the red wire, Pin 1, is closest to the motor, near the center rear of the drive, as shown in Figure A.
9. Plug the four wire power connector to the drive to complete the installation.
10. Replace the computer cover and reconnect any peripherals.
11. For a second drive, complete Steps 1 to 3 above.
12. Remove a floppy disk filler panel at the front of the computer unit.
13. Determine that the interface cable to your existing floppy drive has a second connector near the attached drive. If not, substitute the three-connector interface cable shipped with the Imation kit.
14. Using the screws enclosed in the kit, mount the Imation floppy drive in the space in

the computer. If your computer does not have an extra floppy bay, you will need to acquire a 5-inch bay adapter panel from your computer supplier.

15. Connect the cable to the floppy drives with the red stripe closest to the motor assembly as shown in Figure A above.
16. The floppy drive attached to the end connector will appear as Drive A in My Computer or Windows Explorer. The drive attached to the second connector from the end will appear as Drive B.
17. Connect the a four wire power plug to the back of each floppy drive.
18. Reassemble the computer and power on.
19. Follow Steps 1 – 3 from the above instructions.
20. Determine if the mother board of the PC has a 34 pin floppy disk connector and that a 4 pin power connector is available. If the PC does not have an unused small power connector, you may need to obtain a standard power connector to mini adapter from your computer store.
21. Locate the floppy bay at the front of the machine and remove the cover.
22. Mount the floppy drive using the screws from the kit.
23. Attach the end of the 34 pin interface cable without the twist to the floppy disk connector on the mother board of your computer being sure to align the red stripe of the cable with Pin 1.
24. Connect the other end of the cable to the floppy drive with the red stripe closest to the motor assembly.
25. Reassemble the computer.
26. During power up, it may be necessary to reconfigure the BIOS of your PC to recognize the new floppy drive. Review the documentation that came with your PC or contact the manufacturer for this procedure.

Troubleshooting Floppy Disk Drives

1. The floppy drive is installed, but the LED on the front of the unit is continually on. The connection of the interface from the PC mother board to the drive may be incorrect. Power off and unplug the computer and recheck. Be certain that the red stripe of the interface cable connects to Pin 1 on the mother board of the PC and also to Pin 1 on the floppy drive. Pin 1 on the drive is closest to the drive motor, at the rear center of the unit.
2. The drive is cabled but is not recognized by the Windows operating system.
    - Go to Control Panel.
    - Click on System.
    - Click on Device Manager.

- Click the plus sign in front of Floppy Disk Controllers.
- If there is a yellow exclamation point on the disk controller, highlight the unit and click Remove.
- Power off the computer and unplug.
- With the system off, check the cable connections to the floppy drive.
- Reboot the system and Windows should automatically recognize your drive.

3. After setting up the system BIOS, a message "DISK BOOT FAILURE. INSERT A SYSTEM DISK AND HIT ENTER" appears. After trying several boot disks, the same message keeps appearing. The BIOS is not set up correctly. Obtain the proper settings by contacting your computer manufacturer or the Internet site for the manufacturer of the BIOS of your machine.

10 Processors

Personal Computer Processors

Processor is the main component inside the main system unit. This is the biggest electronic circuit board inside the computer system, on which many other board are attached. The boards that attach to the motherboard are known as daughterboard or expansion board.

The motherboard contains following :

1. **Processor Support:** The motherboard dictates directly your choice of processor for use in the system.
2. **Peripheral Support:** The motherboard determines, what types of peripherals you can use in your PC.
3. **Performance:** The motherboard is a major determining factor in system's performance, the motherboard determines what types of processors, memory,

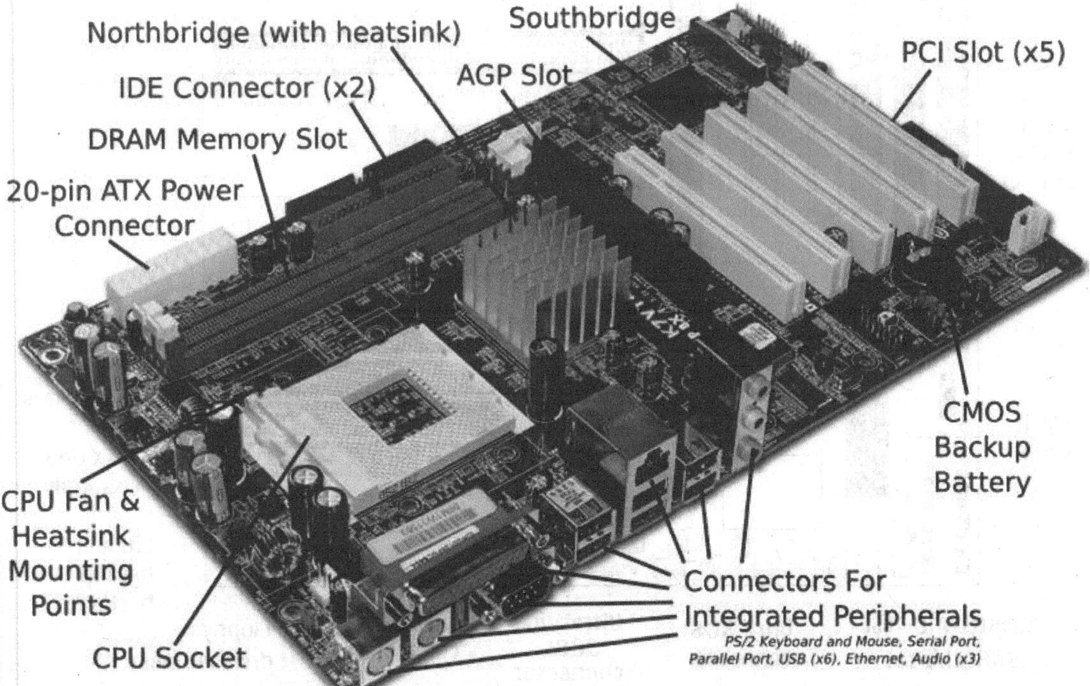

system buses, and hard disk interface speed your system can have, and these components dictate directly your system's performance.

4. **Upgradability:** The capabilities of motherboard dictate to what extent you will be able to upgrade your machine.

5. **Organization:** The way that the motherboard is designed and laid out dictates how the entire computer is going to be organized.

6. **Control:** The motherboard contains the chipset and BIOS program, which control most of the data flow within the computer.

7. **Communication:** All communication between the PC and its peripherals, other PCs, and user, goes through the motherboard.

Various Motherboard Types

PC/XT

It is series of personal computers based on the Intel 8088 processor, introduced by IBM in

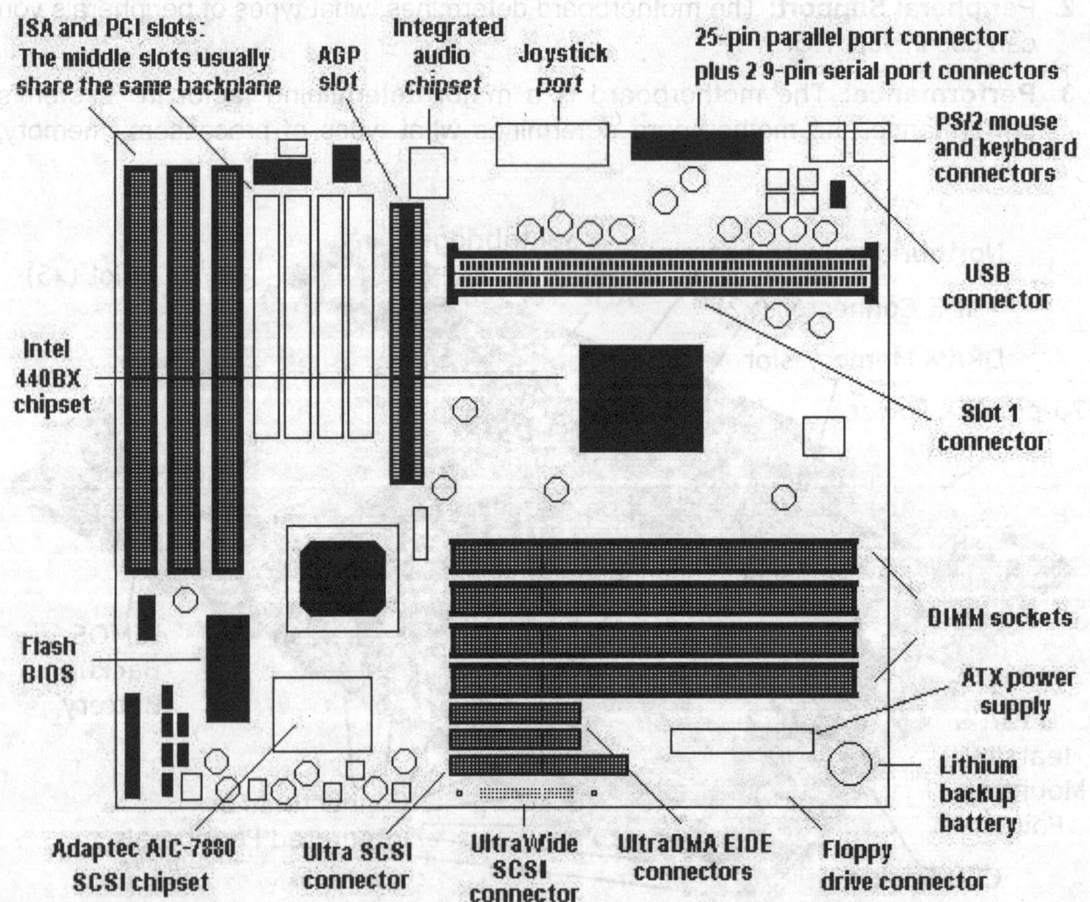

1983. XT stands for eXtended Technology.The PC/XT was the first personal computer to offer a built-in hard disk and the capability to expand memory 640K on the motherboard.

The original PC/XT used an Intel 8088 running at a clock speed of 4.77 MHz . The system was largely intended for business users. It came with 128 kB of memory, a 360 kB double-sided 5 1/4" full-height floppy disk drive, and a 10 MB hard drive, a serial port, eight 8-bit ISA expansion slots, and an Intel 8088 microprocessor running at 4.77 MHz. The eight slots were an increase over the five in the IBM PC, although three were taken up by the floppy drive adapter, the hard drive adapter, and the serial card. Like the original PC, the XT came with a BASIC interpreter in PC and XT keyboards are not compatible with more modern PC.

PC/AT

PC/AT, was IBM's second-generation PC, designed around the Intel 80286 microprocessor running at 6 MHz and released in 1984. AT originally stood for **A**dvanced **T**echnology .The AT represented a significant performance increase over previous computers, up to 75 percent faster than the PC/XT, and the AT bus standard is used in many clones or IBM compatible computers.

It was the most advanced machine in the PC line and featured a new keyboard, a higher-capacity 5.25" floppy (1.2MB) and a 16-bit data bus. AT-class machines ran considerably faster than the earlier 8088-based XT PCs. The motherboard includes connectors for two serial ports, a parallel port, floppy drive, and two IDE chains (for IDE devices such as hard

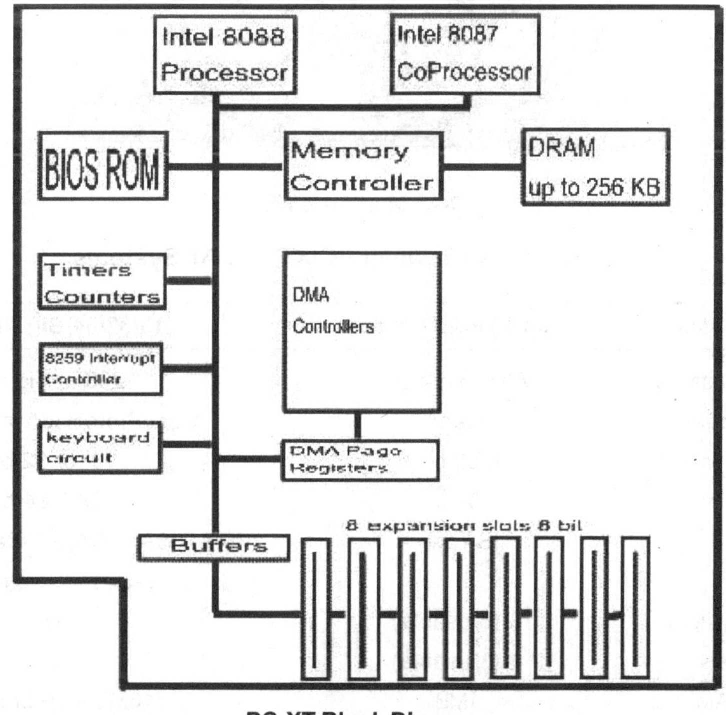

PC-XT Block Diagram

disks and CD-ROM drives). Located just to the left of the keyboard connector, but not pointed out in the photo, is a PS/2 mouse connection on the motherboard.

These connectors will have ribbon cables connected to them that attach to ports on the back of the computer, the floppy drive(s), and hard drives/CD-ROM drives.

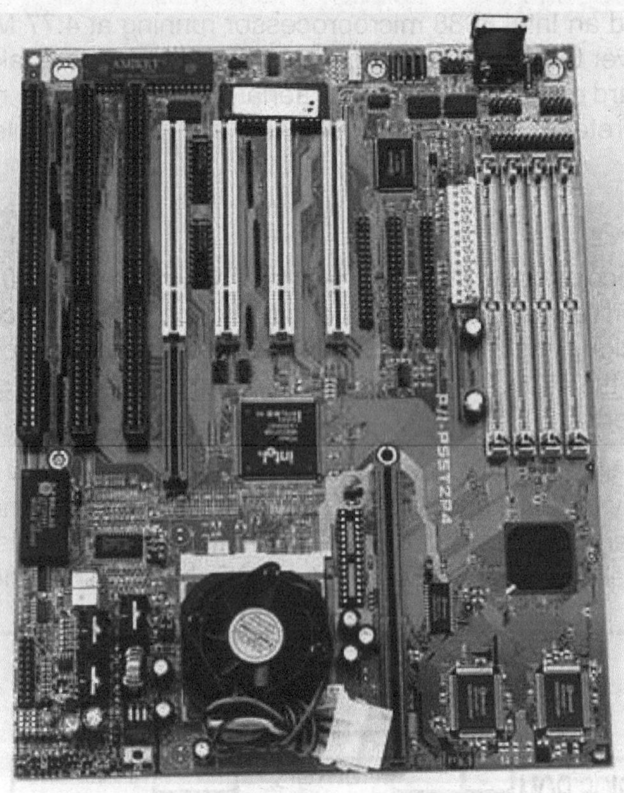

PC-AT Motherboard

Differences Between PC/XT and AT Systems

System Attributes	(8-Bit) PC/XT Type	(16/32/64-Bit) AT Type
Supported processors	All x86 or x88	286 or higher
Processor modes	Real	Real/Protected/Virtual Real
Software supported	16-bit only	16- or 32-bit
Bus slot width	8-bit	16/32/64-bit
Slot type	ISA only	ISA, EISA, MCA, PC-Card, Cardbus, VL-Bus, PCI, and AGP
Hardware interrupts	8 (6 usable)	16
DMA channels	4 (3 usable)	8
Maximum RAM	1MB	16MB/4GB or more

Floppy controller speed	250Kbps	250/300/500/1,000 Kbps
Standard boot drive	360KB or 720KB	1.2MB/1.44MB/2.88MB
Keyboard interface	Unidirectional	Bidirectional
CMOS memory/clock	None standard	MC146818-compatible
Serial-port UART	8250B	16450/16550A or greater

Pentium Motherboard

ATX motherboard

Intel, the primary manufacturer of PC CPUs, has proposed a new motherboard layout called the ATX.

ATX Motherboard

The bus slots are parallel to the short side of the motherboard. Instead of the long side of the motherboard running front to back in the PC, the short side runs front to back. The bus slots are located in the same general location, and the adapters still install in these slots and mount to the back of the computer's chassis. The serial, parallel, keyboard, and mouse connectors are built right onto the motherboard and stick out the back of the chassis when the motherboard is installed. One of the main reasons for the ATX design is to move the CPU closer to the power supply fan for better cooling, which means the CPU will last longer and suffer fewer faults.

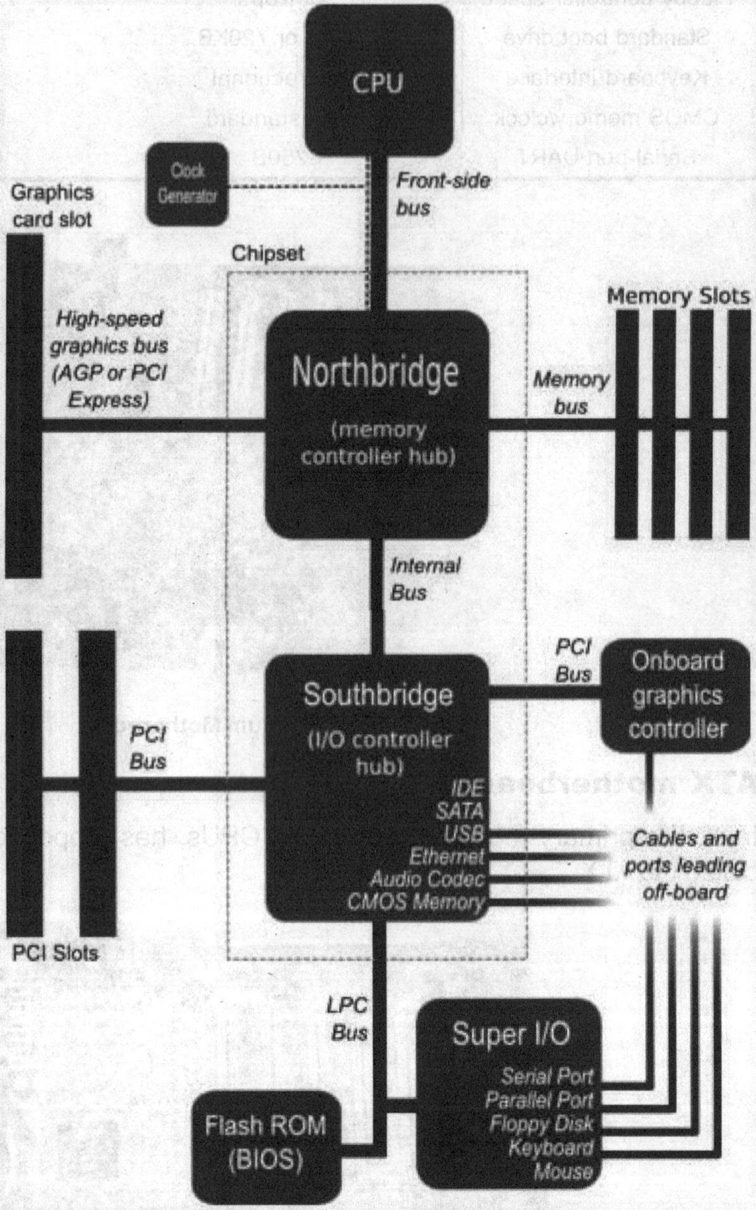

LPX motherboard

It is Low-Profile Extended motherboard introduced in 1997 by Western Digital. Unlike boards for desktop and tower cases that hold the expansion cards perpendicular to the board, cards plug into a riser card on the LPX and are parallel with the board. The LPX form factor is not a standard one but a non-standard proprietary one sometimes found in desktop computer models. This form factor is characterized by an expansion board that runs parallel to the motherboard. A riser card arrangement is used for expansion cards thereby allowing for smaller cases. LPX motherboards are typically integrated and most have the video and sound components built-in.

NLX motherboard

It is New Low-Profile Extended motherboard introduced in 1987. Unlike boards for desktop and tower cases that hold the expansion cards perpendicular to the board, cards plug into a riser card on the NLX and are parallel with the board. NLX has been a form factor in use with desktops for quite some time. It is a compact form factor, often referred to as a "low-profile application". NLX motherboards are easily distinguished by the riser card to which the expansion cards connect. The riser cards allow from two to four expansion cards to be plugged in. These expansion cards sit parallel to the motherboard. The benefit of the NLX form factor is that the bulk of a traditional server is reduced to a space-saving smaller server.

Intel 4 Processor Family

Speed	Cache Size	HT	Speed Step	EM64TF	System Bus	Package	Product Name
2.40 GHz	512 KB	No	No	No	400 MHz	mPGA478	Pentium 4 orocessor 2.40 GHz
2.40A GHz	1MB L2	No	No	No	533 MHz	mPGA478	Pentium 4 processor 2.40A GHz
2.40B GHz	512 KB	No	No	No	533 MHz	mPGA478	Pentium 4 processor 2.40B GHz
2.40C GHz	512 KB	Yes	No	No	800 MHz	mPGA478	Pentium 4 processor with 2.40C GHz
2.60 GHz	512 KB	No	No	No	400 MHz	mPGA478	Pentium 4 processor with 2.60 GHz
2.60C GHz	512 KB	Yes	No	No	800 MHz	mPGA478	Pentium 4 processor with HT 2.60C GHz
2.66 GHz	512 KB	No	No	No	533 MHz	mPGA478	Pentium 4 processor with 2.66 GHz
2.80 GHz	1 MB	Yes	No	No	800 MHz	FCLGA775	Pentium 4 processor 520 GHz with HT
2.80 GHz	512 KB	No	No	No	533 MHz	mPGA478	Pentium 4 processor 2.80 GHz
2.80A GHz	1 MB	No	No	No	533 MHz	mPGA478	Pentium 4 processor 2.80A GHz
2.80C GHz	512 KB	Yes	No	No	800 MHz	mPGA478	Pentium 4 processor with HT 2.80 GHz
2.80E GHz	1 MB	Yes	No	No	800 MHz	mPGA478	Pentium 4 processor with HT 2.80 GHz
3.00 GHz	1 MB	Yes	No	No	800 MHz	FCLGA775	Pentium 4 processor 530 with HT

3.00 GHz	2 MB	Yes	Yes	Yes	800 MHz	FCLGA775	Pentium 4 processor 630 with HT
3.00 GHz	512 MB	Yes	No	No	800 MHz	mPGA478	Pentium 4 processor with HT 3 GHz
3.00E GHz	1 MB	Yes	No	No	800 MHz	mPGA478	Pentium 4 processor with HT 3E GHz
3.06 GHz	512 KB	Yes	No	No	533 MHz	mPGA478	Pentium 4 processor with HT 3.06 GHz
3.20 GHz	1 MB	Yes	No	No	800 MHz	FCLGA775	Pentium 4 processor 540 with HT
3.20 GHz	2 MB	Yes	Yes	Yes	800 MHz	FCLGA775	Pentium 4 processor 640 with HT
3.20 GHz	512 KB	Yes	No	No	800 MHz	mPGA478	Pentium 4 processor with HT 3.20 GHz
3.20E GHz	1 MB	Yes	No	No	800 MHz	mPGA478	Pentium 4 processor with HT 3.20E GHz
3.40 GHz	1 MB	Yes	No	No	800 MHz	FCLGA775	Pentium 4 processor 550 with HT
3.40 GHz	2 MB	Yes	Yes	Yes	800 MHz	FCLGA775	Pentium 4 processor 650 with HT
3.40 GHz	512 KB	Yes	No	Yes	800 MHz	mPGA478	Pentium 4 processor with HT 3.40 GHz
3.40 GHz	512 KB L2 cache 2 MB L3 cache	Yes	No	No	800 MHz	FCLGA775	Pentium 4 processor with HT Extreme Edition 3.40 GHz
3.40E GHz	1 MB	Yes	No	Yes	800 MHz	mPGA478	Pentium 4 processor with HT 3.40E GHz
3.46 GHz	512 KB L2 cache 2 MB L3 cache	Yes	No	No	1066 MHz	FCLGA775	Pentium 4 processor with HT Extreme Edition 3.46 GHz
3.60 GHz	1 MB	Yes	No	No	800 MHz	FCLGA775	Pentium 4 processor 560 with HT
3.60 GHz	2 MB	Yes	Yes	Yes	800 MHz	FCLGA775	Pentium 4 processor 660 with HT
3.73 GHz	2 MB	Yes	No	Yes	1066 MHz	FCLGA775	Pentium 4 processor with HT Extreme Edition 3.73 GHz
3.80 GHz	1 MB	Yes	No	No	800 MHz	FCLGA775	Pentium 4 processor 570 with HT

Advancements in Motherboard Technology

Intel NetBurst microarchitecture delivers a number of innovative features including Hyper-Threading Technology, hyper-pipelined technology, 1066, 800, 533 or 400 MHz system bus, and Execution Trace Cache. It also provides a number of enhanced feature such as Advanced Trnaster Cache, Advanced Dynamic Execution, enhanced floating-point and multimedia unit, and Streaming SIMD Extension, enhanced loating-point and mutimedia unit, and Streaming SIMD Extensions 2 (SSE2). Further enhancements in the 90 nm process-based Pentium 4 processor include Steaming SIMD Extension 3 (SSE3).

Many of these innovations and advances were made possible with improvements in processor technology, process technology, and circuit design and could not previously be implemented in high-volume, manufacturable solutions.

The features and resulting benefits of the microarchitecture are defined below:

Hyper-Threading Technology

Hyper-Threading Technology (HT Technology) is a groundbreaking technology to improve processor performance. It allows software programs to "see" two processors and work more efficiently.

This new technology enables the processor to execute two series, or threads, of instructions at the same time, thereby improving performance and system responsiveness. Hyper-Threading Technology requires a computer system with an Intel Pentium 4 processor supporting HT Technology and a HT Technology enabled chipset, BIOS and operating system.

Hyper-Pipelined Technology

The hyper-pipelined technolgy of the Intel NetBurst microarchitecutre increases the pipeline depth delivering increased performance, frequency and scalabllity of the processor.

Intel Enhanced Memory 64 Technology (Intel EM64T)

Intel EM^$T provides an enhancement to the Intel's 32-bit architecture by enabling the desktop processor platform to access larger amounts of memory. With appropriate 64-bit supporting hardware and software, platforms based on an Intel processor supporting Intel EM64T can enable use of extended virtual and physical memory. EM64T requrires a computer system with a processor, chiset, BIOS, operating system, device drivers and applications enabled for Intel EM64T, Processor will not operate (including 32-bit operation) without an Intel EM64T enabled BIOS.

Integrated 2MB Level 3 Cache on Intel Pentium 4 Processor Extreme Edition 3.46 GHz

The 2-MB L3 cache is available only with the Pentium 4 processor Extreme Edition. The additional third level of cache is located on the processor die and is designed specifically to meet the computer needs of high-end gamers and other power users. The Integrated L3 cache is available in 2 MB and when coupled with either the 1066 MHz or 800 MHz system bus provides a high bandwidth path to memory. The efficient design of the integrated L3 cache proveds a faster path to large data sets stored in cache on the processor. This results in reduced average memory latency and increased throughput for larger workloads.

Integrated 2MB Level 2 Cache on Intel Pentium 4 Processor Extreme Edition 3.73 GHz and 6xx

The 2-MB Advanced Transfer Cache (on-die, full speed Level 2 cache) with 8-way associative and Error Correcting Code (ESS) can improve overall performance by allowing the processor to have faster access to a larger amount of the most often used data.

Advanced Dynamic Execution

The Advance Dynamic Execution engine is a very deep, out-of-order speculative execution engine that keeps the execution units executing instructions. It also includes an enhanced branch prediction algorithm that has the net effect of reducing the number of branch mis-predictions.

Chipsets for the Pentium and Beyond

Pentium chipsets (referred to as fifth-generation chipsets) were more closely tied to the design of the processor than were the 486 chipsets. When Intel created the Pentium processor, it also developed the PCI bus and a chipset to support and integrate the capabilities of these two developments. This PCIset, as it became known, was developed as an exact match for the Pentium processor. Intel chipsets are designated in numbered series: the 420 for 486 chipsets, the 430 for Pentium chipsets, the 440 series for Pentium II and the 450 series for Pentium Pr chipsets (along with the 400FX). The newer 460 and 800 series chipsets just being announced are designed to support the IA-64 (Intel Architecture – 64 bits) processors, such as the Itanium, now emerging.

Here are some of the more common Intel Pentium and above chipsets:

430LX (Mercury): The 430LX was the first Pentium chipset developed to support the 60MHz and 66MHz 5V processors. The Mercury chipset included the PCI bus and supported up to 128MB of RAM. This chipset was made absolute by the chipsets that supported the 90MHz and 100MHz 3.3V processors.

430NX (Neptune): The 430NX was developed to support Intel's second generation Pentium chips. It supported Pentium processors running at 90MHz to 133MHz. Some of the improvements offered over he 430LX chipset are support for dual processors, 512MB of RAM and 512KB of L2 cache.

430FX (Triton I): This was first of the Triton chipsets. It featured support for EDO RAM pipelined burst and synchronous cache, Plug-and-Play and PCI level 2.0 compliance. However, it only supported 128MB of RAM (down from the 512MB supported by the Neptune chipset) and did not have dual processor capabilities.

430MX (Mobile Triton): This is a version of the 430FX designed for laptop, notebook and other portable PCs.

430HX (Triton II): This chipset supported EDO RAM and concurrent PCI buses and was designed for use in business-level servers. It was the next generation of the 430NX and included support for 512MB of RAM and L2 cache.

430VX (Triton III): This chipset was developed to support the home PC market. It featured support for USB, SDRAM and PCI interfaces.

430TX: With this chipset, Intel dropped the Triton label for its chipsets. The 430TX was adaptable for both desktop and mobile use and provided CPI, USB, DMMA and other interfaces.

440LX: Designed for the Pentium II, this AGPset chipset provides support for the LS-120 "superdisk," Ultra DMA, AGP, USB, SDRAM, ECC RAM and the PC97 power management specification. Figure 5-5 shows this chipset.

440LXR: A low-end version of the 440LX chipset.

440BX: Another Pentium II chipset that supports 100MHz bus, dual processors, FireWire and up to 1GB of RAM.

440GX: This chipset is designed for midrange workstations and supports dual CPU and up to 2GB of SDRAM along with dual AGP interfaces. This is an AGPset.

440FX (Natoma): This chipset supported both the Pentium II and the Pentium Pro processors with USB, EDO RAM, ECC memory, dual processors and PCI.

450GX (Orion server): The 450GX chipset and the 450KX share the same basic design. However, the GX version is optimized for the Pentium Pro and supports four processors and 8GB of RAM but FPM memory only.

450KX (Orion workstation): The workstation version of the Orion chipset supports dual processors and 1GB of RAM.

450NX: This is a high-powered chipset designed for Xeon workstations and servers. It supports up to four CPUs, 2MB of L2 cache, 8GB of EDO memory & two 32-bit or one 64-bit PCI interface.

460GX (Merced): This chipset supports very high-end servers and workstations with supports for four CPUs and other high-performance features. You will see this chipset linked to the new high powered Itanium processor.

810: This chipset is designed for value-priced PCs. It includes support for integrated 3-D graphics (AGP) with MPEG-2, 100MHz system bus, two USB ports and the Intel Accelerated Hub, which features a 266MB per second bus speed between memory and peripherals.

810e: This chipset is an extended version of the 810 chipset based on the 440BX chipset and intended for home market and office PCs. Its features are the same as the 9\810 chipset, with added support for 133MHz system bus and the ATA-66 interface.

815: The Intel 815 chipset is specifically designed to work with the Pentium III processor, but it also provides backward compatibility to other Intel processors.

820: Another extension of the 810 chipset designed to support high-end desktops and workstations.

850: The Intel 850 chipset was designed in tandem with the Pentium 4 processor and supports, among many high-performance innovations and features, a 400 MHz system bus that provides over 3 times the bandwidth of previous chipset and processor technologies.

Various Cards on the Motherboards

As we have seen and studied in this chapter, so far, motherboard has various cards. Let us now go through the various cards and their functioning.

1. A Display /video card, is card in computer whose function is to generate and output images to a display. The term is usually used to refer to a separate, dedicated expansion card that is plugged into a slot on the computer's motherboard. A video card consists of a printed circuit board on which the components are mounted. These include:

(*i*) **The GPU:** It is a microprocessor dedicated to manipulating and rendering graphics according to the instructions received from the computer's operating system and the software being used. At their simplest level, GPUs include functions for manipulating two-dimensional graphics, such as blitting. Modern and more advanced GPUs also include functions for generating and manipulating three-dimensional graphics elements, rendering objects with shading, lighting, texture mapping and other visual effects.

(*ii*) **Video Memory:** Unlike integrated video controllers, which usually share memory with the rest of the computer, most video cards have their own separate onboard memory, referred to as video RAM (VRAM). If the video card is integrated in the motherboard, it will use the computer RAM memory (lower throughput). If it is not integrated, the video card will have its own video memory which is called Video RAM or VRAM. The VRAM capacity of most modern video cards range from 128 to 768 MB. In 2006, the VRAM was based on DDR technology, standing out DDR2, GDDR3 and GDDR4.

Video Cards over the Years

	Year	Text Mode	Graphics Mode	Colors	Memory
MDA	1981	80*25	-	1	4 KB
CGA	1981	80*25	640*200	16	16 KB
HGC	1982	80*25	720*348	1	64 KB
EGA	1984	80*25	640*350	16	256 KB
IBM 8514	1987	80*25	1024*768	256	-
MCGA	1987	80*25	320*200	256	-
VGA	1987	720*400	640*480	256	256 KB
SVGA	1989	80*25	1024*768	256	2 MB
XGA	1990	80*25	1024*768	65,536	1 MB

Type	**Clock rate (MHz)**	**Bandwidth (GB/s)**
DDR	166 - 950	1.2 - 30.4
DDR2	533 - 1000	8.5 - 16
GDDR3	700 - 1800	5.6 - 54.4
GDDR4	1600 - 2400	64 - 86.4

The memory clock rate is between 400 MHz and 1.6 GHz. A very important element of the video memory is the Z-buffer, which manages the depth coordinates in 3D graphics.

Pin No.	Function
1	Red Video
2	Green Video
3	Blue Video
4	Monitor ID bit-2
5	Ground
6	Red Return (Ground)
7	Green Retrun (Ground)
8	Blue Return (Ground)
9	Composite Sync.
10	Sync. Return (Ground)
11	Monitor ID bit-0
12	Monitor ID bit-1
13	Horiz. Sync.
14	Vert. Sync.
15	Reserverd

(*iii*) **Video BIOS** chip is a chip that contains the basic program that governs the video card's operations and provides the instructions that allow the computer and software to interface with the card. The video BIOS or firmware chip is a chip that contains the basic program that governs the video card's operations and provides the instructions that allow the computer and software to interface with the card. It contains information on the memory timing, operating speeds and voltages of the processor and ram and other information. It is possible to re-flash a bios although this is typically only done by video card overclockers.

(*iv*) **PCI Express** is the newest slot that most new cards fit into. It comes in a variety of speeds which vary in size proportionate to the speed. Depending on what speed interface used, PCI Express video cards may have a higher speed interface than AGP, leading to increased performance on the high end cards. PCI Express may be up to twice the speed of the AGP interface.

2. A sound card is a computer expansion card that can input and output sound under control of computer programs. Typical uses of sound cards include providing the audio component for multimedia applications such as music composition, editing video or audio,

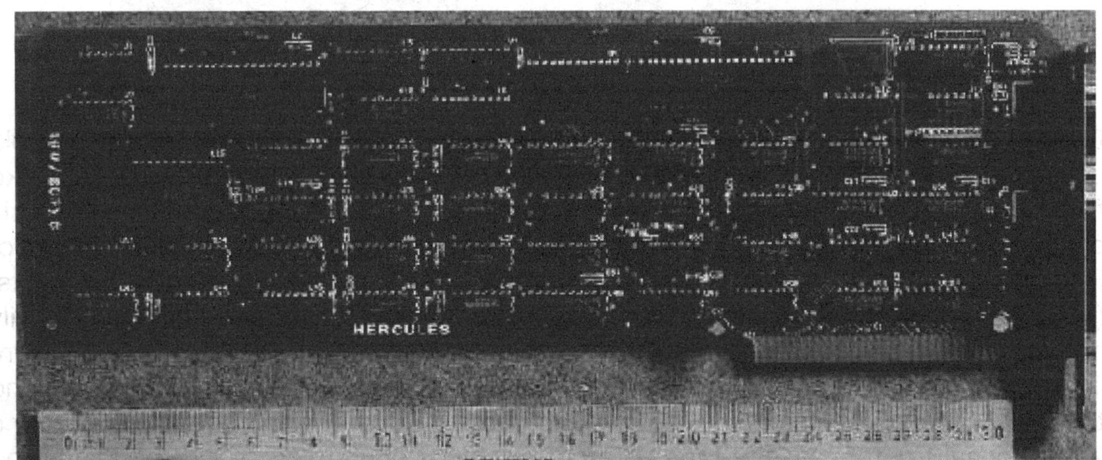

Display Card

presentation/education, and entertainment (games). Many computers have sound capabilities built in, while others require these expansion cards if audio capability is desired. Typical sound card includes a sound chip, usually featuring a digital-to-analog converter, that converts recorded or generated digital waveforms of sound into an analog format. This signal is led to a (typically 1/8-inch earphone-type) connector where an amplifier, headphones, or similar sound destination can be plugged in. More advanced designs usually include more than one sound chip to separate duties between digital sound production and synthesized sounds (usually for real-time generation of music and sound effects utilizing little data and CPU time.

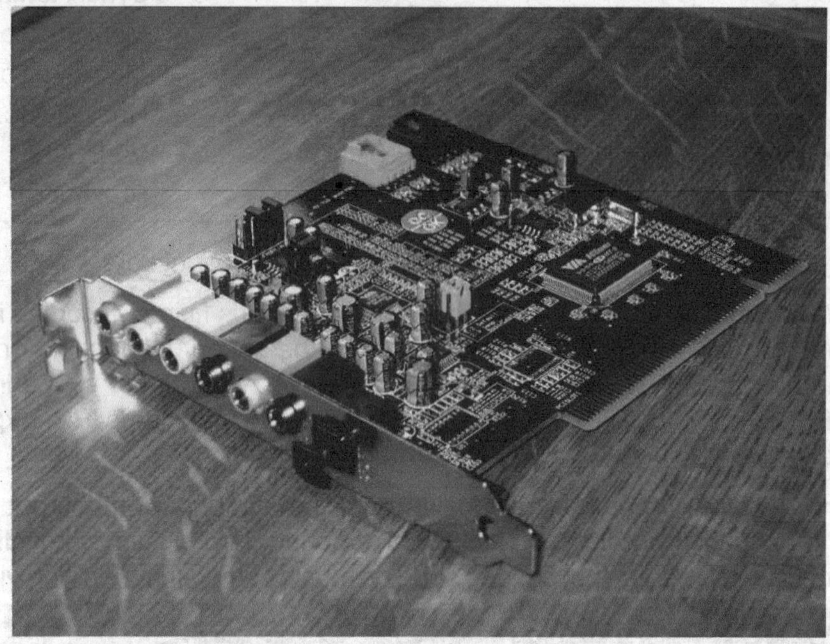

Sound Card

Digital sound reproduction is usually achieved by multi-channel DACs, able to play multiple digital samples at different pitches and volumes, optionally applying real-time effects like filtering or distortion. Multi-channel digital sound playback can also be used for music synthesis if used with a digitized instrument bank of some sort, typically a small amount of ROM or Flash memory containing samples corresponding to the standard MIDI instruments. (A contrasting way to synthesize sound on a PC uses "audio codecs", which rely heavily on software for music synthesis, MIDI compliance and even multiple-channel emulation. This approach has become common as manufacturers seek to simplify the design and the cost of the sound card itself most sound cards have a **line in** connector where the sound signal from a cassette tape recorder or similar sound source can be input. The sound card can digitize this signal and store it (controlled by the corresponding computer software) on the computer's hard disk for editing or further reproduction. Another typical external connector is the **microphone** connector, for connecting to a microphone or other input device that generates a relatively lower voltage than the **line in** connector. Input through a microphone jack is typically used by speech recognition software or Voice over IP applications.

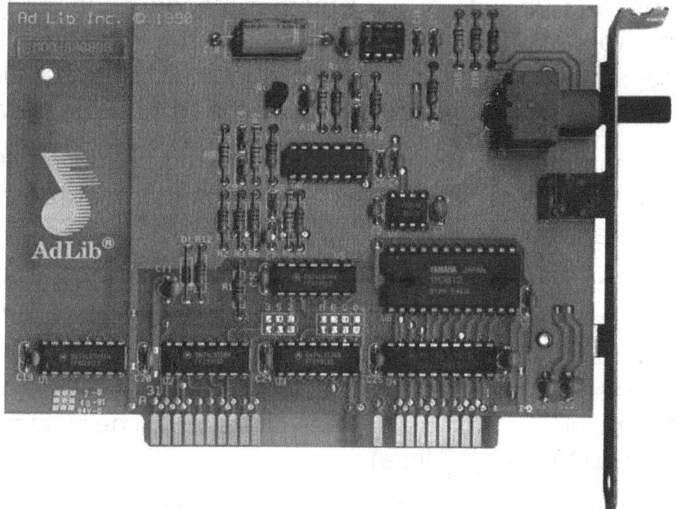

Connections

Most sound cards since 1999 conform to Microsoft's PC 99 standard for color coding the external connectors as follows:

Color	Function
Pink	Analog microphone input.
Light blue	Analog line level input.
Lime green	Analog line level output for the main stereo signal (front speakers or headphones).
Black	Analog line level output for rear speakers.
Silver	Analog line level output for side speakers.
Orange	S/PDIF digital output (sometimes used as an analog line output for a center speaker and subwoofer instead)

3. A network card, **network adapter** or **NIC** (network interface controller) is a piece of computer hardware designed to allow computers to communicate over a computer network. It is both an OSI layer 1 (physical layer) and layer 2 (data link layer) device, as it provides physical access to a networking medium and provides a low-level addressing system through the use of MAC addresses. It allows users to connect to each other either by using cables or wirelessly. Every network card has a unique 48-bit serial number called a MAC address, which is stored in ROM carried on the card. Every computer on a network must have a card with a unique MAC address. No two cards ever manufactured share the same address. This is accomplished by the Institute of Electrical and Electronics Engineers (IEEE), which is responsible for assigning unique MAC addresses to the vendors of network interface controllers.

Whereas network cards used to be expansion cards that plug into a computer bus, the low cost and ubiquity of the Ethernet standard means that most newer computers have a network interface built into the motherboard. These motherboards either have Ethernet capabilities integrated into the motherboard chipset, or implemented via a low cost dedicated Ethernet chip, connected through the PCI (or the newer PCI express bus).

A separate network card is not required unless multiple interfaces are needed or some other type of network is used. Newer motherboards may even have dual network (Ethernet) interfaces built-in.

The card implements the electronic circuitry required to communicate using a specific physical layer and data link layer standard such as Ethernet or token ring. This provides a network card typically has a twisted pair, BNC, or AUI socket where the network cable is connected, and a few LEDs to inform the user of whether the network is active, and whether or not there is data being transmitted on it. The Network Cards are typically available in 10/100/1000 Mbits/s(Mbps).

4. A modem (from **mod**ulate and **dem**odulate) is a device that modulates an analogue carrier signal to encode digital information, and also demodulates such a carrier signal to decode the transmitted information. The goal is to produce a signal that can be transmitted easily and decoded to reproduce the original digital data. Modems can be used over any means of transmitting analog signals, from driven diodes to radio. Experiments have even been performed in the use of modems over the medium of two cans connected by a string. The most familiar example is a voiceband modem that turns the digital '1s and 0s' of a personal computer into sounds that can be transmitted over the telephone lines of Plain Old Telephone Systems (POTS), and once received on the other side, converts those sounds back into 1s and 0s. Modems are generally classified by the amount of data they can send in a given time, normally measured in bits per second, or "bps".

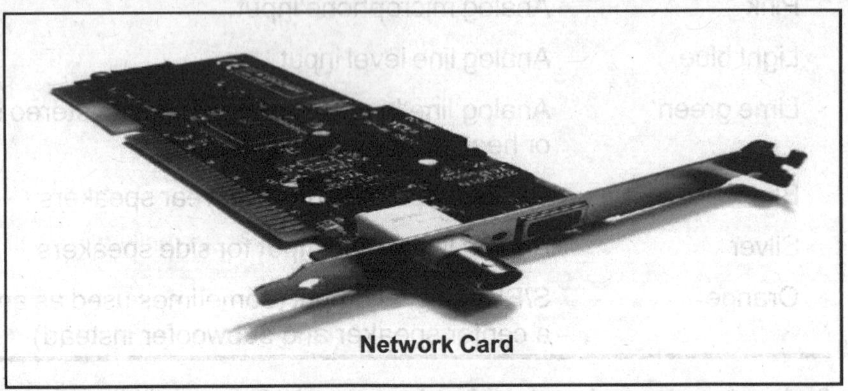

Network Card

Faster modems are used by Internet users every day, notably cable modems and ADSL modems. In telecommunications, "radio modems" transmit repeating frames of data at very high data rates over microwave radio links. Some microwave modems transmit more than a hundred million bits per second. Optical modems transmit data over optic fibers. Most intercontinental data links now use optic modems transmitting over undersea optical fibers. Optical modems routinely have data rates in excess of a billion (1×10^9) bits per second.

Itanium Processor

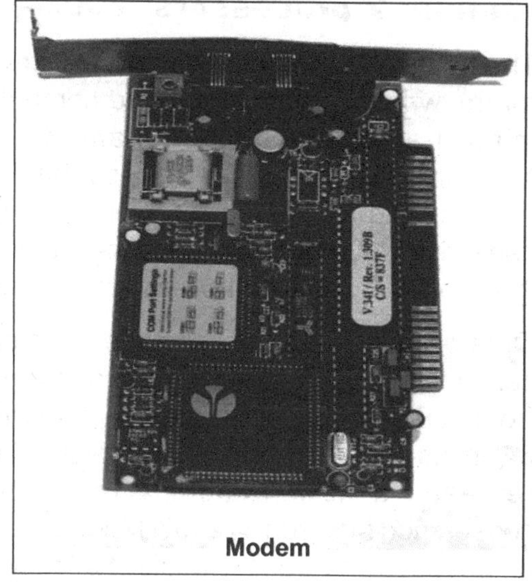
Modem

Itanium is the brand name for 64-bit Intel Microprocessors that implement the Intel Itanium architecture (formerly called IA-64). Intel has released two processor families using the brand: Itanium and Itanium 2. The processors are marketed for use in enterprise servers and high-performance computing systems. The architecture originated at Hewlett-Packard (HP) which was then later developed by HP and Intel together. Itanium's architecture differs dramatically from the x86 and x86-64 architectures used in other Intel processors. The architecture is based on explicit instruction-level parallelism, with the compiler making the decisions about which instructions to execute in parallel. This approach allows the processor to execute up to six instructions per clock cycle. By contrast with other superscalar architectures, Itanium does not need elaborate hardware to keep track of instruction dependencies during parallel execution.

After a protracted development process, the first Itanium was released in 2001, and subsequently more powerful Itanium processors have been released periodically. HP produces most Itanium-based systems, but several other manufacturers have also developed systems based on Itanium. As of 2007 Itanium is the fourth-most deployed microprocessor architecture for enterprise-class systems, behind x86-64, IBM POWER, and SPARC. After a schedule slip of several years, Intel released its newest Itanium 2, codenamed Montecito, in July 2006.

Itanium processor: 2001–2002

By the time Itanium was released in June, 2001, it was no longer superior to contemporaneous RISC and CISC processors. Itanium competed at the low-end (primarily 4-CPU and smaller systems) with servers based on x86 processors, and at the high end with IBM's POWER architecture and Sun Microsystems' SPARC architecture. Intel repositioned Itanium to focus on high-end business and HPC computing, attempting to duplicate x86's successful "horizontal" (i.e., single architecture, multiple systems vendors) market. Its success was limited to replacing PA-RISC and Alpha in HP systems and MIPS in SGI's HPC systems. POWER and SPARC remained strong, while the 32-bit x86 architecture grew into the enterprise space. With economies of scale fueled by its enormous installed base, x86 was the preeminent "horizontal" architecture in enterprise computing. HP and Intel recognized that Itanium was not competitive and replaced it with Itanium 2 a year later, as they had planned. Only a few thousand of the original Itaniums were sold, due to limited availability caused by poor yields, relatively poor performance, and high cost. However, these machines were useful for software development for the Itanium 2 processors that followed. IBM delivered a supercomputer based on this processor.

Itanium 2 processors: 2002–present

The Itanium 2 was released in 2002, and was marketed for enterprise servers rather than for the whole gamut of high-end computing. The initial Itanium 2 was codenamed McKinley. McKinley used a 180 nm process, but it relieved many of the performance problems of the original Itanium. In 2003, AMD released the Opteron, which implemented its x86-64 64-bit architecture.

Opteron gained rapid acceptance in the enterprise server space because it provided an easy upgrade from x86. Intel responded by implementing x86-64 in its Xeon microprocessors in 2004. Intel released a new Itanium 2 family member, codenamed Madison, in 2003. Madison used a 130 nm process and was the basis of all new Itaniums until Montecito was released in June 2006.

Intel Itanium processor	
Central processing unit	
Itanium processor	
Produced:	From June 2001 to June 2002
Manufacturer:	Intel
CPU Speeds:	733 MHz to 800 MHz
FSB Speeds:	266 MT/s to 266 MT/s
Instruction Set:	**Itanium**
Socket:	PAC418
Core Name:	Merced

In March, 2005, Intel announced that it was working on a new Itanium device, codenamed Tukwila, to be released in 2007. Tukwila would have four processors and would replace the Itanium bus with a new Common System Interface, which would also be used by a new Xeon. Intel later said that Tukwila would be delivered in late 2008.

In November 2005, the major Itanium server manufacturers joined with Intel and a number of software vendors to form the Itanium Solutions Alliance to promote the architecture and accelerate software porting. The Alliance announced that its members would invest $10 Billion in Itanium solutions by the end of the decade. As of June 2007, Intel has released seven additional versions of the Itanium 2, and another is expected in late 2007.

Xeon Processors Family

The Xeon brand refers to Intel's x86 multiprocessing CPUs targeted at server and workstation computers. The brand has been maintained over several generations of x86 and x86-64 processors. Older models added the Xeon moniker to the end of the name of their corresponding desktop processor, but more recent models used the name Xeon on its own. The Xeon CPUs generally have more cache than their desktop counterparts in addition to multiprocessing capabilities. Intel's non-x86 IA-64 processors are called Itanium, not Xeon.

Pentium II Xeon

The first Xeon processor was released in 1998 as the Pentium II Xeon (codenamed "Drake") as the replacement of the Pentium Pro. It was based on the 0.25 μm, P6 microarchitecture "Deschutes" Pentium II (sharing its 80523 product code) and used either a 440GX (a dual-processor workstation chipset) or 450NX (quad-processor, or oct with additional logic) chipset, and differed from the desktop Pentium II in that its off-die L2 cache ran at full speed. It also used a larger slot known as slot 2. Cache sizes were 512 KiB, 1 MiB and 2 MiB, and it used a 100 MT/s bus.

Pentium III Xeon

In 1999, the Pentium II Xeon was replaced by the Pentium III Xeon. The initial version, "Tanner", was just like its predecessor except for the addition of Streaming SIMD Extensions (SSE) and a few cache controller enhancements found in the "Katmai" Pentium III. The second version, "Cascades", was based on the "Coppermine" Pentium III core. It was more controversial in that while it had a 133 MT/s bus it only had a 256 KiB on-die L2 cache — in other words, it was the same as the desktop Pentium III whose Slot 1 versions were also capable of dual-processor operation but not quad-processor operation. To improve this situation, Intel released another version, officially also named "Cascades", but often referred to as "Cascades 2 MB". That came in two variants: with 1 MiB or 2 MiB of L2 cache. Its bus speed was fixed at 100 MT/s, though in practice the cache was able to offset this. Product codes for Tanner and Cascades mirrored that of Katmai and Coppermine; 80525 and 80526 respectively.

Xeon & Xeon MP (32-bit)

In mid-2001, the Xeon was introduced ("Pentium" was dropped from the name). The initial variant that used the new NetBurst architecture, "Foster", was slightly different from the desktop Pentium 4 ("Willamette"). It was a decent chip for workstations, but for server applications it was almost always outperformed by the older Cascade 2 MiB core and AMD's Athlon MP. Combined with the need to use expensive Rambus Dynamic RAM, the Foster's sales were somewhat unimpressive.

At most two Foster processors could be accommodated in an SMP system built with a mainstream chipset, so a second version (Foster MP) was introduced with a 1 MiB L3 cache and Jackson Hyper-Threading. This improved performance slightly, but not enough to lift it out of third place. It was also priced much higher than the dual-processor (DP) versions.

In 2002 Intel released a 130 nm version of the Xeon, codenamed "Prestonia". It supported Intel's new Hyper-Threading technology and had a 512 KiB L2 cache. This was based on the "Northwood" Pentium 4 core. A new server chipset, E7500 (which allowed the use of dual-channel DDR SDRAM) was released to support this processor in servers, and soon the bus speed was boosted to 533 MT/s (accompanied by new chipsets: the E7501 for servers and the E7505 for workstations). The new Xeon performed much better than its predecessor and noticeably better than Athlon MP. The support of new features in the

E75xx series also gave it a key advantage over the Pentium III Xeon and Athlon MP (both stuck with rather old chipsets), and it quickly became the top-selling server/workstation processor. The Xeon MP version of the Prestonia was the "Gallatin", which had an L3 cache of 1 MiB or 2 MiB. It also performed much better than Foster MP, and was popular in servers. Later, Intel's experience with the 130 nm process allowed it to port Xeon to the Gallatin core and also create a Xeon MP with 4 MiB cache.

Foster shared the 80528 product code with Willamette; Prestonia and Gallatin Xeons were designated 80532, like Northwood.

Xeon & Xeon MP (64-bit)

Due to a lack of success with Intel's Itanium and Itanium 2 processors, the 90 nm version of the Pentium 4 ("Prescott") was built with support for 64-bit instructions (called Intel 64, Intel's implementation of x86-64), and a Xeon version codenamed "Nocona" was released in 2004. Released with it were the E7525 (workstation), E7520 and E7320 (both server) chipsets, which added support for PCI Express, DDR-II and Serial ATA. The Xeon was noticeably slower than AMD's Opteron, although it could be faster in situations where Hyper-Threading came into play. A slightly updated core called "Irwindale" was released in early 2005, with twice the L2 cache of Nocona and able to reduce its clockspeeds during low processor demand. However, independent tests showed that AMD's Opteron still outperformed Irwindale.

64-bit Xeon MPs were introduced in April 2005. The cheaper "Cranford" was an MP version of Nocona, while the more expensive "Potomac" was a Cranford with 8 MiB of L3 cache. All these Prescott-derived Xeons have the product code 80546.

Cache Memory

In computer science, a cache (pronounced "cash" /kæʃ]) is a collection of data duplicating original values stored elsewhere or computed earlier, where the original data is expensive to fetch (due to slow access time) or to compute, relative to the cost of reading the cache. In other words, a cache is a temporary storage area where frequently accessed data can be stored for rapid access. Once the data is stored in the cache, future use can be made by accessing the cached copy rather than re-fetching or recomputing the original data, so that the average access time is lower. Caches have proven to be extremely effective in many areas of computing because access patterns in typical computer applications have locality of reference. There are several kinds of locality, but this article primarily deals with data that are accessed close together in time (temporal locality). The data might or might not be located physically close to each other (spatial locality).

How cache works?

A cache is a block of memory for temporary storage of data likely to be used again. The CPU and hard drive frequently use a cache, as do web browsers and web servers. A cache is made up of a pool of entries. Each entry has a datum (a nugget of data) which is a copy of the datum in some backing store. Each entry also has a tag, which specifies the

Xeon model	Core 2 Duo model	Speed (GHz)	L2 Cache (MB)	FSB (MHz)
3040	E6300	1.86	2	1066
N/A	E6320	1.86	4	1066
3050	E6400	2.13	2	1066
N/A	E6420	2.13	4	1066
3060	E6600	2.4	4	1066
3070	E6700	2.66	4	1066
3080	X6800	2.93	4	1066
3065	E6550	2.33	4	1333
3075	E6750	2.66	4	1333
3085	E6850	3.00	4	1333

identity of the datum in the backing store of which the entry is a copy. When the cache client (a CPU, web browser, operating system) wishes to access a datum presumably in the backing store, it first checks the cache.

Double Core Processor

The Athlon 64 X2 is the first dual-core desktop CPU manufactured by AMD. It is essentially a processor consisting of two Athlon 64 cores joined together on one die with additional control logic. The cores share one dual-channel memory controller, are based on the E-stepping model of Athlon 64 and, depending on the model, have either 512 or 1024 KiB of L2 Cache per core. The Athlon 64 X2 is capable of decoding SSE3 instructions (except those few specific to Intel's architecture), so it can run and benefit from software optimizations that were previously only supported by Intel chips. This enhancement is not unique to the X2, and is also available in the Venice and San Diego single core Athlon 64s.

In June 2007, AMD released low-voltage variants of their low-end 65 nm Athlon 64 X2, named "Athlon X2". The Athlon X2 processors feature reduced TDP of 45 W

Multithreading

The main benefit of dual-core processors like the X2 is their ability to process more software threads at the same time. The ability of processors to execute multiple threads simultaneously is called thread-level parallelism (TLP). By placing two cores on the same die, the X2 effectively doubles the TLP over a single-core Athlon 64 of the same speed. The need for TLP processing capability is dependent on situation to a great degree, and certain situations benefit from it far more than others. Certain programs are currently only written with one thread, and are therefore unable to utilize the processing power of the second core.

PC—Processor Specifications at a Glance

Processor	Register Size-bit	Data Bus-bit	Address Bus-bit	Int. Cache	Int. FPU	Max. Memory	Trans. Used
8088	16	8	20	No	No	1MB	29,000
8086	16	16	20	No	No	1MB	29,000
286	16	16	24	No	No	16MB	130,000
386SX	32	16	24	No	No	16MB	275,000
386SL	32	16	24	*	No	16MB	855,000
386DX	32	32	32	No	No	4GB	275,000
486SX	32	32	32	8k	No	4GB	1,185,000
486DX	32	32	32	8k	Yes	4GB	1,200,000
486DX2	32	32	32	8k	Yes	4GB	1,100,000
586	32	64	32	8k Data 8k Instr	Yes	4GB	3,100,000
P6	32	64	36	8k Data 8k Instr	Yes	64GB	5,500,000

Programs often written with multiple threads and capable of utilizing dual-cores include many music and video encoding applications, and especially professional rendering programs. High TLP applications currently correspond to server/workstation situations more than the typical desktop. These applications can realize almost twice the performance of a single-core Athlon 64 of the same specifications.

Multi-tasking also runs a sizable number of threads; intense multi-tasking scenarios have actually shown improvements of considerably more than two times. This is primarily due to the excessive overhead caused by constantly switching threads, and could potentially be improved by adjustments to operating system scheduling code.

In the consumer segment of the market as well, the X2 improves upon the performance of the original Athlon 64, especially for multi-threaded software applications. The overall increase in performance of the entry level Athlon 64 X2 chip (the Athlon 64 X2 3800+) over the single-core Athlon 64 3800+ chip is almost 10%. The spread between the latter and the Athlon 64 X2 5000+ is almost 40%.

One can interpret from these numbers that the majority of applications (at least in the benchmark test) are still largely single thread-dominated, hence the absence of a larger gap between the two 3800+ processors. As software programmers begin to take advantage of multi-core processing, the spread between single- and multi-core processors will increase.

11 Motherboards

Motherboards

After microprocessor the next item considered to be most important for the computer is the motherboard. It's the motherboard that ties all parts of the computer together and turns them into a personal computer.

The motherboard or main board, of a PC is a large printed circuit board that is home to many of the most essential parts of the computer, including the microprocessor, chipset, cache, memory sockets, expansion bus, parallel and serial ports, mouse and keyboard connectors and IDE, EIDE or SCSI controllers, among other components of the PC. The motherboard binds the PC's operational components together. Even devices like printers, hard disks, CD-ROMs and the like, either connect to or are controlled by the devices or controllers on the motherboard.

Motherboard Designs

Not all motherboards are created equal. To begin with, two different design approaches are used for PC mainboards: the motherboard style and the backplane style.

Motherboards: A motherboard aggregates all of the PC's primary system components of a single printed circuit board (PCB). In the motherboard's single board design, all of the PC's electronic circuitry that provides the conduit through which all operations flow is located on the motherboard.

Backplanes: Backplane-style mainboards are less popular today than they were in the mid – to late 1980s, but they are still around. Backplane mainboards are common in large PC network servers and on other computers on which the processor is upgraded frequently.

The following table shows the length and width of the various motherboards over the years.

Form	*Width*	*Length*	*Design Type*	*Case Type*
IBM PC	8.5	13	Motherboard	IBM PC
IBM PC XT	8.5	13	Motherboard	IBM PC XT
AT	12	11-13	Motherboard	AT Desktop or Tower
Baby AT	8.5	10-13	Motherboard	Baby AT Desktop or Tower

LPX	9	11-13	Backplane	Low profile
Micro-AT	8.5	8.5	Motherboard	Baby AT Desktop or Tower
ATX	12	9.6	Motherboard	ATX Desktop or Tower
Mini-ATX	11.2	8.2	Motherboard	Smaller ATX Desktop
Mini-LPX	8-9	10-11	Backplane	Low profile
Micro-ATX	9.6	9.6	Motherboard	Low profile
NLX	8-9	10-13.6	Backplane	Low profile
Flex-ATX	9	7.5	Motherboard	Flexible design

Components of the Motherboard

The following figure shows where the major components are found on a typical motherboard. They are:

CPU slot and socket

The CPU mounts to the motherboard through either a slot or socket mounting.

Chipset

Many of the circuit and CPU level functions are contained in the chipset.

Memory Sockets

Depending upon the age of the PC, its memory is mounted on the motherboard as individual memory chips that fit into separate DIP (Dual Inline Packaging) sockets or memory modules, such as SIMM (Single Inline Memory Module) or a DIMM (Dual Inline Memory Module) that snap into edge connector mountings.

BIOS ROM

The BIOS, Basic Input/Output System, is stored as firmware on a read-only memory (ROM) chip. The BIOS is used to start the PC up when the power is turned on and provides a link for the CPU to the PC's peripheral devices.

CMOS Battery

The configuration of PC at the systems level is stored in a type of memory. CMOS, Complementary Metal Oxide Semiconductor, that requires very little power to hold its contents. The CMOS battery supplies a steady power steady power source to store the system configuration for use during the PC's boot sequence.

Power connector

A connection must be made to the power supply so that power is available to the circuitry on the motherboard. Motherboards use different voltages of power for different components on the board.

I/O connectors

The motherboard includes a variety of external I/O connections that allow external devices to communicate with the CPU.

Expansion slots

External peripherals and internal devices are interconnected into the motherboard and CPU through the expansion bus. The motherboard features a variety of expansion slots that usually include three or more of the different expansion buses available.

Chipsets of PC

Among the components on the motherboard contributing to its importance are the chipset and its associated controllers. This group of devices provides much of a PC's functionality and its ability to accept, display and move data. The logic circuits of the chipset and controllers give the motherboard its intelligence and its ability to function. The chipset and controllers also control the movement of data on the system buses so that data and instructions can move about the PC, between the CPU, cache memory and peripherals. The system chipset plays a major role in a PC's function, feature set and speed. Unless data and instructions are able to flow between one component of the PC and another, there isn't much point to even powering up the PC.

The chipset controls the bits (data, instructions and control signals) that flow between the CPU, system memory and over the motherboard's bus. The chipset also manages data transfers between the CPU, memory and peripheral devices and provides support for the expansion bus and any power management features of the system.

Controller Chips

Generally, a chipset does not incorporate all of the controllers used to direct the actions of every peripheral device on the PC. In addition to the chipset, there are at least two and possibly more, controllers mounted directly on the motherboard. In most cases, the motherboard will have at minimum a keyboard controller and an I/O controller (a.k.a. the Super I/O controller). Some expansion cards, such as video adapters, sound cards, network interface cards (NICs) and SCSI (Small Computer System Interface) adapters, have built-in controller chips.

A controller chip controls the transfer of data to and from a peripheral device, such as a disk drive, the monitor, the keyboard or a printer. All of these devices depend on a device controller to interact with the CPU and the rest of the PC. For the most part, PC users don't ever think about controller chips on their systems. In fact, most users probably don't even know they exist. How data gets to and from the keyboard is not of concern, only that it does.

On a PC, a controller is typically is single chip that either mounts directly on the motherboard or on a card that is inserted in an expansion slot on the motherboard. Because they control the flow of data to and from peripheral devices, controllers must be matched to the bus architecture of the PC.

Sockets and Slots

Microprocessors are attached to the motherboard of the computer. There are two general types of mountings used to connect the processor onto the motherboard: sockets and slots. Some processors are available in only one mounting type; others, such as the Intel Celerons are available with both types of mountings. Which type is used is largely a matter of preference on the part of the processor manufacturer. The two types look very different, but functionally their differences are small.

Socket Types

Here are ten of the most commonly used socket types:

Socket 0: A 168-pin inline-layout processor connector for 5V 486DX processors.

Socket 1: A 169-pin inline-layout processor connector for 5V 486DX and 486SX processors.

Socket 2: A 238-pin inline-layout processor connector for 5V 486DX, 486SX and 486DX2 processors.

Socket 3: A 237-pin inline-layout processor connector supporting 3 and 5V 486DX, 486SX, 486DX2 and 486DX4 processors.

Socket 4: A 273-pin inline-layout processor connector supporting 5V Pentium 60 and Pentium 66 processors.

Socket 5: A 320-pin staggered-layout connector supporting early 3V

Socket 6: A 235-pin inline-layout processor connector for 3V 486DX4 processors.

Socket 7: A 321-pin staggered-format socket created to support later Pentium processors. It used a common interface between the L2 cache bus and the main system bus. This common interface typically limited the bus's clock speed. AMD K6, Cyrix 6x86 and IDT processors also use this socket format. This design also provided for a Voltage Regulator Module to allow different voltage levels to be implemented by the socket.

Super 7 Socket: An extension of the Socket 7 design to support 100MHz bus speeds on AMD K6-2 and K6-3 processors allowing them to see an almost 50 percent increase in bandwidth and get around the limitations of the Socket 7.

Socket 8: A 386 pin staggered ZIF-socket format for the Pentium Pro processor.

Socket 370: The original Celeron main board connection. This supported the early Celerons in the Plastic Pin Grid Assembly (PPGA) format.

Slot Types

There are four types of slot mountings used to attach microprocessors to motherboards:

Slot 1 (SC-242 connector): A proprietary Intel connector supporting Celeron SEPP, Pentium II SECC (single-edge contact cartridge), Pentium II SECC2 and Pentium III processors. It has a 242 – pin edge interface and allows higher bandwidth than the original socket designs.

Slot 2 (SC-330 connector): Another Intel processor bus connector styles for the high performance Pentium II Xeon and Pentium III Xeon chips. These processors are designed for Symmetric Multiprocessing (multiple processors working together) and this slot style enhances this interaction.

Slot A: Used by the AMD Athlon processors. It is physically the same as a Slot 1 connector but has incompatible pin-outs.

Slot M: Connectors are planned for the upcoming 64-bit Intel Itanium processor.

Chipsets

One of the fundamental design facts of a PC is that its microprocessor is always faster than the peripheral devices to which it must communicate. This fact has forced designed to develop interfaces that serve as buffers between the slower devices and the faster CPU to match up their speeds and help with the timing of the operations. The very first PCs had an individual chip to control each of the various operations.

It was common for an early PC to have the following separate chips:

Math coprocessor interface: This chip the flow of data between the processor and math coprocessor.

Clock generator: This chip controls the timing of the PC's operations.

Bus controller chip: This chip controls the flow of data on the motherboard's buses.

DMA controller: This chip controls the processes that allowed peripheral devices to interact with memory without involving the processor.

Programmable peripheral interface (PPI): This chip supervises some of the simpler peripheral devices.

Floppy disk controller (FDC): This chip controls the PC's diskette and tape drives.

CRT controller: This chip facilities the PC's display.

UART (universal asynchronous receiver transmitter): This chip is used to send and receive synchronous serial data.

The Windows Device Manger's listing for system devices should list the processor to PCI to ISA bridge controllers and the manufacturers. If these are Intel chips, then you can sure you have an Intel chipset. Another way to check out the chipset on your PC is to open the system unit and find the large square chips, which are usually bigger than most everything else on the motherboard except the microprocessor. A chipset can have only one chip or as many as four separate chips.

Chipset Characteristics

The characteristics of a chipset can be broken down into six categories: host, memory, interfaces, arbitration, south bridge support and power management. Each of these categories defines and differentiates one chipset from another. The characteristics defined in each of these categories are as follows:

Host: This category defines the host processor to which the chipset is matched along with its bus voltage, usually GTL + (Gunning Transceiver Logic Plus) or AGTL + (Advanced Gunning Transceiver Logic Plus) and the number of processors the chipset will support.

Memory: This category defines the characteristics of the DRAM support included in the chipset, including the DRAM refresh technique supported, the amount of memory support (in megabits usually) the type of memory supported and whether memory interleave, ECC (error-correcting code) or parity is supported.

Interfaces: This category defines the type of PCI interface implemented and whether the chipset is AGP-compliant, support integrated graphics, PIPE (pipelining) or SBA (side band addressing).

Arbitration: This category defines the method used by the chipset to arbitrate between different bus speeds and interfaces. The two most common arbitration methods are MTT (Multi-Transition timer) and DIA (Dynamic Intelligent Arbiter).

South bridge support: All Intel chipsets and most of the chipsets for all other manufacturers are two processor sets. In these sets, the north bridge is the main chip and handles CPU and memory interfaces among other tasks, while the sough bridge (or the second chip) handles such things as the USB and IDE interfaces, the RTC (real-time clock) and support for serial and parallel ports.

Power management: All Intel chipsets support both the SMM (System Management Mode) and ACPI (Advanced Configuration and Power Interface) power management standards.

Chipset Built-in Controllers

The controllers and devices included in a chipset are typically those that are common to virtually every PC of the type the chipset is designed to support. The controllers and devices usually included in a chipset are as follows:

Memory controller: This is the logic circuit that controls the reading and writing of data to and from system memory (RAM). Other devices on the PC wishing to access memory must interface with the memory controller. This feature also usually includes error handling to provide for parity checking and ECC (error-correcting code) for every memory word.

EIDE controller: Nearly all mid-to upper-range motherboards now include at least one EIDE connector for hard disks, floppy disks, CD-ROMs, DVDs or other types of internal storage drives. The EIDE controller typically supports devices with ISA, ATA and perhaps an ATA-33 or Ultra – DMA (UDMA) interface.

PCI bridge: Like a network bridge that connects two dissimilar networks, this device logically connects the PCI expansion bus on the motherboard to the processor and other non-PCI devices.

Real-time clock (RTC): This clock holds the date and time on your PC; this is the date and time that is displayed to you on the monitor and is used to date-stamp file activities. This should not be confused with the system clock that provides the timing signal for the processor and other devices.

DMA (Direct Memory Access) controllers: The DMA controller manages the seven DMA channels available for use by ISA/ATA devices on most PCs. DMA channels are used by certain devices, such as floppy disk drives, sound cards, SCSI adapters and some network adapters, to move data into memory without the assistance of the CPU.

IrDA controller: IrDa (Infrared Data Association) is the international organization that has created the standards for short-range, line-of-sight, point-to-point infrared devices, such as a keyboard, mouse and network adapters.

Keyboard controller: A chipset may include the keyboard controller and many of the newer ones do. The keyboard controller is the interface between the keyboard and the processor.

PS/2 mouse controller: When IBM introduced the PS/2 system, the controller for the mouse was included in the keyboard controller. This design has persisted and usually wherever the keyboard controller is, so is the PS/2 mouse controller. This device provides the interface between the Ps/2 mouse and the processor.

Secondary (Level 2 or L2) cache controller: Secondary (L2) cache is located on the motherboard, a daughterboard or as on the Pentium Pro, in the processor package and caches the primary memory (RAM) the hard disk and the CD-ROM drives. The secondary cache controller controls the movement of data to and from the L2 cache and the processor.

CMOS SRAM: The PC's configuration settings are stored in what is called the CMOS memory. The chipset contains the controller used to access and modify this special SRAM area.

BIOS

BIOS, in computing, stands for Basic Input/Output System also incorrectly known as Basic Integrated Operating System and occasionally Built In Operating System. BIOS refers to the firmware code run by an IBM compatible PC when first powered on. The primary function of the BIOS is to prepare the machine so other software programs stored on various media (such as hard drives, floppies, and CDs) can load, execute, and assume control of the PC. This process is known as booting up.

BIOS can also be said to be a coded program embedded on a chip that recognizes and controls various devices that make up the PC. The term BIOS is specific to personal computer vendors. Among other classes of computers, the generic terms boot monitor, boot loader or boot ROM are commonly used. Boot is short for bootstrapping.

The term first appeared in the CP/M operating system, describing the part of CP/M loaded during boot time that interfaced directly with the hardware (CP/M machines usually had a simple boot loader in ROM, and nothing else). Most versions of DOS have a file called "IBMBIO.COM" or "IO.SYS" that is analogous to the CP/M disk BIOS.

How the BIOS boots?

#	Layer
0	Hardware
1	System BIOS
2	Operating system
3	Application

The BIOS runs off the PROM, EPROM or, most commonly, flash memory when the computer is powered on. It initializes several motherboard components and peripherals, including:

- the clock generator,
- the processors and caches,
- the chipset (memory controller and I/O controller),
- the system memory,
- all PCI devices (by assigning bus numbers and resources),
- the primary graphics controller,
- mass storage controllers (such as SATA and IDE controllers),
- various I/O controllers (such keyboard/mouse and USB).

Finally, it loads the boot loader for the operating system, and transfers control to it. The entire process is known as Power-on self-test (POST). On the original IBM PC, the hardware only needed minimal configuration and POST was indeed used for testing; on modern systems, most of POST actually consists of hardware configuration.

Once system memory is initialized, the BIOS typically copies/decompresses itself into that memory and keeps executing from it.

Nearly all BIOS implementations can optionally execute a setup program interfacing the nonvolatile BIOS memory (CMOS). This memory holds user-customizable configuration data (time, date, hard drive details, etc.) accessed by BIOS code. The 80x86 source code for early PC and AT BIOS was included with the IBM Technical Reference Manual.

In most modern BIOS implementations, users select which device boots first: CD, hard disk, floppy disk, flash keydrive and the like. This is particularly useful for installing operating systems or booting to Live CDs, and for selecting the order of testing for the presence of bootable media.

Some BIOS's allow the user to select the operating system to load (e.g. load another OS from the second hard disk), though this is more often handled by a second-stage boot loader.

CMOS

Complementary metal–oxide–semiconductor (CMOS) ("see-moss", is a major class of integrated circuits. CMOS technology is used in chips such as microprocessors, microcontrollers, static RAM, and other digital logic circuits. CMOS technology is also used for a wide variety of analog circuits such as image sensors, data converters, and highly integrated transceivers for many types of communication.

CMOS is also sometimes explained as complementary-symmetry metal–oxide–semiconductor. The words "complementary-symmetry" refer to the fact that the typical digital design style with CMOS uses complementary and symmetrical pairs of p-type and n-type MOSFETs for logic functions.

Two important characteristics of CMOS devices are high noise immunity and low static power supply drain. Significant power is only drawn when its transistors are switching between on and off states; consequently, CMOS devices do not produce as much heat as other forms of logic such as TTL (transistor-transistor logic). CMOS also allows a high density of logic functions on a chip.

The triple compound "metal–oxide–semiconductor" is a reference to the nature of the physical structure of early (and interestingly now, the very latest) field-effect transistors, having a metal gate electrode placed on top of an oxide insulator, which in turn is on top of a semiconductor material. Instead of metal, current gate electrodes (including those up to the 65 nanometer technology node) are almost always made from a different material, polysilicon, but the terms MOS and CMOS nevertheless continue to be used for the modern descendants of the original process. (See also MOSFET.) Metal gates have made a comeback with the advent of high-k dielectric materials in the CMOS transistor as announced by IBM and Intel for the 45 nanometer node and beyond [1].

The combination of MEMS sensors with digital signal processors on one single CMOS chip is sometimes known an CMOSens.

SIMM

A SIMM, or single in-line memory module, is a type of memory module used for random access memory in personal computers. It differs from a DIMM (the most predominant form of memory module today) in that the contacts on a SIMM are redundant on both sides of the module.

Most early PC motherboards (8088 based PCs and XTs) used socketed DIP chips. With the introduction of 80286 based PC/ATs, which could use larger amounts of memory, memory modules evolved from the need of saving motherboard space and to ease memory expansion. Instead of plugging in 8 or 9 single DRAM DIP chips, only one additional memory module was needed to increase the memory of the computer. A few 80286-based computers used (often non-standard) memory modules like SIPP memory (single in-line pin package). SIPP's 30 pins often bent or broke during installation, which is why they were quickly replaced by SIMMs which used contact plates rather than pins.

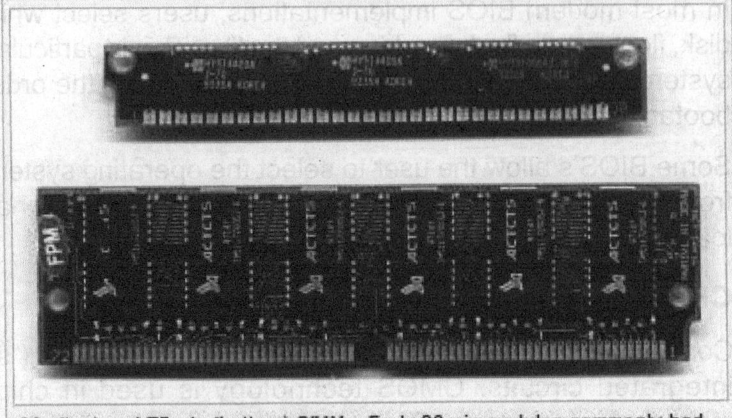

30- (top) and 72-pin (bottom) SIMMs. Early 30-pin modules commonly had either 256 KB or 1 MB of memory.

The first SIMMs appeared on the PS/2 in the mid 1980s, having been first proposed by Skip Coppola while at IBM. They solved several problems at the time, including shrinking motherboard real estate (they took up much less board space than socketed chips) as well as the effects of rapidly advancing memory capacities (a motherboard would quickly become obsolete based on its sockets for a particular RAM chip capacity) This also allowed the manufacturer (IBM at this time) to source RAM chips from different vendors and in different packaging, yet still allow them to be interchangeable through this intermediate form (the SIMM).

The first variant of SIMMs has 30 pins and provides 8 bits of data (9 bits in parity versions). Therefore, systems usually required that 30 pin SIMMs would have to be installed in sets of 4 (because processors such as the 80486 had 32 bit data paths).

The second variant of SIMMs has 72 pins and provides 32 bits of data (36 bits in parity versions). During the mid 90s, 72-pin SIMMs replaced 30-pin SIMMs.

The Macintosh IIfx requires non-standard 64-pin SIMMs.

Due to the differing data bus widths of the memory modules and some processors, sometimes several modules must be installed in identical pairs or in identical groups of four to fill a memory bank. For instance, on 80386 or 80486 systems (data bus width of 32 bits), either four 30-pin SIMMs or one 72-pin SIMM are required for one memory bank. On Pentium systems (data bus width of 64 bits), two 72-pin SIMMs are required.

The earliest SIMM sockets were conventional push-type sockets. These were soon replaced by ZIF (Zero Insertion Force) sockets in which the SIMM was inserted and rotated until it locked into place. To install a SIMM, the module must be placed in the socket at an angle, then rotated (angled) into position. To remove one, the two metal or plastic clips at each end must be pulled to the side, then the SIMM must be tilted back and pulled out. The earlier sockets used plastic retainer clips which were found to break, so steel clips replaced them.

RAM technologies used on SIMMs include EDO and FPM.

SIMM is standardised under JEDEC JESD-21C standard.

DIMM

A DIMM, or dual in-line memory module, comprises a series of random access memory integrated circuits. These modules are mounted on a printed circuit board and designed for use in personal computers. DIMMs began to replace SIMMs (single in-line memory modules) as the predominant type of memory module as Intel's Pentium processors began to control the market.

The main difference between SIMMs and DIMMs is that SIMMs have a 32-bit data path, while DIMMs have a 64-bit data path. Since Intel's Pentium has (as do several other processors) a 64-bit bus width, it required SIMMs installed in matched pairs in order to use them. The processor would then access the two SIMMs simultaneously. DIMMs were introduced to eliminate this inefficiency. Another difference is that DIMMs have separate electrical contacts on each side of the module, while the contacts on SIMMs on both sides are redundant.

The most common types of DIMMs are:

- 72-pin-DIMMs, used for SO-DIMM
- 144-pin-DIMMs, used for SO-DIMM
- 200-pin-DIMMs, used for SO-DIMM
- 168-pin-DIMMs, used for FPM, EDO and SDRAM
- 184-pin-DIMMs, used for DDR SDRAM
- 240-pin-DIMMs, used for DDR2 SDRAM
- 240-pin-DIMMs, used for FB-DIMM

There are 2 notches on the bottom edge of 168-pin-DIMMs, and the location of each notch determines a particular feature of the module.

- The first notch is DRAM key position. It represents RFU (reserved future use), registered, and unbuffered.
- The second notch is voltage key position. It represents 5.0V, 3.3V, and Reserved.
- The upper DIMM in the photo is an unbuffered 3.3V 168-pin DIMM.

A DIMM's capacity and timing parameters may be identified with SPD (Serial Presence Detect), an additional chip which contains information about the module type.

ECC DIMMs are those that have extra data bits which can be used by the system memory controller to detect and correct errors. There are numerous ECC schemes, but perhaps the most common is Single Error Correct, Double Error Detect (SECDED) which uses a 9th extra bit per byte.

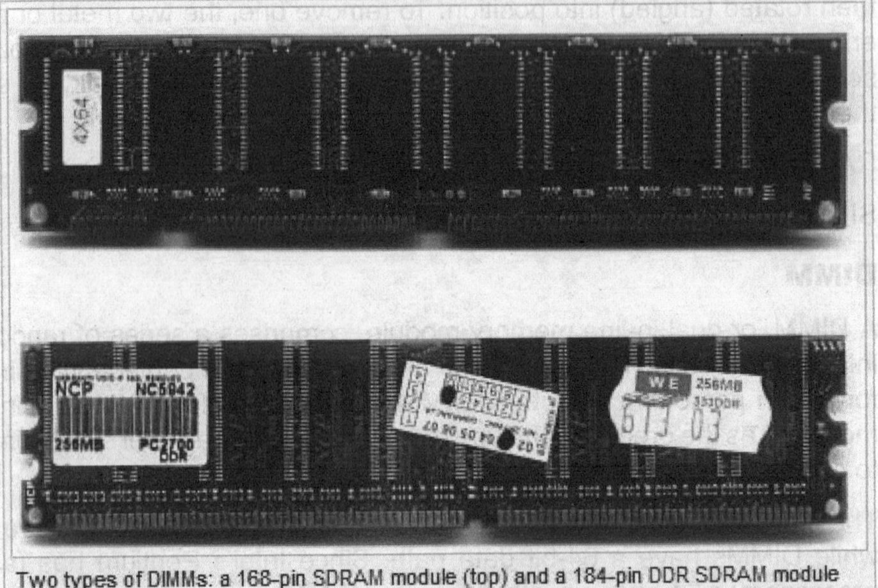

Two types of DIMMs: a 168-pin SDRAM module (top) and a 184-pin DDR SDRAM module (bottom).

Speeds

For various technologies, there are certain bus and device clock frequencies that are standardized. There is also a decided nomenclature for each of these speeds for each type.

SDRAM DIMMs - These first synchronous registered DRAM DIMMs had the same bus frequency for data, address and control lines.

PC66 = 66 MHz

PC100 = 100 MHz

PC133 = 133 MHz

DDR SDRAM (DDR1) SDRAM DIMMs - DIMMs based on Double Data Rate (DDR) DRAM have data but not the strobe at double the rate of the clock. This is achieved by clocking on both the rising and falling edge of the data strobes.

PC1600 = 200 MHz data & strobe / 100 MHz clock for address and control

PC2100 = 266 MHz data & strobe / 133 MHz clock for address and control

PC2700 = 333 MHz data & strobe / 166 MHz clock for address and control

PC3200 = 400 MHz data & strobe / 200 MHz clock for address and control

DDR2 SDRAM SDRAM DIMMs - DIMMs based on Double Data Rate 2 (DDR2) DRAM also have data and data strobe frequencies at double the rate of the clock. This is achieved by clocking on both the rising and falling edge of the data strobes. The power consumption of DDR2 is significantly lower than DDR(1) at the same speed.

PC2-3200 = 400 MHz data & strobe / 200 MHz clock for address and control

PC2-4200 = 533 MHz data & strobe / 266 MHz clock for address and control

PC2-5300 = 667 MHz data & strobe / 333 MHz clock for address and control

PC2-6400 = 800 MHz data & strobe / 400 MHz clock for address and control

RIMM

Rambus Inline Memory Module (RIMM) Rambus Incorporated, founded in 1990, is a provider of high-speed interface technology, most notably their Rambus Dynamic RAM memory technology, which was intended to replace SDRAM and challenge DDR SDRAM as the standard memory used in computers.

Technology

The first PC motherboards with support for RDRAM debuted in 1999. They supported PC800 RDRAM, which operated at 800 MHz and delivered 1600 MB/s of bandwidth over a 16 bit bus using a 184 pin RIMM form factor. This was significantly faster than the previous standard, PC133 SDRAM, which operated at 133 MHz and delivered 1066 MB/s of bandwidth over a 64 bit bus using a 168 pin DIMM form factor.

Some downsides of RDRAM technology, however, included significantly increased latency, heat output, manufacturing complexity, and cost. PC800 RDRAM operated with a latency of 45ns, compared to only 7.5ns for PC133 SDRAM. RDRAM memory chips also put out significantly more heat than SDRAM chips, necessitating heatsinks on all RIMM devices. RDRAM also includes a memory controller on each memory chip, significantly increasing manufacturing complexity compared to SDRAM, which used a single memory controller located on the northbridge chipset. RDRAM was also two to three times the price of PC133 SDRAM due to a combination of high manufacturing costs and high license fees. DDR SDRAM, introduced in 2000, operated at an effective clockspeed of 266 MHz and delivered 2100 MB/s over a 64-bit bus using a 184 pin DIMM form factor.

With the introduction of the i840 chipset, Intel added support for dual-channel PC800 RDRAM, doubling bandwidth to 3200 MB/s by increasing the bus width to 32 bit. This was followed in 2002 by the i850E chipset, which introduced PC1066 RDRAM, increasing total dual-channel bandwidth to 4200 MB/s. Also in 2002, Intel released the E7205 Granitebay chipset, which introduced dual-channel DDR support for a total bandwidth of 4200 MB/s, but at a much lower latency than competing RDRAM. In 2003, Intel released the i875P chipset, and along with it dual-channel DDR400. With a total bandwidth of 6400 MB/s, it marked the end of RDRAM as a technology with competitive performance.

Rambus survived the obsolesence of RDRAM and moved to support DDR and DDR2 in the area of video card technology and in particular, PCI Express. Rambus developed and licensed its XDR RAM technology.

Bus Slots

PCI slots were the first physically-incompatible expansion ports to directly squeeze ISA off of the motherboard. At first, motherboards were largely ISA, including a few PCI slots. By the mid-1990s, the two slot types were roughly balanced, and ISA slots soon were in the minority of consumer systems. Microsoft's PC 97 specification recommended that ISA slots be removed entirely, though the system architecture still required ISA to be present in some vestigial way internally to handle the floppy drive, serial ports, etc. ISA slots remained for a few more years, and it was even possible to see systems with an Accelerated Graphics Port (AGP) sitting near the central processing unit, an array of PCI slots, and one or two ISA slots near the end.

It is also notable that PCI slots are "rotated" compared to their ISA counterparts—PCI cards were essentially inserted "upside-down," allowing ISA and PCI connectors to squeeze together on the motherboard. Only one of the two connectors can be used in each slot at a time, but this allowed for greater flexibility.

8-bit ISA (XT bus architecture)

The XT bus architecture is an eight-bit ISA bus used by Intel 8086 and Intel 8088 systems in the IBM PC and IBM PC XT in the 1980s. The XT bus has four DMA channels, of which three are brought out to the expansion slots. Of these three, two are normally allocated to machine functions:

8 bit ISA or XT bus architecture	
Bus width	8-bit
Compatible with	8 bit ISA
Pins	62
Vcc	+5 V, -5 V, +12 V, -12 V
Clock	4.7727266 MHz

DMA channel	Expansion	Standard function
0	No	Dynamic RAM refresh
1	Yes	Add-on cards
2	Yes	Floppy disk controller
3	Yes	Hard disk controller

The XT bus architecture has single Intel 8259 PIC and eight interrupt lines.

16-bit ISA (AT bus architecture)

The AT bus architecture is an 16-bit version of the ISA bus first in the IBM PC/AT.

PCI Standards

The Peripheral Component Interconnect, or PCI Standard (in practice almost always shortened to PCI) specifies a computer bus for attaching peripheral devices to a computer motherboard. These devices can take any one of the following forms:

- An integrated circuit fitted onto the motherboard itself, called a planar device in the PCI specification.
- An expansion card that fits into a socket.

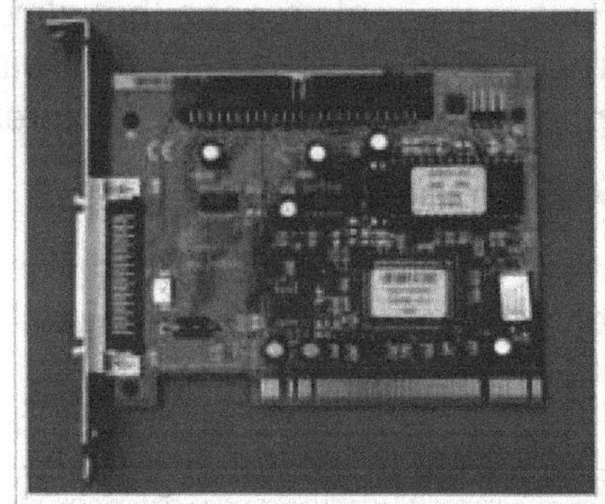

A typical 32-bit PCI card, in this case a SCSI adapter from Adaptec

The PCI bus is common in modern PCs, where it has displaced ISA and VESA Local Bus as the standard expansion bus, but it also appears in many other computer types. The bus will eventually be succeeded by PCI Express, which is standard in most new computers, and other technologies.

The PCI specification covers the physical size of the bus (including wire spacing), electrical characteristics, bus timing, and protocols. The specification can be purchased from the PCI Special Interest Group (PCISIG).

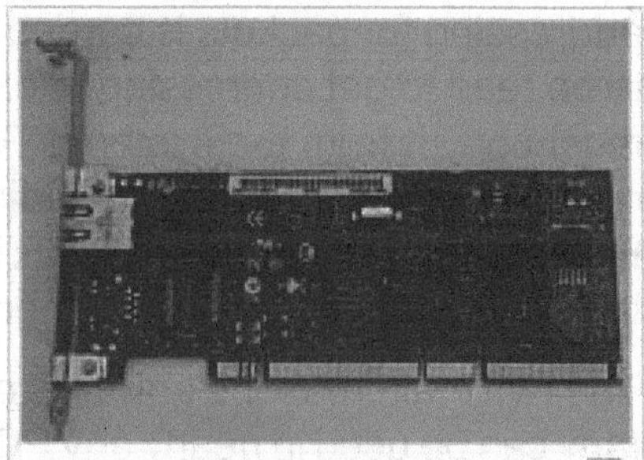

A PCI-X Gigabit Ethernet expansion card

Conventional Hardware Specifications

These specifications represent the most common version of PCI used in normal PCs.

- 33.33 MHz clock with synchronous transfers
- peak transfer rate of 133 MB per second for 32-bit bus width (33.33 MHz × 32 bits ÷ 8 bits/byte = 133 MB/s)
- peak transfer rate of 266 MB/s for 64-bit bus width
- 32-bit or 64-bit bus width
- 32-bit address space (4 gigabytes)
- 32-bit I/O port space (now deprecated)
- 256-byte configuration space
- 5-volt signaling
- reflected-wave switching

AGI Bus

The Accelerated Graphics Port (also called Advanced Graphics Port, often shortened to AGP) is a high-speed point-to-point channel for attaching a graphics card to a computer's motherboard, primarily to assist in the acceleration of 3D computer graphics. AGP is often referred to as a 'bus', however this is a misnomer - a single AGP controller is only capable of controlling a single device.

This is the main reason that almost all mainboards have only a single AGP slot, although motherboards have been built with multiple independent AGP slots. AGP is currently being phased out in favor of PCI Express.

Advantages over PCI

As computers became increasingly graphically oriented, successive generations of graphics adapters began to push the limits of the PCI bus, leading to the development of AGP, dedicated to graphics adapters. Most motherboards manufactured since the late 1990s include either an on-board integrated AGP adapter, or a physical AGP slot into which a separate AGP-based graphics card can be inserted.

For the needs of modern graphics adapters, AGP is superior to PCI because it provides a dedicated pathway between the slot and the processor rather than sharing the PCI bus, allowing for faster communication. AGP also uses sideband addressing, meaning that addressing for packets is carried outside of the packet, so the entire packet does not need to be read to get addressing information. In addition, to load a texture, a PCI graphics card must copy it from the system's RAM into the card's framebuffer, whereas an AGP card is capable of reading textures directly from system RAM using the Graphics Address Remapping Table (GART). GART reapportions main memory for texture storage, allowing the graphics card to access them directly.

The two main reasons graphics cards with the PCI interface are still produced is that, first, they can be used in nearly any PC; because while some motherboards with built-in graphics adapters lack an AGP slot, few, if any, modern desktop PCs do not have PCI slots. Secondly,

a user with an appropriate operating system can use several PCI graphics cards (or several PCI graphics cards in combination with one AGP card) simultaneously — to give many different video outputs (for the use of many screens). This is almost impossible with AGP 1.0 (early AGP 1x and 2x) and AGP 2.0 (AGP 4x) cards, because they do not support more than one AGP Master (video card) per AGP Target (chipset interface); AGP 3.0 (AGP 8x) does support more than one AGP Master per AGP Target, but nonetheless few PC motherboards are equipped with more than one AGP slot. Some server-class computers support having multiple AGP slots in a single system: the HP AlphaServer GS1280 has up to 16 AGP slots, the AlphaServer ES80 up to 4 AGP slots, and the AlphaServer ES47 up to 2 AGP slots.

Versions of AGP

Intel released the first version of AGP; appropriately titled "AGP specification 1.0," in 1997. It included both the 1x and 2x speeds. Specification 2.0 documented AGP 4X and 3.0 documented 8X. Available versions include:

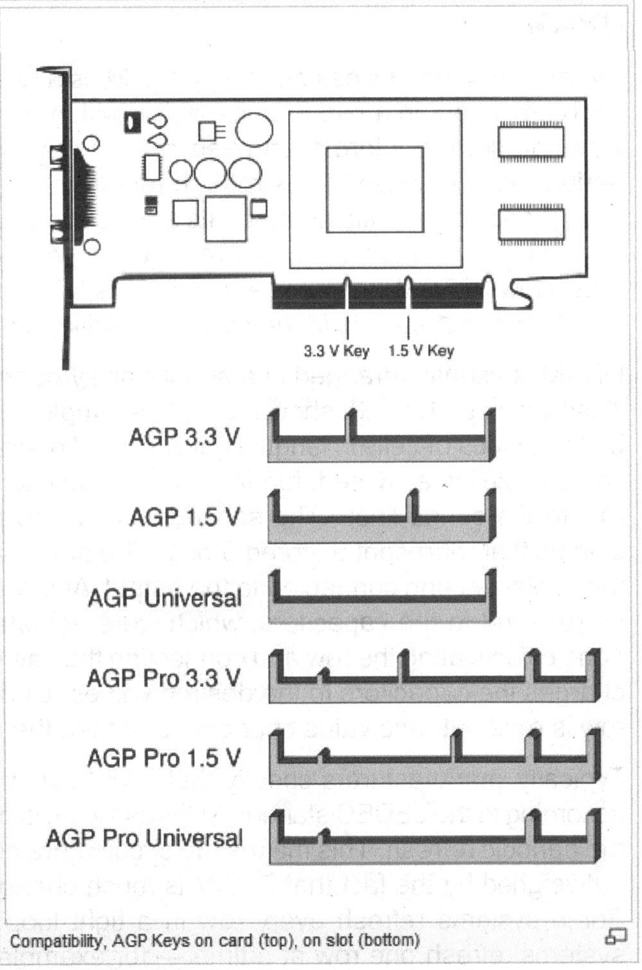

Compatibility, AGP Keys on card (top), on slot (bottom)

AGP 1x: A 32-bit channel operating at 66 MHz resulting in a maximum data rate of 266 megabytes per second (MB/s), doubled from the 133 MB/s transfer rate of PCI bus 33 MHz / 32-bit; 3.3 V signaling.

AGP 2x: A 32-bit channel operating at 66 MHz double pumped to an effective 133 MHz resulting in a maximum data rate of 533 MB/s; signaling voltages the same as AGP 1x;

AGP 4x: A 32-bit channel operating at 66 MHz quad pumped to an effective 266 MHz resulting in a maximum data rate of 1066 MB/s (1 GB/s); 1.5 V signaling;

AGP 8x: A 32-bit channel operating at 66 MHz, strobing eight times per clock, delivering an effective 533 MHz resulting in a maximum data rate of 2133 MB/s (2 GB/s); 0.8 V signaling.

In addition, AGP Pro cards of various types exist. They require more power and are often longer than standard AGP cards (though they only connect to one AGP slot). These cards are usually used to accelerate professional computer-aided design applications employed in the fields of architecture, machining, engineering, simulations, and similar fields. The AGP Pro slot has a few extra pins which supply extra power to the graphics card. However, AGP Pro has not become widely accepted. Instead, modern desktop grade power-hungry video cards are equipped with a separate power source, either through a Molex or peripheral plug for additional power. Generally, there are two types of AGP Pro slots, regarding necessary power: 50 W or 110 W, with or without molex connector on the graphic card (although standard AGP slot is confined to 42 W of power through slot itself).

There are various physical interfaces (i.e. shape of slots), as explained in the Compatibility section below.

AGP version 3.5 is only publicly mentioned by Microsoft under Universal Accelerated Graphics Port (UAGP), which specifies mandatory supports of extra registers once marked optional under AGP 3.0. Upgraded registers include PCISTS, CAPPTR, NCAPID, AGPSTAT, AGPCMD, NISTAT, NICMD. New required registers include APBASELO, APBASEHI, AGPCTRL, APSIZE, NEPG, GARTLO, GARTHI.

DRAM

Dynamic random access memory (DRAM) is a type of random access memory that stores each bit of data in a separate capacitor within an integrated circuit. Since real capacitors leak charge, the information eventually fades unless the capacitor charge is refreshed periodically. Because of this refresh requirement, it is a dynamic memory as opposed to SRAM and other static memory. Its advantage over SRAM is its structural simplicity: only one transistor and a capacitor are required per bit, compared to six transistors in SRAM. This allows DRAM to reach very high density. Since DRAM loses its data when the power supply is removed, it is in the class of volatile memory devices.

DRAM is usually arranged in a square array of one capacitor and transistor per cell. The illustrations to the right show a simple example with only 4 by 4 cells (modern DRAM can be thousands of cells in length/width). A read operation proceeds as follows: the row of the selected cell is activated, turning on the transistors and connecting the capacitors of that row to the sense lines. The sense lines lead to the sense amplifiers, which distinguish signals that represent a stored 0 or 1. The amplified value from the appropriate column is then selected and connected to the output. At the end of a read cycle, the row values must be restored to the capacitors, which were depleted during the read. A write operation is done by activating the row and connecting the values to be written to the sense lines, which charges the capacitors to the desired values. During a write to a particular cell, the entire row is read out, one value changed, and then the entire row is written back int.

Typically, manufacturers specify that each row should be refreshed every 64 ms or less, according to the JEDEC standard. Refresh logic is commonly used with DRAMs to automate the periodic refresh. This makes the circuit more complicated, but this drawback is usually outweighed by the fact that DRAM is much cheaper and of greater capacity than SRAM. Some systems refresh every row in a tight loop that occurs once every 64 ms. Other systems refresh one row at a time — for example, a system with 2^{13} = 8192 rows would require a refresh rate of one row every 7.8 µs (64 ms / 8192 rows). A few real-time systems refresh a portion of memory at a time based on an external timer that governs the operation of the rest of the system, such as the vertical blanking interval that occurs every 10 to 20 ms in video equipment. All methods require some sort of counter to keep track of which row is the next to be refreshed. Some DRAM chips include that counter; other kinds require external refresh logic to hold that counter. (Under some conditions, most of the data in DRAM can be recovered even if the DRAM has not been refreshed for several minutes.)

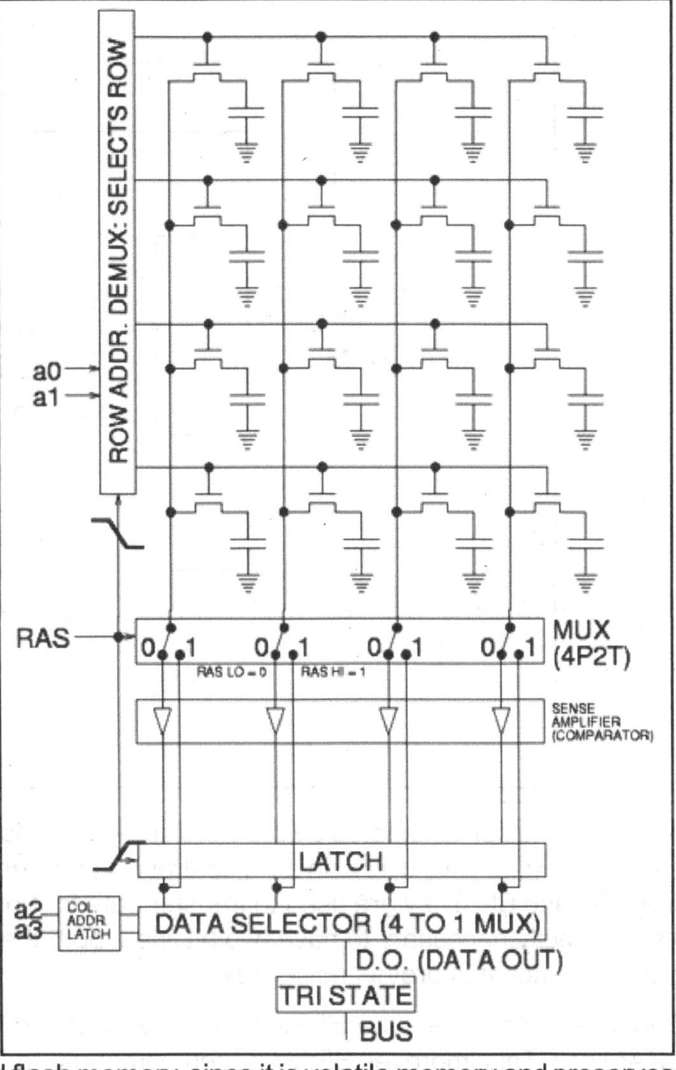

SRAM

Static random access memory (SRAM) is a type of semiconductor memory. The word "static" indicates that the memory retains its contents as long as power remains applied, unlike dynamic RAM (DRAM) that needs to be periodically refreshed (nevertheless, SRAM should not be confused with read-only memory and flash memory, since it is volatile memory and preserves data only while power is continuously applied). SRAM should not be confused with SDRAM, which stands for synchronous DRAM and is entirely different from SRAM, or with pseudostatic RAM (PSRAM), which is DRAM disguised as SRAM.

Random Access

Random access means that locations in the memory can be written to or read from in any order, regardless of the memory location that was last accessed.

Each bit in an SRAM is stored on four transistors that form two cross-coupled inverters. This storage cell has two stable states which are used to denote 0 and 1. Two additional access transistors serve to control the access to a storage cell during read and write operations. It thus typically takes six MOSFETs to store one memory bit.

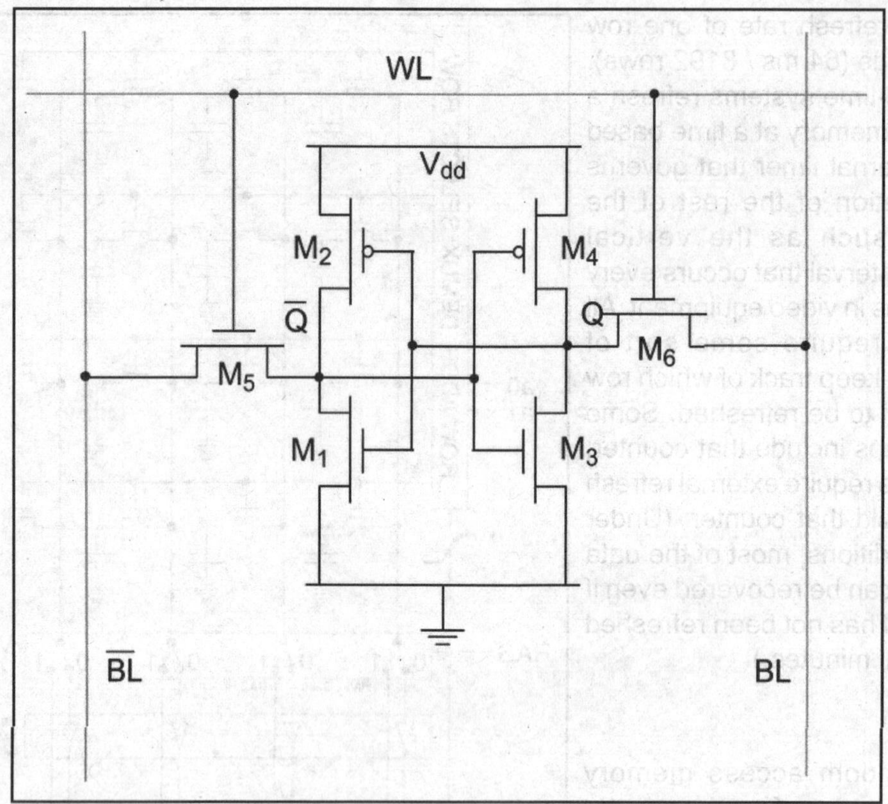

Access to the cell is enabled by the word line (WL in figure) which controls the two access transistors M_5 and M_6 which, in turn, control whether the cell should be connected to the bit lines: BL and BL. They are used to transfer data for both read and write operations. While it's not strictly necessary to have two bit lines, both the signal and its inverse are typically provided since it improves noise margins.

During read accesses, the bit lines are actively driven high and low by the inverters in the SRAM cell. This improves SRAM speed compared to DRAMs—in a DRAM, the bit line is connected to storage capacitors and charge sharing causes the bitline to swing upwards or downwards. The symmetric structure of SRAMs also allows for differential signalling, which makes small voltage swings more easily detectable. Another difference with DRAM that contributes to making SRAM faster is that commercial chips accept all address bits at a time. By comparison, commodity DRAMs have the address multiplexed in two halves, i.e. higher bits followed by lower bits, over the same package pins in order to keep their size and cost down.

The size of an SRAM with m address lines and n data lines is 2^m words, or $2^m \times n$ bits.

Applications and Use

Characteristics: SRAM is a little more expensive, but faster and significantly less power hungry (especially idle) than DRAM. It is therefore used where either speed or low power, or both, are of prime interest. SRAM is also easier to control (interface to) and generally more truly random access than modern types of DRAM. Due to a more complex internal structure, SRAM is less dense than DRAM and is therefore not used for high-capacity, low-cost applications such as the main memory in personal computers.

Clock speed and power: The power consumption of SRAM varies widely depending on how frequently it is accessed; it can be as power-hungry as dynamic RAM, when used at high frequencies, and some ICs can consume many watts at full speed. On the other hand, static RAM used at a somewhat slower pace, such as in applications with moderately clocked microprocessors, draw very little power and can have a nearly negligible power consumption when sitting idle — in the region of a few microwatts.

Static RAM exists primarily as:

- general purpose products
- with asynchronous interface, such as the 28 pin 32Kx8 chips (usually named XXC256), and similar products up to 16 Mbit per chip
- with synchronous interface, usually used for caches and other applications requiring burst transfers, up to 18 Mbit (256Kx72) per chip
- integrated on chip
- as RAM or cache memory in microcontrollers (usually from around 32 bytes up to 128 kibibytes)
- as the primary caches in powerful microprocessors, such as the · x86 family, and many others (from 8 KiB, up to several mebibytes)
- on application specific ICs, or ASICs (usually in the order of kibibytes)
- in FPGAs and CPLDs (usually in the order of a few kilobytes or less)

It may be noted that cpu registers and parts of the state-machines used in microprocessors are also often (not always!) built around static RAM.

Embedded use: Many categories of industrial and scientific subsystems, automotive electronics, and similar, contains static RAM. Some amounts (kibibytes or less) is also embedded in practically all modern appliances, toys, etc that implements an electronic user interface. Several mebibytes may be used in complex products such as digital cameras, cell phones, synthesizers, etc.

SRAM in its dual-ported form is sometimes used for realtime digital signal processing circuits.

In computers: SRAM is also used in personal computers, workstations, routers and peripheral equipment: internal CPU caches and external burst mode SRAM caches, hard disk buffers, router buffers, etc. LCD screens and printers also normally employ static RAM to hold the image displayed (or to be printed). Small SRAM buffers are also found in CDROM and CDRW drives; usually 256 KiB or more are used to buffer track data, which is transferred in blocks instead of as single values. The same applies to cable modems and similar equipment connected to computers. The so called "CMOS RAM" on PC motherboards was originally a battery-powered SRAM chip, but is today more often implemented using EEPROM or Flash.

Hobbyists: Hobbyists often prefer SRAM due to the ease of interfacing. It is much easier to work with than DRAM as there are no refresh cycles and the address and data buses are directly accessible rather than multiplexed. In addition to buses and power connections, SRAM usually require only three controls: Chip Enable (CE), Write Enable (WE) and Output Enable (OE).

DDR SDRAM

While the access latency of DRAM is fundamentally limited by the DRAM array, DRAM has very high potential bandwidth because each internal read is actually a row of many thousands of bits. To make more of this bandwidth available to users, a Double Data Rate interface was developed. This uses the same commands, accepted once per cycle, but reads or writes two words of data per clock cycle. Some minor changes to the SDR interface timing were made in hindsight.

DDR SDRAM doubles the minimum read or write unit; every access refers to at least two consecutive words.

Typical DDR SDRAM clock speeds are 133, 166 and 200 MHz (7.5, 6, and 5 ns/cycle), generally described as DDR-266, DDR-333 and DDR-400 (3.75, 3, and 2.5 ns per beat). Corresponding 184-pin DIMMS are known as PC2100, PC2700 and PC3200. Speeds up to DDR-550 (PC4400) are available for a price.

DDR2 SDRAM

DDR2 SDRAM is very similar to DDR SDRAM, but doubles the minimum read or write unit again, to 4 consecutive words. The bus protocol was also simplified to allow higher speed operation. (In particular, the "burst terminate" command is deleted.) This allows the bus speed of the SDRAM to be doubled without increasing the speed of internal RAM operations; instead, internal operations are performed in units 4 times as wide as SDRAM. Also, an extra bank address pin (BA2) was added to allow 8 banks on large RAM chips.

Typical DDR2 SDRAM clock speeds are 200, 266, 333 or 400 MHz (5, 3.75, 3 and 2.5 ns/cycle), generally described as DDR2-400, DDR2-533, DDR2-667 and DDR2-800 (2.5, 1/875, 1.5 and 1.5 ns per beat). Corresponding 240-pin DIMMS are known as PC2-3200 through PC2-6400. Speeds up to DDR2-1250 (PC2-10000) are available for a price.

Note that because internal operations are at 1/2 the clock rate, DDR2-400 memory (internal clock speed 100 MHz) has somewhat higher latency than DDR-400 (internal clock speed 200 MHz).

DDR3 SDRAM

DDR3 continues the trend, doubling the minimum read or write unit to 8 consecutive words.

This allows another doubling of bandwidth and external bus speed without having to change the speed of internal operations, just the width.

DDR3 memory chips are being made commercially, but computer systems able to use them are not expected until late 2007, with significant usage in 2008. Initial speeds are 400 and 533 MHz, which would be described as DDR3-800 and DDR3-1066, but speeds of 667 and 800 MHz (DDR3-1333 and DDR3-1600) are expected in time. This high speed poses a significant engineering challenge, so the 2008 schedule may be optimistic.

Extended Data Out (EDO) DRAM

EDO DRAM is similar to Fast Page Mode DRAM with the additional feature that a new access cycle can be started while keeping the data output of the previous cycle active. This allows a certain amount of overlap in operation (pipelining), allowing somewhat improved speed. It was 5% faster than Fast Page Mode DRAM, which it began to replace in 1993.

To be precise, EDO DRAM begins data output on the falling edge of /CAS, but does not stop the output when /CAS rises again. It holds the output valid (thus extending the data output time) until either /RAS is deasserted, or a new /CAS falling edge selects a different column address.

Single-cycle EDO has the ability to carry out a complete memory transaction in one clock cycle. Otherwise, each sequential RAM access within the same page takes two clock cycles instead of three, once the page has been selected. EDO's speed and capabilities allowed it to somewhat replace the then-slow L2 caches of PCs. It created an opportunity to reduce the immense performance loss associated with a lack of L2 cache, while making systems cheaper to build. This was also good for notebooks due to difficulties with their limited form factor, and battery life limitations. An EDO system with L2 cache was tangibly faster than the older FPM/L2 combination.

Single-cycle EDO DRAM became very popular on video cards towards the end of the 1990s. It was very low cost, yet nearly as efficient for performance as the far more costly VRAM.

EDO was sometimes referred to as Hyper Page Mode.

Burst EDO (BEDO) DRAM

An evolution of the former, Burst EDO DRAM, could process four memory addresses in one burst, for a maximum of 5-1-1-1, saving an additional three clocks over optimally designed EDO memory. It was done by adding an address counter on the chip to keep track of the next address. BEDO also added a pipelined stage allowing page-access cycle to be divided into two components. During a memory-read operation, the first component accessed the data from the memory array to the output stage (second latch). The second component drove the data bus from this latch at the appropriate logic level. Since the data is already in the output buffer, faster access time is achieved (up to 50% for large blocks of data) than with traditional EDO.

Although BEDO DRAM showed additional optimization over EDO, by the time it was available the market had made a significant investment towards synchronous DRAM, or SDRAM. Even though BEDO RAM was superior to SDRAM in some ways, the latter technology gained significant traction and quickly displaced BEDO.

Multibank DRAM (MDRAM)

Multibank RAM applies the interleaving technique for main memory to second level cache memory to provide a cheaper and faster alternative to SRAM. The chip splits its memory capacity into small blocks of 256 kB and allows operations to two different banks in a single clock cycle.

This memory was primarily used in graphic cards with Tseng Labs ET6x00 chipsets, and was made by MoSys. Boards based upon this chipset often used the unusual RAM size configuration of 2.25 MiB, owing to MDRAM's ability to be implemented in various sizes more easily. This size of 2.25 MiB allowed 24-bit color at a resolution of 1024×768, a very popular display setting in the card's time.

Synchronous Graphics RAM (SGRAM)

SGRAM is a specialized form of SDRAM for graphics adaptors. It adds functions such as bit masking (writing to a specified bit plane without affecting the others) and block write (filling a block of memory with a single colour). Unlike VRAM and WRAM, SGRAM is single-ported. However, it can open two memory pages at once, which simulates the dual-port nature of other video RAM technologies.

SGRAM and SDRAM became the most popular types of DRAM at the end of the 1990s, and well into the first decade of the 2000s.

Battery

The battery inside the PC keeps the clock working when the main power supply to the system is switched off, so that the next time when you switch on the system you will get correct time and date. This battery also provides power to the CMOS memory that keeps the setup information about the system. Usually this battery last for many years, when it eventually fails, your system will lose the setup information saved in the CMOS RAM and also the Real Time Clock (RTC) of your system will stop showing the correct time.

In this condition, every time you switch the correct time and date to the system, to allow the system to show correct time and date as long as machine is on. When the battery inside your system fails you need to replace it with another working battery of the same size and type.

Replacing Battery

To replace the battery, do the following:

1. Switch off system and remove the power supply cable.

2. Remove the main system unit's cover.
3. Remove the battery from the holder and slide in a new battery of the same size and type in the holder.
4. Make sure that it is in correct orientation.
5. Once the battery is replaced, close the cover, switch on the system and run the setup to cofigure the system.

Presently 3V, CR-2030 Lithium battery is commonly used in most of the motherboards.

Super I/O Chip

OnBoard Floppy Controller

Use this item to enable or diable floppy drive controller.

Serial Port Address

Use this item to set the address for the onboard serial port or disable it. Configuration options: [Disabled], [3F8 / IRQ4], [2F8 / IRQ3], [3E8 / IRQ4], [2E8 / IRQ3]

Motherboard Connectors

Several connectors are provided on the motherboard to connect external Reset switche, Power-on LED, Speaker, etc. to the system. When you remove any lead, always remember to note the position and orientation of each of them as some of them are orientation sensitive and will not work when connected in wrong orientation.

Let us see some of these connectors.

External Battery Connector

Pin	Function
1	Battery (+6V DC Input)
2	No Connection
3	Ground
4	Ground

On IBM AT and compatibles, CMOS RAM data is maintained by battery on the motherboard itself and hence do not require any external connection.

Optional Keyboard Connector

Pin	Function
1	Keyboard Clock

2	Keyboard Data
3	No connection
4	Ground
5	+5V

Keyboard connector is a five-pin DIN socket placed towards the rear right hand side of the motherboard.

Power Connector

AT Power Supply

J10	J11
Power Good	Ground
+5V	Ground
+12V	–5V
–12V	+5V
Ground	+5V
Ground	+5V

Power is fed to motherboard from two 6-way non-reversible connectors.

In case you are unsure about which way these two connectors go, always remember that the black wires (ground) of connector J10 and J11 are placed together when connecting them to the motherboard.

ATX Power Supply

Pin	Function	Pin	Function
1	+3.3V	11	+3.3V
2	+3.3V	12	–12V
3	Ground	13	Ground
4	+5V	14	PWR ON
5	Ground	15	Ground
6	+5V	16	Ground
7	Ground	17	Ground

8	PWR GOOD	18	–5V
9	+5V SB	19	+5V
10	+12V	20	+5V

Keylock and Power-on LED Connector

Pin	Function
1	LED+
2	NO CONNECTION
3	LED–
4	KEYLOCK
5	KEYLOCK GROUND

The LED is connected to pin-1 and 3, the keyboard lock switch is connected to pin-4 and 5.

Speaker Connector

Pin	Function
1	+5V
2	Ground
3	Ground
4	SPKR

The loudspeaker is connected by a four-way socket. Only the outer two pins (1 and 4) are used. The loudspeaker is not orientation sensitive and hence it does not matter which way it is connected.

Turbo Mode Selection

Switch Option	System Clock Speed
Open	Turbo
Close	Non-Turbo

"Tubo" switch is nonstandard, so its pin assignments may vary. If you are not sure of its connections, consult the system manual, a wrong connection is unlikely to cause any harm.

Turbo Mode LED Connector

Pin	Function
1	LED
2	LED+

This LED is orientation sensitive and will light only if connected properly.

Reset Connector

Switch Position	Function
Close	Reset the system
Open	Normal operation

The reset button uses a two-pin connector in which pin 1 is the reset line and pin 2 is ground. These two pins are linked when the switch is depressed. The polarization of this switch is unimportant.

Infra-Red (IR) Connector

Pin	Function
1	VCC +5V
2	No Connection
3	IrRx Infrared Receive
4	Ground
5	IrTx Infrared Transmit

This conector provides connection for HP HSDL-1000 compatible infrared (IrDA) transmitter/ receiver.

Front Panel Function Connector

Pin		Function	Pin		Function
1		Power LED	14		Ground
2		No connection	15	IDE LED	IDE LED
3	Key Lock	Ground	16		No connection

4		Key lock	17	SW On	GV VR
5		Ground	18		Push on
6		No connection	19	Ground	Standby 5V
7	Ext SMI	Ext SMI	20	Sleep	VCC
8		Ground	21	LED	Sleep LED
9		No connection	22		Ground
10		Speaker	23	Reset	Reset
11	Speaker	No connection	24		No connection
12		Ground	25	Turbo	VCC
13		Vcc	26	LED	+5V

This connector integrates all system front-panel functions into one single 26-pin connector.

CPU Fan Connector

Pin	Function
1	No Connection
2	+12V
3	Ground

CPU fan connector provides +12V DC supply to the CPU cooling fan. This fan is attached on top of the heatsink element.

CD Audio Input Connector

Pin	Function
1	Left Channel Audio
2	Gound
3	Ground
4	Right Channel Audio

Auxiliary Input Connector

Pin	Function
1	Left Channel Audio

2	Gound
3	Ground
4	Right Channel Audio

Telephony Input Connector

Pin	Function
1	Phone
2	Gound
3	Ground
4	Mono

Integrated Function Connector

Pin		Function	Pin		Function
1		USB +5Volt	11		USB +5Volt
2		USB Port1 –	12		USB Port2 –
3	USB1	USB Port1 +	13	USB2	USB Port2 +
4		Ground	14		Ground
5		No connnection	15		No connection
6		PS/2 Data	16		+5V
7	PS/2 Mouse	PS/2 Clock	17		No connection
8		Ground	18	Infrared	IR Receive
9		No connection	19		Ground
10		+5V	20		IR Transmit

Intel 865G Motherboard

The Intel 865G chipset, designed for the Intel Pentium D processor (compatible with the lead free version of Intel 865G Chipsets supporting socket LGA775) and the Intel Pentium 4 processor supporting Hyper-Threading Technology, is a highly flexible and scalable solution that meets a broad range of demanding computing needs. The 865G chipset offers solid performance through a variety of exciting features, including dual-channel DDR 400 main memory, an 800 MHz system bus, and an integrated graphics controller with Intel Extreme Graphics 2 technology.

Chipset Features

Features	*Benefits*
800/533/400 MHz system bus	Platform longevity with support for Intel® Pentium D processor 805 and 820 sequence, delivering improved system bandwidth.
Supports Hyper-Threading Technology	Delivers increased system responsiveness and performance.
Intel Extreme Graphics 2 technology	Fourth-generation graphics architecture supports the latest APIs, allowing software developers to create real-life environments and characters.
Intel Accelerated Hub Architecture	Dedicated data paths deliver maximum bandwidth for I/O-intensive applications.
Dual-Channel DDR 400/333/266 SDRAM	Flexible memory technology allows a full spectrum of DDR usage from incredible performance to more cost-effective systems.
Intel Dynamic Video Output Interface	Two DVO ports offer added display (digital CRT or TV) flexibility through the standard AGP connector.
AGP 8X interface	Increased bandwidth graphics interface enables upgradeability to latest graphics cards.
Integrated high-speed USB 2.0	Eight ports offer up to 40x greater bandwidth over USB 1.1 for a variety of today's demanding high-speed I/O peripherals
Dual independent Serial ATA controllers	Facilitates high-speed storage transfers and easy hard drive upgrades.
Intel RAID technology[PDF 260 KB]	Enables extreme storage performance for Serial ATA hard disks.
Ultra ATA/100	Takes advantage of the existing industry HDD and optical drive interfaces.
AC '97 controller	Supports Dolby* Digital 5.1 surround-sound[1], delivering up to six channels of enhanced sound quality.
Intel® Communication Streaming Architecture	Wire-speed GbE with Dedicated Network Bus (DNB) for performance network connectivity.
Low-power sleep mode	Saves energy.

Intel 910GL Motherboard

The Intel 910GL Express chipset brings compelling new capabilities to the desktop PC. Designed for the Intel Pentium 4 processor supporting Hyper-Threading Technology, the 910GL chipset features a decade's worth of innovation.

Features

Features	*Benefits*
533 MHz system bus	Front Side Bus (FSB) support for high-performance Intel processors and greater system performance.
Supports Hyper-Threading Technology	Increased system responsiveness for multi-tasking.
LGA775 and 478-pin processor package	Supports the highest performance Intel® desktop processors with the flexibility to support 478-pin Intel processors
Intel Graphics Media Accelerator 900 (Intel GMA 900 graphics)	Stunning media, incredible visuals and new 3D capabilities. For business users, Intel validates the chipset, processor, graphics and software stack to provide a well-tested platform with support for Microsoft* Windows 2000, Windows XP, Linux (top distributions) and OS/2 (SciTech).
PCI Express* bus architecture	PCI Express x1 I/O offers 500 MB/s concurrently, over 3.5 times more bandwidth than PCI at 133 MB/s.
Dual-channel DDR	Dual-channel DDR400/DDR333 memory configurable up to 2 GB RAM.
Direct Media Interface (DMI)	For I/O intensive applications, new serial point-to-point bus delivers up to 2.0 GB/s concurrent bandwidth between the memory and I/O controllers, compared to 266 MB/s with previous generation Intel hub architecture.
Intel High Definition Audio	Support for new consumer audio entertainment formats such as 7.1 surround sound, Dolby* Digital, and DTS*. Audio codec support for 192 kHz quality, multiple streams, and better voice input for speech recognition and voice-over-IP.
Intel® Matrix Storage Technology with ICH6R	Boosts storage performance with RAID 0, while helping to protect your digital memories with

	RAID 1, on the same disks. Advanced Host Controller Interface (AHCI) further boosts performance with Native Command Queuing (NCQ), and provides native hot plug for drive swaps.
Four Serial ATA ports (SATA/150)	Integrated serial ATA controller facilitates high-speed data transfers at up to 150 MB/s for each of 4 ports. Allows easier hard drive upgrades and expansion for new SATA optical drives.
Ultra ATA/100	Supports legacy hard drives and optical drives.
High-speed USB 2.0 ports	Eight ports offer up to 40X greater bandwidth over USB 1.1, for high-speed I/O peripherals such as digital video cameras.
Intel Serial Digital Video Output (SDVO) ports	Dual SDVO ports offer maximum display (digital CRT or TV) flexibility through the existing PCI Express* x16 connector.

Intel 915 Motherboard

Platforms based on the Intel 915P Express Chipset and Intel Pentium 4 processor supporting Hyper-Threading Technology1 deliver innovative features and new benefits for both home and business users. The Intel 915P Express Chipset was designed to support the capabilities of Hyper-Threading Technology, adding intelligence to help manage and prioritize multiple threads received from the processor. An HT Technology-enabled platform can improve system performance and responsiveness.

The Intel 915P Express Chipset, based on a new architecture, innovative technologies and high-bandwidth interfaces, is the newest discrete graphics chipset for the Intel Pentium 4 processor family. It was designed to enable the convergence of digital entertainment, as well as enhance bandwidth-intensive applications, such as audio, video, photography, and gaming. It also offers corporate users a high-performance stable platform that enables new levels of business collaboration.

This highly flexible and scalable solution meets a broad range of demanding computing needs. The Intel 915P Express Chipset can deliver maximum system performance through its high-bandwidth interfaces, such as dual-channel DDR2 main memory, 800-MHz system bus, PCI Express* Graphics and I/O architecture, and Hi-Speed USB 2.0 connectivity. PCI Express architecture enables increased bidirectional bandwidth to the graphics and I/O interfaces. With up to 500 MB/s concurrent data transfer rate, it delivers more than three and a half times the I/O bandwidth of traditional PCI architecture. And with up to 4 GB/s per direction PCI Express Graphics capability, it provides more than three and a half times the graphics bandwidth of previous generation discrete graphics controllers.

To support the faster memory, increased graphics requirements, and I/O bandwidth, the

Intel 915P Express Chipset incorporates a new Memory Controller Hub (MCH) backbone architecture. This new design includes wider internal data buses that support dual-channel DDR2 memory technology at 533 MHz or up to 8.5 GB/s of peak memory bandwidth, for improved platform performance. The new architecture also supports both asynchronous and true isochronous data traffic, with dedicated internal pipelines and specialized arbitration. This enables the Intel 915P Express Chipset to take full advantage of the performance of these new high-speed interfaces.

A high speed serial point-to-point bus architecture, known as Direct Media Interface, links the MCH to the sixthgeneration Intel® I/O Controller Hub (ICH6). This new bus delivers up to 2 GB/s concurrent bandwidth, compared with up to 266-MB/s for the previous Intel® hub architecture. Intel 915P Express Chipset-based platforms also enable system design flexibility, with support for both dual-channel DDR and DDR2 memory, discrete PCI Express graphics, and additional platform capabilities via flexible ICH6 options.

The ICH6 component includes several enhancements and new capabilities, and enables system configuration options for digital home usage and business collaboration. It integrates the Intel® High Definition Audio (Intel® HD Audio) technology, featuring eight independent DMA audio engines that support multiple simultaneous and separate audio input and output streams. This enables high quality integrated audio that rivals the performance of high end discrete solutions. Intel HD Audio is also capable of supporting major consumer entertainment industry formats, such as 7.1 surround sound, Dolby Digital, and DTS. An integrated Serial ATA (SATA) controller supports 4 SATA ports, each providing up to 1.5 GB/s (150 MB/s) transfer rates for SATA optical devices or hard drives. And the Advanced Host Controller Interface (AHCI) provides native hot plug and boosts performance with Native Command Queuing (NCQ) for faster boot times and file transfers. The Intel® ICH6R component elevates SATA storage performance to the next level with Intel® Matrix Storage Technology. Enhanced RAID support allows critical data to be stored on one array that is designed for high reliability, while performance intensive applications like games can reside on separate array designed for maximum performance.

Intel 915P Express Chipset features deliver a compelling solution for both consumer and corporate market segments:

- 800-MHz FSB enables support for today's high-performance Intel Pentium 4 processors.
- Optimized for the Intel Pentium 4 Processor with HT Technology, to enable improved system performance and responsiveness.
- Flexible memory support, with dual-channel DDR2 533/DDR2 400 or DDR400/DDR333 memory.
- PCI Express up to 4 GB/s per direction for graphics bandwidth and up to 500 MB/s concurrent data transfers for I/O.
- Intel Matrix Storage Technology, with integrated Raid 0 and Raid 1 capabilities using the latest SATA interface, for accelerated disk I/O performance.

- Intel HD Audio technology's eight independent DMA audio engines can enable multiple separate, simultaneous audio experiences.

Comparision of Various Motherboards

Part #	Description
MB7759	ASUS A8VE-SE, Socket 939 Athlon 64/64 FX, VIA K8T890, PCI Express ATX-Motherboard
MB7758	Asus A8N32-SLI DELUXE Socket 939 for Athlon 64, Athlon 64FX, nVidia nForce4 SLI x16/RAID/2GbE, ATX Motherboard
MB5707	ASUS P5W-DH DELUXE LGA775 CORE2/975X/XFIRE/A/GLAN ATX-Motherboard

SUPERMICRO MOTHERBOARDS

Part #	Description
MB1254	SuperServer 6025B-8R+B - Super X7DB8+ in SC825S2-R700LPB 2U Rackmount(black), Dual 771-pin LGA for Dual-Core Intel Xeon (Woodcrest/ Dempsey), Intel 5000P, Up to 64GB FBDIMM, 8 x SCA SCSI bays, 700W Redundant PS, Low Profile Slots
MB1255	SuperServer 6025B-TR+B - Super X7DBE+ in SC825TQ-R700LPB 2U Rackmount(black), Dual 771-pin LGA for Dual-Core Intel Xeon (Woodcrest/ Dempsey), Intel 5000P, Up to 64GB FBDIMM, 8 x SATA SCSI bays, 700W Redundant PS, Low Proflle Slots
MB1271	SuperServer 6025B-3B - Super X7DB3 in SC825TQ-560LPB 2U Rackmount(black), Dual 771-pin LGA for Dual-Core Intel Xeon (Woodcrest/ Dempsey), Intel 5000P, Up to 32GB FBDIMM, 8 x SAS bays, 560W PS, Low Profile Slots
MB1252	SuperServer 6025B-8B - Super X7DB8 in SC823S-550LP 2U Rackmount(black), Dual 771-pin LGA for Dual-Core Intel Xeon (Woodcrest/ Dempsey), Intel 5000P, Up to 32GB FBDIMM, 6 x SCA SCSI bays, 550W PS, Low Profile Slots
MB1253	SuperServer 6025B-TB - Super X7DBE in SC823TQ-550LP 2U Rackmount(black), Dual 771-pin LGA for Dual-Core Intel Xeon (Woodcrest/ Dempsey), Intel 5000P, Up to 32GB FBDIMM, 6 x SATA bays, 550W PS, Low Profile Slots
MB1279	SuperServer 6015T-TB - Super X7DBT in SC808T-980B 1U Rackmount(black), Dual Node (twin server design) Dual 771-pin LGA for Quad/Dual-Core Intel Xeon and up to 32GB FBDIMM per server, 2 x SATA bays per server, 980W Shared PS

MB1272 SuperServer 6015B-3B - Super X7DBR-3 in SC815TQ-560B 1U Rackmount(black), Dual 771-pin LGA for Dual or Quad-Core Intel Xeon (Clovertown/Woodcrest/Dempsey), Intel 5000P, Up to 32GB FBDIMM, 4 x SAS/SATA bays, 560W PS, PCI-X or PCI Express x8 slot

MB1250 SuperServer 6015B-8+B - Super X7DBR-8+ in SC815S-700 1U Rackmount(black), Dual 771-pin LGA for Dual-Core Intel Xeon (Woodcrest/Dempsey), Intel 5000P, Up to 64GB FBDIMM, 4 x SCA SCSI bays, 700W PS, PCI-X or PCI Express x8 slot

MB1251 SuperServer 6015B-T+B - Super X7DBR-i+ in SC815TQ-700 1U Rackmount(black), Dual 771-pin LGA for Dual-Core Intel Xeon (Woodcrest/Dempsey), Intel 5000P, Up to 64GB FBDIMM, 4 x SATA bays, 700W PS, PCI-X or PCI Express x8 slot

MB1262 SuperServer 6015P-8RB - Super X7DBP-8 in SC816S-700 1U Rackmount(black), Dual 771-pin LGA for Quad/Dual-Core Intel Xeon (Clovertown/Woodcrest/Dempsey), Intel 5000P, Up to 32GB FBDIMM, 4 x SCSI bays, 700W Redundant PS

MB1261 SuperServer 6015P-TRB - Super X7DBP-i in SC816A-700 1U Rackmount(black), Dual 771-pin LGA for Quad/Dual-Core Intel Xeon (Clovertown/Woodcrest/Dempsey), Intel 5000P, Up to 32GB FBDIMM, 4 x SATA bays, 700W Redundant PS

MB12752 SuperServer 6015V-MRB - Super X7DVL-E in Black SC512F-520 Mini-1U Rackmount, Intel 5000V chipset, Dual Quad-Core/Dual-Core Xeon support, Up to 16GB, 1 Internal SATA drive bay, 520W PS, Integrated graphics, 2 x Intel Gigabit LAN ports, 1 x PCI-X Slot

MB1148 SuperServer 6014A-8B - Super X6DAR-8G in SC813S-500 1U Rack (black), Dual Xeon EM64T, Intel E7525, Up to 32GB LP ECC Reg. DDR, 4 x SCA bays, 500W Cold Swap PS, VGA, PCI Express x16 and PCI Exp. x8 or PCI-X LP Slot, Dual Gigabit LAN, Dual U320 SCSI

MB1120 SuperServer 7044H-X8RB - Super X6DH8-XG2 in SC743S1-R760 in Rackmountable Tower (black), Dual Xeon EM64T, Intel E7520, 8 x SCA bays, Up to 16GB ECC Reg. DDR2, Tri-Red. 760W PS, 1xPCI Express x8, 5xPCI-X slots, Dual Gigabit LAN, VGA, Dual U320 SCSI

MB1114 SuperServer 6034H-X8RB - Super X6DH8-XG2 in SC833S-R760 in 3U Rackmount (black), Dual Xeon EM64T, Intel E7520, 8 x SCA bays, Up to 16GB ECC Reg. DDR2, Tri-Red. 760W PS, 1xPCI Express x8, 5xPCI-X slots, Dual Gigabit LAN, VGA, Dual U320 SCSI

MB1152 SuperServer 6024H-i2B - Super X6DHE-G2 in SC823i-550LP 2U Rack (black), Dual Xeon EM64T support, Intel E7520, 6xFixed IDE HDD, Up to 16GB ECC Reg. DDR2, 550W PS, 3xPCI Express/3xPCI-X LP Slots, Dual Gigabit LAN, VGA

MB1154 SuperServer 6024H-iB - Super X6DHE-G2 in SC823i-550LP 2U Rack (black), Dual Xeon EM64T support, Intel E7520, 6xFixed IDE HDD, Up to 32GB ECC Reg. DDR, 550W PS, 3xPCI Express/3xPCI-X LP Slots, Dual Gigabit LAN, VGA

MB1130 SuperServer 6024H-82RB - Super X6DH8-G2 in SC823S-R500RC 2U Rack (black), Dual Xeon EM64T, Intel E7520, 6xSCA HDD, Up to 16GB ECC Reg. DDR2, 500W Redundant PS, 3 x PCI-X Slot Riser, Dual Gigabit LAN, VGA, Dual U320 SCSI

MB1150 SuperServer 6024H-8RB - Super X6DH8-G in SC823S-R500LP 2U Rack (black), Dual Xeon EM64T, Intel E7520, 6xSCA HDD, Up to 32GB ECC Reg. DDR, 500W Redundant PS, 2xPCI Express/3xPCI-X/1xPCI LP Slots, Dual Gigabit LAN, VGA, Dual U320 SCSI

MB1158 SuperServer 6024H-TRB - Super X6DHT-G in SC823T-R500LP 2U Rack (black), Dual Xeon EM64T, Intel E7520, 6xSATA HDD, Up to 32GB ECC Reg. DDR, 500W Redundant PS, 2xPCI Express/3xPCI-X/1xPCI LP Slots, Dual Gigabit LAN, SATA RAID, VGA

MB1134 SuperServer 6014H-X8B - Super X6DHR-X8G in SC813S-500 1U Rackmount (black), Dual Xeon EM64T, Intel E7520, Up to 32GB LP ECC Reg. DDR, 4 x SCA bays, 500W Cold Swap PS, VGA, 2 x PCI-X Slots (Full + LP), Dual Gigabit LAN, Dual U320 SCSI

MB1133 SuperServer 6014H-82B - Super X6DHR-8G2 in SC813S-500 1U Rackmount (black), Dual Xeon EM64T, Intel E7520, Up to 16GB LP ECC Reg. DDR2, 4 x SCA bays, 500W Cold Swap PS, VGA, PCI Express x8 or PCI-X Slot, Dual Gigabit LAN, Dual U320 SCSI

MB1144 SuperServer 6014H-8B - Super X6DHR-8G in SC813S-500 1U Rackmount (black), Dual Xeon EM64T, Intel E7520, Up to 32GB LP ECC Reg. DDR, 4 x SCA bays, 500W Cold Swap PS, VGA, PCI Express x8 or PCI-X Slot, Dual Gigabit LAN, Dual U320 SCSI

MB1136 SuperServer 6014H-XiB - Super X6DHR-XiG in SC812i-420 1U Rackmount (black), Dual Xeon EM64T, Intel E7520, Up to 32GB LP ECC Reg. DDR, 3 x IDE bays, 420W Cold Swap PS, VGA, 2 x PCI-X Slots (Full + LP), Dual Gigabit LAN

MB1138 SuperServer 6014H-i2B - Super X6DHR-iG2 in SC812i-420 1U Rackmount (black), Dual Xeon EM64T, Intel E7520, Up to 16GB LP ECC Reg. DDR2, 3 x IDE bays, 420W Cold Swap PS, VGA, PCI Express x8 or PCI-X Slot, Dual Gigabit LAN

MB1146 SuperServer 6014H-iB - Super X6DHR-iG in SC812i-420 1U Rackmount (black), Dual Xeon EM64T, Intel E7520, Up to 32GB LP ECC Reg. DDR, 3 x IDE bays, 420W Cold Swap PS, VGA, PCI Express x8 or PCI-X Slot, Dual Gigabit LAN

MB1140 SuperServer 6014H-TB - Super X6DHR-TG in SC813T-500 1U Rackmount (black), Dual Xeon EM64T, Intel E7520, Up to 32GB LP ECC Reg. DDR, 4 x SATA bays, 500W Cold Swap PS, VGA, PCI Express x8 or PCI-X Slot, Dual Gigabit LAN

MB1141 SuperServer 6014P-8RB - Super X6DHP-8G in SC814S-R560 1U Rackmount (black), Dual Xeon EM64T, Intel E7520, Up to 24GB LP ECC Reg. DDR, 4 x SCA bays, 560W Hot Swap Redundant PS, VGA, PCI Express x8 or PCI-X Slot, Dual Gigabit LAN, Dual U320 SCSI

MB1143 SuperServer 6014P-82RB - Super X6DHP-8G2 in SC814S-R560 1U Rack (black), Dual Xeon EM64T, Intel E7520, Up to 16GB LP ECC Reg. DDR2, 4 x SCA bays, 560W Redundant PS, VGA, PCI Express x8 or PCI-X Slot, Dual Gigabit, Dual U320 SCSI

MB1185 SuperServer 6014P-TRB - Super X6DHP-TG in SC814+T-R560 1U Rackmount (black), Dual Xeon EM64T, Intel E7520, Up to 24GB LP ECC Reg. DDR, 4 x SATA bays, 560W Redundant PS, VGA, PCI Express x8 or PCI-X Slot, Dual Gigabit LAN, Marvell 4-port SATA

MB1118 SuperServer 7044A-82RB - Super X6DA8-G2 in SC942i-R760 Rackmountable Tower (black), Dual Xeon EM64T support, Intel E7525, Up to 16GB ECC Reg. DDR2, Tri-Red. 760W PS, PCI Express x16, Dual Gigabit LAN, Audio, Dual U320 SCSI

MB1035 Super P8SGA, Socket 775 P4, 0/4GB Dual Channel DDR400, Intel 915G Express (Grantsdale), Integrated Intel GMA 900 Graphics, (1)PCI Express x16 Slot (3)PCI Exp. x1 Slots (3)32-bit PCI Slots, Intel 82541GI Gig.LAN, (4) Serial ATA ports, ATX

MB1050 Super X6DA8-G2, Dual Socket 604 for Xeon 800MHz (EM64T), 0/16GB DDR2, 8x240-pin DIMM, Intel E7525 chipset, (1)PCI Express x16 Slot (1)PCI Exp. x4 Slot (3)64-bit PCI-X and (1)32-bit PCI Slots, Dual Gigabit LAN, Audio, Dual U320 SCSI, Ext ATX

MB1051 Super X6DAE-G2, Dual Socket 604 for Xeon 800MHz (EM64T), 0/16GB DDR2, 8x240-pin DIMM, Intel E7525 chipset, (1)PCI Express x16 Slot (1)PCI Exp. x4 Slot (3)64-bit PCI-X and (1)32-bit PCI Slots, Intel 82546GB Dual Gigabit LAN, Integrated Audio, Ext ATX

MB1052 Super X6DA8-G, Dual Socket 604 for Xeon 800MHz (EM64T), 0/32GB DDR, 8x184-pin DIMM, Intel E7525 chipset, Adaptec 2-CH Ultra320 SCSI, Gigabit LAN, Ext. ATX - Motherboard only

MB1055 Super X6DAT-G, Dual Socket 604 for Xeon 800MHz (EM64T), 0/32GB DDR, 8x184-pin DIMM, Intel E7525 chipset, Marvell SATA, Gigabit LAN, Ext. ATX - Motherboard only

MB1058 Super X6DAi-G, Dual Socket 604 for Xeon 800MHz (EM64T), 0/32GB DDR,

8x184-pin DIMM, Intel E7525 chipset, IDE, Gigabit LAN, Ext. ATX - Motherboard only

MB1053 Super X6DAL-TG, Dual Socket 604 for Xeon 800MHz (EM64T), 0/24GB DDR, 6x184-pin DIMM, Intel E7525 chipset, Marvell SATA, Gigabit LAN, ATX - Motherboard only

MB1056 Super X6DAL-XTG, Dual Socket 604 for Xeon 800MHz (EM64T), 0/24GB DDR, 6x184-pin DIMM, Intel E7525 chipset, Marvell SATA, Gigabit LAN, ATX - Motherboard only

MB1057 Super X6DAL-XG, Dual Socket 604 for Xeon 800MHz (EM64T), 0/24GB DDR, 6x184-pin DIMM, Intel E7525 chipset, IDE, Gigabit LAN, ATX - Motherboard only

MB1054 Super X6DAL-G, Dual Socket 604 for Xeon 800MHz (EM64T), 0/24GB DDR, 6x184-pin DIMM, Intel E7525 chipset, 2xSATA ports (RAID), (1)PCI Express x16 Slot (1)PCI Exp. x8 Slot (2)64-bit PCI-X and (2)32-bit PCI Slots, 82541GI Gigabit LAN, Audio, ATX

MB1061 Super X6DHE-G2, Dual Socket 604 for Xeon 800MHz (EM64T), Intel E7520 chipset, IDE, Dual Gigabit LAN, Ext. ATX - Motherboard only

MB1062 Super X6DH8-G2, Dual Socket 604 for Xeon 800MHz (EM64T), Intel E7520 chipset, Adaptec 2-CH Ultra320 SCSI, Dual Gigabit LAN, Ext. ATX - Motherboard only

MB1063 Super X6DHE-XG2, Dual Socket 604 for Xeon 800MHz (EM64T), Intel E7520 chipset, IDE, Dual Gigabit LAN, Ext. ATX - Motherboard only

MB1064 Super X6DH8-XG2, Dual Socket 604 for Xeon 800MHz (EM64T), Intel E7520 chipset, Adaptec 2-CH Ultra320 SCSI, Dual Gigabit LAN, Ext. ATX - Motherboard only

MB1065 Super X6DH8-G, Dual Socket 604 for Xeon 800MHz (EM64T), Intel E7520 chipset, Adaptec 2-CH Ultra320 SCSI, Dual Gigabit LAN, Ext. ATX - Motherboard only

MB1066 Super X6DHE-G, Dual Socket 604 for Xeon 800MHz (EM64T), Intel E7520 chipset, IDE, Dual Gigabit LAN, Ext. ATX - Motherboard only

MB1070 Super X6DVA-EG, Dual Socket 604 for Xeon 800MHz (EM64T), Intel E7320 chipset, IDE, Dual Gigabit LAN, ATX - Motherboard only

MB1071 Super X6DVA-4G, Dual Socket 604 for Xeon 800MHz (EM64T)0, Intel E7320 chipset, SCSI, Dual Gigabit LAN, ATX - Motherboard only

MB1008 Super P4SCA, Socket 478 for P4 (Hyper-Threading), 0/4GB Dual-Channel DDR400, 4xDIMMs, Intel E7210 chipset, 800/533/400MHz FSB, 4xPCI/3xISA Slots, Integrated VGA, 2xUSB 2.0, SATA RAID 0, Intel Gigabit LAN, ATX - Motherboard only

TYAN MOTHERBOARDS

Part #	Description
MB7028	Tyan Thunder K8S Pro (S2882G3NR-D) Dual Opteron w/ Dual Core Support, AMD-8131/8111, 0/16GB ECC Reg. DDR333/266, 8x184-pin DIMMs, 4x64-bit PCI-X, 1x32-bit PCI, SATA RAID, Dual Gigabit + 10/100 LAN, Ext. ATX - Motherboard Only
MB7030	Tyan Thunder K8S Pro (S2882UG3NR-D) Dual Opteron w/ Dual Core Support, AMD-8131/8111, 0/16GB ECC Reg. DDR333/266, 8x184-pin DIMMs, 4x64-bit 133MHz PCI-X, 1x32-bit PCI, SATA RAID, Dual Gigabit + 10/100 LAN, AIC7902W U320 SCSI - Motherboard Only

12 Power Supplies

SMPS (Switched Mode Power Supplies)

Power Supplies

Every electronic system, whether it is a laboratory measuring instrument like an oscilloscope or a commercial system like a laser printer, a photocopier or a home entertainment appliance like color TV or personal computer, is invariably powered by a dc source. These dc supplies provide regulated output voltage against mains voltage and load current variations. Commonly power supplies are classified as ac/dc linear power supplies, dc/dc converters and dc/ac inverters, Based on regulation techniques, power supplies are classified as linear and switched mode power supplies.

Linear Power Supplies

ac/dc linear power supply comprises a transformer, rectifier, filter and a regulator. Any change in the output voltage due to change in input voltage or load current will result in a change in voltage drop across the regulator transistor (series type) or a change in the current through the regulator transistor (shunt type) so as to maintain a constant voltage across the load. The transistors in these linear systems dissipate a lot of energy as heat and reduces the efficiency. Elaborate heat sinking provisions are also necessary.

Switched Mode Power Supplies

The primary power received from the ac mains is rectified and filtered as high voltage dc. It is then Chopped at a high frequency (10 to 100 kHz) using a bipolar transistor and fed to the primary side of a step-down transformer. As this transformer is operating at a very high frequency, its size and weight are very small compared to a transformer operating at 50/60 Hz. The transformed chopped waveform is rectified and filtered at the secondary side. A sample of the output voltage is used as feedback signal for driving the switching transistor which provide the regulation.

Most switching power supplies regulate their output using a method called Pulse Width Modulation. The power switch which feeds the primary side of the step-down transformer is driven by a pulse width modulated oscillator, As the load increases, output voltage tends to fall. The PWM control senses the change and increases the torn 'ON' time of the transistor.

Increased turn 'ON' time means increased stored energy i.e. maximum amount of energy will be passed through the transformer and the output voltage will be maintained. Similarly an increase in the output voltage causes a reduction in the 'ON' time and reduces the amount of energy passing through the transformer until the output voltage is maintained at original value.

The width or the 'ON' time of the oscillator is controlled by the voltage feedback from the secondary rectifier output which forms a closed loop regulator, Most switching supplies ate required to produce more than one regulated dc voltage, Example include supplies for television receivers and personal computers.

Switched Mode Power Supply vs Linear Power Supply

Linear power supplies are good at line regulation, load regulation, low output voltage ripples and almost negligible RF interference. The factors in favour of a SMPS are high efficiency as well as small weight and size. High efficiency is obtained because of less wastage of power when supply is regulated. Operations at high frequencies reduce the size of the transformer for the same power operating at mains frequency. RF radiation due to switching of currents and high ripple output are the disadvantages of SMPS. RF radiation can be reduced by shielding the core as well as the entire unit.

The following table shows the comparison.

Sl. No.	*Terms*	*Switched Mode Power Supply*	*Linear Power Supply*
1.	Efficiency	65-75 %	25-50 %
2.	Temperature rise	20-40 deg. cen	50-100 deg cen
3.	Ripple volts	Higher 25 to 50 mV	Even 5 mV possible
4.	Overall regulation	0.3 % is common (% drop of volts)	Even 0.1%possible
5.	RF interference	Can be a problem unless properly shield	None
6.	Magnetic material	Ferrite core	Steel core
7.	Weight	About 60 watts per kg	20-30 watts per kg
8.	Cost	More parts, special ones, increase the cost	Advantage for small units up to 10 W to 15 W, but cost is higher if bigger.
9.	Reliability	Depends on the availability of suitable transistors	More reliable

SMPS for Computers

A PC needs power at two different voltage levels and both positive and negative polarities: +5 V dc, + 12 V dc, -5 V dc and -2 V dc. The power supply has to provide power at ail these

4 voltage levels. Most power is needed at +5 V dc which is needed by most of the electronic circuitry. A fair mount of power is also required at +12 V dc to operate the disk drive motors. The -5 V dc level is designed for dynamic memory bias voltage. The -12 V dc is primarily used by the RS 232C serial port. All four power levels are bused across the system unit expansion slots.

Power Requirements in PCS

The total power requirements of a PC depend upon the components within it. Each component will draw a certain quantity of current at each of the supply voltage it uses. Some components will draw different current depending on what they are doing. For example, a diskette drive will draw more current when die motor is running and when the heads are moving. High capacity disk drives having several platters and heads will draw more current than lower capacity drives.

The following table shows the power requirement in PCs.

Sl. No.	*System Component*	*Power Required*
1.	Motherboard	35 W
2.	Keyboard	2 W
3.	Floppy drive	5 W {during idle)
		10 W (during spinning)
4.	Hard disk drive	35 W
5.	Multi I/O card	4 W
6.	Floppy/Hard disk drive controller	8 W
7.	Display adopter	5 W

AT Power Supply

It outputs a power good signal which is used by the SMPS to indicate the motherboard that all the outputs from power supply are at the correct level and safe for use by the compuer.

ATX Power Supply

It adds two new signals PW_ON (power on) and +5V SB (Standby) for the new generation of computers. Power On signal is used by the motherboard to switch on/off the power supply. This signal allows the motherboard to control the power supply. Motherboard can put the system in stanby by switching off the power supply, and shift back to normal operation by restoring the power.

"+5V standby" is not controlled by the "power on" signal, it is used to provide power to the motherboard when the system is in standby mode and the main voltages from the power supply has been switched off.

Principle

When Power Supply is turned on, it generates a power good signal which indicates that there is adequate power for processing. When the output voltages are above the minimum sense level, a TTL compatible high level (2.4V DC to 5V DC) is generated on the power good line. The power good signal has a turn-on delay of about 100 ms after the output voltages have reached their respective levels.

13 BIOS

Introduction to BIOS

BIOS stands for Basic Input/Output System also incorrectly known as Basic Integrated Operating System and occasionally Built In Operating System. BIOS refers to the firmware code run by an IBM compatible PC when first powered on. The primary function of the BIOS is to prepare the machine so other software programs stored on various media (such as hard drives, floppies, and CDs) can load, execute, and assume control of the PC. This process is known as booting up.

BIOS can also be said to be a coded program embedded on a chip that recognizes and controls various devices that make up the PC. The term BIOS is specific to personal computer vendors. Among other classes of computers, the generic terms boot monitor, boot loader or boot ROM are commonly used. Boot is short for bootstrapping.

The term first appeared in the CP/M operating system, describing the part of CP/M loaded during boot time that interfaced directly with the hardware (CP/M machines usually had a simple boot loader in ROM, and nothing else). Most versions of DOS have a file called "IBMBIO.COM" or "IO.SYS" that is analogous to the CP/M disk BIOS.

CMOS

Complementary metal–oxide–semiconductor (CMOS) is a major class of integrated circuits. CMOS technology is used in chips such as microprocessors, microcontrollers, static RAM, and other digital logic circuits. CMOS technology is also used for a wide variety of analog circuits such as image sensors, data converters, and highly integrated transceivers for many types of communication.

CMOS is also sometimes explained as complementary-symmetry metal–oxide–semiconductor. The words "complementary-symmetry" refer to the fact that the typical digital design style with CMOS uses complementary and symmetrical pairs of p-type and n-type MOSFETs for logic functions.

Two important characteristics of CMOS devices are high noise immunity and low static power supply drain. Significant power is only drawn when its transistors are switching between on and off states; consequently, CMOS devices do not produce as much heat as other forms of logic such as TTL (transistor-transistor logic). CMOS also allows a high density of logic functions on a chip.

The triple compound "metal–oxide–semiconductor" is a reference to the nature of the physical structure of early (and interestingly now, the very latest) field-effect transistors, having a metal gate electrode placed on top of an oxide insulator, which in turn is on top of a semiconductor material. Instead of metal, current gate electrodes (including those up to the 65 nanometer technology node) are almost always made from a different material, polysilicon, but the terms MOS and CMOS nevertheless continue to be used for the modern descendants of the original process. Metal gates have made a comeback with the advent of high-k dielectric materials in the CMOS transistor as announced by IBM and Intel for the 45 nanometer node and beyond.

The combination of MEMS sensors with digital signal processors on one single CMOS chip is sometimes known an CMOSens.

CMOS Setup

Select the Standard CMOS Setup from the AMIBIOS Setup Main Menu. Various options in this Standard Setup are described below:

Floppy Drive A: and B:

Move the cursor to these fields and select the floppy type. The settings are:

360 KB 5¼ inch

1.2 MB 5¼ inch

720 KB 3½ inch

2.88 MB 3½ inch

Primary Master/Primary Slave/Secondary Master/Secondary Slave

Select these options to configure the drive named in the option. Select Auto Detect IDE to let AMIBIOS automatically configure the drive.

A screen with a list of drive parameters appears

Click OK to configure the drive

Type	How to Configure
SCSI	Select Type. Select Not Installed to the drive parameter screen. The SCSI drivers provided by the SCSI manufacturer should allow you to configure the SCSI drive.
IDE	Select Typ. Select Auto to let AMIBIOS determine the parameters, Click on OK when AMIBIOS displays the drive parameters.
	Select LBA Mode. Select On if the drive has a capacity greater than 540 MB.
	Select Block Mode. Select On to allow block mode data transfers.

	Select 32-bit Mode. Select On to allow 32-bit data transfers.
	Select the PIO Mode. It is best to select Auto to allow AMIBIOS to determine the PIO mode. If you select a PIO mode that is not supported by the IDE drive, the drve will not work properly. If you are absolutely certain that you know the drive's PIO mode, select PIO mode 0-4, as appropriate.
CD-ROM	Select Type. Select CD-ROM.
	Click on OK when AMIBIOS displays the drive parameters.
Standard MFM	Select Type. You must know the drive parameters.
	Select the drive type that exactly matches your drive's parameters.
Non-Standard MFM	Select Type. If the drive parameters do not match the drive parameters listed for drive types 1 - 46, select User and enter the correct hard disk drive parameters.

Entering Drive Parameters

Parameter	Description
Type	The number for a drive with certain identification parameters.
Cyclinders	The number of cylinders in the disk drive.
Heads	The number of heads
Write Precompensation	The actual physical size of a sector gets progressively smaller as the track diameter diminishes. Yet each sector must still hold 512 bytes. Write precompensation circuitry on the hard disk compensates for the physical difference in secor size by booting the right current for sectors on inner tracks. This parameter is the track number on the disk surface where write precompensation begins.
Landing Zone	This number is the cylinder location where the heads normally park when the system is shut down.
Sectors	Sectors is the smallest unit of storage on a disk. It is usually 512 bytes in size.
Capacity	The formatted capacity of the drive is the number of heads time sthe number of cylinders times the number of sectors per track times 512 (bytes per sector). Heads x Cylinders x Sectors/track x 512

Advanced CMOS Setup

Under the advanced section, you can setup the following:

Quick Boot: Set this option to Enabled to instruct AMIBIOS to boot quickly when the computer is powered on.

1st Boot Device: This option sets the type of device for the first boot drivers that the AMIBIOS attempts to boot from after AMIBIOS POST completes. The setting are Disabled, Network, Optical, SCSI, CD-ROM, IDE-0, IDE-1, IDE-2 or IDE-3. The Optimal and Fail-Safe default settings are IDE-0.

2nd Boot Device: This option sets the type of device for the second boot drives that the AMIBIOs attempts to boot after AMIBIOS POST completes. The settings are Disabled, Floppy or IDE-0. The Optimal and Fail-Safe default settings are Floppy.

3rd Boot Device: This option sets the type of device for the third boot drives that the AMIBIOS attempts to boot from after AMIBIOS POST completes. The settings are Disabled, CD-ROM or IDE-0. The optimal and Fail-Safe default settings are CD-ROM.

Try Other Boot Devices: Set this option to Yest to instruct AMIBIOS to attempt to boot from any other drive in the system if it cannot find a boot drive among the drives specified in the 1st Boot Device, 2nd Boot Device, 3rd Boot Device options.

Initial Display Mode: Set this option to BIOS for initial display mode by BIOS. Options are BIOS or Silent.

Display Mode at add-on ROM Nit: Set the display mode at add-on ROM Nit. Settings are Force or Keep Current.

Floppy Access Control: This option specifies the Read/Write access that is set when booting from a floppy drive. The settings are Read/Write or Read-only. The Optimal and Fail-Safe default settings are Read/Write.

Hard Disk Access Control: This option specifies the Read/Write access that is set when booting from a hard disk drive. The settings are Read/Write or Read-Only. The Optimal and Fail-Safe default settings are Read/Write.

S.M.A.R.T. for Hard Disks: Set this option to Enable to permit AMIBIS to use the SMART (System Management and Reporting Technologies) protocol for reporting server system information over a network. The settings are Enabled and Disaled. The Optimal and Fail-Safe default settings are Disabled.

Voot Up Num Lock: Set the option to Off to turn the Num Lock Key off when the computer boots up so you can use the arrow keys on both the numeric keyboard and the keypad. The settings are On or Off. The default settings are On.

PS/2 Mosue Support: Set this option to enable AMIBIOS support for a PS/2 mouse. The settings are Enabled or Disabled. The Optimal and Fail-Safe default settings are Enabled

Primary Display: This option configures the type of monitor attached to the computer. The settings are Mono, CGA 40x25, cga 80x25, VGA/EGA or Absent. The Optimal and Fail-Safe default settings are VGA/EGA.

Password Check: This option enables password checking when system boots up or when AMIBIOS Setup is run. Settings are Setup or Always.

Boot To OS/2>64MB: Set this option to Enables if running OS/2 operating system and using more than 64 MB of system memory on the motherboard. The settings are Enabled or Disable. The Optimal and Fail-Safe default settings are Disabled.

CPU Serial Number: Set this option to Enabled to display the CPU Serial Number. The settings are Enabled or Disabled. The Optimal and Fail-Safe default settings are Disabled.

System BIOS Cacheable: When set to Enabled, the contents of the F0000h system memory segment can be read from or written to cache memory. The contents of this memory segment are always copied from the BIOS ROM to System RAM for faster execution. The settings are Enabled or Disabled. The Optimal default setting is Enabled. The Fail-Safe default setting is Disabled.

C000, 16K Shadow, C400, 16K Shadow: This option specifies how the 32 KB of Video ROM at C0000h is treated. The settings are:

Setting	***Description***
Disabled	The contents of the video ROM are not copied to RAM.
Enabled	The contents of the video ROM area from C0000h - C7FFFh are copied (shadowed) from ROM to RAM for faster execution.
Cached	The contents of the video ROM area from C0000h - C7FFFh are copied from ROM to RAM and can be written to or read from cache memory.

C800, 16K Shadow, CC00, 16K Shadow, D000, 16K Shadow, D400, 16K Shadow, D800, 16K Shadow, DC00: These options enable shawoing of the contents of the ROM aread named in the option. The ROM area not used by ISA adapter cards is allocated to PCI adapter cards. The settings are:

Setting	***Description***
Disabled	The contents of the video ROM are not copied to RAM.
Enabled	The contents of the video ROM area from C0000h - C7FFFh are copied (shadowed) from ROM to RAM for faster execution.
Cached	The contents of the video ROM area from C0000h - C7FFFh are copied from ROM to RAM and can be written to or read from cache memory.

Advanced Chipset Setup

Choose Advanced Chipset Setup on the aMIBIOS Setup Main Menu, all Chipset Setup options are then displayed.

DRAM Tras/Trc Cycle Time <SCLKs>: This option specifies the length of the DRAM TRAS/TRC Cycle time. The settings are 5/7 or 6/8. The Optimal and Fail-Safe default settings are 5/7.

Address Setup Time <SCLKs>: This option specifies the address setup time. The settings are Auto (BIOS automtically decide the optimal delay) or Manual. The Optimal and Fail-Safe default settings are Auto.

CAS# Latency <SCLKs>: This option sets the latency period for the CAS signal. The settings are 2 CLKs or 3 CLKs. The Optimal and Fail-Safe default settings are 3 CLKs.

SDRAM RAS# To CAS# delay <SCLKs>: This option specifies the length of the RAS precharge part of the DRAM system memory access. The settings are 2 CLKs or 3 CLKs. The Optimal and Fail-Safe default settings are 3 CLKs.

SDRAM RAS# Precharge: This option specifies the length of the RAS precharge part of the DRAM system memory access cycle when DRAM system memory is installed in this computer. The settings are 2 CLKs or 3 CLKs or Auto. The Optimal and Fail-Safe default settings are 3 CLKs.

DRAM page closing Policy: This option sets the DRAM Page closing Policy. The settings are Closed or Open.

CPU Latency Timer: This option specifies the latency for the Timer. The settings are Disabled or Enabled. The Optimal and Fail-Safe default settings are Disabled.

Memory Hole: This option specifies the location of an area of memory that cannot be addressed on the PCI bus. The settings are Disabled, 15MB - 16 MB. The Optimal and Fail-Safe default settings are Disabled.

CPU BIST Enable: This option specifies the CPU BIST settings. The settings are Disabled and Enabled. The Optimal and Fail-Safe default settings are Disabled.

ICH Delayed Transaction: This option specifies the ICH Delay Transaction settings. The settings are Disabled and Enabled. The Optimal and Fail-Safe default settings are Disabled.

ICH DCB Enable: This option specifies the ICH DCB Enable settings. The settings are Disabled and Enabled. The Optimal and Fail-Safe default settings are Disabled.

Graphic Mode Select: This option specifies the Graphics Mode settings. The settings are UMA, 1MB or UMA 512 KB. The Optimal and Fail-Safe default settings are UMA 1MB.

Display Cache Window Size: This option specifies the Display Windows Size. The settings are 64MB or 32MB. The Optimal and Fail-Safe default settings are 64MB.

Initialize Display Cache Memory: This option specifies the Initialize Display Cache Memory.

The settings are Disabled and Enabled. The Optimal and Fail-Safe default settings are Enabled.

Paging Mode Control: This option specifies the control of Paging Mode. The settings are Close and Open. The Optimal and Fail-Safe default settings are Close.

RAS-to-CAS: This option specifies the RAS-to-CAS settings. The settings are Default or Overdue. The Optimal and Fail-Safe default settings are Default.

CAS Latency: This option specifies the CAS Latency settings. The settings are Slow or Fast. The Optimal and Fail-Safe default settings are Slow.

RAS Timing: This option specifies the RAM Timing settings. The settings are Slow or Fast. The Optimal and Fail-Safe default settings are Slow.

RAS Recharge Timing: This option specifies the RAS Precharge Timing. The settings are Slow or Fast. The Optimal and Fail-Safe default settings are Slow.

BIOS Boot Process

The BIOS runs off the PROM, EPROM or, most commonly, flash memory when the computer is powered on. It initializes several motherboard components and peripherals, including:

- the clock generator,
- the processors and caches,
- the chipset (memory controller and I/O controller),
- the system memory,
- all PCI devices (by assigning bus numbers and resources),
- the primary graphics controller,
- mass storage controllers (such as SATA and IDE controllers),
- various I/O controllers (such keyboard/mouse and USB).

Finally, it loads the boot loader for the operating system, and transfers control to it. The entire process is known as Power-on self-test (POST). On the original IBM PC, the hardware only needed minimal configuration and POST was indeed used for testing; on modern systems, most of POST actually consists of hardware configuration.

Once system memory is initialized, the BIOS typically copies/decompresses itself into that memory and keeps executing from it.

Nearly all BIOS implementations can optionally execute a setup program interfacing the nonvolatile BIOS memory (CMOS). This memory holds user-customizable configuration data (time, date, hard drive details, etc.) accessed by BIOS code. The 80x86 source code for early PC and AT BIOS was included with the IBM Technical Reference Manual.

In most modern BIOS implementations, users select which device boots first: CD, hard disk, floppy disk, flash keydrive and the like. This is particularly useful for installing operating systems or booting to Live CDs, and for selecting the order of testing for the presence of bootable media.

Some BIOS's allow the user to select the operating system to load (e.g. load another OS from the second hard disk), though this is more often handled by a second-stage boot loader.

Boot Disk

A boot disk is a removable digital data storage medium, normally read-only, that can load (boot) an operating system or utility program. Boot disks may create and use a RAM disk for temporary file storage, to eliminate the need to write to the fixed storage media of the computer where the boot disk is used.

Boot disks are used for:

- Operating system installation.
- Data recovery.
- Hardware or software troubleshooting.
- Customizing an operating environment.
- Software demonstration.
- Administrative access in case of lost password (a Windows boot disk does not always permit this, but a Linux or specialist boot disk can sometimes be used for this purpose instead, even if only Windows is installed)

Floppy disks and CD-ROMs are the most common forms of media used, but other media, such as tape drives, zip drives and more recently, USB flash drives can be used. What can be booted depends on whether a computer's BIOS supports booting from that device. For example, some BIOSes do not support booting from a CD-ROM and require a boot floppy to run the software from the CD-ROM.

Boot Floppies

Bootable floppies for PCs usually contain MS-DOS or miniature versions of Linux. The most commonly available floppy disk can hold only 1.44MB of data in its standard format, making it impractical for loading large operating systems. The use of boot floppies is in decline, due to the availability of other higher-capacity options, such as CD-ROMs or USB flash drives.

Booting from a Disk

A modern PC is configured to attempt to boot from various devices in a certain order. If your computer is not booting from the device you desire, such as the floppy drive, you must nter the BIOS setup function, by pressing a special key when the computer is first turned n — Delete, F1, F2, F10 or F12. There will be a menu option for changing the boot order.

lodern Apple computers will boot from an appropriate disk if the user presses the C key hile the machine is starting.

equired Files

Vindows 95/98, Me, NT/2000/XP/2003 Floppy Boot Disk (MS-DOS)

- COMMAND.COM
- IO.SYS
- MSDOS.SYS

long with the boot files, usually a Boot sector is also required. This is generally created ith the same tool that prepares the boot disk, such as SYS.EXE in early Windows systems.

isk Partitioning

 computer operating systems, disk partitioning is the creation of logical divisions upon a ard disk that allows one to apply operating system-specific logical formatting.

 layman's terms, partitioning a hard drive can make it appear to be more than one hard rive. Thus, a single physical hard disk drive may host several logical drives.

artitioning a hard disk drive defines specific areas (the partitions) within the disk. A partition ay constitute an entire logical drive or it may form part of a larger virtual drive which could pan over several partitions and hard disks.

Vithin a partition, a file system may be created for the storage of files, or a partition may be sed for other purposes, such as swap space for those operating systems that support swap partitions".

urpose

artitioning makes it possible to create several file systems (either of the same type or ifferent) on a single hard disk. This has many benefits, including:

- The use of multi-booting setups, which allow users have more than one operating system on a single computer. For example, one could install Linux, Mac OS X, Microsoft Windows or others onto different partitions of the same hard disk (so they don't conflict) and have a choice of booting into any operating system (supported by the hardware) at power-up.
- Sharing swap partitions between multiple Linux distributions, so such partitions use less hard drive space.
- Protecting or isolating files, to make it easier to recover a corrupted file system or operating system installation.

- Raising overall computer performance. For instance, large hard drives with onl one NTFS filesystem typically have a very large Master File Table (MFT), and i generally takes more time to read this MFT than the MFTs of hard drives with multiple partitions (because each partition has fewer files).
- Higher levels of data organization, raising the user efficiency of the system, fo example separate partitions dedicated to digital movie processing, photos, emai mailboxes or browser cache.

Partitions may be customized to different requirements, for example, allowing for read-only partitions to protect data: if one partition is damaged, none of the other file systems are affected, and the drive's data may still be salvageable.

PC BIOS Partition Types

This section describes partitions as used in MS-DOS, Microsoft Windows and Linux or PC compatible computer systems; for examples of partitioning schemes used in othe operating systems, see Slice (disk) and BSD disklabel. Technically, a hard disk shoul contain either as many as four primary partitions, or one to three primaries along with a *single extended partition*. *Each of these partitions* are described by a 16-byte entry in the Partition Table which is located in the Master Boot Record.

The "type" of a partition is identified by a 1-byte code found in its partition table entry. Some of these codes (such as 0x05 and 0x0F) may be used to indicate the presence of a extended partition, but most are used by operating systems that examine partition tables t decide if a partition contains a file system they can mount/access for reading or writin data.

Once a specific partition's type has been identified, additional information about its purpose and probable contents may be found (see: Andries Brouwer. List of partition identifiers fo PCs. as one such resource). For example, some type codes are used to hide a partition's contents from various operating systems. However, if an OS or some partitioning tool ha been programmed to also examine the boot sectors of any partition, then its file system may no longer remain hidden. There are no officially assigned partition types; thus, more than one kind of file system may lay claim to the same code value.

Primary (or Logical)

A primary (or logical) partition contains one file system. In MS-DOS and earlier versions c Microsoft Windows systems, the first partition (C:) must be a "primary partition". Othe operating systems may not share this limitation; however, this can depend on other factors such as a PC's BIOS.

The "partition type" code for a primary or logical partition can either correspond to a fil system contained within (e.g. 0x07 means either an NTFS or an OS/2 HPFS file system or indicate the partition has a special use (e.g. code 0xBC may mean an Acronis Secur Zone and code 0x82 usually indicates a Linux swap file partition). The FAT16 and FAT32 fil systems have made use of quite a number of partition type codes over time due to th limits of various DOS and Windows OS versions. Though a Linux operating system may recognize a number of different file systems (ext2, ext3, reiserfs, etc.), they have all consistently used the same partition type code: 0x83 (Linux native).

Extended

An extended partition is secondary to the primary partition(s). A hard disk may contain only one extended partition; which can then be sub-divided into logical drives, each of which is (under DOS and Windows) assigned additional drive letters. For example, under either DOS or Windows, a hard disk with one primary partition and one extended partition, the latter containing two logical drives, would typically be assigned the three drive letters: C:, D: and E: (in that order).

Extended partitions are useful if you want more than four partitions on a single physical drive. Technically, the number of logical drives is no longer limited in later operating systems, but under Windows there is an effective limit if they are to be assigned drive letters (only 24 letters, C: through Z:, are generally available. Later operating systems may allow more drives to be mounted/accessed by using A-A:, A-B:, A-C:, etc.).

Compressed disks

Hard disks are sometimes compressed to create additional space. Under MS-DOS and early Windows, programs such as STACKER (DR-DOS except 6), SuperStor (DR-DOS 6), DoubleSpace, or DriveSpace (Windows 95) were used. This compression was done by creating a very large file on the partition, then storing the disk's data in this file. At startup, device drivers opened this file and assigned it a separate letter. Frequently, to avoid confusion, the original partition and the compressed drive had their letters swapped, so that the compressed disk is C:, and the uncompressed area (often containing system files) is given a higher name. (SuperStor required a separate device driver to be loaded, DEVSWAP.COM).

Versions of Windows using the NT kernel, including the most recent versions, XP and Vista, contain intrinsic disk compression capability. The use of separate compression utilities has declined sharply.

Partitioning schemes

Microsoft Windows

With Microsoft Windows, the standard partitioning scheme is to create a single active primary partition, the C: drive, where the operating system, user data, applications, and page file all reside. Some users, however, prefer to create multiple partitions so that the operating system can be stored separately from other kinds of data. While this scheme generally results in slightly lower performance due to additional work needing to be done by both the hard drive and the operating system, proponents of multiple partitions generally point to the benefit of being able to erase a single partition (typically the operating system itself) while retaining the other data.

When used in conjunction with 3rd-party partition management programs such as Acroni True Image, Norton PartitionMagic, Norton Ghost, or specialized recovery programs tha come with computers manufactured by most major manufacturers, the use of multipl partitions allows computer users to quickly recover from viruses, rootkits, and trojan horse or an otherwise damaged, corrupt or compromised operating system.

Unix

For Unix-based and Unix-like operating systems such as Linux and Mac OS X, the creatio of separate partitions for /boot, /home, /tmp, /usr, /var, /opt, swap and all remaining file under the "/" (root directory) is possible. (The same is true for Sun-based operating systems except their partitions are called slices.) Such a scheme has a number of potentia advantages: if one file system gets corrupted, the rest of the data (the other file systems stay intact, minimizing data loss; partitions can be accessed read-only and the executio of setuid files disabled thus enhancing security; performance may be enhanced due t less disk head travel.

However, this method has the disadvantage of subdividing the drive into fixed-size partitions so, for instance, a user could run out of hard drive space in his or her /home partition, eve though other partitions still have plenty of usable space. A good implementation require the user to predict how much space each partition will need, which may be a difficult task especially for new users. Logical Volume Management, often used in servers, introduces degree of flexibility by allowing data in these volumes to expand into separate physica disks (which can be added when needed); another option is to resize existing partition when necessary. Typical desktop systems, though, are often comprised of a single " (root directory) containing the entire filesystem plus a much smaller swap partition. separate /home partition, however, can be very useful, since it allows for a clean reinstall c the OS (or a fresh install of another Linux distribution) while leaving the user's data intac

Partition Recovery

When a partition is deleted, in general, only its partition table entry is removed from a table and although the data is no longer accessible, it still remains on the disk until it's overwritten Specialized recovery utilities, (such as TestDisk and gpart), can locate lost file system and recreate a partition table which includes entries for these recovered file systems However, some disk utilities may also overwrite a number of beginning sectors of a partitio they delete. For example, if Windows Disk Management (Windows 2000/XP, etc.) is use to delete a partition, it will overwrite the first sector (relative sector 0) of the partition befor removing it. Hopefully any FAT32 or NTFS partition you wish to recover will still have a available backup boot sector, so the boot sector can be restored.

Disk Formatting

Disk formatting is the process of preparing a hard disk or other storage medium for use including setting up an empty file system. A variety of utilities and programs exist for thi task; pictured to the right is the iconic FORMAT.COM of MS-DOS and PC-DOS.

Large disks can be partitioned, divided into logical sections that are formatted with their own file systems. This is normally only done on hard disks because of the small sizes of other disk types, as well as compatibility issues.

A corrupted operating system can be reverted to a clean state by formatting the disk and reinstalling the OS, as a drastic way of combatting a software problem or malware infection. Obviously, important files should be backed up beforehand.

Two Levels of Formatting

Formatting a disk involves two quite different processes known as low-level and high-level formatting. The former deals with the formatting of disk surfaces and installing characteristics like sector numbers that are visible to, and used by, the disk controller hardware, while the latter deals with file system specific information written by the operating system.

Low-level Formatting of Floppy Disks

The low-level format of floppy disks (and early hard disks) is performed by the disk drive hardware.

The process is most easily described with a standard 1.44 MB floppy disk in mind. Low-level formatting of the floppy normally writes 18 sectors of 512 bytes each on each of 160 tracks (80 on each side) of the floppy disk, providing 1,474,560 bytes of storage on the floppy.

Sectors are actually physically larger than 512 bytes as they include sector numbers, CRC bytes, and other information required in order to identify and verify the sector during reading and writing. These additional bytes do not add to the overall storage capacity of the disk.

To complicate matters, different low-level formats can be used on the same media; for example, large records can be used to cut down on interrecord gap size.

Several freeware, shareware and free software programs (e.g. GParted, FDFORMAT, NFORMAT and 2M) allowed considerably more control over formatting, allowing the formatting of high-density 3 1/2" disks with a capacity up to 2 MB.

Techniques used include:

- head/track sector skew (moving the sector numbering forward at side change and track stepping to reduce mechanical delay),
- interleaving sectors (to minimize sector gap and thereby allowing the number of sectors per track to be increased),
- increasing the number of sectors per track (while a normal 1.44 MB format uses 18 sectors per track, it's possible to increase this to a maximum of 21), and
- increasing the number of tracks (most drives could tolerate extension to 82 tracks – though some could handle more, others jammed).

Linux supports a variety of sector sizes, and DOS and Windows support a large-record-size DMF-formatted floppy format.

Low-level Formatting (LLF) of Hard Disks

User instigated low-level formatting (LLF) of hard disks was common in the 1980s. Typically this involved setting up the MFM pattern on the disk, so that sectors of bytes could be successfully written to it. With the advent of RLL encoding, low-level formatting grew increasingly uncommon, and most modern hard disks are embedded systems, which are low-level formatted at the factory with the physical geometry dimensions and thus not subject to user intervention.

Early hard disks were quite similar to floppies, but low-level formatting was generally done by the BIOS rather than by the operating system. This process involved using the MS-DOS debug program to transfer control to a routine hidden at different addresses in different BIOSs.

Starting in the early 1990s, low-level formatting of hard drives became more complex as technology improved to:

- use RLL encoding,
- store a higher number of sectors on the longer outer tracks (traditionally, all tracks had the same number of sectors, as is still the case with floppy disks),
- encode track numbers into the disk surface to simplify hardware, and
- increase the mechanical speeds of the drive.

Rather than face ever-escalating difficulties with BIOS versioning, disk vendors started doing low-level formatting at the factory. Today, an end-user, in most cases, should never perform a low-level formatting of an IDE or ATA hard drive, and in fact it is often not possible to do so on modern hard drives outside of the factory.

Disk Reinitialization

While it's impossible to perform an LLF on most modern hard drives (since the mid-1990s) outside the factory, the term "low-level format" is still being used (erroneously) for what should be called the reinitialization of an IDE or ATA hard drive to its factory configuration (and even these terms may be misunderstood). Reinitialization should include identifying (and sparing out if possible) any sectors which cannot be written to and read back from the drive, correctly. The term has, however, been used by some to refer to only a portion of that process, in which every sector of the drive is written to; usually by writing a zero byte to every addressable location on the disk; sometimes called zero-filling.

The present ambiguity in the term "low-level format" seems to be due to both inconsistent documentation on web sites and the belief by many users that any process below a "high-level (file system) format" must be called a low-level format. Instead of correcting this mistaken idea (by clearly stating such a process cannot be performed on specific drives), various drive manufacturers have actually described reinitialization software as LLF utilities on their web sites. Since users generally have no way to determine the difference between a true LLF and reinitialization (they simply observe running the software results in a hard disk that must be partitioned and "high-level formatted"), both the misinformed user and mixed signals from various drive manufacturers have perpetuated this error. Note: Whatever possible misuse of such terms may exist (search hard drive manufacturers' web sites for all these terms), many sites do make such reinitialization utilities available (possibly as bootable floppy diskette or CD image files), to both overwrite every byte and check for damaged sectors on the hard disk.

One popular method for performing only the "zero-fill" operation on a hard disk is by writing zero-bytes to the drive using the Unix dd utility (available under Linux as well) with the "/dev/zero" stream as the input file (if=) and the drive itself (either the whole disk, or a specific partition) as the output file (of=).

High-level Formatting

High-level formatting is the process of setting up an empty file system on the disk, and installing a boot sector. This alone takes little time, and is sometimes referred to as a "quick format".

In addition, the entire disk may optionally be scanned for defects, which takes considerably longer, up to several hours on larger harddisks. In the case of floppy disks, both high- and low-level formatting are customarily done in one pass by the software. In recent years, most floppies have shipped preformatted from the factory as DOS FAT12 floppies. It is possible to format them again to other formats, if necessary.

Formatting in DOS

Under MS-DOS and PC-DOS, disk formatting is performed by the FORMAT program. FORMAT usually asks for confirmation beforehand to prevent accidental removal of data, but some versions of DOS had an undocumented /AUTOTEST option; if used, the usual confirmation is skipped and the format begins right away. The WM/FormatC macro virus uses this command to format the C: drive as soon as a document is opened.

There is also the undocumented /U parameter that performs an unconditional format which overwrites the entire partition, preventing the recovery of data through software (but see below).

Recovery of Data from a Formatted Disk

As with regular deletion, data on a disk is not fully destroyed during a high-level format. Instead, the area on the disk containing the data is merely marked as available (in whatever file system structure the format uses), and retains the old data until it's overwritten. If the reformatting is done with a different file system than previously existed in the partition, some data may be overwritten that wouldn't be if the same file system had been used. However, under some file systems (e.g., NTFS; but not FAT), the file indexes (such as $MFTs under NTFS, "inodes" under ext2/3, etc.) may not be written to the same exact locations. And if the partition size is increased, even FAT file systems will overwrite more data at the beginning of that new partition.

From the perspective of preventing the recovery of sensitive data through recovery tools, the data must either be completely overwritten (every sector) with random data before the format, or the format program itself must perform this overwriting; as the DOS FORMAT command did with floppy diskettes, filling every data sector with F6h bytes.

Disk Utility

Disk Utility is the name of a utility created by Apple for performing disk-related tasks in Mac OS X. These tasks include:

- the creation, conversion, compression and encryption of disk images from a wide range of formats read by Disk Utility to .dmg or .cdr, which is identical to the .iso format;
- mounting, unmounting, and ejecting disks (including both · hard disks, removable media and disk images);
- enabling or disabling journaling;
- verifying a disk's integrity, and repairing it if the disk is damaged;
- verifying and repairing permissions;
- disk erasing, formatting and partitioning;
- secure deletion of free space or disk using a 30-pass Gutmann algorithm
- adding or changing partition table between Apple Partition Table and GUID Partition Table;
- creating, destroying, and repairing RAID sets;
- restoring volumes from scanned for ASR images;
- burning disk images to CD or DVD in HFS+ format;
- erasing CD-RWs and DVD-RWs;
- checking the S.M.A.R.T status of a hard disk.

Disk Utility functions may also be accessed from the Mac OS X command line with the diskutil and hdiutil commands.

Disk Utility was updated with Mac OS X v10.3. Prior to v10.3, the functionality of Disk Utility was spread across two applications: Disk Copy and Disk Utility. Disk Copy was used for creating and mounting disk image files, and Disk Utility was used for formatting, partitioning, verifying and repairing file structures. The ability to "zero" all data on a disk was not added until Mac OS X 10.2.3.

Further changes introduced in 10.4.3 allowed Disk Utility to be used to verify the file structure of the current boot drive. However as Apple notes in their public knowledge base doing so can sometimes yield false error messages.

In versions of the Mac OS prior to Mac OS X, similar functionality to the verification features of Disk Utility could be found in the Disk First Aid application. Another application called Drive Setup was used for drive formatting and partitioning, and the application Disk Copy was used for working with disk images.

Computer Software

Computer software, consisting of programs, enables a computer to perform specific tasks, as opposed to its physical components (hardware) which can only do the tasks they are mechanically designed for. The term includes application software such as word processors which perform productive tasks for users, system software such as operating systems, which interface with hardware to run the necessary services for user-interfaces and applications, and middleware which controls and co-ordinates distributed systems.

Terminology

The term "software" is sometimes used in a broader context to describe any electronic media content which embodies expressions of ideas such as film, tapes, records, etc.

Relationship to Computer Hardware

Computer software is so called in contrast to computer hardware, which encompasses the physical interconnections and devices required to store and execute (or run) the software. In computers, software is loaded into RAM and executed in the central processing unit. At the lowest level, software consists of a machine language specific to an individual processor. A machine language consists of groups of binary values signifying processor instructions (object code), which change the state of the computer from its preceding state. Software is an ordered sequence of instructions for changing the state of the computer hardware in a particular sequence. It is usually written in high-level programming languages that are easier and more efficient for humans to use (closer to natural language) than machine language. High-level languages are compiled or interpreted into machine language object code. Software may also be written in an assembly language, essentially, a mnemonic representation of a machine language using a natural language alphabet. Assembly language must be assembled into object code via an assembler.

Types

Practical computer systems divide software systems into three major classes: system software, programming software and application software, although the distinction is arbitrary, and often blurred.

- System software helps run the computer hardware and computer system. It includes operating systems, device drivers, diagnostic tools, servers, windowing systems, utilities and more. The purpose of systems software is to insulate the applications programmer as much as possible from the details of the particular computer complex being used, especially memory and other hardware features, and such accessory devices as communications, printers, readers, displays, keyboards, etc.

- Programming software usually provides tools to assist a programmer in writing computer programs and software using different programming languages in a more convenient way. The tools include text editors, compilers, interpreters, linkers, debuggers, and so on. An Integrated development environment (IDE) merges those tools into a software bundle, and a programmer may not need to type multiple commands for compiling, interpreter, debugging, tracing, and etc., because the IDE usually has an advanced graphical user interface, or GUI.
- Application software allows end users to accomplish one or more specific (non-computer related) tasks. Typical applications include industrial automation, business software, educational software, medical software, databases, and computer games. Businesses are probably the biggest users of application software, but almost every field of human activity now uses some form of application software. It is used to automate all sorts of functions.

Program and Library

A program may not be sufficiently complete for execution by a computer. In particular, it may require additional software from a software library in order to be complete. Such a library may include software components used by stand-alone programs, but which cannot work on their own. Thus, programs may include standard routines that are common to many programs, extracted from these libraries. Libraries may also include 'stand-alone' programs which are activated by some computer event and/or perform some function (e.g., of computer 'housekeeping') but do not return data to their calling program. Programs may be called by one to many other programs; programs may call zero to many other programs.

Three Layers

Users often see things differently than programmers. People who use modern general purpose computers (as opposed to embedded systems, analog computers, supercomputers, etc.) usually see three layers of software performing a variety of tasks: platform, application, and user software.

Platform Software

Platform includes the firmware, device drivers, an operating system, and typically a graphical user interface which, in total, allow a user to interact with the computer and its peripherals (associated equipment). Platform software often comes bundled with the computer, and users may not realize that it exists or that they have a choice to use different platform software.

Application Software

Application software or Applications are what most people think of when they think of software. Typical examples include office suites and video games. Application software is often purchased separately from computer hardware. Sometimes applications are bundled with the computer, but that does not change the fact that they run as independent applications. Applications are almost always independent programs from the operating system, though they are often tailored for specific platforms. Most users think of compilers, databases, and other "system software" as applications.

User-written Software

User software tailors systems to meet the users specific needs. User software include spreadsheet templates, word processor macros, scientific simulations, and scripts for graphics and animations. Even email filters are a kind of user software. Users create this software themselves and often overlook how important it is. Depending on how competently the user-written software has been integrated into purchased application packages, many users may not be aware of the distinction between the purchased packages, and what has been added by fellow co-workers.

BIOS Features

This program lets your operating system and application programs communicate with computer hardware and peripheral devices such as floppy disk, hard disk, printer, display adapter, etc. Reading the keystroke, displaying on the screen, reading/writing of the serial and parallel port, reading/writing to and from the floppy and hard disk, etc., is done under the control of the BIOS.

The BIOS is a set of insructions or software stored inside a PROM (Programmable Read Ony Memory), PROM is a hardware, so a BIOS is not complete software nor a complete hardware that is the reason a new name "firmware" is used to describe the BIOS.

The term "firmware" is used to describe a software stored in read only memory.

When the user program asks the BIOS to read the keyboard it is the job of the BIOS to read the keyboard in a proper manner, so as the data from the keyboard can be made available to the user program.

If you have two different computers, one having keyboard connection at I/O port 60 and the other having keyboard connection at I/O port 62, you don't have to purchase a different program for each of them.

Your program can just give the "read keyboard" command to the BIOS and it will be the job of the BIOS to read proper I/O port:

port 60 on the first computer and

port 62 on the second computer.

Error Messages BIOS

If a nonfatal error occurs during the POST routine, each time the system is powered on, the error message will appear on the screen in the following format:

ERROR Message Line 1

ERROR Message Line 2

Pres <F1> to RESUME

Note down the error message and press the <F1> key to continue with the bootup procedure. For most of the error messages, generally there is no ERROR Message Line 2.

Generally, for those messags containing a line 2 ERROR Message, the line 2 text will be "RUN SETUP UTILITY". Pressing the <F1> will invoke the BIOS SETUP PROGRAM.

A description of some common error messages appears below:

1. CH-2 Timer Error: Most AT standard system boards include two timers. An error with timer #1 is a fatal error. This error message indicates an error with timer #2.
2. INTR #1 Error: Some problem with the interrupt channel #1.
3. INTR #2 Error: Some error with the interrupt channel #2.
4. CMOS Battery State Low: There is a battery in your system which is used for storing CMOS values. This battery appears to be low in power and needs to be replaced.
5. CMOS Checksum Failure: After the CMOS values are saved, a checksum value is generated to provide for error checking. If the previous value is different from the value currently read, this error message appears. To correct this error, you should run the BIOS SETUP Program.
6. CMOS System Options Not Set: The values tored in the cMOS are either corrupt or nonexistent. Run the BIOS SETUP Program to correct this error.
7. CMOS Display Type Mismatch: The type of video stored in CMOS does not match with the type detected by the BIOS. Run the BIOS SETUP Program to correct this error.
8. Display Switch Not Proper: Some systems require that a video swith/jumper on the motherboard be set to either colour or monochrome, depending on the type of video you are using. To correct this situation, set the switch properly. (Remember to shut down the system first). Se the switch to colour for CGA, EGA, VGA, PGA and to monochrome for other display.
9. Keyboard Is Locked . . . . Inlock It: The keyboard lock on the system is engaged. The system must be unlocked to continue the boot up procedure.
10. Keyboard Error: The BIOS has encountered a timing problem with the keyboard. Make sure you have a main BIOS compatible keyboard BIQS installed in your system. You may also set the "keyboard" option in the BIOS SETUP Program's Standard

CMOS Setup option to "Not Installed" which will cause the BIOS to skip the keyboard POST routines.

11. KB/Interface Error: The BIOS has found an error with the keyboard connector on the system board.
12. CMOS Memory Size Mismatch: If the BIOS finds the amount of memory on your system board to be different from the amount stored in CMOS, this error message is generated. Run the BIOS Setup to correct this error.
13. FDD Controller Failure: The BIOS is not able to communicate with the hard disk drive controller. Check all appropriate connections after the system is powered off.
14. HDD Controller Failure: The BIOS is not able to communicate with the hard disk drive controller. Check all appropriate connections after the system is powered down. Also check the drive type in the CMOS setup.
15. C: Drive Error: The BIOS is not receiving any response from hard disk drive C:. It may be necessary to run the Hard Disk Utility to correct this problem. Also, check the type of hard disk selected in the Standard CMOS Setup of the BIOS Setup program.
16. D: Driver Error: The same error has occurred with hard drive D:. Follow the procedures in Error #15 to correct this situation.
17. C: Drive Failure: The BIOS cannot get any response from the hard disk drive C:. It may be necessary to replace the hard disk.
18. D: Drive Failure: The same error as #17 has occurred with hard drive D:.
19. CMOS Time and Date Not Set: Run the Standard CMOS Setup of the BIOS SETUP Program to set the date and time.
20. Cache Memory Bad, Do Not Enable Cache: The BIOS has found the cache memory of the motherboard to be defective.
21. 8042 Gate-A20 Error: The gate-A20 portion of the keyboard controller (8042) has failed to operate correctly. The 8042 chip should be replaced.
22. Address Line Short: An error has occurred in the address decoding circuitry of the motherboard.
23. DMA #2 Error: An error has occurred with the second DMA channel on the motherboard.
24. DMA #1 Error: An error has occurred with the first DMA channel on the motherboard.
25. DMA Error: An error has occurred with the DMA controller on the motherboard.
26. No ROM BASIC: This error occurs when a proper bootable secotr cannot be found on either the floppy diskette drive A: or the hard disk drive C:. The BIOS will try at this point to run ROM BASIC and this error message will be generated when the BIOS does not find it.

27. Diskette Boot Failure: The diskette used to boot-up in floppy drive A: is corrected, you cannot use it to boot-up the system. Use another boot diskette and follow the instructions on the screen.
28. Invalid Boot Diskette: The BIOS can read the diskette in floppy drive A:, but it cannot boot-up the system with it. Use another boot diskette and follow the instructions on the screen.
29. On Board Parity Error: The BIOS has encountered a parity error with some memory installed on the system board. The message will appear as follows:

    ON BOARD PARITY ERROR

    ADDR (HEX) = (XXXX)

    Where XXXX is the address (in hexadecimal) at which the error has occurred. "On Board" means that this memory is part of the memory attached directly to the system board.
30. Off Board Parity Error: The BIOS has encountered a parity error with some memory installed in an I/O (BUS) slot. The message will appear as follows:

    OFF BOARD PARITY ERROR

    ADDR (HEX) = (XXXX)

    Where XXXX is the address (in hexadecimal) at which the error has occurred. "Off Board" means that it is part of the memory installed via an expansion card in an I/O (BUS) slot.
31. Parity Error ????: The BIOS has encountered a parity error with some meory in the system, but it is not able to determine the address of the error. Memory diagnostic software, such as AMIDIAG or QAPLUS, etc., can be used to find and correct memory problems.

Password Protection

To reset the BIOS you have two options:

- either you can use the BIOS reset jumper provided on your motherboard, check the manual of your PC or motherboard for "Clear CMOS Memory".
- or you can remove the CMOS Setup battery and allow ten minutes for the residual power in the CMOS to drain away. The, reconnect or reinstall the battery.

For both of these steps you would be needing the password, if set by the user in the beginning. Without password you cannot reset the anything in the BIOS.

Optimization of BIOS Parameters

A standard BIOS has the following parameters.

Standard CMOS Setup: Sets time, date, hard diks type, types of floppy drive, monitor type, and if keyboard if installed.

Advanced CMOS Setup: Sets thpematic rate and display, above 1MB memory test, memory test tick sound; hit <del> messae display, system boot up sequence, and many other options.

Advanced Chipset Setup

Sets chipset-specific options and features.

Power Management Setup

Controls power conservation options.

PCI/PnP Setup

Sets options related to PCI bus and Plug and Play options.

Peripheral Setup

Controls I/O Controller-related options.

CPU Configuration Setup

This option selects the type of CPU installed in the motherboard.

Password

A password is a form of secret authentication data that is used to control access to a resource. The password is kept secret from those not allowed access, and those wishing to gain access are tested on whether or not they know the password and are granted or denied access accordingly.

The use of passwords goes back to ancient times. Sentries guarding a location would challenge for a password. They would only allow a person in if they knew the password. In modern times, passwords are used to control access to protected computer operating systems, mobile phones, cable TV decoders, automated teller machines (ATMs), etc. A typical computer user may require passwords for many purposes: logging in to computer accounts, retrieving email from servers, accessing files, databases, networks, web sites, and even reading the morning newspaper online.

Despite the name, there is no need for passwords to be actual words; indeed passwords which are not actual words are harder to guess (a desirable property), but are generally harder for users to remember (an undesirable property). Note that password is often used to describe what would be more accurately called a passphrase. Passcode is sometimes taken to imply that the information used is purely numeric, such as the personal identification number (PIN) commonly used for ATM access. Passwords are generally short enough to be memorized.

Designing a personal, user-friendly password

Passwords vary in the degree of public awareness, security protection and frequency of change. The most public, and therefore least secure, password might be one that is given to members of a group, a committee or some other organization. For instance, "publiclibrary", "internet" or "AAAfinancecommittee" are all examples of easily remembered passwords, more or less publicly known passwords.

Less easily attacked passwords might be built from such a basic form, for instance, "smith12nov34street" or "AAAchairpersonSUE". These are slightly more secure, but being relatively easily predictable should not be relied upon to actually block unauthorized access. Effective access control requires passwords which are more difficult to guess or to find automatically, less publicly known (ideally not at all), and these are the subject of much of the rest of this article.

Security and convenience

In controlling access to anything, trade-offs are made between security and convenience. If a resource is protected by a password, then security is increased with a consequent loss of convenience for users. The amount of security and inconvenience inherent in a particular password system or policy are affected by several factors addressed below. However, there is generally no one universal 'best' way to set a balance between security and convenience for all cases.

Some password protected systems pose little or no risk to a user if compromised, for example a password allowing access to a free information web site with no confidential data. Others pose modest economic or privacy risk, as for instance a password used to access e-mail or a security lock code for a mobile telephone. Still others could have very serious consequences if compromised, such as passwords used to limit access to AIDS treatment records, control a power transmission grid, or access to personnel records (consider the risk of identity theft in this instance).

Factors in the security of a password system

The security of a password-protected system depends on several factors. The system must, of course, be designed for sound overall security, without which no password protection can have any significance. Early passwords on many systems were limited to a few numbers, or upper-case-letters, only often in prescribed patterns limiting the number of possible passwords.

Most passwords today usually have fewer such limits. User input is determined by several limiting factors: allowable inputs (numbers / letters, non-visual codes and/or other keys / device inputs), minimum & maximum of time required for input, availability of cut / delete / paste / copy for input, and error/noise tolerance errors in the password or communications input. Some system administrators also enforce other limitations on passwords, such as compulsory change schedules, safe-password analysis feedback, and compulsory length / composition limits.

Here are some password management issues that must be considered:

Rate at which an attacker can try out guessed passwords

The rate at which an attacker can submit guessed passwords to the system is a key factor in determining system security. Some systems impose a long time out (several seconds) after a small number (e.g., a maximum of three) of failed password entry attempts. Absent other vulnerabilities, such systems can be secure with relatively simple passwords, if they are not easily guessed. Examples of passwords that are easily guessed include the name of a relative or pet, an automobile license plate number, and such default passwords as admin, 123456, or letmein.

Other systems store or transmit a cryptographic hash of the password in a manner that makes the hash value accessible to an attacker. When this is done, and it is very common (to most observers' surprise or despair), an attacker can work off-line, rapidly testing candidate passwords against the true password's hash value.

Lists of common passwords are widely available and can further speed the process. (See Password cracking.) A sufficiently complex password used in a system with a good hash algorithm can defeat such attacks as the work factor imposed on such an attacker can be made impossible in practice. Passwords that are used to generate cryptographic keys, e.g. for disk encryption or Wi-Fi security, are also subject to high rate guessing. Stronger passwords are needed in such systems.

Form of stored passwords

Some computer systems store passwords, against which to compare user attempts, as cleartext. If an attacker gains access to such an internal password file, all passwords would be compromised. If some users employ the same password for multiple accounts, those will be compromised as well. More secure systems store each password in a cryptographically protected form, so access to the actual password will be difficult for a snooper who gains internal access to the system, while validation still remains possible.

Email is sometimes used to distribute passwords. Since most email is sent as cleartext, it is available without effort during transport to any eavesdropper. Further, it will be stored on at least two computers as cleartext — the sender's and the receipients's. If it passes through intermediate systems during its travels, it will likely be stored on those as well. Emailed passwords are generally an insecure method of distribution.

A common cryptographically based scheme stores only a "hashed" form of the plaintext password. When a user types in a password on such a system, it is run through the hashing algorithm, and if the hash value generated from the user's entry matches the hash stored in the password database, the user is permitted access.

The hash value is created by applying a cryptographic hash function to a string consisting of the submitted password and, usually, another value known as a salt. The salt prevents attackers from building a list of hash values for common passwords. MD5 and SHA1 are frequently used cryptographic hash functions. A modified version of DES was used in early Unix systems.

The UNIX DES function was iterated to make the hash function slow, to further frustrate automated guessing attacks, and used the password candidate as a key to encrypt a fixed value, thus blocking yet another attack on the password hashing system. A more flexible function for iterated hashed passwords is described in PKCS-5.

If the hash function is well designed, it will be computationally infeasible to reverse it to find the plaintext directly. However, many systems do not protect their hashed passwords adequately, and if an attacker can gain access to hashed values he can use widely available tools which compare the encrypted outcome of every word from some collection, such as a dictionary.

Long lists of possible passwords in many languages are widely available (eg, on the Internet) and the tools try common variations as well. The existence of these dictionary attack tools demonstrates the relative strengths of different password choices against such attacks. Use of a key derivation function can reduce this risk.

14 Beep Codes

Power on Self Test

Power-on self-test (POST) is the common term for a computer's, router's or printer's pre-boot sequence. The same basic sequence is present on all computer architectures. It is the first step of the more general process called initial program load (IPL), booting, or bootstrapping. The term POST has become popular in association with and as a result of the proliferation of the PC. It can be used as a noun when referring to the code that controls the pre-boot phase or when referring to the phase itself. It can also be used as a verb when referring to the code or the system as it progresses through the pre-boot phase. Alternatively this may be called "POSTing."

General Internal Workings

On power up, the main duties of POST are handled by the BIOS, which may hand some of these duties to other programs designed to initialize very specific peripheral devices, notably for video and SCSI initialization. These other duty-specific programs are generally known collectively as option ROMs or individually as the video BIOS, SCSI BIOS, etc. The principal duties of the main BIOS during POST are as follows:

- verify the integrity of the BIOS code itself
- determine the reason POST is being executed
- find, size, and verify system main memory
- discover, initialize, and catalog all system buses and devices
- pass control to other specialized BIOSes (if and when required)
- provide a user interface for system's configuration
- identify, organize, and select which devices are available for booting
- construct whatever system environment that is required by the target OS

The BIOS will begin its POST duties when the CPU is reset. The first memory location the CPU tries to execute is known as the reset vector. In the case of a hard reboot, the northbridge will direct this code fetch (request) to the BIOS located on the system flash memory. For a warm boot, the BIOS will be located in the proper place in RAM and the northbridge will direct the reset vector call to the RAM. During the POST flow of a contemporary BIOS, one of the first things a BIOS should do is determine the reason it is executing. For a cold boot, for example, it may need to execute all of its functionality. If, however, the system supports power savings or quick boot methods, the BIOS may be able to circumvent the standard POST device discovery, and simply program the devices from a preloaded system device table.

Fundamental Structure

In the case of the IBM PC compatible machines, the main BIOS is divided into two basic sections. The POST section, or POST code, is responsible for the tasks mentioned above, and the environment POST constructs for the OS is known as the runtime code, the runtime BIOS, or the runtime footprint. Primarily these two divisions can be distinguished in that POST code should be flushed from memory before control is passed to the target OS while the runtime code remains resident in memory.

Error reporting

The original IBM BIOS reported errors detected during POST by outputting a number to a fixed I/O port address, 80. Using a logic analyzer or a dedicated POST card, an interface card that shows port 80 output on a small display, a technician could determine the origin of the problem. (Note that once an operating system is running on the computer, the code displayed by such a board is often meaningless, since some OSes, e.g. Linux, use port 80 for I/O timing operations.) In later years, BIOS vendors used a sequence of beeps from the motherboard-attached loudspeaker to signal error codes.

AMI BIOS Beep Codes

The AMI BIOS is one of the most popular on the PC, and fortunately is quite consistent in performance, across its different versions.

Beeps	*What does it mean?*
None	You are supposed to hear at least one beep. If you truly don't hear anything, either your computer's power supply, motherboard, or PC speaker has some problem.
1	One beep is good! Everything is Ok, if you see things on the screen. If you don't see anything, check your monitor and video card first. Is everything connected? If they seem fine, your motherboard has some bad chips on it. First reset the SIMMs and reboot. If it still shows the same things, one of the memory chips on the motherboard since these chips are soldered on.
2	Your computer has memory problem. First, check video. If video is working, you'll see an error message. If not, you have a parity error in your first 64K of memory. Check your SIMMs. Reset them and reboot. If this doesn't do it, the memory chips may be bad. You can try switching the first and second banks memory chips. First banks are the memory banks in which your CPU finds its first 64K of base memory. You'll need to consult your manual to see which bank is first. If all of your memory tests are good, you probably need to buy another motherboard.
3	Same as 2 beeps; follow diagnosis above.
4	Same as 2 beeps; follow diagnosis above. Your problem could also be a bad timer.

5	Your motherboard is complaining. Try reseating the memory and rebooting. If that does not help, you should consider another motherboard. You could probably get away with just replacing the CPU, but that's not too cost-effective.
6	The chip on your motherboard that controls your keyboard isn't working. First, try another keyboard. If that doen't help, reseat the chip that controls the keyboard, if it isn't soldered in. If it still beeps, replace the chip is possible. Replace the motherboard if the chip is soldered in.
7	Your CPU could be broken. Either replace the CPU or buy another motherboard.
8	Your video card isn't working. Make sure it is seated well in the bus. If it still beeps, either the whole card is bad or there is problem in the memory. Your best bet is to install another video card.
9	Your BIOS is bad; replace it.
10	Your problem lies deep inside the CMOS. All chips associated with the CMOS will likely have to be replaced. Your best bet is to get a new motheboard.
11	Your cache memory is bad and your computer disabled it for you. You could reactivate it by pressing Ctrl + Alt + Shift + +(Plus), but you probably should not. Instead, replace your chache memory.

Award BIOS Beep Codes

Award is other major BIOS provider today, along with AMI. Award uses by far the fewest beep codes of any of the BIOS manufacturers. In fact, they have only one beep code that can find any reliable documentation on, and two others that have had a couple of people report.

Beeps	*What does it mean?*
1 long, 2 short	Indicates a video error has occurred and the BIOS cannot initialize the video screen to display any additional information.
Others	RAM problem.

Phoenix Beep Codes

Pheonix uses by far the most complicated set of beep codes. The Pheonix BIOS uses groups of beeps; there may be 2 beeps, followed by 1 beep, and then 3 beeps; this is represented as 2-1-3. The older Pheonix BIOS uses three groups of beeps, while the newer one uses four (for example, 2-1-3-1). The newer Pheonix BIOS has over 100 beep codes; the older one had about 40 or so.

Beeps	*What does it mean?*
1-1-3	Your computer can't read the configuration information stored in the CMOS. Replace the motherboard.
1-1-4	Your BIOS needs to replaced.

1-2-1	You have a bad timer chip on the motherboard, you need a new motherboard.
1-2-2	The motheboard is bad.
1-2-3	The motheboard is bad.
1-3-1	The motheboard is bad.
1-3-3	Same as AMI BIOS 2 beeps. Replace the motherboard.
1-3-4	The motheboard is bad.
1-4-1	The motheboard is bad.
1-4-2	Some of your memory is bad.
2-_-_	Any combination of beeps after two beeps means that some of your memory is bad, and unless you want to get real technical, you should probably have the guys in the lab coats test the memory for you. Take your computer to the shop.
3-1-_	One of the chips on your motherboard is not functioning. You will likely need to get another board.
3-2-4	Same as AMI BIOS 6 beeps; keyboard controller failure.
3-3-4	Your computer can't find the ur video card. Is it there? If so, try swapping it with another one and see if it works.
3-4-_	Your video card isn't working. You'll need to replace it.
4-2-1	There's a bad chip on the motherboard. You need to buy another board.
4-2-2	First, check the keyboard for problems. If there are none, you have a bad motherboard.
4-2-3	See 4-2-2.
4-2-4	One of the cards is bad. Try taking out the cards one by one to isolate the culprit. Replace the bad one. The last possibility is to buy another motheboard.
4-3-1	Replace the motherboard.
4-3-2	See 4-3-1
4-3-4	Time and date clock failure. Try running the setup program that comes with the computer, and check the date and time. If that doesn't work, replace the battery; still it doen't work, replace the power supply. You may have to replace the motherboard, but that is rare.
4-4-1	Your serial ports are acting up. Reseat or replace the I/O card. If the I/O is on the motherboard itself, disable it with a jumper (consult your manual to know which one) and then add an I/O card.
4-4-2	See 4-4-1.
4-4-3	Your math co-processor is malfunctioning. Run a test program to double-check it. If it is indeed bad, diable or replace it. Disabling is fine, because you probably don't need it anyway.

15 Buses and Memory

What is a Bus?

Bus is an electronic road along which signals are send from one part of the computer to another.

Thin lines you see on the Motherboard are the buses that take data, address, control signals and power from one place to another on the motherboard.

Depending on their use, bus is divided into three major types:

- Data bus
- Address bus
- Control bus

When someone talks about the bus, without specifying its type, then most probably he is talking about the data bus.

Data Bus

The data bus is used to move data from one place to another. The number of the data lines provided in the bus is very important factor that determines the speed of this data transfer.

Address Bus

The address bus is used to select a particular memory location to read or write the data Maximum memory that CPU can address depends on the size of its address bus.

Addressable locations = $2^{\text{(total address lines)}}$

If you have 3 address lines total addressable locations will be $2^3 = 8$, 32 bit PCI local bus uses 32 address lines and it can address $2^{32} = 4,294,967,296$ different locations or 4096 Mega Bytes of memory.

Control Bus

The control bus is used to send control and timing signals between various parts of the computer.

Factors Affecting Processing Speed

How Registers Affect Speed

The size of the registers (16-bit register or 32-bit register) which is also called the word size indicate the amount of data with which the computer can work. The bigger the size of register, the faster the computer can process a set of data. Registers retain information on a temporary basis. They are not considered part of main memory. Registers have the ability to receive information, hold it temporarily and then pass it on as directed by supervisory control unit.

There are several type of registers:

1. Instruction Register : It holds the instruction which is being executed.
2. Address Register: It holds the storage location address.
3. Accumulator: It collects results.

Memory and Computing Power

More RAM make the computer run faster. The computer does not necesarily have to load anentire program into memory to run it, but the more ofthe program it can fit into memory, the faster theprogram will run. The computer loads only the most essential parts into memory. Whent it needs access to other parts of the program on the disk, it can unload, or swapout non essential parts and swap in program code or data it needs.

Computer's Internal Clock

Every microcomputer has a system clock made up of quartz crystal. The molecules in the crystal vibrate millions of times per second which is constant. The system uses the vibration of the crystal (quartz) in the system clock to time its processing operations. The clock speed is measured in hertz. Pentium CPU today have clock speed from 75 MHz to 200 MHz.

RISC: More Is Not Always Better

An important aspect of computer system is the design of the instruction set for the processor; because it determines the way, machine language programs are constructed. Early computers had small and simple instruction sets; this was because of the high cost of hardware. With the invention of integrated circuits, computer instruction set tend to increase both in number and complexity. For example, the most common microprocessors found in small computers today viz; 80x86 and 680x0 families uses large (from 100 to 200) instruction sets.

A computer with a large number of instructions is classified as a complex instruction set computer (CISC).

CISC Characteristics

The main reason for provision of a complex instruction set is due to the requirement of the simplification of compilation, and the requirement in the improvement of the overall computer performance. The task of a compiler is to generate a sequence of machine instructions for each high level language statement. The task is simplified if there are machine instructions that implement the statements directly.

The essential goal of a CISC architecture is to attempt to provide a single machine instruction for each statement in a high level language.

Examples of CISC architecture are:

IBM 370 and VAX

Another characteristics of CISC architecture is the incorporation of variable-length instruction formats.

RISC Characteristics

A newer theory in the design of microprocessor holds that, if the instruction set is kept small and simple each instruction will execute much faster, allowing the processor to complete more instructions during a given period. This design results in a faster and less expensive processors. CPUs designed around this methodology are called reduced instruction set computers (RISC). The major characteristics of a RISC methodology are:

1. Relatively few instructions
2. Memory access limited to load and store instructions
3. All operations done within the registers of the CPU
4. Fixed length, easily decoded instruction format

RISC technology is used extensively in mid-size computers such as the IBM RS/6000 and high-end UNIX workstations such as those built by Hewlett Packard & Sun Microsystem.

RISC CPus are also used extensively in printers and other intelligent devices that have their own internal CPUs.

RISC technology are designed and manufactured by the same companies that produce CISC technology.

In 1989, Intel introduced i860 RISC Chip of 64-bit, which contains more than 1 million transistors. Newer RISC chip include the Intel i960, the Motorola 88100. Sun Microsystems are also produced a RISC chip known as SPARC, which it uses in its UNIX workstations.

Memory Basics

So far at every stage we have said that computer cannot think on its own and cannot remember anything unless we store in hard disk with save. While working all the information is stored in what is called the memory of the computer till we press the button to save it. Till that point all the information and results are stored in memory. So usually a big memory means a faster and more useful computer.

A PC's memory is made up of electronic components in which the PC temporarily stores data and instructions. Technically, any device that stores data or instructions on the PC can be called memory, including the hard disk, floppy disks, ROM, CMOS, RAM and cache.

However, what is commonly referred to as memory on the PC is its primary storage, which is also known as system memory, temporary storage or RAM. With the exception of ROM, the other forms of storage (hard disk, floppy disk, CD-ROM and the like) are known as secondary storage.

ROM

It's logical then that data stored on read-only memory (ROM) cannot be changed, as its name implies. ROM also has the added feature of being nonvolatile, which means that it can keep its contents even without a power source. This makes it ideal for storing the PC's startup instructions and system BIOS (Basic Input/Output System). While virtually all ROM chips are packed in a DIP (dual inline packaging) form, there are three types of ROM used in a PC:

PROM (programmable read-only memory)

This type of ROM chip is programmed using a special type of programming device called a PROM burner, which permanently stores machine language (binary instructions) code on the PROM chip. A PROM chips is also referred to as OTP (One Time Programmable) memory.

EPROM (erasable programmable read-only memory)

This type of ROM, pronounced "e-prom," is erasable and can be reprogrammed. Unlike a PROM chip that cannot be reused and can only be thrown out when it becomes obsolete, an EPROM chip can be reprogrammed and reused. An EPROM has a quartz window on the face of the chip that exposes the chip's interior circuits. When ultraviolet (UV) light is shined through this window, it causes a chemical reaction that erases the EPROM. In order to reprogram an EPROM, it must be removed from the computer, erased with UV light and then reprogrammed on a PROM programmer.

EEPROM (electronically erasable programmable read-only memory)

Most newer PCs now include an EEPROM (pronounced-e-prom") that can be reprogrammed like an EPROM, but unlike the EPROM doesn't need to be removed from the PC to be reprogrammed. An EEPROM can be reprogrammed, a process called flashing, using specialized software that runs on your PC. An EEPROM is also referred to as flash ROM. Flashing lets you upgrade your computer's BIOS easily without removing and replacing the ROM chip. One thing that all DIP chips suffer from including removable and replaceable PROMs and EPROMs is a condition called chip creep. DIP chips are inserted into what are called through-hole sockets and can and do squirm out of their sockets. Should a ROM chip creep out of its socket, it can cause startup problems. If you have an older motherboard that includes removable DIP ROM or memory chips, you should check them occasionally for creep.

RAM

RAM or Random Access Memory is the main memory inside the computer. It is used to store program, data and results. It is called Random acsess because this memory is organized in such a way that any part of the memory can be accessed without serially going through all the previous memory locations

A better term to describe the RAM would be Read/Write Memory. One can read the information stored inside the RAM as well as write or store information in it.

Two common type of RAM are:

DRAM (Dynamic RAM)

SRAM (Static RAM)

Dynamic RAM (DRAM)

A dynamic RAM (DRAM) is cost wise cheaper than the static RAM (SRAM), and it is the main reason of using the DRAM as the main memory.

DRAM utilizes capacitors to store information, so the problem with the DRAM is once data is stored into it, it can't retain the data for long unless the data is refreshed periodically.

Refreshing of a DRAM memory is done by rewriting the entire content of the memory every few millisecond. For this a special refresh circuitry is used.

Unless the DRAM is refreshed every few milliseconds it loses its content.

Static RAM (SRAM)

Unlike the DRAM, SRAM memory retains the information stored inside it, as long as the power supply is provided to the SRAM chip.

One need not refresh the information stored in the SRAM.

Because the SRAM does not require any refresh circuits, the circuitry required to interface SRAM is very simple compared to the interface circuitry for the DRAM chips. Also, the SRAM is much faster than the DRAM.

SRAM generally use flip-flops to store the information.

DDR SDRAM

DDR SDRAM or double-data-rate synchronous dynamic random access memory is a class of memory integrated circuit used in computers. It achieves greater bandwidth than the preceding single-data-rate SDRAM by transferring data on the rising and falling edges of the clock signal (double pumped). Effectively, it nearly doubles the transfer rate without increasing the frequency of the front side bus. Thus a 100 MHz DDR system has an effective clock rate of 200 MHz when compared to equivalent SDR SDRAM, the "SDR" being a retrospective designation.

With data being transferred 64 bits at a time DDR RAM gives a transfer rate of [mbcr x 2 x 64] / 8; annotated it looks like this: (memory bus clock rate) × 2 (for dual rate) × 64 (number of bits transferred) / 8 (number of bits/byte). Thus with a bus frequency of 100 MHz, DDR-SDRAM gives a max transfer rate of 1600 MB/s.

JEDEC has set standards for speeds of DDR SDRAM, divided into two parts: The first specification is for memory chips and the second is for memory modules.

As DDR is superseded by the newer DDR2, the older version is often now referred to as DDR1.

Chip specification

- DDR-200: DDR-SDRAM memory chips specified to operate at 100 MHz
- DDR-266: DDR-SDRAM memory chips specified to operate at 133 MHz
- DDR-333: DDR-SDRAM memory chips specified to operate at 166 MHz
- DDR-400: DDR-SDRAM memory chips specified to operate at 200 MHz

Chip characteristics

- DRAM density. Size of the chip in mebibits. Example: 256 Mibit — 32 MiB chip.
- DRAM organization. Written in the form of 64M x 4, where 64M is a number of storage units (64 million), x4 (pronounced «by 4») — number of bits per chip, which equals the number of bits per storage unit. There are x4 and x8 DDR chips. The former allows the use of advanced error correction features like Chipkill, memory scrubbing and Intel SDDC, while the latter chips are somewhat more expensive.

Stick/module specification

- PC-1600: DDR-SDRAM memory module specified to operate at 100 MHz using DDR-200 chips, 1.600 GB/s bandwidth
- PC-2100: DDR-SDRAM memory module specified to operate at 133 MHz using DDR-266 chips, 2.133 GB/s bandwidth
- PC-2700: DDR-SDRAM memory module specified to operate at 166 MHz using DDR-333 chips, 2.667 GB/s bandwidth
- PC-3200: DDR-SDRAM memory module specified to operate at 200 MHz using DDR-400 chips, 3.200 GB/s bandwidth

Note: All RAM speeds in-between or above these listed specifications are not standardized by JEDEC — most often they are simply manufacturer optimizations using higher-tolerance or overvolted chips.

The package sizes in which DDR SDRAM is manufactured are also standardised by JEDEC.

There is no architectural difference between DDR SDRAM designed for different clock frequencies, e.g. PC-1600 (designed to run at 100 MHz) and PC-2100 (designed to run at 133 MHz). The number simply designates the speed that the chip is guaranteed to run at. Hence DDR SDRAM can be run at lower clock speeds than it was made for (underclocking) or higher clock speeds than it was made for (overclocking).

DDR SDRAM DIMMs have 184 pins (as opposed to 168 pins on SDR SDRAM, or, 240 pins on DDR-2), and can be differentiated from SDRAM DIMMs by the number of notches (DDR SDRAM has one, SDR SDRAM has two). DDR operates at a voltage of 2.5 V, compared to 3.3 V for SDR SDRAM. This can significantly reduce power usage.

Many new chipsets use these memory types in dual-channel or even quad channel configurations, which doubles or quadruples the effective bandwidth.

Variations of 1 GiB PC2100 Registered DDR SDRAM module

Module size	Number of chips	Chip size	Chip organization	Number of rows (ranks)
1 GiB	36	256 Mibit	64M x 4	2
1 GiB	18	512 Mibit	64M x 8	2
1 GiB	18	512 Mibit	128M x 4	1

DDR2 SDRAM

In electronic engineering, DDR2 SDRAM or double-data-rate two synchronous dynamic random access memory is a random access memory technology used for high speed storage of the working data of a computer or other digital electronic device.

It is a part of the SDRAM (synchronous dynamic random access memory) family of technologies, which is one of many DRAM (dynamic random access memory) implementations, and is an evolutionary improvement over its predecessor, DDR SDRAM (double-data-rate synchronous dynamic random access memory).

Its primary benefit is the ability to run its bus at twice the speed of the memory cells it contains, thus enabling faster bus speeds and higher peak throughputs than earlier technologies. This is achieved at the cost of higher latency.

Like all SDRAM implementations, DDR2 stores memory in memory cells that are activated with the use of a clock signal to synchronize their operation with an external data bus. Like DDR before it, DDR2 cells transfer data both on the rising and falling edge of the clock (a technique called double pumping). The key difference between DDR and DDR2 is that in DDR2 the bus is clocked at twice the speed of the memory cells, so four words of data can be transferred per memory cell cycle. Thus, without speeding up the memory cells themselves, DDR2 can effectively operate at twice the bus speed of DDR.

DDR2's bus frequency is boosted by electrical interface improvements, on-die termination, prefetch buffers and off-chip drivers. However, latency is greatly increased as a trade-off. The DDR2 prefetch buffer is 4 bits deep, whereas it is 2 bits deep for DDR and 8 bits deep for DDR3. While DDR SDRAM has typical read latencies of between 2 and 3 bus cycles, DDR2 may have read latencies between 3 and 9 cycles. Because of this higher latency, DDR SDRAM running at the same bus speed as DDR2 is generally considered superior; DDR2 is, however, able to run at substantially higher bus speeds which equates to an overall increase in throughput. Another cost of the increased speed is the requirement that the chips are packaged in a more expensive and more difficult to assemble BGA package as compared to the TSSOP package of the previous memory generations such as DDR and SDRAM. This packaging change was necessary to maintain signal integrity at higher speeds.

Power savings are achieved primarily due to an improved manufacturing process through die shrinkage, resulting in a drop in operating voltage (1.8 V compared to DDR's 2.5 V). The lower memory clock frequency may also enable power reductions in applications that do not require the highest available speed.

Specification standards

Chips

Standard name	Memory clock	I/O Bus clock	Data transfers per second
DDR2-400	100 MHz	200 MHz	400 Million
DDR2-533	133 MHz	266 MHz	533 Million
DDR2-667	166 MHz	333 MHz	667 Million
DDR2-800	200 MHz	400 MHz	800 Million
DDR2-1066	266 MHz	533 MHz	1066 Million

Modules

For use in PCs, DDR2 SDRAM is supplied in DIMMs with 240 pins and a single locating notch. DIMMs are identified by their peak transfer capacity (often called bandwidth).

Module name	Bus clock	Chip type	Peak transfer rate
PC2-3200	200 MHz	DDR2-400	3.200 GB/s
PC2-4200	266 MHz	DDR2-533	4.264 GB/s

PC2-5300	333 MHz	DDR2-667	5.336 GB/s[1]
PC2-6400	400 MHz	DDR2-800	6.400 GB/s
PC2-8500 (planned)	533 MHz	DDR2-1066	8.500 GB/s

DDR2-xxx (or DDR-xxx) denotes effective clockspeed, whereas PC2-xxxx (or PC-xxxx) denotes theoretical bandwidth (though it is often rounded up or down). Bandwidth is calculated by taking transfers per second and multiplying by eight. This is because DDR2 memory modules transfer data on a bus that is 64 data bits wide, and since a byte is comprised of 8 bits, this equates to 8 bytes of data per transfer.

Optionally implement ECC, which is an extra data byte lane used for correcting minor errors and detecting major errors for better reliability. Modules with ECC are identified by an additional ECC in their designation. PC2-4200 ECC is a PC2-4200 module with ECC.

Be "registered", which improves signal integrity (and hence potentially clock speed) by electrically buffering the signals at a cost of an extra clock of increased latency. Those modules are identified by an additional R in their designation, PC2-4200R is a registered PC2-4200 module, PC2-4200R ECC is the same module but with additional ECC.

DD3 SDRAM

DDR3 SDRAM or double-data-rate three synchronous dynamic random access memory is the name of the new DDR memory standard that is being developed as the successor to DDR2 SDRAM.

The memory comes wlth a promlse of a power consumption reduction of 40% compared to current commercial DDR2 modules, due to DDR3's 90 nm fabrication technology, allowing for lower operating currents and voltages (1.5 V, compared to DDR2's 1.8 V or DDR's 2.5 V). "Dual-gate" transistors will be used to reduce leakage of current.

DDR3's prefetch buffer width is 8 bit, whereas DDR2's is 4 bit, and DDR's is 2 bit.

Theoretically, these modules could transfer data at the effective clockrate of 800-1600MHz (for a single clock bandwidth of 400-800MHz), compared to DDR2's current range of 400-1066 MHz (200-533 MHz) or DDR's range of 200-600 MHz (100-300 MHz). To date, such bandwidth requirements have been mainly on the graphics market, where fast transfer of information between framebuffers is required.

DDR3 sticks maintain the 240-pin DIMM interface of DDR2, allowing DDR3 compatible chipsets to host DDR2 modules (though not both types at once).

Prototypes were announced in early 2005, while the DDR3 specification is expected to be publicly available in mid-2007. Supposedly, Intel has preliminarily announced that they expect to be able to offer support for it in mid 2007 with a version of their upcoming Bearlake chipset. AMD's roadmap indicates their own adoption of DDR3 to come in 2008.

The GDDR3 memory, with a similar name but an entirely dissimilar technology, has been in use for several years in high-end graphic cards such as ones from NVIDIA or ATI Technologies, and as main system memory on the Xbox 360. It is sometimes incorrectly referred to as "DDR3".

Spec standards

Chips

- DDR3-800 : DDR3-SDRAM memory chips specified to run at 100 MHz, I/O clock at 400 MHz
- DDR3-1066: DDR3-SDRAM memory chips specified to run at 133 MHz, I/O clock at 533 MHz
- DDR3-1333: DDR3-SDRAM memory chips specified to run at 166 MHz, I/O clock at 667 MHz
- DDR3-1600: DDR3-SDRAM memory chips specified to run at 200 MHz, I/O clock at 800 MHz

Sticks/Modules

- PC3-6400: DDR3-SDRAM memory stick specified to run at 400 MHz using DDR3-800 chips, 6.40 GB/s bandwidth
- PC3-8500: DDR3-SDRAM memory stick specified to run at 533 MHz using DDR3-1066 chips, 8.53 GB/s bandwidth
- PC3-10600: DDR3-SDRAM memory stick specified to run at 667 MHz using DDR3-1333 chips, 10.67 GB/s bandwidth
- PC3-12800: DDR3-SDRAM memory stick specified to run at 800 MHz using DDR3-1600 chips, 12.80 GB/s bandwidth

Features

DDR3 SDRAM Components:

- Introduction of asynchronous RESET pin
- Support of system level flight time compensation
- On-DIMM Mirror friendly DRAM ballout
- Introduction of CWL (CAS Write Latency) per speed bin

- On-die IO calibration engine
- READ and WRITE calibration

DDR3 Modules

- Fly-by command/address/control bus with On-DIMM termination
- High precision calibration resistors

Advantages compared to DDR2

- Higher bandwidth (up to 1600 MHz)
- Performance increase at low power
- Longer battery life in laptops
- Enhanced low power features and thermal design

Disadvantages compared to DDR2

- Commonly higher CAS Latency
- Lower MFIBS per Quad Cycle

DDR1, DDR2 and DDR4 Memory

DDR SDRAM or double-data-rate synchronous dynamic random access memory is a class of memory integrated circuit used in computers. It achieves greater bandwidth than the preceding single-data-rate SDRAM by transferring data on the rising and falling edges of the clock signal (double pumped). Effectively, it nearly doubles the transfer rate without increasing the frequency of the front side bus.

Thus, a system with a 100 MHz front side bus has an effective clock rate of 200 MHz when DDR SDRAM memory is installed. The same system using SDR (single data rate) SDRAM, will not have its front side bus rate doubled and be limited to a 100 MHz front side bus speed.

With data being transferred 64 bits at a time, DDR SDRAM gives a transfer rate of [mbcr x 2 x 64] / 8; annotated it looks like this: (memory bus clock rate) × 2 (for dual rate) × 64 (number of bits transferred) / 8 (number of bits/byte). Thus with a bus frequency of 100 MHz, DDR-SDRAM gives a max transfer rate of 1600 MB/s.

JEDEC has set standards for speeds of DDR SDRAM, divided into two parts: The first specification is for memory chips and the second is for memory modules. As DDR is superseded by the newer DDR2, the older version is often now referred to as DDR1.

Chips and modules

Standard name	Memory clock	Time between signals	I/O Bus clock	Data transfers per second	Module name	Peak transfer rate
DDR-200	100 MHz	10 ns	100 MHz	200 Million	PC-1600	1.600 GB/s
DDR-266	133 MHz	7.5 ns	133 MHz	266 Million	PC-2100	2.133 GB/s
DDR-333	166 MHz	6 ns	166 MHz	333 Million	PC-2700	2.667 GB/s
DDR-400	200 MHz	5 ns	200 MHz	400 Million	PC-3200	3.200 GB/s

All above listed are specified by JEDEC as JESD79. All RAM speeds in-between or above these listed specifications are not standardized by JEDEC — most often they are simply manufacturer optimizations using higher-tolerance or overvolted chips.

The package sizes in which DDR SDRAM is manufactured are also standardised by JEDEC.

DDR SDRAM memory modules have 184 pins and one notch

There is no architectural difference between DDR SDRAM designed for different clock frequencies, e.g. PC-1600 (designed to run at 100 MHz) and PC-2100 (designed to run at 133 MHz). The number simply designates the speed that the chip is guaranteed to run at. Hence DDR SDRAM can be run at lower clock speeds than it was made for (underclocking) or higher clock speeds than it was made for (overclocking).

DDR SDRAM DIMMs have 184 pins (as opposed to 168 pins on SDRAM, or, 240 pins on DDR2 SDRAM), and can be differentiated from SDRAM DIMMs by the number of notches (DDR SDRAM has one, SDRAM has two). DDR SDRAM operates at a voltage of 2.5 V, compared to 3.3 V for SDRAM. This can significantly reduce power usage. Note: some DIMMs have nominal voltage of 2.6 V.

Many new chipsets use these memory types in dual-channel configurations, which doubles or quadruples the effective bandwidth.

16 I/O Interfaces

I/O PORTS

Most of the Input-Output (I/O) devices like keyboard, mouse, printers, modems and other devices are connected to the computer system through an interfacing facility called I/O ports. The data communications between devices and the system are established through these ports only.

The keyboard, mouse and speakers are connected through special ports. General-purpose I/O ports include serial port, parallel port and game port. Through these I/O ports an I/O device can be connected to the system.

Serial Port

In the Serial Interface Technique, the data is transmitted as 1-bit at a time through a single wire. The parallel data (byte) from the computer bus is converted into serial data (bits) and sent through the serial cable. It slows down the data transfer rate. It enables to communicate date transfer over a distance.

RS232 is the serial communication standard. The system normally supports two Serial ports COM 1 and COM 2. A 9-pin DB9 connector used with COM 1 and 25 pin DB 25 connector is used with COM 2 for connecting devices. An adapted 9 to 25 pin connector can be used to connect devices either to COM 1 or COM 2.

In modern PCs the serial port interface electronics is included in the motherboard chipset itself. Serial port can be enabled by BIOS set-up. The data transfer rate or the communication speed has to be set to match the speed of the devices connected to the system.

Serial Interface Connectors

A 25-pin or 9-pin D-shell subminiature male connector is used on the system as connector for the serial interface. The 25-pin connector was introduced with the PC system, but as not all the 25-pins are used for data transmission, IBM introduced 9-pin connectors with the AT system.

The parallel port also uses 25-pin D type connector but it can be distinguished from the serial port because the parallel port connector is female, whereas the connector for the serial port are male connectors (connectors with pin).

Old style MDA/CGA/EGA video connectors, which use 9-pin D-shell connectors are also female connectors. If the serial cable for your device contains 25-pin connector and the serial port has only 9-pin connector then many 25-pin to 9-pin converters are available in the market, same is true for conecting 9-pin device to a 25-pin port connector you can get a 9-pin to 25-pin converter.

Parallel Port

In a parallel interface technique the data, i.e. the entire byte is transferred to the devices at once as each bit is transmitted much faster than with a serial communication link. Devices like printers, scanners and plotters are connected to the system through female D25 pin connector. A system normally supports one parallel port LPT1 and it can also support more parallel ports.

Parallel ports are not only used to connect printers but also to connect external CD-ROM drives, external hard disk drive, ZIP drives and other mass storage devices. Recent PCs include two new technology parallel ports called External Parallel Ports (EPP) and Extended Capability Port (ECP). These ports are designed to support data transfer in both directions and also the selection of the direction of data flow can be controlled by software.

Working of Parallel Port

In this interfacing system, the signals travel through data cable, eight bits at a time. Other than the data, some control signals are also passed through the cable between the printer and the computer.

The parallel interface is one of the simplest communication system available, in this eight different lines are provided for the eight data lines, for each signal required to control the communication process a new wire is provided. This makes the circuitry required to drive the parallel signals very simple.

However, this simplicity has one drawback that is the cable required for the transmission. The increased numbers of lines make the cable required for the parallel transmission very thick. The number of lines going together have one more problem of cross-talk. When the electrical signals travel together in a cable, these signals start to affect each other as they travel down the cable. This makes the signal from one wire to change the signal on the other wire or the problem of cross-talk (signal crosses over and start talking with other signals) appears.

To prevent this problem of cross-talk it is recommended to keep the length of the parallel cable limited to maximum 10 feet. If the cable length is more than this, there is a chance of cross-talk appearing in the line.

Uni and Bi-directional Parallel Port

The original parallel interfce provided on the initial IBM computer's were designed as printer output port so they were uni-directional, i.e., they could only send the information to the device connected to the port but they could not receive any information from the device.

Later IBM made some changes in the design and made the parallel ports capable of the bi-directional operation.

Enhanced Parallel Port (EPP)

Enhanced Parallel Port or the EPP is a new parallel port specificaion that allows high-speed two-way communication between the computer and the device, other than a printer or scanner.

Extended Capabilities Port (ECP)

Extended Capabilities Port or ECP is also a new high-speed two-way communication parallel port specification, ECP port is mainly used for a printer or scanner.

To connect to a printer to the ECP port you would require:

- EPP/ECP port
- ECP capable printer
- EPP/ECP capable printer cable
- Windows 98/2000/ME/XP operating system

Parallel port provided on the motherboard can be setup as EPP/ECP port using the following procedure

- Enter BIOS setup during computer power on by pressing Del key.
- In the BIOS setup main menu, select Peripheral Setup option.
- Look for Parallel Port Mode.
- Change the mode to EPP/ECP.
- Save and Exit BIOS setup and restart the system.

Game Port

This port in PC is used for connecting game controllers like joystick. The game port adopter is available either in multi I/O cards or in the sound card. Stand alone cards are also available that fit into one of the PC's 8-bit I/O slots.

The game port supports two game controllers at a time using a special split cable. The port is responsible for reporting the X and Y positions of the joystick to the system. It is available through a standard 15-pin D shell connector.

USB Port

Peripheral devices are connected to computers through I/O ports. The devices that support parallel interface standard are connected to parallel ports and devices that support serial interface standard are connected to serial ports.

Normally computers come with one parallel port and two serial ports. Universal Serial Bus

(USB) is a peripheral bus standard that allows a variety of peripheral devices to be connected to computers simultaneously. USB is a single, standardized, easy-to-use way to connect upto 127 USB devices to a computer.

A USB device is connected to computers by plugging it to the USB connector available at the back of the computer. Type A connector and USB port connect the device to the computer. Type B connector and USB port connect individual devices.

USB *Universal Serial Bus*	
The USB "trident" Icon	
Year Created:	January 1996
Width:	1 bits
Number of Devices:	127 per host
Speed:	Up to 480 Mbit/s (USB 2.0)
Style:	Serial
Hotplugging?	Yes
External?	Yes

Features of USB

1. The computer acts as a host.
2. Up to 127 devices can be connected to the host either directly or by way of USB hubs.
3. USB has a data transfer rate of 480 megabits per second.
4. USB devices are hot swappable—the devices can be connected and disconnected at any time.

A USB Series "A" plug

A USB hub with the plastic cover removed

USB Hubs

The USB standard supports upto 127 devices and USB hubs are a part of the standard. A hub has four ports commonly. The hub is plugged to the computer and the devices are plugged to the hub. Hubs can be chained to connect more devices. Hubs can be powered hub or unpowered hub.

The USB standard allows the low powered devices like mice to get their power from the bus i.e. from the powered huh. High power devices like printer or scanner will have their own power supply and hence, unpowered hubs can serve these devices.

USB Cable Connection

Inside the USB cable there are four wires for connections, Red wire for + 5V (power) and brown wire for ground (power). The twisted pair yellow and blue is used for data. The four wires are perfectly shielded.

Different Data Transfer Types Used in USB

There are three modes of data transfers.

They are:

1. **Interrupt:** to transfer little date-devices using this type are keyboard or a mouse.
2. **Bulk:** to transfer data in one big pocket-device like a printer use this type.
3. **Isochronous:** Out streams between the device and the host in real time. Devices like speakers use this mode.

The Hardware

A USB cable has four wires: power, ground, D+ and D–. The signal wires usually operate in differential mode. There are two types of USB devices: high speed and low speed. There are differences in the type, length and connectors that can be used with the two types. Generally the requirements are stricter for high speed devices. A high speed device can transfer data at a maximum of 12 Mbs while low speed is limited to 1.5 Mbs. The PIC 16C745 can only operate at low speed standard. The connector at the computer (A End) is a flattened rectangle while at the device (B end) the connector is square with two cut-off corners. Each USB device is able to draw 100 mA from the cable which allows a device to be bus powered. A device can negotiate up to 500 mA once connected to the USB cable but this power may not be available. If the power is unavailable the device must stay in a low power setting. Obviously devices can be powered externally as well.

The Software

When a device is connected, the computer (or a hub) detects the device by a pullup resister. A pullup resister on the D– wire signals a low speed device, while a high speed device has a pullup on the D+ wire. When detected a series of enumeration steps are started. The enumeration process assigns an identifier number to the device (there can be a maximum of 127 devices on a network) and also tells the host computer what sort of capabilities a device has (input, ouput, etc). The device also informs the computer of its name (Vendor, Product, Version and Serial Number). If the device identifies itself as a HID (Human Interface Device) then the device describes how the data should be interpreted.

USB Hub

A USB hub is a device that allows many USB devices to be connected to a single USB port on the host computer or another hub.

USB hubs are often built into equipment, normally keyboards or, more rarely, monitors or printers. Separate USB hubs come in a wide variety of form factors from boxes that look similar to a network hub to small designs intended to be plugged directly into the USB port on a computer (that is, without a connecting cable).

USB History

- USB 0.7: Released in November 1994.
- USB 0.8: Released in December 1994.
- USB 0.9: Released in April 1995.
- USB 0.99: Released in August 1995.
- USB 1.0 Release Candidate: Released in November 1995.
- USB 1.0: Released in January 1996.

  Specified data rates of 1.5 Mbps (Low-Speed) and 12 Mbps (Full-Speed). Did not anticipate or pass-through monitors. Few such devices actually made it to market.
- USB 1.1: Released in September 1998.

  Fixed problems identified in 1.0, mostly relating to hubs. Earliest revision to be widely adopted.
- USB 2.0: Released in April 2000.

  Added higher maximum speed of 480 Mbps (now called Hi-Speed).
- Mini-B Connector ECN: Released in October 2000.

  Specifications for Mini-B plug and receptable. These should not be confused with Micro-B plug and receptable.
- Errata as of December 2000: Released in December 2000.
- Resistor ECN: Released in May 2002.
- Errata as of May 2002: Released in May 2002.
- Interface Associations ECN: Released in May 2003.

  New standard desriptor was added that allows multiple interfaces to be associated with a single device function.
- Rounded Chamfer ECN: Released in October 2003.
- Unicode ECN: Released in February 2005.
- USB On-The-Go Supplement 1.0: Released in December 2001.
- USB On-The-Go Supplement 1.0a: Released in June 2003.
- USB On-The-Go Supplement 1.2: Released in April 2006.
- USB On-The-Go Supplement 1.3: Released in December 2006. This is the current revision

USB Connectors

Connector types

There are several types of USB connectors, and some have been added as the specification has progressed. From the original USB specification:

- Standard-A plug
- Standard-A receptacle
- Standard-B plug
- Standard-B receptacle

Added in the first engineering change noticed to the USB 2.0 specification:

- Mini-B plug
- Mini-B receptacle

Added in the Universal Serial Bus Micro-USB Cables and Connectors Specification:

- Micro-A plug (white)
- Micro-AB receptacle (gray)
- Micro-B plug (black)
- Micro-B receptacle (black)

Adapters, also from the Universal Serial Bus Micro-USB Cables and Connectors Specification (Note that no other adapters are allowed.):

- Standard-A receptacle to Micro-A plug
- Micro-USB is a connector announced by the USB Implementers Forum (USB-IF) on January 4, 2007. It is intended to replace the Mini-USB plugs used in many new smartphones and PDAs. The Micro-USB plug is rated for 10,000 connect-disconnect cycles. It is about half the height of the mini-USB connector in widespread use today but features a similar width.

USB Device Classes

Devices that attach to the bus can be full-custom devices requiring a full-custom device driver to be used, or may belong to a device class. These classes define an expected behavior in terms of device and interface descriptors so that the same device driver may be used for any device that claims to be a member of a certain class. An operating system is supposed to implement all device classes so as to provide generic drivers for any USB device.

Device classes are decided upon by the Device Working Group of the USB Implementers Forum. If the class is to be set for the entire device, the number is assigned to the bDeviceClass field of the device descriptor, and if it is to be set for a single interface on a device, it is assigned to the bInterfaceClass field of the interface descriptor. Both of these are a single byte each, so a maximum of 254 different device classes are possible (values 0x00 and 0xFF are reserved). If bDeviceClass is set to 0x00, the operating system will look at bInterfaceClass of each interface to determine the device class. Each class also optionally supports a SubClass and Protocol subdefinition. These can be used as the main device classes are continuously revised.

The most used device/interface classes (grouped by assigned class ID) are:

0x00 Reserved value - used in the device descriptor to signify that the interface descriptor holds the device class identifier for each interface.

0x01 USB audio device class, sound card-like devices.

0x02 USB communications device class ("CDC"), used for modems, network cards, ISDN connections, Fax.

0x03 USB human interface device class ("HID"), keyboards, mice, etc.

0x06 Still image capture device class, identical to the Picture Transfer Protocol as used across USB

0x07 USB printer device class, printer-like devices.

0x08 USB mass storage device class used for flash drives, portable hard drives, memory card readers, digital cameras, digital audio players etc. This device class presents the device as a block device (almost always used to store a file system).

0x09 USB hubs.

0x0B Smart card readers.

0x0E USB video device class, webcam-like devices, motion image capture devices.

0xE0 Wireless controllers, for example Bluetooth dongles.

0xFF Custom device class - used to establish that a device or interface does not support any standard device class and requires custom drivers.

USB Flash Drivers or Pen Drive

USB flash drives are NAND-type flash memory data storage devices integrated with a USB (universal serial bus) interface. They are typically small, lightweight, removable and rewritable. As of November 2006, memory capacities for USB Flash Drives currently are sold from 32 megabytes up to 64 gigabytes. Capacity is limited only by current flash memory densities, although cost per megabyte may increase rapidly at higher capacities due to the expensive components. (USB Memory card readers are also available, whereby rather than being built-in, the memory is a removable Flash memory card housed in what is otherwise a regular USB flash drive, as described below.)

USB flash drives offer potential advantages over other portable storage devices, particularly the floppy disk. They are more compact, generally faster, hold more data, and are more reliable (due to both their lack of moving parts, and their more durable design) than floppy disks. These types of drives use the USB mass storage standard, supported natively by modern operating systems such as Linux, Mac OS X, Unix, and Windows.

A flash drive consists of a small printed circuit board encased in a plastic or metal casing, making the drive sturdy enough to be carried about in a pocket, as a key fob, or on a lanyard. Only the USB connector protrudes from this protection, and is usually covered by a removable cap. Most flash drives use a standard type-A USB connection allowing them to be connected directly to a port on a personal computer.

To access the data stored in a flash drive, the drive must be connected to a computer, either by plugging it into a USB host controller built into the computer, or into a USB hub. Flash drives are active only when plugged into a USB connection and draw all necessary power from the supply provided by that connection.

However, some flash drives, especially high-speed drives utilizing the USB 2.0 standard, may require more power than the limited amount provided by a bus-powered USB hub, such as those built into some computer keyboards or monitors. These drives will not work unless plugged directly into a host controller (i.e., the ports found on the computer itself) or a self-powered hub.

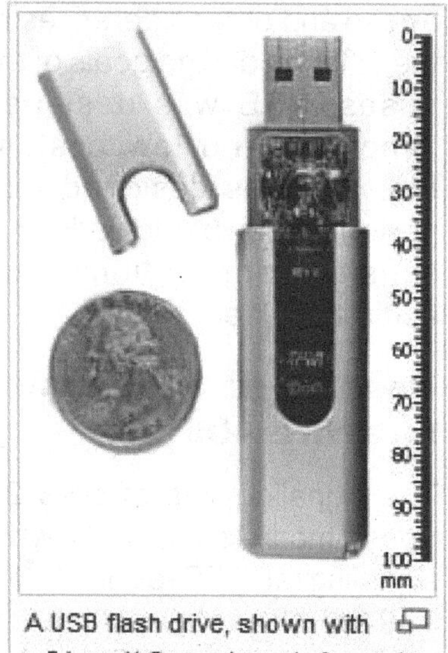

A USB flash drive, shown with a 24 mm U.S. quarter coin for scale.

USB 2.0

Its speed reached a performance level sufficient for consumer equipment while retaining compatibility with older devices. An example of how the popularity of USB displaced FireWire in a commercial device is the Apple iPod. It was originally released with a FireWire connector, which was eventually modified to allow for both USB and FireWire connections when the product was released for Windows. 3rd generation iPods used USB and Firewire for data transfer and only allows a FireWire connection to charge the battery from the main adapter. The iPod does charge via both cables when connected to the host computer. With the 4th generation and newer, iPods use USB for data transfer and both USB and Firewire for charging. The Firewire controller chip set has been removed in favour with reduced costs. The iPod Nano and shuffle don't even support Firewire, only supporting USB.

Today, USB Hi-Speed is used in many consumer products. FireWire, however, retains its popularity in areas such as video and audio production.

Technical differences

The most significant technical differences between FireWire and USB include the following:

- USB networks use a tiered-star topology, while FireWire networks use a repeater-based topology.
- USB uses a "speak-when-spoken-to" protocol; peripherals cannot communicate with the host unless the host specifically requests communication. A FireWire device can communicate with any other node at any time, subject to network conditions.
- A USB network relies on a single host at the top of the tree to control the network. In a FireWire network, any capable node can control the network.

These and other differences reflect the differing design goals of the two buses: USB was designed for simplicity and low cost, while FireWire was designed for high performance, particularly in time-sensitive applications such as audio and video.

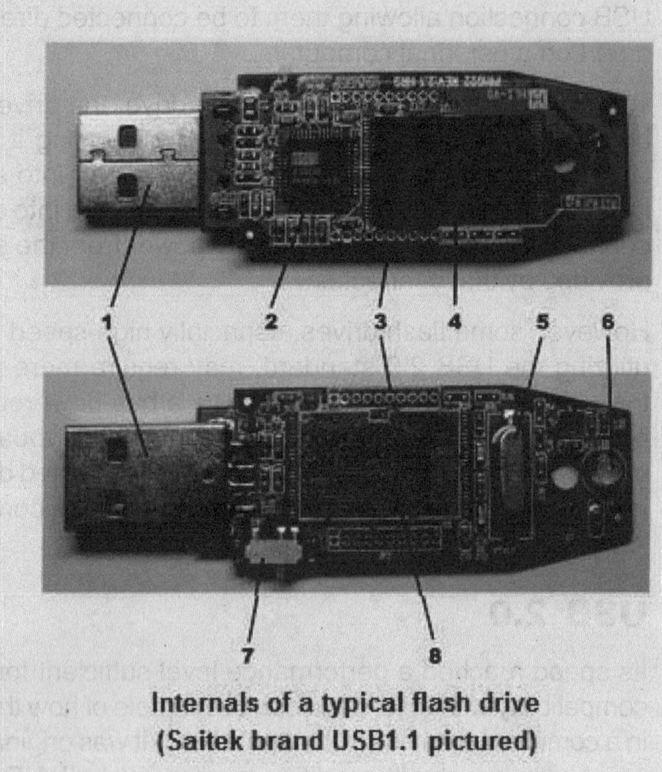

Internals of a typical flash drive (Saitek brand USB1.1 pictured)

USB 2.0 Hi-Speed versus FireWire 400

The signaling rate of USB 2.0 Hi-Speed mode is 480 Mb/s, while the signaling rate of FireWire 400 (IEEE 1394a, the slower, yet more common variant of firewire as of 2007) is 393.216 Mb/s, which would appear to indicate that USB should be slightly faster, but in reality the situation is far more complicated than that and other design factors can dwarf a relatively small difference in signaling rate. USB requires more host processing power than FireWire due to the need for the host to provide the arbitration and scheduling of transactions. USB transfer rates are theoretically higher than FireWire due to the need for FireWire devices to arbitrate for bus access. A single FireWire device may achieve a transfer rate for FireWire 400 as high as 41 MB/s, while for USB 2.0 the rate can theoretically be 55 MB/s (for a single device). In a multi-device environment FireWire rapidly loses ground to USB: FireWire's mixed speed networks and long connection chains dramatically affect its performance.

The peer-to-peer nature of FireWire requires devices to arbitrate, which means a FireWire bus must wait until a given signal has propagated to all devices on the bus. The more devices on the bus, the lower is its peak performance. Conversely, for USB the maximum timing model is fixed and is limited only by the host-device branch (not the entire network). Furthermore, the host-centric nature of USB allows the host to allocate more bandwidth to high priority devices instead of forcing them to compete for bandwidth as in FireWire.

All of the above indicates that USB 2 should be faster than firewire 400 but tests have generally shown that for mass storage using normal consumer equipment firewire is faster often by a significant margin.

17 Computer Installation

Introduction

In this section we shall see how one can assemble a perfect computer. Assembling a computer is a very easy job, one just need to select proper components and then connect them properly. Let us see how to build your dream PC.

First, buy the components required to make the PC and keep them ready.

- Monitor, Main case with Power Supply, keyboard, Mouse
- Motherboard, Procesor, RAM
- Display card, Sound card, Modem card, LAN card
- Floppy drive, Hard Disk drive, CD/DVD drive
- Speaker/Microphone, External, Modem

Keep the following tools handy

- Star/Philips screwdriver set, nose pliers

Before starting the assembly process, touch some metallic grounded object, to make sure that you are free from any static charge. Also, handle the Motherboard, CPU, RAM etc. static sensitive components only from its edges.

Following is a step-by-step procedure to assemble a computer.

Remove Cover of the Main Unit

1. Open the four screws at the back of the system's main unit.
2. Slide the top cover off the main unit.

Remove Base Plate from the Main Unit

1. Remove the screws holding the base plate to the main unit
2. Lift the base plate out of the main unit

Mount the Motherboard to the Base Plate

1. Place the Motherboard on the base plate using the spacers and screws provided (this process is explained later).

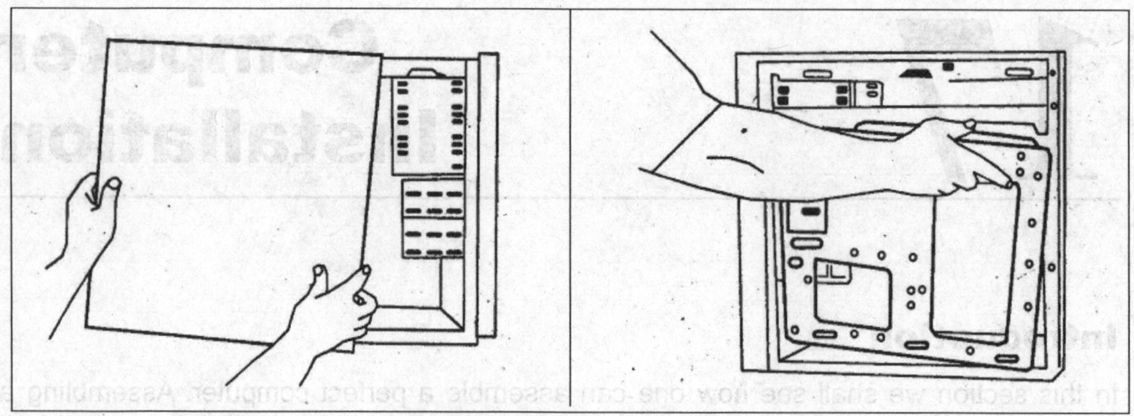

2. Tighten the screws provided to fix the Motherboard to the base plate. Do not completely tighten the screws, leave a little room to make any adjustments when some new expansion card is installed.

   Tighten the screws only after you mount all the cards to the Motherboard. One can place foam pieces or old newspaper between Motherboard and base plate, so that Motherboard components will not touch the base plate and short circuit.

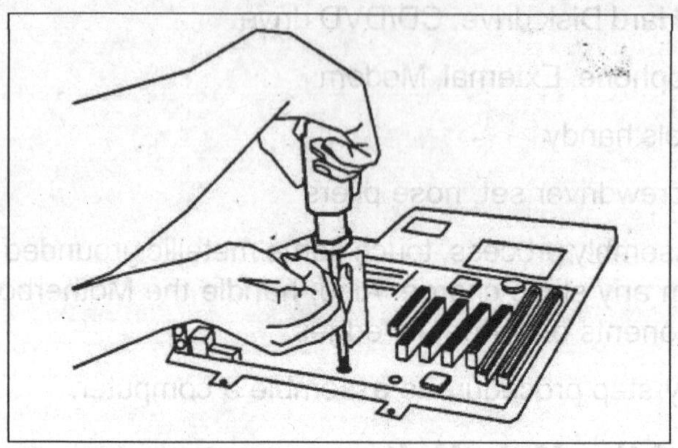

Attach the Processor to the Motherboard

1. Attach the CPU to the Motherboard

   Based on the CPU used, you may use socket-370 or SEC slot socket.

2. Attach CPU fan to the power connector (this is very important, as excessive heat build up may permanently damage the processor)

3. Set any jumpers to configure the Motherboard for the CPU type, this information should be available in the Motherboard manual.

   On most of the new Motherboards, the board automatically detects the processor clock speed and core voltage, without any need for setting up the jumpers

Attach the RAM Modules to the Motherboard

1. To attach RAM module, properly align both ends of the module with the slot given on the Motherboard and push the module into the slot with a smooth push.

   Based on the Motherboard, you may need to install SIMM or DIMM type memory module.

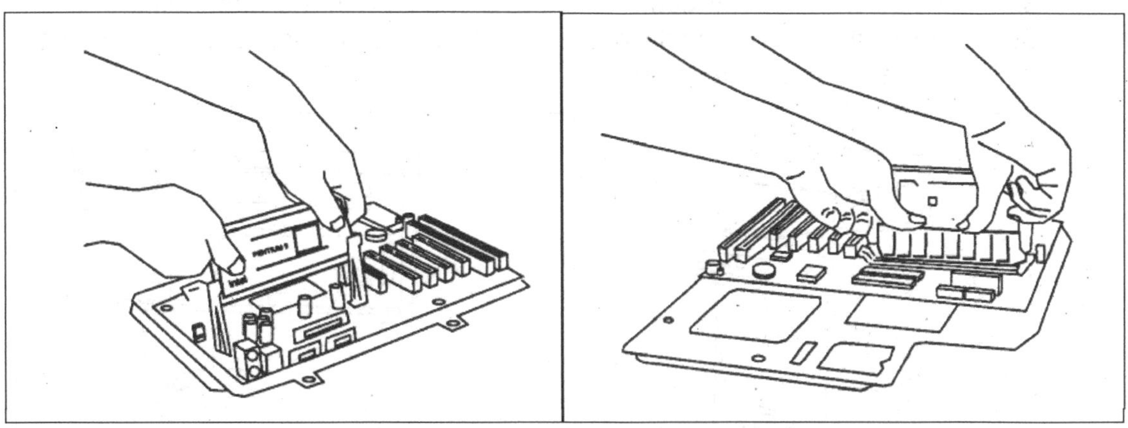

Mount the Motherboard into the Computer Unit

1. Once the CPU and Memory is attached to the Motherboard you can mount the back plate (with the Motherboard) into the main system unit.

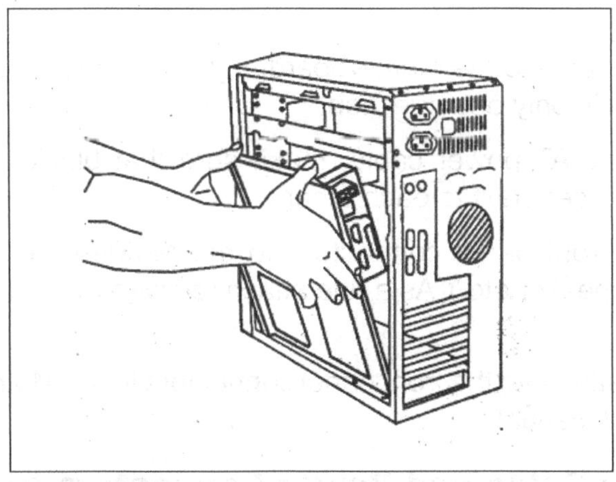

   Remember to tighten the screws only lightly. You can fully tighten them after the expansion cards are mounted on the Motherboard.

Attach Storage Devices (Floppy/HDD/CD drive etc.) to the Main Unit

1. Place the Floppy Disk Drive (FDD), Hard Disk Drive (HDD) and CD/DVD etc. to

their respective bays, tighten the side holding screws only after power and data cables are attached.

CD/DVD and floppy drive need to be inserted into their bays from the opening at the front of the system unit.

If your Motherboard and HDD support ATA/66, then use new ATA/66 cable. Connect Blue Connector of ATA/66 cable to the IDE channel on the Motherboard. Black Connector of this cable should be connected to the master IDE drive, connect White Connector to the slave device.

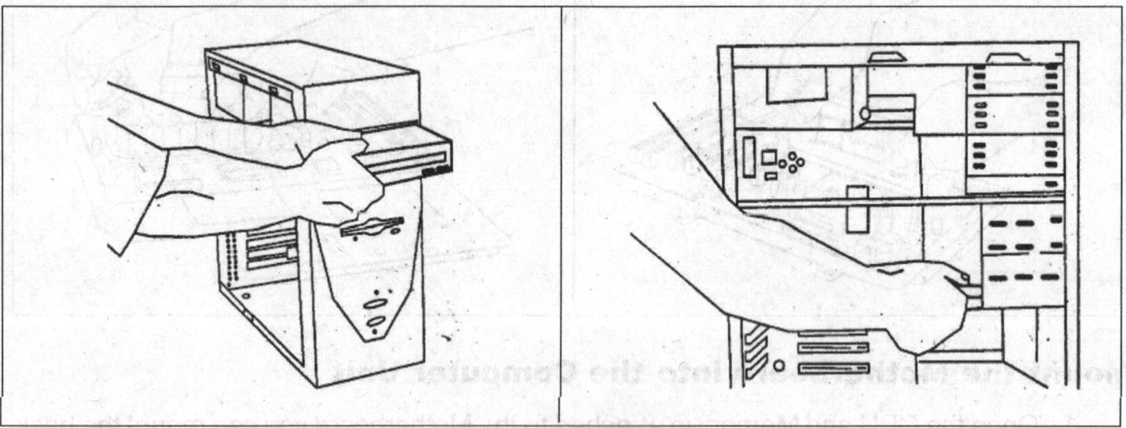

Connect Cables (Reset, Speaker, Power Indicator LED etc.) to the Motherboard

1. Connect power cable to the Motherboard. If you have ATX Power Supply then the connector will fit in only one direction.

   When connecting AT power cable, make sure that black ground lines on both connector are placed next to each other.

2. Attach various front panel connectors to the Motherboard (reset, power/HDD indicator LED, speaker etc.). As a rule attach red wire to pin 1 and black wire to pin 2.

   Information for attaching the front panel connectors to the Motherboard are given in the Motherboard manual.

Attach Drive Data Cable and Power Connectors to the Storage Devices

1. Connect primary IDE channel to the master/boot hard disk drive.

   Primary IDE channel is indicated as Pri-Master or IDEO on the Motherboard. When attaching data cable, red/dotted wire on the cable should align with pin-0 on the connector.

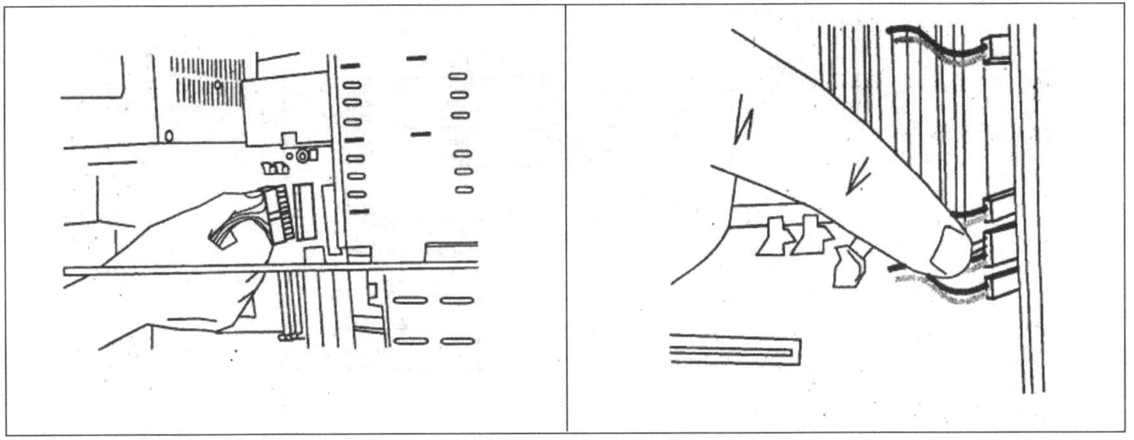

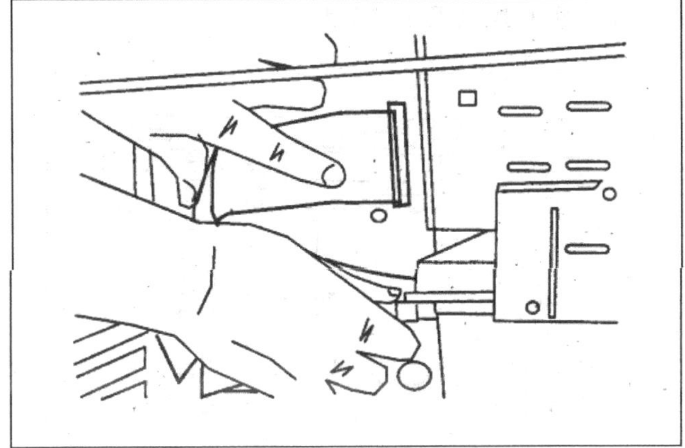

2. Attach power connector to the hard disk drive.

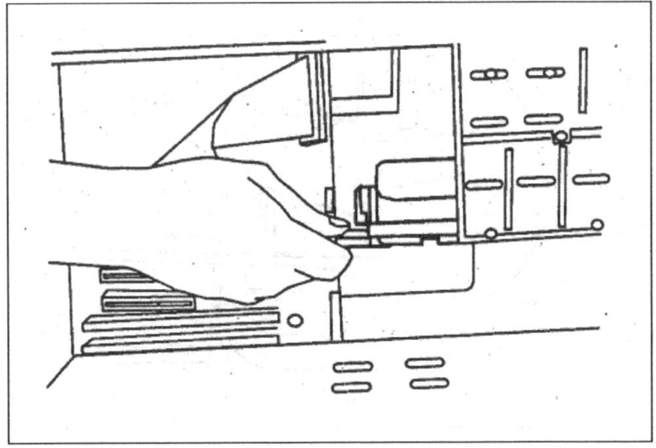

3. Connect secondary IDE channel to the CD/DVD drive.

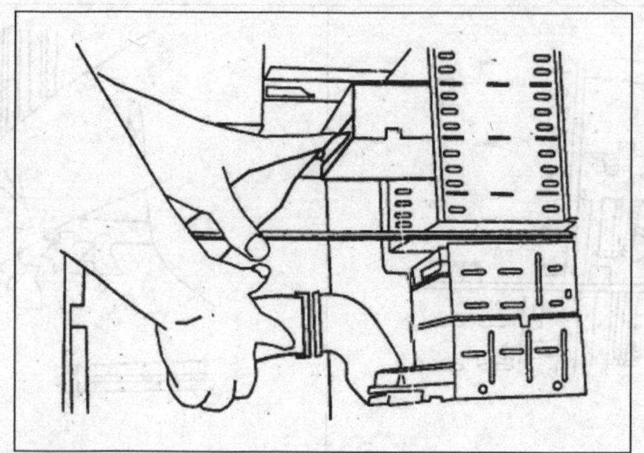

4. Attach power connector the CD/DVD drive.

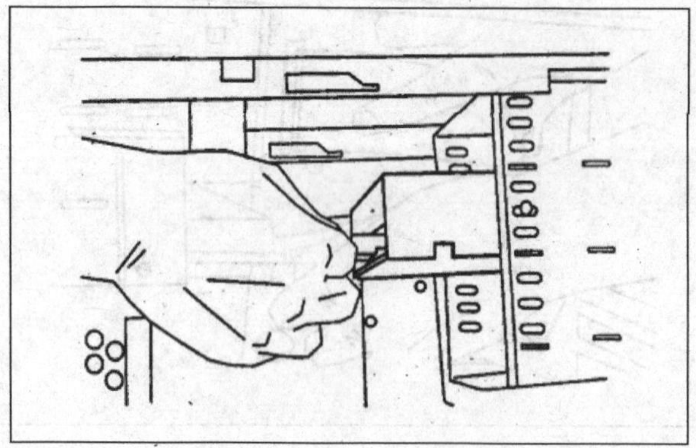

5. Connect floppy drive to the Motherboard connector.

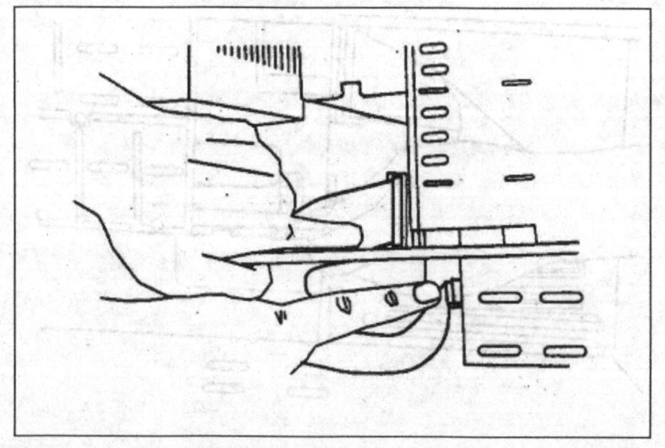

6. Attach power connector to the floppy drive.

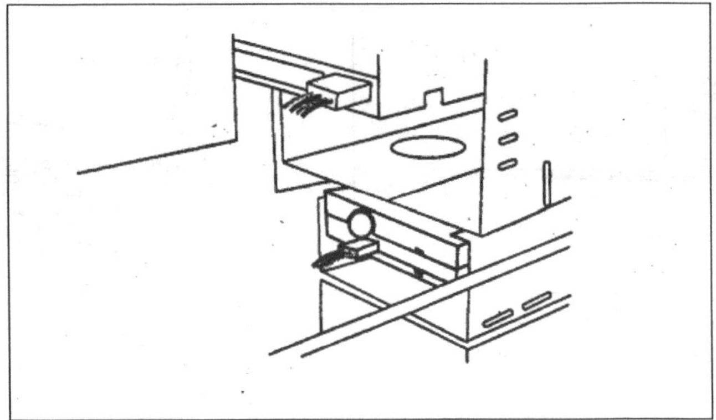

Connecting CD/DVD drive to Secondary IDE channel will improve the speed of the Primary IDE Hard disk drive, compared to connecting the CD/DVD as slave to the Primary IDE channel hard disk drive.

A HDD/CD/DVD can be made master/slave by changing the position of jumper provided on its back.

Once the data cable and power cable is connected to the hard disk and floppy disk drives, use some rubber band or tie-wrap to arrange the data and power cable, so that the air flow inside the system is not blocked.

Connect external port cables

1. Connect Serial, Parallel, Game, Infrared etc. ports to the Motherboard. Connectors for this are provided with the Motherboard. ATX Motherboard does not require this, as these ports are built into the Motherboard itself.

   Position of these connectors, on the Motherboard, is generally provided in the Motherboard manual.

   Arrange these connectors with the help of some rubber band or tie-wrap so that they do not obstruct the airflow inside the system case and keep the system cool.

Connect Display Card and Sound Card

If your Motherboard does not have integrated Display/Sound card then you need to connect these cards to your system.

When handling these cards remember to handle them by edges to prevent any damage due to static charge.

1. To connect the cards find an empty slot
2. Insert the card by first aligning card's edge connectors to the slot on the Motherboard.
3. Slide in the card into the slot by gently rocking the card back and forth and pushing down

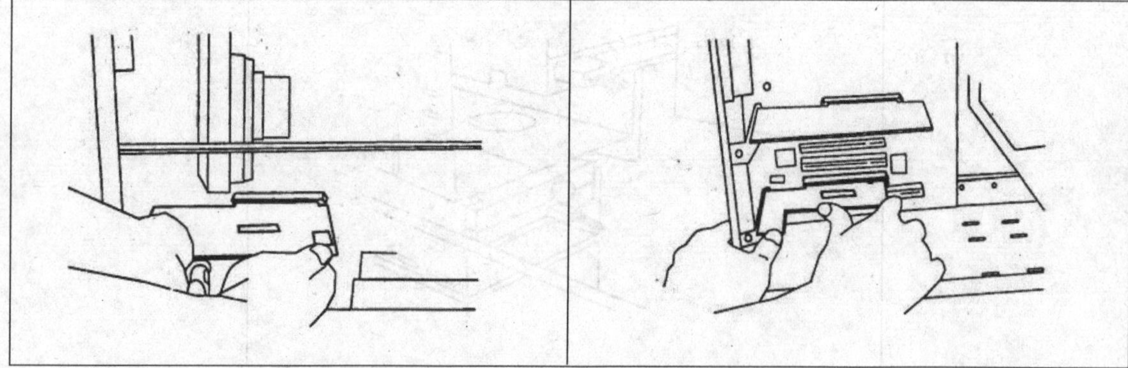

Never try to force a card into the slot

Make sure that the card is firmly seated in the slot

4. Tighten the screw to fix the card to the Motherboard.

Connect CD Audio Cable

1. To use you CD drive to hear Audio CDs, connect Audio Out socket on the CD/DVD drive to the CD-in connector on the Soundcard/Motherboard (if the Motherboard has built in Soundcard)

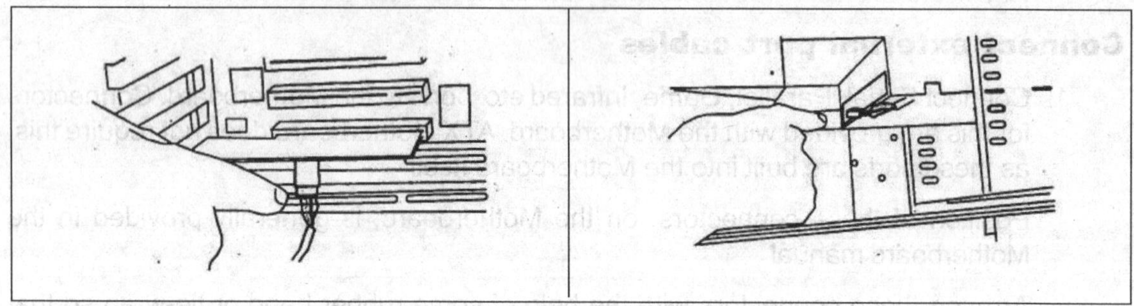

The cable required to make this connection is generally provided with the CD/DVD drive.

Connect Peripherals

1. Connect keyboard to the round opening provided at the back of the system.

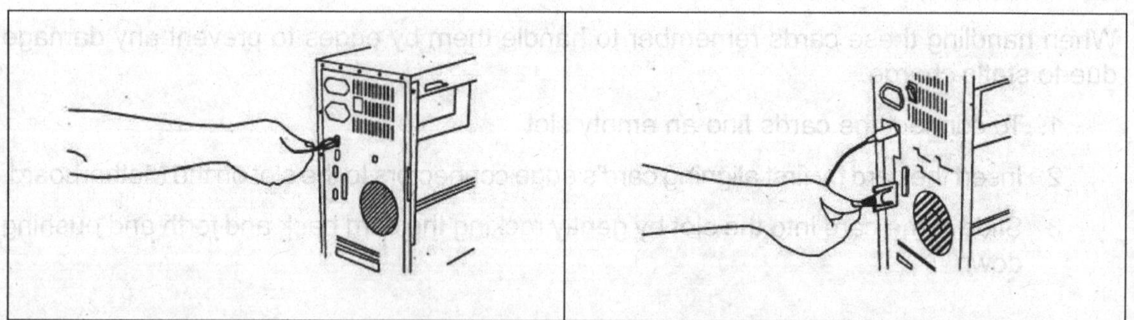

2. Connect mouse to the serial port connector provided at the back of the system.

   If you have PS/2 keyboard then connect it to the lower PS/2 port (port closer to the surface of the Motherboard), upper PS/2 port is used to connect a PS/2 mouse.

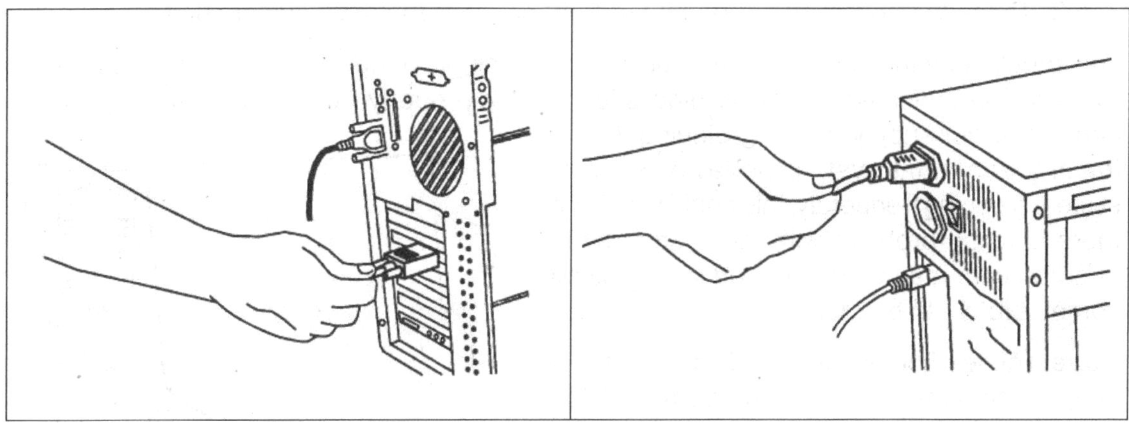

Connect External Cables

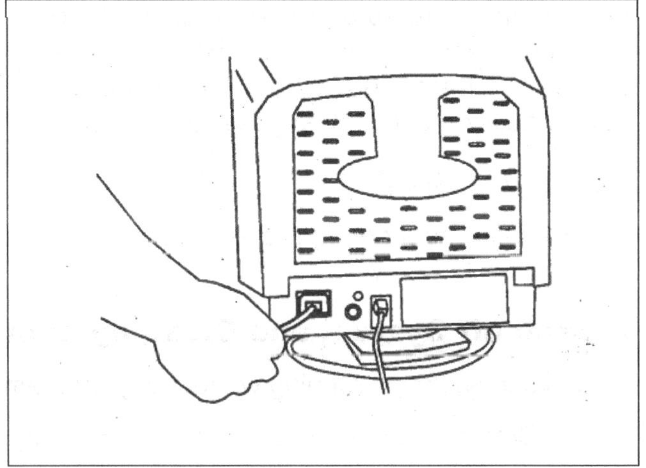

1. Connect Data cable from the monitor to the connector at the back of the display card.
2. Connect mains power cord to the system's power supply.
3. Connect power cord from the monitor to the power supply.

Depending on the type of monitor power cord, the cord may be connected directly to the mains power supply or to a connector provided on the system unit power supply near the mains power connector.

Before connecting computer to a mains power outlet, make sure that the power outlet has proper earthing. This is very important, as improper earthing could permanent damage the computer.

Get the earthing checked by an electrician, without proper earthing, floating voltage on the power line could damage the electronics inside the computer.

Check Connections

Now you are ready to switch on the system, but before switching on the system, check all connections; make sure that there is no loose contact anywhere. Check that all cards are seated properly into their sockets. This is a very important step before switching on the system. One should careful! check all the cards and connectors.

Switch on the System

1. Turn the mains power on
2. Switch on the power supply/UPS etc. if you are using any.
3. Press the power on button on the front panel of the main system unit.

You should hear the hard disk drive spinning and a single beep sound will be heard from the system. This indicates that everything is functioning properly. Make sure that the CPU fan and the power supply fan are spinning. Check for any abnormal system behavior such as system stopping frequently, this could mean that there is some problem with the system setup or some card may be configured incorrectly or some card could be loose.

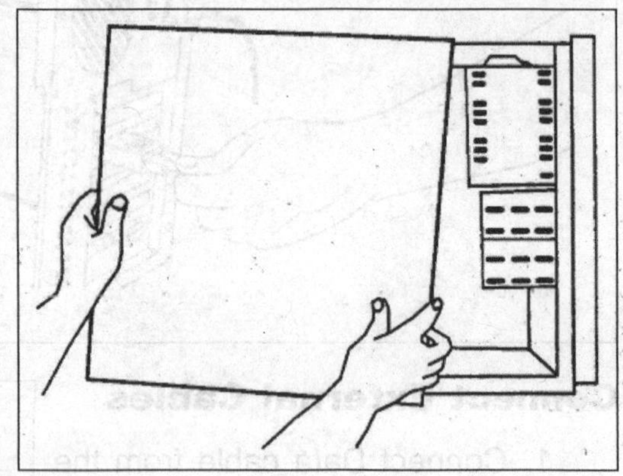

Current generation Motherboards do not require jumper setup they can be setup from the BIOS setup program. Also, most of these Motherboards are auto-jumper type, which do not require any jumper setting. Based on the processor being used the Motherboard automatically required changes in the setup.

Configure BIOS

Ones things are working properly you can make changes in the BIOS Setup to make function in a better way.

Switch off System and Close System Unit's Cover

Once your system is running without any problem, the system cover can be closed.

1. Before closing the cover, switch off the system.
2. Slide the cover on the system unit and fasten the screws at the back of the unit.

Install the required Software/Programs

Ones your machine is ready, you need to install the operating system (Windows 98/NT/2000/XP, Linux etc.) into your system. Ones the operating system is installed, install the software required for your work, such as the Microsoft Office, Tally, DTP software such as CorelDraw, PageMaker, Photoshop, etc. You can also install various regional fonts and their keyboard, if your job requires it.

18 New Computer Devices

Zip Drives

A high-capacity floppy disk drive developed by Iomega Corporation, Zip disks are slightly larger than conventional floppy disks, and about twice as thick. They can hold 100 or 250 MB of data. Because they're relatively inexpensive and durable, they have become a popular media for backing up hard disks and for transporting large files.

A Zip drive is a small, portable disk drive used primarily for backing up and archiving personal computer files. The trademarked Zip drive was developed and is sold by Iomega Corporation. Zip drives and disks come in two sizes. The 100 megabyte size actually holds 100,431,872 bytes of data or the equivalent of 70 floppy diskettes. There is also a 250 megabyte drive and disk. The Iomega Zip drive comes with a software utility that lets you copy the entire contents of your hard drive to one or more Zip disks.

The Zip drive can be purchased in either a parallel or a Small Computer System Interface (SCSI) version. In the parallel version, a printer can be chained off the Zip drive so that both can be plugged into your computer's parallel port.

DVD ROM

DVD stand stands for digital video disc or digital versatile disc, is the next generation of optical disc storage technology. It is bigger, faster CD that can hold cinema-like view, better-than-CD audio, and compatriot CD data. Using a DVD you can have home entertainment, computers, and business information with a single digital format. The DVD will eventually replace audio/video CD, videotape, laserdisc, CD-ROM, and video game cartridges.

There are various variations of DVD; DVD-ROM or DVD-R are physical formats and DVD-Video or DVD-Audio are application formats. DVD-ROM is the base format that holds data. Physical format of DVD-ROM includes recordable variations DVD-R, DVD-RAM, DVD-RW, and DVD-RW. The application formats include DVD-Video, DVD-Video Recording, DVD-Audio, DVD-Audio Recording, DVD Stream Recording, and SACD.

Storage Capacity of DVDs

DVDs are of the same diameter and thickness as CDs, and they are made using some of the same materials and manufacturing methods. Like a CD, the data on a DVD is encoded in the form of small pits and bumps in the track of the disc. A DVD is composed of several layers of plastic, totalling about 1.2 millimeters thick. Each layer is created by injection molding polycarbonate plastic. This process forms a disc that has microscopic bumps arranged as a single, continuous and extremely long spiral track of data.

Once the clear pieces of polycarbonate are formed, a thin reflective layer is sputtered onto the disc, covering the bumps. Aluminium is used behind the inner layers, but a semi-reflective gold layer is used for the outer layers, allowing the laser to focus through the outer and onto the inner layers. After all the layers are made, each one is coated with lacquer, squeezed together and cured under infrared light.

For single-sides discs, the label is silk-screened onto the nonreadable side. Double-sided discs are printed only on the nonredable area near the hold in the middle. If you could lift the data track off a single layer of a DVD, and stretch it out into a straight line, it would be almost 7.5 miles long. A double-sided, double-layer DVD would have 30 miles of data.

Multi-Layer Storage

To increase the storage capacity, a DVD can have up to four layers, two on each side. The laser that reads the disc can actually focus on the second layer through the first layer. Here is a list of the capacities of different forms of DVDs:

DVD disc capacity

	Single layer capacity		Dual/Double layer capacity	
Physical size	**GB**	**GiB**	**GB**	**GiB**
12 cm, single sided	4.7	4.38	8.5	7.92
12 cm, double sided	9.4	8.75	17.1	15.93
8 cm, single sided	1.4	1.30	2.6	2.42
8 cm, double sided	2.8	2.61	5.2	4.84

Note: GB here means gigabyte, equal to 10^9 (or 1,000,000,000) bytes. Many programs will display gibibyte (GiB), equal to 2^{30} (or 1,073,741,824) bytes.

Example: A disc with 8.5 GB capacity is equivalent to: (8.5 × 1,000,000,000) / 1,073,741,824 H" 7.92 GiB.

Size Note: There is a difference in size between + and - DL DVD formats. For example, the 12 cm single sided disk has capacities:

Disk Type	Sectors	bytes	GB	GiB
DVD-R SL	2,298,496	4,707,319,808	4.7	4.384
DVD+R SL	2,295,104	4,700,372,992	4.7	4.378
DVD-R DL	4,171,712	8,543,666,176	8.5	7.957
DVD+R DL	4,173,824	8,547,991,552	8.5	7.961

Capacity Nomenclature

The four basic types of DVD are referred to by their capacity in gigabytes, rounded up to the nearest integer.

DVD type	Name
Single sided, single layer	DVD-5
Single sided, dual layer	DVD-9
Double sided, single layer	DVD-10
Double sided, dual layer	DVD-18

Another format in limited use is a double sided DVD with one side comprising a single layer of data while the opposite side comprises two layers of data (effectively a DVD-5 on one side bonded to a DVD-9 on the other). This format holds approximately 12.3 GB of data and is known as DVD-14.

Web Camera

A web camera is basically a low-end digital video camera with low resolution and fixed focus lens. This camera is suited for webcasting, video messaging, etc., applications. One can use the web camera to make low-grade movies and capture still images.

In recent years, source-data automation has expanded to allow the direct entry of graphic information, as well as text-based information via scanners. In a process called imaging, a scanner converts a drawing, a picture, or any document into computer- recognizable form by shinning a light on the image and sensing the intensity of the reflection at each point of the image. That is, the hard-copy image is translated into an electronic format that can be interpreted by and stored on computers. The electronic version of the image can then be stored, probably on disk, and reproduced on the screen when needed.

The image to be stored can be handwritten notes, a photograph, a drawing, an insurance form - anything that can be digitized. Once an image has been digitized and entered to the computer system, it can be retrieved, displayed, altered, merged with text, stored, and sent via data communications to one or several remote locations. Businesses find imaging particularly useful for documents, since they can view an exact replica of the original document at any time. Professional photo agencies are the another area where imaging is useful. Here the film that was shot with a conventional camera is processed onto optical disk instead of prints or slides. Professional photo agencies keep thousands of images on file, ready to be leased for a fee. Typically a couple of dozen small-size images can be displayed on the screen at one time; a particular image can be enlarged to full screen size with a click of a mouse button.

A digital camera can store many more pictures than an ordinary camera. Pictures taken using a digital camera are stored inside its memory and can be transferred to a computer by connecting the camera to it. A digital camera takes pictures by converting the light passing through the lens at the front into a digital image.

It does not by using a grid of tiny light sensors which concert the light that is falling on them into binary patterns of 0s and 1s. Different binary patterns are used to represent the different colours and shades of light that make up a picture. Pictures taken using a digital camera can be easily saved and transferred from one computer to another where they can be edited using special graphics software.

Some digital camera can also capture short clips of moving images but for longer video clips a digital video camera is needed. However both of these types of camera are still quite expensive.

Modem

The modem is a device which allows you to connect your computer to any other computer, anywhere else in the world using a telephone line. This allows you to communicate with the connected person, transfer data, copy software/programs from the connected computer, sent and received mail using e-mail, etc.

Currently, the modem can also be used to sent and receive fax, for this you use modem as fax device. Also you can use modem to connect to the Internet. There are two main types of modems: Internal and External Modems.

Let us see how modem works?

When the computer is switched on and is ready to transmit data, it sends a Data Terminal Ready (DTR) signal to the modem. When the modem is ready to receive data or instruction from the computer, it sends a Data Set Ready (DSR) signal to the computer. Both these signals must be present before the next step can happen. Next, the computer sends a command to the modem to go "Off Hook", *i.e.*, to open communication with the phone line. Next, the computer issues a command to modem to dial a phone number.

Installing the Modem

There are two ways by which the modem can be installed. One of them is Automatically and the other is Manually.

Automatically

After connecting the modem when you switch on the computer system, Windows 95/98 should automatically detect the modem and ask for the modem driver software. If the auto detection does not work then:

1. Click on the Start/Setting/Controls Panel.
2. In the control panel window double click on Add New Hardware icon.
3. In the next Add New Hardware Wizard screen, to automatically detect new hardware click on Next>option.
4. In the next screen select Yes for Do you want Windows to search for your new hardware? question and click on Next option.
5. Click on Modem to select it.
6. Click on the Next>option, it will start the auto detection process, which may take some time.
7. Finally next screen will appear with an option to click on Details..... button to see the list of detected hardware.
8. Click on Finish option to install the drivers for the detected hardware.

If your modem was not detected during this process then you need to manually install the modem driver software.

Manually

For this, follow the above instructions for step 1 & 2 and in the 3rd, in Add New Hardware Wizard screen, do the following:

1. Click on No, I want to select the hardware for a list, to the Do you want Windows to search for your new hardware? question.
2. Click on Next>option.
3. In the next screen a list of hardware appear, from the list click on Modem.
4. Click on Next>option.
5. Next Windows will try to automatically detect the modem.

To manually install the modem driver,

1. Click on Don't detect my modem; I will select it from a list.
2. Click on Next>option. A list of modem manufacturers and their modem models are shown on the next screen. There is also an option called Have Disk ....., if you have received a modem driver disk or CD with your modem then.
3. Click on the Have Disk . . . . option.
4. Place the driver disk/CD into proper drive and in the next Install From Disk screen select the proper drive. You can also click on Browse . . . . option to search for the driver disk/CD.

5. Once the driver is found on disk, click on OK, this will install the modem driver into the computer system. The driver could be on some sub-directory of the driver disk/CD, check the manual that came with the modem.
6. Restart the computer to make the modem active.

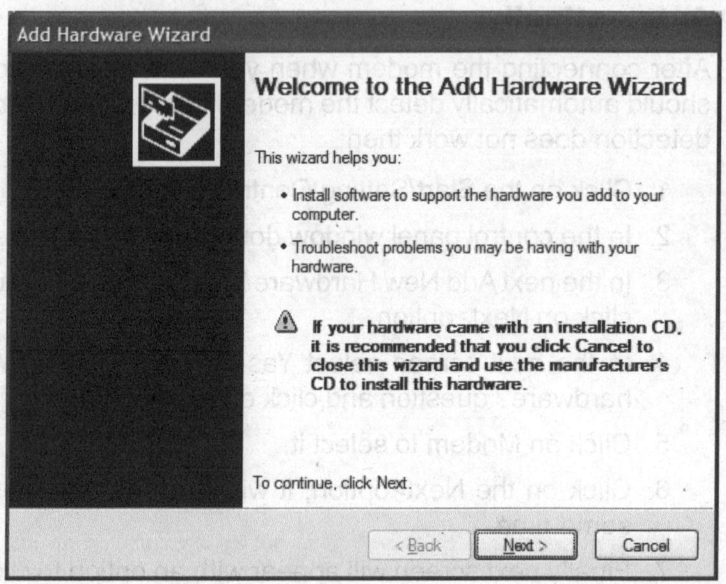

Sometimes the driver disk/CD that comes with the modem contains a SETUP.EXE or INSTALL.EXE program. Running this program will automatically install the modem driver to the Windows.

Flash Disk

A flash drive, related to a solid state drive, is a storage device that uses flash memory rather than conventional spinning platters to store data. Unlike a USB flash drive or keydrive, flash drives tend to physically imitate conventional hard drives in size, shape, and interface so that they may act as a replacement for hard drives.

These products are typically used as low power, rugged replacements for hard drives, especially in installations exposed to extreme conditions. The flash memory cells tend to fail after around a million writes which made early devices unsuitable for storage which is often updated in place, such as swap files. To address this problem, some flash disk vendors have introduced wear-levelling techniques that track usage and transparently relocate the data in highly utilized extents of storage to extents that have been less utilized. Unlike solid state drives, flash drives do not generally require backup battery systems.

Another use for flash drives is running light weight operating systems designed specifically for turning general-purpose PCs into network appliances comparable to more expensive routers and firewalls. In this situation, a write protected flash drive containing the whole operating system is used to boot the system. A similar system could boot from CD, floppy disk or a traditional hard drive but flash memory is a good choice because of very low power consumption and failure rate.

Limited quantities of consumer electronics (such as notebook PCs) have become available including flash drives in place of conventional hard drives. It is widely assumed that this trend will increase over time as the cost of flash drives decreases and the performance needs of consumer electronics continue to increase.

19 Data Recovery and BIOS Updating

DATA Recovery

Data recovery is the process of salvaging data from damaged, failed, corrupted or inaccessible primary storage media when it cannot be accessed normally. Often the data is being salvaged from storage media formats such as hard disk drive, storage tapes, CDs, DVDs, RAID, and other electronics. This can be due to physical damage to the storage device or logical damage to the file system that prevents it from being mounted by the host operating system. Although there is some confusion as to the term, data recovery can also be the process of retrieving and securing deleted information from a storage media for forensic purposes.

Physical Damage

A wide variety of failures can cause physical damage to storage media. CD-ROMs can have their metallic substrate or dye layer scratched off; hard disks can suffer any of several mechanical failures, such as head crashes and failed motors; tapes can simply break. Physical damage always causes at least some data loss, and in many cases the logical structures of the file system are damaged as well. This causes logical damage that must be dealt with before any files can be salvaged from the failed media. Most physical damage cannot be repaired by end users. For example, opening a hard disk in a normal environment can allow dust to settle on the surface, causing further damage to the platters and complicating the recovery process. Furthermore, end users generally do not have the hardware or technical expertise required to make these repairs; therefore, costly data recovery companies are consulted to salvage the data. These firms often use Class 100 cleanroom facilities to protect the media while repairs are being made. The extracted raw image can be used to reconstruct usable data after any logical damage has been repaired. Once that is complete, the files may be in usable form although recovery is often incomplete.

According to research by SrA Cyrus Robinson of the Defense Cyber Crime Institute there are also tools available to law enforcement and government agencies only such as ILook IXimager or open source tools such as DCFLdd v1.3.4-1 installed to a FreeBSD operating system that can usually recover all data with exception of the physically damaged sectors. It is important that DCFLdd v1.3.4-1 be installed on a FreeBSD operating system in that studies by the Defense Cyber Crime Institute have shown that the same program installed to a Linux kernel produces extra “bad sectors”, resulting in the loss of information that is actually available.

On the other hand, there are many accounts of users getting a bad disk going long enough to pull their data off, often via slightly bizarre tricks. These include making the drive cold (in the freezer) or spinning it manually on the ground, both actions being used to unstick a jammed platter.

Examples of physical recovery procedures are: removing a damaged PCB (printed circuit board) and replacing it with a matching PCB from a healthy drive (this often entails the movement of a microchip from the original board to the replacement), changing the original damaged read/write head assembly with matching parts from a healthy drive, removing the hard disk platters from the original damaged drive and installing them into a healthy drive, and often a combination of all of these procedures.

All of the above described procedures are highly technical in nature and should never be attempted by an untrained individual. All of these procedures will almost certainly void the manufacturer's warranty.

Logical Damage

Far more common than physical damage is logical damage to a file system. Logical damage is primarily caused by power outages that prevent file system structures from being completely written to the storage medium, but problems with hardware (especially RAID controllers) and drivers, as well as system crashes, can have the same effect. The result is that the file system is left in an inconsistent state. This can cause a variety of problems, such as strange behavior (e.g., infinitely recursing directories, drives reporting negative amounts of free space), system crashes, or an actual loss of data.

Various programs exist to correct these inconsistencies, and most operating systems come with at least a rudimentary repair tool for their native file systems. Linux, for instance, comes with the fsck utility, Mac OS X has Disk Utility and Microsoft Windows provides chkdsk. Third-party utilities such as The Coroners Toolkit and The Sleuth Kit are also available, and some can produce superior results by recovering data even when the disk cannot be recognized by the operating system's repair utility. Utilities such as TestDisk can be useful for reconstruction corrupted partition tables.

Two main techniques are used by these repair programs. The first, consistency checking, involves scanning the logical structure of the disk and checking to make sure that it is consistent with its specification. For instance, in most file systems, a directory must have at least two entries: a dot (.) entry that points to itself, and a dot-dot (..) entry that points to its parent. A file system repair program can read each directory and make sure that these entries exist and point to the correct directories. If they do not, an error message can be printed and the problem corrected. Both chkdsk and fsck work in this fashion. This strategy suffers from two major problems.

First, if the file system is sufficiently damaged, the consistency check can fail completely. In this case, the repair program may crash trying to deal with the mangled input, or it may not recognize the drive as having a valid file system at all. The second issue that arises is the disregard for data files. If chkdsk finds a data file to be out of place or unexplainable, it may delete the file without asking. This is done so that the operating system may run smoother, but the files deleted are often important user files which cannot be replaced. Similar issues arise when using system restore disks (often provided with proprietary systems like Dell and Compaq), which restore the operating system by removing the previous installation. This problem can often be avoided by installing the operating system on a separate partition from your user data.

The second technique for file system repair is to assume very little about the state of the file system to be analyzed, and using any hints that any undamaged file system structures might provide, rebuild the file system from scratch. This strategy involves scanning the entire drive and making note of all file system structures and possible file boundaries, then trying to match what was located to the specifications of a working file system.

Some third-party programs use this technique, which is notably slower than consistency checking. It can, however, recover data even when the logical structures are almost completely destroyed. This technique generally does not repair the underlying file system, but merely allows for data to be extracted from it to another storage device.

While most logical damage can be either repaired or worked around using these two techniques, data recovery software can never guarantee that no data loss will occur. For instance, in the FAT file system, when two files claim to share the same allocation unit ("cross-linked"), data loss for one of the files is essentially guaranteed.

The increased use of journaling file systems, such as NTFS 5.0, ext3, and XFS, is likely to reduce the incidence of logical damage. These file systems can always be "rolled back" to a consistent state, which means that the only data likely to be lost is what was in the drive's cache at the time of the system failure. However, regular system maintenance should still include the use of a consistency checker. This can protect both against bugs in the file system software and latent incompatibilities in the design of the storage hardware.

One such incompatibility is the result of the disk controller reporting that file system structures have been saved to the disk when it has not actually occurred. This can often occur if the drive stores data in its write cache, then claims it has been written to the disk. If power is lost, and this data contains file system structures, the file system may be left in an inconsistent state such that the journal itself is damaged or incomplete. One solution to this problem is to use hardware that does not report data as written until it actually is written. Another is using disk controllers equipped with a battery backup so that the waiting data can be written when power is restored.

Finally, the entire system can be equipped with a battery backup that may make it possible to keep the system on in such situations, or at least to give enough time to shut down properly.

Some kinds of logical damage can be mistakenly attributed to physical damage. For instance, when a hard drive's read/write head begins to click, most end-users will associate this with internal physical damage. This is not always the case, however. Often, either the firmware on the platters or the controller card will instead need to be rebuilt. Once the firmware on either of these two devices is restored, the drive will be back in shape and the data accessible.

BIOS Upgrade

You may want to upgrade your existing BIOS, if it does not support the device you want to use in your system. Some old BIOS do not have support for 2.88MB 3.5 inch floppy drives, 20GB HDD, booting them from CD-ROM, etc. In this connection you have two options:

Either you can buy a new BIOS or

You can modify your existing BIOS.

Buying a new BIOS and installing it into your system is an easy approach compared to the modification of the exising BIOS. You will need some additional hardware devices and a thorough knowledge of hardware and software to modify your existing BIOS.

BIOS Modification

Other than the BIOS upgrade you can also do the BIOS modification, if you have proper hardware and software knowledge and EPROM programming device. Using these devices you can make any change to the existing BIOS code, you can change the system start up message being displayed, or the error codes displayed, etc.

Copying BIOS

Before making any change in the existing BIOS it is always safe to make a backup copy of your old BIOS code, this will help you if something goes wrong during the modification. The EPROM programmers can read from the EPROM and write to the disk file, this facility can be used to make a disk backup of your BIOS code. You can also copy the disk backup file to an empty EPROM.

Rescue Disks

It is often the case that data recovery and forensics operations cannot be done on a running system; as a result, it is common to use a specialized boot disk, Live CD or Live USB containing a minimal operating system and a set of repair tools.

When floppy drives were still common, the boot disk was typically a very minimal LiveDistro on a floppy disk (such as the Mac OS Classic Disk Tools disk, standard with every system release); however, as operating system complexity has increased, it has become more common for developers to include recovery tools on the same media as the OS installer.

Alternatively, some system administrators use Live CD or Live USB tools such as Knoppix with advanced file management and forensics tools.

Section 3
Networking

This section includes information about the following:

- Communication Technology
- Network Technology
- Designing the Network
- Network Security
- Network Architecture
- Network Connectivity
- Network Administration Security
- Wireless Networking

20 Communication Technology

Introduction

It is not that the Personal Computers are for personal use only. They can be used for sharing of information too with others having similar type of equipments. Logically it sometimes is fisible to have a number of PCs then having a bigger computer which can give the same thoughput as the number of PCs. But, overall it becomes a expensive proposition and sometimes is not fisible, specially for individuals and small businesses or small companies.

Another problem arises for those who are physically placed at a distance. They would need to send messages and receive messages, or use the same data at, or share program at, many different locations. One answer to this problem is to keep separate data files at each location, but this approach is very costly and potentially a dangerous solution. It is very expensive to maintain these redundant files of data and difficult to ensure the continuing accuracy of data at any one location. The solution of both, the need for more power and the ability to receive, send messages and share data, are found in data communication technology.

Communicating Data

When you send data from one location to another using any electronic means, it is called Data communication. Linking one computer to another permits the power and resources of that computer to be tapped. It also makes possible the updating and sharing of data at different location. Computer that are located in the same room office building, can communicate data through a direct cable link. For example, in a multiuser system, a single processing unit is linked by several dumb terminals through direct cables. Since multi-user systems link inexpensive terminals instead of the more expensive personal computers used with other systems, multi-user systems provide cost savings for small companies purchasing a complete system or adding users to a system currently in operation. In general, multi-user systems are most appropriate for companies requiring a shared data base for extensive data input and output. Computer located far away from the processor use a special form of data communication – telecommunication or telegraph. For example, teller and point-of-sale terminals are spotted in location away from computers: airlines, car-rentals, railway reservation systems and hotel reservation systems have thousands of terminals located many miles from the processors. In these cases, the process of using communication facilities such as the telephone system and microwave relays to send data between computers is a form of data communication, sometimes referred to as telecommunication, or tele-processing.

Dr. George Stibitz was the first to link computer and computing devices and send data way back in 1940. He used telegraph lines to send data files from Dartmouth College in New Hampshire, USA to a Bell Laboratories calculator in New York City, USA. An early large-scale business application was the Sabre passenger reservation system, developed in late 1950s and early 1960s by American Airlines. Hundreds of terminals were linked to the central processing unit. Communication usage has grown steadily since then.

Now-a-days minis and larger machines are in constant communication with outlying terminals. With available attachments, computers can use telecommunications channels to link up with information retrieval services, banks and electronic bulletin boards. An electronic-mail message can be sent from one place to another and an answer can be returned by electronic mail as soon as it is received. This service eliminates the hassle of continually trying to return a call, or long mail delays.

Data Transmission Techniques

Telephone lines are used for sending human voice. They were never planned to send Data. So to send data through telephone lines you have to convert the data into the format which can be read by telephone lines. These are called analog signals. For data communication between computers to take place over a telephone line, the digital pulses of the data to be transmitted must be converted to an analog signal before they are transmitted.

After its journey over the telephone lines, the analog signal must be re-converted to digital pulses so that it can be used by the receiving computer. The process of converting digital pulses to an analog signal is called modulation. And the process of re-converting an analog signal to digital pulses is called demodulation. The device that accomplishes modulation-demodulation process is called a modem.

There are 3 basic types of modems used in microcomputers.

Acoustic Coupler Modem

This is used to provide the necessary interface. The acoustic coupler is attached to a portable terminal and a standard telephone handset fits into rubber cups located on the coupler. The acoustic coupler modem sends data through the mouthpiece and receives data through the earpiece of the handset. The digital pulses produced by the terminal are converted into audible tones that are picked up by the handset receiver. The signals from these tones are then sent to the processor location where another modem converts them back to digital pulses.

External Direct-Connect Modem

It is external to the computer and connects directly to computer via RS-232 serial interface cable and to the telephone line via a modular phone jack. An external direct-connect modem may be equipped with microprocessors, storage chips and specialized communication chips. Such intelligent modem is programmed to automatically perform dialing, disconnecting functions, check the operating status using status lights and speakers, self test to verify the modem's ability to correctly transmit data, respond to commands from a communication program and change the speed at which data are transmitted.

Internal Direct-Connect Modem

It has all the needed communication circuitry on a plug-in board that fits into one of the expansion slots inside the computer. Internal direct connect modem also links directly to the telephone line via a modular phone jack.

These modems have many of the same special features as the external direct connect modems.

Communcation Channels

It is actually the media through which data is transmitted from one place to another. There are 3 types of communication channels.

Wire Cable

These are the most popular and widely used channels to transmit data from one location to another. This is so because it is cheaper and easier to use. Wire cable includes telegraph lines, telephone lines and coaxial cables. An advantage of wire cable is that the technology used to transmit data over wire cables is standardized, thus reducing the compatibility problems.

A dlsadvantage of wire cable is that it is subject to electrical interference making it less reliable than other types of communication channels. Another disadvantage is that wire cable must transmit data in analog form. Therefore, digital data must be converted to an analog signal before they reach the wire cable. This conversion not only needs special hardware, i.e., modem but also slows down the transmission of digital data.

Various items used are:

Telephone Lines

Telephone lines may be used to transmit computer data using the modems. The lines themselves may be either leased or switched.

Leased Lines

A leased line is a telephone line that is leased for the express purpose of maintaining a communication channel between two computers. The line is not shared with any other users and is available at all times for data communication between the computers. A leased line is similar to a telephone connection that is always open. Both computers are always listening for a signal to start the communication. Leased lines are used in computer networks where computers or terminals in the network must be in constant contact with one another. For example, leased lines are used in a network employing point-of-sale terminals, as the terminals must be in constant contact with the main computer. Leased lines are often conditioned to limit the level of noise on the line. Conditioned leased lines are usually necessary to carry on high speed data communication. Security requirements often require that leased lines be shielded from outside interference and unauthorized snooping.

Switched Lines

A switched line can be used for either voice or data communication and is switched from user to user, as requirements dictate. When switched lines are used, one computer must establish contact with the other by dialing a telephone number. After the transmission has been completed, the connection between the computers is broken, just as if a telephone receiver were hung up.

Twisted Pair Cable

Twisted pair [YP] is a common scheme for using copper wire as telecommunication cable. Because copper is such a good conductor of electrons, copper wires do not constrain electromagnetic signals well. When two copper wires conduct electric signals in close proximity, a certain amount of electromagnetic interference occurs. This type of interference is called cross-talk. In addition, because of the electromagnetic range used, TP transmits and receives unwanted signals from other sources. Twisting the copper wires reduces cross-talk and signal emissions. Each intertwined strand conducts a current whose emitted waves are cancelled out by the other wire's emissions. Twisted pairs are formed by two insulated 22 to 26 gauge copper wires that are twisted about each other. When one or more twisted pairs are combined within a common jacket, they form a twisted pair cable.

The two types of TP cables are:

Unshielded Twisted Pair Cable

This type of cable is composed of a set of twisted pairs with a simple plastic encasement. You may be familiar with UTP because it is commonly used in telephone systems. It is widely available and has been largely standardized. The Electrical Industries Association (EIA) popularized a category labeling scheme for five different qualities of twisted pair cable.

Category 3 and Category 5 UTP are commonly used in computer networking. While Category 3 is suitable for most contemporary computer networks, Category 5 included some enhancements, such as more twists per foot and a higher grade insulator, to improve the transmission media performance. Category 5 installations also require compatible equipment and more exacting installation techniques. Due to its voice telecommunication heritage, computer network UTP is often installed in the same manner as most telephone installations. A user device contains a port which accommodates a modular RJ-45 (4-pair) or RJ-11 (2-pair) telephone connector. The cost of UTP is extremely low compared to other transmission media. It continues to be mass produced for telecommunications and has become a popular computer network medium.

Some network integrators use existing spare wires from telephone cables to significantly reduce the already low implementation costs. However, this practice is not recommended if the existing UTP cable is lower than Category 3, if the cable drops exceed 100 meters, or if significant crosstalk is already present between the voice wires. UTP installation equipment is also inexpensive, easy to use and widely available.

Installation techniques are so simple that the cable can be adequately installed with very little training. Because voice telecommunication connection techniques have been optimized for easy moves, adds and changes, UTP is easily managed and reconfigured. Using current and emerging techniques, UTP may support data transfer rates from 1 to 100 Mbps at distances up to 100 m. Ten Mbps is the most common transmission rate in use today. All copper wire suffers from rapid attenuation when used as a communication medium. UTP is no exception.

Current technology restricts the effective range of UTP to hundreds of meters.

The copper cable used in UTP is very susceptible to EMI. Although the twists greatly reduce crosstalk, a certain amount of interference exists between pairs of wires.

Also, signals on the pairs are easily influenced by outside emitters of electromagnetic waves. External devices can also be used to intercept signals that are emitted from the pairs, breaching the security of a network.

Shielded Twisted Pair Cable

Though most of the cable is unshielded, but some forms of Shielded Twisted Pair (STP) is also used at some places. STP is insulated cable which included bundled pairs wrapped in a foil shielding. Various transmission media specifications from Apple Computer and IBM use STP cable. STP is more difficult to install than UTP.

Like coaxial cable, an electric ground, created by special connectors and installation techniques, must be provided for the shield. However, STP is more difficult to install than coaxial cable. If you use standardized and pre-configured cables, it makes installation simple. Bulk STP is moderately expensive. It currently costs more than UTP but is less expensive than thick coaxial or fiber optic cable. With the reduction of outside interference, STP can use higher frequencies and more bandwidth-efficient signaling techniques.

It is capable of greater transmission speeds, up to 500 Mbps at 100 m, but has not been widely implemented at data rates higher than 155 Mbps. The most common transmission rate is 16 Mbps. The biggest difference between UTP and STP is the reduction of interference and EMI emissions provided by STP's shielding. However, STP still suffers from relatively low immunity from interference. STP suffers from attenuation at a rate similar to UTP. Current technology also restricts the effective range of STP to hundreds of meters.

Coaxial Cables

This type of cable come in protective cover which shields the cable from physical dangers as well as from electromagnetic interference. Within the cover, the various cables are shielded from interference with one another. Coaxial cables are used in communication networks that require many simultaneous communication links. Each coaxial cable can provide more than 5000 links. The initial installation of coaxial cable is relatively simple. However, current installation techniques usually use a single strand of cable, which may become difficult to manage and reconfigure.

Local drops may be connected to the base cable to make device connections easier. Using current technologies, coax supports data transfer rates between twisted pair and fiber optic cable, although the typical data rate in use today is 10 Mbps. Much greater data rates are available. However, these higher rates are only infrequently used in computer networking. It is important to note that coaxial cable's bandwidth potential increases with the diameter of the inner conductor.

The cost of coaxial cable increases with the diameter and composition of the conductor. The cost of thin coaxial cable is relatively low (less than STP or Category 5 UTP). Thick coaxial cable is moderately expensive (more than STP or Category 5 UTP). Both are more expansive than Category 3 UTP (all comparisons are made in reference to bulk cable with no connectors).

As a copper wire media, coaxial cable suffers from high attenuation, but at a much lower rate than either variety of twisted pair. Using current LAN technology, the effective range of coaxial cable is in the low thousands of meters. While copper wire generally is a poor resistor to EMI, the shielding provided by coaxial cable greatly reduces its effects.

There are two types of coaxial cables: baseband and broadband.

A baseband coaxial cable transmits a single signal at a time at very high speed, while a broadband coaxial cable can transmit many simultaneous signals using different frequencies. A baseband cable transmits a single stream of digital data at a very high communication rate (millions of bits per second) but must be amplified every 1000 feet or so. It is mainly used for local area networks. A baseband coaxial cable can carry only an analog signal, so it must be used in conjunction with a modem. It is more complex to use in a network.

Fiber Optics

They are very reliable communication channels and they transmit data in digital form. They use light impulses that travel through clear flexible tubing (tiny threads of glass or plastic). A single glass fiber is thinner than the size of a human hair and it can transmit all the characters in dozens of books of the same size of this one across the country in a single second. It would take about 21 hours to send the same information over a copper telephone line. Since thousands of these fibers can be fit in the same amount of space required for one wire cable, the future cost of broad band transmission capability should be within the reach of small organizations and individuals.

Fiber optics can transmit data at very high speed with no errors. Unlike wire cables, fiber optic cables are not subject to electrical interference. They do, however, require repeaters to read and boost the signal strength because light pulses will lose signal strength over long distances. Optical fibers support extremely high bandwidths because they are limited by the high-frequency photon properties of light rather than by lower frequency properties of electrical systems.

Current technologies allow data rates from 100 Mbps to over 2 Gbps, at distances from 2 to 25 km. The data rate of a given fiber optic system is dependent upon the fiber composition (glass or plastic), the mode and the wavelength of the light transmitted. The most common LAN installations include glass multi-mode fiber and 850 nm wavelength LEDs. This configuration can sustain a transmission rate of 100 Mbps at distances of approximately 20 km. Historically, bulk fiber and connectors have been relatively expensive compared to copper wire, but these costs are falling rapidly.

However, the extreme cost of installation far outpaces the cost of materials. The nature of fiber optic cable poses installation problems. Every fiber junction, splice, or connection must be made with extreme care to ensure that the light path is unobstructed. Installers must be careful not to excessively stretch or bend the fiber. Fiber optic cables have extremely low attenuation rates. The amount of attenuation varies depending upon the operating wavelength, but effective ranges are usually measured in kilometers. Therefore, fiber optic cable attenuates much less than any copper wire transmission medium. Due to the use of the light spectrum, fiber optic cables do not leak signals and are immune to electromagnetic interference and eavesdropping. Also, the light spectrum does not require electrical grounds, so fiber optic cables do not suffer from potential shifts to the electrical ground not do they produce sparks. These characteristics make fiber ideal for hazardous, high voltage, or eavesdropping sensitive environments.

Microwave

This is also a type of analog communication channel. Microwave signals are transmitted through the atmosphere rather than through wire cables, similar to the way radio and television signals are transmitted. Microwave signals must be transmitted in a straight line, they do not bend around corners or around the curve of the earth. Transmitter stations redirect and boost the signals. The data may be beamed to a communications satellite that acts as a reflector by accepting signals from one point on earth and returning the same signals to some other point on earth.

The satellite appears from the earth to be stationary target for the microwave signals because its precisely positioned 22,300 miles above the equator with an orbit speed that matches the earth's rotation. Dozens of satellites are now in orbit to handle international and domestic data, voice and video communications.

Compared to wire cable, microwave has a much lower error rate, making it more reliable. Also, because there are no physical links between the sending and receiving systems communication links can be made over large distance and rough terrains. The only disadvantage is the high cost of ground stations and satellites to support a microwave network.

Bandwidth Channels

The bandwidth, or grade, of a communication channel determines the rate or speed that data can be transmitted over a channel. The term **bandwidth** is often shortened to **band**.

There are 3 bands for communication channels.

Narrow-band

The narrow-band channel is used where data volume is relatively low and which transmits data at a rate between 40 to 100 bits per second (bps). Telegraph lines are an example of narrow-band channels and their transmission rate is slow.

Voice-band

The voice-band channels are able to speed up the transmission rate between 110 to 9600 bits per second. Telephone lines are an example of voice-band channels. In many cases, a terminal operator at a remote location uses the regular dial-up telephone switching network, calls a number at the control processor location and enters the data. For large volumes of data, it is cheaper for an organization to acquire its own dedicated or leased line which can be used for both voice and data transmissions.

Broad-band

The broad-band channels are used where data volumes are large and which transmit data at rate upto several megabits per second. Microwaves, coaxial cables, fiber optics and communications satellites are examples of broad-band channels.

Data Transmission

The 2 forms of data transmission are discussed below.

Analog Data Transmission

Here the transmission of data is in a continuous wave form. The telephone system, for instance, is designed for analog data transmission.

Waves are measured using one or more of the following 3 characteristics.

Amplitude

You can consider the amplitude of a wave as the signal strength compared to some reference value (measured in volts). Analog signals are based upon amplitude, or strength, shifts which vary constantly from positive to negative values. Amplitude is commonly expressed in volts when measuring electrical potential, amps when measuring electrical current, watts when measuring electrical power, and decibels when measuring the ratio between the power of two signals.

Frequency

The frequency of a wave is the time it takes for a wave to complete one cycle. In other words, if a signal takes one second to make a transition from high amplitude to low and back to high, the frequency of the wave is one second. Frequency is typically measured in hertz[Hz], or cycles per second.

Phase

The phase of a signal refers to the relative state of the wave when timing began. Two signals cross at a slightly different time. Signal phase is measured in degrees. As with digital signals, analog signals can be modulated on encoded to represent binary data.

Current State

The most common analog current state strategies use different signal amplitudes or frequencies to represent data. These are two type of analog signal encoding schemes:

Amplitude-shift keying (ASK)

Amplitude-shift keying encodes binary data by varying the signal's amplitude between two or more levels. For example, a binary 0 might be one volt and a binary 1 might be three volts.

Frequency-shift keying (FSK)

Frequency-shift keying encodes binary data by varying the signal's frequency between two or more values.

For example, a binary 0 would be one frequency or group of frequencies and a binary 1 would be some other frequency or group of frequencies.

Network devices, using current state analog signaling, periodically measure the signal's amplitude, frequency, or both simultaneously.

State Transition

Transitions from one analog phase to another can also encode data on an analog signal. This method of analog signaling is called Phase-Shift Keying (PSK). This encodes binary data by varying the phase of the signal to indicate a value. For example, a 180 degree phase shift could represent 1 and no shift could indicate 0. Network devices periodically measure the analog signal to determine if a phase change has occurred.

Digital Data Transmission

It is the transmission of data using distinct **ON** and **OFF** electrical states. Computer circuitry represents data as a pattern of **ON** or **OFF** electrical states. These two states are represented by a 1 or **ON** and 0 for **OFF**. Digital data communication is faster and more efficient than analog. All the data communication between the computers is in digital form as the computers understand and work only in digital forms.

However, telephone system, an analog data transmission system, is used for a great percentage of data communication because it is the largest and the most widely used communication system in the world. The modem, sometimes referred as interface element, is used to bridge the gap between digital and analog data transmission, or to allow the digital data to be transmitted/received over from the telephone lines.

Buffers and Protocols

Before data are transmitted, a set of traffic rules and procedures, called protocol, must be established. The same protocol must be followed by all devices participating in the communication session. These rules may vary depending on the devices being used. Prearranged signals defining the protocol to be followed when transmitting and receiving data are sent between computers in an exchange called handshaking. Data communication between computers takes place independently of the CPU through the use of buffers at both the receiving and sending ends.

A buffer is a section of RAM which holds the data being transmitted or received. When the sending computer's buffer is almost empty, the CPU is interrupted and asked to refill the buffer. At the receiving end, the receiving buffer interrupts the CPU when it is full and the data are moved to their ultimate destination such as screen, printer or disk.

If the buffer size is large or the communication rate is slow, the buffer may be manipulated without interrupting the transmission of data. If the buffer size is smaller the communication rate is high, the sending and receiving modems use a protocol or prearranged sequence of signals, to interrupt the transmission while the buffer is filled or emptied. When the receiving computer's buffer is full, the receiving modem sends a signal to inform the sending computer to stop. When the buffer has been emptied, the receiving modem sends another signal to inform the sending computer to resume sending.

Error Detection

A number of methods have been used to detect errors while transmitting data. The most popular method for detecting errors is inserting a parity bit alongside the data bits for a character. When the receiving modem detects an incorrect parity bit, it can request the sending modem to retransmit the character.

Serial and Parallel Interface

A parallel interface is the one that uses eight wires to transmit all 8 bits in a byte at the same time. Therefore, parallel interfaces are faster and more expensive than serial interfaces. An interface connection is often called a port. The program instructions used by the computer to communicate with other devices is called driver program. In other words, most data are organised into 8 bit bytes. In some computers, data are further organised into multibyte words. Sometimes data are transmitted, a byte or a word at a time. This is done by using many wires, with one wire carrying each bit, which is known as parallel communication.

Unlike parallel interface, in a serial interface, the 8 bit bytes are lined up into a single stream for bits for transmission to a peripheral device. That is, a serial interface transmits only one bit at a time and hence it is slow. Parallel communication is used primarily for transferring data between devices at the same site. For example, communication between a computer and a printer is mot often parallel, so that an entire byte can be transferred in one operation. Communication between computers is almost always serial.

Rate of Data Transmission

The speed at which data travel over a communication channel is called the communication rate. It is also known as the transmission speed. The rate at which the data are transferred is the baud rate. Baud rate is the number of time per second that the signal being transmitted changes (modulation or demodulation). Baud is often equated with bits per send (bps), however, this comparison is not entirely accurate because a signal does not always carry one bit.

Although higher speeds are possible, typical data transmission speeds are 300, 1200, 2400, 4800 and 9600 bps. Modems used with microcomputers typically use 300, 1200 or 2400 bps. Larger computer systems used for communication in business typically transmit data at speeds of 4800 bps or higher using high-speed modems.

Methods of Data Transmission

There are 3 main methods of data transmission.

Asynchronous Transmission

Here one character is transmitted at a time. The transfer of data is controlled by start bits and stop bits. Each character is surrounded by bits that signal the beginning and end of the character. These characters allow the receiving terminal to synchronize itself with the receipt of data on a character-by-character basis. Asynchronous transmission is often used for low-speed transmission of data in conjunction with narrow-band and few slower speed (less than 1200 bps) voice band channels where the transmitting device operates manually or intermittently. It is least expensive of the two methods. Because the bit strings are relatively short, timing errors between the two device's clocks will not cause the receiving device to mistake the start of a frame.

This type of transmission is often used when characters are generated at random intervals, such as when a user types at a terminal. The start and stop bits not only indicate when a receiver should measure for the presence of bits, but also indicate the beginning and end of the data stream.

Synchronous Transmission

This transmission of data is a method in which blocks of characters are transmitted in timed sequences. Rather than using start and stop bits around each character, each block of characters is marked with synchronization characters. The receiving device accepts data until it detects a special ending character or a predetermined number of characters at which time the device knows the message has come to an end.

Synchronous transmission commonly uses the faster (greater than 1200 bps) voice-band and broad-band channels and is usually used when data-transfer requirements exceed several thousand bits per second. It is much faster than asynchronous transmission. Synchronous transmission is used in direct computer-to-computer communication for large computer systems because of the high data-transfer speeds required. The special characters used by asynchronous (start/stop bits) and synchronous (synchronization characters) transmission to alert the modem when data are being send and when the transmissions are finished are called message characters.

Synchronized transmissions resist timing errors much better than a synchronized transmission because both the transmitter and receiver use the same clock. To maintain framing when no data is being transmitted, synchronous transmission systems use fill bits. The sender can then maintain the integrity of the transmission timing. As with asynchronous transmission, synchronous transmission can perform error detection.

A method known as Cyclic Redundancy Check (CRC) is often used the CRC process subjects the block of data to an algorithm. The result of the computation (called the CRC) is appended to the block of data prior to transmission. On the receiving side, the same algorithm is used and the results are compared with the CRC field. Any difference is assumed to mean frame damage occurred during transmission. CRC is less vulnerable to multiple bit errors than asynchronous error-detection methods.

Isochronous Transmission

These methods use a constant fixed-frequency transmission clock to create set time slots. A clock signal is generated by a designated network device and is passed to all other devices on the network. Using the prescribed media access rules, the network devices monitor the network for free space within the slots and insert data as needed.

Multiple frames can be inserted into each slot until the slot is full. By using this method, a clock signal is not provided for every frame like asynchronous, or provided by the sender at the beginning of a string like synchronous. Rather the clock is provided at a constant rate by a single device for all other devices on the network.

Communication Channel Configurations

The two main communication channel configurations are as follows:

Point-to-point

In a point-to-point channel configuration, a device is connected directly to another devices by a dedicated communication channel. This communication channel configuration can be inefficient and costly if a terminal is not active enough to keep the line busy.

Multi-point

In the multi-point channel configuration, three or more devices, e.g., a terminal or computer, are connected to the same line. Compared to point-to-point configuration, multipoint channel configuration is more efficient and less costly because it reduces the amount of intercabling needed.

Communication Processors

A number of communication processors are used by network designers to achieve their goals. They increase the efficiency of a communication channel. These processors are used for a number of purposes, some of which are as follows:

Multiplexing

It is the process of combining the transmission, character by character, from several devices into a single data stream that can be transmitted over a single communication channel. A multiplexer is a device that produces multiplexing. It is also used at the receiving end to separate the transmissions and send them back in their original order for processing. A multiplexer allows the communication channels to transmit much more data, at any one time, than what a single device can send. Multiplexers are more efficient and less expensive. The equipment that multiplexes and demultiplexes is sometimes called a multiplexer or mux.

The following methods are used by multiplexers to allow multiple devices to communicate concurrently.

Frequency-Division Multiplexing

It uses separate frequencies to establish multiple channels within a broadband medium. To do this, the mux creates special broadband carrier signals that operate on different frequencies. Data signals are added to the carrier signals and are removed, at the opposite end of the media segment, by another mux. FDM is used in broadband LANs to separate different direction traffic on the cable and to provide special services like dedicated connections between machines.

Time-Division Multiplexing

These systems divide a single channel into short time slots. Bits, blocks of bits, bytes, or frames can be placed into each time interval is not exceeded. Time division is a multiplexing technique that you can use on baseband systems. You can also use it on an individual channel of a broadband FDM system. Conventional TDM systems are sometimes called synchronous TDM because the time-divisions are fixed when the muxes are set up. The time slots are always of the same length and are assigned in the same order.

Statistical Time-Division Multiplexing

Conventional synchronous TDM systems waste bandwidth if many of the time slots are left unused. Statistical time-division multiplexing (StatTDM) solves this problem by dynamically allocating time slots to active devices on a first-come, first-served or priority basis. A control field identifies the owners of each slot's data so that the receiving mux can appropriately split out all the individual signals.

Concentration

Very often, it is required to connect more devices (or terminals) to a computer so that the communication channel can handle all at once. Concentration is the process of connecting and serving these devices. A concentrator is hardware that provides concentration. The data are stored in the buffer of concentrator for later transmission, when the number of devices transmitting exceeds the capacity of the communication channel. However, today's micro-processor equipped multiplexers perform much like concentrators. Compared to concentrators, multiplexers are less expensive.

Message Switching

The message switcher receives and analyzes data messages from points in the network, determines the destination and the proper routing and then forwards the messages to other network locations. If needed, a message can be stored till an outgoing line is available.

Front-end Processing

The front-end processor is a computer, which is usually located at a central computer site. It handles all the data communication control functions while the Central Processing Unit (CPU) of the front-end processor handles all the communication tasks. Its purpose is to relieve the main computer – called a host computer – of a number of the functions required to interact with and control the communications network. The two processors interact only when data need to be passed between them.

A typical front-end processor might control scores of communication channels of varying types and speeds coming from a number of diverse remote terminals. The functions of communication processors differ from one network to another and there may be an overlapping of functions. A message switching processor, for example, may also function as a remote concentrator; a front-end processor may perform message-switching function; and, in less complete networks, the host computer may perform most or all of the functions of the front-end processor.

Transmission Modes

Data transmission may occur in one of the following 3 modes.

Simplex Mode

In this mode, data can be transmitted in one direction. A device using the simplex mode of transmission can either send or receive data, but it cannot do both. Simplex mode (circuits) are seldom used because a return path is generally needed to send acknowledgment, control or error signals.

Half-duplex Mode

Here, data can be transmitted back and forth between two stations, but data can only go in one of the directions at any point of time. An example is a citizens band radio where the user must either talk or listen, but cannot do both at the same time.

Full-duplex Mode

The full-duplex mode allows a device to receive and send data simultaneously. A full-duplex mode is faster, since it avoids the delay that occurs in a half-duplex circuit each time the direction of transmission is changed.

Communication Procedures

All communication between computers are managed by data communication software.

The precise procedures used depend on the particular software, but the following account outlines the general procedures.

Communication Between Two Microcomputers

A small business that uses microcomputers has accumulated information that it wants to send to a customer who also uses microcomputers.

The procedure used to send the information is as follows:

1. Both the business and the customer start the communication program, which gives them a menu of options.
2. Both the business and the customer choose the same options, including the number of start and stop bits, the type of parity checking, the communication rate, full-duplex or half-duplex transmission and so on.
3. The communication link is established. The users decide who will originate the telephone call and the originator enters the telephone number. The communication program then instructs the modem to detail the number and reports to the users if a connection has been made.
4. After the connection has been made, the users can have an on-line conversation. They can type messages back and forth to each other and can record their conversation.
5. When the business is ready to transfer the information, it sets its computer to send; the customer sets its computer to receive. The business starts, the transfer. The communication program takes over by reading the information from the disk and sending it through the communication link. The receiving computer stores the incoming information on a disk. The transfer proceeds without any further human attention.
6. When the transfer has been completed, the business and the customer say "goodbye" and terminate the connection.

Communication Between Microcomputer and Larger Computer

The procedure for communication between a microcomputer and a minicomputer or mainframe is similar. The only difference is that the larger computer have safeguards that limit access to files and facilities to authorized users. The most common safeguards are the user identification number and the user password. After the communication link has been established, the receiving computer asks for the user's identification number.

This number is assigned to the microcomputer user by the operators of the larger computer. When requested to do so, the microcomputer user types in the user identification number. The receiving computer checks that the identification number is valid. It then asks for the user's password.

A password is a confidential sequence of characters that allows access to the system.

An example of a password is:

S12$T11

The password is required for the user to obtain access to the larger computer. It also determines exactly which files and facilities the microcomputer user is allowed to read. If the typed password is valid, the microcomputer user is allowed access to the large system.

Going On-Line

Before you establish a communication link, you must adjust various settings to match those of the computer you want to connect with. Called communication parameters, these settings vary with different types of computers and programs. Fortunately, most communication programs let you store and retrieve the parameters that apply to various remote systems. When you connect to a remote system such as an on-line information service, you will probably be asked to reply to one or more on-screen questions.

Generally, you will need to provide some kind of identification, such as your name, an account number and a password. This brief dialogue between you and the remote system is often called a logon procedure. Some remote systems compare your identification with a list of paid subscribers. Obviously, if you are not on the list, you would not be able to access the service.

Other systems use the logon procedure as a security measure, protecting valuable records from tampering. In either case, the remote system maintains a record or log of every caller. Many communication programs support automated logon procedures. When you log on for the first time, the program "records" your entries for later use.

Subsequently, when you access the remote system, these entries are automatically supplied in response to prompts from the remote system. Many communication software packages let you dial, connect and log on to a remote system at the touch of a single function key. Once you have gone through the formalities, the remote system usually welcome you with a greeting and waits for your net command.

At this point, your communication software has turned your computer into a simple video terminal, allowing you to use the remote system's software as if you were connected directly to the system.

File Transfer

Transferring files to and from your disk drive is one of the most common communication applications. These files may be bulletins, electronic mail messages, airline information or even computer programs. In addition to matching communication parameters, file transfer requires that both systems in a communication link agree on a common protocol.

A protocol consists of the technical details that regulate data transmission between computers. Fortunately, you need only a rough idea of how a protocol works in order to use one. The simplest to understand is the text or ASCII protocol. This method sends a file as one uninterrupted stream of ASCII characters.

While this protocol offers transmission of maximum characters in the shortest possible time, it is also the one most likely to produce errors, especially over noisy telephone lines. To combat flaws in file transfer, most protocols offer error correction. Specific methods vary from protocol to protocol, but the basic error correction scheme is the same; breaking up a file into small blocks and then comparing the received blocks to those that were sent to make sure they are identical.

Each block includes an extra character mathematically derived from the ASCII values of the characters it contains. If the receiving computer comes up with a different value for that character after it receives a block, it assumes an error has occurred and requests that block again. While this procedure reduces throughput, error checking and correction virtually assure error free file transfer.

Common error correction programs now include more advanced session level protocols that check for errors throughout an entire communication session, not just during file transfer.

Choosing Parameters

Before loggin on, you must make sure that you and the remote system are using the same communication parameters – the various settings that regulate the means of communication. To clarify this point, baud rate, parity, stop bits and echo are further discussed. Baud rate refers to the rate or "speed" of data transfer. In common parlance, this means the number of bits per second (bps) sent or received.

Technically, baud rate refers to the rate of the phase-shifting method a modem uses to transmit information – which is not necessarily the same as the bps rate. However, most modem manufacturers use baud rate to describe bps and this corruption of the technical term is now commonplace. Since transmitting one character usually takes 10 bits, dividing the baud rate by 10 will give you a rough approximation of how many characters per second are being transferred. Which baud rate you use depends on the capabilities of your modem, as well as the equipment used by the remote system.

Most modems for personal computers transfer data at 300, 1200 or 2400 baud. Whatever baud rate your modem supports, it has to be seen that the rate for your modem and the remote system must be identical. Sometimes a remote system will have different phone access numbers for different baud rates. In general, you should communicate at the highest baud rate possible, since this reduces the amount of connect time you are charged for.

However, some commercial information systems charge premium rates for communication at higher baud rates. Even so, the time saved makes using higher baud rates more economical when transferring large files. Parity refers to a scheme using a single bit along with each character to test for accurate data transfer. The most popular configuration for PC communications uses seven bits for data and the eighth bit for even parity. Using even parity during data transfer means that the eight bit always makes the 1 and 0 bits within a character add up to an even number. If the receiving computer detects an odd number, it either requests re-transmission or ignores the character completely.

Sometimes, however, eight bits are used for data and an additional bit is used for parity, resulting in other common setting; eight bits and no parity. Other parity schemes, such as odd number, space and mark are also used, but they are rather uncommon in PC communications. Stop bits refer to the variable number of bits used to mark the end of each character transferred. Often, you may see parity, the number of data bits and the number of stop bits in one reference. "E-7-1" for example, means even parity, seven data bits and one stop bit.

One stop bit is used almost universally in personal computer communication and many communication programs automatically use this setting unless you specify otherwise. Echo refers to a remote system's practice of sending back the characters you transmit, giving you on-screen verification that the characters have been received.

Mainframe computers and commercial information services often use this procedure, while most PC link-ups omit echo. When you are on-line, it is easy to determine whether to turn the echo function on or off. If you see no characters on the screen as you type, turn echo on; if the characters you type appear in duplicate, turn echo off. Most communication programs let you adjust the echo setting while you are engaged in a communication session.

Logging Off

When you have finished a session with a remote system, you need to formally log off. Usually, the system displays a message on screen confirming that log off procedures have been properly completed. Standard log off commands include log out, Bye, Quit, Off and Exit. If you disconnect without formally logging off the system, the remote system may be fooled into believing that you are still connected. When you are using a commercial service that charges by the minute for connect time, this can be quite an expensive mistake. Therefore, it is a good idea to watch for the remote system's log off confirmation on screen.

Applications of Data Communication

The applications of data communication fall into one of 4 categories.

Electronic Mail

A business depends on the efficient exchange of information between different parts of the business and between the business and the outside world. Much of this exchange has been traditionally carried out through paper documents, delivered by secretary, mail or messenger service. With the growing use of personal computers, a more efficient alternative has emerged, i.e., electronic mail. Electronic mail is usually used to exchange messages and data files. Each user is assigned an electronic mailbox.

Using the appropriate command, the user can scan a list of messages in the mailbox, display the contents of a particular message, send a message to another user and so forth. To send a message, it is not necessary for the recipient to be present at the computer. The message resides in the mailbox until it is read. The sender may restrict delivery of the message to authorised readers by using a password. That is, the recipient must "sign" for the message by typing his or her identifying password. Many other features of standard mail delivery are implemented in electronic mail systems.

For example, mail can be forwarded, stored for delayed delivery and sent to anyone at a particular phone number. In addition, electronic mail systems implement many new features. An electronic mail system can deliver copies of a message to all individuals listed in a certain file. It also allows merging of standard data (from a data file) with a particular message. Now-a-days, several companies have started subscription to electronic mail services. These services are accessed through a modem and allow users to communicate with other subscribers to the service. The service may also accept a message and transmit it to its destination city. There the message is printed out and delivered with the next day's mail. This technique can be used to communicate with people who are not subscribers to the network.

Using External Databases

The most important applications of data communication is the ability to access external databases. There are literally thousands of databases containing information on almost every conceivable subject. Users can subscribe to many of these databases at a cost of the initial fee and a charge for the amount of time spent accessing the database. Users can locate information in an index or can just browse through the database as they would brows through books at a public library.

The types of information available through services vary greatly, as can be seen in the following examples. The Dow Jones News Services provide current news, current stock and commodity prices and securities research data. The stock prices are very nearly the same up-to-the-minute prices that are simultaneously crossing the tape at the major stock exchange. This allows users to use the service for the data on which they base trading decisions. A number of subscription services supply on-line transactions. For example, a number of banks now allow subscribers to bank through a communication link to a personal computer. Some services even allow users to pay bills in this way. Personal computers may also be used to execute stock trades through several on-line brokerage systems. Transaction-oriented services are in their infancy. In the years to come, they will certainly grow in number and sophistication. A number of multiple-listing real estate services offer on-line options.

This allows a broker to find all homes meeting particular criteria, price range, neighbourhood, size and so on, to match client demands. Also in the real estate field, services supply on-line listings of currently available mortgage money, interest rates and restrictive terms. These services allow a prospective home buyer to shop the entire country to obtain the best mortgage terms.

Sharing Data Files

Probably no single data communication application is as important to a large business as is the link between its micro-computers and its mainframe computers. In the last few years, businesses have purchased millions of personal computers to increase their employees productivity. The initial applications of personal computers were stand alone activities, such as word processing and the use of spreadsheets.

To increase productivity further, businesses are taking the additional step of making data stored in mainframe computers available to microcomputer users. The savings including financial ones can be huge. With data communication and networking, the tasks of data collection, analysis, decision making, report writing and data distribution can be integrated into a single, efficient system. In effect, the entire office (or even the entire company) becomes one large communication network.

Bulletin Board Systems

A bulletin board is a communication system that allows users to call in and either leave or retrieve messages. It is similar to an electronic mail system, but there are no private mailboxes, only a single large mailbox. The messages may be directed to all users of the bulletin board or only to particular users. But all messages can be read by all users. Some computer equipment manufactures maintain bulletin boards that users may call to determine the status of company products, corrections to programs and the like. Users may report problems, ask for literature or place orders. Some computer user groups maintain bulletin boards for notifying members of meetings and other group activities. Other bulletin boards are maintained by individuals are meeting places for like-minded people.

Communication Processing

Communication processing is the collective term for all the activities that help to ensure the successful entry, transmission and delivery of information. Just as data processing involves taking raw data and adding value by changing the inherent information content, communication processing adds value to the raw message by ensuring that the message arrives at its destination in a timely manner, in the proper form, at the proper speed, in the proper language and without errors.

The basic responsibilities of communication processing can be divided into three major areas: editorial, conversion and arbitration. Editorial functions include formatting of the message, editing the data and controlling errors. Conversion functions include translating transmission speed and code. Arbitration functions involve network control and message routing. Communication processing can be performed in any intelligent device, using the storage and processing capabilities of that device. In the microcomputer based of LAN, most communication processing occurs within the micro-computer itself. Within a network, communication processing is implemented as protocols, the rules that govern the transmission of information.

The following are sample communication processing services:

- Accommodating different video display characteristics such as screen size, line strength and paging.
- Translating data into the standard network format and subsequently re-translating the data to meet the requirements of the receiving station.
- Controlling the sequence in which messages are sent.

- Assembling and transmitting messages on the basis of time interval, order received, receipt of particular character or other characteristics.
- Alerting users to error conditions and possible problems.

Packets

It is neither practical nor advantageous to transmit long messages as a single entity. Therefore, for the purpose of data transmission, particularly in local area networks, messages are broken down into segments, called packets. Each packet normally contains five parts.

- A start frame, identifying the beginning of the packet.
- A header, containing information for maintaining control of the packet and the network.
- An information field, containing a segment of the total text information or data to be communicated.
- An error control field, permitting the system to verify packet integrity.
- An end frame, signifying the end of the packet.

The control information contained in the header includes the source address, which identifies where the packet originated; the destination address, to which the segment is to be delivered; the packed sequence number, which helps insure that the packets can be reassembled in proper order; and a control block, which helps prevent duplication, loss or looping (in which a packet is routed back and forth in an endless circle) of the packet.

Additional information to insure proper operation of the network under various overload or impaired operating conditions also may be included. Overhead is the additional information that must be transmitted through the network in order to facilitate the proper transmission and delivery of messages. It is created by the system's need to maintain control of all transactions. A percentage of overall network capacity is dedicated to this control information. Overhead information exists on the network in two basic forms; data appended to each user packet, such as the control and error-checking fields named above. The amount of data appended to a basic message varies from one system to another and itself contained acknowledgment and control packets, which are transmitted from one device to another. These packets keep the system advised of the status of the components.

Communication Software

Most computer applications, including data communication, require both appropriate hardware and software. Specialised data communication software is required to set up a communication link between two computers and to transmit data. Data communication software performs a number of jobs. One is to send data at the proper speed; if the receiving and sending computers do not agree on the communication rate, the receiving computer will not be able to understand the communication. Another job is to monitor signals from the receiving computer that indicate any transmission errors. The communication program you choose plays a key role in data exchange between computers. If you are on the receiving end, communication software lets you decide whether you want to save data to disk, send it to a printer or simply let it scroll off the screen.

When you transmit data, most programs let you choose between sending it form a disk file or typing it directly from the keyboard. Software for communication also stores telephone numbers, modem commands and other critical settings. Usually, these parameters reside in a dialing directory, so you do not have to re-enter them each time you want to hook up with a remote system. A well-designed communication program makes it easy to select a remote system from the directory and begin connection procedures. Many communication programs direct modems to dial, hang up and answer incoming calls automatically. While it is modem that actually performs these tasks, the software provides the appropriate instructions. For example, when the program sends the modem a dial command and a phone number. The modem automatically goes off-hook (the same as lifting a telephone handset), waits for a dial tone and proceeds to generate click pulses or tones that dial the number.

Most modems provide an audible indication that dialing is in progress, followed by a signal that a connection has been made. You will hear the modem beeping out tones like fast fingers on a touch-tone phone. Then, if all goes well, you should hear the remote system's line ring and the remote modem "pick up" the call. The remote modem then generates a high-pitched answer tone, to which your modem responds with a burst of tones of its own. This opening interchange is called handshaking. Once two modems are locked on to each other, most communication programs display a 'Connect' message on screen. In the foregoing paragraphs, we listed the rudimentary features of a communication program but a typical one has many additional features. Some programs allow users to redial a number repeatedly (if the line is busy, for example) until a connection is made and others allow users to take remote control of the computer at the other end. That is, the program user can control the other computer from his own keyboard. This allows communication with no one in attendance at the other end. Some programs allow users to dial a sequence of numbers one after the other. These are sometimes used to generate recorded advertising calls.

Micro-to-Mainframe Link

Micro-computers can also be connected to large systems in a micro-to-mainframe link to share data and computing power. As the number of micro-computers used in business increases, this connection is being seen more and more. Line micro-to-micro communication, micro-to-mainframe communication can be accomplished via modem and telephone lines or by hard wiring. However, the connection is not as simple because large systems use different formats for communication and they handle data differently internally. To complicate the problem, the communication and data formats used among the various large systems also differ. Specialized hardware designed for the particular type of computer being used is usually needed to make the data compatible.

For a micro-computer to communicate with a large system, three facts must be known:

1. Type of mainframe to be communicated with;

2. Mainframe's specific data format; and
3. Mainframe's specific communication protocols.

Communication Challeges

The use of data communication is not without its challenges. Data sent over communication channels are subject to various kinds of interference which may alter or destroy some of that data. In addition to ensuring the security of the data, privacy of the data must often be protected. However, unauthorized access to data files can be limited by the use of passwords and access codes. To prevent highly sensitive data from being accessed and used from the communication channels, the data are often encrypted, or scrambled, based on some code before they are sent. Then they are unscrambled using that same code after they are received.

Suppliers of Data Communication Services

Various kind of Data Communication Carriers are:

Common Carriers

To handle large public telephone and telegraph networks, services of common carriers are availed. A common carrier is an organisation that is licensed and regulated by the government to transmit the data communication property of others at regulated rates. There are thousands of licensed common carriers of data communication.

Specialized Common Carriers

In addition to these common carriers that offer a wide range of facilities, there are specialized common carriers whose public networks are often restricted to a more limited number of services. MCI communication corporation is an example of satellite using organizations.

Value Added Carriers

A value added carrier is an organization that leases communication channels from the common carriers (it may not have its own transmission facilities) and adds extra services over and above what the common carriers provide. For example, Tymnet and Telenet both have computer networks that receive customer data coming in over telephone lines. These data are temporarily stored and organized into 'packets' of characters. These packets are then routed and transmitted at high speed over the final data destination. At these offices, data in the packets are reassembled into the complete message for transmission to the final destination. The transmission cost of value-added network (VAN) is less than directly utilizing common carrier channels. Telenet and Tymnet are sometimes referred to as packet-switching networks.

Micro-to-Micro Link

Microcomputers are often connected for data communication in a micro-to-micro link so that microcomputer users with incompatible data formats can share data. For instance, data on an Apple IIc disk cannot be used by an IBM PC/XT drive because the data are not saved on the disk in a format that the IBM can read. However, that data, provided they are in a standard format such as ASCII, can be sent via modem and telephone line to the IBM, saved on the disk by the IBM and used in that format. The reverse, sending data from the IBM to the Apple computer, is also possible. If the two computers are located near each other, another option is to connect directly (hard wire) using a null modem cable. The null modem cable uses a different pin configuration from a modem cable and eliminates the need for a modem by directly matching the data transmit pin from one computer to the data receive pin on the other computer.

The advantages of hard wiring are:

- It allows incompatible computers to transfer data.
- It eliminates the need for modems at each computer.
- It allows data transfer to take place at speeds upto 9600 bps.

However, there are no error dedication capabilities with hard wiring. A small business that uses microcomputers has accumulated information that it wants to send to a customer who also uses microcomputers. The precise procedures used depend on the particular software, but the following account outlines the general procedures:

1. The business and the computer both start the communication program, which gives them a menu of options.

2. The business and computer both, choose the same options, including the number of start and stop bits, the type of parity checking, the communication rate, full-duplex or half-duplex transmission and so on.

3. The communication configuration is made. The users decide who will originate the telephone call and the originator enters the telephone number. The communication program then instructs the modem to dial the number and reports to the users if a connection has been established.

4. When the connection has been established, the users can have an on-line conversation. They can type messages back and forth to each other and can record or capture their conversation.

5. At the business end, if the computer is ready to transfer the information, it sets its computer to send; the customer set its computer to receive. The business starts the transfer. The communication program takes over by reading the information from the disk and sending it through the communication link. The receiving computer stores the incoming information on a disk. When the transfer of a file has been completed, the business and customer sides computers saying “good-bye” and then terminate the connection.

21 Network Technology

Introduction to Networking

Networking is a concept, where 2 or more than 2 computers are joined together to share information. This can be in the form of data or programs. These computers can be within a walking distance or in the same building of the office or in the same city or even across the cities.

But, why is this needed. Have you ever found yourself rushing from one computer to another in your office or home, attending to several different jobs at various locations? Or do you often find yourself moving files that need printing form a PC that you happen to be working on the PC that is connected to the printer? All of these situations can be made easier by allowing the various machines to communicate with each other – by networking the PCs.

The distance between the computers is narrowed down by the telephone lines. The information from the computer is converted to the media understandable by the communication lines and then transferred from one place to another.

With nctworking you can not only share data and programs, but can also share the resources like printers, scanners, etc. In PC technology, such a collection of computers, all located within a few thousand feet of each other, is called Local Area Networking.

Networking Basics

Networking several computers together allows data to be transmitted form one machine to another in rapid and easily managed data streams. This sharing of data allows many of the resources that are located on a single machine to effectively become available to all other machines on the network.

These resources can be physically located on the machine, e.g., as files on the hard disk, or connected logically to the machine. An example of a logically connected resource would be a printer that is connected to a PC, but which is then available over the network to other machines on that network.

An alternative situation would be where access to the Internet is available to all the PCs on a network through a special communication device attached to the network. Access to all external and internal resources are thus made available to PC users on the network.

A network server provides network services to a user workstation (server) on the network. Services can range from sharing database and files, printers; communications or other

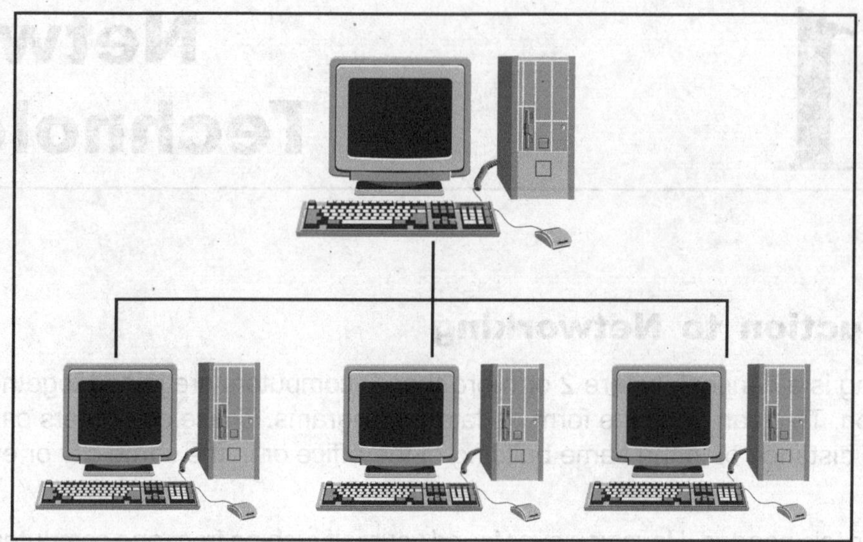

network resources. Thus, the network servers are also called file servers, print servers, communication servers, etc. They can be dedicated to the task of providing network services.

They are then called dedicated network servers. Otherwise, they may be called non dedicated servers. A typical networking is shown on the last page.

Another factor which also favours the networking is the cost factor.

Cost Reduction

If you have 2-3 computers attached in a single networking system, you may go in for a single printer which can be used by all of them. The same goes for other devices like Scanner, Plotter, etc. This results in lots of costs.

The main advantages of Networking can be clubbed as follows:

Resource Sharing

There are two main types of networking systems. The type used for larger networks is known as the Client/Server model. This model involves using a powerful computer that runs a Network Operating System and acts as the 'server'. The Network Operating System then runs the server, supplying network services to the other 'client' computers.

These services might include the management of file transfers, running printing jobs, or even running applications across the network. For example, a word processing software package running on a PC is actually being 'served' form the server across the network, rather than being loaded onto the PC's local hard disk.

The problem with the Client/Server model is that it requires specialised hardware, software and to a large extent skilled networking techniques to configure and maintain the network.

All of this can become expensive.

The second model, the Peer-to Peer system or resource Sharing is fortunately a lot easier to implement and maintain and it is this model that we will use in this book.

Resource Sharing is incorporated into Windows 98 and allows all network users access to all resources such as the hard drives, directories, printers or CD-ROM drives that are available on the network. It also allows access to external resources across the network via special intermediary devices.

Resource Sharing involved each computer on the network taking on equal an equal part in the networking process and is ideally suited to smaller networks.

Security

Being able to have complete access to all resources on the network is not always desirable. It is often the case that certain resources may need to be restricted to certain users.

Resources Sharing within Windows allows for this and incorporates the ability to protect access to particular resources with passwords. These passwords can then be stored within the windows 98 configuration files so that access to protected resources is automatically assigned once the user has gained access to the network; the relevant passwords is therefore only entered once during the network login procedure. This function can also be disabled so that a password is required every single time the user attempts to access a protected resource.

Password access can also be configured to allow the user to read but not to change a particular resource or to allow full access, including the ability to write to a resource (which would be necessary for sending jobs to a printer).

Each individual resource can also be configured separately so that different passwords and access rights can be assigned for different resources

Types of Networking

The three basic types of networks are:

1. Local Area Networks or LAN
2. Metropolitan Area Network or MAN
3. Wide Area Network or WAN

Let us see them in details.

Local Area Network

A local area network (LAN) is two or more computers directly linked within a small well-defined area such as a room, building, or group of closely placed buildings. A LAN may be made up of only microcomputers or any combination of microcomputers and large systems.

A LAN usually consists of the following:

1. Two or more computers
2. Peripheral devices such as printers and hard-disk drives
3. Software to control the operation of the computers or other devices connected to the LAN
4. Special cables, usually coaxial or fibre optic, to connect the computers and other devices
5. A plug-in board to handle the data transmissions.

Some computers require that all the computers be of a certain brand, while others allow a variety of brands to be connected. The number of computers in a LAN varies from smaller LANs that typically connect 2 to 25 computers, to large LANs that can connect as many as 10,000 computers.

The length of the cable connecting a computer to a LAN also varies depending on the LAN. Most LANs allow cables of about 1,000 feet, but some allow cables of several miles to be used. The data transfer speeds range from several thousand bits per second to around 10 million bits per second. The programs that control the LANs also vary in the features they offer. Some programs allow the user of more than on operating system; others allow only one. On some LANs file access is limited to one user at a time; on others, more than one user can access a file simultaneously.

Hardware for LAN

The following are the major hardware components/devices for establishing LAN:

1. Transmission Channel
2. Network Interface Unit or NIU
3. Servers
4. Workstations

Transmission Channel for LAN

Generally four types of channels are used for data transmission in a LAN. These are:

1. Twisted Pair Cables
2. Coaxial Cables
3. Fibre Optic Cables
4. Radio Waves

Interface for LAN

Network interface units connect each devices in the LAN network to shared transmission device. It contain the rules or logic to access the LAN. NIU is also used to implement LAN protocols and for device attachments. Its function depends on the type of topologies (to be told later in the this chapter), used in LAN.

Server and Workstations

One of the major benefits of implementation of LAN is sharing expensive resources such as storage devices, printers, etc. This is achieved through providing servers on the LAN. It is dedicated computer that controls one or more resources. This contains both hardware and software interface for LAN. Three major categories of services used in LANs are:

1. File Server
2. Printer Server
3. Modem Server

In networking, file server is used to share storage for files. Besides providing storage space for files in a LAN environment, it is used for taking periodical backup, and also to provide gateway to other servers with and between LANs. Similarly printer server is used to handle printing works of all workstation connected in the network. In LAN environment also modem is required to get connected to other network or simply to use a telephone. A modem server is used to share this expensive resource by all connected workstations in a network ring.

Software for LAN

LAN operating system is required to operate on the LAN system. It has basically two aspects:

1. Server Software
2. Workstation Software

LAN operating system facilitates :

1. Sharing of expensive resources, e.g., printer, storage space, etc.
2. Security for data
3. Connection to other network

There are various types of LAN operating system. Some popular LAN operating systems are :

— Novel Netware

— Ethernet

— Corvus

— ArcNet

— LAN Server

— Omni Net

— PC Net

— IBM PC LAN

— Etherlink Plus, etc.

Wide Area Networks or WAN

A wide area network is two or more computers that are geographically dispersed, linked by communication facilities such as telephone system or microwave relays. This type of network is usually limited to use by large corporations and government agencies because of the high cost involved in building and maintaining them. A WAN is a network that links separate geographical locations and this network can be a public system or any of the various packet switched services provided by the public telecommunication agencies.

The main difference between a WAN and LAN is under the complete control of the owner, whereas the WAN needs the involvement of another authority like telecom department. LANs are successful and capable of handling very high data transfer rates at low cost because of the small area covered. Besides LANs have a lower error rate than WANs.

Transmission Channel for WAN

Generally 3 types of channels are used for data transmission in a WAN. These are:

1. Radio Waves
2. Micro Waves
3. Communication Satellites

Hardware Requirements for WAN

There are mainly 4 hardware devices which are required to establish linkage between geographically separated computers. These are:

1. Bridges
2. Routers
3. Gateways
4. X.25 Standard Interface

These are explained below.

Bridges

These are used to connect two LANs that use the identical protocols over a wide area. The bridge acts as an address filter which picks up packets from one LAN that are intended for a destination on another LAN and passes these packets on the network. The amount of processing required at the bridge is minimal because all the devices use the same protocols. In case the distance between two LANs is very large then the user is required to employ two identical bridges at either end of the communication link.

Routers

It is a special type of device that can be used to connect networks that may not be similar. Such type of devices provide connectivity between two LANs and two WANs over large geographical distances. These devices operate at the Network Layer of the OSI model. These devices participate in a routing protocol to access the network topology, and on the basis of this information routers compute the best route from a sender to the receiver.

Gateways

These are used to connect two dissimilar LANs. The terms Gateways and Routers are used interchangeably, though there is discriminating difference between the two. A router operates at the network layer whereas a gateway operates on the application layer of the OSI model. A gateway is required to convert data packets from one protocol format to another before forwarding it, as it connects two dissimilar networks.

X.25 Standard Interface

X.25 is a protocol for interfacing to a Public Packet Switched Network. It is not a protocol used for implementing a network. Two systems that support X.25 can't necessarily be connected back-to-back. They can only be connected through a DCE in a Public Packet Switched. International Telegraph and Telephone Consultative Committee (ITTCC) developed X.25 as the standard interface between the Data Terminal Equipment (DTE) and Data Circuit Terminating Equipment (DCTE). This recommendation has been widely accepted as the industry standard for public packet switched networks.

Types of Wide Area Networks

There are mainly two types of WAN:

Public Networks

These are those networks which are installed and run by the telecommunication authorities and are made available to any organization or individual who go for their subscription.

Private Networks

The basic technique used in all forms of private WAN is to use private circuits to link the locations to be served by the network. Between these fixed points the owner of the network has complete freedom to use the circuits in any way they want. They can use the circuits to carry large quantities of data or for high speed transmissions. Private wide area networks can be built using whatever standard technology is available.

Topology

There are ways in which you can connect the various computers for networking. This physical arrangement is called Topology. Different types of topologies are:

The Ring Topology

As the name suggests all the server/nodes are joined together to form a ring. There is no central server in this case. A ring may be unidirectional or bi-directional. A unidirectional ring moves data in one direction only; a bi-directional ring moves data in both directions, but only one direction at a time. In a unidirectional ring, if one computer breaks down, special software is required to keep the network functional. When one node malfunction in a bi-directional ring, a message can usually be sent in the opposite direction still allowing the node to communicate with all the other active nodes in the network.

Advantages of the Ring Network

1. **Short cable length:** the amount of cabling involved in a ring topology is comparable to that of a bus and is small relative to that of a star. This means that less connections will be needed, which will in turn increase network reliability.

2. **No wiring closet space required:** Since there is only one cable connecting each node to its immediate neighbours, it is not necessary to allocate space in the building for wiring closets.

3. **Suitable for optical fibers:** Optical fibers offer the possibility of very high speed transmission. Because traffic on a ring travels in one direction, it is easy to use optical fibers as a medium of transmission. Also, since a ring is made up of nodes connected by short segments of transmission medium, there is a possibility of mixing the types used for different parts of the network. Thus, a manufacturing company's network could use copper cables in the office area and optical fibers in the factory areas, where electrical interference may be a problem.

Disadvantages of the Ring Network

1. **Node failure causes network failure:** the transmission of data on a ring goes

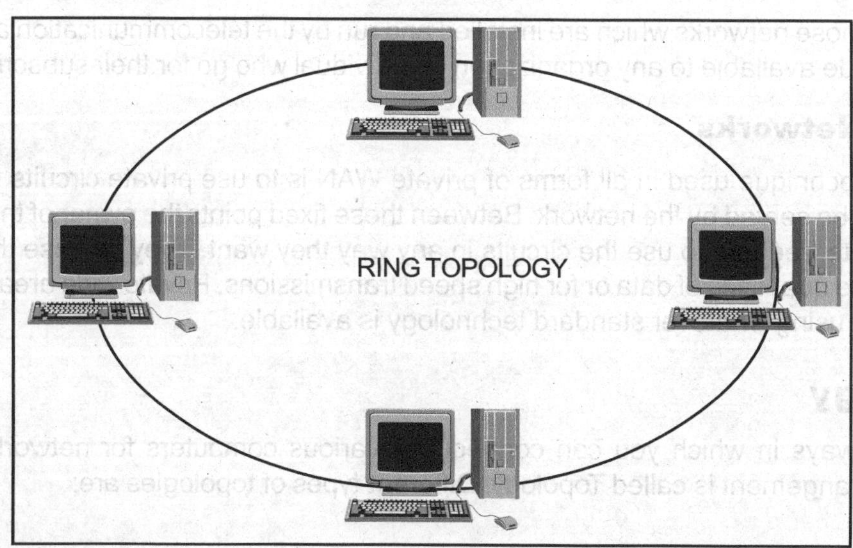

through every connected node on the ring before returning to the sender. If one node fails to pass data through itself, the entire network has failed and no traffic can flow until the defective node has been removed from the ring.

2. **Difficult to diagnose faults:** The fact that failure of one node will affect all other has serious implications for fault diagnosis. It may be necessary to examine a series of adjacent nodes to determine the faulty one. This operation may also require diagnostic facilities to be built into each node.

3. **Network reconfiguration is difficult:** The all or nothing nature of the ring topology can cause problems when one decides to extend or modify the geographical scope of the network. It is not possible to shut down a small section of the ring while keeping the majority of it working normally.

4. **Topology affects the access protocol:** Each node on a ring has a responsibility to pass on data that it receives. This means that the access protocol must take this into account. Before a node can transmit its own data, it must ensure that the medium is available for use.

The Bus Topology

In this case all the server/nodes share a common bus of connecting cables. Every computer can communicate directly with every other computer or device in the network. Each node is given an address.

To access a particular, a user just needs to know its address. This topology is frequently used with local area networks. Going through a hierarchy of nodes is not necessary.

Advantages of the Bus Network

1. **Short cable length and simple wiring layout:** Because there is a single common

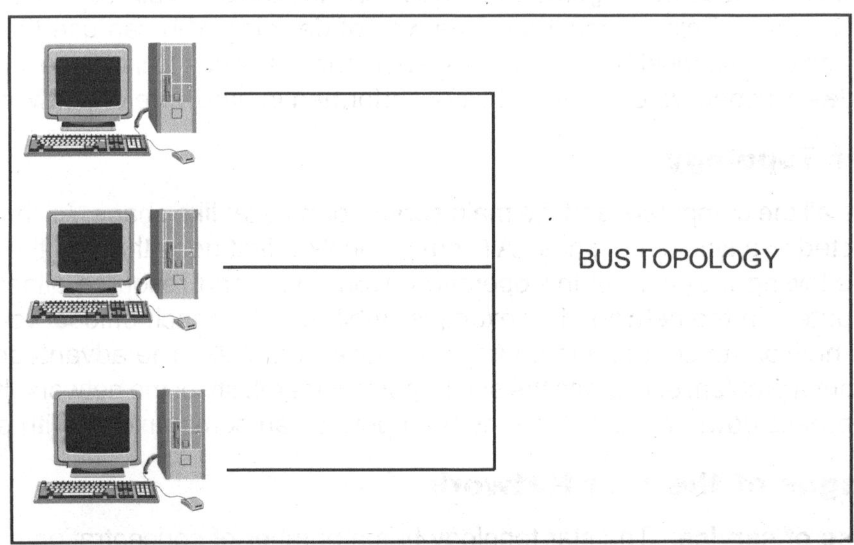

data path connecting all nodes, the bus topology allows a very short cable length to be used. This decreases the installation cost and also leads to a simple, easy to maintain, wiring layout.

2. **Resilient architecture:** The bus architecture has an inherent simplicity that makes it very reliable from a hardware point of view. There is a single cable through which all data passes and to which all nodes are connected.

3. **East to extend:** Additional nodes can be connected to an existing bus network at any point along its length. More extensive additions can be achieved by adding extra segments connected by a type of signal amplifier known as a repeater.

Disadvantages of the Bus Network

1. **Fault diagnosis is difficult:** Although the simplicity of the bus topology means that there is very little that can go wrong, fault detention is not a simple matter. In most LANs based on a bus, control of the network is not centralized in any particular node. This means that detection of a fault may be performed from many points in the network.

2. **Fault isolation is difficult:** In the star topology, a defective node can easily be isolated from the network by removing its connection at the center. If a node is faulty on a bus, it must be rectified at the point where the node is connected to the network. Once the fault has been located the node can simply be removed. In the case where the fault is the network medium itself, an entire segment of the bus must be disconnected.

3. **Repeater configuration:** When a bus-type network has its backbone extended using repeaters, reconfiguration may be necessary. This may involve tailoring cable lengths, adjusting terminators, etc.

4. **Nodes must be intelligent:** Each node on the network is directly connected to the central bus. This means that some way of deciding who can use the network at any given time must be performed in each node. It tends to increase the cost of the nodes irrespective of whether this is performed in hardware of software

The Star Topology

In this case all the computers and the main server form a star like shape. All the computers are connected to a single main host. All communication first goes through the centralized computer allowing it to control the operation, work load, and resource allocation of the other computers in the network. For example, a bank with branch offices would typically use a star network to control and coordinate those branches. The advantage is relative simplicity, but a problem exists with the single-point vulnerability of the network. If the central computer breaks down, none of the other computers can communicate with each other.

Advantages of the Star Network

1. **Ease of service:** The star topology has a number of concentration points, i.e. at

the central node or at intermediate wiring closets. These provide easy access for service of reconfiguration of the network.

2. **One device per connection:** Connection points in any network are inherently prone to failure. In the star topology, failure of a single connection typically involves disconnecting one node from an otherwise fully functional network.

3. **Centralized control/ problem diagnosis:** The fact that the central node is connected directly to every other node in the network means that faults are easily detected and isolated. It is a simple matter to disconnect failing nodes from the system.

4. **Simple access protocols:** Any given connection is a star network involves only the central node and one peripheral node. In this situation, contention for who has control of the medium for transmission purposes is easily solved. Thus in a star network, access protocols are very simple.

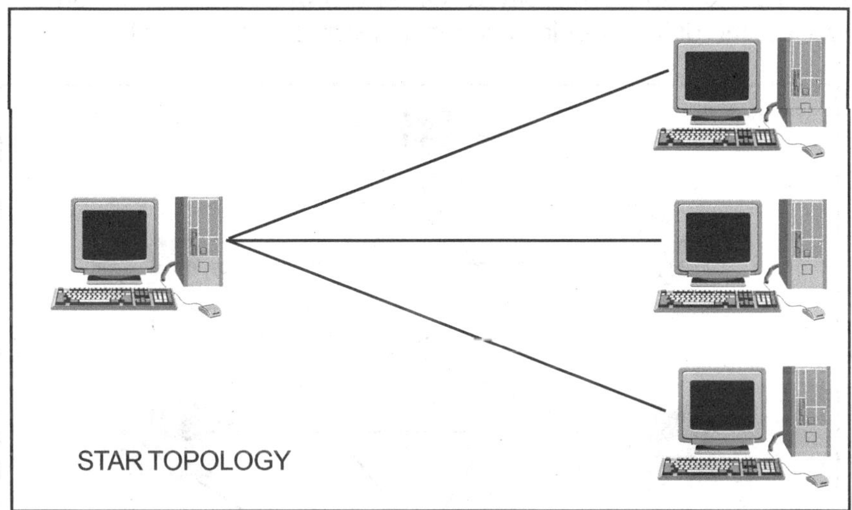

Disadvantages of the Star Network

1. **Long cable length:** Because each node is directly connected to the center, the star topology necessitates a large quantity of cable. While the cost of the cable is often small, congestion in cable ducts and maintenance and installation problems can increase costs considerably.

2. **Difficult to expand:** The addition of a new node to a star network involves a connection all the way to the central node. Expansion is usually catered for by providing large numbers of redundant cables during the initial wiring. However, problems can arise if a longer cable length is needed or an unanticipated concentration of nodes is required.

3. **Central node dependency:** If the central node in a star network fails, the entire network is rendered inoperable. This introduces heavy reliability and redundancy constraints on this node.

Mesh Topology

A network topology featuring a direct path between two nodes. The backbone of this topology looks like this, where most major cities have a direct connection to most major cities.

Advantages and Disadvantages of the Mesh Network

- **Units affected by media failure:** Mesh topologies resist media failure better than other topologies. Implementations that include more than two devices will always have multiple paths to send signals from one device to another. If one path fails, the transmission signals can be routed around the failed link. Theoretically, no units are affected by media failure. However, if all paths normally use the maximum capacity of each link, some performance degradation will occur are signals are routed around a failed link.
- **Ease of installation:** Mesh networks are relatively difficult to install because each device must be linked directly to all other devices. As the number of devices increases, the difficulty of installation increases geometrically.

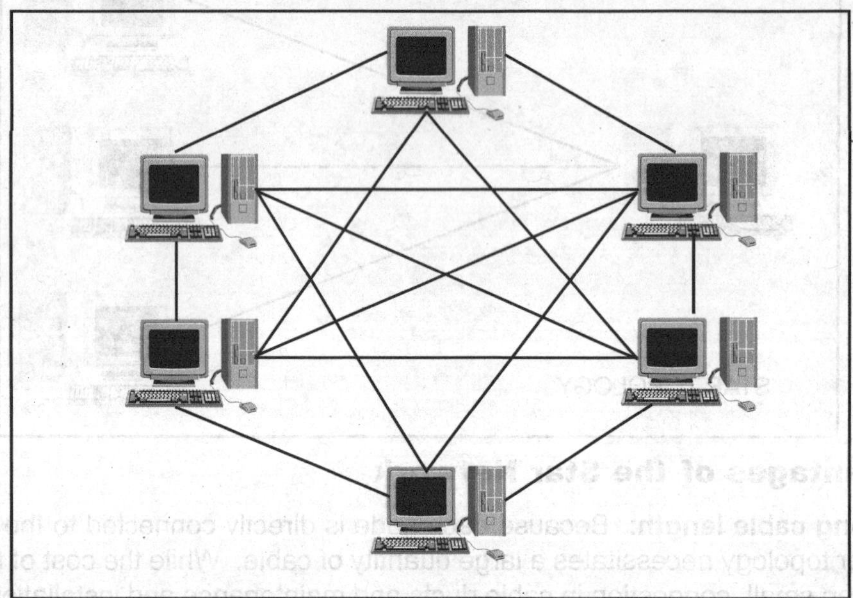

- **Ease of troubleshooting:** Mesh topologies are easy to troubleshoot because each medium link is independent of all others. You can easily identify faults and can isolate the affected link.
- **Ease of reconfiguration:** Mesh topologies are difficult to reconfigure for the same reasons that they are difficult to install.

Hybrid Topology

A combination of two or more network topologies. The resultant is a hybrid network. Although the backbone is mostly a mesh network, each local loop is a star network with the central office at each hub.

Advantages of the Hybrid Network

1. **Fault diagnoses and isolation:** The presence of concentration points in the network greatly eases fault diagnosis. If a fault is detected on the network, the initial problems to find out which concentration point in the ring is to blame. The fact that this ring is quite small in relation to the total size of the network makes this problem more manageable. The offending concentration point can be isolated easily, leaving the network in a fully functional state while further fault diagnosis is carried out.
2. **Ease of expansion:** The modular construction of a star-ring network means that new sections may be easily added. When designing the network originally, each concentration can have extra, unused lobes which can be called upon later, if needed. The next growth step involved adding a new concentration point and wiring it into the ring.
3. **Cabling:** The concentration points in a star-ring are connected via a single cable. This simplifies wiring between areas in an installation and cuts down on the congestion of cable ducts. Also, the wiring practices involved are very similar to that of telephone system installation. These techniques are well understood by building engineers and lend themselves well to the prewiring of buildings.

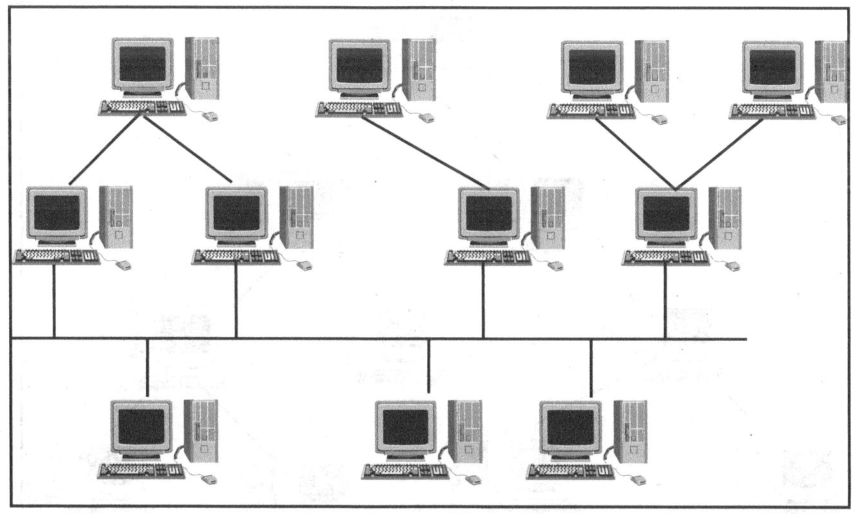

Disadvantages of the Hybrid Network

1. **Intelligent concentration points required:** Depending on the implementation used, the concentration points may need to have built in intelligence/processing ability. This will be necessary if it is to assist in network fault diagnosis, node isolation or conversion from one form of transmission medium to another.

2. **Cabling:** The intercloset cabling in a star ring is critical to its operation. This may mean that redundant cabling in the form of one or more back up rings may be necessary to meet reliability requirements. The largest section of the network (i.e. between the concentration points and the nodes) is laid out in a star. This means that a considerable amount of cable may be required.

Tree Topology

From a purely topological viewpoint, this network resembles a interconnection of star networks. Individual peripheral nodes must transmit to and receive from one other node only, toward a central node. An advantage of a tree structure is that functional groupings can be created.

For example, one branch could contain all the general ledger terminals, another branch all the accounts receivable terminals, and so on. If one branch stops functioning, the other branches in a tree network are not affected. However, data movement through this network can be slow.

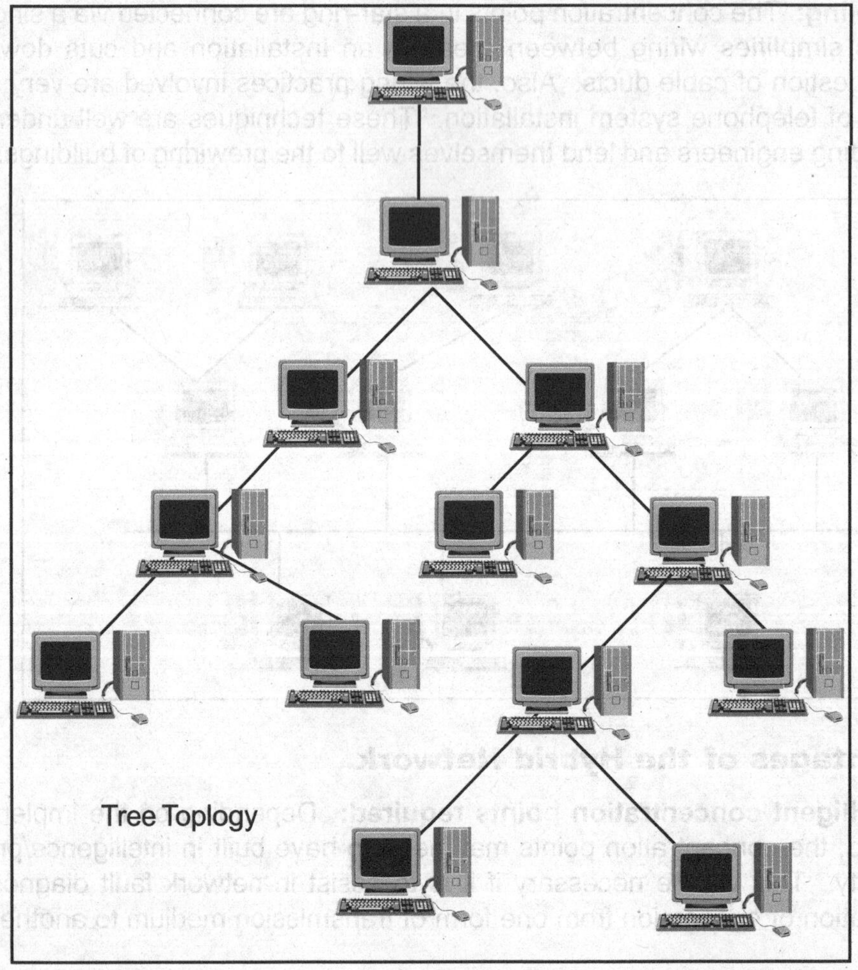

Tree Toplogy

Advantages of the Tree Network

1. **Easy to extend:** Because the tree is of its very nature, divided into subunits, it is easier to add new nodes or branches to it.
2. **Fault isolation:** It is possible to disconnect whole branches of the network from the main structure. This makes it easier to isolate a defective node.

Disadvantages of the Tree Network

1. **Dependant on the root:** If the "headend" device fails to operate, the entire network is rendered inoperable. In this respect, the tree suffers from the same reliability problems as the star.

Applications of Networking

In business, government organizations, universities and many other organizations networks of all types of computers provide tremendous benefits. Four of the most compelling benefits are as follows:

Simultaneous Access

In business computing, most office workers use the same software package. With a network, business can save a lot by purchasing special network versions of the most commonly used software rather than buying separate copies for each machine. When employees need to use the software, they simply load it from a shared storage device into their own desktop computer. Since a single network copy of the software can serve the needs of large number of users simultaneously, all the employees also save the storage space that the software program would occupy on his computer's disk drive. The same is true of data that multiple employees need access to at the same time. Another major area of computer network advantage is access to remote databases.

Shared Peripheral Devices

The best incentive for small businesses from computers networking is sharing of peripheral devices, especially expensive ones such as laser printer and scanners.

Easier Backup

In business, data can be extremely valuable, so making sure that employees backup their data is critical. One way to address this problem is to keep all valuable data on a shared storage device that employees access through a network. That way, one person can be charged with making regular backup of the data on the shared storage device.

Electronic Mail

Computer networking has helped in increasing the speed of the message transfer tremendously. With the help of e-mail, messages can be transferred through computer network within a short span of time. User can send written message without worrying about whether the other user is currently using his/her computer or not. Over centralized networks, the message is delivered almost instantaneously. E-mail cross time zones, can reach many people with the same message, reduces the paper flood and does not interrupt meetings the way a ringing phone does.

Voice Mail

It releases workers from the tyranny of the telephone. In it, if the person being called does not answer, the called is given instructions to dictate a message to the system. The voice mail computer system stores the message in the recipient's Voice mailbox. Later when the recipient dials the mailbox, the system delivers the message. A voice mail system translates the word of a message into digital impulses, which it then stores on disk, just as any other data. Later this message is reconverted to audio form.

The Ethernet Protocol

Ethernet is the most popular protocol used for LAN communications. In essence it uses a digital 'packet' that can contain any other digital information. Every computer that uses this protocol contains an Ethernet Network Interface Card (NIC) that has a unique address code embedded into a microchip on the NIC. This address is used by the protocol to identify each individual computer. This allows every electronic packet that is sent from one machine to another to contain the destination address for which the packet is intended.

Every computer on the network 'listens' for packets that contain its own address. When a packet is placed on a network, that packet is broadcast to and received by every other computer on the network but only the computer which corresponds to the destination address is allowed to claim that packet and receive the digital information contained within it. Only a single packet is allowed onto the network at any one time, but the process operates at such a high speed that effectively the packet is delivered to the destination within milliseconds, allowing the next packet access to the network almost immediately.

The Ethernet protocol also provides a means of preventing two computers from trying to place packets onto the network at the same time. When a NIC tries to place a packet onto the network, it first 'listens' to see if there is already a packet being transmitted to and from other machines, If so, then it is forced to wait for a random amount of time (milliseconds), before trying again. This continues until a 'gap' is found and then the packet can be successfully transmitted onto the network. The Ethernet protocol provides a means of delivering data from any PC on the network to any other on the same network at a theoretical rate of up to 10 Mega bits per second. Ethernet can also be used to connect remotely located PCs, but this requires special communications links to be set up over specialised equipment.

Fast Ethernet

It is a new standard of the Ethernet protocol, based on the existing 10 Mhz standard, but designed to operate at the much faster data rate of 100 Mhz. Mhz stands for megahertz or a million cycles per second and represents the operating frequency of the protocol. The terms 'Mhz' and 'Mega bits per second' are often used interchangeably, but this is only true where one cycle represents one bit (a bit being a unit of data). For many protocols, this direct relationship holds true, but it is not always the case and so the terms should be used with caution.

The TCP/IP Protocol

TCP/IP is actually two protocols. These two protocols are almost invariably use together, hence the term TCP/IP has come to be accepted as describing a single system. We will be using this assumption here. TCP/IP is the networks protocol that is used throughout the Internet. It was originally developed in American academic institutions as a means of communicating between university computer systems, first locally and then nationally across America and internationally between universities, that formed the basis of what is now know as the Internet.

It is the capability for being used over existing telephone systems that gives TCP/IP (and hence the Internet) its enormous potential for worldwide data communication. Ethernet is designed to run over relatively short distances at a very high data rate, but the physical limitations of the public phone systems mean that this high data rate cannot normally be sustained, except perhaps over the larger truck routes between countries and major cities. TCP/IP however is independent of the various data rates associated with different communication media and so can be used over both very slow and very high speed systems. Like Ethernet, the TCP/IP protocol uses an addressing system to determine the intended destinations for a data packet, but unlike Ethernet TCP/IP also includes a source address in the data packet. This system of addresses is used to route the data packet across the Internet, very much like the address on a envelope is used to route a letter across the various national postal systems.

However, unlike Ethernet, each packet is not broadcast cross the entire network, but is routed individually using the addressing system to a single destination. This system is known as 'packet switching'.

Packet Switching

When one computer communicates with another using the TCP/IP protocol, it breaks the information it needs to send into 'chunks' small enough for the TCP/IP packet to be handle and then attaches a destination address and a source address. The packet is then sent out across the Internet, containing all of the information it needs to navigate its way to a remote destination. It is a feature of the Internet that each individual packet can then take one of many different routes via the thousands of intermediate computer systems across the world to reach its final destination. Each computer along the way reads the destination address of he packet and routes it according to certain sets of rules to the next computer system on the Internet. This fragmenting of information and use of many alternative routes means that the receiving computer may well receive the packets in a different order to that in which they were sent. It must therefore have some means of making sure that it reads the incoming packets in the correct order.

The job of the 'TCP' part of TCP/IP is to ensure that each packet reaches its destination intact and that the packets are numbered effectively so that the receiving computer can put the incoming packets back into the correct order. It is the 'IP' part TCP/IP that looks after the addressing. Because TCP/IP packets contain a source address as well as a destination address, the receiving computer system also has a way or replying automatically to the sender by simply reading the source address and then generating another TCP/IP packet using this source address as the destination address for the new packet.

Another feature that is very useful part of the TCP/IP protocol is that because each packet is essentially self-sufficient in its journey across the Internet, many packets from different sources can share a single communication channel, allowing perhaps hundreds of thousands of channels to share a single cable at the same time.

Basic Elements in Networking

All networks require the following three elements:

1. **Network Services**: At least two individuals who have something to share.
2. **Transmission Media**: A method or pathway for contacting each other.
3. **Protocols**: Rules so that two or more individuals can communicate.

Network Services

Network services are provided by numerous combinations of computer hardware and software. Depending upon the task, network services require data, input/output resources and processing power to accomplish their goals.

In the computer industry, the following 3 types of service providers and requestor are as follows:

Servers: Servers are only allowed to provide services.

Clients: Clients are only allowed to request services from others.

Peers: Peers may do both concurrently.

Computer networks are often classified as one of the following two types:

Peer-to-peer

Server-centric

Peer-to-Peer Networks

This type of networks allow any entity to both request and provide network services. Peer-to-peer network software is designed so that peers perform the same or similar functions for each other.

Server-Centric Networks

This network involves strictly defined roles. By definition, a server-centric network places restrictions upon which entity may make requests or service them. Currently, the most popular personal computer networks are server-centric.

Transmission Media

It is the pathway by which networked entities use to contact each other. Computer transmission media includes cable and wireless technologies that allow networked devices to contact each other. Transmission media cannot guarantee that other network devices will understand a message. It can, however, guarantee a message delivery path.

Protocols

A protocol can be one rule or a complete set of rules and standards that allow different devices to hold conversations. For example, human communication would be impossible without language, grammar and cultural rules. The following is an example of set of rules and standards in which network service requesters and service providers can communicate:

- How is the transmission media physically set up?
- How do network entities contact one another?
- How do network entities know how much data can be transmitted?
- How are network entities guaranteed that a message has been received correctly?
- How is a message passed to the Intended recipient(s)?
- How are bits transmitted on the media?
- How do network entities, with disparate languages, communicate?
- How do network entities know when to transmit data?

When you formally agree that you will both use the same language in future communications, you have established a communication protocol.

Value Added Networks

Another type of network is the value added network. This is an established data communication network that owns a leases communication facilities and computers to manage communication. The facilities may include microwave antennas and communication satellites. The owners design and maintain the value added network. They then rent the network simultaneously to many subscribers, who link their own equipment tot he facilities. Using value added network saves organizations the time and cost of designing and maintaining their own networks. The concept of value added common carriers was important in the development of computer networking.

A value added carrier leases communications facilities from conventional common carriers and uses these in conjunction with computers to build a network which offers new types of communications services and tariffs. These are called Value Added Networks (VANs). Graphnet offered services for delivery of documents, often in facsimile form. Telenet built a network for the interconnection of data processing machines, like the ARPA network although the software and hardware mechanisms eventually became substantially different from ARPANET. Telnet delivers packets of data between computers or terminals in a fraction of a second and charges by the packet. TYMNET offering similar services evolved from a private time sharing network to a value added common carrier. In 1971 the United States Office of Telecommunications Policy recommended a policy of first tier second tier common carriers.

The first tier carriers construct and own telecommunications links and lease channels to their customer. They typically own 50% to 100% of the channel miles in service and lease the remainder from another carrier. The second tier carriers are the value added carriers. They add equipment including multiplexers and computers, to channels leased from first tier carriers and sell services that they create in this way, including message delivery services, computer networks and possibly information retrieval services and computer timesharing devices. It seems likely that second markets will develop in may telecommunications areas. The second tier carrier may minimize investment in terminals by letting the customer provide these. Legislation in favour of second tier carriers has increased the diversity and competitiveness of the telecommunications industry in those countries where it has been passed.

In most countries, such legislation does not yet exist. Telecommunication systems use computer in different ways. Some use them for switching; some for sorting messages which are transmitted; some for processing the data transmitted. At one extreme the computer merely switches the circuits; at the other the circuits are merely linked into a data processing system. The term "computer utility" became used for describing public access to computer networks and in 1966 the United States Federal Communications Commission (FCC) initiated a lengthy inquiry to determine whether public computing services should be regulated. Hybrid communication services must be completely tariffed and regulated by the FCC. Common carriers may not offer data processing services (hybrid or otherwise) except through a separate corporation with separate facilities, officers and accounting. AT&T has been excluded from offering any such unregulated services under an earlier consent decree. Most countries do not have these legislative problems because the state telecommunications authority rigorously enforces its absolute monopoly over all telecommunications, no matter how bad its service may be.

Public Networks

During the mid 1970's the need for building a public data network was realised by the telecommunication administration of various countries, with two specified objectives. One was to provide better services to the computer community and the other was to earn revenue which was enormous. This is the revenue from the switches, concentrators, multiplexers polling equipment, line control equipment, etc., - the various devices used in the interconnection of machines.

Common carriers operate (this term includes the telecommunication administrations of countries with government-controlled telecommunications – the PTT's) the equipment for switching and routing telephone calls; it seemed natural that they should operate the new equipment for switching routing data. One computers were used for switching the desire grew to use them for other functions also. AT&T developed its plans for ACS (Advanced Communications Service) in which the nodes would not only switch data but provide a variety of functions which need processing and storage. The British Post Office created its Viewdata scheme (subsequently called Prestel) for operating public data bank accessible with television sets in homes or offices, initially via the telephone network.

Private Networks

Some networks are designed specifically for and used completely by individual organizations. They are called private networks. The communication equipment that forms the network is purchased or leased in the name of the organization. The first WAN to be designed and developed was the private network, ARPANET, a United States network. The objective was to make the interesting and unique computer facilities available in some computer centers accessible to a large community of users. It has grown from a four-site experimental network to a nationwide communication system interconnecting more than fifty universities and research centers. A few computer networks link computer centers in multiple locations. To operate these multicorporate networks, a separate service organization is usually set up and that organization will take care of creating and operating the network. A leading example is the SWIFT electronic fund transfer network that passes financial transactions between banks. SWIFT (Society for Worldwide Interbank Financial Transactions) is a non-profit organization set up and wholly owned by the banks connected to it. The objective of this network is to replace mail, cable and telex and work for 24 hours a day and 7 days a week. It handles over a million transactions per day. It is used to send money, messages and bank statements at high speed between banks and the transaction time is drastically reduced.

SWIFT connects about 3000 financial institutions in more than 600 countries. Citibank Corp. in New York, was the first one to opt for the system and over 40 banks in India have joined the network. The computer based terminals of these banks are hooked with SWIFT's access center in Bombay, which is maintained by CMC Ltd. From here, messages are relayed to the overseas communication center of VSNL and then transmitted to SWIFT's international receiving centers based in London or Singapore, depending on the location of the receiver, through VSNL's GPSS services. The software needed for the operations has been supplied by SWIFT terminal services, a wholly owned subsidiary of SWIFT and the hardware is being supplied by Tata Unisys, Digital Equipment (India) Ltd. The participating banks finance the system and a tariff structure has been built based on the message, connection charge and annual charge.

Common Network Services

The following common network services are available:

File Services

The network file services improve the efficient storage and retrieval of computer data, they are one of the primary services offered on computer networks. The following file service functions are :

- File transfer – Rapidly move files from place to place.
- File storage and data migration – Use storage hardware efficiently.
- File update synchronization – Manage multiple copies of the same file.
- File archiving – Back up critical data

File Transfer

Before computer networks were widely implemented, users physically moved storage media from computer to computer. This inefficient practice has been called "sneaker-net" (because users hand carried data from machine to machine). Organizationally, it is relatively expensive and time consuming to employ people to move computer storage media. The network file service file transfer refers to any service that saves, retrieves, or moves files for a network client. This service allows you to handle data much more efficiently. The major advantage of Computer Networks is, file transfers can be performed with relative ease regardless of file size, distance and often even the local operating systems. This service increases the organization's efficienty, as well as it also provided access to data and information that were previously inaccessible. File services may also coordinate access rights because of the increased information access that the file transfer service provides. An organization may allow network transfer of sensitive information, but only by authorized individuals. During file transfer, network file services often use passwords to control access to systems and files. They use data encryption schemes to encode data so that it can only been read by appropriate individuals.

File Storage and Data Migration

The rapidly increasing amount of computerized data has caused the development of numerous online, nearline and offline storage devices. Hard disk drive, tape jukebox and removable storage is an example of online storage, nearline storage and offline storage respectively. Computers store data on a variety of magnetic and optic disks, diskettes and tapes. Each storage medium exhibits characteristics that make it suitable for a specific use. Because the efficient use of each storage device requires continuous management of multiple devices, network application are well suited to control data storage activities on different storage systems. In addition, if you are working with high end equipment, such as magnetic tape banks or optical libraries, you can use the network's economy of scale to justify the equipment purchase, operation and maintenance. Using file storage and data migration functions, all networked computers can take advantage of the data storage device that is appropriate for their access time, reliability and longevity needs. As data ages and becomes less used, it can be moved from expensive online hard disk drives to less expensive and longer life offline storage media. Moving data from one storage media or location to another is call data migration. Through data migration, you can set up file services to move files based on age, user, size or various other criteria.

File Update Synchronization

File update synchronization is a service that compares the time and date corresponding files were saved and determines which is most current. It may also keep track of who has a specific file and if intermediary changes have been made. Using this information, it automatically updates all file locations with latest version. For examples, mobile computers are not always connected or available to the network. If you are a mobile computer user and you want access to a file that is on a network file server, you would normally save a copy of the file to your computer' shard drive. However, someone else may access and change the original file in the meantime. If that person does make changes, your copy now contains out of date information. Somehow you need to recognize when changes have occurred and take the appropriate action.

File Archiving

Many organizations create duplicate copies of important data on magnetic tape or some other offline storage media in case of emergency. This practice is called file archiving or file backup. The original file can be kept in addition to the backup copy, or it can be removed from online storage media so that the offline media contains the only copy. When file storage devices are interconnected on a network, file archiving becomes much easier. Computer operators use the network to traverse great distances, saving the organization time and money.

Print Services

These are network applications that control and manage access to printers and fax equipment. Print services accept print job request, interpret print job formats and printer configurations, manage print queues and interact with networkable printers and fax equipment for network clients.

The following are print service functions:

- Provide multiple access from limited interfaces – Reduce the number of printers your organization needs.
- Eliminate distance constraints – place printers wherever is most convenient.
- Handle simultaneous requests – Queue print jobs to reduce the time your computer spends sending a print job.
- Share specialized equipment – share specialized printers efficiently.
- Network fax service – Computerize the transmission and reception of fax images.

Providing Multiple Access from Limited Interfaces

Reducing the total number of printers can save your organization a substantial amount of money having fewer printers reduces the number of devices to buy, maintain and manage.

Most modern printer provide multiple ports or interfaces. However, the number of interfaces is finite and relatively small. Typically, only two or three computers may be directly connected to each printer. On the other hand, a network connection requires only one interface. Through this interface, many computers may send data to the printer.

Therefore, print services allow numerous clients to be serviced by a single printer. Managing access to printers, or other devices with limited interfaces, is a major use of modern computer networks.

Eliminating Distance Constraints

Printer ports are often based on cable interface specification that limit the distance between the printer and attached computers. Network cable systems and devices allow longer distances for cable specifications. Organizations can use the network to place printers in strategic locations throughout a building or campus.

Handling Simultaneous Request (Queuing)

Print servers can often handle simultaneous request for print services. When two users try to send data to a printer at the same time, both applications compete for the printer's limited ability to accept and store print request. Queuing solves this bottleneck problem. A print queue is the part of the print server which captures and stores computer print jobs. Depending upon each implementation's specific features, print queues can hold, prioritize, and manage print jobs. When printing with network printing services, your application sends print requests and data to what it believes is a printer. These requests are actually routed to a print queue. The print requests remain in the queue until the desired printer is available. Print queuing increases the efficiency of network print services by organizing the interaction between printers and their clients. In addition, because multiple clients may send data simultaneously to the print queue at full network speeds, each may complete print request rapidly and return to other tasks.

Sharing Specialized Equipment

Some printer are designed for specific use, such as high speed output, large format paper, or color printing. Specialized equipment may be expensive or may not be frequently used by end users. The economies of scale produced by networking each device with numerous clients can reduce the effective cost per user and optimize printer use.

Network Fax Service

Network fax allows users to send and receive faxes using special network hardware and software. This service is becoming increasingly popular because it reduces the time and paper handling normally involved in traditional fax transmissions. Traditional fax machines use computer modem, scanner and printer technologies to send a digital document image to remote locations. Network fax systems use the same computer technologies and computer networks to better integrate fax service with the rest of the network's print and message services.

Message Services

Message services include storing, accessing and delivering text, binary, graphic, digitized video and audio data. Message services are similar to file services. However, unlike file services, message services deal actively with the communication interactions between computer users, user applications, network applications, or documents. Instead of simply storing data files, message services transport data from point to point.

The following are the message services functions:

- Electronic Mail
- Integrated electronic mail and voice mail
- Object oriented applications
- Workgroup applications

Electronic Mail

A business depends on the efficient exchange of information between different parts of the business and between the business and the outside word. Much of this exchange has been traditi0onally carried out through paper documents, delivered by secretary, mail or messenger service. With the growing use of personal computers, a more efficient alternative has emerged, i.e., electronic mail. Electronic mail is usually used to exchange messages and data files. Each user is assigned an electronic mailbox.

Using the appropriate command, the user can scan a list of messages in the mailbox, display the contents of a particular message, send a message to another user and so forth. To send a message, it is not necessary for the recipient to be present at the computer. The message resides in the mailbox until it is read. The sender may restrict delivery of the message to authorized readers by using a password. That is, the recipient must "sign" for the message by typing his or her identifying password. Many other features of standard mail delivery are implemented in electronic mail systems. For example, mail can be forwarded, stored for delayed delivery and sent to anyone at a particular phone number. In addition, electronic mail systems implement many new features. An electronic mail system can deliver copies of a message to all individuals listed in a certain file. It also allow merging of standard data (from a data file) with a particular message. Now-a-days, several companies have started subscription to electronic mail services. These services are accessed through a modem and allow users to communicate with other subscribers to the service. The service may also accept a message and transmit it to its destination city. There the message is printed out and delivered with the next day's mail. This technique can be used to communicate with people who are not subscribers to the network.

Integrated Electronic Mail and Voice Mail

Message services that integrate E-Mail and voice mail are also being developed. Voice mail is a service offered by specialized computer hardware and software that answers telephone calls and records audio messaged. Because voice mail systems are simply specialized computers, thy can be incorporated into computer networks. Computer network and voice mail vendors are currently developing ways to make voice mail system cooperate on computer networks. Eventually, user could retrieve messages from whatever type of device is convenient.

Object Oriented Applications

Object oriented application are computer programs that combine smaller applications to accomplish complex tasks. Message services often facilitate communications between objects on a computer network. Messaging application accomplish this by acting as the object's agent, so every object does not meet to contact every other object. The object simply communicates with an agent from the local messaging service. The agent then become responsible for communicating the message to the destination object.

Workgroup Applications

Message service have also been used to create a new class of applications called workgroup applications. The following are common types of workgroup applications:

Workflow management

Workflow management application intelligently forms, route notices and documents among network clients. These service providers are designed to handle multiuser distributed business processes. For example, assume that you want to convert a payroll process using workflow management. The old manual process required that employees fill out a paper based time card. The time card was then signed by a manager and sent to the payroll department. Upon receipt payroll employees entered the information from the time card, calculated the employee's pay and benefits and generated a check. At each point along the path, an auditor verified that the steps were completed correctly and that errors did not occur. In addition, all of these steps had to take place hurriedly to meet employee expectations and government regulations. Message services are ultimately responsible for making workflow routing and delivery decisions. Workflow management can improve this process by intelligently routing electronic forms to each individual. The form can contain data provided previously by other users that is customized to represent the formats required by each individual. In addition, data can now be moved, stored, manipulated, verified and presented to each user much faster than similar manual processes.

Linked object documents

The computer industry is moving towards the linked object model for creating compound documents. Linked object documents, similar to object oriented applications, incorporate independent data objects into larger structures. For example, a single electronic document could contain text, spreadsheets, graphics, voice and video elements which are linked to other files, objects, or parts. Although this technology is still in development, network message services may act as agents on behalf of the data objects that comprise linked object documents. Conceptually each object includes the intelligent required to pass messages between a document element and its originating application of file. A single document serves as the integrator of the various pieces.

Application Services

Application services are network services that run software for network clients. They are different from file services because they allow computers to share processing power, not just share data. The two other aspects normally associated with application services are:

Specialization of Servers

The greatest benefit of application serves is that they can employ specialized equipment to increase speed, data integrity and security. However, how much processing should be handled by a server and how much is left to the client? Application servers have more computing power than user workstations and they often use special operating systems that have been optimized to perform a specific operation. For example, a personal computer user wants to perform a complex mathematical calculation to create a graph. Using a personal computer (PC), the calculation would take an extremely long time. To accomplish the task more rapidly, the PC sends out the math portion of the calculation to be processed by a mainframe computer. The mainframe quickly processes the request and sends back the results. The PC is only required to collect the resulting data set and generate the graph. What would normally take a very long time can now be accomplished much more rapidly.

Scalability and Growth

Network application services can also provide organizations with relatively inexpensive upgrade paths. If more computing power is required, only the network application server is upgraded. For example, assume that you use an extremely complex modeling application and that the application server software currently runs on a minicomputer. As your company grows, the minicomputer becomes overworked and response time gets worse and worse. To improve response times you simply move the application software to a faster computer, or add another server. You can improve the processing power of your computer while leaving other client and server computer totally unaffected.

Database Services

Network database services provide server based database storage and retrieval that allow network clients to control data manipulation and presentation. A special term has been created to describe database applications that allow clients to request data from these specialized servers: client server databases. Client server database applications divide and optimize the tasks involved in requesting and providing data. Depending upon the design goal, the client is given a portion of the tasks involved in formulating the request and processing the response, while database servers typically evaluate incoming requests and return data.

Network database provide the following services:

- Optimize the computers which store, search and retrieve database records.
- Control where data is stored geographically
- Organize data logically between organizational departments.

- Provide data security.
- Reduce database client access time.

The following aspects of network database services are:

Coordinating Distributed Data

Large organizations often segregate tasks and information between multiple departments. When data access is shared, concerns arise about who controls what data and where it should be stored. Network database services employ a tactic called distributed data to achieve seamless data sharing. They divide control over the pieces of the database among the various departments' computer systems. The database management system is responsible for making the database appear as one logical unit while coordinating changes that occur on various computer systems.

Replication

Data from local databases may typically be retrieved much more rapidly than from remote databases. Therefore, users prefer to work on local data. However, when more than two copies of a database exist, organizations run the risk of making decisions based upon out-of-data or incorrect information. Replication creates and synchronizes multiple copies of a database over the network. Presently, the leading database software uses two different methods to perform replication. One method uses a master database, which is the repository of all additions and changes. The database management system is responsible for making sure that the changes recorded in the master are sent to all copies of the database. The second method gives several local databases responsibility for recording adds and changes. In addition, the local portion of the management system must then coordinate adds and changes with all the other copies.

22 Designing the Network

Introduction

Given the recent surge in networking, it might be possible to believe that you could build a network simply by purchasing the parts and following the instructions that explain how to insert tab A into slot B and so forth. It is possible to purchase the parts and assemble them into a network.

However, if you are working with a business or organizational network, and you want to get started on the right foot, it is necessary to approach the various sets of instructions you will receive, with products, in books, advice from friends, etc.

Identifying the Uses of Your Network

Every network is different. Just as every human being is different. Once created a network grows its own way. No matter what your organization does, its network has to accomplish only one task to be considered successful. It has to ensure that what your organization does, it can do better, faster, more efficiently, and more reliably with the assistance of a network.

If the network does not work do that, it will be a failure, regardless of the quantity of premium technology and quality of service. Keep this is mind as you progress, it is the single most important fact here.

The network is not about technology, no matter how much a techo-fanatic may want it to be. Networks are about getting things done, primarily by people who could not care less whether they do their work on a network or not.

Deciding What Happens at Which Computer

The next step in the network-design process seems obvious. This is knowing which applications and tasks have to preformed at each of the computers on your network. There can be various options under it. Some of them are:

Many-User Computer

Computers used by many users can be built minimally or with all the bells and whistles As with any other system, the amount of power and features depends on the application.

Single-User Computers

It generally occurs in offices. Whether an office is physical or virtual, an increasing number of office workers use computers on a day-to-day basis. This shift in computer has created a new class of office workers called knowledge workers because their currency is dealing with information and formatting, managing, and analyzing data.

Given the increasing focus on high-tech jobs and high-tech workforces, it is easy to lose sight of the fact that knowledge workers are not a homogeneous mass.

Depending on the nature of their jobs, they tend to require higher-end computers to begin with, but they also have widely varying connectivity requirements. For example, some workers may be able to leave their work behind at the end of the day and require no remote access; other users may require two or more computers to be able to do their jobs.

Naturally, this is a rightsizing issue, if you have to provide more than one computer for some users, it is going to affect your capacity planning to a great degree.

Determining the Degree of Centralization

There are times to centralize administration and security, and there are times not to. There are times when it is worthwhile to go the whole nine yards toward establishing a central administrative authority, and times when the return from doing so is not worth the effort or expense. When you are designing a network, you must determine whether or not you want the ability to administer your network from a central point.

Clearly, you would not necessarily want to administer every system if your network consists of only a few computers (less than 10 or so) in the same location. The cost of network management software, that can handle configuration management and software distribution, among other tasks, is altogether too high to justify on a small, local network.

On the other hand, even for a small network, you may want to find some way of centralizing some functions such as file services, security, and backup.

Client/server networks, by contrast, are secure. Their files are usually stored in a central location and backed up on a regular basis. User tends to be controllable. As a result, there are myriad upsides of even basic centralization.

1. Easier access to files
2. Stronger security
3. Easier backup
4. Easier configuration management and standardization of workstations.

Easier access to files

Files stored across multiple workstations can present a problem for network users. If the user has to put together a contract, he or she might have to find a contract file stored on server's machine. To centralize access to files, you have to build a file server, or a server dedicated to sharing its disk space with a collection of users for file storage.

Typically, a file server requires a powerful processor, a lot of memory, and as much disk space as you can afford.

Stronger Security

File servers usually have some security built in so that they can ensure that access to files is limited to those users who should have access to them.

Typically, file server security for PC-based operating systems follow some fairly simple rules:

1. Security inheritance works similarly to financial inheritance; what a parent has can by a child unless it is blocked by third parties. In security a user gets access to a particular directory. Whatever access a user has to this directory is inherited by any and all subdirectories of this directory. Inheritance is a useful tool to ensure that a user has as much access as he or she requires to a given part of the server's disk.
2. In general, uses are limited to 3 levels of access to a given file or directory on a file server:

   No Access, which often means that users cannot even see the file or directory.

   Read-only Access, which means that users can view the contents of a file or directory but cannot modify it.

   Read-write Access, which means that a user has the access rights to view and modify files and directories.

Easier Backup

If all the network user's files are stored on a centralized server, they can be backed up simply by duplicating the server's hard drive to tape. Assuming that your network has 50 user workstations. If all the users store their files on their workstations, you will have to back up all or part of their hard drives to ensure that no data is lost if a system crashes.

Further suppose that each user has 25 megabytes of files on their workstation's hard drives. Backing up this quantity of files across the network for this many users could take 10 or 12 hours and be a nightmare to manage.

On the other hand backing up to a server's drive with an attached tape drive can take as little as an hour or so. Clearly, backing up files from a single server to a tape drive takes less time is more controllable.

Easier Configuration Management

It is an art of using a central console to ensure that user workstations have the correct hardware and software installed, and that the software and hardware are set up according to consensus and preset standards. Its software is however, little complex. It is usually composed of a highly complex database with a proprietary front end that allows a network administrator to view and modify the configurations workstations.

Most management software requires that each system have an agent installed on the workstation, often, agents can be installed automatically as a user logs on the network.

Drawing the Network

By this time you have gained knowledge about:

- ☐ The purpose of the network
- ☐ The specifies of the network's use
- ☐ The quantity of both users and computers
- ☐ Whether or not the network will be centralised or decentralised
- ☐ The network topology you plant to use

Drawing the Logical Diagram

The first drawing you make is the logical diagram. It details the applications that have to run on workstations have to be able to access.

1. Start by drawing a workstation for each type of user (for example, one warehouse floor computer, one analyst's computer, one accounting computer, one secretary's computer and so on).

   Just make a circle for each computer; draw them in a line across the top of the whiteboard or page.

2. Below each computer, list the applications it has to run. This could include word processing, spreadsheets, emails, scheduling and more for a user's desktop computer, or a single application for a dedicated machine, such as a factory or warehouse inventory computer or an in-office computer dedicated to routing email.
3. Make a list of the resources each workstation computer will share. In general, peer networking has a lot of these shared resources (such as printers, scanners, shared modems and so on); client/server networks will have fewer shared resources. No matter whether you've elected to use client/server or peer, add these resources into your diagram.
4. If the system will participate in a network-wide security scheme, note which group of users has login access to the various pieces of the system. For example, business desktop users can log into the file server, warehouse supervisors can log into the transaction server and administrators can log in to anything anywhere. This step helps ensure that you provide the correct levels of security.
5. Add the workstation operating system to the bottom of the list. The Operating System

is usually something like MS-DOS, Windows, or Macintosh. Although Unix can be used as a client, outside of academic computing centers and high-end engineering workstations, it is not common as a workstation Operating System, ensure that you have more than one computer drawn–each workstation Operating System should be shown on a separate machine.

6. Add the quantity of each type of workstation to the bottom of the list.

   Now your workstations are quantified. If you are going to build a client/server network and will require one or more servers, add the servers in at the bottom of the diagram and list the applications and resources each server provides to the network. If you are building a WAN and have to incorporate routers and so forth to hook the LANs together, draw the routers in at the side.

   Now comes the fun part. Draw lines from each workstation type to each system to which that workstation type requires access. In other words, if an accounting PC requires file storage resources on a file server, select a colored marker, draw a line between the two systems and write the name of the resource the workstation client will use.

   If a workstation has a shared printer, ensure that other systems that have to use it are connected to it using lines of a different color than the first.

   If a router provides connectivity between the network and the workstations, but must first route data through a server, draw that full path as well in yet another color.

Drawing the Physical Network Diagram

Drawing the physical network really isn't as hard as it sounds. If you already know which clients have to be connected to specific resources and which topology you'll be using, you're halfway there,

1. Start by drawing the physical center of your network. If you're using a star configuration (such as Ethernet, Token Ring or FDDI), the center of your network is the concentrator: a hub, MAU or switch of some sort. If your network needs only one hub, draw a box and label it as the hub.

2. Draw as many boxes as you will have shared media hubs. (Keep in mind that hubs are measured by the number of ports they have; an 8-port hub supports eight workstations, 16 ports support 16 workstations, and so forth).

   For performance reasons, it's a good idea to divide the network into single hubs with no more than 16 ports per segment. Connect lines between the switch and the segments; each of these lines represents a crossover cable, or a specially made cable that can be used to connect concentrators together.

3. Draw the servers and mark them as connected directly to the switch. A server connected directly to a switch offers compelling advantages in terms of performance at the workstation because the server has a direct connection to the port to which the workstation is connected.

This holds true even if a workstation is connected through a hub connected to a switch port; the collision domain of individual hubs are usually fairly small, so there isn't much competition for bandwidth.

4. Refer to the drawing of the logical network and do some analysis. Look at which workstations require access to which servers and try to group them together.
5. Once you analyze the relative bandwidth requirements of your users, you're ready to start figuring out which class of user has to connect to which device.

Take the time to think about this. If users don't have sufficient bandwidth initially, they will have network problems and consequently lose faith in the network. It's important to roll out systems that work for the users, otherwise the network has no credibility.

Writing Specification & Getting Other's Input

Once you've gotten this far, you have enough data to write a document that includes the following:

- ☐ The organisational purpose of the network
- ☐ The specifics of the network's use
- ☐ The quantity of both users and computers
- ☐ Whether or not the network will be centralized or decentralized
- ☐ The network topology you plan to use

You also have a pair of diagrams that portray the logical and physical connections required by network. Pat yourself on the back – you deserve it.

You've created the basis for an initial specification document, which enumerates all the preceding points and includes the diagrams.

Writing the Specification Document

Now is the time to actually write your specification for the network. The specification document should take into account all the points in the preceding section and list, quite specifically, the various users of the network. Specifications do not have to be long, but they must be complete and clear; as English teachers are prone to say, "It should be as long as it needs to be – but no longer."

Specifying Hardware

Until this point, the network-planning process has dealt entirely with use and software application issues. At this point, you should know what the network needs to do, but you haven't begun looking at hardware products …at least, not specifically.

Selecting Hardware

Networking hardware typically comes in two configurations: the latest and greatest hub/

switch/chasis that costs. If the network you are building is small and not slated to expand, the cheaper is acceptable; it will provide basic connectivity and adequate performance.

If your network is expanding, try to get as much capacity as possible because doing so buys you breathing space. Because networking technology changes so rapidly, purchasing excess capacity is often the only way to get a full, useful life span out of equipment.

It's not a terribly platable decision to make, but unfortunately it's the dirty little secret of networking hardware capacity planning.

The following list provides a baseline for the physical part of your network. This list doesn't provide specific recommendations because hardware changes so rapidly. But it does tell you the features you're like to find useful.

Network Interface Cards

For each computer, you need at least one network card. NICs can cost as little as Rs.2000 or as much as Rs.15000. Make certain that your network cards are the correct topology; even through Token-Ring cards have the same network-cable connector as Ethernet 10BASE-T cards, Ethernet cards won't work on Token-Ring networks and vice versa.

Concentrators (MAUs, hubs and switches)

Once you know how many computers will be on your network, you know how many ports you need. Once you know how many ports you require, it's a matter of determining whether they will be switched or shared media, as detailed (in the abstract) in the specification you've already created.

Wiring

If you're using a star-configuration network, you'll have to run cables from the wiring closet in which the hubs are stored to each workstation's location. Ensure that you use at least Category 5 or better twisted-pair wire; even at twice the price of the lower cable certifications such as Category 3, it's cheap because it has a longer useful life span.

If you're using a bus-configuration network, you'll have to run coaxial cable serially between workstations. If you decide to install the cable yourself, remember to handle it gently, regardless of whether it's coax or twisted pair.

Treating the wire gently (that is, not crimping or breaking it) helps ensure that you'll get a better connection.

A better solution, if your organisation has the finances, is to hire someone who runs cable for a living. Electricians are often smaller cable installers because they run so many cables through walls and other inaccessible locations.

Workstation computers

Once you have specified your network cards, hubs and cables, you're ready to spec out your computers. Refer to the specification you wrote to determine which users need powerful workstations and which ones can use lower-end systems and specify them. Because hardware changes so rapidly, it's pointless to create a fixed specification here, but as of 2001, the fastest chips are reaching 1 gigahertz speeds, so workstations in the 600 to 850 Mhz range are fine for now.

Don't consider this recommendation to be a standard; see what the market is offering. What constitutes a powerful PC changes incredibly fast, so do research to find out what's currently available in the market and that too at a reasonable price.

Server computers

By the same token, overbuild your servers. Get as much power a machine as you can afford and add as much memory as possible. No matter what your application, the power and memory you provide will be used in six months or less and will be tight in a year or so.

Figure out your server's disk-space requirements (a good minimum is 100 Mb per user; more is always better) and then double it if possible. Don't worry; the disk space will be used – probably sooner than you expect.

Management features

When you purchase your hardware, ensure that it can support the SNMP or RMON network-management standard. Even if you don't use the management features immediately, as your network grows, SNMP and RMON capability can extend the useful life of a piece of equipment by ensuring that it can be managed as part of a greater network.

Other features

Likewise, try to find working hardware that can support advanced features like VLANs. Having the capability is crucial because it ensures that you have options.

The more options your hardware has, the more it prevents your networking hardware from becoming quickly obsolete.

Building the Network

Once you've settled on the hardware; you're ready to begin building the network.

23 Network Security

Security in TCP/IP Networks

Allowing access to your hosts for only the users that you intended is the goal of security in a TCP/IP network. As discussed previously, once a user is logged into a system, the security within that system is all that prevents the user from accessing information that user should not be able to access. Thus, the first level of security in a network is to make sure that all the security on the various hosts themselves is carefully policed. Unfortunately, security in UNIX hosts is based on userid and password.

Thus, userids and passwords need to be very difficult to guess. The most effective method used to create a truly secure system is to have userids that are not personal names or initials but computer-generated in some reasonable random style and to have passwords that are likewise computer-generated. Users will not like having userids and passwords that are not easy to remember. But, if someone trespassed into your system, that person will be able to work out userids if it appears that some form of a person's name is being used as a userid. If you find using computer-generated userids to difficult, you should at least force people to change their passwords regularly.

Further, you should regularly use password scanning software to make sure people aren't using simple, easy-to-guess passwords like their name or car type. A second level of security is to ensure that only users whom you want are even accessing your network. If your network is completely disconnected from the outside world, you only need to concentrate on the security of your individual hosts. But if you are part of the Internet community and have linked up to the outside world, you need to consider measures to isolate your network from the rest of the Internet. One method is to place a "wall" between your network and the outside networks.

This mechanism is often called a firewall because a "fire" in the outside network will not be allowed enter your network. Routers can be programmed to analyze the network address of a user attempting to access your network and exclude those addresses that are allowed. Thus, routers can be used as firewalls to filter out the network addresses of users whom you do not want to access your system. Another issue is security: The **rlogin** command is sometimes used in place of the **telnet** command because system administrators can set up user validation so that no password is needed for a user to log in on another host. The **telnet** command always requires a password to be entered. Unfortunately, this approach while convenient for users, opens a security hole on the remote system when you use it.

With access to the outside world via the Internet a reality for many networks, you should not have any passwordless userids.

If you need to provide a guest password for a short period of time, you should create a special account for this purpose and then only assign a password when you want to provide access to that guest. By the way, userids on most UNIX systems can be set up not to allow login on that userid at all. These userids are normally present in the system for allowing ownership of system files. Another issues of security involve permitting the use of anonymous file transfers. You can set up your system so that a file can be transferred between your system and another system without the user having a userid registered on your system. This is accomplished by setting up the FTP user with a special home directory for that user.

Then a user can log in using the user anonymous and any password will be accepted for that user. Once logged in, the anonymous user will have access to those files that are in the home directory of the anonymous user. With careful attention to the permissions on other directories, only this one directory can be made available to outside users.

LAN Security

Security for microcomputer LANs has increased in importance and more vendors are supplying LAN security systems. As end-users become more aware of the value of the vast amounts of data being accumulated and the need to protect that data, more users adopt such systems. Newspapers carry stories almost every week about some computer network being penetrated, either for financial gain or as a prank. Most of these break-ins involve large corporate networks and wide area networks. As local area networks proliferate and tap into national and international data communication systems, these local networks will also become targets. Companies that do sensitive work, such as those with defense contracts are often heavily involved in data security.

Other companies may be aware only of the threat, but not of their own vulnerability. Most analysts agree that businesses and institutions, such as schools will have to suffer a loss through theft or vandalism before they actually establish measures to protect their data. A computing network like any other valuable shared resources is subject to branches of security. Such breaches can be accidental or intentional and their effects on network operations can range from harmless to irritating to devastating. Security is a critical issue to those planning, managing or using a LAN. It is also a very complex issue. Security is a component of overall network reliability. However, reliability depends largely upon the dependability of network hardware, software and technology. In contrast, the security of a network depends almost exclusively upon the behaviour of that network's authorized users, managers and their guests.

Security is best addressed as part of an overall network strategy. Security concerns must be balanced by other factors that affect the network and its users. Users and managers must therefore discover and implement methods that improve network security without infringing upon user's work patterns or implying that all users are suspected violators of security. Users have other concerns that network security methods must address as well. Users must be reassured that they can collaborate on projects and share information without being spied upon by managers or other users. Well-implemented password protection schemes can provide much of this reassurance.

Managers must also demonstrate to users that procedures for tracking user work patterns on the network are used to improve security and reliability and not merely to keep a closer eye on users or their activities. Security methods must be selected with care and implemented with the full cooperation and knowledge of authorized users if security is to be assured. A first step towards these goals is a definition of network security.

LAN Security

1. Security cannot exist without a management policy.
2. LAN users should be positively identifiable before they have access to network resources.

   Prevention: passwords, passkeys authorization measures.
3. Data, hardware and software should be protected from unauthorized and/or accidental modification, destruction, theft or disclosure.

   Prevention: locks
4. Data should be recontrcutible.

   Prevention: frequent, regular backup of files.
5. Equipment must be protected from fire, dirt and natural disasters.

   Prevention: smoke detectors, sprinklers, air conditioning.

What Network Security Means

All the features of electromagnetic media which are desirable to a user also make this media vulnerable to theft and damage. Information stored on disk is easily copied, altered and erased. As larger amounts of critical data rare stored in this way, the significance of the problem grows. A stand-alone personal computers is easy to secure. You simply put your diskettes in a safe and store your computer in a locked closet. But when you attach that computer to a network of computers, security becomes more complicated.

Even a "local" network probably will spread out through several offices, with connecting cables running in ceilings and floors and in halls and basements. A thief or vandal can tap into any one of a dozen or more spots on the network, many secluded from normal observation. But tapping into the network from some secluded spot on the cable is not usually necessary. A person can simply log-on to a convenient PC and steal or damage data at will. Unfortunately, the easier a system is to use, the easier it is to misuse. Like any other kind of insurance, data security involves trade-offs. You must weigh the cost of the potential loss against the cost of protection as well as any inconvenience the security measures may cause.

The first thing to do in planning your data security programme is to put a value on the data you are going to protect. In general, a secure network is one that is resistant to disruptions caused by unauthorized network use. Such a network is designed and operated to minimize unauthorized use and can recover from disruptions easily and completely should unauthorized users evade safeguards. Network, security can be defined as the protection of network resources against unauthorized disclosure, modification, utilization, restriction or destruction. Security has long been an object of concern and study for both data processing systems and communication facilities.

With computer networks, these concerns are combined. And for local networks, the problems may be most acute. Consider a full-capacity local network, with direct terminal access to the network and data files and applications distributed among a variety of processors. The local network may also provide access to and from long-haul communication and be part of an internet. The complexity of the task of providing security in such an environment is clear.

The subject is a broad one and encompasses physical and administrative controls as well as automated ones. This general definition of a secure network is the foundation upon which you must build a definition that fits your work group's specific requirements and constraints. An effective definition requires careful assessment of needs by you, your colleagues and your managers.

Risk Analysis

Before you can realistically decide how much time and money to invest in data security, you must quantify the risk. Risk analysis has been elevated to a precise discipline. For out purposes, we would not need to examine formulas or other exact methods of quantifying every risk associated with networked data. But we can look briefly at some of the elements of risk analysis. These can help you to develop a preliminary description you your data's value and potential for loss. First, you will want to determine two values, in rupees, for the information stored in your data system.

One is the cost of re-creating the data; the other is the value of lost business if a competitor should gain access to your data.

These two figures should be easy to obtain or at last to estimate. Many smaller companies have never considered the potential loss of their stored data. If noting else, such an appraisal should encourage the use of data back up and the insistence n serious password security procedures. Next, you should identify and possible threats to your data. If your data has little or no monetary value to a computer, then there is probably little risk of theft.

On the other hand, the value of your data to a competitor may be great, with the risk of theft proportionally high. The physical volume of valuable data is another element is consider. If the volume and diversity of the data are extensive the chance of a total loss by theft is reduced. A related calculation is the frequency of potential thefts. This figure can be difficult to predict unless you have compiled a history of losses over some period of time.

Law enforcement agencies and some trade associations keep extensive records of thefts, defined by type of business, kind of penetration and value of loss. Contacting these groups may turn up sufficient data to allow you to make an intelligent prediction of risk. In addition, you should make a detailed study of any active attacks on your data so that your can estimate the cost of countering a similar attack. Vandalism is another threat, possibly more serious than theft because the frequency of vandalism is often greater.

A discontented employee may decide to "get even" by destroying or altering important files. Or an act of vandalism may be done simply as a prank or game, just to see if it can be done. After you calculate the value of your data and the types of risks, the final element in risk analysis is the data's vulnerability. Remote access is one factor that causes data to be come more easily available and vulnerable.

When people can access your network remotely, the potential for loss increases. On a local basis, the risk to data goes up when the network's contents are generally known. The capability to see those contents (for example, files servers and other resources) is controlled partially by the operation system and partially by the site administration. Making a risk analysis will enable you to answer many questions about where risks are greatest and how much money and procedural inconveniences are necessary to thwart these threats. Next, you should consider steps for building a secure data network.

Types of Threats

A publication of the National Bureau of Standards identified some of the threats that have stimulated the upsurge of interest in security:

1. Organized and intentional attempts to obtain economic or market information from competitive organizations in the private sector.
2. Organized and intentional attempts to obtain economic information from government agencies.
3. Inadvertent acquisition of economic or market information.
4. Inadvertent acquisition of information about individuals.
5. International fraud through illegal access to computer data bank with emphasis, in decreasing order of importance, on acquisition of founding data, economic data, law enforcement data and data about individuals.
6. Government intrusion on the rights of individuals.
7. Invasion of individual rights by the intelligence community.

These are examples of specific threats that an organization (or an individual for an organization on behalf of its employees) may feel the need to counter. The nature of the threat that concerns an organization will vary greatly from one set of circumstances to another. Fortunately, we can approach the problem from a different angle by looking at the generic types of threats that might be encountered. The following table lists the types of threats that might be faced in the context of network security.

The threats can be divided into the categories of passive threats and active threats.

Potential network security threats

PASSIVE THREATS

The monitoring and/or recording of data while the data are being transmitted over a communications facility.

RELEASE OF MESSAGE CONTENTS

Attack can read the user data in messages.

TRAFFIC ANALYSIS

The attacker can read packet headers to determine the location and identity of communication hosts. The attacker can also observe the length and frequency of messages.

ACTIVE THREATS

The unauthorized use of a device attached to a communication facility to alter transmitting data or control signals or to generate spurious data or control signals.

MESSAGE-STREAM MODIFICATION

The attacker can selectively modify, delete, reorder and duplicate real messages.

The attacker can also insert counterfeit messages.

DENIAL OF MESSAGE SERVICE

The attacker can destroy or delay most or all messages.

MASQUERAGE

The attacker can pose as a real host or switch and communicate with another host or switch to acquire data or service.

Passive Threats

These are in the nature of eavesdropping or monitoring of the transmissions of an organization. The goal of the attacker is to obtain information that is being transmitted. Two types of threats are involved here: release of message contents and traffic analysis. The threat of release of message contents is clearly understood by most managers. A telephone conversation, an electronic mail message or a transferred file may contain sensitive or confidential information.

We would like to prevent the attacker from learning the contents of these transmissions. The second passive threat, traffic analysis is more subtle and often less applicable. Suppose that we had a way of masking the contents of messages or other information traffic so that an attacker, even if he or she captured the message, would be unable to extract the information from the message. The common technique for doing this is encryption, discussed at length subsequently. If we had such protection in place, it might still be possible for an attacker to observe the pattern of these messages.

The attacker can determine the location and identity of communicating hosts and can also observe the frequency and length of messages being exchanged. This information might be useful in guessing the nature of the communication that is taking place. Passive threats are very difficult to detect since they do not involve any alteration of the data. However, it is feasible to prevent these attacks from being successful. Thus, the emphasis in dealing with passive threats is on prevention and not detection.

Active Threats

The second major category of threat is active threats. These involve some modification of the data stream or the creation of a false stream. We can subdivide these threats into three categories; message stream modification, denial of message service and masquerade.

Message-stream modification simply means that some portion of a legitimate message is altered, or that messages are delayed, replayed or reordered, in order to produce an unauthorized effect. For example, a message meaning "Allow J. N. Saxena to read confidential file accounts."

The **denial of service** prevents or inhibits the normal use or management of communication facilities. This attack may have a specific target; for example, an entity may suppress all messages directed to a particular destination (e.g. the security audit service). Another form of service denial is the disruption of an entire network, either by disabling the network or by overloading it with messages so as to degrade performance.

A **masquerade** takes place when one entity pretends to be a different entity. A masquerade attack usually includes one of the other two forms of active attack. Such an attack can take place, for example, by capturing and replaying an authentication sequence.

Active threats present the opposite characteristics of passive threats. Whereas passive attacks are difficult to detect, measures are available to prevent their success. On the other hand, it is quite difficult t absolutely prevent active attacks, since this would require physical protection of all communication facilities an paths at all times. Instead, the goal with respect to active attacks is to detect these attacks and to recover from any disruption or delays caused by the attack. Because the detection has a deterrent effect, this may also contribute to prevention.

Determining what secure means to You & Your LAN

To arrive at a specific definition of security for your LAN, you and your colleagues must first examine your current network or network plans to identify points of vulnerability. Where points of vulnerability occur depends greatly on the work and network use patterns of every member of your work group. An initial challenge, thus, is to determine these patterns accurately without interfering with them. If you already have a network, your group will have to decide whether written surveys, personal interviews, software that tracks network access by user, or some other method is best for gathering this information.

If you are still in the planning stages, you and your group will have to gather the same information about each independent personal computer (PC) user and use the data to hypothesise points of network vulnerability. A consultant may be helpful with this step. Every network environment is different, with a different list of specific points of vulnerability. However, most environments have certain vulnerable points. Be sure not to overlook these areas in determining you own environment's particular potential weaknesses.

Securing Workstations and Servers

Like LANs themselves, strategies that address security begin on user's desktops, with their workstations. To protect against both accidental and intentional breaches of network security, users must develop good workstation-protection habits. One simple habit is turning of workstations when leaving for the evening or weekend, so the screens do not attract wandering eyes and hands. Keeping boot (start-up) disks in a non-obvious drawer instead of a desk or in the workstations' floppy drive also reduces the likelihood of unauthorized access via an authorized user's workstation. Physical locks are also available for disk drive doors, keyboards and workstations or PC system units.

Some of these locks impede both access and theft. LAN users in large or open-office environments should be encouraged to use these additional security measures and not to defeat them by keeping the keys in their unlocked desks. It is important to note that in many organizations, the most serious threat to workstation security is not unauthorized users with malicious intent. A larger problem is unauthorized access to user workstations by guests or children or authorized users.

These legitimate users often sit their charges in front of an absent user's workstation, to play or explore while the worker works. This problem is most acute during off hours, when network supervision is minimal or absent. Some companies report a similar problem with after-hours office cleaning staff bringing in and playing unauthorized games on PCs connected to a network. Practices like these must be detected and discouraged to prevent serious network problems caused by well-intended but untrained people. Servers represent another point of potential vulnerability, especially if they are non-dedicated and also used as workstations. A single-user problem on a combined workstation-server can become a network-wide problem. In addition, even a dedicated server can be mistaken for a workstation if it has a keyboard, floppy disk drive and a screen attached. The more critical your network is to your business, the more seriously you and your colleagues must work to secure your servers. Removal of the keyboard from each PC-based server is a good first step.

You may also want to put waning signs on servers or to secure them behind locked doors, depending upon their configuration and susceptibility to unauthorized access.

Securing Network Passwords

Another point of vulnerability under direct user supervision is the passwords that allow access to the network itself, as well as to specific resources, such as particular servers, programmers or files. Users remember their passwords better when they choose their own, so assignment of random passwords is to be avoided in most situations. However, users must be encouraged to use a bit of creativity when selecting their passwords to make them difficult for unauthorized users to guess or discover accidentally. You and your colleagues should choose as passwords random numbers or word combination that are not obvious, but have enough personal significance to be remembered easily.

Such a password is less likely to be guessed or discovered and is a more effective security measure than a password based on your telephone number, your birthday or a loved one's name. You and your colleagues must also implement routines for changing your passwords regularly. Some network managers automatically invalidate any passwords more than 30 days old, forcing users to select new ones at least once a month.

Your network's security and reliability could be enhanced simultaneously if you and your colleague changed your personal passwords each time you made complete back-up copies of your network files. Needless to say, some users write down their passwords or store them in some electronic note file. If these users leave the notes where other can find them, all the security you and your colleagues are trying to implement can be rendered useless. Encourage your co-workers to treat their network passwords like credit card numbers or access codes for automated teller-machines and to protect them with at least as much vigilance.

Securing Files and Programmes

Users can also help protect against unauthorized access to network files and programmes. Keep master and boot copies of programmes on write-protected disks and, if possible, use passwords to protect your work group's network or application software. When copies of important files are stored on easily removable media such as floppy disks or tape cartridges, restrict access to these media by using locks and keys, sign-in and sign-out lists, supervisor monitoring or other measures.

These practices reduce the possibility of accidental or malicious erasure or modification of important files. File must also be protected while they are in use on a network. Users must strive always to open and close files according to the procedures required by their network and application software. Otherwise, network file directories can become incorrect or corrupted, and larger problems can result. Most network software offers some protection against these problems, but good user habits are the best safeguards. Some network programmes require the insertion of key disks into workstation floppy drives to qualify legitimate users for access to programmes and files. Where these disks are in use, they must be protected and not widely distributed or duplicated.

The use of third-party programmes that eliminate the need for key disks must also be weighed against the increased security risk that these disks can represent. Networks must also be protected from unauthorized programmes, such as programmes or other personal software. Unauthorized programmes can contaminate your network with annoying or highly destructive software viruses. You and your colleagues should avoid bringing unauthorized software into contract with your network. Whether a harmless game or our own copy of a programme your work group uses, any software not supplied through your network's usual channels should be viewed as a potential source of harm to your network.

Levels of Security

There is no such thing as 100% security. With enough skill and thought time to complete the job, a perpetrator can defeat any security measure.

Of the two security elements of skill and time, the most dependable protection is time. If you can make certain that a break-in will be time-consuming project for a thief, you have gone a long way in protecting your data. Therefore, all serious security systems are layered with not one but several security measures. For a local area network the following strategies should be considered:

1. Physical security
2. Access Control
3. Personal identification
4. Encryption
5. The diskless PC
6. Protection against cable radiation
7. Call-back security

Physical Security

Data security can take many forms. The simplest is physical security, which may be a lock on the computer or a guard at the door. With physical security, a would- be thief must attack and defeat your security measures before becoming a threat to the data. Locks can set up barriers from the back door to the office door to the computer itself. Key locks are now provided for IBM PC/ATs and compatible.

The lock interrupts the power to the display and keyboard, while still allowing the terminal to remain on-line. Turning the key powers up the user interfaces: the key cannot be removed while the system is on. This kind of physical security is available for personal computers. An alarm system works in partnership with your physical security measures. Locking devices are designed to increase the time needed for penetration. Alarms put an effective limit on the amount of time available.

Professional criminals do not run when they hear an alarm or when they think they have tripped a silent alarm. Most know precisely how much time they have before the police arrive. If they cannot get through the security system's physical barriers in the time available, then the criminals will abandon the effort.

Access Controls

The purpose of access controls is to ensure that only authorized users have access to the system and its individual resources and that access to and modification of particular portions of data is limited to authorized individuals and programmes. The control of access by user is referred to an authentication. A quite common example of this one a time-sharing system is the user log-on, which requires both a user ID and a password. The system will only allow a user to logon if that user's ID is known to the system and if the user knows the password associated by the system with the ID.

This ID/password system is a notoriously unreliable method of access control. Users can forget their passwords and accidentally or intentionally reveal their password. Also, the ID/password file is subject to penetration attempts. No cost-effective method of overcoming this problem exists. Exotic techniques such as voice prints fingerprints and hand geometry analysis may be foolproof but are at present prohibitively expensive. Simple measures that can be taken now are to change passwords frequently and to maintain tight multiple measures of security over the ID/password directory. One additionally measure that is cost effective is to associate ID's with terminals rather than users and hard wire the code into the terminal.

This changes an administrative/software security problem into a physical security problem. However, if it is desirable to allow one-to-many and/or many-to-one relationships between users and terminals, this technique is ineffective. The problem of authentication is compounded over a multi-access medium LAN. The log-on dialogue must take place over the communication medium and eavesdropping is a potential threat. One approach to protection would be to certify that each NIU can capture only data addressed to it. This is no easy task. Another approach is to encrypt the ID/password data. User and user group authentication can be either centralized or distributed. In a centralized approach the network provides a log-on service.

Distributed authentication treats the network as a transparent communication link and the usual log-on procedure is carried out by the destination host. Of course, the security concerns for multi-access media must still be addressed. In fact, in many local networks, two levels of authentication will probably be used. Individual hosts may be provided with log-on facility to protect host-specific resources and applications. In addition, the network as a whole may have protection to restrict network access to authorized users.

This two-level facility is desirable currently for the common case, in which the local network connects disparate hosts and simply provides a convenient means of terminal-host access. Future integrated networks (in the OSI sense) may require only a network-level scheme. Following successful authentication, the user has been granted access to one or a set of hosts and/or processes. This is generally not sufficient for a system that includes sensitive data in its database. Through the authentication procedure, a user can be identified together with a profile that specifies permissible operations and file accesses. The operating system can enforce rules based on the user profile. The database management system, however, must control access to specific portions of records.

For example, it may be permissible for anyone in administration to obtain a list of company personnel, but only selected individuals may have access to salary information. The issue is more than just one of level of detail. Whereas the operating system may grant a user permission to access a file or use an application, following which there are each individual access attempt. That decision will depend not only on the user's identity but also on the specific parts of the record being accessed and even on the information already divulged to the user. A general model of access control as exercised by a data base management system is that of an access matrix. One axis of the table consists of identified subjects that may attempt data access.

Typically, this list will consist of individual users or user groups, although access could be controlled for terminals, hosts or processes instead of or in addition to users. The other axis lists the objects that may be accessed. At the greatest level of detail, objects may be individual data fields. More aggregate groupings, such as records, record types, or even the entire database may also be objects in the matrix indicates the access rights of that subject for that object. In practice, an access matrix is usually sparse and is implemented by decomposition in one of the two ways. The matrix may be decomposed by columns, yielding access control lists. Thus for each object, an access control list users and their permitted access opportunities. Decomposition by rows yield capability tickets. A capability ticket specifies authorized objects and operations for a user. Each user has a number of tickets and may be authorized to loan or give them to others. Because tickets may be dispersed around the system, they present a greater security management problem than access control lists. Network considerations for access control parallel those for authentication. Encryption may be needed to provide secure communications on a LAN. Typically, access control is decentralized, that is, controlled by host-based data management systems. However, if a network data base server exists on a LAN, access control becomes a network service.

Personal Identification

A local area network presents some additional security problems because of its dispersed nature and because many people have access to the network. Remote access through modems and telephone lines is used widely on LANs, which makes dispersion essentially infinite. Dispersion thwarts one of the best types of personal-identifications security systems. On most networks the first line of security is personal identification. You physically recognize people who are authorized to be in your office, sitting at a PC. With remote access this kind of identification is impossible.

Companies must rely on passwords and classified access schemes to protect their data. Several techniques can be used to restrict access to authorized users. All these techniques are based on some kind of identification: personal, such as ID badge; key word such as a log-n name and password; or key number. Badges and personal recognition may not be successful in large companies where everyone is not personally known. In a company with many employees, a counterfeit badge may, in fact, be all that is necessary to penetrate a security system based widely on identification.

Passwords

Password security adds no cost to the network and it's potentially a useful security measure.

After logging onto the network, the user must type a password. Theoretically, if users must give a password, unauthorized access is prevented. But often the password system is misused and ineffective. Passwords usually are chosen because they are easily remembered. This, however, also makes them easily guessed. Common assignments include first name for-log-in name and last name or title for password. The value of passwords is further diluted when employees give their passwords to others in the organization.

A password often is given out because another employee needs to read a particular file or to perform some tasks for an absent employee. Password protection can be improved through both systematized procedures and more sophisticated operating system password utilities. Passwords should be assigned by a network manager, not by the individual. This assignment method reduces the likelihood that someone will identify the password in half a dozen guesses.

Many network operating systems have a password utility that allows authorized users to change their own passwords. Such a utility should be deleted from all users directories and given only to the network supervisor. Over time, passwords will become generally known, particularly within a small office or department. This decaying security can be stopped by periodically issuing new passwords, say, on a monthly basis.

One additional advantage of changing passwords regularly is that employees will take more seriously both the password system and the subject of security.

Security in Log-in

The network operating system should be designed to thwart attempts to break into the system. For one thing, the password should not be "echoed" back to the screen when the user types it during log-in. The number of times that a password can be attempted should be limited to no more than three tries. After that, the log-in name should be invalidated temporarily and the network supervisor notified of a failed log-in.

An audit tail can also be provided to record the number of password attempts from a given user to station. The presence of the audit trail utility that monitors the password system is a deterrent in itself, especially to malicious or casual vandals. A sophisticated thief, however, can collect log-in routines and password as they are entered often simply by tapping into the network. The network operating system can be enhanced to make this activity more difficult for the thief.

Passwords can be encrypted at the workstation and decrypted at the central processor so that the data on the cable is unusable through a tap. As part of security planning and implementation, an independent analyst should evaluate the security measures, even to the extent of attempting to steal or corrupt a prearranged target file.

Encryption

Earlier, we referred to one of the major security risks on LANs, which uses a multi-access medium-the risk of eavesdropping. Eavesdropping can be accomplished by programming the NIU to accept packets other than those addressed to it or by physically tapping into the medium. One counter measure that, properly used, is very effective is to encrypt the data in each packet, i.e., send the data in code. Encryption is the process of changing intelligible data into unintelligible data; decryption reverses the process.

For most local area networks, data encryption is used only when the security threat is substantial. Ensuring that data is secure in a network environment is more difficult than ensuring the security of physical documents. Typically, data in a network is held in a common storage facility, and anyone authorized to use the central storage has the potential to access classified files. The best solution to this potential problem is to store the data in an encrypted form.

Then, any unauthorized person accessing the file would not be able to read its contents. Encryption techniques cover a broad range, from simple encryption that guards against accidental disclosure to sophisticated methods which protect against all but the highly trained criminal with an in-depth knowledge of cryptanalysis and considerable deciphering equipment. Most encryption schemes are based on mathematical operations that are "computationally in-feasible".

That is, they are based on prime numbers which are so large that even the computational power of a mainframe computer cannot break the code within a practical time period. Two primary types of encryption exist: link and end-to-end. Link encryption is used to make data unreadable while it is on a point-to-point link, such as between two PCs. Link encryption prevents the causal reading of data. End-to-end encryption protects data anywhere on the system. This type of encryption corresponds to Layer 4 (the Transport Layer) in the OSI model. Because Layer 4 is end-to-end, encryption here can provide protection to any number of communication links or intermediate networks.

Encryption Keys

Encryption key systems are commonly found on dial-up networks but are also available on LANs. A key is essentially a formula for coding and decoding a message. Keys are carefully distributed to authorized users. In fact, the security of the distribution channel for keys often establishes the security level of a system. Such a system of secret keys is very difficult and expensive to maintain, especially as the number of participants increases. To overcome these disadvantages, a new key called a "public key" was devised. Public keys may be published openly and they permit virtually any individual to use a personal public key to code a message and send it to another person.

To decode the message, however, the receiver must use a secret key. A secret key consists of two prime numbers that are not published. One other application of public keys is to authenticate messages. You can use your secret key to encrypt a message and send it to a second person. That person will take your public key and use it to decode the message. If your public key does decode an encoded message, presumably sent by you, then proof has been provided that you did indeed send the message.

In other words, the public key is an electronic signature. All keys are factorable and, therefore, limited in their level of security. Over the last few years, a debate has been going on about how complex a key should be. Generally, any encryption system provides file privacy against casual perusal. But encryption systems can go far beyond providing file privacy. The Data Encryption Standard (DES) is an encryption system designed by IBM and adopted by the National Bureau of Standards in 1977. Using an encryption system that conforms to the DES standard generally is considered sufficient protection against unauthorized access.

That is, most criminals and vandals would not be able to break into a communication system and steal or alter data which has been encrypted according to the DES standard. With the largest and fastest computers available today, however, DES encryption schemes probably are breakable. A number of schemes for encryption have been proposed. In this section, we describe two techniques that are good candidates for local network use.

Conventional Encryption

The encryption process consists of an algorithm and a key. The key is a relatively short bit string that controls the algorithm. The algorithm will produce a different output depending on the specific key being used at the time. Changing the key radically changes the output of the algorithm. Once the ciphertext is produced, it is transmitted.

Upon reception, the ciphertext can be transformed back to the original plaintext by using a decryption algorithm and the same key that was used for encryption. The security of conventional encryption depends on several factors. First, the encryption algorithm must be powerful enough to make it impractical to decrypt a message on the basis of the ciphertext alone. Beyond that, the security of conventional encryption depends on the secrecy of the key, not the secrecy of the algorithm. That is, it assumed that it is impractical to decrypt a message on the basis of the ciphertext plus knowledge of the encryption/decryption algorithm. In other words, we do not need to keep the algorithm secret; we only need to keep the key secret. This feature of conventional encryption is what makes it feasible for widespread use. The fact that the algorithm need not be kept secret means that manufactures can and have, developed low-cost chip implementations of data encryption algorithm. These chips are widely available and incorporated into a number of products. With the use of conventional encryption, the principal security problem is maintaining the secrecy of the key. This issue is addressed here.

The Data encryption Standard

The most widely used encryption scheme is based on the data encryption standard (DES), adopted in 1977 by the National Bureau of Standards. For DES, data are encrypted in 64-bit blocks using a 56-bit key. Using the key, the 64-bit input is transformed in a series of steps involving transposition and exclusive-or operations. The result is a 64-bit output in which each bit of output is a function of each bit of the input and each bit of the key. At the receiver, the plaintext is recovered by using the same key and reversing the steps. The DES has enjoyed widespread use. Unfortunately, it has also been the subject of much controversy as to how secure the DES is. The main concern is in the length of the key, which some observers of consider to be to short. To appreciate the nature of the controversy, let us quickly review the history of the DES.

The DES is the result of the request for proposals for a national cipher standard released by the NBS in 1973. At that time, IBM was in the final stages of a project called Lucifer to develop its own encryption capability. IBM proposed the Lucifer scheme, which was by far the best system submitted. It was, in fact, so good that it considerably upset some people at the National Security Agency (NSA), which until that moment had considered itself comfortably ahead of the rest of the world in the still arcane art of cryptography. DES, as eventually adopted, was essentially the same s Lucifer, with one crucial difference; Lucifer's key size was originally 128 bits, whereas the final standard use a key of 56 bits. What is the significance of the 72 dropped bits? There are basically two ways to break a cipher. One way is to exploit properties of whatever mathematical functions form the basis of the encryption algorithm to make a "cryptoanalytic" attack on it.

It is generally assumed that DES is immune to such attacks, although the role of NSA in shaping the final DES standard leaves lingering doubts. The other way is a brute force attack in which you try all possible keys in an "exhaustive search". That is, you attempt to decrypt ciphertext with every possible 56-bit key until something intelligible pops out. With only 56 bits in the Des key, there are 2x56 different keys—a number that is uncomfortably small, and becoming smaller as computers get faster. Whatever, the merits of the case, DES has flourished in recent years and is widely used, especially in financial applications. Except in areas of extreme sensitivity, the use of DES in commercial applications should not be a cause for concern by the responsible managers.

Commercial Communications Security Endorsement Programme

Although DES still has a reasonably useful life ahead of it, it is likely that non-government organizations will begin to look for replacements for what is seen as an increasingly vulnerable algorithm. The most likely replacement is a family of algorithms developed under the NSA commercial COMSEC (communications security) Endorsement Program (CCEP). CCEP is a joint NSA-industry effort to produce a new generation of encryption devices that are more secure than DES, that are low-cost and that are capable of operating at high data rates. Features of the new OCCEP algorithms are:

1. The CCEP algorithm are developed by NSA and are classified. Thus the algorithm themselves remain secret and are subject to change from time to time.
2. Industry participants will produce chip implementation of the algorithms, but the NSA maintains control over the design, fabrication and dissemination of chips.

Two types of algorithms come under the CCEP heading. Type 1 algorithms are designed to protect classified government information. Equipment using Type I CCEP will be available only to government agencies and their designated contractors. Type II algorithms are designed to protect sensitive but unclassified information. Type II gear is intended to replace DES gear. Unlike the Type I modules, which will handle classified information, the Type II equipment is controlled only to the point of sale.

Presumably, after a Type II module is build into a computer or communication device and sold by a vendor, the customer can do with it as he or she pleases—short of exporting it overseas. Although the purpose of developing the Type II equipment, as with the Type I equipment, was to provide a means of protecting government information, the Type II modules are available for use in non-government, private sector applications. As this equipment becomes more widely available, it is likely to become more widely used, at the expense of DES.

Key Distribution

For conventional encryption to work, then two parties to an exchange must have the same key and that key must be protected from access by others. Furthermore, frequent key changes are usually desirable to limit the amount of data compromised if an attacker learns the key. Therefore, the strength of any cryptographic system rests with the key distribution, technique, a term that refers to the means of delivering a key to two parties that wish to exchange data, without allowing other to see the key.

Key distribution can be achieved in a number of ways. For two parties A and B;

1. A key could be selected by A and physically delivered to B.
2. A third party could select the key and physically deliver it to A and B.
3. If A and B have previously and recently used a key, one party could transmit the new key to the other, encrypted using the old key.
4. If A and B each have an encrypted connection to a third party C, C could deliver a key on the encrypted links to A and B.

Options 1 and 2 call for manual delivery of a key, which is awkward. In a distributed system, any given host or terminal may need to engage in exchanges with many other hosts and terminals over time. Thus, each device needs a number of keys, supplied dynamically. The difficulty with option 3 is that if an attacker ever succeeds in gaining access to one key, then all subsequent keys are revealed. Option 4 is the most attractive and could be handled from a host facility or network control center. Two kinds of keys are identified.

— **Session Key:** When two end-systems (hosts, terminals, etc) wish to communicate, they establish a logical connection, e.g., LLC connection or transport connection. For the duration of that logical connection, al user data are encrypted with a one-time session key. At the conclusion of the session or connection, the key is destroyed.

Permanent Key: A permanent key is one used between entities for the purpose of distributing session keys.

The configuration consists of the following elements:

Access control center: The access control center determines which systems are allowed to communicate with each other.

Key distribution center: When permission is granted by the access control center for two systems to establish a connection, the key distribution center provides a one-time session key for that connection.

Network interface unit: The NIU performs end-to-end encryption and obtains session keys on behalf of its host or terminal.

Several variations on this scheme are possible. The functions of access control and key distribution could be combined into a single-system. The separation makes the two functions clear and may provide a slightly enhanced level of security. If we wish to let any two devices communicate at will, then the access control function is not needed at all. When two devices wish to establish a connection, one of them applies to the key distribution center for a session key. The automated key distribution approach provides the flexibility and dynamic characteristics needed to allow a number of terminal users to access a number of hosts and for the hosts to exchange data with each other. A number of LAN vendors offer some version of the scheme. It is a powerful and reasonably inexpensive means of enhancing network security.

Public Key Encryption

As we have seen, one of the major difficulties with conventional encryption schemes is the need to distribute the keys in a secure manner. A clever way around this requirement is an encryption scheme that, surprisingly, does not require key distribution. For conventional encryption schemes, the keys used for encryption and decryption are the same. This is not a necessary condition. Instead it is possible to develop an algorithm that uses one key for encryption and a companion but different key for decryption.

Furthermore, it is possible to develop algorithms such that knowledge of the encryption algorithm plus the encryption key is not sufficient to determine the decryption key. Thus the following technique will work.

1. Each end-system in a network generates a pair of keys to be used for encryption and decryption of messages that it will receive.
2. Each system publishes its encryption key by placing it in a public register or file. This is the public key. The companion key is kept private.
3. If A wishes to send a message to B, it encrypts the message using B's private key.
4. When B receives the message, it decrypts it using B's private key, No other recipient can decrypt the message since only B knows B's private key.

As you can see, public-key encryption solves the key distribution problem, since there are no keys to distribute! All participants have access to public keys and private keys are generated locally by each participant and therefore need never be distributed. As long as a system controls its private key, its incoming communication is secure. At any time, a system can change its private key and publish the companion public key to replace its old public key. A further refinement is needed. Since anyone can transmit a message to A using A's public key, a means is needed to prevent impostors.

To develop this scheme, you need to know that public key encryption algorithms are such that the two keys can be used in either order. That is, one can encrypt with the public key and decrypt with the matching private key, or encrypt with the private key and decrypt with the matching private key and then encrypts the result with A's public key. On the other end, A first uses its private key and then uses B's public key in a double decryption. Since it was also encrypted with A's private key, it could only come from B. Since it was also encrypted with A's public key, it can only be read by A. With this technique, any two stations can at any time set up a secure connection without a prior secret distribution of keys. A main disadvantage of public-key encryption compare to conventional encryption is that algorithm for the former are much more complex. Thus, for comparable size and cost of hardware, the public-key scheme will provide much lower throughput. One possible application of public-key encryption is to use it for the permanent key portion, with conventional keys used for sessions keys. Since there are few control messages relative to the amount of user data traffic, the reduced throughput should not be a handicap. The following table summarises some of the important aspects of conventional and public-key encryption.

On-Line Orders

The easiest measure to take for LAN security is to attach an encryption device at either end of a communication link. Several companies make such devices and will modify them for specific applications. After the devices are installed, the system is fully transparent to the user. With each person using an encryption box, the message sent between parties will be encrypted while it is on the line. Another way to set up a system is to place an encryption box between each PC and the network. Then all the data that goes out on the network and all data stored on the hard disk will be encrypted. Ideally, the device can be modified and tuned to provide the speed and security needed. If necessary, a public key system can also be built in.

To show how such a security system might work, let us suppose that we have three groups on a network: administration, accounting and sales. All the data on the network can be encrypted. The administrator can read everything, but accounting and sales can read only their respective files. Each user encrypts the data on an optional basis. With each transmission the encryption device will ask the user whether to transmit in the clear or with encryption. The administrator's device will also ask the administrator, "Which key do you want admin, accounting or sales?"

The Diskless PC

The power of the PC itself is a potential security threat that should be considered. One of the advantages that the personal computer has over dumb terminals is its local storage capability. Information can be locally manipulated and stored on a PC's floppy diskettes, then transferred to the central storage. From central storage the information can be made available to other users and maintained and backed up properly. With local storage devices, users can maintain their own back-up systems, independent of the central system.

The degree of autonomy associated with a personal set of data diskettes is appealing to many users. At the same time, such autonomy creates two threats to data security. One threat is unintentional. Because two copies of data exist, one on the central disk and one locally, the copies may be updated independently. Eventually, unique data on one version may be lost when the two "copies" are merged. The other threat is that local disk drive 'permits data theft. A person with access to the network and with a local disk drive can copy large amounts of data onto floppy disks in just minutes.

The data, then, can be easily hidden and removed from even reasonably secure buildings. Most network vendors now provide the capability of booting a local PC workstation from a central server so that diskless PCs can be used on the network. Since machine require full-time networking and permit no local storage, a common reason for using diskless PCs is cost. Because diskless PCs require no local floppy controller or disk drive, the cost of a workstation is reduced. But equally important is the increased security offered by a diskless PC. Take away the disk drive and you take away the means for stealing the data. But you also reduce the power of the PC.

In many instances local storage is desirable so that the PC can be used as a stand-alone workstation in the event of a network failure. One answer is to exchange a local floppy for a local hard disk. Then not only would the user have all the benefits of local storage, but local speed and efficiency would improve also. No ready way, however, would be available to copy or remove data. Diskless PCs have been hampered by software problems. Many application programmes are designed to run only from a local floppy disk drive.

Diagnostics and the operating system itself have usually required at least one local drive. Increasingly, however, software vendors are providing some mechanism for their application packages to be stored on a hard disk and used in a multi-user environment. A company can then make its own decisions about how to configure PCs. Probably the answer will be a variety of configurations to fit particular circumstances.

Protection Against Cable Radiation

Any time information is transmitted, even through cable, that information can potentially be intercepted by unauthorised persons. The possibility also exists that a vandal can tamper with data or destroy data files. Several methods may be used for protecting data while it is on the cable. The first thing to do is to put the cable out of sight. This step should be taken anyway, to prevent damage to the cable and to meet building codes.

Security is a secondary benefit. Install cables in protective raceways in areas where penetration is less likely. A radio-signal that is broadcast onto the air waves can easily be intercepted and the information stolen. Such emissions, however, are not limited to broadcasted radio signals. A data cable also radiates intelligible signals, just as a transmitting antenna does. Simple intercept equipment located near the cable can pick up and record these transmissions. More sophisticated devices can intercept the signals a considerable distance from the cable. The likelihood of signal interception can be eliminated by using a shielded cable, which is a cylinder of braided copper wire that encases the intelligence carrying wires.

If one shield does not reduce emissions to satisfactory levels, more shields can be added. Frequently, cable with the necessary electrical characteristics is available in only one version. If additional shielding is needed, special shielding conduit is available that meets security standards. Another way to eliminate the cable radiation problem entirely is by using fiber-optic cable. Fiber optics technology uses a glass fiber to carry a beam of light. Information is passed when the light is modulated. With fiber optics no signal is emitted outside the cable; therefore, data cannot be intercepted. Because fiber optic cable is also extremely difficult to tap into physically, it is ideal for security purposes.

Call-Back Security

Remote access to networks is a significant threat to data security. Remote workstations are part of many LAN environments, enabling a user to access networks remotely, log into the network, and use the system as if the user were local. Securing this type of access requires special measures. Call-back security and user management are part of dial-up systems and can be used with remote PC-to-network traffic. With call-back security, when you want to access a computer, you can call into a different number instead of calling in directly. You indicate that you want to access the network and the security device arranges for a call-back to your location. In other words, the system has embedded within batter-supported memory to complete listing for every allowed user. Included in this file is a ID number that you must punch in when you want to access the file, a telephone number at which you can be reached and the host systems to which you are allowed access. This security device also keeps track of user priorities. If all available lines are busy, the device sets up a queue based on the priority of the user. The device will inform the caller regarding queue position. When a line becomes available, the device contact the user. Therefore, the user never has to get busy signals. The device also keeps accounting information for traffic statistics and call-backs.

Management Level Concerns

Managers have a sensitive role in network security. They must help users implement and execute measures like those discussed here and integrate these into network-wide policies that are followed rigorously. These policies also must go beyond the measures that users can implement, but without interfering with users' work. Managers of sensitive LANs need tó address the possibility o9f their LANs being tapped like telephone lines. With relatively simple electrical devices and a little time, an interloper can tap a LAN cable with little or no immediate evidence.

Some LANs can even be tapped from a distance, with devices that monitor the radio-frequency emissions that almost all LANs produce. LANs that permit dial-up connections are particularly susceptive to such taps. LANs based on fiber-optic cable are the most tap resistant. Call-back modems are a security measure used by many managers of dial-up LAN connections. These modems and their software accept user's calls and then instruct users to enter identifying information and to hang up. The modem then checks the user's access information and calls the user back only after the information is verified.

Users who enter information that they system cannot verify are refused to access network. Managers must also monitor connections between their LANs and other networks and computers. Managers must periodically audit access to and from network bridges, routers and other links and they must regularly update the passwords and other security measures associated with these links.

Managers may also have to help users implement more complex personal security measures as their LANs gain access to other networks and systems and security risks increase. Managers' must also implement measures that provide as much information as possible about network security and about attempted and successful breaches. Ideally, some combination of hardware, software, and physical procedures should be used to provide a near-constant audit of network access and use.

This audit will not only help trace the paths of any breaches, but will aid in recovery from any problems these breaches may cause. Software and procedures that increase accountability can be of great value to a LAN manager and to that manager's organization. Sufficient information about accountability can limit the liability of an individual, a work group or an organization, should an accidental or malicious breach of network security result in a loss of tangible assets or in a law-suit for some other reason. LAN managers are also ultimately responsible for maintaining a constant balance between security measures that are effective and security measures that interfere with users' work pattern or make users feel that their every move is being monitored.

The best way to maintain this balance is to involve users actively and positively in the implementation of any security measures. Users should also be encouraged to see enhanced security as a way of protecting their own livelihoods and works environments, as well as the assets of their enterprise. The LAN manager has primary responsibility for getting both network users and financial decision makers to see network security as a strategic benefit as well as a basic necessity. In many cases, the best way to enhance network security is to include security-bolstering procedures and tools alongside aids to other aspects of network operation and management.

There are LAN software products which enhances security gracefully. These LAN packages are designed to be invisible to LAN users and can be used to control access to programme and files, to audit network software for changes, to protect network against viruses and to facilitate raped recovery from disk drive and server failures.

Firewall Friendly FTP

The FTP protocol uses a secondary TCP connection for actual transmission of files. By default, this connection is set up by an active open from the FTP server to the FTP client. However, this scheme does not work well with packet filter-based firewalls, which in general cannot permit incoming calls to random port numbers. If, on the other hand, clients use the PASV command, the data channel will be an outgoing call through the firewall. Such calls are more easily handled and present fewer problems. An active open is done by the server, from its port 20 to the same port on the client machine as was used for the control connection. The client does a passive open. For better or worse, most current FTP clients do not behave that way.

A new connection is used for each transfer; to avoid running afoul of TCP's TIMEWAT state, the client picks a new port number each time and sends a PORT command announcing that to the server. If a packet filter is used (as, for example, provided by most modern routers), the data channel requests appear as incoming calls to unknown ports. Most firewalls are constructed to allow incoming calls only to certain believed-to-be-safe ports, such as SMTP. The usual compromise is to block only the "server" area, i.e., port numbers below 1024. But that strategy is risky; dangerous services such as X Windows live at higher-numbered ports.

Outgoing calls, on the other hand, present fewer problems, either for the firewall administrator or for the packet filter. Any TCP packet with the ACK bit set cannot be the packed used to initiate a TCP connection; filters can be configured to pass such packets in the outbound direction only.

We thus want to change the behaviour of FTP so that the data channel is implemented as a call from the client to the server. Fortunately, the necessary mechanisms already exist in the protocol. If the client sends a PASV command, the server will do a passive TCP open on some random port and inform the client of the port number. The client can then do an active open to establish the connection.

Recommendation

It is recommended that vendors convert their FTP client programs (including FTP proxy agents such as Gopher) to use PASV instead of PORT. There is no reason not to use it even for non-firewall transfers, and adopting it as standard behaviour will make the client more useful in a firewall environment.

Security Considerations

Few people feel that packet filters are dangerous, since they are very hard to configure properly. But they are quite popular. Another common complaint is that permitting arbitrary outgoing calls is dangerous, since it allows free export of sensitive data through a firewall. Some firewalls impose artificial bandwidth limits to discourage this. While a discussion of the merits of this approach is beyond the scope of this memo, we note that the sort of application-level gateway necessary to implement a bandwidth limiter could be implemented just as easily using PASV as with PORT. Using PASV does enhances the security of gateway machines, since they no longer need to create ports that an outsider might connect to before the real FTP client.

More importantly, the protocol between the client host and the firewall can be simplified, if there is no need to specify a "create" operation. Concerns have been expressed that this use of PASV just trades one problem for another. With it, the FTP server must accept calls to random ports, which could pose an equal problems for its firewall, believe that this is not a serious issue, for several reasons. First, there are many fewer FTP servers than there are clients. It is possible to secure a small number of special purpose machines, such as gateways and organizational FTP servers. The firewall's filters can be configured to allow access to just these machines.

Further precautions can be taken by modifying the FTP server so that it only uses ver high-numbered ports for the data channel. It is comparatively easy to ensure that n dangerous services live in a given port range. Again, this is feasible because of the sma number of servers.

Circuit Gateways

Just as the packet-filtering gateways operate at the network-layer level of a TCP/IP networ a circuit-gateway firewall operates at the transport-layer lever – specifically for TC connections. As discussed, packet-filtering gateways establish an electronic barrier th examines every network packet as the packet passes through the firewall. A circuit gatewa on the other hand, only creates an electronic barrier when two Internet hosts initially establis a TCP connection. When a client program tires to connect to a server on a host that circuit gateway protects, the circuit gateway firewall (rather than the server) actually accep the connection using a special type of relay software. In other words, a circuit gatewa firewall sits as a barrier between both ends of a TCP connection; the gateway's rel software transfers data between the client and server programs on either side of the gatewa

As you might suspect, only client programs that know how to talk to the circuit gateway ca reach the server on the other side of the firewall. In other words, circuit gateways requi the use of special client programs. Clients that want access to the server must negotiate connection with the circuit gateway relay that let the data transfer occur. The relay softwa intercepts connection requests that occur at all protocol ports the network security manag defines. After a client successfully negotiates a connection with the relay software, t circuit gateway becomes essentially invisible. In other words, the circuit gateway firew establishes a security barrier only during connection negotiations. After the relay softwa validates the connection request, data transfer proceeds as though the relay software c not exist; the relay does not examine the content of the packets that pass through t firewall.

After the security negotiations complete, the relay software acts much like a wire. In oth words, the relay software becomes another part of the transmission medium. Rememb the relay software on the circuit gateway handles the security negotiations which initia occur and then essentially makes itself invisible. In other words, after the connecti negotiations complete, the circuit gateway becomes invisible. Obviously, since it's yo circuit gateway, you will have the special client software necessary to negotiate t connection. The custom client software makes the security negotiations relative transparent.

24 Network Architecture

ARCnet Specifications

RCnet is an acronym for *Attached Resource Computer NETwork* , which was founded y the Datapoint Corporation. Novell uses the term RX-Net to denote its form of this rchitecture and TRX-Net for the Turbo version. ARCnet uses a *token-bus* packet passing cheme.

RCnet operates at 2.5 Mbps throughput and can be connected using RG-62 A/U coax able or unshielded twisted pair (UTP) wiring. Although ARCnet can support up to 255 ode numbers on a single network, systems of this size are not practical.

ypical ARCnet coax cable specifications:

- RG-62 A/U, solid conductor, CL2, 90%+ braided shield, PVC jacket, nominal 93 ohm impedance, 15.5 nominal capacitance/ft.
- RG-62 A/U, solid conductor, CL2P, 90%+ braided shield, plenum jacket, nominall 93 ohm impedance, 12.5 nominal capacitance/ft.

RCnet was one of the topologies used early on in networking and is rarely used as the pology of choice in current LAN environments. ARCnet, however, still is a solid, functional nd cost-effective means of networking.

ne diagram next shows the components of a typical ARCnet card. This card is configured r use with twisted pair wiring. ARCnet cards for use with coax cable have a BNC (*Bayonne eil Councelman* also commonly called *British Naval Connector*). You will find jumpers or IP switches for setting the following characteristics:

- Node number
- Base I/O address
- Memory address
- Interrupt
- Network timeout.

The node number and network timeout are characteristics unique to ARCnet.

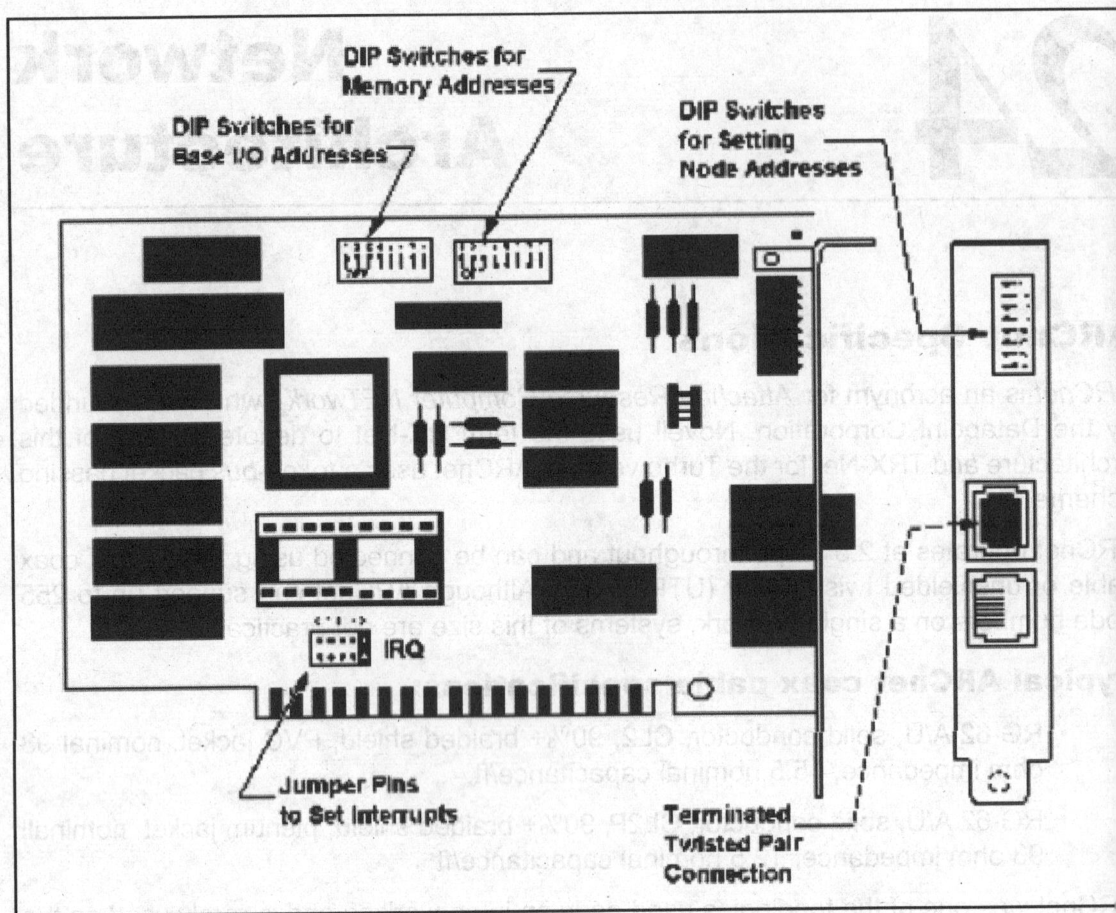

Each network interface card (NIC) on an ARCnet network is assigned a *node number*. Th number must be unique on each network and in the range of 1 to 255.

ARCnet manages network access with a *token passing bus* mechanism. The toke (permission to speak on the LAN) is passed from the lowest number node to higher numbe nodes in ascending order. Lower numbered addresses get the token before the high numbered addresses.

Network traffic is made more efficient by assigning sequential numbers to nodes using th same order in which they are cabled. Choosing random numbers can create a situation which a node numbered 23 can be a whole building away from the next number, 46, but the same room as numbers 112 and 142. The token has to travel in a haphazard mann that is less effective than if you numbered the three workstations in the same offic sequentially, 46, 47, and 48, and the workstation in the other building 112. With th configuration, the packet stays within the office before venturing on to other stations.

ARCnet Board Settings

Depending on the vendor design specifications of your ARCnet card, most *base I/*

addresses, node addresses, and *memory addresses* are set by DIP switches. The addresses are set using a binary mode calculation with an on or off setting in the requir switch block. *Interrupt settings* are made by jumper combinations at marked locations the network interface card (NIC). Many types and brands of ARCnet cards are on t market today. Refer to the documentation for the NIC or call the technical support group the specific vendor of the component.

Most ARCnet cards require a *shared memory address*. Many manufacturers use the ar of D000:0 to DFFF:0 as the default. Standard DOS memory is limited to the first 640 KB a PC's memory. However, extended or expanded memory managers can be used to ma memory above 640 KB available for use by DOS programs. If memory above the 640 K line (above hex address A000:0) is used for network boards, however, the memory becom unavailable for use by a memory manager. This makes it difficult to optimize a PC's upp memory area. If a network card requires a memory area such as D000:0-DFFF:0, t memory available for use by DOS memory managers is reduced by 64 KB. This is usua accomplished with an optional switch setting such as X=D000-DFFF to exclude the shar memory address range.

ARCnet Cabling

The ARCnet topology uses coax, twisted pair, or fiber optic cabling to connect netwo devices. An ARCnet network is used primarily with either coax or twisted pair cable. Mc older ARCnet installations are coax and use RG-62 A/U type cable terminated with 93 Oh terminators. Twisted pair (UTP) installations are newer and use stranded 24 or 26 gaug wire, or solid core 22, 24, or 26 gauge type cable terminated with 100 Ohm terminator Many ARCnet networks use a mix of both coax and UTP cabling. UTP cable is simple install and provides a reliable connection to the workstations, whereas coax provides means to span longer distances.

Typical ARCnet installations are wired as a star. ARCnet can run off a linear bus topolog using coax or twisted pair as long as the cards specifically support BUS. The most popul star-wired installations of ARCnet run off two types of hubs:

- *Passive hubs* cannot amplify signals. Each hub has four connectors. Because the characteristics of passive hubs, unused ports must be equipped with a terminatc a connector containing a resistor that matches the ARCnet cabling characteristic: A port on a passive hub can only connect to an active device (an active hub or a NIC). Passive hubs can never be connected to passive hubs.
- *Active hubs* have active electronics that amplify signals and split them to multipl ports. The number of ports on an active hub varies with the manufacturer, but eigh is typical. A port on an active hub can be connected to a port on another activ device (such as another active hub or an NIC) or to a passive hub.

One of the greatest flexibilities of ARCnet is that you can integrate connections from activ hubs to a linear bus connection as long as you terminate at the last connection point.

A maximum time limit of 31 microseconds is allotted for an ARCnet signal. This is als ed a *time-out setting*. Signals on an ARCnet can travel up to 20,000 feet during the *31 :rosecond* default time-out period. You can sometimes extend the range of an ARCnet increasing the time out value. However, 20,000 feet is the distance at which ARCnet nals begin to seriously degrade. Extending the network beyond that distance can result nreliable or failed communication. Therefore, the time-out parameter and cabling distance ommendations should be increased only with great caution.

e maximum cable distances between individual components in an ARCnet network are pendent on how the components are connected.

cabling ARCnet networks with coax cable, you must follow these rules:

- Never connect a passive hub to another passive hub directly.
- Passive hubs should never be used to connect two active hubs.
- Passive hubs are only used to connect an active hub and a node.
- Unused connectors on active hubs do not need to be terminated.
- Unused connectors on passive hubs must be terminated using a 93 Ohm terminator.

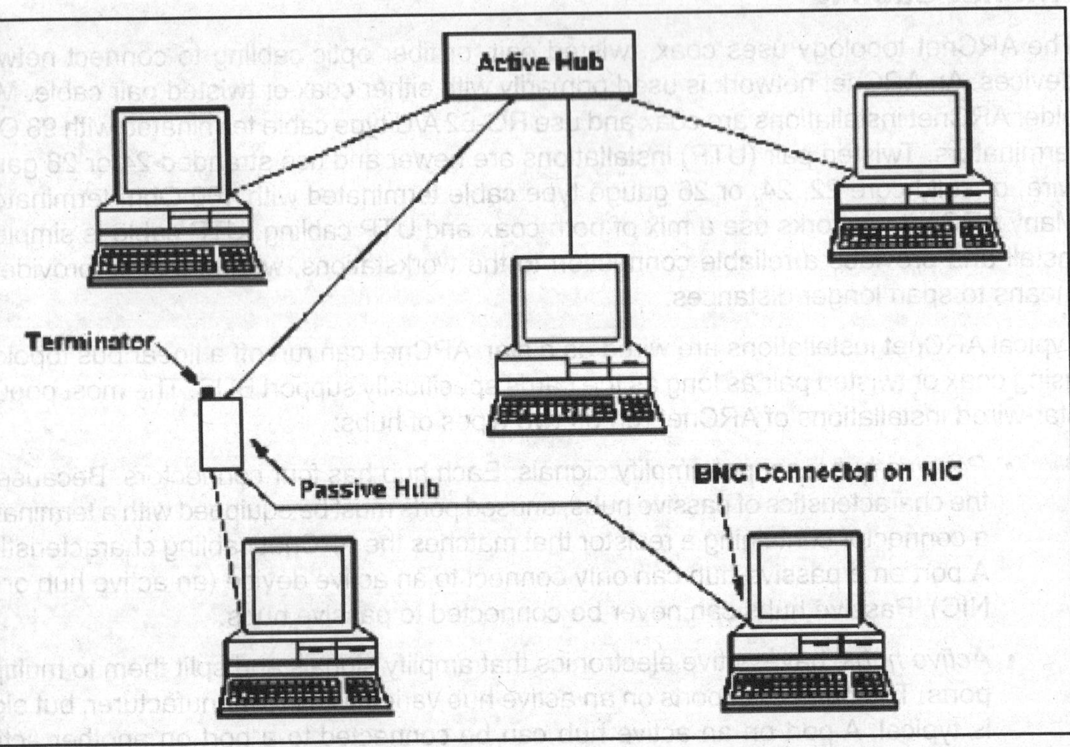

he figure above shows an ARCnet configuration using active and passive hubs. Active ubs are required to extend the network for long distances and to configure networks that ave more than four nodes. Passive hubs are used as an economical means of splitting a ort on an active hub to support three devices.

ARCnet Trouble shooting

Common sources of problems on ARCnet networks are as follows:

- Duplicate addresses. No more than one node can have a given node address the same network. If two or more nodes share an address, one of the workstations will either lose its network connection or will not be able to fin network.
- Missing terminators

Missing terminators may not present visible problems on a small network. Missing terminators cause data retransmits on smaller systems, eventually appearing as transmit time out errors or network errors.

- Using a terminator with an incorrect rating. Coax uses 93 Ohm; UTP must use Ohm terminators.

A terminator's value in ohms depends on the impedance of the cable. The cable's impedance and the terminator's value should always match.

- Failed NICs
- Failed active hubs (or a port on that hub)
- Cable lengths that exceed specifications. Twisted pair, cabled in a bus rather th a star, cannot have more than ten NICs per segment. This number varies w different manufacturers.

ARCnet UTP installed in a bus configuration is generally used only in very small networks of six nodes or less. This configuration has the major drawback of halting the network if a single cable is disconnected. In an ARCnet bus configuration, the network must be brought down to make any changes or service to the ARCnet cards.

- Coax connector not built and/or crimped correctly. Twist-on connectors a responsible for more intermittent errors on a network than most other failures becau of their design.

Twist-on coax connectors became popular in the IBM 3XXX systems. These systems used RG-62 coax cable and operated at 1.5 Mbps throughput. The twist-on connectors are not recommended for use on any modern LAN cable system because of the higher data rates employed.

Maximum ARCnet Cable Distances

Maximum Distance	From	To
2,000 feet	Network node	Active hub
2,000 feet	Active Hub	Active hub
100 feet	Active Hub	Passive hub
Not supported	Passive Hub	Passive hub
100 feet	Network node	Passive hub
2,000 feet	Network node	Network node
20,000 feet	Farthest node	Farthest node

e primary characteristics of ARCnet are:

- ARCnet operates at 2.5 Mbps throughput using a token-passing-bus scheme.
- ARCnet is cabled with RG-62 A/U coax with 93 Ohm terminators or the newer UTP with 100 Ohm terminators.
- The maximum time it takes for the ARCnet signal to travel the length of the network is 31 microseconds.
- The maximum distance an ARCnet signal can travel between the two nodes farthest away from each other is 20,000 feet.
- The absolute maximum number of ARCnet nodes that can occupy a given network segment is 255. An ARCnet segment consists of all cabling and nodes that share a given network address.

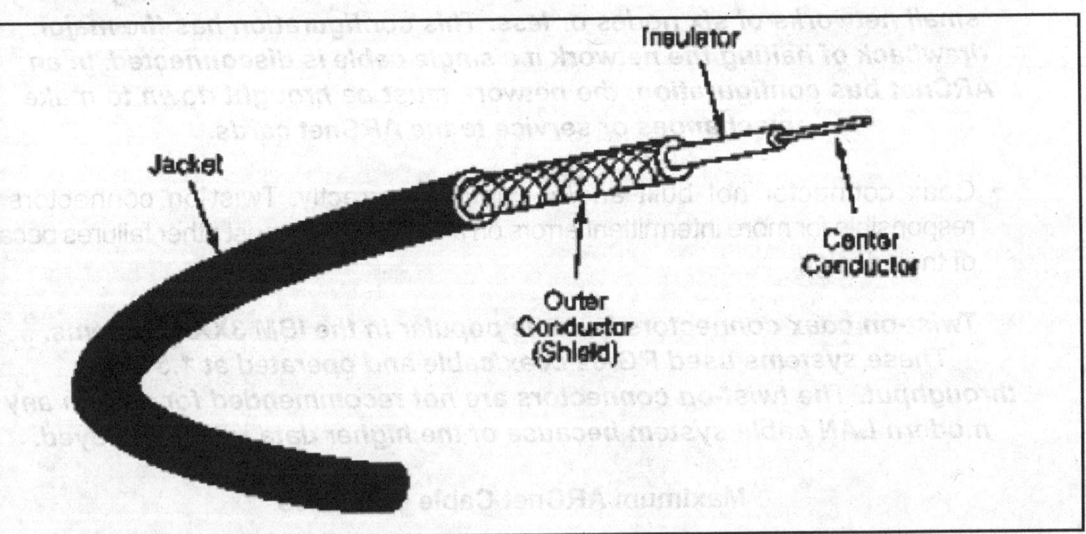

plication:

will be building a typical ARCnet coax cable for our hands-on lab project for this lesson.

n your LAN-Wire materials kit locate the:

- 6' length of RG-62 A/U coax cable
- RG-62 A/U crimp-on BNC connectors (Qty. 3).

rication Instructions:

1. Set the Coax wire stripper to the RG-59 setting. (RG-59 & RG-62 are the same diameter)
2. The dual-set blades of the coax wire stripper will strip the end of the coax cable with a precise two-stage cut. Strip the ends of your RG-62 cable using a rotary motion with the coax stripper.
3. Crimp the center pin of the BNC connector onto the end of the center conductor.
4. Slide the crimp ferrule over the coax cable.
5. Slip the body of the BNC connector under the braided shield as far as it will go.
6. Slide the crimp ferrule over the braided shield up to the BNC body shoulder.
7. Use the ratchet crimping tool to evenly and completely crimp the ferrule to the BNC body.
8. Repeat for the other end of the cable.
9. Use a digital multimeter to test your cable for shorts. (any Ohm reading other than infinity)
10. Using a BNC butt-splice and terminating resistor, also test for a perfect 93 Ohm reading.

nernet Specification

ernet was originally developed by DIX - the Digital Corporation, the Intel Corporation, the Xerox Corporation in the early 1970s. Ethernet is known as a *spanning tree topology* ause the networks expand by branching in tree structures that do not allow redundant s between nodes. Ethernet uses the *CSMA/CD* (Carrier Sense Multiple Access with ision Detection) media contention access method and supports a maximum throughput) or 100 Mbps. The original Ethernet and later *IEEE 802.3 protocols* are similar but not ally interchangeable.

origins of Ethernet are commemorated in the initials *DIX*, which is a 15-pin connector d to interface Ethernet components (also called the *AUI* - Attachment Unit Interface). acronym "DIX" is derived from the combination of leading letters of the founding Ethernet dors — Digital, Intel, and Xerox.

The term Ethernet commonly refers to original Ethernet (now most frequently identifi *Ethernet II*) as well as the *IEEE 802.3 standards*. However, Ethernet and the IEEE standards differ in ways significant enough to make standards incompatible in ter packet formats. At the Physical Layer, Ethernet and IEEE 802.3 are generally compati terms of cables, connectors, and electronic devices.

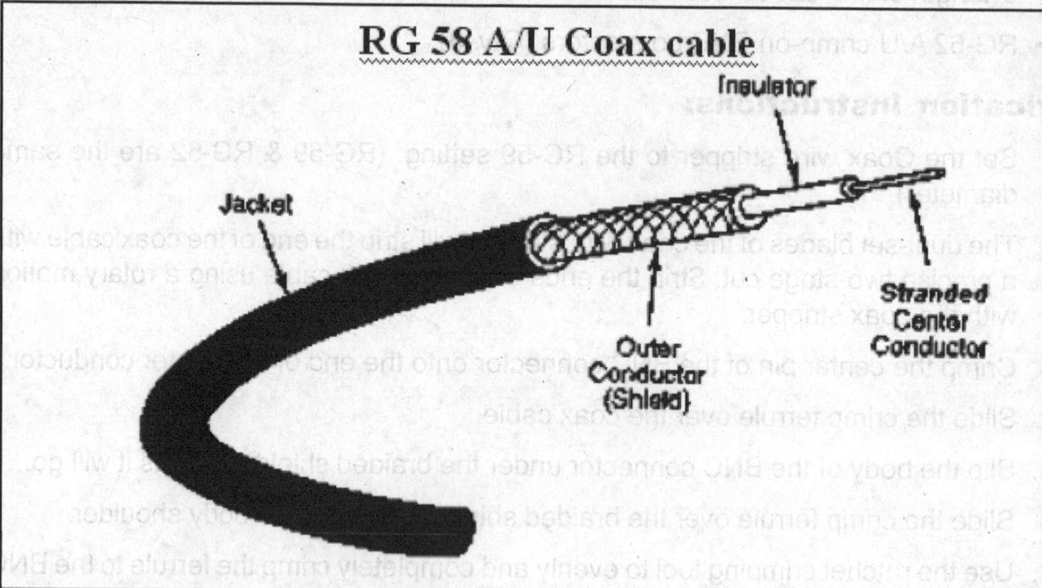

RG 58 A/U Coax cable

Ethernet is generally used on light to medium traffic networks, and performs best wh network's data traffic is sent in short bursts. Ethernet is the most popular network stan It has become especially popular in many university and government installations.

Ethernet Board Settings

Most versions of Ethernet NICs are configured using jumpers to set *addresses* and *inter* Certain models of newer type *Network Interface Cards* (NICs) can be configured us diagnostic program that allows changing of interrupt and memory address settings s in a special memory chip on the NIC.

An example of an Ethernet NIC is shown above. Some of the features of these cards

- Shared memory address selection *(most Ethernet cards do not require the u shared memory)*
- I/O address
- Interrupt
- Connectors (DIX/AUI, BNC, RJ-45)
- Active connector selection jumpers

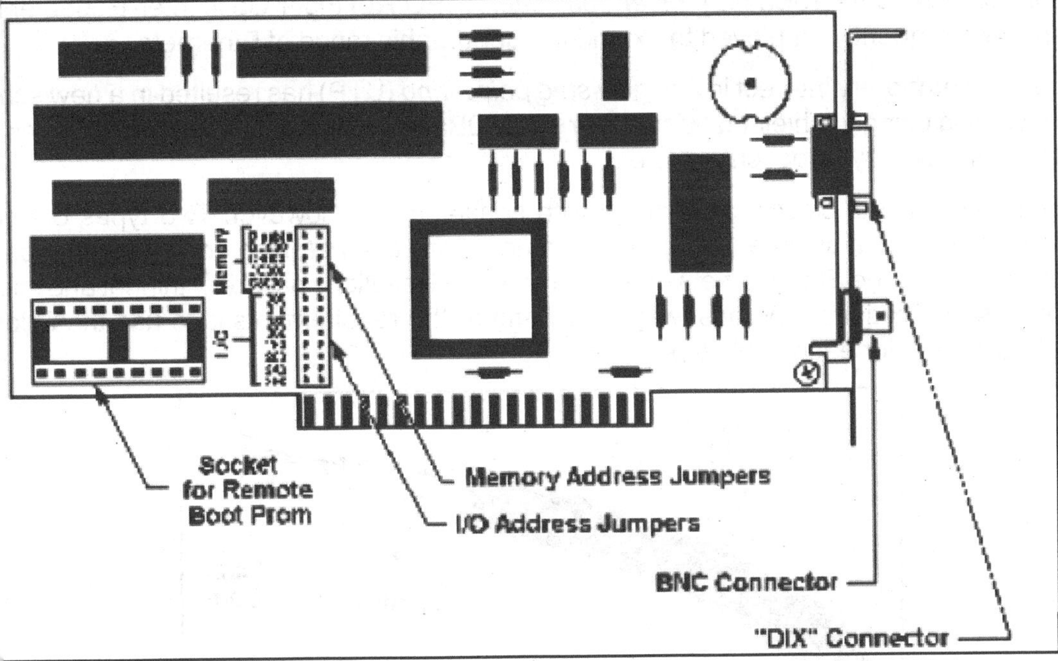

- Socket for a remote boot PROM.

rnet cards can have one, two, or possibly all three of the following *connectors*:

- DIX/AUI connectors support 10Base5 external transceivers
- BNC connectors support 10Base2 coax cabling
- RJ-45 connectors support 10Base-T/100Base-TX (UTP) cabling.

any cases, DIP switches or blocks of jumpers are used to select the active connector. some cards, however, the active connector can be selected with configuration software.

itation of 1,024 nodes (physical addresses) per network address exists on an Ethernet ork. Addresses are assigned by IEEE to the vendor for the first three bytes of a six- address. The vendor is responsible for assigning the rest of the address and ensuring ue IDs. These unique addresses are called *Burned-In Addresses* (BIA).

ith the Token Ring cards, the card's manufacturer *"burns in"* a unique node address a ROM on each NIC. Unless you override the *burned-in address* (using what are called lly administered Addresses - LAA), address conflicts should not occur on an Ethernet. dors sometimes label their cards with the node address. If the address is not visible, the diagnostic disk supplied by the vendor.

ernet Cabling

riety of cables can be used to implement Ethernet networks. Traditionally, Ethernets been cabled with *coax cables* of several different types (similar to RG 8 for 10Base5 and RG 58 A/U for 10Base2). *Fiber optic cables* (FOIRL) Fiber Optic Inter-Repeater are now frequently employed to extend the geographic range of Ethernets.

The contemporary interest in using *twisted pair wiring* (UTP) has resulted in a new sch for cabling using unshielded twisted pair. The 10Base-T cabling standard, which uses in a star topology, is described later.

Ethernet remains closely associated with coaxial cable, however. Two types of co cable still used in small and large environments are *thin net* (also known as cheape and *thick net*. The Ethernet networks have different limitations based on thinnet and thic cable specifications. The best way to remember the requirements is to use the follo rule of thumb for each cable type.

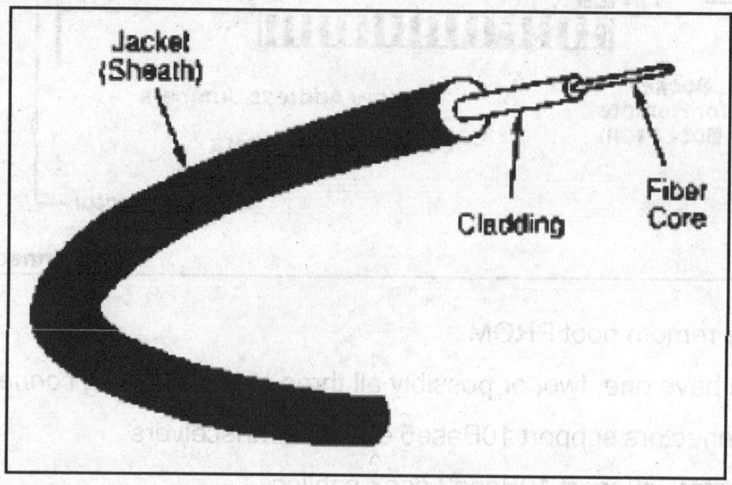

Typical Ethernet Coax Cable Specifications:

- RG-58 A/U, stranded conductor, CL2, 95%+ copper braided shield, PVC jac nominal 50 ohm impedance, 29.5 nominal capacitance/ft.
- RG-58 A/U, stranded conductor, CL2P, 95%+ copper braided shield, Plenum jac nominal 50 ohm impedance, 27.0 nominal capacitance/ft.
- RG-58/U, solid conductor, CL2, 90%+ copper braided shield, PVC jacket, nom 50 ohm impedance. 26.0 nominal capacitance/ft.
- Thick Ethernet Yellow Trunk Cable, solid conductor, CL2, double foil and brai shield, PVC jacket, nominal 50 ohm impedance, 26.0 nominal capacitance /ft.

The 5-4-3 Rule

The 5-4-3 rule states that between any two nodes in the Ethernet network can be:

- Up to (5) five segments in a series
- Up to (4) four concentrators or repeaters
- Up to (3) three populated segments (coax only).

10Base2 (ThinNet)

The 10Base2, *thinnet* topology generally uses the *on-board transceiver* of the network interface card to translate the signals to and from the rest of the network. Thin net cabling uses RG-58 A/U coaxial type cable, 50 Ohm terminators, and BNC T-connectors that directly attach to the connector on the NIC. A *grounded terminator* must be used on only one end of the network segment. The components of a *thin net network* are shown below.

> ***A* transceiver *is a device that takes the digital signal from the node and translates it to communicate on a baseband cabling system. NICs that support thinnet or 10Base-T/100Base-TX cable have* built-in transceivers. *External transceivers are used for 10Base5 thick Ethernet.***

Several additional rules must be adhered to in 10Base2 thinnet Ethernet environments, including the following:

- The minimum cable distance between workstations must be 1.5 feet or .5 meters.
- Pig tails, also known as drop cables, from BNC T-connectors should <u>*not*</u> be used to connect to the BNC connector on the NIC. The BNC T-connector on the coax must be connected directly to the NIC.

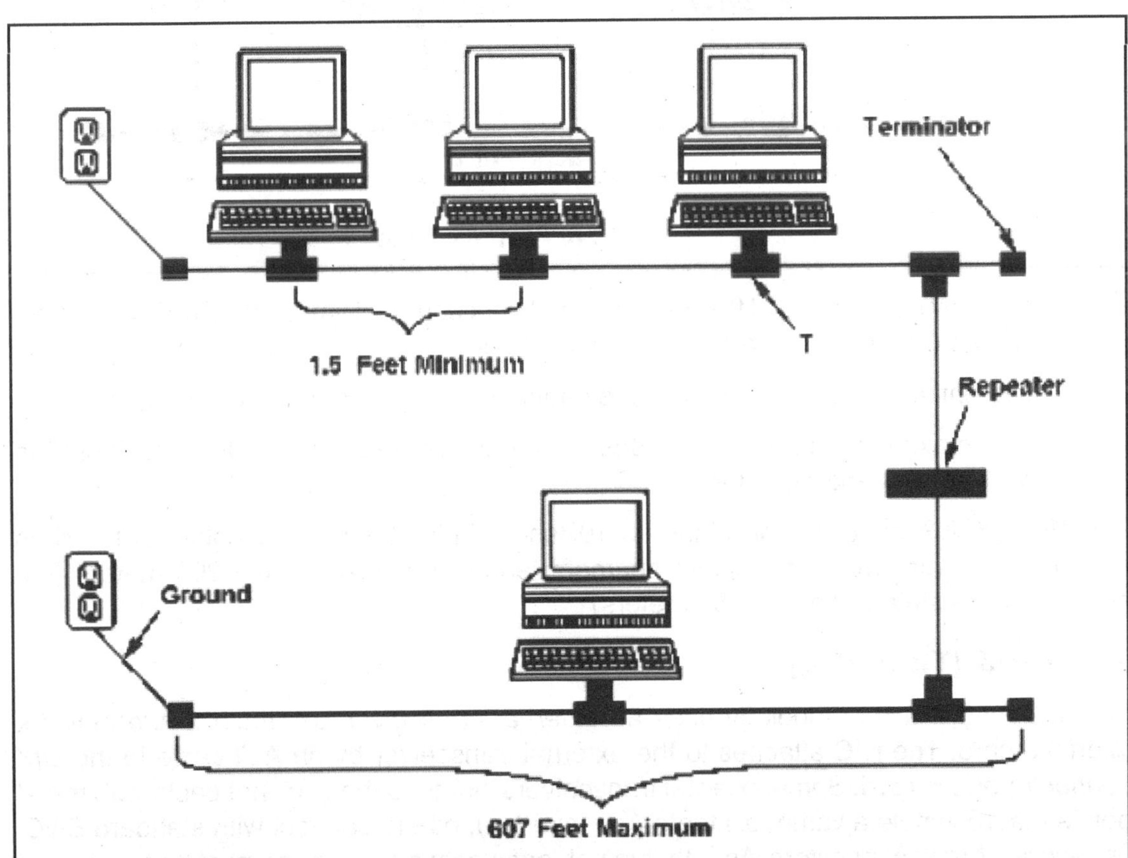

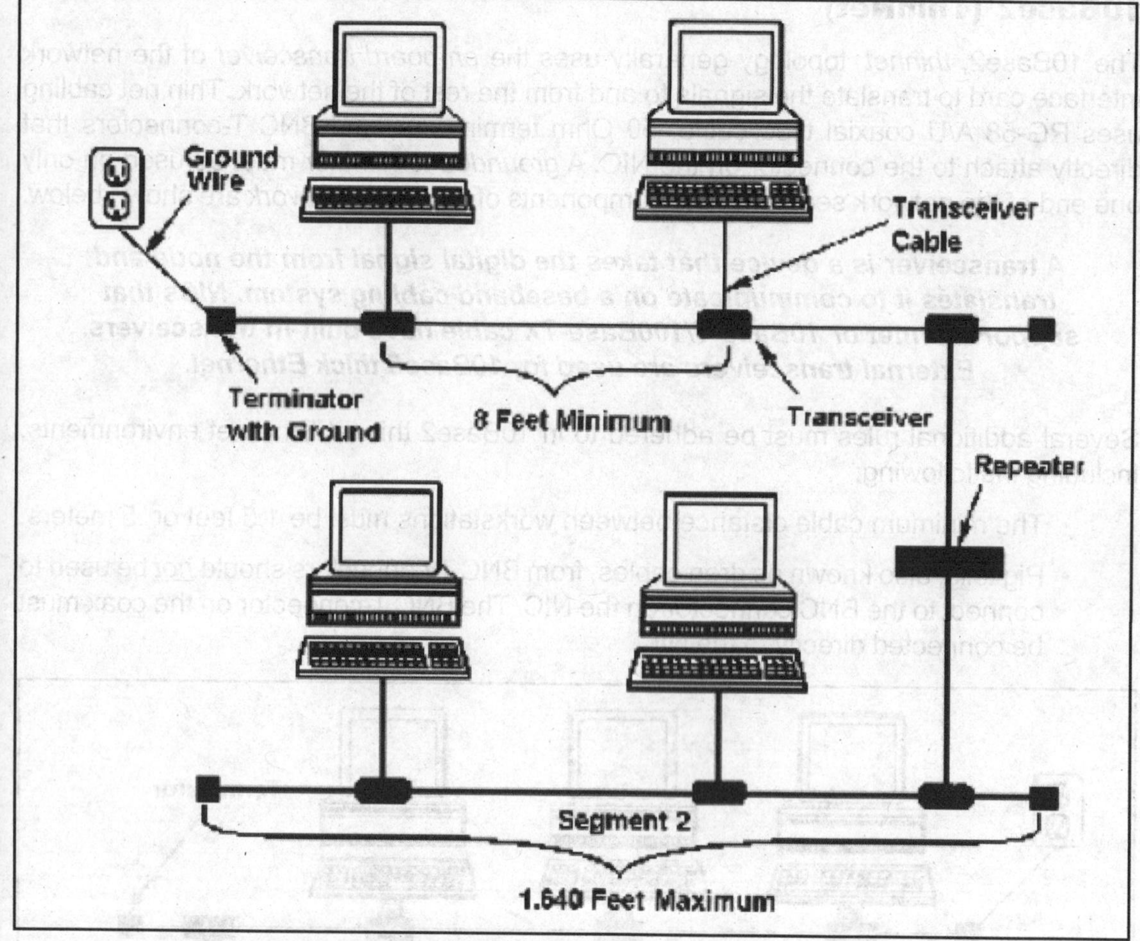

- You may not go beyond the maximum network segment limitation of 607 feet or 185 meters (not the 200 meters commonly stated).
- The entire network cabling scheme cannot exceed 3,035 feet or 925 meters.
- The maximum number of nodes per network segment is 30 (this includes workstations and repeaters).

The *IEEE 802.3 standard* for thinnet is 10Base2. This standard describes a 10 Mbps baseband network with a maximum segment length of approximately 200 meters (the actual limit, as stated above is 185 meters).

10BASE5 (ThickNet)

The 10Base5, *thicknet* topology uses an *external transceiver* to attach to the network interface card. The NIC attaches to the external transceiver by an *AUI cable* to the *DIX connector* on the card. Some external transceivers clamp to the thick net cable with metal points that resemble a vampire's teeth *(vampire tap)*, others connect with standard *BNC* or *N-series barrel connectors*. As with thin net, each network segment must be terminated at both ends with one end using a grounded terminator. The components of a *thicknet network* are shown in the figure below.

Several additional guidelines along with the 5-4-3 rule must be followed in 10Base5 thicknet Ethernet networks:

- The minimum cable distance between transceivers is eight feet or 2.5 meters.
- You may not go beyond the maximum network segment length of 1,640 feet or 500 meters.
- The entire network cabling scheme cannot exceed 8,200 feet or 2,500 meters.
- One end of the terminated network segment must be grounded.
- The maximum number of nodes per network segment is 100. (This includes all repeaters.)

The *IEEE 802.3 standard* that describes thicknet is 10Base5. This standard describes a 10 Mbps baseband network that can have segments up to 500 meters long.

The 10Base5 cabling scheme and components are shown next.

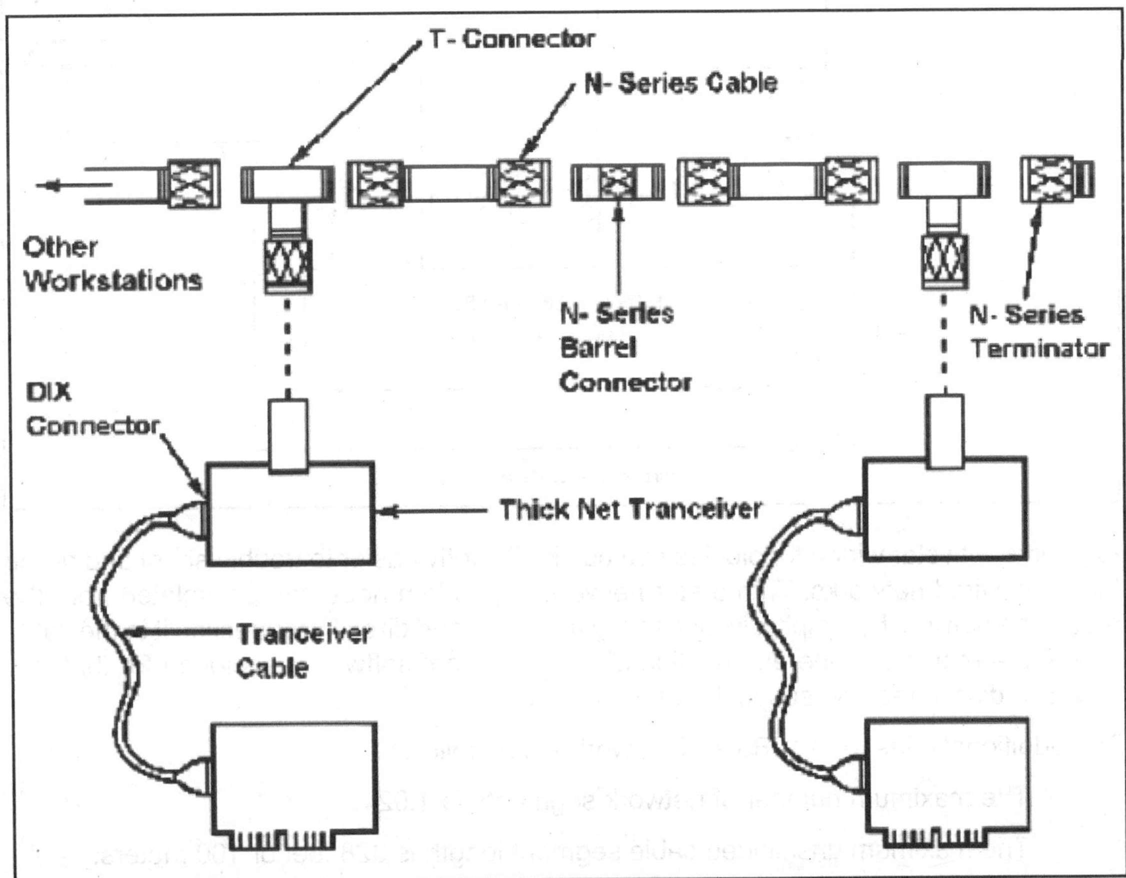

10Base-T/100Base-TX (Twisted Pair Ethernet)

The trend in wiring Ethernet networks is to use unshielded twisted pair (UTP) cable. UTP cable has a lower cost than coax. Another significant advantage is that UTP is smaller than coax, which relieves congestion of wiring conduits. *UTP Ethernet* is wired in a star-shaped design and is referred to in the technical world as 10BaseT. The cable uses *RJ-45 connectors*, and the network interface card can have RJ-45 jacks built into the back of the cards. External transceivers attached to a DIX connector can also be used to connect standard Ethernet cards into a twisted pair topology.

The figure next shows 10Base-T Ethernet cabled using twisted pair and a concentrator.

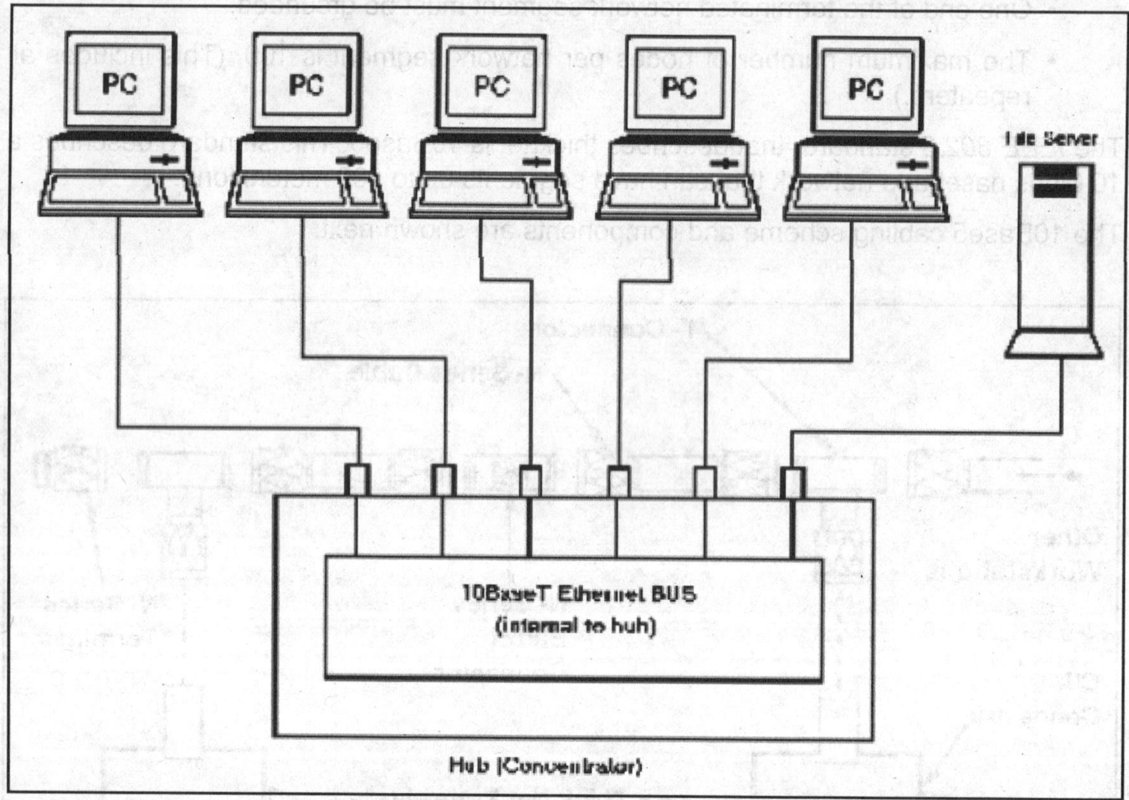

Networks with star wiring topologies can be significantly easier to trouble shoot and repair than bus wired networks. With a star network, a problem node can be isolated from the rest of the network by simply disconnecting the cable and directly connecting it to the cable hub. If the hub is considered "intelligent", management software developed for that hub type can disconnect the suspect port.

The additional rules for a 10Base-T network are as follows:

- The maximum number of network segments is 1,024.
- The maximum unshielded cable segment length is 328 feet or 100 meters.

10Base-T requires that the UTP cable system be compliant with a minimum rating of Category 3. RJ-45 connectors wired with two pairs (4 wires) on pins 1,2,3, & 6 are used with 10Base-T. Level IV is cable certified to operate at 10Base-T required throughput.

Fast Ethernet

An extension of the popular 10Base-T Ethernet standard, **Fast Ethernet** transports data at 100 Mbps. With rules defined by the **IEEE 802.3u** standard, Fast Ethernet leverages the familiar Ethernet technology and retains the CSMA/CD protocol of 10 Mbps Ethernet. Three types of Fast Ethernet are available: **100Base-TX**, which runs over Category 5 UTP; **100Base-T4** which runs over existing Category 3 UTP; and **100Base-FX**, which operates over multimode fiber optic cabling.

EIA/TIA T568B Colour Codes & Pin-out for the 10Base-T & 100Base-TX RJ-45 connector

1	2	3	4	5	6	7	8
TD+	TD-	RD+	N/C	N/C	RD-	N/C	N/C

Pins 1 & 2 - Pair #1 Transmit Data

Pins 3 & 6 - Pair #2 Receive Data

Pins 4, 5, 7, & 8 - Not Connected

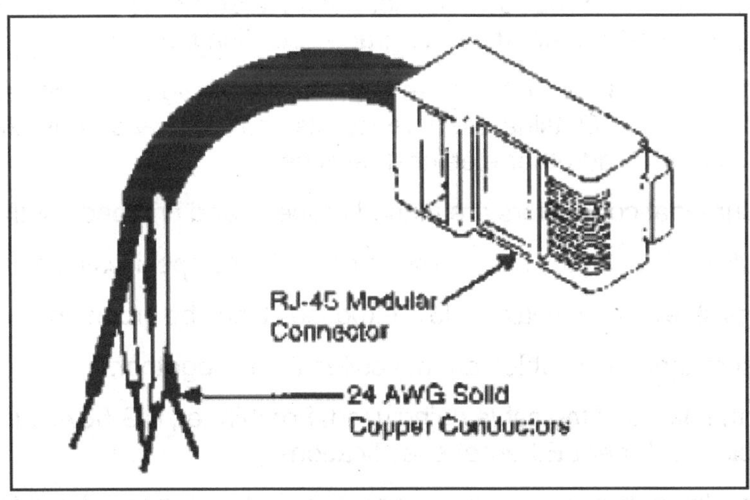

As specified for 10Base-T (CAT3 minimum) & 100Base-TX (CAT5 minimum), cables should be 100 Ohm unshielded or shielded twisted pair (UTP or STP) wire of AWG gauge 24, 26, or 28. Maximum length is 100 meters. IBM Type-1 cable and other 150 Ohm STP cables are not suitable.

Categories for UTP cable:

Category 3 - The characteristics are specified up to 16 MHz. They are typically used for

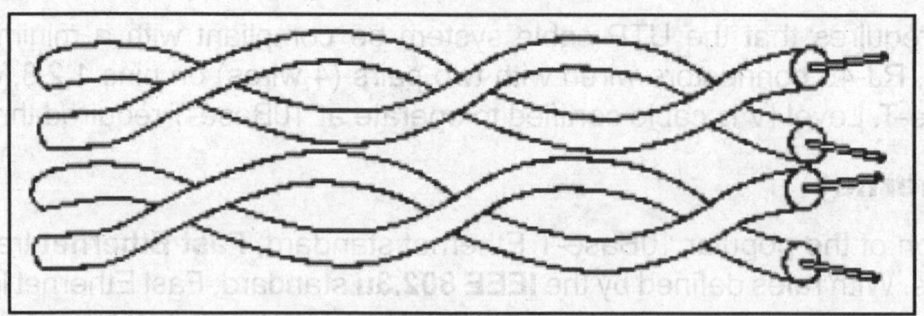

voice and data transmission rates up to and including 10 Mbps, e.g. IEEE 802.5 4-Mbps UTP (Token Ring) and IEEE 802.3 10Base-T (Ethernet).

Category 4 - The characteristics are specified up to 20MHz. They are typically used for voice and data transmission rates up to and including 16 MHz, e.g. IEEE 802.5 16-Mbps UTP (Token Ring).

Category 5 - The characteristics are specified up to 100 MHz. They are typically used for voice and data transmissions up to and including 100 Mbps e.g. the 100Base-TX Fast Ethernet, 100 Mbps Fast ARCnet, and others.

Ethernet Trouble shooting

Look for the following things when trouble shooting Ethernets:

- With 10Base-T & 100Base-TX, make sure that the cable used has the correct number of twists to meet the data grade specifications.
- Electrical interference can be caused by tying the network cable together with monitor and power cords. Outside interference also can be caused by fluorescent lights, electric motors, and other electrical devices.
- Make sure that connectors are pinned properly and crimped tightly.
- Check the cable lengths to make sure that distance specifications are not exceeded.
- If excess shielding on coax cable is exposed, it may be grounding out the connector.
- Make sure that coax cables are not coiled tightly together.
- Check the grade of the cable being used. For thinnet, RG-58 A/U is required. Thick net cable must meet Ethernet specifications.
- If using a linear bus setup, make sure that the topology rules are followed.
- Check for missing terminator or terminators with improper impedance ratings.
- Make sure that all the component cables in a segment are connected together. A user who moves his workstation and removes the T-connector incorrectly can cause a broken segment.

10Base2, thinnet and 10Base5, thick net cable can be combined to extend the distance of an Ethernet network topology (spanning tree topology). The following formula can be used to define the maximum amount of thinnet cable that can be used in one network segment combination:

Maximum length of thinnet that can be used =

1,640 feet (length of new networksegment to be added)

A linear bus topology is economical to wire because it is not necessary to have a separate cable run for each workstation. However, some local problems on a linear bus have the capability of bringing the entire network down.

If a break is in the cable or a streaming (beaconing) NIC is in the channel, the entire network can go down. Streaming is more frequently referred to as a broadcast storm. This occurs when a network card fails, and the transmitter floods the cable with traffic, just like a faucet that is stuck open. At this point, the network becomes unusable.

Application Projects:

We will be building a typical coax cable for 10Base2 thinnet for our first hands-on lab project for this lesson. We will then build a typical UTP patch-cable for 10Base-T & 100Base-TX Ethernet for our second project. Then we will build a cross-cable (sometimes called a 10Base-T / 100Base-TX null-modem cable) for directly connecting two 10Base-T or 100Base-TX NICs together without the need for a concentrator.

From your LAN-Wire materials kit locate the:

- 6' length of RG-58A/U coax cable
- RC-58 A/U crimp-on BNC connectors (Qty. 3)
- Two 6' lengths of four-pair (8 wire) UTP cable
- RJ-45 crimp-on connectors (Qty. 6).

Project #1 - 10Base2 coax cable

1. Set the Coax wire stripper to the RG-58 setting. (RG-59 & RG-62 are the same diameter).
2. The dual-set blades of the coax wire stripper will strip the end of the coax cable with a precise two-stage cut. Strip the ends of your RG-58 cable using a rotary motion with the coax stripper.
3. Crimp the center pin of the BNC connector onto the end of the center conductor.
4. Slide the crimp ferrule over the coax cable.
5. Slip the body of the BNC connector under the braided shield as far as it will go.
6. Slide the crimp ferrule over the braided shield up to the BNC body shoulder.
7. Use the ratchet crimping tool to evenly and completely crimp the ferrule to the BNC body.

8. Repeat for the other end of the cable.
9. Use a digital multimeter to test your cable for shorts. (any Ohm reading other than infinity).
10. Using a BNC butt-splice and terminating resistor, also test for a perfect 50 Ohm reading.

Project #2 - 10Base-T/100Base-TX patch-cable

Technically, as long as you build your 10Base-T/100Base-TX patch-cable with straight-through connections for pins 1, 2, 3, & 6 it will work. But there is a EIA/TIA 568 standard that specifies minimum recommendations for telecommunications wiring within a structure, including telecommunication outlets, and between structures in a campus environment. It specifies a wiring system with a recommended topology and distances. It specifies media by parameters which determine performance and specifies connectors and their pin assignments to ensure interconnectability.

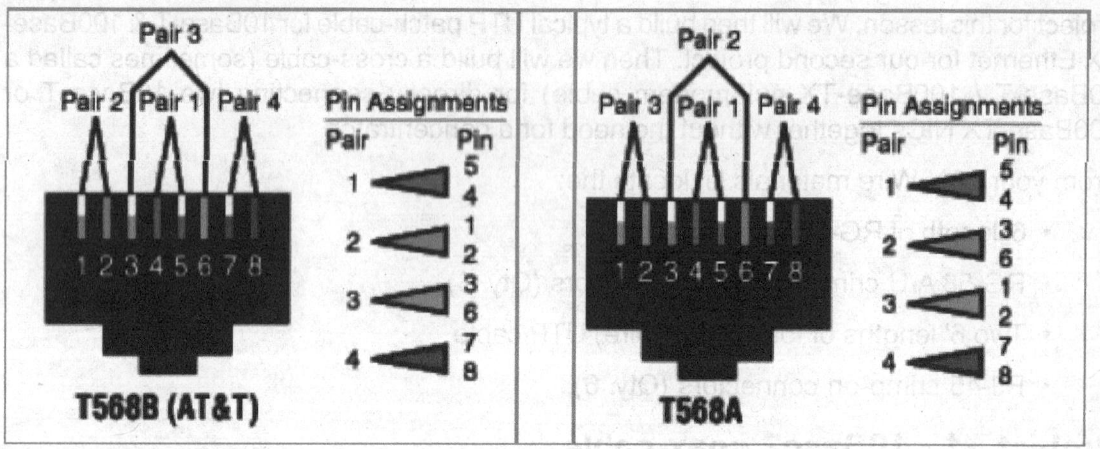

Using the USOC/PDS wiring pair colour codes and the EIA/TIA T568B (AT&T 258A) wiring scheme assemble a *standard* 10BaseT cable with straight-through wiring using pins 1, 2, 3 & 6. Use the Paladin twisted pair tester to insure connection integrity.

Universal Service Ordering Codes (USOC): are a series of Registered Jack (RJ) wiring configurations developed by the Bell System for connection of customer premise equipment to the public network.

Banded & Solid / Wiring Pair Colour Codes:

Pair #	ID	Pin #T568B	Bandcode	Pin #USOC	Solidcode
1	T1	5	White/Blue	5	Red
	R1	4	Blue(White)	4	Green

2	T2	1	White/Orange	6	Black
	R2	2	Orange(White)	3	Yellow
3	T3	3	White/Green	7	Orange
	R3	6	Green(White)	2	Blue
4	T4	7	White/Brown	8	Gray (or White)
	R4	8	Brown(White)	1	Brown

Project #3 - 10Base-T/100Base-TX Cross-cable

To direct-connect two 10BaseT NIC's for testing or trouble shooting you will assemb 10Base-T/100Base-TX cross-cable (sometimes called a UTP null-modem cable or p to-jack cable). This cable will allow you to connect two 10Base-T or 100Base-TX no together without the need for a concentrator. This can create a two-node LAN. Be sur check the wiring with the Padadin test tool.

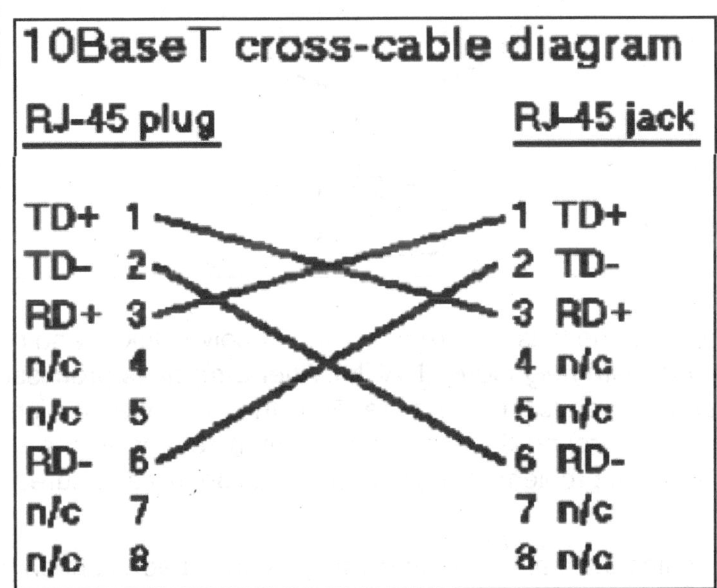

Token Ring Specifications

Token Ring uses a non-contention *token-passing* architecture that adheres to the *IE 802.5* standard. The topology is physically a star, but logically uses a ring to pass the to from station to station. Each node must be attached to a hub/concentrator calle *multistation access unit* (MAU or MSAU).

Token Ring network interface cards (NICs) can run at *4 Mbps or 16 Mbps*. 4 Mbps ca can run only at that data rate. However, 16 Mbps cards can be configured to run at 4 o Mbps. All cards on a given network ring must be running at the same rate.

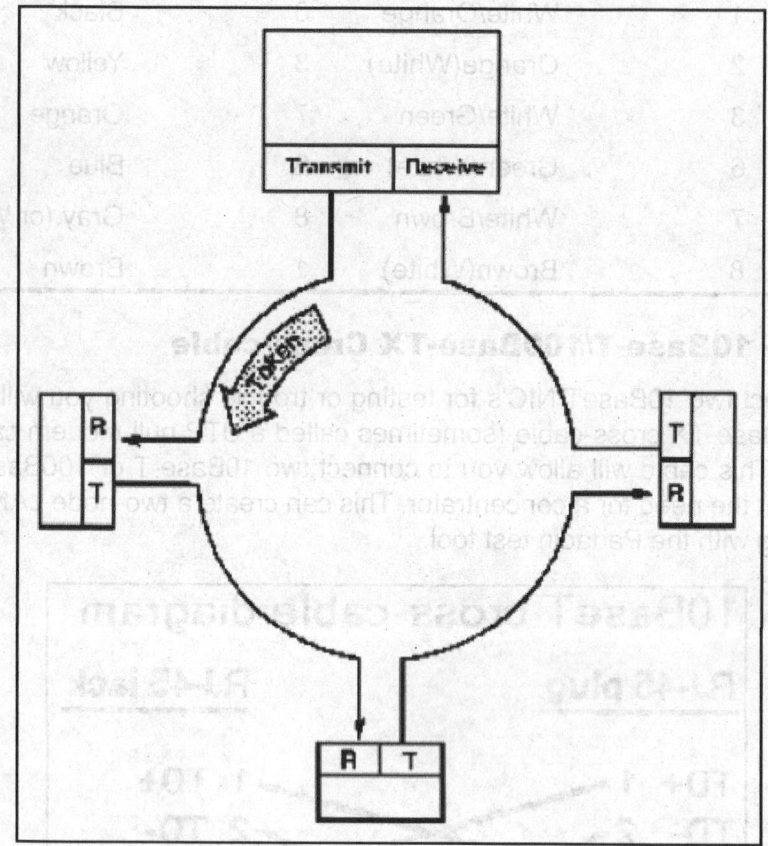

hown below, each node acts as a *repeater* that receives token and data frames from *earest active upstream neighbour* (NAUN). After a frame is processed by the node, frame is passed (rebroadcast) downstream to the next attached node. Each token es at least one trip around the entire ring. It then returns to the originating node. kstations that indicate problems send a *"beacon"* to identify an address of the potential re.

a Novell LAN, to find out if any beacon messages have been sent on your Token Ring vork, review your System Error Log found in SYSCON through Supervisor Options.

ken Ring Board Settings

vith the Ethernet cards, the node address on each NIC is *"burned in"* (BIA) at the ufacturer and is unique to each card. The node address in some cases can be ridden by vendor specified software instructions *(this is called a Locally Administered ress - LAA)*. A maximum of two Token Ring cards can be installed in any node, with n card being defined as the primary or alternate Token Ring card in the machine. A cal Token Ring card is shown below.

common features of a Token Ring NIC are:

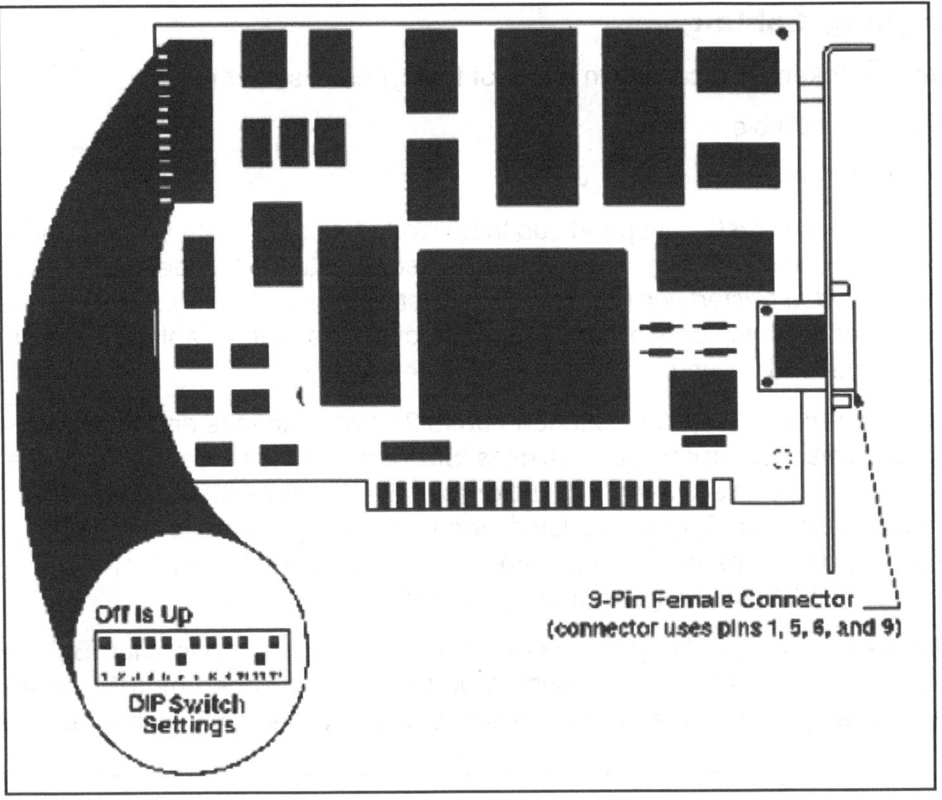

- Interrupt (IRQ)
- I/O address (Primary or Secondary)
- Shared RAM address
- Shared RAM size
- Data Rate (4Mbps or 16Mbps)
- DMA channel
- 9-pin female connector
- (optional RJ-45 connector)
- Remote boot PROM socket.

The *interrupt* (IRQ), *I/O address*, and *shared memory address* on each Token Ring must be set to avoid conflicts with all other components. The *DMA channel* may or not be sharable depending on your system.

Each Token Ring card comes with a diagnostic disk that provides testing for the ada Refer to the appropriate documentation for your card for more detailed instructions.

ken Ring Cabling

defines Token Ring cabling in terms of two types of systems:

- Small movable
- Large non-movable.

small movable system supports up to 96 workstations and file servers and 12 MAUs. ses *Type 6* cable to attach workstations and servers to IBM Model *8228 MAUs*. Type 6 le is a *shielded twisted pair* (STP) cable with *stranded conductors*. This cable is flexible, has limited distance capabilities. The characteristics of this cable make it suitable for ll networks and for *patch cords* (wiring closet jumpers).

large non-movable system supports up to 260 workstations and file servers, with up 3 MAUs. This network configuration uses IBM *Type 1* or *Type 2* cable. These are shielded ted pair cables with *solid-wire conductors* suitable for carrying signals greater distances are possible with *Type 6*. The large non-movable system also involves other wiring ds such as punch panels or distribution panels, equipment racks for MAUs, and wiring ets to contain the previously listed components.

Multistation Access Unit (MAU) is the central cabling component for IBM Token Ring vorks. The *8228 MAU* was the original wiring hub developed by IBM for Token Ring vorks. The figure above shows an example of a network cabling several workstations

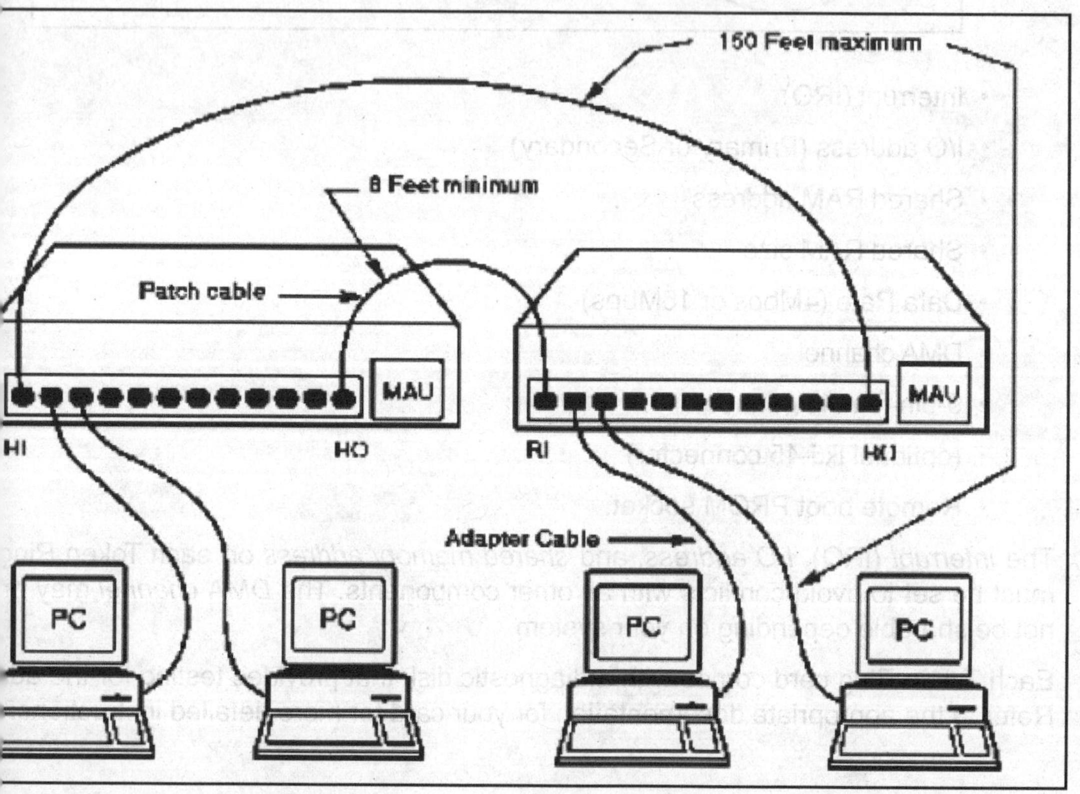

228 MAUs. The distances noted in the figure are based on the rules for the small, ɔle cabling system. Each 8228 has *ten connectors*, eight of which accept cables to tations or servers. The other connectors are labeled *RI* (ring in) and *RO* (ring out). I and RO connectors are used to connect multiple 8228s to form larger networks.

are mechanical devices that consist of relays and connectors. Their purpose is to workstations in and out of the network. Each port is controlled by a *relay* powered by ge sent to the MAU from the NIC. When an 8228 is first set up, each of these relays ɔe initialized with a *setup tool* (sometimes referred to as a phaser) shipped with the he setup tool is inserted into each port and held there until a light indicates that the properly initialized (charged).

member that when talking about Token Ring; MAU and MSAU both refer to Multistation Access Units.

ken Ring networks use two (or three) types of connectors. NICs are equipped with a *(DB-9)* nine-pin connector (only four pins are used) and/or an RJ-45 connector. , repeaters, and most other equipment use a special *IBM Type-1 unisex data ctor*. (Newer Token Ring cards and MAUs use *RJ-45 connectors* and CAT5 UTP g).

IBM STP Cable

PAIRS	AWG	USE
Solid twisted	22	Data
Type 1 *plus*(4) voice pairs	22	Data &Voice
Stranded twisted	26	Patch
Solid parallel	26	Undercarpet
Solid twisted	26	Plenum

andard types of cables are employed as follows:

Patch cables have IBM data connectors at both ends. These cables interconnect MAUs, repeaters, and most other Token Ring components.

Token Ring adapter cables have an IBM Type-1 unisex data connector at one end and a nine-pin connector at the other. Adapter cables connect workstation and server NICs to other network components that use IBM data connectors.

you are connecting a Token Ring network, make sure that you do the following:

Initialize each port in the 8228 MAU by using the setup tool shipped with the MAU (wait for the click) before connecting a cable.

If using more than one MAU, connect the ring out (RO) port of each MAU with the ring in (RI) port of the next MAU in the loop. This must physically *complete the ring*.

Node/Distance/MAU limitations

A variety of rules must be observed when configuring a Token Ring LAN. The fo rules apply to Token Ring networks:

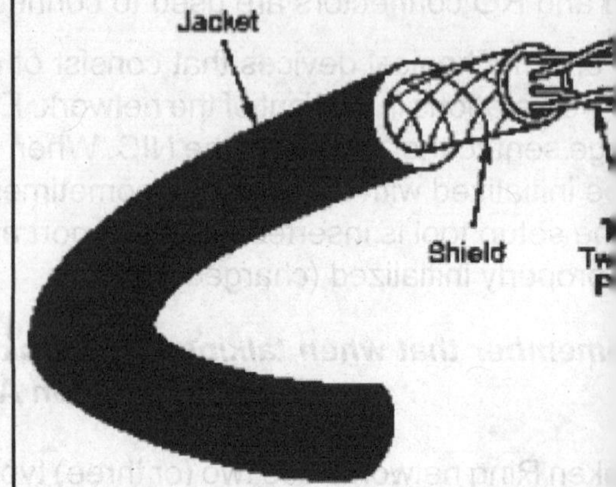

- The minimum patch cable distance between two MAUs is eight feet.
- The maximum patch cable distance between two MAUs is 150 feet. Patch cables come in standard lengths of 8, 30, 75, and 150 for Type 6.
- The maximum patch cable distance connecting all MAUs is 400 feet.
- The maximum patch cable distance between a MAU and a node is 150 fee

These additional configuration rules apply to a small movable Token-Ring cable s

- Maximum 96 nodes
- Maximum 12 MAUs
- Uses Type 6 cable.

A large non-movable Token-Ring cable system is subject to the following rules:

- Maximum 260 nodes
- Maximum 33 MAUs
- Uses Type 1 or Type 2 cable.

Token Ring networks also can be cabled using UTP (CAT5) cable. The IEEE 802.5 s describes 4 Mbps Token Ring using IBM Type 3 UTP cable (equivalent to CAT3). H CAT4 or CAT5 cable must be used for 16 Mbps Token Ring.

When using UTP wiring with older non-UTP cards, a *media filter* must be installed b the NIC and the UTP cable. Some newer Token Ring NICs have built-in media filt RJ-45 jacks ready to interface with UTP wiring.

Token-Ring Trouble Shooting

When trouble shooting Token Ring networks, look for the following:

- Any base I/O, DMA shared memory, or Interrupt conflicts with other board
- The version of the workstation or server software driver to make sure that its level is compatible with your NIC. Drivers are different for file serv workstations.

Make sure that the MAUs are connected properly, with ring out ports connecting to ring in ports throughout the ring.

Some MAUs other than the 8228 are active and require a power supply. These MAUs fail if they have a blown fuse or a bad power source.

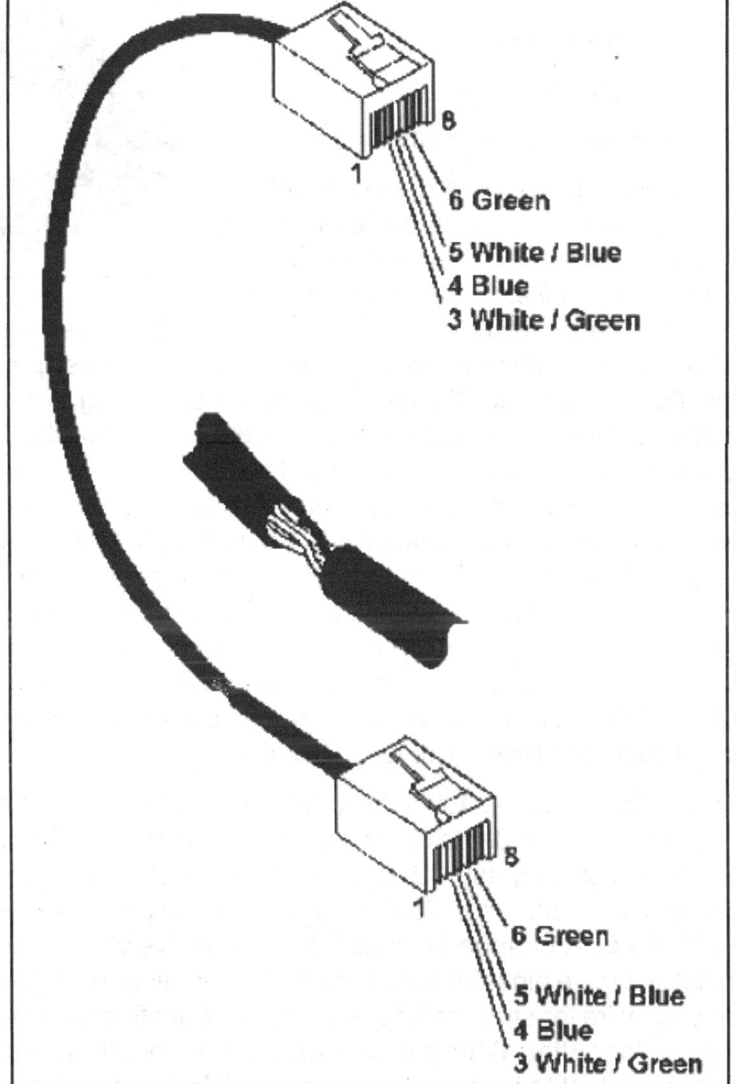

Check that patch cables are correctly attached to the adapter cable. Patch cables connect MAUs together. Another type of connecting cable is called an adapter cable which connects the NIC to the MAU.

You may have a failed NIC. Try substituting another one known to work properly.

Determine if the MAU or the MAU port is bad. Ports may need to be reinitialized with the setup tool.

Check to see if a 16 Mbps card is inserted into a 4 Mbps ring or vice versa. Neither situation is correct.

Determine if the wrong type of cable for speed of network is used.

Examine the pins on the adapter cable to see if they are bent or broken.

If you are overriding the burned-in network addresses, it is possible that duplicate node addresses may be set.

If connecting to a 4 Mbps twisted pair network, check the Type 3 media filter.

cation Project:

be building a typical Token Ring adapter cable for this lesson project.

From your LAN-Wire materials kit locate the:

- 6' length of IBM Type 6 cable
- 1 IBM unisex data connector
- 1 DB-9 male (pin) connector
- 1 DB-9 hood
- 4 (or more) DB male pins
- 1 DB Insertion/Extraction tool.

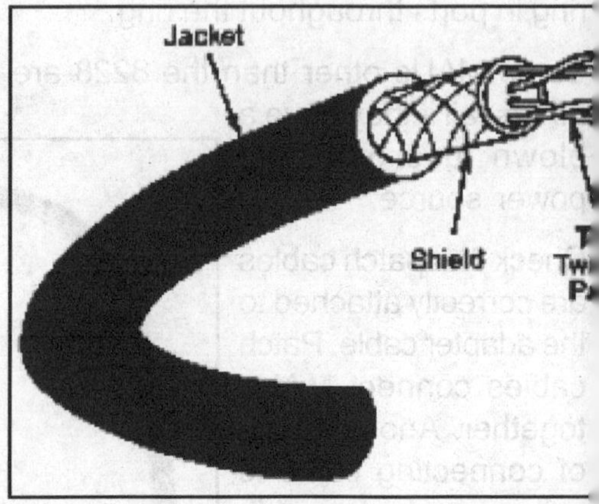

The unisex IBM Type-1 data connector is on both sides of a patch cable or on one side of an adapter cable. This unique IBM connector is *unisex* in that two of the same connector will attach to each other. You will find these connectors on the standar 8228 MAU, in patch panels, and in the walls of most pre-wired token-ring installa Installing the unisex IBM data connector is a learning experience even for the most cable installer. Some data connector kits come with 45, 90, and 180 degree cab strain reliefs. You will only use one. This snap-together kit looks easy to assemble a and *is* easy after you develop a little finesse. Do make sure that the cable colour wire pairs for the "Christmas Pair" (receive) and "Halloween Pair" (transmit) are co inserted into the built-in punch-down block (use the punch-down block slide as a code guide). A common mistake is to leave out the metal ferrule strain relief or the relief collar. You may have to assemble/disassemble this data connector several When done properly the snap-together unit looks clean and is very rigid. Two pieces kit can be ignored until after assembly, the dust cover (with attachment loop) a installation lock (usually beige in colour).

The node side of the Token Ring adapter cable is a standard DB-9 male connector only pins 1, 5, 6, & 9 (the outside narrow edge pins). Assembling this end of the cable same as installing any DB type connector. Make sure you follow the wiring diagra connect the "Christmas Pair" (Red & Green) to pins 1 & 6 respectively and the "Hall Pair" (**Black** & Orange) to pins 5 & 9 respectively. You will need to use a pin crimp install the male pins. Be sure to crimp the rear fingers of the pin around the insulation stripped wire for strain relief and crimp the front fingers around the conductor for a p connection. After all four pins have been crimped on and inspected, use the Ins Extraction tool to insert the pins into the DB-9 connector as per the colour code dia Be sure to inspect and re-inspect the colour coding at the data connector end and th 9 end. After the pins have been inserted and inspected, attach the DB-9 hood. Be s secure the strain relief of the hood.

We will test the Token Ring adapter cable two ways. First, you will use the digital mult to test for continuity and correct wiring. Second, you will disconnect one of the a cables from one of the nodes on the Token-Ring LAN, reconnect *your* cable, power workstation, and log on to the file server.

25 Network Connectivity

Network Connectivity Devices

Network connection devices connect the various segments of network media that make up a network or internetwork. A segment is one section of network transmission media that is assigned a specific network address; it provides servers and clients on the network with access to network resources.

A network interface board attaches a device, such as a computer, to a transmission medium. Network interface cards (NICs) are circuit boards that provide the means to change a computer's electric signals to those used by the transmission medium.

The transceiver is the basic component of a NIC, this is what enables the NIC to send and receive data.

Hubs

A hub is a wiring concentrator for a LAN or WAN that provides a central attachment point for network cabling. Coaxial cable doesn't use hubs.

An active hub can regenerate or amplify a signal, it connects multiple media segments, extends cable length and thereby increases transmission length.

A passive hub connects multiple media segments together, it does not regenerate or amplify a signal.

Switches - Data Link - Switching hubs (Switches)

These are intelligent hubs which contain circuitry that very quickly routes signals between ports on the hub. This method reduced bandwidth waste because only the device which needs to receive the packet does rather than the entire network segment.

Switch filters traffic through MAC addresses. A switch receives a transmission and retransmits it using only that port through which the intended receiver can be reached.

Repeater - Physical

Regenerates signals for retransmission. Moves packets from one physical media to another. Will pass broadcast storms. Cannot connect different network topologies or access methods.

Repeaters work in the Physical layer of the OSI model to provide fast signal regeneration. In digital computer networks, repeaters aren't simply amplifiers; repeaters deal with attenuation by receiving and evaluating the data then immediately re-transmitting a clean copy of the signal on to the next segment of the network cable.

Bridge - Data Link (MAC Sublayer)

Bridges are used to segment networks. They forward packets based on address of destination node. Uses RAM to build a routing table based on hardware addresses. Will connect dissimilar network topologies. Will forward all protocols. Regenerates the signal at the packet level.

A bridge, like a repeater, extends a network's transmission distance, however, a bridge is used to connect segments on different networks.

Bridges are used to segment networks. They forward packets based on address of destination node. Uses RAM to build a routing table based on hardware addresses. Some bridge types are capable of connecting dissimilar network topologies. Will forward all protocols. A hub is a single point where media segments can connect.

Remote Bridge - Data Link (MAC Sublayer)

Same as bridge, but used for telephone communications. Uses STA (Spanning Tree Algorithm).

Router - Network

Routes packets across multiple networks. Uses RAM to build a routing table based on network addresses (i.e. TCP address). Shares status and routing information to other routers to provide better traffic management and bypass slow connections. Will not pass broadcast traffic. Are slower than bridges due to complex functions. Strips off Data Link Layer source and destination addresses and then recreates them for packets. Routers can accommodate multiple active paths between LAN segments. Will not pass unroutable protocols.

Routers, operating in the Network layer, use network address information to move data through the best path to its destination. To connect different networks, routers must be aware of network addresses. Because routers can determine network addresses, they can be "intelligent" about routing data through a complex internetwork involving multiple networks.

Multiplexers

Multiplexers (mux) enable several devices to simultaneously share a high-bandwidth line.

half-duplexing - each device in the configuration can send and receive information, but only one at a time; while sending the device cannot receive, very much like walkie-talkies.

full-duplexing - each device in the configuration can send and receive simultaneously. The best example of this is the telephone.

Brouter - Data Link and Network

Will act as a router for specified protocols and as a bridge for other specified protocols. Brouters are a hybrid of routers and bridges. Brouters function like routers, relaying data transmissions between networks, but when they encounter a data unit that uses a protocol with which they are unfamiliar, they work like a bridge and forward the data to the next segment by using a physical address. Because of this ability, you can use brouters for networks on which there is mixed-protocol traffic and for networks that use protocols that do not support routing.

Channel Service Unit/Digital Service Unit (CSU/DSU)

The units are designed to shield network users from electric voltages as well as electrical interference. They also ready data for transmission by adhering to any network rules.

Both units are parts of a data communications equipment (DCE) device and are collectively referred to as a CSU/DSU. A CSU/DSU operates like a modem; however, it is a digital-to-digital device rather than digital-to-analog. It readies digital signals and guarantees that they have sufficient strength and the proper format to be transmitted over digital WAN links.

Gateway - Transport, Session, Presentation and Application. Used for communications between different NOS's. Takes the packet, strips off the old protocol and repackages it for the receiving network. A gateway basically grants a workstation a direct connection to the host computer and acts as a messenger between the two systems. Gateways operate between the OSI Transport layer through the Application Layer.

Transmission Media Adapter - - Adapter used to connect dissimilar NIC and cable connections (i.e. RJ-45 to RS-232 adapter).

MAUs - (Multistation Access Unit) an access device used to connect the main cabling structure to devices in use on a Token Ring network. This device adds fault tolerance to the network so that a single failure doesn't stop the whole network.

Broadband and Baseband

Baseband transmissions use the entire medium's capacity for a single channel over digital signaling. Since only one signal at a time can occupy a channel, the use of a MUX will allow multiple devices to send multiple signals using a single transmission medium. Provide excellent throughput because the digital signal occupies the entire channel.

Broadband transmissions share the medium's bandwidth over multiple analog channels unidirectionally. This is performed using different frequencies and a process known as FDM (frequency division multiplexing). Since these transmission work very well over long distances, WAN communications take advantage of this technology.

NICs

A **network card, network adapter** or **NIC** (network interface card) is a piece of computer hardware designed to allow computers to communicate over a computer network. It is both an OSI layer 1 (physical layer) and layer 2 (data link layer) device, as it provides physical access to a networking medium and provides a low-level addressing system through the use of MAC addresses. It allows users to connect to each other either by using cables or wirelessly.

Although other network technologies exist, Ethernet has achieved near-ubiquity since the mid-1990s. Every Ethernet network card has a unique 48-bit serial number called a MAC address, which is stored in ROM carried on the card. Every computer on an Ethernet network must have a card with a unique MAC address.

No two cards ever manufactured share the same address.

This is accomplished by the Institute of Electrical and Electronics Engineers (IEEE), which is responsible for assigning unique MAC addresses to the vendors of network interface controllers.

Whereas network cards used to be expansion cards that plug into a computer bus, the low cost and ubiquity of the Ethernet standard means that most newer computers have a network interface built into the motherboard. These motherboards either have Ethernet capabilities integrated into the motherboard chipset, or implemented via a low cost dedicated Ethernet chip, connected through the PCI (or the newer PCI express bus). A separate network card is not required unless multiple interfaces are needed or some other type of network is used. Newer motherboards may even have dual network (Ethernet) interfaces built-in.

The card implements the electronic circuitry required to communicate using a specific physical layer and data link layer standard such as Ethernet or token ring. This provides a base for a full network protocol stack, allowing communication among small groups of computers on the same LAN and large-scale network communications through routable protocols, such as IP. There are four techniques used to transfer data, the NIC may use one or more of these techniques.

- Polling is where the microprocessor examines the status of the peripheral under program control.
- Programmed I/O is where the microprocessor alerts the designated peripheral by applying its address to the system's address bus.
- Interrupt-driven I/O is where the peripheral alerts the microprocessor that it's ready to transfer data.
- DMA is where the intelligent peripheral assumes control of the system bus to access memory directly. This removes load from the CPU but requires a separate processor on the card.

A network card typically has a twisted pair, BNC, or AUI socket where the network cable is connected, and a few LEDs to inform the user of whether the network is active, and whether or not there is data being transmitted on it. The Network Cards are typically available in 10/

100/1000 Mbit/s(Mbit/s). This means they can support a transfer rate of 10 or 100 or 1000 Megabits per second.

Notable manufacturers

3Com

AEI Intelligent Technologies

AMD

ASIX Electronics

Belkin

Broadcom

Cisco

Digital Equipment Corporation (DEC)

Intel

Marvell Technology Group

National Semiconductor

Netgear

Novell

Realtek

VIA Networking.

Hubs

An **Ethernet hub** or **concentrator** is a device for connecting multiple twisted pair or fiber optic Ethernet devices together, making them act as a single segment. Hubs work at the physical layer (layer 1) of the OSI model. The device is thus a form of multiport repeater. Ethernet hubs are also responsible for forwarding a jam signal to all ports if it detects a collision.

Hubs also often come with a BNC and/or AUI connector to allow connection to legacy 10BASE2 or 10BASE5 network segments. The availability of low-priced Ethernet switches has largely rendered hubs obsolete but they are still seen in older installations and more specialist applications.

Technical information

A hubbed Ethernet network behaves like a shared-medium, that is, only one device can successfully transmit at a time and each host remains responsible for collision detection and retransmission. With 10BASE-T and 100BASE-T links (which generally account for most or all of the ports on a hub) there are separate pairs for transmit and receive but they are used in half duplex mode in which they still effectively behave like shared medium links. An Ethernet hub, or repeater, is a fairly unsophisticated broadcast device. Hubs do not manage any of the traffic that comes through them, and any packet entering any port is broadcast out on every other port (every port other than the port of entry). Since every packet is being sent out through every other port, packet collisions result—which greatly impedes the smooth flow of traffic.

The need for hosts to be able to detect collisions limits the number of hubs and the total size of the network. For 10 Mbit/s networks, up to 5 segments (4 hubs) are allowed between any two end stations. For 100 Mbit/s networks, the limit is reduced to 3 segments (2 hubs) between any two end stations, and even that is only allowed if the hubs are of the low delay variety.

Some hubs have special (and generally manufacturer specific) stack ports allowing them to be combined in a way that allows more hubs than simple chaining through Ethernet cables, but even so a large Fast Ethernet network is likely to require switches to avoid the chaining limits of hubs.

Most hubs detect typical problems, such as excessive collisions on individual ports, and *partition* the port, disconnecting it from the shared medium. Thus, hub-based Ethernet is generally more robust than coaxial cable-based Ethernet, where a misbehaving device can disable the entire segment. Even if not partitioned automatically, a hub makes troubleshooting easier because status lights can indicate the possible problem source or, as a last resort, devices can be disconnected from a hub one at a time much more easily than a coaxial cable. They also remove the need to troubleshoot faults on a huge cable with multiple taps.

Hub-based Ethernet is generally more robust than coaxial cable-based Ethernet

Dual speed hubs

In the early days of Fast Ethernet, Fast Ethernet switches were relatively expensive devices. However, hubs suffered from the problem that as simple repeaters they could only support a single speed. Whilst normal PCs with expansion slots could be easily upgraded to Fast Ethernet with a new network card, computers with less common expansion mechanisms, or no expansion bus at all, and other equipment, such as printers, could be expensive or impossible to upgrade.

Therefore, a compromise between a hub and a switch appeared known as a dual speed hub. These split the network into two segments, each acting like a hubbed network at its respective speed with a two-port switch between them. Therefore, they allowed mixing of the two speeds without the cost of a Fast Ethernet switch.

Usefulness

Historically, the main reason for purchasing hubs rather than switches was price. This has largely been eliminated by reductions in the price of switches, but hubs can still be useful in special circumstances:

- A protocol analyzer connected to a switch does not always receive all the desired packets since the switch separates the ports into different segments. Connecting the protocol analyzer to a hub allows it to see all the traffic on the segment. (Expensive switches can be configured to allow one port to listen in on traffic on another port. However, these cost much more than a hub.)
- Some computer clusters require each member computer to receive all of the traffic going to the cluster. A hub will do this naturally; using a switch requires implementing special tricks.
- When a switch is accessible for end users to make connections, for example, in a conference room, an inexperienced or careless user (or saboteur) can bring down the network by connecting two ports together, causing a loop. This can be prevented by using a hub, where a loop will break other users on the hub, but not the rest of the network. (It can also be prevented by buying switches that can detect and deal with loops, for example by implementing the Spanning Tree Protocol.)
- A cheap hub with a 10BASE2 port is probably the cheapest and easiest way to connect devices that only support 10BASE2 to a modern network (cheap switches don't tend to come with 10BASE2 ports). The same goes for linking in an old thicknet network segment using an AUI port on a hub (individual devices that were intended for thicknet can be linked to modern Ethernet by using an AUI-10BASE-T transceiver).

Repeaters

A **repeater** is an electronic device that receives a weak or low-level signal and retransmits it at a higher level or higher power, so that the signal can cover longer distances without degradation.

The term "repeater" originated with telegraphy and referred to an electromechanical device used to regenerate telegraph signals.

Use of the term has continued in telephony and data communications.In telecommunication, the term **repeater** has the following standardized meanings:

1. An analog device that amplifies an input signal regardless of its nature (analog or digital).
2. A digital device that amplifies, reshapes, retimes, or performs a combination of any of these functions on a digital input signal for retransmission.

Because repeaters work with the actual physical signal, and do not attempt to interpret the data being transmitted, they operate on the Physical layer, the first layer of the OSI model.

A digipeater is a blend meaning "digital repeater", particularly used in amateur radio. Digipeaters generally receive a transmission and then retransmit it on the same frequency, unlike repeaters that receive on one and transmit on another frequency.

Repeaters are often used in trans-continental and trans-oceanic cables, because the attenuation (signal loss) over such distances would be completely unacceptable without them. Repeaters are used in both copper-wire cables carrying electrical signals, and in fibre optics carrying light.

Repeaters are used in radio communication services. Radio repeaters often transmit and receive on different frequencies. A special subgroup of those repeaters is those used in amateur radio.

Repeaters are also used extensively in broadcasting, where they are known as translators or boosters.

When providing a point-to-point telecom link using radio beyond line of sight, one uses repeaters in a microwave radio relay. A reflector, often on a mountain top, that relays such signals around an obstacle, is called a **passive repeater.**

In optical communications the term **repeater** is used to describe a piece of equipment that receives an optical signal, converts that signal into an electrical one, regenerates it, and then retransmits an optical signal. Since such a device converts the optical signal into an electrical one, and then back to an optical signal, they are often known as Optical-Electrical-Optical (OEO) repeaters.

Before the invention of electronic amplifiers, mechanically coupled carbon microphones were used as amplifiers in telephone repeaters. The invention of the audion tube made transcontinental telephony practical. In the 1930s vacuum tube repeaters using hybrid coils became common place, allowing the use of thinner wires.

In the 1950s negative impedance gain devices were more popular, and a transistorized version called the E6 repeater was the final major type used in the Bell System before the low cost of digital transmission made all voice band repeaters obsolete.

Multiplexers

A **multiplexer** or **mux** (*occasionally the term* ***muldex*** *is also found, for a combination multiplexer-demultiplexer*) is a device that selects one of many data-sources and outputs that source into a single channel.

A demultiplexer (or demux) is a device taking a single input that selects one of many data-output-lines and connects the single input to the selected output line. A multiplexer is often used with a complementary demultiplexer on the receiving end.

In electronics, multiplexers function as multiple-input, single-output switches. A multiplexer has multiple inputs and a selector that connects a specific input to the single output. The schematic symbol for a multiplexer is an isosceles trapezoid with the longer parallel side containing the input pins and the short parallel side containing the output pin. The schematic on the right shows a 2-to-1 multiplexer on the left and an equivalent switch on the right. The *sel* wire connects the desired input to the output.

In digital signal processing (DSP), the multiplexer takes several separate digital data streams and combines them together into one data stream of a higher data rate. This allows multiple data streams to be carried from one place to another over one physical link, which saves cost.

Modes and Routers

Router is a computer networking device that buffers and forwards data packets across an internetwork toward their destinations, through a process known as routing. Routing occurs at layer 3 (the Network layer e.g. IP) of the OSI seven-layer protocol stack.

Router acts as a junction between two or more networks to buffer and transfer data packets among them. A router is different from a switch and a hub: a router is working on layer 3 of OSI model, a switch on layer 2 and a hub on layer 1. This makes them work for different situations: a switch connects devices to form a Local area network (LAN) (which might, in turn, be connected to *another* network via a router).

One easy illustration for the different functions of routers and switches is to think of switches as neighbourhood streets, and the router as the intersections with the street signs. Each house on the street has an address within a range on the block. In the same way, a switch connects various devices each with their own IP address(es) on a LAN. However, the switch knows nothing about IP addresses except its own management address. Routers connect networks together the way that on-ramps or major intersections connect streets to both highways and freeways, etc. The street signs at the intersection (routing table) show which way the packets need to flow.

So for example, a router at home connects the Internet Service Provider's (ISP) network (usually on an Internet address) together with the LAN in the home (typically using a range of private IP addresses, see network address translation) and a single broadcast domain. The switch connects devices together to form the LAN. Sometimes the switch and the router are combined together in one single package sold as a multiple port router.

In order to route packets, a router communicates with other routers using routing protocols and using this information creates and maintains a routing table. The routing table stores the best routes to certain network destinations, the "routing metrics" associated with those routes, and the path to the next hop router. See the routing article for a more detailed discussion of how this works.

Routing is most commonly associated with the Internet Protocol, although other less-popular routed protocols are in use.

History

The first Internet router was developed at BBN as part of their contract to build out the original Arpanet. The first multiprotocol router was created at Stanford University by a staff researcher named William Yeage in January of 1980. His boss at the time told him that he was the "network guy" and to find a way to connect the computers in the computer science department, medical center and department of electrical engineering. He first wrote a network operating system and routing code to run on a DEC PDP11/05. He used Alan Snyder's Portable C compiler but it generated too much code so he modified the compiler to improve the code generators.That still wasn't good enough so he wrote an optimizer for PDP11/05 assembler that reduced the code size further.

Types of routers

In the origin era of routing (from the mid-1970s through the 1980s), general-purpose mini-computers served as routers. Although general-purpose computers can perform routing, modern high-speed routers are highly specialized computers, generally with extra hardware added to accelerate both common routing functions such as packet forwarding and specialised functions such as IPsec encryption.

Other changes also improve reliability, such as using DC power rather than line power (which can be provided from batteries in data centers), and using solid-state rather than magnetic storage for program loading.

Large modern routers have thus come to resemble telephone switches, with whose technology they are currently converging and may eventually replace, whilst small routers have become a common household item.

A router that connects clients to the Internet is called an *edge router*. A router that serves solely to transmit data between other routers, e.g. inside the network of an Internet service provider, is called a *core router*.

A router is normally used to connect at least two networks, but a special variety of router is the one-armed router, used to route packets in a virtual LAN environment. In the case of a one-armed router, the multiple attachments to different networks are all over the same physical link.

In mobile ad-hoc networks every host performs routing and forwarding by itself, while in wired networks there is usually just one router for a whole broadcast domain.

26 Network Administration Security

Server Chief Technology and Server Management

Server (also called a server application) is “an application program that accepts connection in order to service requests by sending back responses.” (RFC 2616 (Hypertext Transfe Protocol — HTTP/1.1)) A server application can run on the same computer as the clier application using it, or they can connect through a computer network. Examples includ file server, database server, backup server, print server, mail server, web server, FTP serve application server, VPN server, DHCP server, DNS server, WINS server, logon serve security server, domain controller, backup domain controller, proxy server, firewall, etc.

Server is an adjective in the term server operating system.

A server operating system is *intended*, *enabled*, or *better able* to run server application The differences between the server version and the “workstation” version of an operatin system vary. Sometimes (as in the case of Windows 2000 and Windows 2000 Server the primary difference is the removal of arbitrary license-dependent limits on the number c network file share connections accepted. Some server editions include additional serve applications bundled with the operating system. Some server applications (e.g. Microso IIS) impose arbitrary limits on the number of HTTP connections they will accept, dependin on whether they are running under a server operating system or not.

A server computer (often called server for short) is a computer system that has been designated for running a specific server application or applications.

A computer that is designated for only one server application is often named for th application. For example, when Apache HTTP Server (software) is a company's web serve the computer running it is also called the web server. Server applications can be divide among server computers over an extreme range, depending upon the workload. Unde light loading, every server application can run concurrently on a single computer. Unde heavy loading, multiple server computers may be required for each application. Unde medium loading, it is common to use one server computer per server application, in orde to limit the amount of damage caused by failure of any single server computer or securit breach of any single server application. Any server computer can also be used as workstation, but it is avoided in practice, again to contain risk.

Server or server computer is also a designation for computer models intended for use running server applications, often under heavy workloads, unattended, for extended time. While any "workstation" computer can run server operating systems and server applications, a server computer usually has special features intended to make it more suitable. Distinctions often include faster processor and memory, more RAM, larger hard drives, higher reliability, redundant power supplies, redundant hard drives (RAID), compact size and shape, modular design (e.g., blade servers often used in server farms), rack or cabinet mountability, serial console redirection, etc.

The name server or server appliance also applies to network-connected computer appliances or "appliance hardware" that provides specific services onto the network. Though the appliance is a server computer, loaded with a server operating system and a server application, the user need not configure any of it. It is a black box that does a specific job. The simplest servers are most often sold as appliances, for example switches, routers, gateways, print servers, net modems.

Server Hardware

Although servers can be built from commodity computer components—particularly for low-load and/or non-critical applications—dedicated, high-load, mission-critical servers use specialized hardware that is optimized for the needs of servers.

For example, servers may incorporate "industrial-strength" mechanical components such as disk drives and fans that provide very high reliability and performance at a correspondingly high price. Aesthetic considerations are ignored, since most servers operate in unattended computer rooms and are only visited for maintenance or repair purposes. Although servers usually require large amounts of disk space, smaller disk drives may still be used in a trade-off of capacity vs. reliability.

CPU speeds are far less critical for many servers than they are for many desktops. Not only are typical server tasks likely to be delayed more by I/O requests than processor requirements, but the lack of any graphical user interface (GUI) in many servers frees up very large amounts of processing power for other tasks, making the overall processor power requirement lower. If a great deal of processing power is required in a server, there is a tendency to add more CPUs rather than increase the speed of a single CPU, again for reasons of reliability and redundancy.

The lack of a GUI in a server (or the rare need to use it) makes it unnecessary to install expensive video adapters. Similarly, elaborate audio interfaces, joystick connections, USB peripherals, and the like are usually unnecessary.

Because servers must operate continuously and reliably, noisy but efficient and trustworthy fans may be used for ventilation instead of inexpensive and quiet fans; and in some cases, centralized air-conditioning may be used to keep servers cool, instead of or in addition to fans. Special uninterruptible power supplies may be used to ensure that the servers continue to run in the event of a power failure.

ɔical servers include heavy-duty network connections in order to allow them to handle large amounts of traffic that they typically receive and generate as they receive and ly to client requests.

ə major difference between servers and desktop computers is not in the hardware but in software. Servers often run operating systems that are designed specifically for use in vers. They also run special applications that are designed specifically to carry out server ks.

rvers have a unique property where the more powerful and complex the system, the ger it takes for the hardware to turn on and begin loading the operating system. Servers ən do extensive pre-boot memory testing and verification, along with starting up remote nagement services. The hard drive controllers then start up banks of drives in sequence as not to overload the power supply with the sudden surge of everything turning on at ce, then followed by RAID system prechecks for correct operation of redundancy. It is uncommon for all these preboot hardware checks to take several minutes, but then for machine to run continuously for months at a time.

rver Operating Systems

ə Microsoft Windows operating system is predominant among desktop computers, but he world of servers, the most popular operating systems—such as FreeBSD, Solaris, d GNU/Linux—are derived from or similar to the UNIX operating system. UNIX was originally ninicomputer operating system, and as servers gradually replaced traditional nicomputers, UNIX was a logical and efficient choice of operating system for the servers.

rver-oriented operating systems tend to have certain features in common that make m more suitable for the server environment, such as the absence of a GUI (or an optional I); the ability to be reconfigured (in both hardware and software) to at least some extent hout stopping the system; advanced backup facilities to permit online backups of critical a at regular and frequent intervals; facilities to enable the movement of data between erent volumes or devices in such a way that is transparent to the end user; flexible and vanced networking capabilities; features (such as daemons in UNIX or services in ndows) that make unattended execution of programs more reliable; tight system security, h advanced user, resource, data, and memory protection, and so on.

Server-oriented operating systems in many cases can interact with hardware sensors to detect conditions such as overheating, processor and disk failure, and either alert an operator, take remedial action, or both, depending on the configuration.

cause the requirements of servers are, in some cases, almost diametrically opposed to se of desktop computers, it is extremely difficult to design an operating system that ndles both environments well; thus, operating systems that are well suited to the desktop y not be ideal for servers and vice versa. Nevertheless, certain versions of Windows also used on a minority of servers as are recent versions of the popular Mac OS X (which is Unix-based, and gives users complete access to the Unix operating syst family of desktop operating systems and even some proprietary mainframe opera systems (such as z/OS); but the dominant operating systems among servers contin to be UNIX versions or clones. Even in the case of GNU/Linux, a popular UNIX-like opera system frequently used on servers, configurations that are ideal for servers may unsatisfactory for desktop use, and configurations that perform well on the desktop leave much to be desired on servers.

The rise of the microprocessor-based server was facilitated by the development of sev versions of the Unix operating system to run on the Intel x86 microprocessor architect including Solaris, GNU/Linux and FreeBSD. The Microsoft Windows family of opera systems also runs on Intel hardware, and versions beginning with Windows NT h incorporated features making them suitable for use on servers.

Whilst the role of server and desktop operating systems remains distinct, improvemen both hardware performance and reliability and operating system reliability have blurred distinction between these two classes of system, which at one point remained lar separate in terms of code base, hardware and vendor providers. Today, many desktop server operating systems share the same code base, and differ chiefly in term configuration. Furthermore, the rationalisation of many corporate applications towards w based and middleware platforms has lessened the demand for specialist application serv

Servers on the Internet

Almost the entire structure of the Internet is based upon a client-server model. Many milli of servers are connected to the Internet and run continuously throughout the world.

Among the many services provided by Internet servers are: the Web; the Domain Na System; electronic mail; file transfer; instant messaging; streaming audio and video, or gaming, and countless others. Virtually every action taken by an ordinary Internet u requires one or more interactions with one or more servers.

There are also technologies that operate on an inter-server level.

Servers in Daily Life

Remember that any computer or device serving out applications or services can technic be called a server. In an office or enterprise environment, the network server is eas identify. However, if you are reading this, you probably have a server in your home. Y DSL/Cable router is a server as it provides your computer with application services s as assigning an IP address via Dynamic Host Configuration Protocol, DHCP), and Netw Address Translation (NAT) services which is the firewall that protects your computer f the internet.

Your iTunes software on your computer acts as your music server for your iPod. When share your printer or a folder on your computer, your computer suddenly becomes a ser It is these instances, often, that can cause security problems in homes. Your wire access point, if not secured properly, can also serve out your network connection to y ghbour who then can see the folder you shared out to your wife's computer with all the ncial information she needs to do your taxes. Hence why securing home networks has ome so important.

id Management and Mirroring

omputing, specifically computer storage, a Redundant Array of Independent Drives (or ks), also known as Redundant Array of Inexpensive Drives (or Disks) (RAID) is an rella term for data storage schemes that divide and/or replicate data among multiple d drives. They offer, depending on the scheme, increased data reliability and/or I/O formance.

st schemes are numbered and referred to as levels. RAID began as a collection of five h levels but has since grown to include many more, notably several nested levels and ny non-standard levels (mostly proprietary).

sic Functions

damentally, RAID combines multiple hard disks into a single logical unit. There are two s this can be done: in hardware and in software. Hardware combines the drives into a cal unit in dedicated hardware which then presents the drives as a single drive to the rating system. Software does this within the operating system and presents the drives a single drive to the users of the system.

RAID is typically used on servers but can be used on workstations. This is especially true in storage-intensive computers such as those used for video and audio editing.

story

man Ken Ouchi at IBM was awarded a 1978 U.S. patent 4,092.732 titled "System for overing data stored in failed memory unit." The claims for this patent describe what uld later be termed RAID 5 with full stripe writes. This 1978 patent also mentions that mirroring or duplexing (what would later be termed RAID 1) and protection with dedicated ity (that would later be termed RAID 4) were prior art at that time.

term RAID was first defined by David A. Patterson, Garth A. Gibson and Randy Katz at University of California, Berkeley in 1987. They studied the possibility of using two or re drives to appear as a single device to the host system and published a paper: "A se for Redundant Arrays of Inexpensive Disks (RAID)" in June 1988 at the SIGMOD ference.

s specification suggested a number of prototype "RAID levels", or combinations of drives. ch had theoretical advantages and disadvantages. Over the years, different lementations of the RAID concept have appeared. Most differ substantially from the inal idealized RAID levels, but the numbered names have remained. This can be confusing, since one implementation of RAID 5, for example, can differ substantially fr another. RAID 3 and RAID 4 are often confused and even used interchangeably.

Their paper formally defined RAID levels 1 through 5 in sections 7 to 11:

- "First Level RAID: Mirrored drives"
- "Second Level RAID: Hamming Code for Error Correction"
- "Third Level RAID: Single Check Disk Per Group"
- "Fourth Level RAID: Independent Reads and Writes"
- "Fifth Level RAID: Spread data/parity over all drives (no single check disk)"

RAID levels have been recently standarized by SNIA.

Standard RAID levels

A quick summary of the most commonly used RAID levels (N.B This summary assum you have your system partition on another disk i.e. Raid 5 Requires 3 Disks Min for RAIL 1 for System Partiton):

- RAID 0: Striped Set (2 disks minimum) without parity. Provides improv performance and additional storage but no fault tolerance from disk errors or d failure. Any disk failure destroys the array, which becomes more likely with m disks in the array. The reason a single disk failure destroys the entire array is becau when data is written to a RAID 0 drive, the data is broken into "fragments". T number of fragments is dictated by the number of disks in the drive. Each of the fragments are written to their respective disks simultaneously on the same sec This allows the entire chunk of data to be read off the drive in parallel, giving t type of arrangement huge bandwidth. When one sector on one of the disks fa though, the corresponding sector on every other disk is rendered useless becau part of the data is now corrupted. RAID 0 does not implement error checking so a error is unrecoverable. More disks in the drive means higher bandwidth, but grea risk of data loss.

- RAID 1: Mirrored Set (2 disks minimum) without parity. Provides fault toleran from disk errors and single disk failure. Increased read performance occurs wh using a multi-threaded operating system that supports split seeks, very sm performance reduction when writing. Array continues to operate so long as at le one drive is functioning.

- RAID 3 and RAID 4: Striped Set (3 disks minimum) with Dedicated Parity, the pa bits represent a memory location each, they have a value of 0 or 1, whether t given memory location is empty or full, thus enhancing the speed of read and wr Provides improved performance and fault tolerance similar to RAID 5, but wit dedicated parity disk rather than rotated parity stripes. The single disk is a bott neck for writing since every write requires updating the parity data. One minor ben is that the dedicated parity disk allows the parity drive to fail and operation will continue without parity or performance penalty.

- RAID 5: Striped Set (3 disks minimum) with Distributed Parity. Distributed parity requires all but one drive to be present to operate; drive failure requires replacement, but the array is not destroyed by a single drive failure. Upon drive failure, any subsequent reads can be calculated from the distributed parity such that the drive failure is masked from the end user. The array will have data loss in the event of a second drive failure and is vulnerable until the data that was on the failed drive is rebuilt onto a replacement drive.
- RAID 6: Striped Set (4 disks minimum) with Dual Distributed Parity. Provides fault tolerance from two drive failures; array continues to operate with up to two failed drives. This makes larger RAID groups more practical. This is becoming a popular choice for SATA drives as they approach 1 Terabyte in size. This is because the single parity RAID levels are vulnerable to data loss until the failed drive is rebuilt. The larger the drive, the longer the rebuild will take. With dual parity, it gives the array time to rebuild onto a large drive with the ability to sustain another drive failure.

Nested RAID levels

Many storage controllers allow RAID levels to be nested. That is, one RAID can use another as its basic element, instead of using physical drives. It is instructive to think of these arrays as layered on top of each other, with physical drives at the bottom.

Nested RAIDs are usually signified by joining the numbers indicating the RAID levels into a single number, sometimes with a '+' in between. For example, RAID 10 (or RAID 1+0) conceptually consists of multiple level 1 arrays stored on physical drives with a level 0 array on top, striped over the level 1 arrays. In the case of RAID 0+1, it is most often called RAID 0+1 as opposed to RAID 01 to avoid confusion with RAID 1. However, when the top array is a RAID 0 (such as in RAID 10 and RAID 50), most vendors choose to omit the '+', though RAID 5+0 is more informative.

Common nested RAID levels

- RAID 0+1: Striped Set + Mirrored Set (4 disks minimum; Even number of disks) provides fault tolerance and improved performance but increases complexity. The key difference from RAID 1+0 is that RAID 0+1 creates a second striped set to mirror a primary striped set. The Array continues to operate with one or more drives failed in the same mirror set, but if two or more drives fail on different sides of the mirroring, the data on the RAID system is lost.
- RAID 1+0: Mirrored Set + Striped Set (4 disks minimum; Even number of disks) provides fault tolerance and improved performance but increases complexity. The key difference from RAID 0+1 is that RAID 1+0 creates a striped set from a series of mirrored drives. The array can sustain multiple drive losses as long as no two drives lost comprise a single pair of one mirror.

- RAID 5+0: A stripe across distributed parity RAID systems.
- RAID 5+1: A mirror striped set with distributed parity (some manufacturers label this as RAID 53).

Non-standard RAID levels

Given the large amount of custom configurations available with a RAID array, many companies, organizations, and groups have created their own non-standard configurations, typically designed to meet at least one but usually very small niche groups of arrays. Most of these non-standard RAID levels are proprietary.

Some of the more prominent modifications are:

- ATTO Technology's DVRAID™ adds parity RAID protection to systems which demand performance for 4K film, 2K film, high-definition audio and video.
- The Storage Computer Corporation uses RAID 7, which adds caching to RAID 3 and RAID 4 to improve performance.
- EMC Corporation offers RAID S as an alternative to RAID 5 on their Symmetrix systems.
- RAID-Z in the zfs file system of Open Solaris solves the "write hole" problem of RAID-5.

RAID Implementations

Hardware and/or software RAID based solutions: The distribution of data across multiple drives can be managed either by dedicated hardware or by software. Additionally, there are hybrid RAIDs that are partially software and hardware-based solutions.

Software RAID

Software implementations are provided by most operating systems. A software layer sits above the (generally block based) disk device drivers and provides an abstraction layer between the logical drives (RAID arrays) and physical drives. Software RAID is typically limited to RAID 0 (striping across multiple drives for increased space and performance), RAID 1 (mirroring two drives) and RAID 5 (data striping with parity).

In a multi-threaded operating system (such as Linux, FreeBSD, Mac OS X, Windows NT/2000/XP/Vista and Novell NetWare) the operating system can perform overlapped I/O, allowing multiple read or write requests to be initiated without waiting for completion on each request. This is the capability that makes RAID 0/1 possible in an operating system. However, most operating systems do not support RAID 0/1 striping or mirroring with parity, due to the substantial processing demands of calculating parity.

Software implementations require some very small amount of processing time, which is provided by the main CPU in the host system. Since SCSI, PATA, and SATA drives all support asynchronous read/write, any multi-threaded operating system can support non-parity RAID on multiple hard drives with only a one percent increase in CPU overhead.

Software implementations can exceed the performance levels of hardware-based RAID due to the high-performance of modern CPUs[citation needed]. Since the software must run on a host server attached to storage, the processor (as mentioned above) on that host must dedicate processing time to run the RAID software. Like hardware-based RAID, if the server experiences a hardware failure, the attached storage could be inaccessible for a period of time.

Software implementations can allow RAID arrays to be created from partitions rather than entire physical drives.

Hardware RAID

A hardware implementation of RAID requires at a minimum a special-purpose RAID controller. On a desktop system, this may be a PCI expansion card, or might be a capability built in to the motherboard. In industrial applications the controller and drives are provided as a stand alone enclosure. The drives may be IDE/ATA, SATA, SCSI, SSA, Fibre Channel, or any combination thereof. The using system can be directly attached to the controller or, more commonly, connected via a SAN. The controller hardware handles the management of the drives, and performs any parity calculations required by the chosen RAID level.

Most hardware implementations provide a non-volatile read/write cache which, depending on the I/O workload, will improve performance. Cached RAID controllers are most commonly used in industrial applications.

Hardware implementations provide guaranteed performance, add no overhead to the local CPU complex and can support many operating systems, as the controller simply presents a logical disk to the operating system.

Hardware implementations also typically support hot swapping, allowing failed drives to be replaced while the system is running.

Hybrid RAID

Hybrid RAID implementations have become very popular with the introduction of inexpensive RAID controllers, implemented using a standard disk controller and then implementing the RAID in the controllers BIOS extension (for early boot-up/real mode operation) and the operating system driver (for after the system switches to protected mode). Since these controllers actually do all calculations typically proprietary to a given RAID controller manufacturer and typically cannot span multiple controllers. The only advantages over software RAID are that the BIOS can boot from them, and the tighter integration with the device driver may offer better error handling.

Both hardware and software implementations may support the use of hot spare drives, a pre-installed drive which is used to immediately (and almost always automatically) replace a drive that has failed. This reduces the mean time to repair period during which a second drive failure in the same RAID redundancy group can result in loss of data. It also prevents data loss when multiple drives fail in a short period of time, as is common when all drives in an array have undergone very similar use patterns, and experience wear-out failures.

Reliability of RAID configurations

Failure Rate

The mean time to failure (MTTF) or the mean time between failure (MTBF) of a given RAID may be lower or higher than those of its constituent hard drives, depending on what type of RAID is employed.

Mean Time to Data Loss (MTTDL)

In this context, the average time before a loss of data in a given array.

Mean Time to Recovery (MTTR)

In arrays that include redundancy for reliability, this is the time following a failure to restore an array to its normal failure-tolerant mode of operation. This includes time to replace a failed disk mechanism as well as time to re-build the array (i.e. to replicate data for redundancy).

Unrecoverable Bit Error Rate (UBE)

This is the rate at which a disk drive will be unable to recover data after application of cyclic redundancy check (CRC) codes and multiple retries. This failure will present as a sector read failure. Some RAID implementations protect against this failure mode by remapping the bad sector, using the redundant data to retrieve a good copy of the data, and rewriting that good data to the newly mapped replacement sector. The UBE rate is typically specified at 1 bit in 1015 for enterprise class disk drives (SCSI, FC, SAS) , and 1 bit in 1014 for desktop class disk drives (IDE, ATA, SATA). Increasing disk capacities and large RAID 5 redundancy groups have led to an increasing inability to successfully rebuild a RAID group after a disk failure because an unrecoverable sector is found on the remaining drives. Double protection schemes such as RAID 6 are attempting to address this issue, but suffer from a very high write penalty.

Atomic Write Failure

Also known by various terms such as torn writes, torn pages, incomplete writes, interrupted writes, non-transactional, etc. This is a little understood and rarely mentioned failure mode for redundant storage systems that do not utilize transactional features. Database researcher Jim Gray wrote “Update in Place is a Poison Apple” during the early days of relational database commercialization. However, this warning largely went unheeded and fell by the wayside upon the advent of RAID, which many software engineers mistook as solving all data storage integrity and reliability problems. Many software programs update a storage object “in-place”; that is, they write a new version of the object on to the same disk addresses as the old version of the object. While the software may also log some delta information elsewhere, it expects the storage to present “atomic write semantics,” meaning that the write of the data either occurred in its entirety or did not occur at all.

However, very few storage systems provide support for atomic writes, and even fewer specify their rate of failure in providing this semantic. Note that during the act of writing an object, a RAID storage device will usually be writing all redundant copies of the object in parallel, although overlapped or staggered writes are more common when a single RAID processor is responsible for multiple drives. Hence an error that occurs during the process of writing may leave the redundant copies in different states, and furthermore may leave the copies in neither the old nor the new state. The little known failure mode is that delta logging relies on the original data being either in the old or the new state so as to enable backing out the logical change, yet few storage systems provide an atomic write semantic on a RAID disk.

Since transactional support is not universally present in hardware RAID, many operating systems include transactional support to protect against data loss during an interrupted write.

Novell Netware, starting with version 3.x, included a transaction tracking system. Microsoft introduced transaction tracking via the journalling feature in NTFS.

To mitigate this problem, some high-end RAID cards use a battery-backed write cache. If an "atomic" write only partially completes because of power failure, the controller flushed the unwritten data to disk when the power is restored. Some provide the capability of testing the battery periodically (however, this leaves the system without a fully charged battery for several hours). This solution still has potential failure cases: the battery may have worn out, the power may be off for too long, the disks could be moved to another controller, the controller itself could fail in the middle of a write, etc. However, on a well-maintained machine it probably prevents corruption in most incidents.

Hauffman Code and Cryptography

Cryptography is the study of message secrecy. In modern times, cryptography is considered to be a branch of both mathematics and computer science, and is affiliated closely with information theory, computer security, and engineering. Cryptography is used in many applications encountered in everyday life; examples include the security of ATM cards, computer passwords, and electronic commerce, all of which depend on cryptography.

Terminology

Until modern times, cryptography referred almost exclusively to encryption, the process of converting ordinary information (plaintext) into unintelligible gibberish (ie, ciphertext). Decryption is the reverse, moving from unintelligible ciphertext to plaintext. A cipher (or cypher) is a pair of algorithms which perform this encryption and the reversing decryption. The detailed operation of a cipher is controlled both by the algorithm and, in each instance, by a key. This is a secret parameter (known only to the communicants) for a specific message exchange context. Keys are important as ciphers without variable keys are trivially breakable and so rather less than useful for most purposes. Historically, ciphers were often used directly for encryption or decryption, without additional procedures such as authentication or integrity checks.

In colloquial use, the term "code" is often used to mean any method of encryption or concealment of meaning. However, in cryptography, code has a more specific meaning; it means the replacement of a unit of plaintext (i.e., a meaningful word or phrase) with a code word (for example, apple pie replaces attack at dawn). Codes are no longer used in serious cryptography—except incidentally for such things as unit designations (eg, 'Bronco Flight' or Operation Overlord) — since properly chosen ciphers are both more practical and more secure than even the best codes, and better adapted to computers as well.

Some use the English terms cryptography and cryptology interchangeably, while others use cryptography to refer to the use and practice of cryptographic techniques, and cryptology to refer to the subject as a field of study. In this respect, English usage is more tolerant of overlapping meanings and word origins than are several European languages in which meanings of cognate words are more restricted.

History of Cryptography and Cryptanalysis

The Ancient Greek scytale probably much like this modern reconstruction, may have been one of the earliest devices used to implement a cipher.

Before the modern era, cryptography was concerned solely with message confidentiality (i.e., encryption) — conversion of messages from a comprehensible form into an incomprehensible one, and back again at the other end, rendering it unreadable by interceptors or eavesdroppers without secret knowledge (namely, the key needed for decryption of that message). In recent decades, the field has expanded beyond confidentiality concerns to include techniques for message integrity checking, sender/receiver identity authentication, digital signatures, interactive proofs, and secure computation, amongst others.

The earliest forms of secret writing required little more than local pen and paper analogs, as most people could not read. More literacy, or opponent literacy, required actual cryptography. The main classical cipher types are transposition ciphers, which rearrange the order of letters in a message (e.g. 'help me' becomes 'ehpl em' in a trivially simple rearrangement scheme), and substitution ciphers, which systematically replace letters or groups of letters with other letters or groups of letters (e.g., 'fly at once' becomes 'gmz bu podf' by replacing each letter with the one following it in the alphabet). Simple versions of either offered little confidentiality from enterprising opponents, and still don't.

The Enigma machine, used in several variants by the German military between the late 1920s and the end of World War II, implemented a complex electro-mechanical polyalphabetic cipher to protect sensitive communications. Breaking the Enigma cipher at the Biuro Szyfrów, and the subsequent large-scale decryption of Enigma traffic at Bletchley Park, was an important factor contributing to the Allied victory in WWII.

Although frequency analysis is a powerful and general technique, encryption was still often effective in practice; many a would-be cryptanalyst was unaware of the technique. Breaking a message without frequency analysis essentially required knowledge of the cipher used, thus encouraging espionage, bribery, burglary, defection, etc. to discover it. It was finally recognized in the 19th century that secrecy of a cipher's algorithm is not a sensible or practical safeguard; in fact, any adequate cryptographic scheme (including ciphers) should remain secure even if the adversary knows the cipher algorithm itself. Secrecy of the key should alone be sufficient for confidentiality when under attack — for good ciphers. This fundamental principle was first explicitly stated in 1883 by Auguste Kerckhoffs and is generally called Kerckhoffs' principle; alternatively and more bluntly, it was restated by Claude Shannon as Shannon's Maxim — 'the enemy knows the system'.

Various physical devices and aids have been used to assist with ciphers. One of the earliest may have been the scytale of ancient Greece, a rod supposedly used by the Spartans as an aid for a transposition cipher. In medieval times, other aids were invented such as the cipher grille, also used for a kind of steganography. With the invention of polyalphabetic ciphers came more sophisticated aids such as Alberti's own cipher disk, Johannes Trithemius' tabula recta scheme, and Thomas Jefferson's multi-cylinder (invented independently by Bazeries around 1900). Early in the 20th century, several mechanical encryption/decryption devices were invented, and many patented, including rotor machines — most famously the Enigma machine used by Germany in World War II. The ciphers implemented by better quality examples of these designs brought about a substantial increase in cryptanalytic difficulty after WWI.

The development of digital computers and electronics after WWII made possible much more complex ciphers.

Furthermore, computers allowed for the encryption of any kind of data that is represented by computers in any binary format, unlike classical ciphers which only encrypted written language texts, dissolving the utility of a linguistic approach to cryptanalysis in many cases. Many computer ciphers can be characterized by their operation on binary bit sequences (sometimes in groups or blocks), unlike classical and mechanical schemes, which generally manipulate traditional characters (i.e., letters and digits) directly.

However, computers have also assisted cryptanalysis, which has compensated to some extent for increased cipher complexity. Nonetheless, good modern ciphers have stayed ahead of cryptanalysis; it is usually the case that use of a quality cipher is very efficient (i.e., fast and requiring few resources), while breaking it requires an effort many orders of magnitude larger, making cryptanalysis so inefficient and impractical as to be effectively impossible. A credit card with smart card capabilities. The 3 by 5 mm chip embedded in the card is shown enlarged in the insert. Smart cards attempt to combine portability with the power to compute modern cryptographic algorithms.

Extensive open academic research into cryptography is relatively recent — it began only in the mid-1970s with the public specification of DES (the Data Encryption Standard) by the NBS, the Diffie-Hellman paper, and the public release of the RSA algorithm. Since then, cryptography has become a widely used tool in communications, computer networks, and computer security generally. The present security level of many modern cryptographic techniques is based on the difficulty of certain computational problems, such as the integer factorisation problem or the discrete logarithm problem. In many cases, there are proofs that cryptographic techniques are secure if a certain computational problem cannot be solved efficiently.With one notable exception—the one-time pad—these proofs are contingent, and thus not definitive, but are currently the best available for cryptographic algorithms and protocols.

As well as being aware of cryptographic history, cryptographic algorithm and system designers must also sensibly consider probable future developments in their designs. For instance, the continued improvements in computer processing power have increased the scope of brute-force attacks when specifying key lengths. The potential effects of quantum computing are already being considered by some cryptographic system designers; the announced imminence of small implementations of these machines is making the need for this pre-emptive caution fully explicit.

Essentially, prior to the early 20th century, cryptography was chiefly concerned with linguistic patterns. Since then the emphasis has shifted, and cryptography now makes extensive use of mathematics, including aspects of information theory, computational complexity, statistics, combinatorics, abstract algebra, and number theory. Cryptography is also a branch of engineering, but an unusual one as it deals with active, intelligent, and malevolent opposition most other kinds of engineering need deal only with neutral natural forces. There is also active research examining the relationship between cryptographic problems and quantum physics.

Modern Cryptography

The modern field of cryptography can be divided into several areas of study. The chief ones are discussed here;

Symmetric-key Cryptography

Symmetric-key cryptography refers to encryption methods in which both the sender and receiver share the same key (or, less commonly, in which their keys are different, but related in an easily computable way). This was the only kind of encryption publicly known until 1976.

One round (out of 8.5) of the patented IDEA cipher, used in some versions of PGP for high-speed encryption of, for instance, e-mail.

The modern study of symmetric-key ciphers relates mainly to the study of block ciphers and stream ciphers and to their applications. A block cipher is, in a sense, a modern embodiment of Alberti's polyalphabetic cipher: block ciphers take as input a block of plaintext and a key, and output a block of ciphertext of the same size. Since messages are almost always longer than a single block, some method of knitting together successive blocks is required. Several have been developed, some with better security in one aspect or another than others. They are the mode of operations and must be carefully considered when using a block cipher in a cryptosystem.

The Data Encryption Standard (DES) and the Advanced Encryption Standard (AES) are block cipher designs which have been designated cryptography standards by the US government (though DES's designation was finally withdrawn after the AES was adopted). Despite its deprecation as an official standard, DES (especially its still-approved and much more secure triple-DES variant) remains quite popular; it is used across a wide range of applications, from ATM encryption to e-mail privacy and secure remote access. Many other block ciphers have been designed and released, with considerable variation in quality. Many have been thoroughly broken.

Stream ciphers, in contrast to the 'block' type, create an arbitrarily long stream of key material, which is combined with the plaintext bit-by-bit or character-by-character, somewhat like the one-time pad. In a stream cipher, the output stream is created based on an internal state which changes as the cipher operates. That state's change is controlled by the key, and, in some stream ciphers, by the plaintext stream as well. RC4 is an example of a well-known stream cipher.

Cryptographic hash functions (often called message digest functions) do not use keys, but are a related and important class of cryptographic algorithms. They take input data (often an entire message), and output a short, fixed length hash, and do so as a one-way function. For good ones, collisions (two plaintexts which produce the same hash) are extremely difficult to find.

Message authentication codes (MACs) are much like cryptographic hash functions, except that a secret key is used to authenticate the hash value on receipt.

Public-key Cryptography

Symmetric-key cryptosystems typically use the same key for encryption and decryption, though this message or group of messages may have a different key than others. A significant disadvantage of symmetric ciphers is the key management necessary to use them securely. Each distinct pair of communicating parties must, ideally, share a different key, and perhaps each ciphertext exchanged as well. The number of keys required increases as the square of the number of network members, which very quickly requires complex key management schemes to keep them all straight and secret. The difficulty of establishing a secret key between two communicating parties, when a secure channel doesn't already exist between them, also presents a chicken-and-egg problem which is a considerable practical obstacle for cryptography users in the real world.

In addition to encryption, public-key cryptography can be used to implement digital signature schemes.

A digital signature is reminiscent of an ordinary signature; they both have the characteristic that they are easy for a user to produce, but difficult for anyone else to forge. Digital signatures can also be permanently tied to the content of the message being signed; they cannot be 'moved' from one document to another, for any attempt will be detectable. In digital signature schemes, there are two algorithms: one for signing, in which a secret key is used to process the message (or a hash of the message, or both), and one for verification, in which the matching public key is used with the message to check the validity of the signature. RSA and DSA are two of the most popular digital signature schemes. Digital signatures are central to the operation of public key infrastructures and many network security schemes (SSL/TLS, many VPNs, etc).

Public-key algorithms are most often based on the computational complexity of "hard" problems, often from number theory. For example, the hardness of RSA is related to the integer factorization problem, while Diffie-Hellman and DSA are related to the discrete logarithm problem. More recently, elliptic curve cryptography has developed in which security is based on number of theoretic problems involving elliptic curves. Because of the difficulty of the underlying problems, most public-key algorithms involve operations such as modular multiplication and exponentiation, which are much more computationally expensive than the techniques used in most block ciphers, especially with typical key sizes.

As a result, public-key cryptosystems are commonly hybrid cryptosystems, in which a fast high-quality symmetric-key encryption algorithm is used for the message itself, while the relevant symmetric key is sent with the message, but encrypted using a public-key algorithm. Similarly, hybrid signature schemes are often used, in which a cryptographic hash function is computed, and only the resulting hash is digitally signed.

Cryptanalysis

The goal of cryptanalysis is to find some weakness or insecurity in a cryptographic scheme, thus permitting its subversion or evasion. Cryptanalysis might be undertaken by a malicious attacker, attempting to subvert a system, or by the system's designer (or others) attempting to evaluate whether a system has vulnerabilities, and so it is not inherently a hostile act. In modern practice, however, cryptographic algorithms and protocols must be carefully examined and tested to offer any assurance of the system's security (at least, under clear — and hopefully reasonable — assumptions).

There are a wide variety of cryptanalytic attacks, and they can be classified in any of several ways. A common distinction turns on what an attacker knows and what capabilities are available. In a ciphertext-only attack, the cryptanalyst has access only to the ciphertext (good modern cryptosystems are usually effectively immune to ciphertext-only attacks). In a known-plaintext attack, the cryptanalyst has access to a ciphertext and its corresponding plaintext (or to many such pairs). In a chosen-plaintext attack, the cryptanalyst may choose a plaintext and learn its corresponding ciphertext (perhaps many times); an example is gardening, used by the British during WWII. Finally, in a chosen-ciphertext attack, the cryptanalyst may choose ciphertexts and learn their corresponding plaintexts. Also important, often overwhelmingly so, are mistakes (generally in the design or use of one of the protocols) involved;

Cryptanalysis of symmetric-key ciphers typically involves looking for attacks against the block ciphers or stream ciphers that are more efficient than any attack that could be against a perfect cipher. For example, a simple brute force attack against DES requires one known plaintext and 255 decryptions, trying approximately half of the possible keys, to reach a point at which chances are better than even the key sought will have been found. But this may not be enough assurance; a linear cryptanalysis attack against DES requires 243 known plaintexts and approximately 243 DES operations. This is a considerable improvement on brute force attacks.

Public-key algorithms are based on the computational difficulty of various problems. The most famous of these is integer factorization (eg, the RSA algorithm is based on a problem related to factoring), but the discrete logarithm problem is also important. Much public-key cryptanalysis concerns numerical algorithms for solving these computational problems, or some of them, efficiently. For instance, the best known algorithms for solving the elliptic curve-based version of discrete logarithm are much more time-consuming than the best known algorithms for factoring, at least for problems of more or less equivalent size. Thus, other things being equal, to achieve an equivalent strength of attack resistance, factoring-based encryption techniques must use larger keys than elliptic curve techniques. For this reason, public-key cryptosystems based on elliptic curves have become popular since their invention in the mid-1990s.

While pure cryptanalysis uses weaknesses in the algorithms themselves, other attacks on cryptosystems are based on actual use of the algorithms in real devices, and are called side-channel attacks. If a cryptanalyst has access to, say, the amount of time the device took to encrypt a number of plaintexts or report an error in a password or PIN character, he may be able to use a timing attack to break a cipher that is otherwise resistant to analysis. An attacker might also study the pattern and length of messages to derive valuable information; this is known as traffic analysis,and can be quite useful to an alert adversary. And, of course, social engineering, and other attacks against the personnel who work with cryptosystems or the messages they handle (e.g., bribery, extortion, blackmail, espionage, ...) may be the most productive attacks of all.

Cryptographic Primitives

Unsolved problems in computer science: One-way functions are functions that are easy to compute but hard to invert. Can one-way functions be proved to exist?

Much of the theoretical work in cryptography concerns cryptographic primitives — algorithms with basic cryptographic properties — and their relationship to other cryptographic problems. For example, a one-way function is a function intended to be easy to compute but hard to invert. In a very general sense, for any cryptographic application to be secure (if based on such computational feasibility assumptions), one-way functions must exist. However, if one-way functions exist, this implies that $P \neq NP$. Since the P versus NP problem is currently unsolved, we don't know if one-way functions really do exist. For instance, if one-way functions exist, then secure pseudorandom generators and secure pseudorandom functions exist.

Currently known cryptographic primitives provide only basic functionality. These are usually noted as confidentiality, message integrity, authentication, and non-repudiation. Any other functionality in a cryptosystem must be built in using combinations of these algorithms and assorted protocols. Such combinations are called cryptosystems and it is they which users will encounter. Examples include PGP and its variants, SSH, SSL/TLS, all PKIs, digital signatures, etc

Other cryptographic primitives include the encryption algorithms themselves, one-way permutations, trapdoor permutations, etc.

Cryptographic Protocols

In many cases, cryptographic techniques involve back and forth communication among two or more parties in space (eg, between the home office and a branch office) or across time (e.g., cryptographically protected backup data). The term cryptographic protocol captures this general idea.

Cryptographic protocols have been developed for a wide range of problems, including relatively simple ones like interactive proofs, secret sharing, and zero-knowledge, and much more complex ones like electronic cash and secure multiparty computation.

When the security of a good cryptographic system fails, it is rare that the vulnerability leading to the breach will have been in a quality cryptographic primitive. Instead, weaknesses are often mistakes in the protocol design (often due to inadequate design procedures, or less than thoroughly informed designers), in the implementation (e.g., a software bug), in a failure of the assumptions on which the design was based (e.g., proper training of those who will be using the system), or some other human error. Many cryptographic protocols have been designed and analyzed using ad hoc methods, but they rarely have any proof of security. Methods for formally analyzing the security of protocols, based on techniques from mathematical logic and more recently from concrete security principles, have been the subject of research for the past few decades. Unfortunately, to date these tools have been cumbersome and are not widely used for complex designs.

The study of how best to implement and integrate cryptography in applications is itself a distinct field.

27 Wireless Networking

Basics of Wireless LAN

A wireless LAN or WLAN is a wireless local area network, which is the linking of two or more computers without using wires. WLAN utilizes spread-spectrum or OFDM (802.11a) modulation technology based on radio waves to enable communication between devices in a limited area, also known as the basic service set. This gives users the mobility to move around within a broad coverage area and still be connected to the network.

For the home user, wireless has become popular due to ease of installation, and location freedom with the gaining popularity of laptops. Public businesses such as coffee shops or malls have begun to offer wireless access to their customers; some are even provided as a free service. Large wireless network projects are being put up in many major cities. Google is even providing a free service to Mountain View, California and has entered a bid to do the same for San Francisco. New York City has also begun a pilot program to cover all five boroughs of the city with wireless Internet access.

History

In 1970 University of Hawaii, under the leadership of Norman Abramson, developed the world's first computer communication network using low-cost ham-like radios, named ALOHAnet.

The bi-directional star topology of the system included seven computers deployed over four islands to communicate with the central computer on the Oahu Island without using phone lines.

"In 1979, F.R. Gfeller and U. Bapst published a paper in the IEEE Proceedings reporting an experimental wireless local area network using diffused infrared communications. Shortly thereafter, in 1980, P. Ferrert reported on an experimental application of a single code spread spectrum radio for wireless terminal communications in the IEEE National Telecommunications Conference. In 1984, a comparison between Infrared and CDMA spread spectrum communications for wireless office information networks was published by Kaveh Pahlavan in IEEE Computer Networking Symposium which appeared later in the IEEE Communication Society Magazine. In May 1985, the efforts of Marcus led the FCC to announce experimental ISM bands for commercial application of spread spectrum technology. Later on, M. Kavehrad reported on an experimental wireless PBX system using code division multiple access. These efforts prompted significant industrial activities in the development of a new generation of wireless local area networks and it updated several old discussion in the portable and mobile radio industry.

The first generation of wireless data modems was developed in the early 1980's by amateur communication groups. They added a voice band data communication modem, with data rates below 9600 bit/s, to an existing short distance radio system such as a walkie talkie. The second generation of wireless modems was developed immediately after the FCC announcement in the experimental bands for non-military use of the spread spectrum technology. These modems provided data rates on the order of hundreds of kbit/s. The third generation of wireless modem then aimed at compatibility with the existing LANs with data rates on the order of Mbit/s. Several companies developed the third generation products with data rates above 1 Mbit/s and a couple of products had already been announced by the time of the first IEEE Workshop on Wireless LANs."

The first of the IEEE Workshops on Wireless LAN was held in 1991. At that time early wireless LAN products had just appeared in the market and the IEEE 802.11 committee had just started its activities to develop a standard for wireless LANs. The focus of that first workshop was evaluation of the alternative technologies. By 1996, the technology was relatively mature, a variety of applications had been identified and addressed and technologies that enable these applications were well understood. Chip sets aimed at wireless LAN implementations and applications, a key enabling technology for rapid market growth, were emerging in the market. Wireless LANs were being used in hospitals, stock exchanges, and other in building and campus settings for nomadic access, point-to-point LAN bridges, ad-hoc networking, and even larger applications through internetworking. The IEEE 802.11 standard and variants and alternatives, such as the wireless LAN interoperability forum and the European HIPERLAN specification had made rapid progress, and the unlicensed PCS [Unlicensed Personal Communications Services] and the proposed SUPERNet [,later on renamed as UNII,] bands also presented new opportunities."

On July 21, 1999, AirPort debuted at the Macworld Expo in New York City with Steve Jobs picking up an iBook supposedly to give the cameraman a better shot as he surfed the Web. Applause quickly built as people realized there were no wires. This was the first time Wireless LAN became publicly available at consumer pricing and easily available for home use. Before the release of the Airport, Wireless LAN was too expensive for consumer use and used exclusively in large corporate settings.

Originally WLAN hardware was so expensive that it was only used as an alternative to cabled LAN in places where cabling was difficult or impossible.

Early development included industry-specific solutions and proprietary protocols, but at the end of the 1990s these were replaced by standards, primarily the various versions of IEEE 802.11 (Wi-Fi). An alternative ATM-like 5 GHz standardized technology, HIPERLAN has so far not succeeded in the market, and with the release of the faster 54 Mbit/s 802.11a (5 GHz) and 802.11g (2.4 GHz) standards, almost certainly never will.

In November 2006, the Australian Commonwealth Scientific and Industrial Research Organisation (CSIRO) won a legal battle in the US federal court of Texas against Buffalo Technology which found the US manufacturer had failed to pay royalties on a US WLAN patent CSIRO had filed in 1996. CSIRO are currently engaged in legal cases with computer companies including Microsoft, Intel, Dell, Hewlett-Packard and Netgear which argue that the patent is invalid and should negate any royalties paid to CSIRO for WLAN-based products.

Benefits

The popularity of wireless LANs is a testament primarily to their convenience, cost efficiency, and ease of integration with other networks and network components. The majority of computers sold to consumers today come pre-equipped with all necessary wireless LAN technology. The benefits of wireless LANs include:

- **Convenience**: The wireless nature of such networks allows users to access network resources from nearly any convenient location within their primary networking environment (home or office). With the increasing saturation of laptop-style computers, this is particularly relevant.
- **Mobility**: With the emergence of public wireless networks, users can access the internet even outside their normal work environment. Most chain coffee shops, for example, offer their customers a wireless connection to the internet at little or no cost.
- **Productivity**: Users connected to a wireless network can maintain a nearly constant affiliation with their desired network as they move from place to place. For a business, this implies that an employee can potentially be more productive as his or her work can be accomplished from any convenient location.
- **Deployment**: Initial setup of an infrastructure-based wireless network requires little more than a single access point. Wired networks, on the other hand, have the additional cost and complexity of actual physical cables being run to numerous locations (which can even be impossible for hard-to-reach locations within a building).
- **Expandability**: Wireless networks can serve a suddenly-increased number of clients with the existing equipment. In a wired network, additional clients would require additional wiring.
- **Cost**: Wireless networking hardware is at worst a modest increase from wired counterparts. This potentially increased cost is almost always more than outweighed by the savings in cost and labour associated to running physical cables.

Disadvantages

Wireless LAN technology, while replete with the conveniences and advantages described above, has its share of downfalls. For a given networking situation, wireless LANs may not be desirable for a number of reasons. Most of these have to do with the inherent limitations of the technology.

- **Security**: Wireless LAN transceivers are designed to serve computers throughout a structure with uninterrupted service using radio frequencies. Because of space and cost, the antennas typically present on wireless networking cards in the end computers are generally relatively poor. In order to properly receive signals using such limited antennas throughout even a modest area, the wireless LAN transceiver utilizes a fairly considerable amount of power. What this means is that not only can the wireless packets be intercepted by a nearby adversary's poorly-equipped computer, but more importantly, a user willing to spend a small amount of money on a good quality antenna can pick up packets at a remarkable distance; perhaps hundreds of times the radius as the typical user. In fact, there are even computer users dedicated to locating and sometimes even hacking into wireless networks, known as wardrivers. On a wired network, any adversary would first have to overcome the physical limitation of tapping into the actual wires, but this is not an issue with wireless packets. To combat this consideration, wireless networks users usually choose to utilize various encryption technologies available such as Wi-Fi Protected Access (WPA). Some of the more older encryption methods, such as WEP are known to have weaknesses that a dedicated adversary can compromise.
- **Range**: The typical range of a common 802.11g network with standard equipment is on the order of tens of meters. While sufficient for a typical home, it will be insufficient in a larger structure. To obtain additional range, repeaters or additional access points will have to be purchased. Costs for these items can add up quickly. Other technologies are in the development phase, however, which feature increased range, hoping to render this disadvantage irrelevant.
- **Reliability**: Like any radio frequency transmission, wireless networking signals are subject to a wide variety of interference, as well as complex propagation effects (such as multipath, or especially in this case Rician fading) that are beyond the control of the network administrator. In the case of typical networks, modulation is achieved by complicated forms of phase-shift keying (PSK) or quadrature amplitude modulation (QAM), making interference and propagation effects all the more disturbing. As a result, important network resources such as servers are rarely connected wirelessly.
- **Speed**: The speed on most wireless networks (typically 1-108 Mbit/s) is reasonably slow compared to the slowest common wired networks (100 Mbit/s up to several Gbit/s). There are also performance issues caused by TCP and its built-in congestion avoidance. For most users, however, this observation is irrelevant since the speed bottleneck is not in the wireless routing but rather in the outside network connectivity itself. For example, the maximum ADSL throughput (usually 8 Mbit/s or less) offered by telecommunications companies to general-purpose customers is already far slower than the slowest wireless network to which it is typically connected. That is to say, in most environments, a wireless network running at its slowest speed is still faster than the internet connection serving it in the first place. However, in specialized environments, the throughput of a wired network might be necessary.

Newer standards such as 802.11n are addressing this limitation and will support peak throughputs in the range of 100-200 Mbit/s.

Architecture

Stations

All components that can connect into a wireless medium in a network are referred to as stations. All stations are equipped with wireless network interface cards (WNICs). Wireless stations fall into one of two categories: access points and clients.

- **Access points:** Access points (APs) are base stations for the wireless network. They transmit and receive radio frequencies for wireless enabled devices to communicate with.
- **Clients:** Wireless clients can be mobile devices such as laptops, personal digital assistants, IP phones, or fixed devices such as desktops and workstations that are equipped with a wireless network interface.

Basic service set

The basic service set (BSS) is a set of all stations that can communicate with each other. There are two types of BSS: independent BSS and infrastructure BSS. Every BSS has an identification (ID) called the BSSID, which is the MAC address of the access point servicing the BSS.

- Independent basic service set

  An independent BSS is an ad-hoc network that contains no access points, which means they can not connect to any other basic service set.
- Infrastructure basic service set

  An infrastructure BSS can communicate with other stations not in the same basic service set by communicating through access points.

Extended service set

An extended service set (ESS) is a set of connected BSSes. Access points in an ESS are connected by a distribution system. Each ESS has an ID called the SSID which is a 32-byte (maximum) character string. For example, "linksys" is the default SSID for Linksys routers.

Distribution system

A distribution system connects access points in an extended service set.

Types of wireless LANs

Peer-to-Peer or ad-hoc wireless LAN

A peer-to-peer (P2P) allows wireless devices to directly communicate with each other. Wireless devices within range of each other can discover and communicate directly without involving central access points. This method is typically used by two computers so that they can connect to each other to form a network.

If a signal strength meter is used in this situation, it may not read the strength accurately and can be misleading, because it registers the strength of the strongest signal, which may be the closest computer.

802.11 specs define the physical layer (PHY) and MAC (Media Access Control) layers. However, unlike most other IEEE specs, 802.11 includes three alternative PHY standards: diffuse infrared operating at 1 Mbit/s in; frequency-hopping spread spectrum operating at 1 Mbit/s or 2 Mbit/s; and direct-sequence spread spectrum operating at 1 Mbit/s or 2 Mbit/s. A single 802.11 MAC standard is based on CSMA/CA (Carrier Sense Multiple Access with Collision Avoidance).

The 802.11 specification includes provisions designed to minimize collisions. Because two mobile units may both be in range of a common access point, but not in range of each other. The 802.11 has two basic modes of operation: Ad hoc mode enables peer-to-peer transmission between mobile units. Infrastructure mode in which mobile units communicate through an access point that serves as a bridge to a wired network infrastructure is the more common wireless LAN application the one being covered. Since wireless communication uses a more open medium for communication in comparison to wired LANs, the 802.11 designers also included a shared-key encryption mechanism, called wired equivalent privacy (WEP), or Wi-Fi Protected Access, (WPA, WPA2) to secure wireless computer networks.

Bridge

A bridge can be used to connect networks, typically of different types. A wireless Ethernet bridge allows the connection of devices on a wired ethernet network to a wireless network. The bridge acts as the connection point to the Wireless LAN.

Wireless distribution system

When it is difficult to connect all of the access points in a network by wires, it is also possible to put up access points as repeaters.

Bluetooth

Bluetooth is an industrial specification for wireless Personal Area Networks (PANs). Bluetooth provides a way to connect and exchange information between devices such as mobile phones, laptops, PCs, printers, digital cameras, and video game consoles over a secure, globally unlicensed short-range radio frequency.

The Bluetooth specifications are developed and licensed by the Bluetooth Special Interest Group.

Uses

Bluetooth is a radio standard and communications protocol primarily designed for low power consumption, with a short range (power-class-dependent: 1 meter, 10 meters, 100 m) based on low-cost transceiver microchips in each device.

Bluetooth lets these devices communicate with each other when they are in range. The devices use a radio communications system, so they do not have to be in line of sight of each other, and can even be in other rooms, as long as the received transmission is powerful enough.

Class	Maximum Permitted	Power Range (mW/dBm) (approximate)
Class 1	100 mW (20 dBm)	~100 meters
Class 2	2.5 mW (4 dBm)	~10 meters
Class 3	1 mW (0 dBm)	~1 meter

Bluetooth profiles

In order to use Bluetooth, a device must be compatible with certain Bluetooth profiles. These define the possible applications and uses.

List of applications

More prevalent applications of Bluetooth include:

- Wireless control of and communication between a cell phone and a hands-free headset or car kit. This was one of the earliest applications to become popular.
- Wireless networking between PCs in a confined space and where little bandwidth is required.
- Wireless communications with PC input and output devices, the most common being the mouse, keyboard and printer.
- Transfer of files between devices with OBEX.
- Transfer of contact details, calendar appointments, and reminders between devices with OBEX.
- Replacement of traditional wired serial communications in test equipment, GPS receivers, medical equipment and traffic control devices.
- For controls where infrared was traditionally used.
- Sending small advertisements from Bluetooth enabled advertising hoardings to other, discoverable, Bluetooth devices.
- Seventh-generation game consoles—Nintendo Wii, Sony PlayStation 3—use Bluetooth for their respective wireless controllers.

Bluetooth vs. Wi-Fi in networking

Bluetooth and Wi-Fi both have their places in today's offices, homes, and on the move: setting up networks, printing, or transferring presentations and files from PDAs to computers.

Bluetooth

Bluetooth is implemented in a variety of new products such as phones, printers, modems, and headsets. Bluetooth is acceptable for situations when two or more devices are in proximity to each other and don't require high bandwidth. Bluetooth is most commonly used with phones and hand-held computing devices, either using a Bluetooth headset or transferring files from phones/PDAs to computers.

Bluetooth also simplifies the discovery and setup of services. Bluetooth devices advertise all services they provide. This makes the utility of the service that much more accessible, without the need to worry about network addresses, permissions and all the other considerations that go with typical networks.

Wi-Fi

Wi-Fi is more analogous to the traditional Ethernet network and requires configuration to set up shared resources, transmit files, set up audio links (for example, headsets and hands-free devices). It uses the same radio frequencies as Bluetooth, but with higher power output resulting in a stronger connection. Wi-Fi is sometimes called "wireless Ethernet." Although this description is inaccurate, it provides an indication of its relative strengths and weaknesses. Wi-Fi requires more setup, but is better suited for operating full-scale networks because it enables a faster connection, better range from the base station, and better security than Bluetooth.

One method for comparing the efficiency of wireless transmission protocols such as Bluetooth and Wi-Fi is spatial capacity, or bits per second per square meter.

Computer Requirements

A personal computer must have a Bluetooth adapter in order to be able to communicate with other Bluetooth devices (such as mobile phones, mice and keyboards).While some portable computers and fewer desktop computers already contain an internal Bluetooth dongle, most PCs require an external USB Bluetooth dongle. Most Macs come with built-in Bluetooth adapters.

Unlike its predecessor, IrDA, in which each device requires a separate dongle, multiple Bluetooth devices can communicate with a computer over a single dongle.

Operating system support

Linux provides two Bluetooth stacks, with the BlueZ stack included with most Linux kernels. It was originally developed by Qualcomm and Affix. BlueZ supports all core Bluetooth protocols and layers.

Only Microsoft Windows XP Service Pack 2 and later versions of Windows have native support for Bluetooth. Previous versions required the users to install their Bluetooth adapter's own drivers, which was not directly supported by Microsoft. Microsoft's own Bluetooth dongles (that are packaged with their Bluetooth computer devices) have no external drivers and thus require at least Windows XP Service Pack 2. Mac OS X has supported Bluetooth since version 10.2 released in 2002.

Specifications and features

The Bluetooth specification was developed in 1994 by Sven Mattisson and Jaap Haartsen, who were working for Ericsson Mobile Platforms in Lund, Sweden. The specifications were formalized by the Bluetooth Special Interest Group (SIG). The SIG was formally announced on May 20, 1998. Today it has over 7000 companies worldwide. It was established by Ericsson, Sony Ericsson, IBM, Intel, Toshiba, and Nokia, and later joined by many other companies. Bluetooth is also known as IEEE 802.15.1.

Bluetooth 1.0 and 1.0B

Versions 1.0 and 1.0B had many problems, and manufacturers had difficulties making their products interoperable. Versions 1.0 and 1.0B also had mandatory Bluetooth hardware device address (BD_ADDR) transmission in the Connecting process, rendering anonymity impossible at a protocol level, which was a major setback for services planned to be used in Bluetooth environments, such as Consumerium.

Bluetooth 1.1

- Many errors found in the 1.0B specifications were fixed.
- Added support for non-encrypted channels.
- Received Signal Strength Indicator (RSSI).

Bluetooth 1.2

This version is backward-compatible with 1.1 and the major enhancements include the following:

- Faster Connection and Discovery.
- Adaptive frequency-hopping spread spectrum (AFH), which improves resistance to radio frequency interference by avoiding the use of crowded frequencies in the hopping sequence.
- Higher transmission speeds in practice, up to 721 kbit/s, as in 1.1.
- Extended Synchronous Connections (eSCO), which improve voice quality of audio links by allowing retransmissions of corrupted packets.
- Host Controller Interface (HCI) support for three-wire UART.

Bluetooth 2.0

This version, specified in November 2004, is backward-compatible with 1.1. The main enhancement is the introduction of an enhanced data rate (EDR) of 3.0 Mbit/s. This has the following effects:

- Three times faster transmission speed—up to 10 times in certain cases (up to 2.1 Mbit/s).
- Lower power consumption through a reduced duty cycle.
- Simplification of multi-link scenarios due to more available bandwidth.
- Further improved (bit error rate) performance.

Bluetooth 2.1

Bluetooth Core Specification Version 2.1 + EDR, is fully backward-compatible with 1.1, and will be adopted by the Bluetooth SIG once interoperability testing has completed. This specification includes the following features:

- **Extended inquiry response**: provides more information during the inquiry procedure to allow better filtering of devices before connection. This information includes the name of the device, a list of services the device supports, as well as other information like the time of day, and pairing information.
- **Sniff subrating**: reduces the power consumption when devices are in the sniff low-power mode, especially on links with asymmetric data flows. Human interface devices (HID) are expected to benefit the most, with mouse and keyboard devices increasing the battery life from 3 to 10 times those currently used.
- **Encryption Pause Resume**: enables an encryption key to be refreshed, enabling much stronger encryption for connections that stay up for longer than 24 hours.
- **Secure Simple Pairing**: radically improves the pairing experience for Bluetooth devices, while increasing the use and strength of security. It is expected that this feature will significantly increase the use of Bluetooth.
- **NFC cooperation**: automatic creation of secure Bluetooth connections when NFC radio interface is also available. For example, a headset should be paired with a Bluetooth 2.1 phone including NFC just by bringing the two devices close to each other (a few centimeters). Another example is automatic uploading of photos from a mobile phone or camera to a digital picture frame just by bringing the phone or camera close to the frame.

Future of Bluetooth

- **Broadcast Channel: enables** Bluetooth information points. This will drive the adoption of Bluetooth into cell phones, and enable advertising models based around users pulling information from the information points, and not based around the object push model that is used in a limited way today.
- **Topology Management**: enables the automatic configuration of the piconet topologies especially in scatternet situations that are becoming more common today. This should all be invisible to the users of the technology, while also making the technology just work.

- **Alternate MAC PHY**: enables the use of alternative MAC and PHY's for transporting Bluetooth profile data. The Bluetooth Radio will still be used for device discovery, initial connection and profile configuration, however, when lots of data needs to be sent, the high speed alternate MAC PHY's will be used to transport the data. This means that the proven low power connection models of Bluetooth are used when the system is idle, and the low power per bit radios are used when lots of data needs to be sent.
- **QoS improvements**: enable audio and video data to be transmitted at a higher quality, especially when best effort traffic is being transmitted in the same piconet.

Bluetooth technology already plays a part in the rising Voice over IP (VOIP) scene, with Bluetooth headsets being used as wireless extensions to the PC audio system. As VOIP becomes more popular, and more suitable for general home or office users than wired phone lines, Bluetooth may be used in cordless handsets, with a base station connected to the Internet link.

Bluetooth 3.0

The next version of Bluetooth after v2.1, code-named *Seattle*, that will be called Bluetooth 3.0, has many of the same features, but is most notable for plans to adopt ultra-wideband (UWB) radio technology. This will allow Bluetooth use over UWB radio, enabling very fast data transfers of up to 480 Mbit/s, while building on the very low-power idle modes of Bluetooth.

High Speed Bluetooth

On 28 March 2006, the Bluetooth Special Interest Group announced its selection of the WiMedia Alliance Multi-Band Orthogonal Frequency Division Multiplexing (MB-OFDM) version of UWB for integration with current Bluetooth wireless technology.

UWB integration will create a version of Bluetooth wireless technology with a high-speed/high-data-rate option. This new version of Bluetooth technology will meet the high-speed demands of synchronizing and transferring large amounts of data, as well as enabling high-quality video and audio applications for portable devices, multi-media projectors and television sets, and wireless VOIP. At the same time, Bluetooth technology will continue catering to the needs of very low power applications such as mice, keyboards, and mono headsets, enabling devices to select the most appropriate physical radio for the application requirements, thereby offering the best of both worlds.

Ultra Low Power Bluetooth

On 12 June 2007, Nokia and Bluetooth SIG announced that Wibree will be a part of the Bluetooth specification as an ultra low power Bluetooth technology. Expected user cases includes watches displaying Caller ID information, sports sensors monitoring your heart rate during exercise, as well as medical devices. The Medical Devices Working Group is also creating a medical devices profile and associated protocols to enable this market.

The main contributer to the development of the Wibree standard is the world known Norwegian company Nordic Semiconductor.

Technical information

Communication and Connection

A master Bluetooth device can communicate with up to seven devices. This network group of up to eight devices is called a piconet. A piconet is an ad-hoc computer network, using Bluetooth technology protocols to allow one master device to interconnect with up to seven active devices. Up to 255 further devices can be inactive, or parked, which the master device can bring into active status at any time.

At any given time, data can be transferred between the master and one other device. However, the master switches rapidly from device to another in a round-robin fashion. (Simultaneous transmission from the master to multiple other devices is possible, but not used much.) Either device can switch roles and become the master at any time.

Bluetooth specification allows connecting two or more piconets together to form a scatternet, with some devices acting as a bridge by simultaneously playing the master role and the slave role in one piconet. These devices are planned for 2007.

Setting up Connections

Any Bluetooth device will transmit the following sets of information on demand:

- Device name.
- Device class.
- List of services.
- Technical information, for example, device features, manufacturer, Bluetooth specification, clock offset.

Any device may perform an inquiry to find other devices to which to connect, and any device can be configured to respond to such inquiries. However, if the device trying to connect knows the address of the device, it always responds to direct connection requests and transmits the information shown in the list above if requested. Use of device services may require pairing or acceptance by its owner, but the connection itself can be started by any device and held until it goes out of range.

Some devices can be connected to only one device at a time, and connecting to them prevents them from connecting to other devices and appearing in inquiries until they disconnect from the other device.

Every device has a unique 48-bit address. However, these addresses are generally not shown in inquiries. Instead, friendly Bluetooth names are used, which can be set by the user. This name appears when another user scans for devices and in lists of paired devices. Most phones have the Bluetooth name set to the manufacturer and model of the phone by default. Most phones and laptops show only the Bluetooth names and special programs that are required to get additional information about remote devices. This can be confusing as, for example, there could be several phones in range named T610 .

Pairing

Pairs of devices may establish a trusted relationship by learning (by user input) a shared secret known as a passkey. A device that wants to communicate only with a trusted device can cryptographically authenticate the identity of the other device. Trusted devices may also encrypt the data that they exchange over the air so that no one can listen in. The encryption can, however, be turned off, and passkeys are stored on the device file system, not on the Bluetooth chip itself. Since the Bluetooth address is permanent, a pairing is preserved, even if the Bluetooth name is changed.

Pairs can be deleted at any time by either device. Devices generally require pairing or prompt the owner before they allow a remote device to use any or most of their services. Some devices, such as Sony Ericsson phones, usually accept OBEX business cards and notes without any pairing or prompts.

Certain printers and access points allow any device to use its services by default, much like unsecured Wi-Fi networks. Pairing algorithms are sometimes manufacturer-specific for transmitters and receivers used in applications such as music and entertainment.

Air interface

The protocol operates in the license-free ISM band at 2.45 GHz. To avoid interfering with other protocols that use the 2.45 GHz band, the Bluetooth protocol divides the band into 79 channels (each 1 MHz wide) and changes channels up to 1600 times per second. Implementations with versions 1.1 and 1.2 reach speeds of 723.1 kbit/s. Version 2.0 implementations feature Bluetooth Enhanced Data Rate (EDR) and reach 2.1 Mbit/s. Technically, version 2.0 devices have a higher power consumption, but the three times faster rate reduces the transmission times, effectively reducing power consumption to half that of 1.x devices (assuming equal traffic load).

Bluetooth differs from Wi-Fi in that the latter provides higher throughput and covers greater distances, but requires more expensive hardware and higher power consumption. They use the same frequency range, but employ different multiplexing schemes. Bluetooth is often thought of as wireless USB, whereas Wi-Fi is wireless Ethernet, both operating at much lower bandwidth than the cable systems they are trying to replace. However, this analogy is not entirely accurate since any Bluetooth device can, in theory, host any other Bluetooth device—something that is not universal to USB devices.

While Bluetooth is a cable replacement for a variety of applications, Wi-Fi is a cable replacement only for local area network access.

Many USB Bluetooth adapters are available, some of which also include an IrDA adapter. Older (pre-2003) Bluetooth adapters, however, have limited services, offering only the Bluetooth Enumerator and a less-powerful Bluetooth Radio incarnation.

Such devices can link computers with Bluetooth, but they do not offer much in the way of services that modern adapters do.

Security

Bluetooth implements authentication and key derivation with custom algorithms based on the SAFER+ block cipher. The initialization key and master key are generated with the E22 algorithm.

The E0 stream cipher is used for encrypting packets. This makes eavesdropping on Bluetooth-enabled devices more difficult.

Social Concerns

2003:

In November 2003, Ben and Adam Laurie from A.L. Digital Ltd. discovered that serious flaws in Bluetooth security may lead to disclosure of personal data. It should be noted, however, that the reported security problems concerned some poor implementations of Bluetooth, rather than the protocol itself.

In a subsequent experiment, Martin Herfurt from the trifinite.group was able to do a field-trial at the CeBIT fairgrounds, showing the importance of the problem to the world. A new attack called BlueBug was used for this experiment.

2004:

In April 2004, security consultant firm @stake (now Symantec) revealed a security flaw that makes it possible to crack conversations on Bluetooth based wireless headsets by reverse engineering the PIN. This is one of a number of concerns that have been raised over the security of Bluetooth communications. In 2004 the first purported virus using Bluetooth to spread itself among mobile phones appeared on the Symbian OS. The virus was first described by Kaspersky Lab and requires users to confirm the installation of unknown software before it can propagate.

The virus was written as a proof-of-concept by a group of virus writers known as 29A and sent to anti-virus groups. Thus, it should be regarded as a potential (but not real) security threat to Bluetooth or Symbian OS since the virus has never spread in the wild.

In August 2004, a world-record-setting experiment showed that the range of Class 2 Bluetooth radios could be extended to 1.78 km (1.08 mile) with directional antennas. This poses a potential security threat because it enables attackers to access vulnerable Bluetooth-devices from a distance beyond expectation. However, such experiments do not work with signal amplifiers. The attacker must also be able to receive information from the victim to set up a connection. No attack can be made against a Bluetooth device unless the attacker knows its Bluetooth address and which channels to transmit on.

2005:

In April 2005, Cambridge University security researchers published results of their actual implementation of passive attacks against the PIN-based pairing between commercial Bluetooth devices, confirming the attacks to be practicably fast and the Bluetooth symmetric key establishment method to be vulnerable. To rectify this vulnerability, they carried out an implementation which showed that stronger, asymmetric key establishment is feasible for certain classes of devices, such as handphones.

In June 2005, Yaniv Shaked and Avishai Wool published the paper "Cracking the Bluetooth PIN1," which shows both passive and active methods for obtaining the PIN for a Bluetooth link. The passive attack allows a suitably equipped attacker to eavesdrop on communications and spoof if they were present at the time of initial pairing. The active method makes use of a specially constructed message that must be inserted at a specific point in the protocol, to make the master and slave repeat the pairing process. After that, the first method can be used to crack the PIN. This attack's major weakness is that it requires the user of the devices under attack to re-enter the PIN during the attack when the device prompts them to. Also, this active attack probably requires custom hardware, since most commercially available Bluetooth devices are not capable of the timing necessary.

In August 2005, police in Cambridgeshire, England, issued warnings about thieves using Bluetooth-enabled phones to track other devices left in cars. Police are advising users to ensure that any mobile networking connections are de-activated if laptops and other devices are left in this way.

2006:

In April 2006, researchers from Secure Network and F-Secure published a report that warns of the large number of devices left in a visible state, and issued statistics on the spread of various Bluetooth services and the ease of spread of an eventual Bluetooth worm.

In October 2006, at the Luxemburgish Hack.lu Security Conference, Kevin Finistere and Thierry Zoller demonstrated and released a remote root shell over Bluetooth on Mac OSX 10.3.9 and 10.4. They also demonstrated the first Bluetooth PIN and Link-keys cracker, which is based on the research of Wool and Shaked.

Health concerns

Bluetooth uses the microwave radio frequency spectrum in the 2.4 GHz to 2.4835 GHz range. Maximum power output from a Bluetooth radio is 1mW, 2.5mW, and 100mW for Class 3, Class 2, and Class 1 devices respectively, which puts Class 1 at roughly the same level as cell phones, and the other two classes much lower. Accordingly, Class 2 and Class 3 Bluetooth devices are considered less of a potential hazard than cell phones, and Class 1 may be comparable to that of cell phones, which are of little concern.

Origin of the name and the logo

Bluetooth was named after a late tenth century king, Harald Bluetooth King of Denmark and Norway. He is known for his unification of previously warring tribes from Denmark (including Scania, present-day Sweden, where the Bluetooth technology was invented), and Norway.

Bluetooth likewise was intended to unify different technologies, such as computers and mobile phones.

The name may have been inspired less by the historical Harald than the loose interpretation of him in The Long Ships by Frans Gunnar Bengtsson, a Swedish Viking-inspired novel.

The Bluetooth logo merges the Nordic runes analogous to the modern Latin H and B: (haglaz) and (berkanan) forming a bind rune.

Bluetooth Consortium

In 1998, Ericsson, IBM, Intel, and Nokia, formed a consortium and adopted the code name Bluetooth for their proposed open specification. In December 1999, 3Com, Lucent Technologies, Microsoft, and Motorola joined the initial founders as the promoter group. Since that time, Lucent Technologies transferred their membership to their spinoff Agere Systems, and 3Com has left the promoter group.